COLONIAL AMERICAN WRITING

COLONIAL

AMERICAN

WRITING

Edited with Introductions by

ROY HARVEY PEARCE

Rinehart & Company, Incorporated

Third Printing, November 1958

Introduction copyright, 1950, by Roy Harvey Pearce
Typography and Cover Design by Stefan Salter
Printed in the United States of America

INTRODUCTION

The selections in this volume illustrate main aspects of American intellectual and imaginative origins and growth through the third quarter of the eighteenth century. Exhibiting not so much colonial social, institutional, and political forms, as ideas and attitudes which made for such forms, they embody the thought and imagination of those colonial Americans who were to become Revolutionary Americans. These writings, in fact, point immediately toward the American mind of the Revolutionary period—a mind of the Enlightenment, one which was to center on the notion of the free, rational personality and which was to know that freedom and rationality were embodied in the very nature of things American.

There are represented in this volume some of the origins of that mind and of its drive toward freedom. The Pilgrim idea of freedom through private and separate devotion, the Puritan idea of freedom through work and facing one's fate as a sinful individual, the Virginia idea of freedom through the responsibilities of the ruling gentleman, the Quaker idea of freedom through the inviolable sacredness of the individual, and the frontier idea of freedom through violent self-assertion—all these ultimately found their largest realization in the thoughts, beliefs, and actions of enlightened Americans of the Revolution and beyond. In the writings here selected, we can know these ideas as they came into being and began to be explored and tested and as they made for characteristic attitudes toward life and living.

There is little of what we may, properly speaking, call "literature" in this collection, as there was little of the sustained æsthetic attitude in colonial America. Colonial Americans were determined to make a new way of life in a new world—or rather to realize in the best possible way, in the best possible circumstances, the best aspects of the old life which they had left behind them. They had little or no time for that disinterested contemplation which is essential in making works of art. When they did write poetry, it was poetry which had a public, commemorative value, which would recall to them something significant; or it was poetry which showed them that when and if they wished, they could write as well as any gentlemanly Englishman. In their various ways, in their various conditions, with their various beliefs, they took the arts as seriously as they could.

Because they had first of all to survive, they took life with deadly seriousness. And in their seriousness they were able to record memorably life and living as they knew it. When their writing has distinguished style, as it often does, it is style which serves a higher purpose than itself; it is style which expresses the very seriousness of the colonial enterprise. Indeed, when one studies stylistically the best of colonial writing, one is studying the quality of colonial seriousness. The very forms of expression—sermons, histories, diaries, poems, and the like—themselves characterize the men who write, the society to which they write, and the occasion for writing. The difference between the writing of a Mather and of a Byrd, between that of a Sewall and of a Woolman, is in the style and form as well as the content. One can see not only what each believes in, but the quality of the belief. Theirs is the style and form which develop when an idea or an attitude is seriously put into action.

Consideration of style and form thus returns us to idea and attitude. Basic to that idea and attitude is a search for freedom through order. We can see in these selections widely varying conceptions of what order is and for whom freedom exists, and we can look ahead to the development of such conceptions in the Revolutionary period. Freedom was to come more and more to be the right of all men; a Revolution was to be fought and won; a new world, a new way of thinking, and a new literature were to come into being; new liberties, new responsibilities, new goods and evils, were to develop. The selections here printed show evidence of the beginnings of that development. They should remind us, as we struggle in our time to find freedom through order, that the struggle is eternal; only the conditions of struggle change. They should let us know the past well enough at once to profit from it and to free ourselves from it. Not the least advantage of coming to know these colonial writings is that which accrues when we try to understand our present, for good and bad, as it takes its origins in our past.

BIBLIOGRAPHICAL NOTE

Bibliographical notes on specific areas will be found following the introductions to each section of this anthology, and bibliographical headnotes precede the individual selections. For a general overview, the best inclusive account of American colonial history is C. M. Andrews, *The Colonial Period of American History,* 4 vols. (New Haven: 1934-1938). A valuable short account is L. B. Wright, *The Atlantic Frontier* (New York: 1947). Social history is treated in the second and third volumes of *The History of American Life,* T. J. Wertenbaker's *The First Americans, 1607-1690* (New York: 1927) and J. T. Adam's *Provincial Society, 1690-1732* (New York: 1927). Intellectual history is treated in the opening sections of Merle Curti, *The Growth of American Thought* (New York: 1943) and of Herbert Schneider, *A History of American Philosophy* (New York: 1946). Still the most adequate survey of colonial American literature (understanding "literature" in the broadest sense) is M. C. Tyler, *A History of American Literature, 1607-1765,* 2 vols. (rev. ed., New York: 1897). The first volume of V. L. Parrington, *Main Currents in American Thought* (New York: 1927) suffers most from Parrington's special populist, Jeffersonian bias, but it remains an important and stimulating book, perhaps now a literary work in its own right. The studies of colonial writing in H. M. Jones, *Ideas in America* (Cambridge: 1944) suggest important ways and means of analysis and revaluation. The relevant sections in the first volume of the *Literary History of the United States* (New York:

1948) offer an invaluable summary of our knowledge of our colonial literature, but do not go very far toward analysis and revaluation; the bibliographies in the third volume, however, supersede all others and may be called definitive for all but the specialist. The essays by Clarence Faust and Leon Howard in *Transitions in American Literary History,* ed. H. H. Clark (Durham, N. C., 1953) do much to suggest the form which future understanding of the period will take.

TEXTUAL NOTE

Whenever possible, texts here printed have been drawn from modern scholarly editions. Where such versions are lacking, texts have been drawn from early editions. Although typographical practice has been modernized, spellings, usages, and locutions have been allowed to stand as in the originals. Obvious errors and omissions have been silently corrected. Unless otherwise noted, dates following titles are those of first publication.

Annotation has been kept to a minimum. Passages in foreign languages have been translated. References to persons, places, and events have been expanded when knowledge of such references is necessary to make sense of passages involved. Proper names occurring in common works of reference, like *Webster's New Collegiate Dictionary* and *The American College Dictionary*, have not been annotated. It has been assumed that the texts can best exhibit themselves without extended commentaries by the editor. Annotation has been directed toward this end.

Grateful acknowledgment is owed the following for permission to reprint versions of texts occurring in books which they have copyrighted: American Book Company, publishers of *The Puritans,* edited by Perry Miller and Thomas Johnson and of *Jonathan Edwards: Representative Selections,* edited by Clarence Faust and Thomas Johnson; American Antiquarian Society, publishers of *The First Century of New England Verse,* edited by Harold Jantz; Princeton University Press, publishers of *The Poetical Works of Edward Taylor,* edited by Thomas Johnson; Yale University Press, publishers of Jonathan Edwards, *Images or Shadows of Divine Things,* edited by Perry Miller; University of North Carolina Press, publishers of Robert Beverly, *The History and Present State of Virginia,* edited by L. B. Wright; The Arthur

H. Clark Company, publishers of *Early Western Travels,* edited by R. G. Thwaites; Harvard University Press, publishers of *Handkerchiefs from Paul,* edited by K. B. Murdock; Harcourt Brace and Company, publishers of *Selections from Cotton Mather,* edited by K. B. Murdock; L. B. Wright and Marion Tinling, editors of *The Secret Diary of William Byrd of Westover, 1709-1712;* Barnes and Noble Inc., publishers of the *Original Narratives of Early American History* series; Columbia University Press, publishers of Mather Byles, *Poems on Several Occasions,* edited by C. L. Carlson and William Dawson, *Poems on Several Occasions,* edited by R. L. Rusk.

Note on the Second Printing

For the second printing of this collection, I have corrected a number of typographical errors, tried, so far as space would permit, to bring the Bibliographical Notes up to date, and made one change in the contents: I have, for reasons of significance and merit, replaced John James' "Of John Bunyan's Life &c." with John Fiske's anagrammatic poem on Thomas Hooker.

August, 1956   R. H. P.

CONTENTS

SECTION I
THE VOYAGER

SECTION II
THE PILGRIM

SECTION III
THE PURITAN

PURITAN POETRY

SECTION IV

THE VIRGINIA GENTLEMAN

SECTION V

THE QUAKER

SECTION VI
THE AMERICAN AS AUGUSTAN POET

SECTION VII
THE FRONTIERSMAN

COLONIAL AMERICAN WRITING

THE VOYAGER

Elizabethan and Stuart voyagers saw in America a land in need of exploitation and a people in need of God and civilization. They felt no contradiction in the union of their ideas of religion and empire; for only in terms of such a union could the voyager—and the planter he became or who came after him—assure himself that his world was ordered and intelligible. It was, as one contemporary editor of voyage narratives said, a "union of spirituals and temporals." The voyager's obsession—a Renaissance obsession—was to make the new world part of the old. If the voyage narratives seldom testify directly to this obsession, they nonetheless furnish us occasional explicit statements of and abundant circumstantial evidence for it. We have to analyze out of the narratives such a valuation of life, its duties, and pleasures precisely because such a valuation is so deeply and integrally imbedded in them.

John Smith is a case in point. A professional soldier turned pamphleteer, not the most modest of men, he published various accounts of his life and adventures, descriptions of lands he had seen, and prescriptions for Englishmen who would go to America. Obviously he is no philosopher. Yet he has a kind of philosophy. And it is that philosophy—one which propagandizes for progress, order, religion, and empire—which holds together his excited accounts of the possibilities of life in a brave new world.

Bibliographical Note. The great collections of voyage narratives are Richard Hakluyt's *Principal Navigations* (1598-1600), available in a modern edition in 12 vols. (Glasgow, 1903-1905);

and Samuel Purchas's continuation, *Hakluytus Posthumus; or, Purchas His Pilgrimes* (1625), available in a modern edition in 20 vols. (Glasgow, 1905-1907). On the idea of colonization see L. B. Wright, *Religion and Empire* (Chapel Hill, 1943).

CAPTAIN JOHN SMITH

(*1580-1631*)

Bibliographical Note. Smith's writings are collected in E. Arber and A. Bradley, eds., *Travels and Works of Captain John Smith,* 2 vols. (Edinburgh, 1910); the text of the following selection is taken from this edition, I, 187-191 and 208-217. The best account of Smith is in S. E. Morison, *Builders of the Bay Colony* (Boston, 1930), pp. 3-20.

from A DESCRIPTION OF NEW ENGLAND (1616)

In the moneth of Aprill, 1614. with two Ships from *London,* of a few Marchants, I chanced to arrive in *New-England,* a parte of *Ameryca;* at the Ile of *Monahigan,* in 43½ of Northerly latitude: our plot was there to take Whales and make tryalls of a Myne of Gold and Copper. If those failed, Fish and Furres was then our refuge, to make our selves savers howsoever. We found this Whale-fishing a costly conclusion: we saw many, and spent much time in chasing them; but could not kill any: they beeing a kinde of Jubartes, and not the Whale that yeelds Finnes and Oyle as wee expected. For our Golde, it was rather the Masters device to get a voyage that projected it, then any knowledge hee had at all of any such matter. Fish and Furres was now our guard: and by our late arrival, and long lingring about the Whale[s], the prime of both those seasons were past ere wee perceived it; we thinking that their seasons, served at all times: but wee found it otherwise; for, by the midst of Iune, the fishing failed. Yet in July and August some was taken, but not sufficient to defray so great a charge as our stay required. Of dry fish we made about 40000., of Cor fish about 7000.

Whilest the sailers fished, my selfe with eight or

My first voyage to New England.

nine others of them [that] might best bee spared;
Ranging the coast in a small boat, wee got for
trifles neer 1100 Beuer skinnes, 100 Martins [skins],
and neer as many Otters; and most of them within
the distance of twenty leagues.

We ranged the Coast both East and West much
furder; but Eastwards our commodities were not
esteemed, they were so neare the French who
affords them better: and right against us in the
Main [*the mainland*] was a Ship of Sir *Frances
Popphames,* that had there such acquaintance, having many yeares used onely that porte, that the
most parte there, was had by him. And 40 leagues
westwards were two French Ships, that had made
there a great voyage by trade; during the time we
tryed those conclusions, not knowing the Coast,
nor Salvages habitation.

With these Furres, the Traine [*train oil*], and
Cor-fish, I returned for *England* in the Bark: where
within six monthes after our departure from the
Downes, we safe arrived back. The best of this fish
was solde for five pound the hundreth, the rest by
ill usage betwixt three pound and fifty shillings.

The other ship staied to fit herselfe for *Spaine*
with the dry fish: which was sould, by the Sailers
reporte that returned, at forty ryalls [*20s.*] the quin-
tall, each hundred [weight] weighing two quintalls
and a halfe.

The situation
of New Eng-
land.

New England is that part of *America* in the
Ocean Sea opposite to *Nova Albyon* [*California*]
in the South Sea, discovered by the most memorable Sir *Francis Drake* in his voyage about the
worlde. In regarde whereto this is stiled *New
England,* beeing in the same latitude. *New France,*
off it, is Northward: Southwardes is *Virginia,* and

all the adioyning Continent, with *New Granado,*
New Spain, New Andolosia, and the *West Indies.*

Now because I have beene so oft asked such
strange questions, of the goodnesse and greatnesse
of those spatious Tracts of land, how they can bee
thus long unknown, or not possessed by the *Spaniard,* and many such like demands; I intreat your
pardons, if I chance to bee too plaine, or tedious in
relating my knowledge for plaine mens satisfaction.

Florida is the next adioyning to the *Ind[i]es,*   Notes of
which unprosperously was attempted to bee planted   Florida.
by the *French.* A Country farre bigger then
England, Scotland, France, and *Ireland,* yet little
knowne to any Christian but by the wonderful
ende[a]vours of *Ferdinando de Soto,* a valiant
Spaniard: whose writings in this age is the best
guide knowne to search those parts.

Virginia is no Ile (as many doe imagine) but   Notes of
part of the Continent adioyning to *Florida;* whose   Virginia.
bounds may be stretched to the magnitude thereof
without offence to any Christian inhabitant. For
from the degrees of 30. to 45. his Majestie hath
granted his Letters patents, the Coast extending
South-west and North-east aboute 1500 miles; but
to follow it aboard, the shore may well be 2000. at
the least: of which, 20 miles is the most [that] gives
entrance into the Bay of *Chisapeak,* where is the
London plantation: within which [entrance] is a
Country (as you may perceive by the description in
a Booke and Map printed in my name of that little
I there discovered) [that] may well suffice 300000
people to inhabit.

And Southward adioyneth that part discovered
at the charge of Sir *Walter Rawley,* by Sir *Ralph*

Lane, and that learned Mathematician Master
Thomas Heryot.

Northward six or seaven degrees is the River
Sadagahock, where was planted the Westerne Col-
ony, by that Honourable Patrone of vertue, Sir
Iohn Poppham, Lord chief Justice of *England.*

Ther[e] is also a relation printed by Captaine
Bartholomew Gosnould, of *Elizabeths Isles:* and an
other by Captaine *Waymouth,* of *Pemmaquid.*

From all these diligent observers, posterity may
be bettered by the fruits of their labours. But for
divers others that, long before and since, have
ranged those parts, within a kenning sometimes
of the shore, some touching in one place, some in
another, I must entreat them [to] pardon me for
omitting them; or if I offend in saying that their
true descriptions are concealed, or [were] never
well observed, or died with the Authors: so that
the Coast is yet still but even as a Coast unknowne
and undiscovered.

I have had six or seaven severall plots of those
Northern parts, so unlike each to other, and most
so differing from any true proportion or resemblance of the Countrey, as they did mee no more
good then so much waste paper, though they cost
me more. It may be it was not my chance to see the
best; but at least others may be deceived as I was,
or thro[u]gh dangerous ignorance hazard themselves as I did, I have drawen a Map from Point to
Point, Ile to Ile, and Harbour to Harbour, with
the Soundings, Sands, Rocks, and Land-marks as I
passed close aboard the Shore in a little Boat; although there be many things to be observed which
the haste of other affaires did cause me [to] omit.
For being sent more to get present commodities
then knowledge by discoveries for any future

good, I had not power to search as I would: yet it will serve to direct any [that] should goe that waies, to safe Harbours and the Salvages habitations. What marchandize and commodities for their labour they may finde, this following discourse shall plainely demonstrate.

Thus you may see, of this 2000. miles more then halfe is yet unknowne to any purpose: no, not so much as the borders of the Sea are yet certainly discovered. As for the goodness and true substances of the Land, wee are for [the] most part yet altogether ignorant of them, unlesse it bee those parts about the Bay of *Chisapeack,* and *Sagadahock:* but onely here and there wee touched or have seene a little the edges of those large dominions, which doe stretch themselves into the Maine, God doth know how many thousand miles; whereof we can yet no more judge, then a stranger that saileth betwixt *England* and *France* can describe the Harbors and dangers, by landing here or there in some River or Bay, tell thereby the goodnesse and substances of *Spaine, Italy, Germany, Bohemia, Hungaria* and the rest. By this you may perceive how much they erre, that think every one which hath bin at *Virginia,* understandeth or knowes what *Virginia* is: Or that the *Spaniards* know one half quarter of those Territories they possesse; no, not so much as the true circumference of *Terra Incognita,* whose large dominions may equalize the greatnesse and goodnes of *America,* for any thing yet known. It is strange with what small power hee hath raigned in the *East Ind[i]es;* and few will understand the truth of his strength in *America:* where he having so much to keepe with such a pampered force, they neede not greatly feare his furie in the *Bermudas, Virginia, New France,* or *New England.* Beyond whose bounds, *America* doth stretch many thousand miles: into the frozen partes whereof, one Master *Hutson* [*Hudson*], an English Mariner, did make the greatest discoverie of any Christian I know of, where he unfortunately died. For *Affrica,* had not the industrious Portugales ranged her unknowne parts, who would have sought for wealth among those fryed Regions of blacke brutish Negers; where notwithstanding all the wealth and admirable adventures and endeavours more then 140 years [1476-1616], they knowe not one third of those blacke habitations.

But it is not a worke for every one, to manage such an affaire as makes a discoverie, and plants a Colony. It requires all the best parts of Art, Judgement, Courage, Honesty, Constancy, Diligence, and Industrie, to doe but neere well. Some are more proper for one thing then another; and therein are to be imployed: and nothing breedes more confusion then misplacing and misimploying men in their undertakings. *Columbus, Cortez, Pitzara, Soto, Magellanes,* and the rest served more than a prentiship to learne how to begin their most memorable attempts in the *West Ind*[*i*]*es:* which to the wonder of all ages successfully they effected, when many hundreds of others, farre above them in the worlds opinion, beeing instructed but by relation, came to shame and confusion in actions of small moment, who doubtlesse in other matters, were both wise, discreet, generous, and couragious. I say not this to detract any thing from their incomparable merits, but to answer those questionlesse questions that keep us back from imitating the worthinesse of their brave spirits that advanced themselves from poore Souldiers to great Captaines, their posterity to great Lords, their King to be one of the greatest Potentates on earth, and the fruites of their labours, his greatest glory, power, and re-nowne.

. . . . .

Who can desire more content, that hath small meanes; or but only his merit to advance his for-tune, then to tread, and plant that ground hee hath purchased by the hazard of his life? If he have but the taste of virtue and magnanimitie, what to such a minde can bee more pleasant, then planting and building a foundation for his Posteritie, gotte from the rude earth, by Gods blessing and his owne in-dustrie, without preiudice to any? If hee have any graine of faith or zeale in Religion, what can hee doe lesse hurtfull to any: or more agreeable to God, then to seeke to convert those poore Salvages to know Christ, and humanitie, whose labors with discretion will triple requite thy charge and paines? What so truly su[i]tes with honour and honestie, as the discovering things unknowne? erecting Townes, peopling Countries, informing the igno-rant, reforming things unjust, teaching virtue; and gaine to our Natiue mother-countrie a kingdom to attend her: finde imployment for those that are idle, because they know not what to doe: so farre from wronging any, as to cause Posteritie to re-member thee; and remembring thee, ever honour that remembrance with praise?

A note for men that have great spirits, and smal meanes.

Consider: What were the beginnings and end-ings of the Monarkies of the *Chaldeans,* the *Syr-ians,* the *Grecians,* and *Romanes,* but this one rule; What was it they would not doe, for the good of the commonwealth, or their Mother-citie? For ex-ample: *Rome,* What made her such a Monarchesse, but onely the adventures of her youth, not in riots

at home; but in dangers abroade? and the justice
and judgement out of their experience, when they
grewe aged. What was their ruine and hurt, but
this; The excesse of idlenesse, the fondnesse of Parents, the want of experience in Magistrates, the admiration of their undeserved honours, the contempt
of true merit, their unjust jealo[u]sies, their poli-
ticke incredulities, their hypocriticall seeming goodnesse, and their deeds of secret lewdnesse? finally, in
fine, growing onely formall temporists, all that their
predecessors got in many years, they lost in few
daies. Those by their pain and vertues became
Lords of the world; they by their ease and vices became slaves to their servants. This is the difference
betwixt the use of Armes in the field, and on the
monuments of stones; the golden age and the
leaden age, prosperity and miserie, justice and corruption, substance and shadowes, words and deeds,
experience and imagination, making Common-
wealths and marring Commonwealths, the fruits
of vertue and the conclusions of vice.

Then, who would live at home idly (or thinke
in himselfe any worth to live) onely to eate, drink,
and sleepe, and so die? Or by consuming that care-
lessly, his friends got worthily? Or by using that
miserably, that maintained vertue honestly? Or for
being descended nobly, pine with the vaine vaunt
of great kindred, in penurie? Or (to maintaine a
silly shewe of bravery) toyle out thy heart, soule,
and time, basely; by shifts, tricks, cards, and dice?
Or by relating newes of others actions, sharke here
or there for a dinner, or supper; deceive thy friends,
by faire promises and dissimulation, in borrowing
where thou never intendest to pay; offend the
lawes, surfeit with excesse, burden thy Country,
abuse thy selfe, despaire in want, and then couzen

thy kindred, yea even thine owne brother, and wish thy parents death (I will not say damnation) to have their estates? though thou seest what honours, and rewards, the world yet hath for them [who] will seeke them and worthily deserve them.

I would be sor[r]y to offend, or that any should mistake my honest meaning: for I wish good to all, hurt to none. But rich men for the most part are growne to that dotage, through their pride in their wealth, as though there were no accident could end it, or their life.

And what hellish care do such take to make it their owne miserie, and their Countries spoile, especially when there is most neede of their imployment? drawing by all manner of inventions, from the Prince and his honest subiects, even the vitall spirits of their powers and estates: as if their Bagges, or Bragges, were so powerfull a defence, the malicious could not assault them; when they are the onely baite, to cause us not to be onely assaulted; but betrayed and murdered in our owne security, ere we well perceive it.

May not the miserable ruine of *Constantinople,* their impregnable walles, riches, and pleasures [at] last taken by the *Turke* (which are but a bit, in comparison of their now mightines) remember us of the effects of private covetousness? at which time the good *Emperour* held himselfe rich enough, to have such rich subjects, so formall in all excesse of vanity, all kinde of delicacie and prodigalitie. His povertie when the *Turke* besieged, the citizens (whose marchandizing thoughts were onely to get wealth, little conceiving the desperate resolution of a valiant expert enemy) left the Emp[erour] so long to his conclusions, having spent all he had to pay his young, raw, discontented Souldiers; that

An example
of secure
coveteousness.

sodainly he, they, and their citie were all a prey to
the devouring *Turke*. And what they would not
spare for the maintenance of them who adventured
their lives to defend them, did serve onely their
enemies to torment them, their friends, and countrey, and all Christendome to this present day. Let
this lamentable example remember you that are
rich (seeing there are such great theeves in the
world to robbe you) not [to] grudge to lend some
proportion, to breed them that have little, yet [are]
willing to learne how to defend you: for, it is too
late when the deede is a-doing.

The *Romanes* estate hath beene worse then this:
for, the meere covetousnesse and extortion of a few
of them, so mooved the rest, that not having any
imployment but contemplation; their great judgements grew to so great malice, as themselves were
sufficient to destroy themselves by faction: Let this
moove you to embrace imployment for those whose
educations, spirits, and judgements want but your
purses; not onely to prevent such accustomed dangers, but also to gaine more thereby then you have.

And you fathers, that are either so foolishly fond,
or so miserably covetous, or so willfully ignorant,
or so negligently carelesse, as that you will rather
maintaine your children in idle wantonness, till
they grow your masters; or become so basely un-
kinde, as they wish nothing but your deaths; so
that both sorts grow dissolute: and although you
would wish them any where to escape the gallowes,
and ease your cares; though they spend you here
one, two, or three hundred pound[s] a yeer; you
would grudge to give halfe so much in adventure
with them, to obtaine an estate, which in a small
time, but with a little assistance of your providence,
might be better then your owne. But if an Angell

should tell you, [that] any place yet unknowne can afford such fortunes; you would not beleeve him, no more then *Columbus* was beleeved there was any such Land as is now the well knowne abounding *America;* much lesse such large Regions as are yet unknowne, as well in *America,* as in *Affrica,* and *Asia,* and *Terra incognita;* where were courses for gentlemen (and them that would be so reputed) more suiting their qualities, then begging from their Princes generous disposition, the labours of his subiects, and the very marrow of his maintenance.

I have not beene so ill bred, but I have tasted of *Plenty* and *Pleasure,* as well as *Want* and *Miserie:* nor doth necessitie yet, or occasion of discontent, force me to these endeavors: nor am I ignorant what small thanke I shall have for my paines; or that many would have the Worlde imagine them to be of great judgement, that can but blemish these my designes, by their witty objections and detractions: yet (I hope) my reasons with my deeds, will so prevaile with some, that I shall not want imployment in these affaires, to make the most blinde see his owne senselessnesse, and incredulity; Hoping that gaine will make them affect that, which Religion, Charity, and the Common good cannot. It were but a poore device in me, To deceive my selfe; much more the King, State, my Friends and Countrey, with these inducements: which, seeing his Majestie hath given permission, I wish all sorts of worthie, honest, industrious spirits, would understand: and if they desire any further satisfaction, I will doe my best to give it: Not to perswade them to goe onely; but goe with them: Not leave them there; but live with them there.

The Authors conditions.

I will not say, but by ill providing and undue managing, such courses may be taken, [that] may make us miserable enough: But if I may have the execution of what I have projected; if they want to eate, let them eate or never digest Me. If I performe what I say, I desire but that reward out of the gaines [which] may su[i]te my paines, quality, and condition. And if I abuse you with my tongue, take my head for satisfaction. If any dislike at the yeares end, defraying their charge, by my consent they should freely returne. I feare not want of companie sufficient, were it but knowne what I know of those Countries; and by the proofe of that wealth I hope yearely to returne, if God please to blesse me from such accidents, as are beyond my power in reason to prevent: For, I am not so simple to thinke, that ever any other motive then wealth, will ever erect there a Commonweale; or draw companie from their ease and humours at home, to stay in *New England* to effect my purposes.

The planters pleasures, and profits.

And lest any should think the toile might be insupportable, though these things may be had by labour, and diligence: I assure my selfe there are who delight extreamly in vaine pleasure, that take much more paines in *England,* to enjoy it, then I should doe heere [*New England*] to gaine wealth sufficient: and yet I thinke they should not have halfe such sweet content: for, our pleasure here is still gaines; in *England* charges and losse. Heer nature and liberty affords us that freely, which in *England* we want, or it costeth us dearely. What pleasure can be more, then (being tired with any occasion a-shore, in pianting Vines, Fruits, or Hearbs, in contriving their owne Grounds, to the pleasure of their owne mindes, their Fields, Gardens, Orchards, Buildings, Ships, and other works,

&c.) to recreate themselves before their owne doores, in their owne boates upon the Sea; where man, woman and childe, with a small hooke and line, by angling, may take diverse sorts of excellent fish, at their pleasures? And is it not pretty sport, to pull up two pence, six pence, and twelve pence, as fast as you can ha[u]le and veare a line? He is a very bad fisher [that] cannot kill in one day with his hooke and line, one, two, or three hundred Cods: which dressed and dried, if they be sould there for ten shillings the hundred, though in England they will give more than twentie, may not both the servant, the master, and marchant, be well content with this gaine? If a man worke but three dayes in seaven, he may get more then hee can spend, unlesse he will be excessive. Now that Carpenter, Mason, Gardiner, Taylor, Smith, Sailer, Forgers, or what other, may they not make this a pretty recreation though they fish but an houre in a day, to take more then they eate in a weeke? or if they will not eate it, because there is so much better choice; yet sell it, or change it, with the fisher men, or marchants, for any thing they want. And what sport doth yeeld a more pleasing content, and lesse hurt or charge then angling with a hooke; and crossing the sweete ayre from Ile to Ile, over the silent streames of a calme Sea? Wherein the most curious may finde pleasure, profit, and content.

Thus, though all men be not fishers: yet all men, whatsoever, may in other matters doe as well. For necessity doth in these cases so rule a Commonwealth, and each in their severall functions, as their labours in their qualities may be as profitable, because there is a necessary mutuall use of all.

For Gentlemen, what exercise should more delight them, then ranging dayly those unknowne

Imployments for gentlemen.

parts, using fowling and fishing, for hunting and hawking? and yet you shall see the wilde-haukes give you some pleasure, in seeing them stoope (six or seaven after one another) an houre or two together, at the skuls of fish in the faire harbours, as those a-shore at a foule; and never trouble nor torment yourselues, with watching, mewing, feeding, and attending them: nor kill horse and man with running and crying, *See you not a hawk?* For hunting also: the woods, lakes, and rivers affoord not onely chase sufficient, for any that delights in that kinde of toyle, or pleasure; but such beasts to hunt, that besides the delicacy of their bodies for food, their skins are so rich, as may well recompence thy dayly labour, with a Captains pay.

Employments for labourers.

For labourers, if those that sowe hemp, rape, turnups, parsnips, carrats, cabidge, and such like; give 20, 30, 40, 50 shillings yearely for an acre of ground, and meat drinke and wages to use it, and yet grow rich; when better, or at least as good ground, may be had, and cost nothing but labour; it seems strange to me, any such should there grow poore.

My purpose is not to perswade children from their parents; men from their wives; nor servants from their masters: onely, such as with free consent may be spared: But that each parish, or village, in Citie or Countrey, that will but apparell their fatherlesse children, of thirteene or fourteene years of age, or young mar[r]ied people, that have small wealth to live on; heere by their labour may live exceeding well: provided alwaies that first there bee a sufficient power to command them, houses to receive them, meanes to defend them, and meet provisions for them; for, any place may bee overlain: and it is most necessarie to have a fortresse (ere this grow to practice) and sufficient masters (as, Carpenters, Masons, Fishers, Fowlers, Gardiners, Husbandmen, Sawyers, Smiths, Spinsters, Taylors, Weavers, and such like) to take ten, twelve, or twentie, or as ther is occasion, for Apprentises. The Masters by this may quicklie growe rich; these may learne their trades themselves, to doe the like; to a generall and an incredible benefit, for King, and Countrey, Master, and Servant.

It would bee an historie of a large volume, to recite the adventures of the *Spanyards,* and *Portugals,* their affronts and defeats, their dangers and miseries; which with such incomparable honour and constant resolution, so farre beyond beleefe, they have attempted and indured in their discoveries and plantations, as may well condemne us, of too much imbecillitie, sloth, and negligence: yet the Authors of those new inventions, were held as ridiculous, for a long time, as now are others, that doe but seek to imitate their unparalleled vertues. And though we see daily their mountaines of wealth (sprong from the plants of their generous indevours) yet is our sensualitie and untowardnesse such, and so great, that wee either ignorantly beleeve nothing, or so curiously contest to prevent wee knowe not what future events; that wee either so neglect, or oppresse and discourage the present, as wee spoile all in the making, crop all in the blooming; and building upon faire sand, rather then rough rockes, judge that wee knowe not, governe that wee have not, feare that which is not; and for feare some should doe too well, force such against their willes to be idle or as ill. And who is he [that] hath iudgement, courage, and any industrie or qualitie with understanding, will leave his Countrie, his hopes at home, his certaine estate,

Example of the Spanyards.

his friends, pleasures, libertie, and the preferment
sweete *England* doth afford to all degrees, were it
not to advance his fortunes by injoying his deserts?
whose prosperitie once appearing will incourage
others: but it must be cherished as a childe, till it
be able to goe, and understand it selfe, and not corrected nor oppressed above it[s] strength, ere it
knowe wherefore.

A child can neither performe the office, nor
deedes of a man of strength, nor indure that affliction He is able; nor can an Apprentice at the first
performe the part of a Maister. And if twentie
yeeres bee required to make a child a man, seven
yeares limited [to] an apprentice for his trade, if
scarce an age be sufficient to make a wise man a
States man, and commonly a man dies ere he hath
learned to be discreet: If perfection be so hard to
be obtained, as of necessitie there must bee practice,
as well as theorick: Let no man much condemne
this paradox opinion, to say, that halfe seaven yeeres
is scarce sufficient, for a good capacitie, to learne in
these affaires, how to carrie himselfe: and who ever
shall trie in these remote places the erecting of a
Colony, shall finde at the ende of seaven yeares
occasion enough to use all his discretion: and, in
the *Interim* all the content, rewardes, gaines, and
hopes will be necessarily required, to be given to
the beginning, till it bee able to creepe, to stand,
and goe, yet time enough to keepe it from running:
for there is no feare it wil grow too fast, or ever to
any thing; excepte libertie, profit, honor, and prosperitie there found, more binde the planters of
those affaires, in devotion to effect it; then bondage,
violence, tyranny, ingratitude and such double dealing, as bindes freemen to become slaves, and honest
men [to] turne knaves: which hath ever bin the

ruine of the most popular common-weales; and is verie unlikelie ever well to begin in a new.

Who seeth not what is the greatest good of the *Spanyard,* but these new conclusions, in searching those unknowne parts of the unknowne world? By which meanes hee dives even into the verie secrets of all his Neighbours, and the most part of the world: and when the *Portugale* and *Spanyard* had found the *East* and *West Indies;* how many did condemn themselves, that did not accept of that honest offer of Noble *Columbus?* who, upon our neglect, brought them to it, perswading our selves the world had no such places as they had found: and yet ever since wee finde, they still (from time to time) have found new Lands, new Nations, and trades, and still daily dooe finde both in *Asia, Africa, Terra Incognita,* and *America;* so that there is neither Soldier nor Mechanick, from the Lord to the beggar, but those parts afforde them all imploiment; and discharge their Native soile, of so many thousands of all sorts, that else, by their sloth, pride, and imperfections, would long ere this have troubled their neighbours, or have eaten the pride of *Spaine* it selfe.

The blisse of Spaine.

Now he knowes little, that knowest not *England* may well spare many more people then *Spaine,* and is as well able to furnish them with all manner of necessaries. And seeing, for all they have, they cease not still to search for that they have not, and know not; It is strange we should be so dull, as not [to] maintaine that which wee have, and pursue that wee know.

Surely I am sure many would taste it ill, to bee abridged of the titles and honours of their predecessors: when if but truly they would judge themselves; looke how inferior they are to their noble vertues, so much they are unworthy of their honours and livings: which never were ordained for showes and shadowes, to maintaine idlenesse and vice; but to make them more able to abound in honor, by heroycall deeds of action, judgement, pietie, and vertue. What was it, they would not doe both in purse and person, for the good of the Commonwealth? which might move them presently to set out their spare kindred in these generous designes.

Religion, aboue all things, should move us (especially the Clergie) if wee were religious, to shewe our faith by our workes; in converting those poore salvages, to the knowledge of God, seeing what paines the *Spanyards* take to bring them to their adulterated faith. Honor might move the Gentrie, the valiant, and industrious; and the hope and assurance of wealth, all; if wee were that we would seeme, and be accounted. Or be we so far inferior to other nations, or our spirits so far dejected, from our aunicent predecessors, or our mindes so [set] upon spoile, piracie, and such villany, as to serve the *Portugall, Spanyard, Dutch, French,* or *Turke,* (as to the cost of *Europe,* too many dooe) rather then our God, our King, our Country, and our selves? excusing our idlenesse, and our base complaints, by want of imploiement; when heere is such choise of all sorts, and for all degrees, in the planting and discovering these North parts of *America.*

THE PILGRIM

In 1609 a small congregation of Separatists from the village of Scrooby in the west of England managed to flee to Holland, where the members hoped to practice their religion free from all ecclesiastical authority. Hardships, discontent, and fear drove them in 1620 to bargain for land in Virginia; bad seamanship and mismanagement took them, and some adventurers who came along for luck and financial gain, to New England; courage and necessity forced them to take over land to which they had no legal right. Virtually apotheosized in the nineteenth century, they became for us the Pilgrim Fathers. As Separatists, however, they were a minority sect in the Puritan movement. They wanted, simply enough, to be left alone to live and worship as they felt they must. After some early setbacks, their little colony prospered; they raised their crops, dealt in beaver pelts, got along with the Indians, and worshipped as they would; they were even able to buy out London investors in their enterprise. Theirs was to be an independent, communal, almost patriarchal society. But they were gradually drawn into the orbit of the colony established by orthodox Puritans at Massachusetts Bay. They joined the New England Confederacy in 1643, were merged with the Massachusetts Bay Colony in 1684, and so lost their separateness.

What the Plymouth colonists came to be for nineteenth-century Americans is made clearest by the narrative history, *Of Plymouth Plantation,* written by their perennial governor, William Bradford. When it was first printed in 1856, its very grace, dignity, matter-of-fact self-assurance, and simple yet practical idealism made, above all, for the myth and the cult of the Pilgrim Fathers. Myth and cult, however, and attendant snobbishness, sentimentality, and ancestor-worship cannot destroy the strength of Bradford and his fellows. This remains in *Of Plymouth Plantation*.

———————

Bibliographical Note. Of Plymouth Plantation (generally called *The History of Plymouth Plantation*) remains the great account of the Pilgrim enterprise; the best edition is that of W. C. Ford, in 2 vols. (Boston, 1912). A more freely, but nonetheless precisely, edited version is *Of Plymouth Plantation, 1620-1647,* ed. Samuel Eliot Morison (New York, 1953). A recent account, valuable because it sets Bradford's narrative in its historical-cultural context, is George F. Willison, *Saints and Strangers* (New York, 1945); it contains a detailed critical bibliography.

WILLIAM BRADFORD
(*1590-1657*)

Bibliographical Note. The most complete edition of *The History of Plymouth Plantation* is that of W. C. Ford, in 2 vols. (Boston, 1912); a more readily accessible scholarly edition is that of W. T. Davis (New York, 1908). The text of the following selections follows that of the Davis edition, pp. 44-48, 92-97, 106-111, 146-147, 390-391. On Bradford, see the article by S. E. Morison in *The Dictionary of American Biography;* on the *History,* see E. F. Bradford, "Conscious Art in Bradford's *History of Plymouth Plantation," New England Quarterly.* I (1928), 133-157.

from THE HISTORY OF PLYMOUTH PLANTATION
(*written 1620-1651*)

["REASONS AND CAUSES OF THEIR REMOVALL," 1609-1617]

After they had lived in this citie [Leyden] about some 11. or 12. years, (which is the more observable being the whole time of that famose truce[1] between that state and the Spaniards,) and sundrie of them were taken away by death, and many others begane to be well striken in years, the grave mistris Experience haveing taught them many things, those prudent governours with sundrie of the sagest members begane both deeply to apprehend their present dangers, and wisely to foresee the future, and thinke of timly remedy. In the agitation of their thoughts, and much discours of things hear aboute, at length they began to incline to this conclusion, of remoovall to some other place. Not out of any newfanglednes, or other such like giddie humor, by which men are oftentimes transported to their great hurt and danger, but for sundrie weightie and solid reasons; some of the cheefe of which I will hear breefly touch. And first, they saw and found by experience the hardnes of the place and countrie to be such, as few in comparison would come to them, and fewer that would bide it out, and continew with them. For many that came to them, and many more that desired to be with them, could not

---

[1] This truce, signed April 9, 1609, was to expire in 1621.—*Davis.*

25

endure that great labor and hard fare, with other inconveniences which they underwent and were contented with. But though they loved their persons, approved their cause, and honoured their sufferings, yet they left them as it weer weeping, as Orpah did her mother in law Naomie, or as those Romans did Cato in Utica, who desired to be excused and borne with, though they could not all be Catoes. For many, though they desired to injoye the ordinances of God in their puritie, and the libertie of the gospell with them, yet, alass, they admitted of bondage, with danger of conscience, rather than to indure these hardships; yea, some preferred and chose the prisons in England, rather then this libertie in Holland, with these afflictions. But it was thought that if a better and easier place of living could be had, it would draw many, and take away these discouragments. Yea, their pastor would often say, that many of those who both wrote and preached now against them, if they were in a place wher they might have libertie and live comfortably, they would then practise as they did.

2^{ly}· They saw that though the people generally bore all these difficulties very cherfully, and with a resolute courage, being in the best and strength of their years, yet old age began to steale on many of them, (and their great and continuall labours, with other crosses and sorrows, hastened it before the time,) so as it was not only probably thought, but apparently seen, that within a few years more they would be in danger to scatter, by necessities pressing them, or sinke under their burdens, or both. And therfore according to the devine proverb, that a wise man seeth the plague when it cometh, and hideth him selfe, Pro. 22. 3., so they like skillfull and beaten souldiers were fearfull either to be intrapped or surrounded by their enimies, so as they should neither be able to fight nor flie; and therfor thought it better to dislodge betimes to some place of better advantage and less danger, if any such could be found. Thirdly; as necessitie was a taskmaster over them, so they were forced to be such, not only to their servants, but in a sorte, to their dearest children; the which as it did not a litle wound the tender harts of many a loving father and mother, so it produced likwise sundrie sad and sorowful effects. For many of their children, that were of best dispositions and gracious inclinations, haveing lernde to bear the yoake in their youth, and willing to bear parte of their parents burden, were, often times, so oppressed with their hevie labours, that though their minds were free and willing, yet their bodies bowed under the weight of the same, and became decreped in their early youth; the vigor of nature being consumed in the very budd as it were. But that which was more lamentable, and of all sorowes most heavie to be borne, was that many of their children, by these occasions, and the great licentiousness of youth in that countrie, and the manifold temptations of the place, were drawne away by evill examples into extravagante and dangerous courses, getting the raines off their neks, and departing from their parents. Some became souldiers, others tooke upon them farr viages by sea, and other some worse courses, tending to dissolutnes and the danger of their soules, to the great greefe of their parents and dishonour of God. So that they saw their posteritie would be in danger to degenerate and be corrupted.

Lastly, (and which was not least), a great hope and inward zeall they had of laying some good foundation, or at least to make some way therunto, for the propagating and advancing the gospell of the kingdom of Christ in those remote parts of the world; yea, though they should be but even as stepping-stones unto others for the performing of so great a work.

These, and some other like reasons, moved them to undertake this resolution of their removall; the which they afterward prosecuted with so great difficulties, as by the sequell will appeare.

The place they had thoughts on was some of those vast and unpeopled countries of America, which are frutfull and fitt for habitation, being devoyd of all civill inhabitants, wher ther are only salvage and brutish men, which range up and downe, litle otherwise then the wild beasts of the same. This proposition being made publike and coming to the scaning of all, it raised many variable opinions amongst men, and caused many fears and doubts amongst them selves. Some, from their reasons and hops conceived, laboured to stirr up and incourage the rest to undertake and prosecute the same; others, againe, out of their fears, objected against it, and sought to diverte from it, aledging many things, and those neither unreasonable nor unprobable; as that it was a great designe, and subjecte to many unconceivable perills and dangers; as, besids the casulties of the seas (which none can be freed from) the length of the vioage was such, as the weake bodies of women and other persons worne out with age and traville (as many of them were) could never be able to endure. And yet if they should, the miseries of the land which they should be exposed unto, would be to hard to be borne; and lickly, some or all of them togeither, to consume and utterly to ruinate them. For ther they should be liable to famine, and nakednes, and the wante, in a maner, of all things. The chang of aire, diate, and drinking of water, would infecte their bodies with sore sickneses, and greevous diseases. And also those which should escape or overcome these difficulties, should yett be in continuall danger of the salvage people, who are cruell, barbarous, and most trecherous, being most furious in their rage, and merciles wher they over- come; not being contente only to kill, and take away life, but delight to tormente men in the most bloodie manner that may be; fleaing[2] some alive with the shells of fishes, cutting of the mem- bers and joynts of others by peesmeale, and broiling on the coles, eate the collops of their flesh in their sight whilst they live; with other cruelties horrible to be related. And surely it could not be thought but the very hearing of these things could not but move the very bowels of men to grate within them, and make the weake to quake and tremble. It was furder objected, that it would re- quire greater summes of money to furnish such a voiage, and to fitt them with necessaries, then their consumed estats would amounte too; and yett they must as well looke to be seconded with supplies,[3] as presently to be transported. Also many presidents of ill success, and lamentable misseries befalne others in the like designes, were easie to be found, and not forgotten to be aledged; besids their owne experience, in their former troubles and hard-

---

[2] Flaying.—*Davis.*
[3] *I. e.,* reinforcements.—*Davis.*

ships in their removall into Holand, and how hard a thing it was for them to live in that strange place, though it was a neighbour countrie, and a civill and rich comone wealth.

It was answered, that all great and honourable actions are accompanied with great difficulties, and must be both enterprised and overcome with answerable courages. It was granted the dangers were great, but not desperate; the difficulties were many, but not invincible. For though their were many of them likly, yet they were not cartaine; it might be sundrie if the things feared might never befale; others by providente care and the use of good means, might in a great measure be prevented; and all of them, through the help of God, by fortitude and patience, might either be borne, or overcome. True it was, that such atempts were not to be made and undertaken without good ground and reason; not rashly or lightly as many have done for curiositie or hope of gaine, etc. But their condition was not ordinarie; their ends were good and honourable; their calling lawfull, and urgente; and therfore they might expecte the blessing of God in their proceding. Yea, though they should loose their lives in this action, yet might they have comforte in the same, and their endeavors would be honourable. They lived hear but as men in exile, and in a poore condition; and as great miseries might possibly befale them in this place, for the 12. years of truce were now[4] out, and ther was nothing but beating of drumes, and preparing for warr, the events wherof are allway uncertaine. The Spaniard might prove as cruell as the salvages of America, and the famine and pestelence as sore hear as ther, and their libertie less to looke out for remedie. After many other perticuler things answered and aledged on both sids, it was fully concluded by the major parte, to put this designe in execution, and to prosecute it by the best means they could.

. . . . .

[THE VOYAGE, 1620]

. . . now all being compacte togeather in one shipe, they put to sea againe with a prosperus winde, which continued diverce days

---

[4] The truce between the Dutch and Spain would end in April, 1621.—*Davis.*

togeather, which was some incouragmente unto them; yet according to the usuall maner many were afflicted with seasicknes. And
I may not omite hear a spetiall worke of Gods providence. Ther
was a proud and very profane yonge man, one of the sea-men, of
a lustie, able body, which made him the more hauty; he would
allway be contemning the poor people in their sicknes, and cursing them dayly with greevous execrations, and did not let to tell
them, that he hoped to help to cast halfe of them over board
before they came to their jurneys end, and to make mery with
what they had; and if he were by any gently reproved, he would
curse and swear most bitterly. But it plased God before they came
halfe seas over, to smite this yong man with a greevous disease,
of which he dyed in a desperate maner, and so was him selfe the
first that was throwne overbord. Thus his curses light on his owne
head; and it was an astonishmente to all his fellows, for they
noted it to be the just hand of God upon him.

After they had injoyed faire winds and weather for a season,
they were incountred many times with crosse winds, and mette
with many feirce stormes, with which the shipe was shroudly[5]
shaken, and her upper works made very leakie; and one of the
maine beames in the midd ships was bowed and craked, which
put them in some fear that the shipe could not be able to performe
the vioage. So some of the cheefe of the company, perceiveing the
mariners to feare the suffisiencie of the shipe, as appeared by their
mutterings, they entred into serious consulltation with the m[r] and
other officers of the ship, to consider in time of the danger; and
rather to returne then to cast them selves into a desperate and inevitable perill. And truly ther was great distraction and differance
of opinion amongst the mariners them selves; faine would they
doe what could be done for their wages sake, (being now halfe
the seas over,) and on the other hand they were loath to hazard
their lives too desperately. But in examening of all opinions, the
m[r] and others affirmed they knew the ship to be stronge and firme
under water; and for the buckling of the maine beame, ther was

---

[5] Shrewdly, severely.—*Davis.*

a great iron scrue the passengers brought out of Holland, which would raise the beame into his place; the which being done, the carpenter and m[r] affirmed that with a post put under it, set firme in the lower deck, and otherways bounde, he would make it sufficiente. And as for the decks and uper workes they would calke them as well as they could, and though with the workeing of the ship they would not longe keepe stanch, yet ther would otherwise be not great danger, if they did not overpress her with sails. So they commited them selves to the will of God, and resolved to proseede. In sundrie of these stormes the winds were so feirce, and the seas so high, as they could not beare a knote of saile, but were forced to hull,[6] for diverce days togither. And in one of them, as they thus lay at hull, in a mighty storme, a lustie yonge man (called John Howland) coming upon some occasion above the grattings, was, with a seele[7] of the shipe throwne into [the] sea; but it pleased God that he caught hould of the top-saile halliards, which hunge over board, and rane out at length; yet he held his hould (though he was sundrie fadomes under water) till he was hald up by the same rope to the brime of the water, and then with a boat hooke and other means got into the shipe againe, and his life saved; and though he was something ill with it, yet he lived many years after, and became a profitable member both in church and commone wealthe. In all this viage ther died but one of the passengers, which was William Butten, a youth, servant to Samuell Fuller, when they drew near the coast. But to omite other things, (that I may be breefe,) after longe beating at sea they fell with that land which is called Cape Cod; the which being made and certainly knowne to be it, they were not a litle joyfull. After some deliberation had amongst them selves and with the m[r] of the ship, they tacked aboute and resolved to stande for the southward (the wind and weather being faire) to finde some place aboute Hudsons river for their habitation. But after they had sailed that course aboute halfe the day, they fell amongst deangerous shoulds and roring breakers, and they were so farr intangled

---

[6] To drift.—*Davis.*

[7] The "seele" of a ship is the toss in a rough sea.—*Davis.*

ther with as they conceived them selves in great danger; and the wind shrinking upon them withall, they resolved to bear up againe for the Cape, and thought them selves hapy to gett out of those dangers before night overtooke them, as by Gods providence they did. And the next day they gott into the Cape-harbor wher they ridd in saftie. A word or too by the way of this cape; it was thus first named by Capten Gosnole and his company, An°: 1602, and after by Capten Smith was caled Cape James; but it retains the former name amongst seamen. Also that pointe which first shewed those dangerous shoulds unto them, they called Pointe Care, and Tuckers Terrour; but the French and Dutch to this day call it Malabarr, by reason of those perilous shoulds, and the losses they have suffered their.

Being thus arived in a good harbor and brought safe to land, they fell upon their knees and blessed the God of heaven, who had brought them over the vast and furious ocean, and delivered them from all the periles and miseries therof, againe to set their feete on the firme and stable earth, their proper elemente. And no marvell if they were thus joyefull, seeing wise Seneca was so affected with sailing a few miles on the coast of his owne Italy; as he affirmed, that he had rather remaine twentie years on his way by land, then pass by sea to any place in a short time; so tedious and dreadfull was the same unto him.

But hear I cannot but stay and make a pause, and stand half amased at this poore peoples presente condition; and so I thinke will the reader too, when he well considers the same. Being thus passed the vast ocean, and a sea of troubles before in their prepara-tion (as may be remembred by that which wente before), they had now no friends to wellcome them, nor inns to entertaine or refresh their weatherbeaten bodys, no houses or much less townes to repaire too, to seeke for succoure. It is recorded in scripture[8] as a mercie to the apostle and his shipwraked company, that the bar-barians shewed them no smale kindnes in refreshing them, but these savage barbarians, when they mette with them (as after will

8 "Act. 28."—*Bradford*.

appeare) were readier to fill their sids full of arrows than otherwise. And for the season it was winter, and they that know the
winters of that cuntrie know them to be sharp and violent, and
subjecte to cruell and feirce stormes, deangerous to travill to
known places, much more to serch an unknown coast. Besids,
what could they see but a hidious and desolate wildernes, full of
wild beasts and willd men? and what multituds ther might be of
them they knew not. Neither could they, as it were, goe up to
the tope of Pisgah, to vew from this willdernes a more goodly
cuntrie to feed their hops; for which way soever they turnd their
eys (save upward to the heavens) they could have litle solace or
content in respecte of any outward objects. For summer being
done, all things stand upon them with a wetherbeaten face; and
the whole countrie, full of woods and thickets, represented a wild
and savage heiw. If they looked behind them, ther was the mighty
ocean which they had passed, and was now as a maine barr and
goulfe to seperate them from all the civill parts of the world. If it
be said they had a ship to sucour them, it is trew; but what heard
they daly from the m^r and company? but that with speede they
should looke out a place with their shallop, wher they would be
at some near distance; for the season was shuch as he would not
stirr from thence till a safe harbor was discovered by them wher
they would be, and he might goe without danger; and that victells
consumed apace, but he must and would keepe sufficient for them
selves and their returne. Yea, it was muttered by some, that if
they gott not a place in time, they would turne them and their
goods ashore and leave them. Let it also be considred what weake
hopes of supply and succoure they left behinde them, that might
bear up their minds in this sade condition and trialls they were
under; and they could not but be very smale. It is true, indeed,
the affections and love of their brethren at Leyden was cordiall
and entire towards them, but they had litle power to help them,
or them selves; and how the case stode betweene them and the
marchants at their coming away, hath allready been declared.
What could now sustaine them but the spirite of God and his
grace? May not and ought not the children of these fathers rightly

say: *Our faithers were Englishmen which came over this great ocean, and were ready to perish in this willdernes; but they cried unto the Lord, and he heard their voyce, and looked on their adversitie, etc. Let them therfore praise the Lord, because he is good, and his mercies endure for ever. Yea, let them which have been redeemed of the Lord, shew how he hath delivered them from the hand of the oppressour. When they wandered in the deserte willdernes out of the way, and found no citie to dwell in, both hungrie, and thirstie, their sowle was overwhelmed in them. Let them confess before the Lord his loving kindnes, and his wonderfull works before the sons of men.*

. . . . .

[THE MAYFLOWER COMPACT, EARLY HARDSHIPS, AND INDIAN AFFAIRS, 1620-1621]

I shall a litle returne backe and begine with a combination made by them before they came ashore, being the first foundation of their govermente in this place; occasioned partly by the discontented and mutinous speeches that some of the strangers amongst them had let fall from them in the ship—That when they came a shore they would use their owne libertie; for none had power to command them, the patente they had being for Virginia, and not for New-england, which belonged to an other Goverment, with which the Virginia Company had nothing to doe. And partly that shuch an acte by them done (this their condition considered) might be as firme as any patent, and in some respects more sure.

The forme was as followeth.

In the name of God, Amen. We whose names are under-writen, the loyall subjects of our dread soveraigne Lord, King James, by the grace of God, of Great Britaine, Franc, and Ireland king, defender of the faith, etc., haveing undertaken, for the glorie of God, and advancemente of the Christian faith, and honour of our king and countrie, a voyage to plant the first colonie in the Northerne parts of Virginia, doe by these presents solemnly and mutualy in the presence

of God, and one of another, covenant and combine our selves togeather into a civill body politick, for our better ordering and preservation and furtherance of the ends aforesaid; and by vertue hearof
to enacte, constitute, and frame such just and equall lawes, ordinances, acts, constitutions, and offices, from time to time, as shall be
thought most meete and convenient for the generall good of the
Colonie, unto which we promise all due submission and obedience.
In witnes wherof we have hereunder subscribed our names at Cap-
Codd the 11. of November, in the year of the raigne of our soveraigne
lord, King James, of England, France, and Ireland the eighteenth,
and of Scotland the fiftie fourth. An°: Dom. 1620.

After this they chose, or rather confirmed, Mr. John Carver (a
man godly and well approved amongst them) their Governour
for that year. And after they had provided a place for their goods,
or comone store, (which were long in unlading for want of boats,
foulnes of winter weather, and sicknes of diverce,) and begune
some small cottages for their habitation, as time would admitte,
they mette and consulted of lawes and orders, both for their civill
and military Govermente, as the necessitie of their condition did
require, still adding therunto as urgent occasion in severall times,
and as cases did require.

In these hard and difficulte beginings they found some dis-
contents and murmurings arise amongst some, and mutinous
speeches and carriags in other; but they were soone quelled and
overcome by the wisdome, patience, and just and equall carrage
of things by the Govr and better part, which clave faithfully togeather in the maine. But that which was most sadd and lamentable was, that in 2. or 3. moneths time halfe of their company
dyed, espetialy in Jan: and February, being the depth of winter,
and wanting houses and other comforts; being infected with the
scurvie and other diseases, which this long vioage and their in-
acomodate condition had brought upon them; so as ther dyed
some times 2. or 3. of a day, in the foresaid time; that of 100. and
odd persons, scarce 50. remained. And of these in the time of most
distres, ther was but 6. or 7. sound persons, who, to their great
comendations be it spoken, spared no pains, night nor day, but

with abundance of toyle and hazard of their owne health, fetched them woode, made them fires, drest them meat, made their beads, washed their lothsome cloaths, cloathed and uncloathed them; in a word, did all the homly and necessarie offices for them which dainty and quesie stomacks cannot endure to hear named; and all this willingly and cherfully, without any grudging in the least, shewing herein their true love unto their freinds and bretheren. A rare example and worthy to be remembred. Tow of these 7. were Mr. William Brewster, ther reverend Elder, and Myles Standish, ther Captein and military comander, unto whom my selfe, and many others, were much beholden in our low and sicke condition. And yet the Lord so upheld these persons, as in this generall calamity they were not at all infected either with sicknes, or lamnes. And what I have said of these, I may say of many others who dyed in this generall vissitation, and others yet living, that whilst they had health, yea, or any strength continuing, they were not wanting to any that had need of them. And I doute not but their recompense is with the Lord.

But I may not hear pass by an other remarkable passage not to be forgotten. As this calamitie fell among the passengers that were to be left here to plant, and were hasted a shore and made to drinke water, that the sea-men might have the more bear,[9] and one in his sicknes desiring but a small cann of beere, it was answered, that if he were their owne father he should have none; the disease begane to fall amongst them also, so as allmost halfe of their company dyed before they went away, and many of their officers and lustyest men, as the boatson, gunner, 3. quarter-maisters, the cooke, and others. At which the m^r was something strucken and sent to the sick a shore and tould the Govr he should send for beer for them that had need of it, though he drunke water homward bound. But now amongst his company ther was farr another kind of carriage in this miserie then amongst the passengers; for they that before had been boone companions in drinking and joyllity in the time of their health and wellfare,

---

[9] "Which was this author him selfe."—*Bradford*.

begane now to deserte one another in this calamitie, saing they would not hasard ther lives for them, they should be infected by coming to help them in their cabins, and so, after they came to dye by it, would doe litle or nothing for them, but if they dyed let them dye. But such of the passengers as were yet abord shewed them what mercy they could, which made some of their harts relente, as the boatson (and some others), who was a prowd yonge man, and would often curse and scofe at the passengers; but when he grew weak, they had compassion on him and helped him; then he confessed he did not deserve it at their hands, he had abused them in word and deed. O! saith he, you, I now see, shew your love like Christians indeed one to another, but we let one another lye and dye like doggs. Another lay cursing his wife, saing if it had not ben for her he had never come this unlucky viage, and anone cursing his felows, saing he had done this and that, for some of them, he had spente so much, and so much, amongst them, and they were now weary of him, and did not help him, having need. Another gave his companion all he had, if he died, to help him in his weaknes; he went and got a litle spise and made him a mess of meat once or twise, and because he dyed not so soone as he expected, he went amongst his fellows, and swore the rogue would cousen him, he would see him choaked before he made him any more meate; and yet the pore fellow dyed before morning.

All this while the Indians came skulking about them, and would sometimes show them selves aloofe of, but when any aproached near them, they would rune away. And once they stoale away their tools wher they had been at worke, and were gone to diner. But about the 16. of March a certaine Indian came bouldly amongst them, and spoke to them in broken English, which they could well understand, but marvelled at it. At length they understood by discourse with him, that he was not of these parts, but belonged to the eastrene parts, wher some English-ships came to fhish, with whom he was aquainted, and could name sundrie of them by their names, amongst whom he had gott his language. He became proftable to them in aquainting them with many things concerning the state of the cuntry in the east-parts wher he lived, which was afterwards profitable unto them; as also of the people hear, of their names, number, and strength; of their situation and distance from this place, and who was cheefe amongst them. His name was Samaset; he tould them also of another Indian whos name was Squanto, a native of this place, who had been in England and could speake better English then him selfe. Being, after some time of entertainmente and gifts, dismist, a while after he came againe, and 5. more with him, and they brought againe all the tooles that were stolen away before, and made way for the coming of their great Sachem, called Massasoyt; who, about 4. or 5. days after, came with the cheefe of his freinds and other attendance, with the aforesaid Squanto. With whom, after frendly entertainment, and some gifts given him, they made a peace with him (which hath now continued this 24. years) in these terms.

1. That neither he nor any of his, should injurie or doe hurte to any of their peopl.

2. That if any of his did any hurte to any of theirs, he should send the offender, that they might punish him.

3. That if any thing were taken away from any of theirs, he should cause it to be restored; and they should doe the like to his.

4. If any did unjustly warr against him, they would aide him; if any did warr against them, he should aide them.

5. He should send to his neighbours confederats, to certifie them of this, that they might not wrong them, but might be likewise comprised in the conditions of peace.

6. That when ther men came to them, they should leave their bows and arrows behind them.

After these things he returned to his place caled Sowams,[10] some 40. mile from this place, but Squanto continued with them, and was their interpreter, and was a spetiall instrument sent of God for their good beyond their expectation. He directed them how to set their corne, wher to take fish, and to procure other

---

[10] On the present site of Warren, R. I.—*Davis*.

comodities, and was also their pilott to bring them to unknowne places for their profitt, and never left them till he dyed. He was a native of this place, and scarce any left alive besids him selfe.

. . . . .

[SOCIAL AND ECONOMIC PROBLEMS, 1623]

. . . they begane to thinke how they might raise as much corne as they could, and obtaine a beter crope then they had done, that they might not still thus languish in miserie. At length, after much debate of things, the Govr (with the advise of the cheefest amongst them) gave way that they should set corne every man for his owne perticuler, and in that regard trust to them selves; in all other things to goe on in the generall way as before. And so assigned to every family a parcell of land, according to the pro- portion of their number for that end, only for present use (but made no devission for inheritance), and ranged all boys and youth under some familie. This had very good success; for it made all hands very industrious, so as much more corne was planted then other waise would have bene by any means the Govr or any other could use, and saved him a great deall of trouble, and gave farr better contente. The women now wente willingly into the feild, and tooke their litle-ons with them to set corne, which before would aledg weaknes, and inabilitie; whom to have compelled would have bene thought great tiranie and oppression.

The experience that was had in this commone course and con- dition, tried sundrie years, and that amongst godly and sober men, may well evince the vanitie of that conceite of Platos and other ancients, applauded by some of later times;—that the taking away of propertie, and bringing in communitie into a comone wealth, would make them happy and florishing; as if they were wiser then God. For this comunitie (so farr as it was) was found to breed much confusion and discontent, and retard much imploy- ment that would have been to their benefite and comforte. For the yong-men that were most able and fitte for labour and service did repine that they should spend their time and streingth to worke for other mens wives and children, with out any recompence. The strong, or man of parts, had no more in devission of victails and cloaths, then he that was weake and not able to doe a quarter the other could; this was thought injuestice. The aged and graver men to be ranked and equalised in labours, and victails, cloaths, etc., with the meaner and yonger sorte, thought it some indignite and disrespect unto them. And for mens wives to be commanded to doe servise for other men, as dresing their meate, washing their cloaths, etc., they deemd it a kind of slaverie, neither could many husbands well brooke it. Upon the poynte all being to have alike, and all to doe alike, they thought them selves in the like condition, and one as good as another; and so, if it did not cut of those relations that God hath set amongst men, yet it did at least much diminish and take of the mutuall respects that should be preserved amongst them. And would have bene worse if they had been men of another condition. Let none objecte this is men's corruption, and nothing to the course it selfe. I answer, seeing all men have this corruption in them, God in his wisdome saw another course fiter for them.

But to returne. After this course setled, and by that their corne was planted, all ther victails were spente, and they were only to rest on Gods providence; at night not many times knowing wher to have a bitt of any thing the next day. And so, as one well observed, had need to pray that God would give them their dayly brade, above all people in the world. Yet they bore these wants with great patience and allacritie of spirite, and that for so long a time as for the most parte of 2. years; which makes me remember what Peter Martire writs, (in magnifying the Spaniards) in his 5. Decade, pag. 208.[11] *They* (saith he) *led a miserable life for 5. days togeather, with the parched graine of maize only, and that not to saturitie;* and then concluds, *that shuch pains, shuch labours, and shuch hunger, he thought none living which is not a Spaniard could have endured.* But alass! these, when they had maize (that is, Indean corne) they thought it as good as a feast, and wanted not only for 5. days togeather, but some time 2. or 3.

---

[11] Peter Martyr of Anghiera, *Decades de Rebus Oceanicis et Novo Orbe,* the great Spanish history of America, translated into English by Richard Eden.—*Davis.*

months togeather, and neither had bread nor any kind of corne.
Indeed, in an other place, in his 2. Decade, page 94. he mentions
how others of them were worse put to it, wher they were faine
to eate doggs, toads, and dead men, and so dyed almost all. From
these extremities they [the] Lord in his goodnes kept these his
people, and in their great wants preserved both their lives and
healthes; let his name have the praise. Yet let me hear make use
of his conclusion, which in some sorte may be applied to this people: *That with their miseries they opened a way to these new-
lands; and after these stormes, with what ease other men came to
inhabite in them, in respecte of the calamities these men suffered;
so as they seeme to goe to a bride feaste wher all things are provided for them.*

. . . . .

[THE WEAKENING OF THE PILGRIM WAY, 1644]

Many having left this place (as is before noted) by reason of
the straightnes and barrennes of the same, and their finding of
better accommodations elsewher, more sutable to their ends and
minds; and sundrie others still upon every occasion desiring their
dismissions, the church begane seriously to thinke whether it
were not better joyntly to remove to some other place, then to be
thus weakened, and as it were insensibly dissolved. Many meetings and much consultation was held hearaboute, and diverse
were mens minds and opinions. Some were still for staying togeather in this place, aledging men might hear live, if they would
be contente with their condition; and that it was not for wante
or necessitie so much that they removed, as for the enriching of
them selves. Others were resolute upon removall, and so signified
that hear they could not stay; but if the church did not remove,
they must; insomuch as many were swayed, rather then ther
should be a dissolution, to condescend to a removall, if a fitt place
could be found, that might more conveniently and comfortablie
receive the whole, with such accession of others as might come to
them, for their better strength and subsistence; and some such
like cautions and limitations. So as, with the afforesaide provissos,

the greater parte consented to a removall to a place called Nawsett, which had been superficially viewed and the good will of the purchassers (to whom it belonged) obtained, with some addition thertoo from the Courte. But now they begane to see their errour, that they had given away already the best and most commodious places to others, and now wanted them selves; for this place was about 50. myles from hence, and at an outside of the countrie, remote from all society; also, that it would prove so straite, as it would not be competente to receive the whole body, much less be capable of any addition or increase; so as (at least in a shorte time) they should be worse ther then they are now hear. The which, with sundery other like considerations and inconveniences, made them chaing their resolutions; but such as were before resolved upon removall tooke advantage of this agreemente, and wente on notwithstanding, neither could the rest hinder them, they haveing made some beginning. And thus was this poore church left, like an anciente mother, growne olde, and forsaken of her children, (though not in their affections,) yett in regarde of their bodily presence and personall helpfullness. Her anciente members being most of them worne away by death; and these of later time being like children translated into other families, and she like a widow left only to trust in God. Thus she that had made many rich became her selfe poore.

THE PURITAN

The world which Puritans made in New England was under the firm and absolute control of an inscrutable God. It was a world which existed solely for the glorification of that God, a world in which men had to find their place, accept it, and thereby glorify Him. God was all; man had fallen into nothingness and could hope to rise again only if God should so decree. Each man was predestined for eternal salvation or damnation. Although man might feel himself elected to eternal salvation, he could never feel absolutely sure. He could only work and worship, watch and wait, live in this world as God had decreed.

Such was the Puritan's understanding of the world and his place in it. Behind this understanding lay the individualizing forces of the Protestant revolution, the rise of a class of self-made enterprising men, and a revival—principally in the work of Calvin and his followers—of the theology of Saint Augustine. In their sense of themselves as individuals, Puritans were aware of the immense and terrifying gulf between man and God, of human incompleteness and imperfection. This was the sense of sin, and of humility and abasement in the face of that sin. The whole effort of Puritan thinking and living was so to comprehend sin as to live bravely, resignedly, and intelligently with it; so to understand the necessity of living hard in this world, with perhaps only hell in view, as to live righteously; so to justify God's way to man as to build His Commonwealth on the Massachusetts earth.

The devout, upper middle-class Englishmen—headed by learned humanists from Cambridge University—who went to Massachusetts in the 1630's knew that it was their special mission to purify the Church and to restore it to its proper place at the center of society; it was only through the Church and its ministers and teachers that men could learn of their individual sinfulness, of the place of that sinfulness in God's scheme of things, and of the necessity to work and worship in this world. They were so sure of their rightness that they refused to call themselves Separatists (as had the Pilgrims) and insisted that only they were members of the True Church—and thus of the True Holy Commonwealth. All others had somehow been separated, as they said, from the path of righteousness. If the Puritans were denying the authority of the English Church, its rituals, and its government, they were denying from within the Church, not from without; they could say that their Church had been contaminated and that they would purify it. They were not revolutionaries; they feared and hated dissenters and dissidence. If they were moving away from the authoritarianism of the English Church as the English Church had moved away from the authoritarianism of the Roman Catholic Church, they were not moving into libertarian thinking. Their true church was an absolute church. They could countenance no way but their own.

What the New England Puritans had found was a new principle of order and authority which was to take the place of the old, which should be all the more rigorously held to because it was so much truer than the old. Their new principle stemmed from a new understanding of the nature of the sinful individual and his role in society and in religion. If the individual was free of one kind of external authority, he was in the power of another. This was the authority expressed in the Puritan Theocratic State, certainly as oppressive as the Stuart state which it tried to escape, certainly more oppressive than the Cromwellian state which was its English counterpart. Politically, the record of Puritan New England is one of righteous oppression rising out of righteous authority. Yet, viewed in a twentieth-century perspective, it is the psychological and philosophical source of this authority—the notion of the sinful individual and his duties and destiny, not its expression in social and political forms, which is our heritage from

Puritanism and which we should remark as we read the Puritan record.

The Puritans possessed a myth which contained the germ of all their truths—theological, philosophic, scientific, political, and esthetic. This was Covenant Theology—a synthesis of their Augustinian, Calvinist Christianity and their sense of social and economic necessity. In the beginning, according to the myth, God had contracted with Adam in a Covenant of Works; Adam had only to perform certain duties in order to live in his paradise. But, as God had foreknown, Adam willfully broke this contract, gained knowledge but lost his simple clarity of understanding, and so doomed all men after him. Then God's Son contracted with His Father in a Covenant of Grace, by the terms of which He would sacrifice Himself so that God would save a few sons of Adam. As a result, some men were visited with God's irresistible Grace and so elected for eternal salvation. Men had no choice in the matter, only hope. Paradoxically, they might learn more of their hope if they would refine the very instruments of knowledge which, imperfect and misleading, had been gained by Adam in his fall. So it was the duty of men to study, to hope, to wait, and to work—to make themselves more and more aware of their worthlessness, to know that worthlessness so well as to find it overpoweringly right. Thus the sweetness, as it was said, of the sense of sin; thus the hope against hope of election; thus the obligation to accept the authority of those elect in Puritan society; thus the fierce optimism and fortitude—even in the face of damnation; thus the intense and exhilarating certainty that all was right in the world, that everything made sense, that good and bad, sin and sinning, life and death, all were part of that eternal order which glorified God.

New England Puritan society as it took shape was held firmly together by a Civil Covenant which was taken to duplicate the Holy Covenant. Conditions of environment and situation pulled men together into urban and semirural settlements and prospered them in their trading, fishing, farming, and shipbuilding. Theocratically organized, that society was ruled by the Elect who were full church members and who could vote. Practically, worldly goods seemed to go along with spiritual goods; somehow the Elect were also the well-to-do, and work was obviously worship. One who newly felt himself to be of the Elect was required to undergo rigorous examination to prove that he was. Here, if ever, was a stable society.

Yet in the 1650's, as even men who were not of the Elect began to prosper in the new world, work and worship inevitably came to be dissociated; unfranchised Massachusetts citizens felt dissatisfied with the oppressive rule of theocrats; proving oneself to be of the Elect seemed less and less a dire necessity; evidence of eternal salvation and the right to vote no longer seemed necessarily related. A new world of reasonable men, the world of the Enlightenment, of the Royal Society, Newton, and Locke, began slowly but surely to come into the Puritan view. Puritans tried to compromise with that world; but compromise ultimately meant the death of Puritanism, absolute separation of church and state, an optimistic view of human nature, and the birth of democratic liberalism. The initial Puritan move away from religious authority could not itself be halted. Puritanism had established not only the possibility of the primacy of the individual, but even of secular individualism as it was to develop in eighteenth-century America. The existence of a man like Benjamin Franklin was made possible, perhaps necessary.

So the enlightened New Englander of the later eighteenth century could not be a Puritan. It was he, not his Puritan ancestors, who was to help write the Declaration of Independence. In rationalizing Puritan theology and the Puritan sense of sin out of existence, he was to discover a new non-theological basis for individualism and a faith in the possibility of freedom for all; and he was to help found a nation officially and optimistically dedicated to such individualism and such freedom. We can say now what he could not: that the drive towards individualism and freedom was his—and our—heritage from Puritanism. Moreover, recently we have discovered that even if we, like our Revolutionary ancestors, cannot accept the Puritan mythical, theological explanation of the origins of individualism and freedom, we are once more finding it rather easy to accept the Puritan analysis of the risks and uncertainties in them. We are perhaps recovering even something of the Puritan sense of sin.

The selections here printed manifest the Puritan spirit in various forms and in various stages. Winthrop's speech on liberty and the Hooker and Oakes sermons exhibit the Puritan certainty of the role of sinful individuals in God's world. The piece from the Cotton-Williams debate and the letter of Williams to the townspeople of Providence push the libertarian implications of Puritan individualism to an extreme which, so Puritans felt, would make life in society impossible; it was Williams' glory that he fully comprehended those implications and their difficulties. Sewall's diary shows us the Puritan as an eminently practical, full-blooded man, striving, above all, to be honest with his sinful self. Mrs. Rowlandson's narrative makes out of the horrors of her captivity a full and deep religious experience. The selections from Cotton Mather's *Magnalia* show the Puritan of the third generation looking back to his noble ancestors, trying to face down the iniquities of his fellows who will not be proper Puritans; the selection from his *Christian Philosopher* shows an attempt to prove that the world revealed by the new science only demonstrates eternal Christian truth—in short, a Puritan view of the argument from design. The Puritan poems illustrate variously the Puritan faith in the meaningful order of the world. The anagram drawn from a proper name, the structure of theology, a natural event, or a Biblical text —each is to be expanded poetically so as to draw out its full religious significance; the richness of the world—felt fully—contains in itself such a religious significance; esthetics functions as a form of theology; and the poems vary from Wigglesworth's widely known public doggerel to Taylor's unpublished private and sensitive improvisation. Finally, the selections from Wise and Edwards show the Puritan mind discovering the world of the Enlightenment. Wise embraces it; and Edwards fights it to a stand-still. It is fitting to end with Edwards since his is the last and greatest of Puritan minds. The *Personal Narrative* outlines his own ultimately mystical sense of religion and religious values; and the rest of the writings show him demonstrating in sermonizing rhetoric or in rational, psychological analysis the existence and absolute primacy of such a mystical sense. In Edwards we can know most fully the Puritan sense of the imperfection of the individual who strives, in his human imperfection, to understand himself and his destiny. In Edwards we can know most fully the basic truths of the Puritan insight into the nature of the individual.

Bibliographical Note. The best guide to the voluminous literature of Puritanism is the collection of texts, with introduction and critical bibliographies, edited by Perry Miller and Thomas Johnson, *The Puritans* (Cincinnati, 1938). Substantially the same selection of texts has been edited by Miller as *The American Puritans* (New York, 1956). Miller has studied Puritan intellectual history in three basic books, *Orthodoxy in Massachusetts* (Cambridge, 1933), *The New England Mind: The Seventeenth Century* (New York, 1939), and *The New England Mind from Colony to Province* (Cambridge, 1953). An earlier study, to be modified by Miller's work, is Herbert Schneider, *The Puritan Mind* (New York, 1930). The later history of Puritan theology is examined in Joseph Haroutunian, *Piety and Morality* (New York, 1932). A brilliant brief study of American and English Puritanism, bringing to focus all recent studies of the subject, is Alan Simpson, *Puritanism in Old and New England* (Chicago, 1955). The great study of the religious-economic significance of Puritanism in western European history is Max Weber, *The Protestant Ethic and the Spirit of Capitalism,* trans. Talcott Parsons (London, 1930); Weber's work is followed by one focused particularly on English (and, incidentally, American) Puritanism, R. H. Tawney, *Religion and the Rise of Capitalism* (New York, 1926). New England Puritan society is best to be seen in two studies by Samuel Eliot Morison, *Builders of the Bay Colony* (Boston, 1930) and *The Puritan Pronaos* (New York, 1936). On the nature and achievement of Puritan literature, see Kenneth Murdock, *Literature and Theology in Colonial New England* (Cambridge, 1949).

JOHN WINTHROP

(*1588-1649*)

[*Bibliographical Note.* Winthrop's *Journal,* which covers his lifetime, is available in a two-volume edition, ed. James Savage (Boston,
1853) and in another two-volume edition, ed. J. K. Hosmer (New
York, 1908); it is now being printed definitively as part of the *Winthrop Papers,* published by the Massachusetts Historical Society. The
text of this selection from the *Journal* follows that in Perry Miller
and Thomas Johnson, eds., *The Puritans* (New York, 1938), pp. 205-
207, which in turn derives from Savage's text of the *Journal.* On
Winthrop see R. C. Winthrop, *Life and Letters of John Winthrop,*
2 vols. (Boston 1864-1867); S. E. Morison, *Builders of the Bay Colony*
(Boston, 1930), pp. 51-104; and S. Gray, "The Political Thought of
John Winthrop," *New England Quarterly,* III (1930), 681-705.]

from THE JOURNAL*

[SPEECH TO THE GENERAL COURT, JULY 3, 1645]

I suppose something may be expected from me, upon this
charge that is befallen me,[1] which moves me to speak now to you;
yet I intend not to intermeddle in the proceedings of the court,
or with any of the persons concerned therein. Only I bless God,
that I see an issue of this troublesome business. I also acknowledge
the justice of the court, and, for mine own part, I am well satisfied, I was publicly charged, and I am publicly and legally acquitted, which is all I did expect or desire. And though this be
sufficient for my justification before men, yet not so before the
God, who hath seen so much amiss in my dispensations (and even
in this affair) as calls me to be humble. For to be publicly and
criminally charged in this court, is matter of humiliation, (and I
desire to make a right use of it,) notwithstanding I be thus acquitted. If her father had spit in her face, (saith the Lord con-

---

* Reprinted from *The Puritans,* edited by Perry Miller and Thomas Johnson
and used with permission of the American Book Company.

[1] Winthrop had been acquitted of charges that he had exceeded his authority as
a magistrate.

cerning Miriam,) should she not have been ashamed seven days?
Shame had lien upon her, whatever the occasion had been. I am
unwilling to stay you from your urgent affairs, yet give me leave
(upon this special occasion) to speak a little more to this assembly. It may be of some good use, to inform and rectify the judgments of some of the people, and may prevent such distempers
as have arisen amongst us. The great questions that have troubled the country, are about the authority of the magistrates and
the liberty of the people. It is yourselves who have called us to this
office, and being called by you, we have our authority from God,
in way of an ordinance, such as hath the image of God eminently
stamped upon it, the contempt and violation whereof hath been
vindicated with examples of divine vengeance. I entreat you to
consider, that when you choose magistrates, you take them from
among yourselves, men subject to like passions as you are. Therefore when you see infirmities in us, you should reflect upon your
own, and that would make you bear the more with us, and not be
severe censurers of the failings of your magistrates, when you
have continual experience of the like infirmities in yourselves and
others. We account him a good servant, who breaks not his covenant. The covenant between you and us is the oath you have taken
of us, which is to this purpose, that we shall govern you and judge
your causes by the rules of God's laws and our own, according to
our best skill. When you agree with a workman to build you a ship
or house, etc., he undertakes as well for his skill as for his faithfulness, for it is his profession, and you pay him for both. But when
you call one to be a magistrate, he doth not profess nor undertake to have sufficient skill for that office, nor can you furnish him
with gifts, etc., therefore you must run the hazard of his skill and
ability. But if he fail in faithfulness, which by his oath he is bound
unto, that he must answer for. If it fall out that the case be clear
to common apprehension, and the rule clear also, if he transgress
here, the error is not in the skill, but in the evil of the will: it
must be required of him. But if the case be doubtful, or the rule
doubtful, to men of such understanding and parts as your magis-

trates are, if your magistrates should err here, yourselves must bear it.

For the other point concerning liberty, I observe a great mistake in the country about that. There is a twofold liberty, natural (I mean as our nature is now corrupt) and civil or federal. The first is common to man with beasts and other creatures. By this, man, as he stands in relation to man simply, hath liberty to do what he lists; it is a liberty to evil as well as to good. This liberty is incompatible and inconsistent with authority, and cannot endure the least restraint of the most just authority. The exercise and maintaining of this liberty makes men grow more evil, and in time to be worse than brute beasts: omnes sumus licentia deteriores. This is that great enemy of truth and peace, that wild beast, which all the ordinances of God are bent against, to restrain and subdue it. The other kind of liberty I call civil or federal, it may also be termed moral, in reference to the covenant between God and man, in the moral law, and the politic covenants and constitutions, amongst men themselves. This liberty is the proper end and object of authority, and cannot subsist without it; and it is a liberty to that only which is good, just, and honest. This liberty you are to stand for, with the hazard (not only of your goods, but) of your lives, if need be. Whatsoever crosseth this, is not authority, but a distemper thereof. This liberty is maintained and exercised in a way of subjection to authority; it is of the same kind of liberty wherewith Christ hath made us free. The woman's own choice makes such a man her husband; yet being so chosen, he is her lord, and she is to be subject to him, yet in a way of liberty, not of bondage; and a true wife accounts her subjection her honor and freedom, and would not think her condition safe and free, but in her subjection to her husband's authority. Such is the liberty of the church under the authority of Christ, her king and husband; his yoke is so easy and sweet to her as a bride's ornaments; and if through forwardness or wantonness, etc., she shake it off, at any time, she is at no rest in her spirit, until she take it up again; and whether her lord smiles upon her, and embraceth her in his arms, or whether he frowns, or rebukes, or smites her, she apprehends the sweetness of his love in all, and is refreshed, supported, and instructed by every such dispensation of his authority over her. On the other side, ye know who they are that complain of this yoke and say, let us break their bands, etc., we will not have this man to rule over us. Even so, brethren, it will be between you and your magistrates. If you stand for your natural corrupt liberties, and will do what is good in your own eyes, you will not endure the least weight of authority, but will murmur, and oppose, and be always striving to shake off that yoke; but if you will be satisfied to enjoy such civil and lawful liberties, such as Christ allows you, then will you quietly and cheerfully submit unto that authority which is set over you, in all the administrations of it, for your good. Wherein, if we fail at any time, we hope we shall be willing (by God's assistance) to hearken to good advice from any of you, or in any other way of God; so shall your liberties be preserved, in upholding the honor and power of authority amongst you.

ROGER WILLIAMS
(*c. 1603-1683*)

Bibliographical Note. Williams' writings have been collected in *Publications of the Narragansett Club*, I-VI (1866-1874). The texts here printed follow this edition, IV, 493-501 and VI, 278-280. The best biography of Williams is S. H. Brockunier, *The Irrepressible Democrat: Roger Williams* (New York, 1940); the best study of his thought, although it is too unsympathetic towards Williams' adversaries, is J. E. Ernst, *The Political Thought of Roger Williams* (Seattle, 1929). The best balanced, though brief, study is Perry Miller, *Roger Williams* (Indianapolis, 1953).

from THE BLOODY TENENT YET MORE BLOODY
(1651)

["THE PORTRAITURE OF THE BLOUDIE TENENT"]

Truth. Christ Jesus the *Sun* of *Righteousnesse* hath broke forth, and dayly, will, to a *brighter* and *brighter Discoverie* of this deformed *Ethiopian:* And for my selfe I must proclaime, before the most holy *God, Angells* and *Men,* that (what ever other *white* and heavenly *Tenents* Mr *Cotton* houlds)[1] yet this is a *fowle*, a *black*, and a *bloudie Tenent.*

The Portraiture of the Bloudie Tenent.

A *Tenent* of high *Blasphemie* against the *God* of *Peace,* the *God* of *Order,* who hath of one *Bloud,* made all *Mankinde,* to dwell upon the face of the Earth, now, all *confounded* and *destroyed* in their *Civill Beings* and *Subsistences,* by mutuall flames of *warre* from their feverall respective *Religions* and *Consciences.*

---

[1] This passage, in which Truth and Peace speak, concludes the tract, which is itself the last in a series of debates between Williams and John Cotton on freedom of belief and worship. Cotton had defended Puritan persecution of those who would not conscientiously subscribe to Puritan beliefs. Williams here is searching out the full implications of this "bloudie tenent of persecution for cause of conscience."

A *Tenent warring* against the *Prince* of *Peace, Christ Jesus,* denying his *Appearance* and *Comming* in the *Flesh,* to put an end to, and *abolish* the *shadowes* of that *ceremoniall* and *typicall* Land of *Canaan.*

Luc. 9.
Prov. 9.

A *Tenent* fighting against the sweete *end* of his *comming,* which was not to destroy mens *Lives,* for their *Religions,* but to save them, by the meeke and peaceable *Invitations* and *perswasions* of his peaceable *wisdomes Maidens.*

A *Tenent* fowly charging his *Wisedome, Faithfullnes* and *Love,* in so poorly providing such *Magistrates* and *Civill Powers* all the *World* over, as might effect so great a *charge* pretended to be committed to them.

A *Tenent* lamentably guilty of his most precious *bloud,* shed in the *bloud* of so many hundreth thousand of his poore *servants* by the *civill powers* of the *World,* pretending to suppresse *Blasphemies, Heresies, Idolatries, Superstition,* &c.

A *Tenent* fighting with the *Spirit* of *Love, Holines,* and *Meeknes,* by kindling fiery *Spirits of false zeale* and *Furie,* when yet such *Spirits* know not of what *Spirit* they are.

A *Tenent* fighting with those mighty *Angels* who stand up for the peace of the *Saints,* against *Persia, Grecia,* &c. and so consequently, all other *Nations,* who fighting for their severall *Religions,* and against the *Truth,* leave no *Roome* for such as feare and love the *Lord* on the Earth.

A *Tenent*, against which the blessed *Soules* under the *Altar* cry loud for *vengeance*, this *Tenent* having cut their *Throats*, torne out their *Hearts*, and powred forth their *Bloud* in all *Ages*, as the onely *Hereticks* and *Blasphemers* in the World.

A *Tenent* which no *Uncleannes*, no *Adulterie*, *Incest*, *Sodomie*, or *Beastialitie* can equall, this *ravishing* and forcing (*explicitly* or *implicitly*) the very *Soules* and *Consciences* of all the *Nations* and *Inhabitants* of the *World*.

A *Tenent* that puts out the very *eye* of all true *Faith*, which cannot but be as free and voluntarie as any *Virgin* in the *World*, in *refusing* or *embracing* any *Spirituall offer* or *object*.

A *Tenent* loathsome and ugly (in the eyes of the *God* of *Heaven*, and serious sonnes of men) I say, loathsome with the palpable *filths* of *grosse dissimulation* and *hypocrisie:* Thousands of *Peoples* and whole *Nations*, compelld by this *Tenent* to put on the sowle *vizard* of *Religious hypocrisie*, for feare of *Lawes*, *losses* and *punishments*, and for the keeping and hoping for of *favour*, *libertie*, *wordly commoditie*, &c.

A *Tenent* wofully guiltie of hardning all false and *deluded Consciences* (of whatsoever *Sect*, *Faction*, *Heresie*, or *Idolatrie*, though never so *horrid* and *blasphemous*) by *cruelties* and *violences* practiced against them: all false *Teachers* and their *Followers* (ordinarily) contracting a *Brawnie* and *steelie hardnesse* from their *sufferings* for their *Consciences*.

A *Tenent* that shuts and bars out the gracious *prophecies* and *promises* and *discoveries* of the most glorious *Sun* of *Righteousnes, Christ Jesus,* that burnes up the holy *Scriptures,* and forbids them (upon the point) to be read in *English,* or that any *tryall* or *search,* or (truly) free *disquisition* be made by them: when the most able, diligent and conscionable *Readers* must pluck forth their own *eyes,* and be forced to reade by the (which foever *prædominant*) *Cleargies Spectacles.*

A *Tenent* that *seales up* the spirituall *graves* of all men, *Jewes* and *Gentiles,* (and consequently stands guiltie of the *damnation* of all men) since no *Preachers,* nor *Trumpets of Christ* himselfe may call them out, but such as the severall and respective *Nations* of the *World* themselves allow of.

A *Tenent* that fights against the *common principles* of all *Civilitie,* and the very *civill being* and *combinations* of men in *Nations, Cities,* &c. by commixing (*explicitly* or *implicitly*) a *spirituall* and *civill State* together, and so confounding and overthrowing the *puritie* and *strength* of both.

A *Tenent* that kindles the devouring *flames* of *combustions* and *warres* in most *Nations* of the *World,* and (if *God* were not infinitely gracious) had almost ruind the *English, French,* the *Scotch* and *Irish,* and many other *Nations, Germane, Polonian, Hungarian, Bohemian,* &c.

A *Tenent* that bowes downe the *backs* and *necks* of all *civill States* and *Magistrates, Kings* and *Emperours,* under the proud feete of that *man* and *monster* of *sinne* and *pride* the *Pope,* and all *Popish* and proud *Cleargie-men* rendring such *Laicks* and *Seculars* (as they call them) but slavish *Executioners* (upon the point) of their most imperious *Synodicall Decrees* and *Sentences*.

A *Tenent* that renders the highest *civill Magistrates* and *Ministers* of *Justice* (the *Fathers* and *Gods* of their *Countries*) either odious or lamentably grievous unto the very best *Subjects* by either clapping or keeping on, the *iron yoakes* of *cruellest oppression*. No *yoake* or *bondage* comparably so grievous, as that upon the Soules necke of mens *Religion* and *Consciences*.

A *Tenent*, all besprinckled with the *bloudie murthers, stobs, poysonings, pistollings, powderplots*, &c. against many famous *Kings, Princes,* and *States*, either actually performed or attempted, in *France, England, Scotland, Low-Countries,* and other *Nations*.

A *Tenent* all *red* and *bloudie* with those most *barbarous* and *Tyger*-like *Massacres,* of so many thousand and ten thousands formerly in *France,* and other parts, and so lately and so horribly in *Ireland:* of which, what ever causes be assigned, this chiefly will be found the true, and while this continues (to wit, *violence* against *Conscience*) this *bloudie Issue,* sooner or later, must *breake forth* againe (except *God* wonderfully stop it) in *Ireland* and other places too.

A *Tenent* that *stunts* the *growth* and *flourishing* of the most likely and hopefullest *Commonweales* and *Countries*, while *Consciences*, the *best*, and the *best* deserving *Subjects* are forct to flie (by enforced or voluntary *Banishment*) from their native *Countries;* The lamentable proofe whereof *England* hath felt in the flight of so many worthy *English*, into the *Low Countries* and *New England*, and from *New England* into old againe and other forraigne parts.

A *Tenent* whose grosse partialitie denies the *Principles of common Justice*, while *Men* waigh out to the *Consciences* of all others, that which they judge not fit nor right to be waighed out to their owne: Since the *persecutours Rule* is, to take and persecute all *Consciences*, onely, *himselfe* must not be touched.

A *Tenent* that is but *Machevilisme*, and makes a *Religion*, but a *cloake* or *stalking horse* to *policie* and *private Ends* of *Jeroboams Crowne*, and the *Priests Benefice*, &c.

A *Tenent* that *corrupts* and *spoiles* the very *Civill Honestie* and *Naturall Conscience* of a *Nation*. Since *Conscience* to *God* violated, proves (without *Repentance*) ever after, a very *Jade*, a *Drug*, loose and *unconscionable* in all converse with men.

Lastly, a *Tenent* in *England* most unseasonable, as powring *Oyle* upon those *Flames* which the high *Wisdome* of the *Parliament*, (by easing the yoakes on Mens *Consciences*) had begun to quench.

Peace her Repose and Tabernacle.

In the sad Consideration of all which (Deare *Peace*) let *Heaven* and *Earth* judge of the *washing* and *colour* of this *Tenent*. For thee *sweete heavenly Guest*) goe lodge thee in the *breasts* of the *peaceable* and humble *Witnesses* of *Jesus,* that love the *Truth* in *peace!* Hide thee from the Worlds *Tumults* and *Combustions,* in the breasts of thy truely *noble children,* who professe and *endeavour* to breake the *irony* and insupportable *yoakes* upon the *Soules* and *Consciences* of any of the sonnes of Men.

Peace. Me-thinkes (Deare *Truth*) if any of the least of these deepe charges be found against this *Tenent,* you doe not wrong it when you stile it *bloudie:* But since, in the wofull proofe of all *Ages* past, since *Nimrod* (the *Hunter* or *persecutour* before the *Lord*) these and more are lamentably evident and undeniable: it gives me wonder that so many and so excellent *eyes* of *Gods* servants should not espie so fowle a *monster,* especially considering the *universall opposition* this *Tenent* makes against *Gods Glory,* and the *Good* of all mankinde.

Truth. There hath been many fowle *opinions,* with which the *old Serpent* hath infected and bewitched the sonnes of men (touching *God, Christ,* the *Spirit,* the *Church,* against *Holines,* against *Peace,* against *civill Obedience,* against *chastitie*) in so much, that even *Sodomie* it selfe hath been a *Tenent* maintained in print by some of the very *pillars* of the *Church* of *Rome:* But this *Tenent* is so universally opposite to *God* and *man,* so pernicious and destructive to both (as hath been declared) that like the *Powder-plot,* it threatens to blow up all *Religion,* all *civilitie,* all *humanitie,* yea the very *Being* of the *World,* and the *Nations* thereof at once.

Peace. He that is the *Father* of *Lies,* and a *murtherer* from the beginning, he knowes this well, and this ugly *Blackmore* needs a *maske* or *vizard.*

The *Bloudie Tenent* of persecution compared.

The maskes
and vizards
of the *blou-
die Tenent.*

Truth. Yea the *bloudines* and *inhumantie* of it is such, that not onely Mr *Cottons* more tender and holy Breast, but even the most bloudie *Bonners* and *Gardiners* have been forced to arme themselves with the faire *shewes* and glorious *pretences,* of the *Glory* of *God,* and *zeale* for that *Glory,* the *Love* of his *Truth,* the *Gospel* of *Christ Jesus, love* and *pitie* to mens soules, the *peace* of the *Church, uniformitie, Order,* the *peace* of the *Common-weale,* the *Wisedome of the State,* the *Kings, Queenes* and *Parliaments* proceedings, the *odiousnesse* of *Sects, Heresies, Blasphemies, Novelties, Seducers,* and their *Infections:* the *obstinacie* of *Hereticks,* after all *Meanes, Disputations, Examinations, Synods,* yea and after *Conviction* in the poore *Hereticks* owne *Conscience:* Add to these the flattring sound of those glosing *Titles,* the *Godly Magistrate,* the *Christian Magistrate,* the *Nurcing Fathers* and *Mothers* of the *Church, Christian Kings* and *Queenes.* But all other *Kings* and *Magistrates* (even all the *Nations* of the *World* over, as Mr *Cotton* pleads) must suspend and hould their hands, and not meddle in *matters* of *Religion,* untill they be informed, &c.

Peace. The dreadfull righteous hand of *God,* the *Eternall* and avenging *God,* is pulling off these *maskes* and *vizards,* that *thousands,* and the *World* may see this *bloudie Tenents Beautie.*

Truth &
Peace, their
meetings sel-
dome and
short.

Truth. But see (my *heavenly Sister* and true *stranger* in this Sea-like restles, raging World) see here what *Fires* and *Swords* are come to part us! Well; Our *meetings* in the Heavens shall not thus be interrupted, our *Kisses* thus *distracted,* and our *eyes* and *cheekes* thus *wet, unwiped:* For me, though *censured, threatned, persecuted,* I must *professe,* while *Heaven* and *Earth lasts,* that no one *Tenent* that either *London, England,* or the *World* doth harbour, is so *hereticall, blasphemous, seditious,* and *dangerous* to the *corporall,* to the *spirituall,* to the *present,* to the *Eternall* Good of all Men, as the *bloudie Tenent* (how ever *wash't* and *whited*) I say, as is the *bloudie Tenent* of *persecution* for cause of *Conscience.*

[LETTER TO THE TOWN OF PROVIDENCE, JANUARY 1655, ON THE LIMITS OF FREEDOM]

That ever I should speak or write a tittle, that tends to such an infinite liberty of conscience, is a mistake, and which I have ever disclaimed and abhorred. To prevent such mistakes, I shall at present only propose this case: There goes many a ship to sea, with many hundred souls in one ship, whose weal or woe is common, and is a true picture of a commonwealth, or a human combination or society. It hath fallen out sometimes, that both papists and protestants, Jews and Turks, may be embarked in one ship; upon which supposal I affirm, that all the liberty of conscience, that ever I pleaded for, turns upon these two hinges—that none of the papists, protestants, Jews, or Turks, be forced to come to the ship's prayers or worship, nor compelled from their own particular prayers or worship, if they practice any. I further add, that I never denied, that notwithstanding this liberty, the commander of this ship ought to command the ship's course, yea, and also command that justice, peace and sobriety, be kept and practiced, both among the seamen and all the passengers. If any of the seamen refuse to perform their services, or passengers to pay their freight; if any refuse to help, in person or purse, towards the common charges or defence; if any refuse to obey the common laws and orders of the ship, concerning their common peace or preservation; if any shall mutiny and rise up against their commanders and officers; if any should preach or write that there ought to be no commanders or officers, because all are equal in Christ, therefore no masters nor officers, no laws nor orders, nor corrections nor punishments;—I say, I never denied, but in such cases, whatever is pretended, the commander or commanders may judge, resist, compel and punish such transgressors, according to their deserts and merits. This if seriously and honestly minded, may, if it so please the Father of lights, let in some light to such as willingly shut not their eyes.

I remain studious of your common peace and liberty.

ROGER WILLIAMS

THOMAS HOOKER

(1586-1647)

Bibliographical Note. There is no collection of Hooker's writings. The text which is printed here follows that printed in Perry Miller and Thomas Johnson, eds., *The Puritans* (New York, 1938), pp. 292-301; Miller and Johnson's text is printed from Hooker's *Application of Redemption* (London, 1659), pp. 52-66. The best life of Hooker is G. L. Walker, *Thomas Hooker* (New York, 1891). A significant study of Hooker's supposed liberal tendencies is Perry Miller, "Thomas Hooker and the Democracy of Early Connecticut," *New England Quarterly,* IV (1931), 663-712.

A TRUE SIGHT OF SIN (1659)*

WHEREIN THIS TRUE SIGHT, AND APPREHENSION OF SIN PROPERLY DISCOVERS IT SELF.

I answer, A true sight of sin hath two Conditions attending upon it; or it appears in two things: We must see sin, 1. Cleerly. 2. Convictingly, what it is in it self, and what it is to us, not in the appearance and paint of it, but in the power of it; not to fadam it in the notion and conceit only, but to see it with Application.

We must see it cleerly in its own Nature, its Native color and proper hue: It's not every slight conceit, not every general and cursorie, confused thought or careless consideration that will serve the turn, or do the work here, we are all sinners; it is my infirmity, I cannot help it; my weakness, I cannot be rid of it; no man lives without faults and follies, the best have their failings, *In many things we offend all.* But alas all this wind shakes no Corn, it costs more to see sin aright than a few words of course; It's one thing to say sin is thus and thus, another thing to see it to be such; we must look wis[e]ly and steddily upon our distempers, look sin in the face, and discern it to the full; the want whereof is the cause of our mistaking our estates, and not redressing of our hearts and waies, *Gal.* 6. 4. *Let a man prove his own work.* Be-

* Reprinted from *The Puritans,* edited by Perry Miller and Thomas Johnson and used with the permission of the American Book Company.

fore the Goldsmith can sever and see the Dross asunder from the Gold, he must search the very bowels of the Mettal, and try it by touch, by tast, by hammer, and by fire; and then he will be able to speak by proof what it is; So here. We perceive sin in the crowd and by hearsay, when we attend some common and customary expressions taken up by persons in their common converse, and so report what others speak, and yet never knew the Truth, what either others or we say, but we do not single out our corruptions and survey the loathsomness of them, as they come naked in their own Natures; this we ought to do: There is great ods betwixt the knowledg of a Traveller, that in his own person hath taken a view of many Coasts, past through many Countries, and hath there taken up his abode some time, and by Experience hath been an Eye-witness of the extream cold, and scorching heats, hath surveyed the glory and beauty of the one, the barrenness and meanness of the other; he hath been in the Wars, and seen the ruin and desolation wrought there; and another that sits by his fire side, and happily reads the story of these in a Book, or views the proportion of these in a Map, the ods is great, and the difference of their knowledg more than a little: the one saw the Country really, the other only in the story; the one hath seen the very place, the other only in the paint of the Map drawn. The like difference is there in the right discerning of sin; the one hath surveyed the compass of his whol course, searched the frame of his own heart, and examined the windings and turnings of his own waies, he hath seen what sin is, and what it hath done, how it hath made havock of his peace and comfort, ruinated and laid wast the very Principles of Reason and Nature, and Morality, and made him a terror to himself, when he hath looked over the loathsom abominations that lie in his bosom, that he is afraid to approach the presence of the Lord to bewail his sins, and to crave pardon, lest he should be confounded for them, while he is but confessing of them; afraid and ashamed lest any man living should know but the least part of that which he knows by himself, and could count it happy that himself was not, that the remembrance of those hideous evils of his might be no more; Another happily hears the like preached or repeated, reads them writ or recorded in some Authors, and is able to remember and relate them. The ods is marvelous great. The one sees the History of sin, the other the Nature of it; the one knows the relation of sin as it is mapped out, and recorded; the other the poyson, as by experience he hath found and proved it. It's one thing to see a disease in the Book, or in a mans body, another thing to find and feel it in a mans self. There is the report of it, here the malignity and venom of it.

But how shall we see cleerly the Nature of sin in his naked hue?

This will be discovered, and may be conceived in the Particulars following. Look we at it: First, As it respects God. Secondly, As it concerns our selves. As it hath reference to God, the vileness of the nature of sin may thus appear.

It would dispossess God of that absolute Supremacy which is indeed his Prerogative Royal, and doth in a peculiar manner appertayn to him, as the Diamond of his Crown, and Diadem of his Deity, so the Apostle, *He is God over all blessed for ever,* Rom. 9. 5. All from him and all for him, he is the absolute first being, the absolute last end, and herein is the crown of his Glory. All those attributes of Wisdom, Goodness, Holiness, Power, Justice, Mercy, the shine and Concurrency of all these meeting together is to set out the unconceivable excellency of his Glorious name, which exceeds all praise, *Thyne is the kingdom, the power and the glory,* the right of all and so the rule of all and the Glory of all belongs to him.

Now herein lyes the unconceavable hainousness of the hellish nature of sin, it would justle the Almighty out of the Throne of his Glorious Soveraignty, and indeed be above him. For the will of man being the chiefest of all his workmanship, all for his body, the body of the soul, the mind to attend upon the will, the will to attend upon God, and to make choyce of him, and his wil, that is next to him, and he onely above that: and that should have been his Throne and Temple or Chair of State, in which he would have Set his Soveraignty for ever. He did in an Especial manner intend to meet with man, and to communicate himself to man in his righteous Law, as the rule of his Holy and righteous will, by which the will of *Adam* should have been ruled and guided to him, and made happie in him; and all Creatures should have served God in man, and been happy by or through him, serving of God being happy in him; But when the will went from under the government of his rule, by sin, *it would be above God, and be happy without him,* for the rule of the law in each command of it, holds forth a three-fold expression of Soveraignty from the Lord, and therein the Soveraignty of all the rest of his Attributes.

1. The Powerful Supremacy of his just will, as that he hath right to dispose of all and authority to command all at his pleasure; *What if God will? Rom.* 9. 22 *My Counsel shall stand and I wil do all my pleasure, Isa.* 46. 10. And as its true of what shal be done upon us, so his wil hath Soveraignty of Command in what should be done by us we are to say *the will of the Lord be done; Davids* warrant was *to do all Gods wils Acts.* 13. 22. and our Saviour himself professeth, *John.* 6. 38. *that he came not to do his own will but the will of him that sent him,* and therfore his wrath and jealousie and judgment will break out in case that be disobeyed.

2. There is also a fulness of wisdom in the law of God revealed to guide & direct us in the way we should walk, *Psal.* 19. 7. *the law of God makes wise the simple, 2. Tim.* 3. 15. *it's able to make us wise unto Salvation.*

3. There's a Sufficiency of God to content and satisfy us. *Blessed are they who walk in his wayes, and blessed are they that keep his Testimonies. Psal.* 119. 1. 2. *Great prosperity have they that love the law, and nothing shal offend them,* ver. 16. and in truth there can be no greater reward for doing wel, than to be enabled to do well, he that hath attayned his last end he cannot go further, he cannot be better;

Now by sin we justle the law out of its place, and the Lord out of his Glorious Soveraignty, pluck the Crown from his head, and the Seepter out of his hand, and we say and profess by our practice, there is not authority and power there to govern, nor wisdom to guide, nor good to content me, but I will be swayed by mine own wil and led by mine own deluded reason and satisfied with my own lusts. This is the guise of every graceless heart in the commission of sin; *so Pharaoh who is the Lord? I know not the Lord, nor will I lett Israel go. Exod.* 5. 2. in the time of their prosperity see how the Jews turn their backs and shake off the authority of the Lord, *we are Lords* (say they) *we will come no more at thee. Jer.* 2. 31. *and our tongues are our own who shal be Lords over us? Psal.* 12. 4. So for the wisdom of the world, see how they set light by it as not worth the looking after it *Jer.* 18. 12. *we wil walk after our own devices & we wil every one do the imagination of his own evil heart, yea they sett up their own traditions,* their own Idols and delusions, and Lord it over the law, *making the command of God of none effect Math.* 15. 8. 9. So for the goodness of the word; *Job.* 22. 17. *Mat.* 3. 14. *It is in vayn to serve God and what profit is there that we have kept his ordinances, yea his Commandements are ever grievous,* Its a grievous thing to the loose person he cannot have his pleasures but he must have his guilt and gall with them; Its grievous to the worlding that he cannot lay hold on the world by unjust means, but Conscience layes hold upon him as breaking the law. Thou that knowest and keepest thy pride and stubbornness and thy distempers, know assuredly thou dost justle God out of the Throne of his glorious Soveraignty and thou dost profess, Not Gods wil but thine own (which is above his) shall rule thee, thy carnal reason and the folly of thy mind, is above the wisdome of the Lord and that shal guide thee; to please thine own stubborn crooked pervers spirit, is a greater good than to please God and enjoy happines, for this more Contents, thee; That when thou considerest but thy Course, dost thou not wonder that the great and Terrible God doth not pash such a poor insolent worm to pouder, and send thee packing to the pitt every moment.

2. It smites at the Essence of the Almighty and the desire of the sinner, is not only that God should not be supream but that indeed he should *not be at all,* and therefore it would destroy the being of Jehovah. *Psal.* 81. 15. Sinners are called *the haters of the Lord.* John. 15. 24. *they hated both me and my Father.* Now he that hates endeavours if it be possible the annihilation of the thing

hated, and its most certain were it in their power, they would
pluck God out of Heaven the light of his truth out of their Consciences, and the law out of the Societies and Assemblies where
they live, that they might have elbow room to live as they list.
Nay what ever they hate most and intend, and plott more evil
against in al the' world, they hate God most of all, and intend
more evil against him than against all their Enemies besides, because they hate all for his sake, therefore wicked men *are said to
destroy the law Psal.* 126. 119 the Adulterer loaths that law that
condemns, uncleaness; the Earthworm would destrow that law
that forbids Covetousness, they are sayd to *hate the light* John 3.
21. to hate the Saints and Servants of the Lord John 15. 18. *the
world hates you,* he that hates the Lanthorn for the lights sake,
he hates the light much more, he that hates the faithful because
of the Image of God, and the Grace that appears there, he hates
the God of all, Grace and Holiness, most of all, so God to *Zena-
charib,* Isa. 37. 28. *I know thy going out and thy Comming in,
and thy rage against me,* Oh it would be their content, if there
was no God in the world to govern them, no law to curbe them,
no justice to punish, no truth to trouble them, Learn therfore to
see how far your rebellions reach, It is not arguments you gain-
say, not the Counsel of a Minister you reject, the command of a
Magistrate ye oppose, evidence of rule or reason ye resist; but be
it known to you, you fly in the very face of the Almighty, and it
is not the Gospel of Grace ye would have destroyed, but the spirit
of Grace, the author of Grace the Lord Jesus, the God of all
Grace that ye hate.

It crosseth the whol course of Providence, perverts the work of
the Creature and defaceth the beautiful frame, and that sweet
correspondence and orderly usefulness the Lord first implanted in
the order of things; The Heavens deny their influence, the Earth
her strength, the Corn her nourishment, thank sin for that. Weeds
come instead of herbs, Cockle and Darnel instead of Wheat,
thank sin for that, *Rom.* 8. 22. *The whol Creature* (or Creation)
grones under vanity, either cannot do what it would or else miss-
eth of that good and end it intended, breeds nothing but vanity,

brings forth nothing but vexation, It crooks all things so as that none can straiten them, makes so many wants that none can supply them, *Eccles.* 1. 15. This makes crooked Servants in a family no man can rule them, crooked inhabitants in towns, crooked members in Congregations, ther's no ordering nor joynting of them in that comly accord, and mutual subjection; know they said, *the adversary sin hath done all this.* Man was the mean betwixt God and the Creature to convey all good with all the constancy of it, and therefore when Man breaks, Heaven and Earth breaks all asunder, the Conduit being cracked and displaced there can be no conveyance from the Fountain.

In regard of our selves, see we and consider nakedly the nature of sin, in Four particulars.

Its that which makes a separation between God and the soul, breaks that Union and Communion with God for which we were made, and in the enjoyment of which we should be blessed and happie, *Isai.* 59. 1. 2. *Gods ear is not heavy that it cannot hear nor his hand that it cannot help, but your iniquities have separated betwixt God and you & your sins have hid his face that he wil not hear for he professeth,* Psal. 5. 4. *that he is a God that wills not wickedness neither shal iniquity dwell with him. Into the new Jerusalem shal no unclean thing enter, but without shal be doggs Rev.* 21. 27. The Dogs to their Kennel, and Hogs to their Sty and Mire: but if an impenitent wretch should come into Heaven, the Lord would go out of Heaven; *Iniquity shall not dwell with sin.* That then that deprives me of my greatest good for which I came into the world, and for which I live and labor in the world, and without which I had better never to have been born; nay, that which deprives me of an universal good, a good that hath all good in it, that must needs be an evil, but have all evil in it: but so doth sin deprive me of God as the Object of my will, and that wills all good, and therefore it must bring in Truth all evil with it. Shame takes away my Honor, Poverty my Wealth, Persecution my Peace, Prison my Liberty, Death my Life, yet a man may still be a happy man, lose his Life, and live eternally: But sin takes away my God, and with him all good goes; Prosperity without

God will be my poyson, Honor without him my bane; nay, the word without God hardens me, my endeavor without him profits nothing at all for my good. A Natural man hath no God in any thing, and therefore hath no good.

It brings an incapability in regard of my selfe to receive good, and an impossibility in regard of God himself to work my spiritual good, while my sin Continues, and I Continue impenitent in it. An incapability of a spiritual blessing, *Why trangress ye the Commandement of the Lord that ye cannot prosper do what* ye can, 2 Chron. 24. 20. And *He that being often reproved hardens his heart, shal be consumed suddenly and there is no remedy,* He that spils the Physick that should cure him, the meat that should nourish him, there is no remedy but he must needs dye, so that the Commission of sin makes not only a separation from God, but obstinate resistance and continuance in it, maintains an infinit and everlasting distance between God and the soul: So that so long as the sinful resistance of thy soul continues; God cannot vouchsafe the Comforting and guiding presence of his grace; because it's cross to the Covenant of Grace he hath made, which he will not deny, and his Oath which he will not alter. So that should the Lord save thee and thy Corruption, carry thee and thy proud vnbeleeving heart to heaven he must nullify the Gospel, (Heb. 5. 9. *He's the Author of Salvation to them that obey him*) and forswear himself, (Heb. 3. 18. *He hath sworn unbeleevers shall not enter into his rest*) he must cease to be just and holy, and so to be God. As *Saul* said to *Jonathan* concerning *David,* 1 Sam. 20. 30, 31. *So long as the Son of* Jesse *lives, thou shalt not be established, nor thy Kingdom:* So do thou plead against thy self, and with thy own soul; So long as these rebellious distempers continue, Grace and Peace, and the Kingdom of Christ can never be established in thy heart For this obstinate resistance differs nothing from the plagues of the state of the damned, when they come to the highest measure, but that it is not yet total and final, there being some kind of abatement of the measure of it, and stoppage of the power of it. Imagine thou sawest the Lord Jesus coming in the clouds, and heardest the last trump blow, *Arise ye dead, and come to Judgment:* Imagine thou sawest the Judg of all the World sitting upon the Throne, thousands of Angels before him, and ten thousands ministring unto him, the Sheep standing on his right hand, and the Goats at the left: Suppose thou heardest that dreadful Sentence, and final Doom pass from the Lord of Life (whose Word made Heaven and Earth, and will shake both) *Depart from me ye cursed;* How would thy heart shake and sink, and die within thee in the thought thereof, wert thou really perswaded it was thy portion? Know, that by thy dayly continuance in sin, thou dost to the utmost of thy power execute that Sentence upon thy soul: It's thy life, thy labor, the desire of thy heart, and thy dayly practice to depart away from the God of all Grace and Peace, and turn the Tomb-stone of everlasting destruction upon thine own soul.

It's the Cause which brings all other evils of punishment into the World, and without this they are not evil, but so far as sin is in them. The sting of a trouble, the poyson and malignity of a punishment and affliction, the evil of the evil of any judgment, it is the sin that brings it, or attends it, *Jer.* 2. 19. *Thine own wickedness shall correct thee, and thy back slidings shall reprove thee, know therefore that it is an evil, and bitter thing that thou hast forsaken the Lord.* Jer. 4. 18. *Thy waies and doings have procured these things unto thee, therefore it is bitter, and reacheth unto the heart.* Take miseries and crosses without sin, they are like to be without a sting, the Serpent without poyson, ye may take them, and make Medicines of them. So *Paul* 1 *Cor.* 15. 55. he plaies with death it self, sports with the Grave. *Oh death, where is thy sting? Oh Grave where is thy Victory? the sting of death is sin.* All the harmful annoyance in sorrows and punishments, further than either they come from sin, or else tend to it, they are rather improvements of what we have than parting with any thing we do enjoy, we rather lay out our conveniences than seem to lose them, yea, they encrease our Crown, and do not diminish our Comfort. *Blessed are ye when men revile you, and persecute you, and speak all manner of evil of you for my sake, for great is your reward in Heaven:* Matth. 5. 11. There is a blessing in

persecutions and reproaches when they be not mingled with the
deserts of our sins; yea, our momentary short affliction for a good
cause, and a good Conscience, works an excessive exceeding
weight of Glory. If then sin brings all evils, and makes all evils
indeed to us, then is it worse than all those evils.

It brings a Curse upon all our Comforts, blasts all our blessings,
the best of all our endeavors, the use of all the choycest of all Gods
Ordinances: it's so evil and vile, that it makes the use of all good
things, and all the most glorious, both Ordinances and Improvements evil to us. *Hag.* 2. 13. 14. When the Question was made to
the Priest; *If one that is unclean by a dead Body touch any of the
holy things, shall it be unclean? And he answered, Yea. So is this
People, and so is this Nation before me, saith the Lord; and so is
every work of their hands, and that which they offer is unclean:*
If any good thing a wicked man had, or any action he did, might
be good, or bring good to him, in reason it was the Services and
Sacrifices wherein he did approach unto God, and perform Service to him, and yet *the Sacrifice of the wicked is an abomination
to the Lord,* Prov. 28. 9. and Tit. 1. 15. *To the pure all things are
pure; but to the unbeleeving there is nothing pure, but their very
Consciences are defiled.* It is a desperate Malignity in the temper
of the Stomach, that should turn our Meat and diet into Diseases,
the best Cordials and Preservatives into Poysons, so that what in
reason is appointed to nourish a man should kill him. Such is the
venom and malignity of sin, makes the use of the best things become evil, nay, the greatest evil to us many times; *Psal.* 109. 7. *Let
his prayer be turned into sin.* That which is appointed by God to
be the choycest means to prevent sin, is turned into sin out of the
corrupt distemper of these carnal hearts of ours.

Hence then it follows; *That sin is the greatest evil in the world,
or indeed that can be.* For, That which separates the soul from
God, that which brings all evils of punishment, and makes all
evils truly evil, and spoils all good things to us, that must needs be
the greatest evil, but this is the nature of sin, as hath already appeared.

But that which I will mainly press, is, Sin is only opposite to

God, and cross as much as can be to that infinite goodness and holiness which is in his blessed Majesty; it's not the miseries or distresses that men undergo, that the Lord distasts them for, or estrangeth himself from them, he is with *Joseph* in the Prison, with the three Children in the Furnace, with *Lazarus* when he lies among the Dogs, and gathers the Crums from the rich Mans Table, yea with *Job* upon the dung-hil, but he is not able to bear the presence of sin: yea, of this temper are his dearest servants, the more of God is in them, the more opposite they are to sin where ever they find it. It was that he commended in the Church of *Ephesus, That she could not bear those that were wicked*, Rev. 2. 3. As when the Stomach is of a pure temper and good strength, the least surfet or distemper that befals, it presently distasts and disburdens it self with speed. So *David* noted to be *a man after Gods own heart.* He professeth, 101. *Psal.* 3. 7. *I hate the work of them that turn aside, he that worketh deceit shall not dwell in my house, he that telleth lyes, shall not tarry in my sight.* But when the heart becomes like the Stomach, so weak it cannot help it self, nor be helped by Physick, desperate diseases and dissolution of the whol follows, and in reason must be expected. Hence see how God looks at the least connivance, or a faint and feeble kind of opposition against sin, as that in which he is most highly dishonored, and he follows it with most hideous plagues, as that indulgent carriage of *Ely* towards the vile behavior of his Sons for their grosser evils, 1 *Sam.* 2. 23. *Why do you such things, It's not well my Sons that I hear such things: It is not well,* and is that all? why, had they either out of ignorance not known their duty or out of some sudden surprisal of a temptation neglected it, it had not been well, but for them so purposedly to proceed on in the practice of such gross evils, and for him so faintly to reprove: The Lord looks at it as a great sin thus feebly to oppose sin, and therefore verse 29. he tells him, *That he honored his Sons above God,* and therefore he professeth, *Far be it from me to maintain thy house and comfort, for he that honors me I wil honor, and he that despiseth me shall be lightly esteemed,* verse 30. Hence it is the Lord himself is called *the holy one of Israel,* 1. Hab. 12.

Who is of purer eyes than to behold evil, and cannot look upon iniquity, no not in such as profess themselves Saints, though most deer unto him, no, nor in his Son the Lord Jesus, not in his Saints, *Amos,* 8. 7. *The Lord hath sworn by himself, I abhor the excellency of* Jacob; what ever their excellencies, their priviledges are, if they do not abhor sin, God will abhor them, *Jer.* 22. 24. *Though* Coniah *was as the Signet of my right hand, thence would I pluck him.* Nay, he could not endure the appearance of it in the Lord Christ, for when but the reflection of sin (as I may so say) fell upon our Savior, even the imputation of our transgressions to him, though none iniquity was ever committed by him, the Father withdrew his comforting presence from him, and let loose his infinite displeasure against him, forcing him to cry out, *My God, my God, why hast thou forsaken me?*

Yea, Sin is so evil, (that though it be in Nature, which is the good Creature of God) that there is no good in it, nothing that God will own; but in the evil of punishment it is otherwise, for the torments of the Devils, and punishments of the damned in Hell, and all the plagues inflicted upon the wicked upon Earth, issue from the righteous and revenging Justice of the Lord, and he doth own such execution as his proper work, *Isa.* 45. 7. *Is there any evil in the City,* viz. of punishment, *and the Lord hath not done it? I make peace, I create evil, I the Lord do all these things:* It issues from the Justice of God that he cannot but reward every one according to his own waies and works; those are a mans own, the holy one of Israel hath no hand in them; but he is the just Executioner of the plagues that are inflicted and suffered for these; and hence our blessed Savior becoming our Surety, and standing in our room, he endured the pains of the Second death, even the fierceness of the fury of an offended God; and yet it was impossible he could commit the least sin, or be tainted with the least corrupt distemper. And it's certain it's better to suffer all plagues without any one sin, than to commit the least sin, and to be freed from all plagues. Suppose that all miseries and sorrows that ever befel all the wicked in Earth and Hell, should meet together in one soule, as all waters gathered together in one Sea: Suppose thou heardest the Devils roaring, and sawest Hell gaping, and flames of everlasting burnings flashing before thine eyes; it's certain it were better for thee to be cast into those inconceivable torments than to commit the least sin against the Lord: Thou dost not think so now, but thou wilt find it so one day.

URIAN OAKES

(*1631-1681*)

Bibliographical Note. The text which is here printed follows that in Perry Miller and Thomas Johnson, *The Puritans* (New York, 1938), pp. 350-368; Miller and Johnson's text follows that of the original edition (Boston, 1682), pp. 5-22, 32-37.

from THE SOVERAIGN EFFICACY OF DIVINE PROVIDENCE

(DELIVERED 1677)*

Doct. *That the Successes and Events of Undertakings and Affairs are not determined infallibly by the greatest Sufficiency of Men, or Second Causes; but by the Counsel and Providence of God ordering and governing Time and Chance according to his own good Pleasure.*

I have endeavoured to comprize and grasp the substance of *Solomon's* Intendment, in this Doctrinal Conclusion: and shall explicate and demonstrate the Truth of it (as God shall help) in the following Propositions.

Prop. 1. *Second Causes may have a sufficiency in their Kind, to produce these and those Effects:* an hability, a congruous disposition, or an aptness, yea, a kind of sufficiency in order to the putting forth this and that Act, and the giving Existence to these and those Effects: not indeed an absolute and universal Sufficiency (which can be affirmed of none but Him that is Allsufficient and Omnipotent) but a limited sufficiency, or a sufficiency in their *Kind,* and order: The Sun, to *shine;* the Fire, to *burn* that which is combustible; the Rational Creature to act or effect this or that in a way of *counsel,* and with *freedom of will;* the Swift, to *run;* the strong and valiant, and well-instructed Souldier, to *fight well;* the wise man, to *get his bread* to gather *riches,* to gain *acceptance* among those with whom he hath to do. This is no more than to say, that created Agents and Second Causes, may have the active

* Reprinted from *The Puritans,* edited by Perry Miller and Thomas Johnson and used with permission of the American Book Company.

power and virtue of causes, all that is requisite on their parts in order to the production of their peculiar and appropriate Effects, all that sufficiency that *dependent Beings,* and *second Causes* are capable of. And indeed it belongs to the Infinite Wisdom and Goodness of God to furnish his Creatures with sufficient Ability for the operations and effects He hath made them for: and so He did at *first,* when He made every thing good in its *Kind;* and whatever Defect there is *now* in this respect, it is the fruit & punishment of Sin. Though God is *able* to give Being to things in an immediate way, yet it is his *pleasure* in the course of his Providence to use Means, and to produce many things by the mediation and Agency of second Causes, and so gives *causal virtue* and ability to these and those things in order to the producing of such and such Effects. It is a good observation, that the Lord is pleased, not through any *defect of power* in Himself but out of *the abundance of his goodness* to communicate causal power and virtue to his Creatures, & to honour them with that Dignity that they may be his Instruments, by which He will produce these and those Effects: whereby He takes them, as it were, into partnership & fellowship with Himself in the way of his providential Efficiency, that they may be *Vnder-workers* to, yea *Co-vorkers* with Himself. Hence He gives them an aptitude and sufficiency in their *kind* in order to their respective operations and effects: though some have a greater aptitude & sufficiency than others. But without some degree of such *sufficiency,* nothing can deserve the name of a *Cause;* the very essence whereof consists in its *power, virtue* & *ability* to produce an *Effect.* A *cause* cannot be a *cause* without an *active power,* or *sufficiency* to give *being* to this or that *Effect.*

Prop. 2. *The Successes, and Events of Affairs and Undertakings do ordinarily depend in some respects upon the Sufficiency of Second Causes.*

I do not say in the *Observation;* nor is it the meaning of *Solomon,* that Successes and Events of Affairs and Undertakings do not depend at all in an ordinary course, on the sufficiency of Second Causes. For this were to deny and destroy their *causality,* and to make nothing of their *efficiency.* Second causes have their pe-

culiar Influence into their *Effects,* and contribute something to
their *Existence:* and to assert the contrary, were to say that Causes
are no Causes, and to speak a flat Contradiction. This would be
to suppose that the Lord hath set up an Order and course in Nature, in vain; and given to Second Causes a sufficiency *in their
Kind,* for *Action,* to no purpose; and to deny the ordinary Providence of God, which is that whereby the Lord observes the Order
which He hath set, and that course of Nature which is originally
of his own Appointment, whereby one thing depends upon, and
receives Being from another. Though the Lord is pleased sometimes upon great and important Occasions, to leave the ordinary
Road of Providence, and act beyond and above the usual, stated
course of Things; and not to concurre with, and shine upon the
endeavours of created Agents, so as to crown them with that success which according to an ordinary course of Providence, might
be rationally expected; yet it is not to be imagined that He should
ordinarily dispence with the course, and methods of his ordinary
Providence: For why then should it be called *ordinary?* God who
is the Lord of Hosts, the great Leader Commander & Ruler of
Nature, not only *permits,* but also *effectually commands* and
causes his whole *Militia,* ordinarily, to *move* and *act* according
to their *Natures* and *natural Properties* respectively, without
Countermanding them, or turning them out of their way. For
(as I remember One argues) He will not shew such a dislike to
his own workmanship, as ordinarily to cross the Order, and alter
the course He hath set in the World. Therefore the meaning of
the Text is not, that *Swiftness* conduces nothing to the *winning
of the Race,* or *Strength,* to the winning of the *Battel;* or *Wisdom
& Vnderstanding,* to the getting of *Bread* and *Riches;* or *Prudence, Art,* or *Skill,* to the getting of the *Favour* and *goodwill* of
Princes, or *People:* nor, that the *Race* is *never* to the *Swift,* or the
Battel never to the *Strong;* no nor yet, that the *Race* is not *more
frequently* to the *Swift,* and the *Battel usually* to the *Strong, &c.*
For the Lord doth most ordinarily award *Success* unto causes of
greatest *Sufficiency,* rather than *Disappointment & Defeatment.*
Otherwise, it would be a very *heartless,* if not a *foolish* Thing (in

the eye of Reason) to *use means,* or to think to get the *Race* by *Swiftness,* or *Bread* by *Labour* and *Diligence,* or *Favour* by *dexterous & prudent Behaviour;* or *Learning,* by *Study* and *Industry;* or to *win the Battel* by good *Conduct,* and *Courage,* and *numbers of men.* Yet then *Wisdom* would not be better than *Folly;* nor *Strength* more desirable than *Weakness;* nor *Diligence* more benefical & available than *Idleness,* and *sitting still.* This therefore is evident, that the Issues and Events of Undertakings do *in some respect, ordinarily,* depend upon the *Sufficiency* of *Second Causes;* insomuch as the greatest probability of Success (according to an ordinary providence, and in the eye of Reason) is ordinarily on the side of Causes that are most sufficient in their kind of Efficiency.

Prop. 3. *Second Causes, though of greatest Sufficiency in their kind, have not the certain Determination of Successes & Events in their own Hands: but may be frustrated & disappointed.*

Though the Successes and Events of Undertakings ordinarily depend upon the sufficiency of Second Causes; yet they are not infallibly determined thereby. Created Agents have not Events in their own Hands, but may be disappointed: they cannot warrant the Events of their Undertakings, or Success of their Counsels and Endeavours; but may be defeated of their Hopes and Expectations. Thus no man hath the absolute command of the Issue & success of his own Undertakings. He may be sure of this or that Event, if the Lord *Promise* it to him, or *Reveal* it to be *His Pleasure* to give such Success to such Endeavours: but he cannot be secured of it from, or by any *Sufficiency* of his own. He may, as a wise man, forsee & say, what in an ordinary course of Providence is rationally to be expected; but cannot warrant the Success of his Undertakings, or carv out what Event he pleases, to himself. His Prudence, and Providence, and Diligence, and *Sufficiency for Action,* cannot assure him of the *Event,* or determin the Success on his side. And there is that Demonstration of it, that created Agents of the greatest *Sufficiency,* are sometimes disappointed. Two Things I would say here,

1. *Agents of greatest Sufficiency are subject to Disappointment,*

as well (I do not say, as much, or as ordinarily and often, but as well) *as Agents of less sufficiency.* The Ablest Men in any kind may miss of the Success they expect, as well as weaker men. That Men of great Sufficiency in this or that way, may be defeated of their Ends and Hopes, *Solomon* from his own Experience, assures us, in the Text: and who is it that upon his own observation cannot set his Seal to what He asserts? He gives five Instances. 1. *The Race is not to the Swift:* not profitable, or successful to him always; but sometimes pernicious, & destructive. Many a good Runner runs Himself into mischief and Ruine. Thus *Asahel,* that is said to be as light of foot as a wild Roe, ran after *Abner* so fast, that he lost his Life in that overhasty pursuit. 2 *Sam.* 2. 18-23. There are Times when men that are swift would run from danger, and cannot: they have neither power to run, nor success in attempting it, *Jer.* 46, 6. Sometimes the Flight perisheth from the Swift, and he that is swift of foot, or that rideth the Horse, though it be at full speed, cannot deliver himself, *Amos* 2. 14, 15. It is not absolutely in the power of the swiftest man to escape danger, or win the prize by Running. 2. *The Battel is not to the Strong.* There is *in Bello Alea, the Chance of Warre,* as they use to speak. There is, as it were, a kind of Lottery, a great Uncertainty in Warre. Great Armies are sometimes defeated by small and inconsiderable Forces; the great Host of *Midian,* by *Gideon's* three hundred men; the Garrison of the *Philistines* by *Jonathan,* and his Armour-Bearer. This hath been often observed in the World. Sometimes strong and valiant Men are overthrown by those that are in strength farre inferiour to them; *great Goliah,* by *little David.* Well might *David* say, as *Psal.* 33. 16, 17. *There is no King saved by the multitude of an host: a mighty man is not delivered by much strength. An Horse is a vain thing for safety: neither shall he deliver any by his great strength.* There are Times, when *the mighty Ones are beaten down,* Jer. 46. 5. & *The mighty cannot deliver himself, or the strong strengthen himself; but the couragious among the mighty is put to flight,* Amos 2. 14, 16. Sometimes the strong melt like water at approaching danger, and the stouthearted are spoiled and sleep their sleep, and the men of might cannot find their hands, to make the least Defence, or Resistance, *Psal.* 76. 5.

3. *Bread is not to the Wise.* Wise men are not able to get their Livelihood, but have much adoe to make a shift to get a bare Subsistence in the world; and, it may be, are forc'd to beg for it, or be beholding to the Charity of others. There have been strange Instances of very wise, and worthy Persons, that have been reduced to such a Condition. Some of you know the famous Story, *Date Obolum,* or (as others have it) *Panem Belisario. David* was put to beg his Bread of *Nabal,* 1. *Sam.* 25. & *Paul* was often in Hunger and Thirst, 2 *Cor.* 11. 27.

4. *Riches are not to men of Understanding.* Sometimes indeed, wise men get Estates and gather Riches; and one would think they should be best accomplish'd for it: and yet it so falls out, that some understanding Men cannot thrive in the World and grow rich, notwithstanding all their Endeavours. So it is, that many men of great Understanding and rational Forecastings and Contrivances to gather wealth, though they lay out their Parts and their Hearts this way, and would be rich, yet they cannot; but are strangely defeated. You read of the *poor* wise man, *Eccles.* 9. 15. Many men of great Understandings are too wise, and of too great Spirits to labour after wealth; or if they do, their designs are unsuccessful. 5. *Favour is not to men of Skill.* Many very wise, and knowing, & skillful men, and experienced in Affairs, and prudent also in their Deportment, yet cannot get, or keep the *Favour* of Princes or People. Some Expositors on the Place, instance in *Joseph,* that was envied, and hated, and sold by his Brethren, & also lost the favour of *Potiphar* (though He managed the Affairs of his House prudently and prosperously, and deserved well at his Hands) and was cast into Prison by him. *David,* that was hated and persecuted by *Saul; Daniel,* that was cast into the Lions Den, though *an excellent Spirit was found in Him,* and great Prudence and Faithfulness in managing the Affairs of the Empire; and before that, though He had been in great Favour and Esteem in *Nebuchadnezzar*'s time, yet afterwards in the Reign of *Belshazzar,* He lived obscure, and as it were buried at

Court, as Mr. *Cartwright* gathers from *Dan*. 5. 11, 12, 13. Many wise, and learned, and Ingenious Men cannot get the Favour of men, or keep it, when they have. The *poor* wise man delivered the City, and yet no man remembred that same poor man, *Eccl.* 9. 15. *Belisarius* (whom I mentioned before) was a most prudent, experienced, faithful General under the Emperour *Justinian,* that had won Him many Battels, reduced many Cities & Countryes to his Obedience and approved Himself for a most loyal, and worthy Subject, & yet after all his Services, even in *that* Emperour's Time, was through Envy, falsely accused, for ought appears by the Story, had his Eyes put out, and was forced to stand daily in the Temple of *Sophia,* where He held out his wooden dish, begging his Bread, and useing those words, *Give a little Bread to* Belisarius, *whom his Virtue & Valour hath raised; and Envy depressed, & cast down again.* Other Scripture Testimonies and Instances, besides those in the Text, might be produced, if it were needful. But every observing man's experience may furnish him with Demonstrations of his Truth, *That Agents of greatest Sufficiency among men are subject to Disappointments, as well as those of less Sufficiency.* Again,

2. *Agents of little, or no Sufficiency, succeed sometimes in their Undertakings; when those of greater Sufficiency, miscarry & meet with Disappointment.* There is many times one Event to both as *Solomon* speaks *Eccl.* 9. 2. when the ablest Agents are frustrated, as well as the weakest: and there is sometimes a better Event to weaker Agents, & Instruments; they prosper in their way, when abler men are disappointed. The Race is *sometimes* to the Slow, and the Swift lose the Prize. The Battel is *sometimes* to the Weak; and the Strong are put to flight: as we have many Instances both in Scripture and common History. Weak and simple people have bread enough sometimes, when wise men are in want of their daily bread. *Nabal* had good store, when *David* was hard put to it. Men of shallow heads grow rich and get great Estates, when men of understanding can thrive at no Hand. *Solomon* tells us of the *poor* wise man; and our Saviour in that Parable, *Luk.* 12. 16, 20. tells us of a *rich Fool.* It is ordinarily seen in the World,

that the thriving men in Estates, are none of the most understanding & judicious. Many a man hath this world-craft, that yet
is a man of no deep or solid Understanding. So, many weak,
worthless, ignorant, empty Persons find Favour with Princes and
People: when men of Skill, & Learning, & great worth are neglected and despised. This is an Evil under the Sun, & an Error that
proceeds from the Ruler, a great miscarriage in Government, that
Folly is set in great dignity (Fools are favoured and advanced)
and the Rich, i.e. men of rich Endowments for Wisdom and
Piety, *sit in low places,* i.e. are depressed and discountenanced;
Servants are upon Horses, men of poor servile Spirits and Conditions, are set up and honoured, *and Princes,* i.e. men of great
worth, *walking as Servants upon the Earth.* Eccl. 10. 5, 6, 7. So
that it appeares plainly, that Success doth not alwayes wait upon
the Counsels and Actions of Persons of great Sufficiency; but
they may suffer Disappointment, when others are prosperous:
Which demonstrates that the Issues and Events of Undertakings
and Affairs are not determined infallibly by the Qualifications &
accomplishments of created Agents, and Second Causes.

Prop. 4. *The Defeat & Disappointment of Agents of great Sufficiency in their kind, is from the Hapning of* Time *&* Chance
unto them.

Some read it (and the Original will bear it) *because,* or *for*
Time and Chance happeneth to them all. For Explication.

1. By *Time,* understand not barely the *Duration,* or *spate* of
Time, which hath no such determining Influence into humane
Affairs. But Time *so & so Circumstanced.* Time is sometimes as
much as a special *Season* or *Opportunity,* when there is a concurrence of Helps, means, and advantages for the furthering the
Designs and undertakings of men. By *Time* sometimes, we are
to understand such a *Nick,* or *Juncture* of time, wherein there is
a coincidence of Difficulties, disadvantages, & hindrances to the
effecting of any Business. And this seems the meaning of *Solomon* in the Text. An adverse or *evil Time,* Ec. 9. 12. Sometimes
the Times favour the Enterprizes of men, Sometimes they frown
upon them. At one time, wise and good men stand up for the

Defence of their Country and Liberties thereof, and prosper in it;
the Times favour them, there is a concurrence of all manner of
Furtherances and advantages: at another time, they may endeavour it, and the Times frown upon them, the Spirit and Humour of
the People is degenerated; and they swim against the stream, &
are lost in the Attempt. And we say, *Such a Man was worthy of
better Times,* had been a brave man, if He had lived in better
Times, his worth had been more known and prized, and He
would have had better success. So when the Time of Judgment
upon a People, is come, then wrath ariseth against them without
remedy; and then the *strong man* may fight for the defence of
such a Country; and *the wise man* endeavour to deliver the City:
but all in vain; they shall miscarry in the Undertaking. *Aben
Ezra* (as *Mercer* tells us) referres this to the *Conjunctions,* and
Aspects of the Starres, by which He apprehended these inferiour
Things were governed. We are sure there are certain Periods, and
Revolutions of Time, respecting the Prosperity, or Adversity of
Nations, Countries, Cities, Churches, Families, Persons. As Time
is set to all the Successes, so to all the Defeats and disappoint-
ments of men; and when this Time comes, no Sufficiency of man
can withstand Disappointments.

2. By *Chance,* Understand contingent and casual Events. Many
things fall out between the *Cup,* and the *Lip;* or otherwise than
expect or imagine, or can possibly foresee. Some Event chops in,
and interposeth unexpectedly, to cross a man's Designs, & defeat
his Hopes & rational Expectations. When *Saul* and his men were
compassing *David* and his men, and ready to take them, then
comes a Messenger to *Saul,* saying, *Haste & come: for the* Philistines *have Invaded the Land.* 1 Sam. 23. 27. When *Haman* had
plotted the Ruine of the *Jews,* and brought his Design near to an
Issue, then the King cannot sleep but calls for the Book of the
Records of the Chronicles, and they read to Him of the good Service of *Mordecai,* in discovering the Treason that was plotted
against his Person; and one thing falls in after another, to defeat
Haman's cruel design, and ruine the whole fabrick of his strong

built, and almost perfected Contrivance. In this sence *Time* and *Chance* happens to men of greatest Sufficiency, which they cannot either foresee, (*Eccl* 9. 12.) or prevent, or help themselves against them when they come upon them: and hereby their Counsels, and Undertakings are defeated and ruined sometimes.

Prop. 5. *Time and Chance which happens to men in the way of their Vndertakings, is effectually ordered & governed by the Lord.* God is the Lord of Time, and Orderer, and Governour of all Contingences. Time and Chance that further or hinder the Designs of men, are under the Rule and Management of the Lord. His Counsel sets the *Times,* appoints the *Chances;* His Providence dispenses the *Times,* and frames the *Chances,* that befall men. The Lord hath in his own power the Dispensation of *Times,* Eph. 1. 10. *The Times and Seasons He hath put in his own power,* Act. 1. 7. He hath such a Dominion over the Times, that *He changeth Times and Seasons,* according to his own pleasure. *Dan.* 2. 31. *My Times* (saith *David,* Ps. 31. 15. *are in thy Hands.* He means the state and condition of his *Times;* his Prosperities, and Adversities; his Successes, and Disappointments; and universally, whatever should befall him in the Times that should pass over Him. Moreover, all the Chances that happen to men, as the Scripture but now mentioned shews, are in the Hand of God. *My Times* i.e. the Chances of my Times. No Contingency, or Emergency, or Accident so casual, but it is ordered & governed by the Lord. The Arrow that was shot at a venture, and smote *Ahab* throw the joints of his Harness, was directed at him by the Hand of God. So in that case of Man-slaughter, and killing a man casually, as if a man be hewing Wood, and his hand fetcheth a stroke with the Axe, to cut down a Tree, and the head slippeth from the helve, and lighteth upon his Neighbour, that he die, *Deut.* 19. 5. God is said in that case, to *deliver* that man that is slain, *into his hand,* Exod. 21. 13. God ordered that sad event. All Casualties in the World, are guided by the steady Hand of the great God. *Thou* (saith *David*, Ps. 16. 5.) *maintainest my Lot.* The Lord makes and disposes the Lot, or Chance of every man, whatever it is. He hath appointed all Times and Chances in his *Eternal* Counsel; and in *Time* executes accordingly, in the course of his Providence.

Prop. 6. *The great God hath the absolute and infallible Determination of the Successes and Events of all the Operations & Undertakings of created Agents & Second Causes, in his own Power.* His Counsel and soveraign Will appoints what they shall be, and his Providence (which is not determined by any Second Cause: but is the Determiner of them all) Executes accordingly. And it must needs be so, if you consider these two Particulars,

1. *God is the Absolute First Cause, and Supream Lord of all.* Of Him, and to Him, and through Him are all Things, *Rom.* 11. 36. He that understands any thing of God indeed, knows this to be a Truth. Here we might be large; as they that are acquainted with the Doctrine of *Creation* and *Providence,* in *Conservation* and *Gubernation* of all Things, will readily apprehend: for here we might shew you, 1. That God is the absolute first Cause of all the causal power and virtue that is in Creatures. He gives them power to act, furnisheth them with a Sufficiency for their operations. He gives Swiftness to the Runner; Skill, and Strength, and Courage, to the Souldier.

2. That He supports, and continues the active power of the creature. He continues Swiftness, Wisdom, Strength, Courage, as He pleaseth. If He withdraw, all is gone. The Swift is lame, or slow-footed, the Strong is weak & timorous, the Wise is foolish and besotted, the man of Skill, is a meer Bungler at any thing. 3. That He doth by a *previous Influx* excite and stirre up, and actuate the active power of the Creature, and set all the wheels agoing. For the most operative, active created Virtue, is not a *pure Act:* but hath some *Potentiality* mixed with it; and therefore cannot put forth it self into Action, unless it be set agoing by the *first Cause.* And the creature cannot be the absolute *first Cause* of any *physical action.* In Him we live, and move, *Act.* 17. 28. Again. 4. That He determines and applyes Second Causes to the Objects of their Actions. When they stand, as it were, *in Bivio,* as it is said of *Nebuchadnezzar,* when he was marching with his

Army He *stood at the parting of the way, at the head of the two wayes, to use Divination,* as doubting which way he had best to march; whether to *Jerusalem,* or some other way, *Ezek.* 21. 21, 22. Then the Lord casts the Scale and the Lot, & determines them this way, and not another. He doth not only stir up Second Causes to act at large, and set them agoing, and leave it to their own Inclination, whither they shall go, & what they shall do: but He leads them forth, and determines them to this, or that Object. 5. That He *cooperates,* and workes *jointly* with Second Causes, in producing their Effects. As He *predetermins* Second Causes, so He *concurres* with them in their Operations. And this *Præ-determination,* and *Concurse* is so necessary; that there can be no real Effect produced by the Creature without it. And it is a Truth also, that when God Improves Second Causes for the production of any Effect, He so concurres with them, that He doth withall most immediately, intimously, and without Dependence upon these Causes by which He acts, produce the *Entity,* or *Esse* of the Effect. If this be considered, it will appear that created Agents, are as it were, God's Instruments, that act as they are acted by Him; and cannot move of themselves. The busy, bustling, proud *Assyrian* was so, *Is.* 10. 15. 6. *That all the Ataxy, Disorder, Irregularity, moral Evil that is found in the Actions of Rational Agents, is by His Permission.* If it were not the Pleasure of God to permit it, no Sin should be in the World, nor in the Actions of Men. Though there is no *Legal* Permission, or allowance of it; (for the Law of God forbids it) yet there is a *Providential* Permission of it. God could have kept it out of his World. 7. *That He limits and sets Bounds to the Actions of Second Causes: what they shall do, and how farre they shall proceed in this or that way.* He set bounds to Satan, when he had Commission to afflict *Job.* He limits, and restrains the Eruptions of the Wrath & Rage of the Churches Adversaries, *Ps.* 76. 10. He sets bounds to the sinfull Actions of Men: He regulates and governs all the Actions of Second Causes, as to time, place, degrees, and all manner of Circumstances. He is not the *Author:* but He is the *Orderer* of Sin it self. 8. *That He serves Himself, and his own Ends of all Second*

Causes. He makes them all in all their Operations subservient to his own Designs: and that not only natural, but rational Agents, that act by Counsel. And not only such of them as are his professed willing Servants. Many serve God's ends beside their Intentions, and against their wills. I will do this and that saith God, by the *Assyrian, howbeit he meaneth not so,* Is. 10. 6, 7. Wicked men and Devils do God's will against their own will, and beside their Intentions. *Ye thought Evil against me* (saith *Joseph* to his Brethren) *but God meant it for good &c.* Gen. 50. 20. God elicites what good He pleases out of the actions of his Creatures. Whatever this or that Agent proposeth to himself, yet God alwayes attaineth His Ends. He serves Himself of the very Sins of his Creatures, and brings good out of them. He makes that which is not *Bonum honestum,* to be *Bonum conducibile:* and though Sin is not good; yet, as God orders the matter, it is good, in order to many holy Ends, that Sin should be in the World, as *Austin observes.*

9. *That He useth means in themselves* unfit, *and improves Agents of themselves* insufficient, *to bring about his own Purposes & produce marveilous Effects.* Yea, and it is as easy with Him to do any thing by weak and insufficient, as by the ablest & most accomplished Instruments. *There is no restraint to the Lord to Save by many, or by few.* 1 Sam. 14. 6. *It is nothing with Him to help, whether with many, or with them that have no power.* 2 Chron. 14. 11. Despicable Instruments, sometimes, do great Things in His Hand. 10. *That He renders the aptest means ineffectual, and the Vndertakings of the most sufficient Agents unsuccessful, when He pleases.* He hath a *Negative Voice* upon all the Counsels and Endeavours, and Active Power of the Creature. He can stop the Sun in its course, and cause it to withdraw its shining; He can give check to the Fire, that it shall not burn; & to the hungry Lions, that they shall not devour: and He can order it so, that the men of might shall *sleep their sleep, and not find their Hands.* He can break the Ranks of the most orderly Souldiers, take away courage from the stoutest hearts, send a pannick

Fear into a mighty Host, and defeat the Counsels of the wisest
Leaders and Conducters. He can blow upon, and blast the likeliest
Undertakings of the ablest Men. In a word: the Lord being the
Absolute First Cause, and supream Governour of all his Creatures, and all their Actions; though He hath set an Order among
his Creatures, this shall be the cause of that effect, &c. yet He himself is not tied to that Order; but Interrupts the course of it, when
He pleases. The Lord reserves a Liberty to Himself to interpose,
and to Umpire matters of Success and Event, contrary to the
Law and common Rule of Second Causes. And though He ordinarily concurreth with Second Causes according to the Law given
and Order set; yet sometimes there is in his Providence a Varia-
tion and Digression. Though He hath given Creatures power to
act; and Man, to act as *a Cause by Counsel,* and hath furnished
him with active Abilities; yet He hath not made any Creature
Master of Events; but reserves the Disposal of Issues, and Events
to Himself. Herein the absolute Soveraignty and Dominion of
God appears.

2. *Otherwise, the Lord might possibly suffer real Disappointment, and be defeated of his Ends in some Instances.* He might
be cross'd in his Designs, if any of his Creatures could doe what
they will, without absolute Dependence upon Him. He could not
be sure of his Ends, & what He designs in the World, if He had
not command of all Events that may further or hinder them. If
there were any active power in Creatures that He cannot controll;
or any one event that is out of his Reach, and absolutely in the
Creature's power, exempted from his providential Command, it
would be possible that He might be defeated of his Ends, and so
far unhappy, as to his *voluntary Happiness,* which results from
his having his *Pleasure done* in the World, and compassing all his
Ends in the works of Creation and Providence. God hath made
all Things, ruleth all Things, and manageth all Things according
to the Counsel of his Will, in a way of subserviency to Himself,
and his own Occasions: which He could not do universally and
infrustrably, if He had not the absolute and infallible Determina-

tion of all Events in his own Hand. *But His Counsel shall stand, and He will do all his Pleasure:* Is. 46. 10. Thus much for the Explication, and Confirmation of the Doctrine.

USE I. Of Instruction, in these Particulars.

1. *We see what a poor dependent, nothing-Creature Proud Man is:* Depending absolutely upon God for his Being, Actions, and the Success of them. Men of greatest Sufficiency cannot get their own Bread, or bring any thing to effect in their own strength. Let their Abilities be what they will (*Swiftness,* for the *Race; Strength,* for the *Battel; Wisdom,* for getting their *Bread, &c.*) yet they shall stand them in no stead without the concurrence and Blessing of God. Man saith, he will do this and that: but he must ask God leave first. He saith, To day or to morrow I will go to such a place, and buy and sell, & get gain; whereas he knows not what shall be: but it shall certainly be as the Lord will. *The way of man is not in himself; it is not in man that walketh to direct his steps,* nor perform any thing that he purposeth, without divine Concurrence, or Permission. He hath not the Success of any of his actions in his own power; nor doth he know that any thing he doth shall prosper. One would wonder poor *dependent* man should be so *proud!* Any little thing lifts him up. When the Souldier on such occasions as these, is in his Bravery, in his military Garb drest up for the purpose, with his *Buffe Coat,* his *Scarfe,* his *rich Belt,* his *Arms, a good Horse under him,* O what a goodly Creature is he in his own Eyes! and what wonders can he do in his own conceit! and yet he hath as absolute need of God's Assistance, if he go forth to Battel, as any naked, unarmed man. He cannot move a step, or fetch his next breath, or bring his hand to his mouth, or leap over a straw, or do any thing, without help from God, *in whose hand his breath is, and whose are all his wayes* Dan. 5. 23. It's strange to see how the hearts of men are lifted up with nothing! *O cease ye from Man: for wherein is he to be accounted of?*

2. *We see that there is, and there is not* Chance *in the World.* Chance there is, in respect of Second Causes: (so some things fall

out Κατα Συγχυριαν as our Saviour speaks *Luk*. 10. 31.) but no
Chance as to the first Cause. That piece of *Atheism,* and *Hea-
thenism* ascribing things to *Fortune* and *Chance,* is hardly rooted
out of the minds of men, that are or should be better instructed
and informed. The *Philistines* when they were plagued, could not
tell whether *God* had done it, or a meer *Chance* happened to
them, 1 *Sam*. 6. 9. They understood not, that what was *a Chance
to them,* was ordered by the *Providence of God*. Truth is, Chance
is something that falls out beside the Scope, Intention, and fore-
sight of *Man,* the Reason and cause whereof may be hid from
him; and so it excludes the Counsel of *Men;* but it doth not ex-
clude the Counsel and Providence of *God;* but is ordered and
governed thereby. And it is so farre from being *Chance* to God,
that there is as much (if not more) of the Wisdom, and Will,
and Power of God appearing in matters of Chance and Contingency, as in any other Events.

3. *We see here something of the Power, and Greatness, and
Glory of God appearing in his Efficiency, whereby He works all
in all.* As He is himself Independent, so all Things have an absolute Dependence on Him. He gives Success, or causeth Disappointment, as he pleaseth. So that men are wholly beholden to
Him for all the good they enjoy: for Victory, for Bread, for
Riches, for Favour and Acceptance, for all. Nothing comes to pass
without his permission, if it be *moral Evil;* without his Concurse
and cooperation, yea, Predetermination, if it be *moral* or *physical
Good,* or *penal Evil*. In him we live and move, and have our
Being. The Counsels of the ablest Statesmen, how rational soever,
shall not prosper without him: Ministers, how sufficient soever,
pious, learned, industrious, zealous, shall convert no man, edify
no man, comfort & establish no man, without Him. 1 *Cor*. 3. 6, 7.
Though Scholars study hard, they shall make no proficiency without the Blessing of God. The Merchant may trade, and project
rationally, and yet shall not grow rich upon it, unless God give
him success. It is God that maketh *Zebulum rejoice in his Going
out, and Issachar in his Tents:* that crowns the labours of Seamen,
Merchants, and Husbandmen with Success. *Except the Lord build*

the House &c Ps. 127. 1. *Training Days, Artillery Days,* tho' of great use, and very necessary; yet are all in vain, unless the Lord bless. He must instruct, and teach, and accomplish you; otherwise the help of your expert Officers, and your own endeavours to learn War, will signify nothing. And when valiant Souldiers come to fight; whatever Skill, and Strength, and Courage, and Conduct, and Advantages they have, yet they will be worsted, if the Lord do not give Success. We should learn hence to admire the Power and Greatness of God. It is a lamentable thing, that He that doth all, is thought to do nothing! He can work without Means, by insufficient Means; & blast the ablest Instruments: and yet is little minded in the World. God gives forth a Challenge to Idols, *Do good,* if you can, *or do evil.* Isai. 41. 23. It is God's Prerogative to do good or evil, i.e. not the evil of *Sin* (which argues Defect and Impotency; and comes not within the compass of Omnipotency to do it) but of *Punishment.* God only can give good, or award bad Success; and *Reward* or *Correct* and punish his Creatures that way. *Who is he that saith* (what Man or Angel?) *& it* cometh to pass, when the Lord commandeth it not? Lam. 3. 37. O see, and adore the Greatness of God in this respect! He works all in all. . . .

First, Whatever your own Sufficiencie may be, yet acknowledge God thankfully, as if you had been wholly Insufficient: for your Sufficiencie is of God, and He could have disappointed notwithstanding. The ground of our Unthankfulness for all good Issues and Events of Affairs and Undertakings, is, because we do not see the good Hand of God dispensing all to us. We make too *little* of God, and too *much* of our selves; either by thinking we deserve better than God hath done for us (Hence a proud Heart is never thankful to God or Man) or by thinking we have done all, or more than we have done, toward the getting of this or that Mercy. We put our selves too much in the place of God; as if it were in our power to make our Endeavours Successful, and to give a good Effect and Issue to them, according to *our* Desire. We get up into God's Throne, and usurp upon his Prerogative, and assume that which is peculiar to Him, when we presume we can bring any thing to pass, or do any thing successfully in our Own strength. If we make our selves the only and absolute *first Causes* of our good Success; no marvel we make our selves the *last End* also, and deny God the glorie. O do not ascribe good Success to your own Wit, and Parts, and Policy, and Industrie, and say, my Nimbleness hath won the Race; my Conduct and Courage hath won the Battel; my Wisdom hath gotten me this Bread; my Understanding hath heaped up this Wealth; my Dexteritie, and Skill, and Complaisance, and agreeable Conversation hath procured me the Favour of Rulers or People; my Parts or Study hath given me this Learning. Say not with the Vapouring *Assyrian, By the Strength of My Hand I have done it, and by My Wisdom: for I am Prudent.* Isa. 10. 13. Let not this be so much as the secret Language of your Hearts. Say not, as *Nebuchadnezzar, This is great Babylon, which I have built,* and so derogate from God that works all in all; lest He turn you a grazing, as He did him, with the Beasts of the Field, and teach you better Manners by some severe Correction. Do not *Sacrifice to your own Nets, and burn Incense to your Drags; as if by them your portion were fat, and meat plenteous* (Hab. 1. 16.) but ascribe all to God. There is that deep Wickedness in the Hearts of Men, that if they get any thing by any Fraud, and crafty fetches, and overreaching of their Brethren, in a sinful way, they will be too readie to attribute *that* to the Providence and Blessing of God, and say, it was God's Providence that cast it in upon them; when they have been craftily and sinfully designing it, and bringing it about: but when they have gotten any thing honestly, by their Wisdom and Prudence, and Industrie, they are too ready to forget Providence, and ascribe all to themselves. See the Evil of this, and remember that no People in the World have greater cause of Thankfulness than we have to God, who hath governed *Time* and *Chance* on our behalf marvellously. O Bless Him for good Success, not only when you cannot but acknowledge your own *Insufficiency;* but also when you have apprehensions of the greatest *Sufficiency* of Second Causes. And *Blessed for ever be the Lord, who hath Pleasure in the Prosperity of his Servants,* Psal. 35. 27.

Secondly, *Acknowledge God also in all your Frustrations and Disappointments, so as to resent his Disposals and Dispensations towards you in a* gracious *manner.* We have met with manie Disappointments in the late Warre, and in other respects. We should see God in all. When He blasts our *Corn,* defeats our *Souldiers,* frowns upon our *Merchants,* and we are *disappointed;* now acknowledge the Hand of God, Ordering *Time,* and *Chance* according to his Good Pleasure, Justifie God in all, and bear such Frustrations patientlie. When you have done your Dutie, be quiet, though the Event doth not answer your Endeavours, and Hopes. Take heed of quarrelling at GOD's Disappointments. Do you know VVhom you have to do with? *I was dumb, I opened not my mouth; because Thou didst it.* Psal. 89. 9. If we look at faultie Instruments, or at meer Chance onely, we shall be apt to murmur. It is the observation of One, *That the Reason why men are more apt to fly out into Cursings and Blasphemies for their bad Luck (as they call it) in those Vnlawful Games of* Cards, and Dice, *than in other Exercises, that are governed by Art and Skill, ariseth partly from the very nature of those Games: because when they have tried their Lot or Chance over and over, and their Expectation is deceived, they think that that Power that governs the Lot or Chance, is Adverse to them. They cannot blame their own Art or Skill, when no Art can infallibly determine the Event; but curse their bad Fortune.* And if we look at Disappointments, as our bad *Fortune* and *Chance* onely, looking no further, we shall be apt to fret and quarrel: but if we do indeed see God ordering our Lot for us, it may and ought to silence us. When Magistrates have done their Duty, according to the Law of God, and of the Country, and endeavoured faithfully to give check & stop to the Inundation of *Profaneness* and *Heresy;* and yet the bad Genius of the Times, and degenerous Humour of the People, and this or that Emergency happens, that frustrates the Success of their Counsels and Endeavours; truly they may sit down and mourn indeed; but yet humbly submit to the All-disposing Providence of God. When Ministers have laboured faithfully, and yet Israel is not gathered, and their Labours seem to be in vain, not successful in converting Sinners; they may weep in secret indeed; but yet patiently bear the Unsuccessfulness of their Ministry from the Hand of God. When Souldiers have shewed themselves valiant, and faithful, and done what they can; and yet are worsted: They must acknowledge God's Hand in it, and that *the Battel is the Lord's.* I Sam. 17. 47. who governeth the Warre, and determins the Victory on what side He pleaseth. All men have *Briars* and *Thorns* springing up in the way of their Callings, as well as Husbandmen; and meet with Difficulties and Crosses therein. Get the Spirit *David* had 2 *Sam.* 15. 25, 26. and so acknowledge God in every thing, as to submit humbly to his Disposals, even when they are Adverse, and cross to your Desires and Expectations.

Thirdly, *Be always Prepared for Disappointments.* Do not promise your selves Success from the Sufficiency of Second Causes: God may determine otherwise. . . . Events are not in the Creatures power. The Lord sometimes disappoints men of greatest Sufficiency, overrules and controlls their Counsels and Endeavours, and blasts them strangely. *Time* and *Chance* happens to them. If *Adam* had stood; though he would not have had the Determination of Events & Successes in his own hand; yet God would have determined them for him according to his heartsdesire: and he should never have been disappointed. But since the Fall, as no Man hath power to determine Events (which is God's Prerogative) so it is just with God that every man should meet with Crosses and Disappointments; and this is the Fruit of the Curse, under which all natural men ly: and as for the People of God; though they are delivered from the Curse of the Law, in the *Formality* of it; so that nothing befalls them *as a Curse,* how *cross* soever it be: yet they are not yet absolutely delivered from the *Matter* of the Curse, as appears by the Afflictions they meet with, and Death it self. And indeed it makes sometimes for the glory of God, to disappoint Men of greatest Abilities. When men do not see and own God; but attribute Success to the Sufficiency of Instruments, It's time for God to maintain his own Right (as Dr. *Preston* speaks) and shew that He gives, or denies Success, according to His own good Pleasure. God is much seen in Controlling the ablest Agents, & blasting their Enterprizes; yea more, many times, than in backing them, & blessing their Endeavours in an ordinary Course of Providence. Herein the *Wisdom* of God is much seen. It is best, sometimes, it should be so, with respect to God's Int'rest and Glory. His *Power* also appears in giving Check to the Ablest Instruments, and turning all their Designs another way than they Intended. His Mercy also to his People, is seen herein; for it is best for them, in some Cases, to be defeated and disappointed. His *Justice* also appears herein, in his correcting and punishing the Self-confident, sinful Creature with unexpected Disappointments. So that it is our Wisdom, to look for Changes and Chances, some Occurrents and Emergencies that may blast our Undertakings, that Faith and Prayer may be kept agoing, and lest if such Frustrations befall us unexpectedly, we either fly out against God, or faint and sink in Discouragements. At the first going out of our Forces, in the beginning of the Warre, what great Apprehensions were there of speedy Success and ending of the Warre; that it was but going and Appearing, and the Enemy would be faced down: As if the first News from our Souldiers should be, *Venimus, Vidimus, Vicimus*. And several times after, great probability of concluding that unhappy War; and yet all disappointed, contrary to Expectation. VVhen there is therefore greatest Probability of Success, yet remember there may be Disappointment; and provide for it, that you may not be surprised thereby. This may be good Counsel to men of projecting Heads, that are wont to be very confident that they see their way farre before them: but they do not know what *Time* and *Chance* may happen: This may check the Confidence of Man, and teach us not to promise our selves great Things, or build upon this or that Event or Enjoyment for time to come. Labour to be prepared and provided for Disappointments.

SAMUEL SEWALL

(*1652-1730*)

Bibliographical Note. Sewall's diary is printed in the *Collections of the Massachusetts Historical Society,* 5th ser., V-VII (1878-1882). The selections here printed follow that text; V, 44, 342, 369-370, 419-420, 442-445, VI, 343, VII, 262-276. The best general account of Sewall is N. H. Chamberlain, *Samuel Sewall and the World He Lived In* (Boston, 1897). The diarist, however, reveals himself as no one else can.

from THE DIARY

[WRITTEN 1673-1729]

Jan. 13, 167⁶⁄₇. Giving my chickens meat, it came to my mind that I gave them nothing save Indian corn and water, and yet they eat it and thrived very well, and that that food was necessary for them, how mean soever, which much affected me and convinced what need I stood in of spiritual food, and that I should not nauseat daily duties of Prayer, &c.

. . . . .

March 19, 169⁰⁄₁. Mr. C. Mather preaches the Lecture from Mat. 24., and appoint his portion with the Hypocrites: In his proem said, *Totus mundus agit histrionem.* Said one sign of a hypocrit was for a man to strain at a Gnat and swallow a Camel. Sign in 's Threat discovered him; To be zealous against an iñocent fashion, taken up and used by the best of men; and yet make no Conscience of being guilty of great Immoralities. Tis supposed means wearing of Perriwigs: said would deny themselves in any thing but parting with an ōportunity to do God service; that so might not offend good Christians. Meaning, I suppose, was fain to wear a Perriwig for his health. I expected not to hear a vindication of Perriwigs in Boston Pulpit by Mr. Mather; however, not from that Text. The Lord give me a good Heart and help to know, and not only to know but also to doe his Will; that my Heart and Head may be his.

Nov. 6. Joseph threw a knop of Brass and hit his Sister Betty on the forhead so as to make it bleed and swell; upon which, and for his playing at Prayer-time, and eating when Return Thanks, I whipd him pretty smartly. When I first went in (call'd by his Grandmother) he sought to shadow and hide himself from me behind the head of the Cradle: which gave me the sorrowfull remembrance of Adam's carriage.

.   .   .   .   .

Nov. 22, 1692. I prayd that God would pardon all my Sinfull Wanderings, and direct me for the future. That God would bless the Assembly in their debates, and that would chuse and assist our Judges, &c., and save New England as to Enemies and Witch-crafts, and vindicate the late Judges, consisting with his Justice and Holiness, &c., with Fasting. Cousin Anne Quinsy visited me in the Evening, and told me of her children's wellfare. Now about, Mercy Short grows ill again, as formerly.

[Jan. 13, 169⅚.]

.   .   .   .   .

When I came in, past 7. at night, my wife met me in the Entry and told me Betty had surprised them. I was surprised with the abruptness of the Relation. It seems Betty Sewall had given some signs of dejection and sorrow; but a little after diñer she burst out into an amazing cry, which caus'd all the family to cry too; Her Mother ask'd the reason; she gave none; at last said she was afraid she should goe to Hell, her Sins were not pardon'd. She was first wounded by my reading a Sermon of Mr. Norton's, about the 5ᵗʰ. of Jan. Text Jnᵒ 7. 34. Ye shall seek me and shall not find me. And those words in the Sermon, Jnᵒ 8. 21. Ye shall seek me and shall die in your sins, ran in her mind, and terrified her greatly. And staying at home Jan. 12. she read out of Mr. Cotton Mather—Why hath Satan filled thy heart, which increas'd her Fear. Her Mother ask'd her whether she pray'd. She answer'd, Yes; but feared her prayers were not heard because her Sins not pardon'd. Mr. Willard though sent for timelyer, yet not being told of the message, till bruised Dinsdals [?] was given him; He came not till after I came home. He discoursed with Betty who could not give a distinct account, but was confused as his phrase was, and as had experienced in himself. Mr. Willard pray'd excellently. The Lord bring Light and Comfort out of this dark and dreadful Cloud, and Grant that Christ's being formed in my dear child, may be the issue of these painfull pangs.

. . . . .

Decr. 21 [1696.] A very great Snow is on the Ground. I go in the morn to Mr. Willard, to entreat him to chuse his own time to come and pray with little Sarah: He comes a little before night, and prays very fully and well. Mr. Mather, the President, had pray^d with her in the time of the Courts sitting. Decr. 22. being Catechising day, I give Mr. Willard a note to pray for my daughter publickly, which he did. Note, this morn Madam Elisa Bellingham came to our house and upbraided me with setting my hand to pass Mr. Wharton's acc^o- to the Court, where he obtain'd a Judgm^t for Eustace's farm. I was wheadled and hector'd into that business, and have all along been uneasy in the remembrance of it: and now there is one come who will not spare to lay load. The Lord take away my filthy garments, and give me change of Rayment. This day I remove poor little Sarah into my Bed-chamber, where about Break of Day Decr. 23. she gives up the Ghost in Nurse Cowell's Arms. Born, Nov. 21, 1694. Neither I nor my wife were by: Nurse not expecting so sudden a change, and having promis'd to call us. I thought of Christ's Words, could you not watch with me one hour! and would fain have sat up with her: but fear of my wives illness, who is very valetudinarious, made me to lodge with her in the new Hall, where was call'd by Jane's Cry, to take notice of my dead daughter. Nurse did long and pathetically ask our pardon that she had not call'd us, and said she was surpriz^d. Thus this very fair day is rendered fowl to us by reason of the general Sorrow and Tears in the family. Master Chiever was here the evening before, I desir'd him to pray for my daughter. The Chapt^r read in course on Decr. 23. m. was Deut. 22. which made me sadly reflect that I had not been so thorowly tender of my daughter; nor so effectually carefull of her Defence and preservation as I should have been. The good Lord pity and pardon and help for the future as to those God has still left me.

Dec^r- 24. Sam. recites to me in Latin, Mat. 12. from the 6th. to the end of the 12th. v. The 7th. verse did awfully bring to mind the Salem Tragedie.

6th. day, Decr. 25, 1696. We bury our little daughter. In the chamber, Joseph in course reads Ecclesiastes 3^d. a time to be born and a time to die—Elisabeth, Rev. 22. Hanah, the 38th- Psalm. I speak to each, as God helped, to our mutual comfort I hope. I order'd Sam. to read the 102. Psalm. Elisha Cooke, Edw. Hutchinson, John Baily, and Josia Willard bear my little daughter to the Tomb.

Note. Twas wholly dry, and I went at noon to see in what order things were set; and there I was entertain'd with a view of, and converse with, the Coffins of my dear Father Hull, Mother Hull, Cousin Quinsey, and my Six Children: for the little posthumous was now took up and set in upon that that stands on John's: so are three, one upon another twice, on the bench at the end. My Mother ly's on a lower bench, at the end, with head to her Husband's head: and I order'd little Sarah to be set on her Grandmother's feet. 'Twas an awfull yet pleasing Treat; Having said, The Lord knows who shall be brought hither next, I came away.

.   .   .   .   .

[Jan. 14, 1697.]

.   .   .   .   .

Copy of the Bill I put up on the Fast day;[1] giving it to Mr. Willard as he pass'd by, and standing up at the reading of it, and bowing when finished; in the Afternoon.

Samuel Sewall, sensible of the reiterated strokes of God upon himself and family; and being sensible, that as to the Guilt con-

---

[1] This day was officially appointed as one of public fasting, prayer, and contrition over the Witchcraft Trials of 1692, in which Sewall had participated.

tracted upon the opening of the late Comission of Oyer and Terminer at Salem (to which the order for this Day relates) he is, upon many accounts, more concerned than any that he knows of, Desires to take the Blame and shame of it, Asking pardon of men, And especially desiring prayers that God, who has an Unlimited Authority, would pardon that sin and all other his sins; personal and Relative: And according to his infinite Benignity, and Sovereignty, Not Visit the sin of him, or of any other, upon himself or any of his, nor upon the Land: But that He would powerfully defend him against all Temptations to Sin, for the future; and vouchsafe him the efficacious, saving Conduct of his Word and Spirit.

. . . . .

Sixth-day, April, 11 [1712]. I saw Six Swallows together flying and chipering very rapturously.

. . . . .

Sept. 30, 1720. Mr. Colman's Lecture: Daughter Sewall acquaints Madam Winthrop that if she pleas'd to be within at 3. p.m. I would wait on her. She answer'd she would be at home.

Oct. 1, 1720. Satterday, I dine at Mr. Stoddard's: from thence I went to Madam Winthrop's just at 3. Spake to her, saying, my loving wife died so soon and suddenly, 'twas hardly convenient for me to think of Marrying again; however I came to this Resolution, that I would not make my Court to any person without first Consulting with her. Had a pleasant discourse about 7 Single persons sitting in the Fore-seat 7^r 29th, viz. Mad^m Rebekah Dudley, Catharine Winthrop, Bridget Usher, Deliverance Legg, Rebekah Loyd, Lydia Colman, Elizabeth Bellingham. She propounded one and another for me; but none would do, said Mrs. Loyd was about her Age.

Oct. 3, 1720. Waited on Madam Winthrop again; 'twas a little while before she came in. Her daughter Noyes being there alone with me, I said, I hoped my Waiting on her Mother would not be disagreeable to her. She answer'd she should not be against that

that might be for her Comfort. I Saluted her, and told her I per-
ceiv'd I must shortly wish her a good Time; (her mother had told
me, she was with Child, and within a Moneth or two of her
Time). By and by in came Mr. Airs, Chaplain of the Castle, and
hang'd up his Hat, which I was a little startled at, it seeming as
if he was to lodge there. At last Madam Winthrop came too. After
a considerable time, I went up to her and said, if it might not be
inconvenient I desired to speak with her. She assented, and spake
of going into another Room; but Mr. Airs and Mrs. Noyes presently rose up, and went out, leaving us there alone. Then I usher'd
in Discourse from the names in the Fore-seat; at last I pray'd that
Katharine [Mrs. Winthrop] might be the person assign'd for me.
She instantly took it up in the way of Denyal, as if she had catch'd
at an Opportunity to do it, saying she could not do it before she
was asked. Said that was her mind unless she should Change it,
which she believed she should not; could not leave her Children.
I express'd my Sorrow that she should do it so Speedily, pray'd her
Consideration, and ask'd her when I should wait on her agen. She
setting no time, I mention'd that day Sennight. Gave her Mr.
Willard's Fountain open'd with the little print and verses; saying,
I hop'd if we did well read that book, we should meet together
hereafter, if we did not now. She took the Book, and put it in her
Pocket. Took Leave.

Oct. 6, 1720. A little after 6. p.m. I went to Madam Winthrop's.
She was not within. I gave Sarah Chickering the Maid 2^s, Juno,
who brought in wood, 1^s. Afterward the Nurse came in, I gave
her 18^d, having no other small Bill. After awhile Dr. Noyes came
in with his Mother; and quickly after his wife came in: They sat
talking, I think, till eight a-clock. I said I fear'd I might be some
Interruption to their Business: Dr. Noyes reply'd pleasantly: He
fear'd they might be an Interruption to me, and went away.
Madam seem'd to harp upon the same string. Must take care of
her Children; could not leave that House and Neighbourhood
where she had dwelt so long. I told her she might doe her children as much or more good by bestowing what she laid out in
Hous-keeping, upon them. Said her Son would be of Age the

7th of August. I said it might be inconvenient for her to dwell
with her Daughter-in-Law, who must be Mistress of the House.
I gave her a piece of Mr. Belcher's Cake and Ginger-Bread
wrapped up in a clean sheet of Paper; told her of her Father's
kindness to me when Treasurer, and I Constable. My Daughter
Judith was gon from me and I was more lonesom—might help
to forward one another in our Journey to Canaan.—Mr. Eyre
came within the door; I saluted him, ask'd how Mr. Clark did,
and he went away. I took leave about 9 aclock. I told [her] I
came now to refresh her Memory as to Monday-night; said she
had not forgot it. In discourse with her, I ask'd leave to speak with
her Sister; I meant to gain Mad^m Mico's favour to persuade her
Sister. She seem'd surpris'd and displeas'd, and said she was in the
same condition!

Oct. 10, 1720. In the Evening I visited Madam Winthrop, who
treated me with a great deal of Curtesy; Wine, Marmalade. I gave
her a News-Letter about the Thanksgiving Proposals, for sake of
the verses for David Jeffries. She tells me Dr. Increase Mather
visited her this day, in Mr. Hutchinson's Coach.

Oct. 11, 1720. I writ a few Lines to Madam Winthrop to this
purpose: "Madam, These wait on you with Mr. Mayhew's Sermon, and Account of the state of the Indians on Martha's Vin-
yard. I thank you for your Unmerited Favours of yesterday; and
hope to have the Happiness of Waiting on you to-morrow before
Eight a-clock after Noon. I pray God to keep you, and give you a
joyfull entrance upon the Two Hundred and twenty ninth year
of Christopher Columbus his Discovery; and take Leave, who am,
Madam, your humble Servt. S.S.

Oct. 12, 1720. Mrs. Anne Cotton came to door (twas before 8.)
said Madam Winthrop was within, directed me into the little
Room, where she was full of work behind a Stand; Mrs. Cotton
came in and stood. Madam Winthrop pointed to her to set me a
Chair. Madam Winthrop's Countenance was much changed from
what 'twas on Monday, look'd dark and lowering. At last, the
work, (black stuff or Silk) was taken away, I got my Chair in
place, had some Converse, but very Cold and indifferent to what

'twas before. Ask'd her to acquit me of Rudeness if I drew off her Glove. Enquiring the reason, I told her twas great odds between handling a dead Goat, and a living Lady. Got it off. I told her I had one Petition to ask of her, that was, that she would take off the Negative she laid on me the third of October; She readily answer'd she could not, and enlarg'd upon it; She told me of it so soon as she could; could not leave her house, children, neighbours, business. I told her she might do som Good to help and support me. Mentioning Mrs. Gookin, Nath, the widow Weld was spoken of; said I had visited Mrs. Denison. I told her Yes! Afterward I said, If after a first and second Vagary she would Accept of me returning, Her Victorious Kindness and Good Will would be very Obliging. She thank'd me for my Book, (Mr. Mayhew's Sermon), But said not a word of the Letter. When she insisted on the Negative, I pray'd there might be no more Thunder and Lightening, I should not sleep all night. I gave her Dr. Preston, The Church's Marriage and the Church's Carriage, which cost me 6^s at the Sale. The door standing open, Mr. Airs came in, hung up his Hat, and sat down. After awhile, Madam Winthrop moving, he went out. Jno Eyre look'd in, I said How do ye, or, your servant Mr. Eyre: but heard no word from him. Sarah fill'd a Glass of Wine, she drank to me, I to her, She sent Juno home with me with a good Lantern, I gave her 6^d and bid her thank her Mistress. In some of our Discourse, I told her I had rather go to the Stone-House adjoining to her, than to come to her against her mind. Told her the reason why I came every other night was lest I should drink too deep draughts of Pleasure. She had talk'd of Canary, her Kisses were to me better than the best Canary. Explain'd the expression Concerning Columbus.

Oct. 13. I tell my Son and daughter Sewall, that the Weather was not so fair as I apprehended.

Oct. 17. In the Evening I visited Madam Winthrop, who Treated me Courteously, but not in Clean Linen as sometimes. She said, she did not know whether I would come again, or no. I ask'd her how she could so impute inconstancy to me. (I had not visited her since Wednesday night being unable to get over the Indisposition received by the Treatment received that night, and *I must* in it seem'd to sound like a made piece of Formality.) Gave her this day's Gazett. Heard David Jeffries say the Lord's Prayer, and some other portions of the Scriptures. He came to the door, and ask'd me to go into Chamber, where his Grandmother was tending Little Katee, to whom she had given Physick; but I chose to sit below. Dr. Noyes and his wife came in, and sat a Considerable time; had been visiting Son and dâter Cooper. Juno came home with me.

Oct. 18, 1720. Visited Madam Mico, who came to me in a splendid Dress. I said, It may be you have heard of my Visiting Madam Winthrop, her Sister. She answered, Her Sister had told her of it. I ask'd her good Will in the Affair. She answer'd, If her Sister were for it, she should not hinder it. I gave her Mr. Homes's Sermon. She gave me a Glass of Canary, entertain'd me with good Discourse, and a Respectfull Remembrance of my first Wife. I took Leave.

Oct. 19, 1720. Midweek, Visited Madam Winthrop; Sarah told me she was at Mr. Walley's, would not come home till late. I gave her Hannah 3 oranges with her Duty, not knowing whether I should find her or no. Was ready to go home: but said if I knew she was there, I would go thither. Sarah seem'd to speak with pretty good Courage, She would be there. I went and found her there, with Mr. Walley and his wife in the little Room below. At 7 a-clock I mentioned going home; at 8. I put on my Coat, and quickly waited on her home. She found occasion to speak loud to the servant, as if she had a mind to be known. Was Courteous to me; but took occasion to speak pretty earnestly about my keeping a Coach: I said 'twould cost £100. per annum: she said twould cost but £40. . . . Exit. Came away somewhat late.

Oct. 20, 1720. . . . Madam Winthrop not being at Lecture, I went thither first; found her very Serene with her dâter Noyes, Mrs. Dering, and the widow Shipreev sitting at a little Table, she in her arm'd Chair. She drank to me, and I to Mrs. Noyes. After awhile pray'd the favour to speak with her. She took one of the Candles, and went into the best Room, clos'd the shutters, sat down upon the Couch. She told me Madam Usher had been there, and said the Coach must be set on Wheels, and not by Rusting. She spake somthing of my needing a Wigg. Ask'd me what her Sister said to me. I told her, She said, If her Sister were for it, She would not hinder it. But I told her, she did not say she would be glad to have me for her Brother. Said, I shall keep you in the Cold, and asked her if she would be within to morrow night, for we had had but a running Feat. She said she could not tell whether she should, or no. I took Leave. As were drinking at the Governour's, he said: In England the Ladies minded little more than that they might have Money, and Coaches to ride in. I said, And New-England brooks its Name. At which Mr. Dudley smiled. Govr said they were not quite so bad here.

Oct. 21, 1720. Friday, My Son, the Minister, came to me p.m by appointment and we pray one for another in the Old Chamber; more especially respecting my Courtship. About 6. a-clock I go to Madam Winthrop's; Sarah told me her Mistress was gon out, but did not tell me whither she went. She presently order'd me a Fire; so I went in, having Dr. Sibb's Bowels with me to read. I read the two first Sermons, still no body came in: at last about 9. a-clock Mr. Jn° Eyre came in; I took the opportunity to say to him as I had done to Mrs. Noyes before, that I hoped my Visiting his Mother would not be disagreeable to him; He answered me with much Respect. When twas after 9. a-clock He of himself said he would go and call her, she was but at one of his Brothers: A while after I heard Madam Winthrop's voice, enquiring something about John. After a good while and Clapping the Garden door twice or thrice, she came in. I mentioned something of the lateness; she banter'd me, and said I was later. She receiv'd me Courteously. I ask'd when our proceedings should be made publick: She said They were like to be no more publick than they were already. Offer'd me no Wine that I remember. I rose up at 11 a-clock to come away, saying I would put on my Coat, She offer'd not to help me. I pray'd her that Juno might light me home, she open'd the Shutter, and said twas pretty light abroad; Juno was weary and gon to bed. So I came hôm by Star-light as

well as I could. At my first coming in, I gave Sarah five Shillings.
I writ Mr. Eyre his Name in his book with the date Octob^r 21.
1720. It cost me 8^s. Jehovah jireh! Madam told me she had visited
M. Mico, Wendell, and Wm Clark of the South [Church].

Oct. 22, 1720. Dâter Cooper visited me before my going out of
Town, staid till about Sun set. I brought her going near as far as
the Orange Tree. Coming back, near Leg's Corner, Little David
Jeffries saw me, and looking upon me very lovingly, ask'd me if
I was going to see his Grandmother? I said, Not to-night. Gave
him a peny, and bid him present my Service to his Grandmother.

Oct. 24, 1720. I went in the Hackny Coach through the Common, stop'd at Madam Winthrop's (had told her I would take
my departure from thence). Sarah came to the door with Katee
in her Arms: but I did not think to take notice of the Child.
Call'd her Mistress. I told her, being encourag'd by David Jeffries
loving eyes, and sweet Words, I was come to enquire whether
she could find in her heart to leave that House and Neighbourhood, and go and dwell with me at the Southend; I think she said
softly, Not yet. I told her It did not ly in my Lands to keep a
Coach. If I should, I should be in danger to be brought to keep
company with her Neighbour Brooker, (he was a little before
sent to prison for Debt). Told her I had an Antipathy against
those who would pretend to give themselves; but nothing of their
Estate. I would a proportion of my Estate with my self. And I
suppos'd she would do so. As to a Perriwig, My best and greatest
Friend, I could not possibly have a greater, began to find me with
Hair before I was born, and had continued to do so ever since;
and I could not find in my heart to go to another. She commended
the book I gave her, Dr. Preston, the Church Marriage; quoted
him saying 'twas inconvenient keeping out of a Fashion commonly used. I said the Time and Tide did circumscribe my Visit.
She gave me a Dram of Black-Cherry Brandy, and gave me a
lump of the Sugar that was in it. She wish'd me a good Journy. I
pray'd God to keep her, and came away. Had a very pleasant
Journy to Salem.

Oct. 31, 1720. At night I visited Madam Winthrop about 6. p.m.

They told me she was gon to Madam Mico's. I went thither and found she was gon; so return'd to her house, read the Epistles to the Galatians, Ephesians in Mr. Eyre's Latin Bible. After the Clock struck 8. I began to read the 103. Psalm. Mr. Wendell came in from his Warehouse. Ask'd me if I were alone? Spake very kindly to me, offer'd me to call Madam Winthrop. I told him, She would be angry, had been at Mrs. Mico's; he help'd me on with my Coat and I came home: left the Gazett in the Bible, which told Sarah of, bid her present my Service to Mrs. Winthrop, and tell her I had been to wait on her if she had been at home.

Nov. 1, 1720. I was so taken up that I could not go if I would.

Nov. 2, 1720. Midweek, went again, and found Mrs. Alden there, who quickly went out. Gave her about ½ pound of Sugar Almonds, cost 3ˢ per £. Carried them on Monday. She seem'd pleas'd with them, ask'd what they cost. Spake of giving her a Hundred pounds per anum if I dy'd before her. Ask'd her what sum she would give me, if she should dy first? Said I would give her time to Consider of it. She said she heard as if I had given all to my Children by Deeds of Gift. I told her 'twas a mistake, Point-Judith was mine &c. That in England, I own'd, my Father's desire was that it should go to my eldest Son; 'twas 20 £ per annum; she thought 'twas forty. I think when I seem'd to excuse pressing this, she seem'd to think twas best to speak of it; a long winter was coming on. Gave me a Glass or two of Canary.

Nov. 4, 1720. Friday, Went again about 7. a-clock; found there Mr. John Walley and his wife: sat discoursing pleasantly. I shew'd them Isaac Moses's [an Indian] Writing. Madam W. serv'd Comfeits to us. After awhile a Table was spread, and Supper was set. I urg'd Mr. Walley to Crave a Blessing; but he put it upon me. About 9. they went away. I ask'd Madam what fashioned Necklace I should present her with, She said, None at all. I ask'd her Whereabout we left off last time; mention'd what I had offer'd to give her; Ask'd her what she would give me; She said she could not Change her Condition: She had said so from the beginning; could not be so far from her Children, the Lecture. Quoted the Apostle Paul affirming that a single Life was better than a Married. I answer'd That was for the present Distress. Said she had not pleasure in things of that nature as formerly: I said, you are the fitter to make me a Wife. If she hald in that mind, I must go home and bewail my Rashness in making more haste than good Speed. However, considering the Supper, I desired her to be within next Monday night, if we liv'd so long. Assented. She charg'd me with saying, that she must put away Juno, if she came to me: I utterly deny'd it, it never came in my heart; yet she insisted upon it; saying it came in upon discourse about the Indian woman that obtained her Freedom this Court. About 10. I said I would not disturb the good orders of her House, and came away. She not seeming pleas'd with my Coming away. Spake to her about David Jeffries, had not seen him.

Nov. 7, 1720. My Son pray'd in the Old Chamber. Our time had been taken up by Son and Daughter Cooper's Visit; so that I only read the 130th and 143 Psalm. Twas on the Account of my Courtship. I went to Mad. Winthrop; found her rocking her little Katee in the Cradle. I excus'd my Coming so late (near Eight). She set me an arm'd Chair and Cusheon; and so the Cradle was between her arm'd Chair and mine. Gave her the remnant of my Almonds; She did not eat of them as before; but laid them away; I said I came to enquire whether she had alter'd her mind since Friday, or remained of the same mind still. She said, Thereabouts. I told her I loved her, and was so fond as to think that she loved me: She said had a great respect for me. I told her, I had made her an offer, without asking any advice; she had so many to advise with, that twas a hindrance. The Fire was come to one short Brand besides the Block, which Brand was set up in end; at last it fell to pieces, and no Recruit was made: She gave me a Glass of Wine. I think I repeated again that I would go home and bewail my Rashness in making more haste than good Speed. I would endeavour to contain myself, and not go on to sollicit her to do that which she could not Consent to. Took leave of her. As came down the steps she bid me have a Care. Treated me Courteously. Told her she had enter'd the 4th year of her Widowhood. I had given her the News-Letter before; I did not bid her draw off her Glove as sometime I had done. Her Dress was not so clean as somtime it had been. Jehovah jireh!

Nov. 9, 1720. Dine at Bro^r Stoddard's: were so kind as to enquire of me if they should invite M^{rm} Winthrop; I answer'd No. Thank'd my Sister Stoddard for her Courtesie; . . . She sent her servant home with me with a Lantern. Madam Winthrop's Shutters were open as I pass'd by.

MRS. MARY ROWLANDSON

(C. 1635-c. 1678)

Bibliographical Note. The text printed below follows that of the second edition "Corrected and amended." No copy of the first edition, issued the same year as the second, is known. On Mrs. Rowlandson and the tradition of the captivity narrative, see R. H. Pearce, "The Significances of the Captivity Narrative," *American Literature,* XIX (1947), 1-20.

from THE SOVERAIGNTY AND GOODNESS OF GOD, TOGETHER WITH THE FAITHFULNESS OF HIS PROMISES DISPLAYED; BEING A NARRATIVE OF THE CAPTIVITY AND RESTAURATION OF MRS. MARY ROWLANDSON (1682)

On the tenth of February 1675, Came the Indians with great numbers upon Lancaster: Their first coming was about Sunrising; hearing the noise of some Guns, we looked out; several Houses were burning, and the Smoke ascending to Heaven. There were five persons taken in one house, the Father, and the Mother and a sucking Child, they knockt on the head; the other two they took and carried away alive. Their were two others, who being out of their Garison upon some occasion were set upon; one was knockt on the head, the other escaped: Another their was who running along was shot and wounded, and fell down; he begged of them his life, promising them Money (as they told me) but they would not hearken to him but knockt him in head, and stript him naked, and split open his Bowels. Another seeing many of the Indians about his Barn, ventured and went out, but was quickly shot down. There were three others belonging to the same Garison who were killed; the Indians getting up upon the roof of the Barn, had advantage to shoot down upon them over their Fortification. Thus these murtherous wretches went on, burning, and destroying before them.

At length they came and beset our own house, and quickly it was the dolefullest day that ever mine eyes saw. The House stood upon the edg of a hill; some of the Indians got behind the hill, others into the Barn, and others behind any thing that could shelter them; from all which places they shot against the House, so that the Bullets seemed to fly like hail; and quickly they wounded one man among us, then another, and then a third, About two hours (according to my observation, in that amazing time) they had been about the house before they prevailed to fire it (which they did with Flax and Hemp, which they brought out of the Barn, and there being no defence about the House, only two Flankers at two opposite corners and one of them not finished) they fired it once and one ventured out and quenched it, but they quickly fired it again, and that took. Now is the dreadful hour come, that I have often heard of (in time of War, as it was the case of others) but now mine eyes see it. Some in our house were fighting for their lives, others wallowing in their blood, the House on fire over our heads, and the bloody Heathen ready to knock us on the head, if we stirred out. Now might we hear Mothers and Children crying out for themselves, and one another, Lord, What shall we do? Then I took my Children (and one of my sisters, hers) to go forth and leave the house: but as soon as we came to the dore and appeared, the Indians shot so thick that the bulletts rattled against the House, as if one had taken an handfull of stones and threw them, so that we were fain to give back. We had six stout Dogs belonging to our Garrison, but none of them would stir, though another time, if any Indian had come to the door, they were ready to fly upon him and tear him down. The Lord hereby would make us the more to acknowledge his hand, and to see that our help is always in him. But out we must go, the fire increasing, and coming along behind us, roaring, and the Indians gaping before us with their Guns, Spears and Hatchets to devour us. No sooner were we out of the House, but my Brother in Law (being before wounded, in defending the house, in or near the throat) fell down dead, wherat the Indians scornfully shouted, and hallowed, and were presently upon him, stripping off his cloaths, the bulletts flying thick, one went through my side, and the same (as would seem) through the bowels and hand of my dear Child in my arms. One of my elder Sisters Children, named William, had then his Leg broken, which the Indians perceiving, they knockt him on head. Thus were we butchered by those merciless Heathen, standing amazed, with the blood running down to our heels. My eldest Sister being yet in the House, and seeing those wofull sights, the Infidels haling Mothers one way, and Children another, and some wallowing in their blood: and her elder Son telling her that her Son William was dead, and my self was wounded, she said, And, Lord, let me dy with them; which was no sooner said, but she was struck with a Bullet, and fell down dead over the threshold. I hope she is reaping the fruit of her good labours, being faithful to the service of God in her place. In her younger years she lay under much trouble upon spiritual accounts, till it pleased God to make that precious Scripture take hold of her heart, 2 Cor. 12. 9. *And he said unto me, my Grace is sufficient for thee.* More then twenty years after I have heard her tell how sweet and comfortable that place was to her. But to return: The Indians laid hold of us, pulling me one way, and the Children another, and said, Come go along with us; I told them they would kill me: they answered, If I were willing to go along with them, they would not hurt me.

Oh the dolefull sight that now was to behold at this House! *Come, behold the works of the Lord, what dissolations he has made in the Earth.* Of thirty seven persons who were in this one House, none escaped either present death, or a bitter captivity, save only one, who might say as he, Job 1. 15, *And I only am escaped alone to tell the News.* There were twelve killed, some shot, some stab'd with their Spears, some knock'd down with their Hatchets. When we are in prosperity, Oh the little that we think of such dreadfull sights, and to see our dear Friends, and Relations ly bleeding out their heart-blood upon the ground. There was one who was chopt into the head with a Hatchet, and stript naked, and yet was crawling up and down. It is a solemn sight to see so many Christians lying in their blood, some here, and some there, like a company of Sheep torn by Wolves, All of them stript naked by a company of hell-hounds, roaring, singing, ranting and insulting, as if they would have torn our very hearts out; yet the Lord by his Almighty power preserved a number of us from death, for there were twenty-four of us taken alive and carried Captive.

I had often before this said, that if the Indians should come, I should chuse rather to be killed by them then taken alive but when it came to the tryal my mind changed; their glittering weapons so daunted my spirit, that I chose rather to go along with those (as I may say) ravenous Beasts, then that moment to end my dayes; and that I may the better declare what happened to me during that grievous Captivity, I shall particularly speak of the severall Removes we had up and down the Wilderness.

THE FIRST REMOVE

Now away we must go with those Barbarous Creatures, with our bodies wounded and bleeding, and our hearts no less than our bodies. About a mile we went that night, up upon a hill within sight of the Town, where they intended to lodge. There was hard by a vacant house (deserted by the English before, for fear of the Indians). I asked them whither I might not lodge in the house that night to which they answered, what will you love English men still? this was the dolefullest night that ever my eyes saw. Oh the roaring, and singing and danceing, and yelling of those black creatures in the night, which made the place a lively resemblance of hell. And as miserable was the wast that was there made, of Horses, Cattle, Sheep, Swine, Calves, Lambs, Roasting Pigs, and Fowl (which they had plundered in the Town) some roasting, some lying and burning, and some boyling to feed our merciless Enemies; who were joyful enough though we were disconsolate. To add to the dolefulness of the former day, and the dismalness of the present night: my thoughts ran upon my losses and sad bereaved condition. All was gone, my Husband gone (at least separated from me, he being in the Bay; and to add to my grief, the Indians told me they would kill him as he came homeward) my Children gone, my Relations and Friends gone, our house and home and all our comforts within door, and without, all was gone, (except my life) and I knew not but the next moment that might go too. There remained nothing to me but one poor wounded Babe, and it seemed at present worse than death that it was in such a pitiful condition, bespeaking Compassion, and I had no refreshing for it, nor suitable things to revive it. Little do many think what is the savageness and brutishness of this barbarous Enemy, I even those that seem to profess more than others among them, when the English have fallen into their hands.

Those seven that were killed at Lancaster the summer before upon a Sabbath day, and the one that was afterward killed upon a week day, were slain and mangled in a barbarous manner, by one-ey'd John, and Marlborough's Praying Indians, which Capt. Mosely brought to Boston, as the Indians told me.

THE SECOND REMOVE

But now, the next morning, I must turn my back upon the Town, and travel with them into the vast and desolate Wilderness, I knew not whither. It is not my tongue, or pen can express the sorrows of my heart, and bitterness of my spirit, that I had at this departure: but God was with me, in a wonderfull manner, carrying me along, and bearing up my spirit, that it did not quite fail. One of the Indians carried my poor wounded Babe upon a horse, it went moaning all along, I shall dy, I shall dy. I went on foot after it, with sorrow that cannot be exprest. At length I took it off the horse, and carried it in my arms till my strength failed, and I fell down with it: Then they set me upon a horse with my wounded Child in my lap, and there being no furniture upon the horse back, as we were going down a steep hill, we both fell over the horses head, at which they like inhumane creatures laught, and rejoyced to see it, though I thought we should there have ended our dayes, as overcome with so many difficulties. But the Lord renewed my strength still, and carried me along, that I might see more of his Power; yea, so much that I could never have thought of, had I not experienced it.

After this it quickly began to snow, and when night came on, they stopt: and now down I must sit in the snow, by a little fire, and a few boughs behind me, with my sick Child in my lap; and calling much for water, being now (through the wound) fallen into a violent Fever. My own wound also growing so stiff, that I could scarce sit down or rise up, yet so it must be, that I must sit all this cold winter night upon the cold snowy ground, with my sick Child in my armes, looking that every hour would be the last of its life; and having no Christian friend near me, either to comfort or help me. Oh, I may see the wonderfull power of God, that my Spirit did not utterly sink under my affliction: still the Lord upheld me with his gracious and mercifull Spirit, and we were both alive to see the light of the next morning.

THE THIRD REMOVE

The morning being come, they prepared to go on their way. One of the Indians got up upon a horse, and they set me up behind him, with my poor sick Babe in my lap. A very wearisome and tedious day I had of it; what with my own wound, and my Childs being so exceeding sick, and in a lamentable condition with her wound. It may be easily judged what a poor feeble condition we were in, there being not the least crumb of refreshing that came within either of our mouths, from Wednesday night to Saturday night, except only a little cold water. This day in the afternoon, about an hour by Sun, we came to the place where they intended, *viz.* an Indian Town, called Wenimesset, Norward of Quabaug. When we were come, Oh the number of Pagans (now merciless enemies) that there came about me, that I may say as David, Psal. 27. 13, *I had fainted, unless I had believed,* etc.[1] The next day was the Sabbath: I then remembered how careless I had been of Gods holy time, how many Sabbaths I had lost and mispent, and how evily I had walked in Gods sight; which lay so close unto my spirit, that it was easie for me to see how righteous it was with God to cut off the thread of my life, and cast me out of his presence for ever. Yet the Lord still shewed mercy to me, and

---

[1] "Unless I had believed to see the goodness of the Lord in the land of the living."—*1682 edition.*

upheld me; and as he wounded me with one hand, so he healed
me with the other. This day there came to me one Robbert Pep-
per (a man belonging to Roxbury) who was taken in Captain
Beers his Fight, and had been now a considerable time with the
Indians; and up with them almost as far as Albany, to see king
Philip, as he told me, and was now very lately come into these
parts. Hearing, I say, that I was in this Indian Town, he obtained
leave to come and see me. He told me, he himself was wounded
in the leg at Captain Beers his fight; and was not able some time
to go, but as they carried him, and as he took Oaken leaves and
laid to his wound, and through the blessing of God he was able
to travel again. Then I took Oaken leaves and laid to my side,
and with the blessing of God it cured me also; yet before the
cure was wrought, I may say, as it is in Psal. 38. 5, 6. *My wounds
stink and are corrupt, I am troubled, I am bowed down greatly,
I go mourning all the day long.* I sat much alone with a poor
wounded Child in my lap, which moaned night and day, having
nothing to revive the body, or cheer the spirits of her, but in stead
of that, sometimes one Indian would come and tell me one hour,
that your Master will knock your Child in the head, and then a
second, and then a third, your Master will quickly knock your
Child in the head.

This was the comfort I had from them, miserable comforters
are ye all, as he said. Thus nine dayes I sat upon my knees, with
my Babe in my lap, till my flesh was raw again; my Child being
even ready to depart this sorrowfull world, they bade me carry
it out to another Wigwam (I suppose because they would not be
troubled with such spectacles) Whither I went with a very heavy
heart, and down I sat with the picture of death in my lap. About
two houres in the night, my sweet Babe like a Lambe departed
this life, on Feb. 18, 1675. It being about six yeares, and five
months old. It was nine dayes from the first wounding, in this
miserable condition, without any refreshing of one nature or
other, except a little cold water. I cannot, but take notice, how at
another time I could not bear to be in the room where any dead
person was, but now the case is changed; I must and could ly

down by my dead Babe, side by side all the night after. I have thought since of the wonderfull goodness of God to me, in preserving me in the use of my reason and senses, in that distressed time, that I did not use wicked and violent means to end my own miserable life. In the morning, when they understood that my child was dead they sent for me home to my Masters Wigwam: (by my Master in this writing, must be understood Quanopin, who was a Saggamore, and married King Phillips wives Sister; not that he first took me, but I was sold to him by another Narrhaganset Indian, who took me when first I came out of the Garison). I went to take up my dead child in my arms to carry it with me, but they bid me let it alone: there was no resisting, but goe I must and leave it. When I had been at my masters wigwam, I took the first opportunity I could get, to go look after my dead child: when I came I askt them what they had done with it? then they told me it was upon the hill: then they went and shewed me where it was, where I saw the ground was newly digged, and there they told me they had buried it: There I left that Child in the Wilderness, and must commit it, and my self also in this Wilderness-condition, to him who is above all.

·   ·   ·   ·   ·

THE SEVENTH REMOVE

After a restless and hungry night there, we had a wearisome time of it the next day. The Swamp by which we lay, was, as it were, a deep Dungeon, and an exceeding high and steep hill before it. Before I got to the top of the hill, I thought my heart and legs, and all would have broken, and failed me. What through faintness, and soreness of body, it was a grievous day of travel to me. As we went along, I saw a place where English Cattle had been: that was comfort to me, such as it was: quickly after that we came to an English Path, which so took with me, that I thought I could have freely lyen down and dyed. That day, a little after noon, we came to Squaukheag, where the Indians quickly spread themselves over the deserted English Fields, gleaning what they could find; some pickt up ears of Wheat that were crickled down, some found ears of Indian Corn, some found Ground-nuts, and others sheaves of Wheat that were frozen together in the shock, and went to threshing of them out. My self got two ears of Indian Corn, and whilst I did but turn my back, one of them was stolen from me, which much troubled me. There came an Indian to them at that time, with a basket of Horse-liver. I asked him to give me a piece: What, sayes he, can you eat Horse-liver? I told him, I would try, if he would give a piece, which he did, and I laid it on the coals to rost; but before it was half ready they got half of it away from me, so that I was fain to take the rest and eat it as it was, with the blood about my mouth, and yet a savoury bit it was to me: *For to the hungry Soul every bitter thing is sweet.* A solemn sight methought it was, to see Fields of wheat and Indian Corn forsaken and spoiled: and the remainders of them to be food for our merciless Enemies. That night we had a mess of wheat for our Supper.

THE EIGHTH REMOVE

On the morrow morning we must go over the River, *i.e.* Connecticot, to meet with King Philip; two Cannoos full, they had carried over, the next Turn I my self was to go; but as my foot was upon the Cannoo to step in, there was a sudden out-cry among them, and I must step back; and instead of going over the River, I must go four or five miles up the River farther Northward. Some of the Indians ran one way, and some another. The cause of this rout was, as I thought, their espying some English Scouts, who were thereabout. In this travel up the River, about noon the Company made a stop, and sate down; some to eat, and others to rest them. As I sate amongst them, musing of things past, my Son Joseph unexpectedly came to me: we asked of each others welfare, bemoaning our dolefull condition, and the change that had come upon uss. We had Husband and Father, and Children, and Sisters, and Friends, and Relations, and House, and Home, and many Comforts of this Life: but now we may say, as Job, *Naked came I out of my Mothers Womb, and naked shall I return: The Lord gave, and the Lord hath taken away, Blessed*

be the Name of the Lord. I asked him whither he would read;
he told me, he earnestly desired it, I gave him my Bible, and he
lighted upon that comfortable Scripture, Psal. 118. 17, 18. I shall
not dy but live, and declare the works of the Lord: the Lord hath
chastened me sore, yet he hath not given me over to death. Look
here, Mother (says he) did you read this? And here I may take
occasion to mention one principall ground of my setting forth
these Lines: even as the Psalmist sayes, To declare the Works of
the Lord, and his wonderful Power in carrying us along, preserving us in the Wilderness, while under the Enemies hand, and
returning of us in safety again, And His goodness in bringing to
my hand so many comfortable and suitable Scriptures in my distress. But to Return, We travelled on till night; and in the morning, we must go over the River to Philip's Crew. When I was in
the Cannoo, I could not but be amazed at the numerous crew of
Pagans that were on the Bank on the other side. When I came
ashore, they gathered all about me, I sitting alone in the midst:
I observed they asked one another questions, and laughed, and
rejoyced over their Gains and Victories. Then my heart began to
fail: and I fell a weeping which was the first time to my remembrance, that I wept before them. Although I had met with so
much Affliction, and my heart was many times ready to break,
yet could I not shed one tear in their sight: but rather had been
all this while in a maze, and like one astonished: but now I may
say as, Psal. 137. 1. *By the Rivers of Babylon, there we sate down:
yea, we wept when we remembered Zion.* There one of them
asked me, why I wept, I could hardly tell what to say: yet I answered, they would kill me: No, said he, none will hurt you. Then
came one of them and gave me two spoon-fulls of Meal to comfort
me, and another gave me half a pint of Pease; which was more
worth than many Bushels at another time. Then I went to see
King Philip, he bade me come in and sit down, and asked me
whether I woold smoke it (a usual Complement nowadayes
amongst Saints and Sinners) but this no way suited me. For
though I had formerly used Tobacco, yet I had left it ever since
I was first taken. It seems to be a Bait, the Devil layes to make

men loose their precious time: I remember with shame, how formerly, when I had taken two or three pipes, I was presently ready for another, such a bewitching thing it is: But I thank God, he has now given me power over it; surely there are many who may be better imployed than to ly sucking a stinking Tobacco-pipe.

Now the Indians gather their Forces to go against North-Hampton: over-night one went about yelling and hooting to give notice of the design. Whereupon they fell to boyling of Ground-nuts, and parching of Corn (as many as had it) for their Provision: and in the morning away they went. During my abode in this place, Philip spake to me to make a shirt for his boy, which I did, for which he gave me a shilling: I offered the mony to my master, but he bade me keep it: and with it I bought a piece of Horse flesh. Afterwards he asked me to make a Cap for his boy, for which he invited me to Dinner. I went, and he gave me a Pancake, about as big as two fingers; it was made of parched wheat, beaten, and fryed in Bears grease, but I thought I never tasted pleasanter meat in my life. There was a Squaw who spake to me to make a shirt for her *Sannup,* for which she gave me a piece of Bear. Another asked me to knit a pair of Stockins, for which she gave me a quart of Pease: I boyled my Pease and Bear together, and invited my master and mistress to dinner, but the proud Gossip, because I served them both in one Dish, would eat nothing, except one bit that he gave her upon the point of his knife. Hearing that my son was come to this place, I went to see him, and found him lying flat upon the ground: I asked him how he could sleep so? he answered me, That he was not asleep, but at Prayer; and lay so, that they might not observe what he was doing. I pray God he may remember these things now he is returned in safety. At this Place (the Sun now getting higher) what with the beams and heat of the Sun, and the smoak of the Wigwams, I thought I should have been blind. I could scarce discern one Wigwam from another. There was here one Mary Thurston of Medfield, who seeing how it was with me, lent me a Hat to wear: but as soon as I was gone, the Squaw (who owned that Mary Thurston) came running after me, and got it away again. Here was the Squaw that gave me one spoonfull of Meal. I put it in my Pocket to keep it safe: yet notwithstanding some body stole it, but put five Indian Corns in the room of it: which Corns were the greatest Provisions I had in my travel for one day.

The Indians returning from North-Hampton, brought with them some Horses, and Sheep, and other things which they had taken: I desired them, that they would carry me to Albany, upon one of those Horses, and sell me for Powder: for so they had sometimes discoursed. I was utterly hopless of getting home on foot, the way that I came. I could hardly bear to think of the many weary steps I had taken, to come to this place.

·   ·   ·   ·   ·

THE SIXTEENTH REMOVE

We began this Remove with wading over Baquag River: the water was up to the knees, and the stream very swift, and so cold that I thought it would have cut me in sunder. I was so weak and feeble, that I reeled as I went along, and thought there I must end my dayes at last, after my bearing and getting thorough so many difficulties; the Indians stood laughing to see me staggering along: but in my distress the Lord gave me experience of the truth, and goodness of that promise, Isai. 43. 2. *When thou passest thorough the Waters, I will be with thee, and through the Rivers, they shall not overflow thee.* Then I sat down to put on my stockins and shoos, with the teares running down mine eyes, and many sorrowfull thoughts in my heart, but I gat up to go along with them. Quickly there came up to us an Indian, who informed them, that I must go to Wachusit to my master, for there was a Letter come from the Council to the Saggamores, about redeeming the Captives, and that there would be another in fourteen dayes, and that I must be there ready. My heart was so heavy before that I could scarce speak or go in the path; and yet now so light, that I could run. My strength seemed to come again, and recruit my feeble knees, and aking heart: yet it pleased them to go but one mile that night, and there we stayed two dayes. In that time came a company of Indians to us, near thirty, all on horseback. My heart skipt within me, thinking they had been English-men at the first sight of them, for they were dressed in English Apparel, with Hats, white Neckcloths, and Sashes about their wasts, and Ribbonds upon their shoulders: but when they came near, their was a vast difference between the lovely faces of Christians, and the foul looks of those Heathens, which much damped my spirit again.

. . . . .

THE EIGHTEENTH REMOVE

We took up our packs and along we went, but a wearisome day I had of it. As we went along I saw an English-man stript naked, and lying dead upon the ground, but knew not who it was. Then we came to another Indian Town, where we stayed all night. In this Town there were four English Children, Captives; and one of them my own Sisters. I went to see how she did, and she was well, considering her Captive-condition. I would have tarried that night with her, but they that owned her would not suffer it. Then I went into another Wigwam, where they were boyling Corn and Beans, which was a lovely sight to see, but I could not get a taste thereof. Then I went to another Wigwam, where there were two of the English Children; the Squaw was boyling Horses feet, then she cut me off a little piece, and gave one of the English Children a piece also. Being very hungry I had quickly eat up mine, but the Child could not bite it, it was so tough and sinewy, but lay sucking, gnawing, chewing and slabbering of it in the mouth and hand, then I took it of the Child, and eat it my self, and savoury it was to my taste. Then I may say as Job, Chap. 6. 7. *The things that my soul refused to touch, are as my sorrowfull meat.* Thus the Lord made that pleasant refreshing, which another time would have been an abomination. Then I went home to my mistresses Wigwam; and they told me I disgraced my master with begging, and if I did so any more, they would knock me in head: I told them, they had as good knock me in head as starve me to death.

THE TWENTIETH REMOVE

It was their usual manner to remove, when they had done any mischief, lest they should be found out: and so they did at this time. We went about three or four miles, and there they built a great Wigwam, big enough to hold an hundred Indians, which they did in preparation to a great day of Dancing. They would say now amongst themselves, that the Governour would be so angry for his loss at Sudbury, that he would send no more about the Captives, which made me grieve and tremble. My Sister being not far from the place where we now were, and hearing that I was here, desired her master to let her come and see me, and he was willing to it, and would go with her: but she being ready before him, told him she would go before, and was come within a Mile or two of the place; Then he overtook her, and began to rant as if he had been mad; and made her go back again in the Rain; so that I never saw her till I saw her in Charlestown. But the Lord requited many of their ill doings, for this Indian her Master, was hanged afterward at Boston. The Indians now began to come from all quarters, against their merry dancing day. Among some of them came one Goodwife Kettle: I told her my heart was so heavy that it was ready to break: so is mine too said she, but yet said, I hope we shall hear some good news shortly. I could hear how earnestly my Sister desired to see me, and I as earnestly desired to see her: and yet neither of us could get an opportunity. My Daughter was also now about a mile off, and I had not seen her in nine or ten weeks, as I had not seen my Sister since our first taking. I earnestly desired them to let me go and see them: yea, I intreated, begged, and perswaded them, but to let me see my Daughter; and yet so hard hearted were they, that they would not suffer it. They made use of their tyrannical power whilst they had it: but through the Lords wonderfull mercy, their time was now but short.

On a Sabbath day, the Sun being about an hour high in the afternoon, came Mr. John Hoar (the Council permitting him, and his own foreward spirit inclining him) together with the two forementioned Indians, Tom and Peter, with their third Letter from the Council. When they came near, I was abroad: though I saw them not, they presently called me in, and bade me sit down and not stir. Then they catched up their Guns, and away they ran, as if an Enemy had been at hand; and the Guns went off apace. I manifested some great trouble, and they asked me what was the matter? I told them, I thought they had killed the English-man (for they had in the mean time informed me that an English-man was come) they said, No; They shot over his Horse and under, and before his Horse; and they pusht him this way and that way, at their pleasure: shewing what they could do: Then they let them come to their Wigwams. I begged of them to let me see the English-man, but they would not. But there was I fain to sit their pleasure. When they had talked their fill with him, they suffered me to go to him. We asked each other of our welfare, and how my Husband did, and all my Friends? He told me they were all well, and would be glad to see me. Amongst other things which my Husband sent me, there came a pound of Tobacco: which I sold for nine shillings in Money: for many of the Indians for want of Tobacco, smoaked Hemlock, and Ground-Ivy. It was a great mistake in any, who thought I sent for Tobacco: for through the favour of God, that desire was overcome. I now asked them, whither I should go home with Mr. Hoar? They answered No, one and another of them: and it being night, we lay down with that answer; in the morning, Mr. Hoar invited the Saggamores to Dinner; but when we went to get it ready, we found that they had stollen the greatest part of the Provision Mr. Hoar had brought, out of his Bags, in the night. And we may see the wonderfull power of God, in that one passage, in that when there was such a great number of the Indians together, and so greedy of a little good food; and no English there, but Mr. Hoar and my self: that there they did not knock us in the head, and take what we had: there being not only some Provision, but also Trading-cloth, a part of the twenty pounds agreed upon: But instead of doing us any mischief, they seemed to be ashamed of the fact, and said, it were some Matchit Indian[2] that did it. Oh,

---

[2] I.e., bad Indian.—*1682 edition.*

that we could believe that there is no thing too hard for God! God shewed his Power over the Heathen in this, as he did over the hungry Lyons when Daniel was cast into the Den. Mr. Hoar called them betime to Dinner, but they ate very little, they being so busie in dressing themselves, and getting ready for their Dance: which was carried on by eight of them, four Men and four Squaws: My master and mistress being two. He was dressed in his Holland shirt, with great Laces sewed at the tail of it, he had his silver Buttons, his white Stockins, his Garters were hung round with Shillings, and he had Girdles of Wampom upon his head and shoulders. She had a Kersey Coat, and covered with Girdles of Wampom from the Loins upward: her armes from her elbows to her hands were covered with Bracelets; there were handfulls of Necklaces about her neck, and severall sorts of Jewels in her ears. She had fine red Stokins, and white Shoos, her hair powdered and face painted Red, that was alwayes before Black. And all the Dancers were after the same manner. There were two other singing and knocking on a Kettle for their musick. They keept hopping up and down one after another, with a Kettle of water in the midst, standing warm upon some Embers, to drink of when they were dry. They held on till it was almost night, throwing out Wampom to the standers by. At night I asked them again, if I should go home? They all as one said No, except my Husband would come for me. When we were lain down, my Master went out of the Wigwam, and by and by sent in an Indian called James the Printer, who told Mr. Hoar, that my Master would let me go home to morrow, if he would let him have one pint of Liquors. Then Mr. Hoar called his own Indians, Tom and Peter, and bid them go and see whither he would promise it before them three: and if he would, he should have it; which he did, and he had it. Then Philip smeling the business cal'd me to him, and asked me what I would give him, to tell me some good news, and speak a good word for me. I told him, I could not tell what to give him, I would any thing I had, and asked him what he would have? He said, two Coats and twenty shillings in Mony, and half a bushel of seed Corn, and some Tobacco. I thanked him for his love: but I knew the good news as well as the crafty Fox. My Master after he had had his drink, quickly came ranting into the Wigwam again, and called for Mr. Hoar, drinking to him, and saying, He was a good man: and then again he would say, Hang him Rogue: Being almost drunk, he would drink to him, and yet presently say he should be hanged. Then he called for me. I trembled to hear him, yet I was fain to go to him, and he drank to me, shewing no incivility. He was the first Indian I saw drunk all the while that I was amongst them. At last his Squaw ran out, and he after her, round the Wigwam, with his mony jingling at his knees: But she escaped him: But having an old Squaw he ran to her: and so through the Lords mercy, we were no more troubled that night. Yet I had not a comfortable nights rest: for I think I can say, I did not sleep for three nights together. The night before the Letter came from the Council, I could not rest, I was so full of feares and troubles, God many times leaving us most in the dark, when deliverance is nearest: yea, at this time I could not rest night nor day. The next night I was overjoyed, Mr. Hoar being come, and that with such good tidings. The third night I was even swallowed up with the thoughts of things, *viz*. that ever I should go home again; and that I must go, leaving my Children behind me in the Wilderness; so that sleep was now almost departed from mine eyes.

On Tuesday morning they called their General Court (as they call it) to consult and determine, whether I should go home or no: And they all as one man did seemingly consent to it, that I should go home; except Philip, who would not come among them.

But before I go any further, I would take leave to mention a few remarkable passages of providence, which I took special notice of in my afflicted time.

1. Of the fair opportunity lost in the long March, a little after the Fort-fight, when our English Army was so numerous, and in pursuit of the Enemy, and so near as to take several and destroy them: and the Enemy in such distress for food, that our men might track them by their rooting in the earth for Ground-nuts,

whilest they were flying for their lives. I say, that then our Army should want Provision, and be forced to leave their pursuit and return homeward: and the very next week the Enemy came upon our Town, like Bears bereft of their whelps, or so many ravenous Wolves, rending us and our Lambs to death. But what shall I say? God seemed to leave his People to themselves, and order all things for his own holy ends. *Shal there be evil in the City and the Lord hath not done it? They are not grieved for the affliction of Joseph, therefore shal they go Captive, with the first that go Captive.* It is the Lords doing, and it should be marvelous in our eyes.

2. I cannot but remember how the Indians derided the slowness, and dulness of the English Army, in its setting out. For after the desolations at Lancaster and Medfield, as I went along with them, they asked me when I thought the English Army would come after them? I told them I could not tell: It may be they will come in May, said they. Thus did they scoffe at us, as if the English would be a quarter of a year getting ready.

3. Which also I have hinted before, when the English Army with new supplies were sent forth to pursue after the enemy, and they understanding it, fled before them till they came to Baquaug River, where they forthwith went over safely: that that River should be impassable to the English. I can but admire to see the wonderfull providence of God in preserving the heathen for farther affliction to our poor Countrey. They could go in great numbers over, but the English must stop: God had an over-ruling hand in all those things.

4. It was thought, if their Corn were cut down, they would starve and dy with hunger: and all their Corn that could be found, was destroyed, and they driven from that little they had in store, into the Woods in the midst of Winter; and yet how to admiration did the Lord preserve them for his holy ends, and the destruction of many still amongst the English! strangely did the Lord provide for them; that I did not see (all the time I was among them) one Man, Woman, or Child, die with hunger.

Though many times they would eat that, that a Hog or a Dog

would hardly touch; yet by that God strengthened them to be a scourge to his People.

The chief and commonest food was Ground-nuts: They eat also Nuts and Acorns, Harty-choaks, Lilly roots, Ground-beans, and several other weeds and roots, that I know not.

They would pick up old bones, and cut them to pieces at the joynts, and if they were full of wormes and magots, they would scald them over the fire to make the vermine come out, and then boile them, and drink up the Liquor, and then beat the great ends of them in a Morter, and so eat them. They would eat Horses guts, and ears, and all sorts of wild Birds which they could catch: also Bear, Vennison, Beaver, Tortois, Frogs, Squirrels, Dogs, Skunks, Rattle-snakes; yea, the very Bark of Trees; besides all sorts of creatures, and provision which they plundered from the English. I can but stand in admiration to see the wonderful power of God, in providing for such a vast number of our Enemies in the Wilderness, where there was nothing to be seen, but from hand to mouth. Many times in a morning, the generality of them would eat up all they had, and yet have some forther supply against they wanted. It is said, Psal. 81. 13, 14. *Oh, that my People had hearkned to me, and Israel had walked in my wayes, I should soon have subdued their Enemies, and turned my hand against their Adversaries.* But now our perverse and evil carriages in the sight of the Lord, have so offended him, that instead of turning his hand against them, the Lord feeds and nourishes them up to be a scourge to the whole Land.

5. Another thing that I would observe is, the strange providence of God, in turning things about when the Indians was at the highest, and the English at the lowest. I was with the Enemy eleven weeks and five dayes, and not one Week passed without the fury of the Enemy, and some desolation by fire and sword upon one place or other. They mourned (with their black faces) for their own lossess, yet triumphed and rejoyced in their inhumane, and many times devilish cruelty to the English. They would boast much of their Victories; saying, that in two hours time they had destroyed such a Captain, and his Company at such

a place; and such a Captain and his Company in such a place; and such a Captain and his Company in such a place: and boast how many Towns they had destroyed, and then scoffe, and say, They had done them a good turn, to send them to Heaven so soon. Again, they would say, This Summer that they would knock all the Rogues in the head, or drive them into the Sea, or make them flie the Countrey: thinking surely, Agag-like, *The bitterness of Death is past.*[3] Now the Heathen begins to think all is their own, and the poor Christians hopes to fail (as to man) and now their eyes are more to God, and their hearts sigh heavenward: and to say in good earnest, *Help Lord, or we perish:* When the Lord had brought his people to this, that they saw no help in any thing but himself: then he takes the quarrel into his own hand: and though they had made a pit, in their own imaginations, as deep as hell for the Christians that Summer, yet the Lord hurll'd them selves into it. And the Lord had not so many wayes before to preserve them, but now he hath as many to destroy them.

But to return again to my going home, where we may see a remarkable change of Providence: At first they were all against it, except my Husband would come for me; but afterwards they assented to it, and seemed much to rejoyce in it; some askt me to send them some Bread, others some Tobacco, others shaking me by the hand, offering me a Hood and Scarfe to ride in; not one moving hand or tongue against it. Thus hath the Lord answered my poor desire, and the many earnest requests of others put up unto God for me. In my travels an Indian came to me, and told me, if I were willing, he and his Squaw would run away, and go home along with me: I told him No: I was not willing to run away, but desired to wait Gods time, that I might go home quietly, and without fear. And now God hath granted me my desire. O the wonderfull power of God that I have seen, and the experience that I have had: I have been in the midst of those roaring Lyons, and Salvage Bears, that feared neither God, nor Man, nor the Devil, by night and day, alone and in company:

---

[3] I Samuel xv. 32.—*1682 edition.*

sleeping all sorts together, and yet not one of them ever offered me the least abuse of unchastity to me, in word or action. Though some are ready to say, I speak it for my own credit; But I speak it in the presence of God, and to his Glory. Gods Power is as great now, and as sufficient to save, as when he preserved Daniel in the Lions Den; or the three Children in the fiery Furnace. I may well say as his Psal. 107. 12, *Oh give thanks unto the Lord for he is good, for his mercy endureth for ever.* Let the Redeemed of the Lord say so, whom he hath redeemed from the hand of the Enemy, especially that I should come away in the midst of so many hundreds of Enemies quietly and peaceably, and not a Dog moving his tongue. So I took my leave of them, and in coming along my heart melted into tears, more then all the while I was with them, and I was almost swallowed up with the thoughts that ever I should go home again.

. . . . .

I can remember the time, when I used to sleep quietly without workings in my thoughts, whole nights together, but now it is other wayes with me. When all are fast about me, and no eye open, but his who ever waketh, my thoughts are upon things past, upon the awfull dispensation of the Lord towards us; upon his wonderfull power and might, in carrying of us through so many difficulties, in returning us in safety, and suffering none to hurt us. I remember in the night season, how the other day I was in the midst of thousands of enemies, and nothing but death before me: It is then hard work to perswade my self, that ever I should be satisfied with bread again. But now we are fed with the finest of the Wheat, and, as I may say, With honey out of the rock: In stead of the Husk, we have the fatted Calf: The thoughts of these things in the particulars of them, and of the love and goodness of God towards us, make it true of me, what David said of himself, Psal. 6. 5. *I watered my Couch with my tears.* Oh! the wonderfull power of God that mine eyes have seen, affording matter enough for my thoughts to run in, that when others are sleeping mine eyes are weeping.

I have seen the extreme vanity of this World: One hour I have been in health, and wealth, wanting nothing: But the next hour in sickness and wounds, and death, having nothing but sorrow and affliction.

Before I knew what affliction meant, I was ready sometimes to wish for it. When I lived in prosperity, having the comforts of the World about me, my relations by me, my Heart chearfull, and taking little care for any thing; and yet seeing many, whom I preferred before my self, under many tryals and afflictions, in sickness, weakness, poverty, losses, crosses, and cares of the World, I should be sometimes jealous least I should have my portion in this life, and that Scripture would come to my mind, Heb. 12. 6. *For whom the Lord loveth he chasteneth, and scourgeth every Son whom he receiveth.* But now I see the Lord had his time to scourge and chasten me. The portion of some is to have their afflictions by drops, now one drop and then another; but the dregs of the Cup, the Wine of astonishment, like a sweeping rain that leaveth no food, did the Lord prepare to be my portion. Affliction I wanted, and affliction I had, full measure (I thought) pressed down and running over; yet I see, when God calls a Person to any thing, and through never so many difficulties, yet he is fully able to carry them through and make them see, and say they have been gainers thereby. And I hope I can say in some measure, As David did, *It is good for me that I have been afflicted.* The Lord hath shewed me the vanity of these outward things. That they are the Vanity of vanities, and vexation of spirit; that they are but a shadow, a blast, a bubble, and things of no continuance. That we must rely on God himself, and our whole dependance must be upon him. If trouble from smaller matters begin to arise in me, I have something at hand to check my self with, and say, why am I troubled? It was but the other day that if I had had the world, I would have given it for my freedom, or to have been a Servant to a Christian. I have learned to look beyond present and smaller troubles, and to be quieted under them, as Moses said, Exod. 14. 13. *Stand still and see the salvation of the Lord.*

COTTON MATHER

(1663-1728)

Bibliographical Note. There is no collected edition of Mather's 444 known printed works; these are listed masterfully, however, in T. J. Holmes, *Cotton Mather: A Bibliography of His Works,* 3 vols. (Cambridge, 1940). The only scholarly edition of Mather's writings is Kenneth Murdock, ed. *Selections from Cotton Mather* (New York, 1926). The selections here printed follow Murdock's text, pp. 1-36, 40-51, 58-84, 285-302, 349-362.* The best biographies of Mather are Barrett Wendell, *Cotton Mather: The Puritan Priest* (1891) and Kenneth Murdock's sketch in the *Dictionary of American Biography.* Murdock's introduction to his *Selections* is the most adequate study of Mather as a man of letters.

from THE MAGNALIA CHRISTI AMERICANA[1] (1702)

A GENERAL INTRODUCTION

Ἐρῶ δὲ τοῦτο, τῆς τῶν ἐντευξαμένων ᾿ωφελείας ἕνεκα.

Dicam hoc propter utilitatem eorum qui Lecturi sunt hoc opus.
Theodorit.[2]

§ 1. I write the *Wonders* of the CHRISTIAN RELIGION, flying from the Depravations of *Europe,* to the *American Strand:* And, assisted by the Holy Author of that *Religion,* I do, with all Conscience of *Truth,* required therein by Him, who is the *Truth* it self, Report the *Wonderful Displays* of His Infinite Power, Wisdom, Goodness, and Faithfulness, wherewith His Divine Providence hath *Irradiated* an *Indian Wilderness.*

I Relate the *Considerable Matters,* that produced and attended the First Settlement of COLONIES, which have been Renowned

---

* Notes by Kenneth Murdock, copyright, 1926, by Harcourt, Brace and Company, Inc., and used with their permission.

[1] The American Annals of Christ, i.e., American Ecclesiastical History.

[2] "I say this for the benefit of those who are readers of this book." Theodoret was one of the early fathers of the Church, c. 393-457.—*Murdock.*

for the Degree of REFORMATION, Professed and Attained by *Evangelical Churches,* erected in those *Ends of the Earth:* And a *Field* being thus prepared, I proceed unto a Relation of the *Considerable Matters* which have been acted thereupon.

I first introduce the *Actors,* that have, in a more exemplary manner served those *Colonies;* and give *Remarkable Occurrences,* in the exemplary LIVES of many *Magistrates,* and of more *Ministers,* who so *Lived,* as to leave unto Posterity, *Examples* worthy of *Everlasting Remembrance.*

I add hereunto, the *Notables* of the only *Protestant University,* that ever *shone* in that Hemisphere of the *New World;* with particular Instances of *Criolians,*[3] in our *Biography,* provoking the *whole World,* with vertuous Objects of Emulation.

I introduce then, the *Actions* of a more Eminent Importance, that have signalized those *Colonies;* Whether the *Establishments,* directed by their *Synods;* with a Rich Variety of *Synodical* and *Ecclessiastical* Determinations; or, the *Disturbances,* with which they have been from all sorts of *Temptations* and *Enemies* Tempestuated; and the *Methods* by which they have still weathered out each *Horrible Tempest.*

And into the midst of these *Actions,* I interpose an entire *Book,* wherein there is, with all possible Veracity, a *Collection* made, of *Memorable Occurrences,* and amazing *Judgments* and *Mercies,* befalling many *particular Persons* among the People of *New-England.*

Let my Readers expect all that I have promised them, in this *Bill of Fare;* and it may be they will find themselves entertained with yet many other Passages, above and beyond their Expectation, deserving likewise a room in *History:* In all which, there will be nothing, but the *Author's* too mean way of preparing so great Entertainments, to Reproach the Invitation.

§ 2. The Reader will doubtless desire to know, what it was that

---

[3] Criolians or Creolians, an obsolete word for persons born or naturalized in America but of European race. . . . —*Murdock.*

————*tot Volvere casus*
Insignes Pietate Viros, tot adire Labores,
Impulerit.[4]

And our *History* shall, on many fit Occasions which will be therein offered, endeavour, with all *Historical* Fidelity and Simplicity, and with as little Offence as may be, to satisfy him. The Sum of the Matter is, That from the very Beginning of the REFORMATION in the *English Nation,* there hath always been a Generation of *Godly Men,* desirous to pursue the *Reformation of Religion, according to the word of God, and the Example of the best Reformed Churches;* and answering the Character of *Good Men,* given by *Josephus,* in his Paraphrase on the words of *Samuel* to *Saul,* μηδὲν ἄλλο πραχθήσεσθαι καλῶς ὑφ' ἑαυτῶν νομίζοντες ἢ ὅτι ἂν ποιήσωσι τοῦ θεοῦ κεκελευκότος. *They think they do nothing Right in the Service of God, but what they do according to the Command of God.* And there hath been another Generation of Men, who have still employed the *Power* which they have generally still had in their Hands, not only to stop the Progress of the Desired *Reformation,* but also, with Innumerable Vexations, to Persecute those that most Heartily wished well unto it. There were many of the *Reformers,* who joyned with the Reverend *JOHN FOX,* in the *Complaints* which he then entred in his *Martyrology,* about the *Baits of Popery* yet left in the Church; and in his *Wishes, God take them away, or ease us from them, for God knows, they be the Cause of much Blindness and Strife amongst Men!* They Zealously decried the *Policy* of complying always with the *Ignorance* and *Vanity* of the *People;* and cried out earnestly for *Purer Administrations* in the House of God, and more *Conformity* to the *Law of Christ,* and *Primitive Christianity:* While others would not hear of going any further than the *First Essay of Reformation.* 'Tis very certain, that the *First Reformers* never intended, that what *They* did, should be the

---

[4] "Drove men eminent in piety to endure so many calamities and to undertake so many hardships." The quotation is slightly altered from the *Æneid,* I, 9-11.— *Murdock.*

Absolute Boundary of Reformation, so that it should be a Sin to proceed any further; as, by their own going beyond *Wicklift,* and *Changing* and *Growing* in their own *Models* also, and the Confessions of *Cranmer,* with the *Scripta Anglicana* of *Bucer,* and a thousand other things, was abundantly demonstrated. But after a Fruitless Expectation, wherein the truest Friends of the *Reformation* long waited, for to have that which *Heylin* himself [5] owns to have been the Design of the *First Reformers,* followed as it should have been, a Party very unjustly arrogating to themselves, the Venerable Name of, *The Church of* England, by Numberless Oppressions, grievously *Smote those their Fellow-Servants.* Then 'twas that, as our Great *OWEN* hath expressed it,[6] *Multitudes of Pious, Peaceable Protestants, were driven, by their Severities, to leave their Native Country, and seek a Refuge for their Lives and Liberties, with Freedom, for the Worship of God, in a Wilderness, in the Ends of the Earth.*

§ 3. It is the History of these PROTESTANTS, that is here attempted: PROTESTANTS that highly honoured and affected *The Church of* ENGLAND, and humbly Petition to be a *Part* of it: But by the Mistake of a few powerful *Brethren,* driven to seek a place for the Exercise of the *Protestant Religion,* according to the Light of their Consciences, in the Desarts of *America.* And in this Attempt I have proposed, not only to preserve and secure the Interest of *Religion,* in the Churches of that little Country *NEW-ENGLAND,* so far as the Lord Jesus Christ may please to Bless it for that End, but also to offer unto the Churches of the *Reformation,* abroad in the World, some small *Memorials,* that may be serviceable unto the Designs of *Reformation,* whereto, I believe, they are quickly to be awakened. I am far from any such Boast, concerning these Churches, *That they have Need of Nothing,* I wish their *Works* were more *perfect before God.* Indeed,

---

[5] Peter Heylin, 1600-1662, an Anglican divine and historian, defended Bishop Laud, and wrote often against the Puritans. . . . —*Murdock.*

[6] John Owen, 1616-1683, usually called one of the three greatest English Puritans. . . . —*Murdock.*

that which *Austin* called *The Perfection of Christians,* is like to be, until the Term for the *Antichristian Apostasie* be expired, *The Perfection of Churches* too; *Ut Agnoscant se nunquam esse perfectas.*[7] Nevertheless, I perswade my self, that *so far as they have attained,* they have given *Great Examples* of the *Methods* and *Measures,* wherein an *Evangelical Reformation* is to be prosecuted, and of the *Qualifications* requisite in the Instruments that are to prosecute it, and of the *Difficulties* which may be most likely to obstruct it, and the most likely *Directions* and *Remedies* for those Obstructions. It may be, 'tis not possible for me to do a greater Service unto the Churches on the *Best Island* of the Universe, than to give a distinct Relation of those *Great Examples* which have been occurring among Churches of *Exiles,* that were driven out of that *Island,* into an horrible *Wilderness,* meerly for their being Well-willers unto the *Reformation.* When that Blessed Martyr *Constantine* was carried, with other Martyrs, in a *Dung-Cart,* unto the place of Execution, he pleasantly said, *Well, yet we are a precious Odour to God in Christ.* Tho' the *Reformed Churches* in the *American Regions,* have, by very Injurious Representations of their Brethren (all which they desire to Forget and Forgive!) been many times thrown into a *Dung-Cart;* yet, as they have been a *precious Odour to God in Christ,* so, I hope, they will be a *precious Odour* unto *His People;* and not only *Precious,* but *Useful* also, when the *History* of them shall come to be considered. A *Reformation of the Church* is coming on, and I cannot but thereupon say, with the dying *Cyrus* to his Children in *Xenophon,* Ἐκ τῶν προγεγεννημένων μανθάνετε αὐτὴ γὰρ ἀρίστη διδασκαλία. *Learn from the things that have been done already, for this is the best way of Learning.* The Reader hath here an Account of *The Things that have been done already. Bernard* upon that Clause in the *Canticles,* [*O thou fairest among Women*] has this ingenious Gloss, *Pulchram, non omnimode quidem, sed pulchram inter mulieres eam docet, videlicet cum Distinctione, quatenus ex hoc amplius reprimatur, & sciat quid*

---

[7] "That they may acknowledge themselves to be by no means perfect."—*Murdock.*

desit sibi.[8] Thus I do not say, That the Churches of *New-England*
are the most *Regular* that can be; yet I do say, and am sure, That
they are very like unto those that were in the *First Ages* of Christianity. And if I assert, That in the *Reformation* of the Church,
the State of it in those *First Ages,* is to be not a little considered,
the Great *Peter Ramus,*[9] among others, has emboldened me. For
when the Cardinal of *Lorrain,* the *Mæcenas* of that Great Man,
was offended at him, for turning *Protestant,* he replied, *Inter Opes*
illas, quibus me ditasti, has etiam in æternum recordabor, quod
Beneficio, Poessiacæ Responsionis tuæ didici, de Quindecim a
Christo sæculis, primum vere esse aureum, Reliqua, quo longius
abscederent esse nequiora, atque deteriora: Tum igitur cum fieret
optio, Aureum sæculum delegi.[10] In short, The *First Age* was the
Golden Age: To return unto *That,* will make a Man a *Protestant,*
and I may add, a *Puritan.* 'Tis possible, That our Lord Jesus
Christ carried some Thousands of *Reformers* into the Retire-
ments of an *American Desert,* on purpose, that, with an opportunity granted unto many of his Faithful Servants, to enjoy the
precious *Liberty* of their *Ministry,* tho' in the midst of many
Temptations all their days, He might there, *To* them first, and
then *By* them, give a *Specimen* of many Good Things, which He
would have His Churches elsewhere aspire and arise unto: And
This being done, He knows whether there be not *All done,* that
New-England was planted for; and whether the Plantation may
not, soon after this, *Come to Nothing.* Upon that Expression in
the Sacred Scripture, *Cast the unprofitable Servant into Outer*
Darkness, it hath been imagined by some, That the *Regiones*
Exteræ of America, are the *Tenebræ Exteriores,* which the *Un-*

---

[8] "He teaches that she is fair, not in a universal sense, but fair among women,
plainly with a distinction, to which extent his praise is qualified, and she may
know what is lacking to her."—*Murdock.*

[9] This opponent of Aristotelianism, an educational reformer, who lived 1515-
1572, was much read by the Puritans. . . . —*Murdock.*

[10] "Among those riches, with which you enriched me, this I was mindful of
always, which I learned from your reply at Poissy—that of the fifteen centuries
since Christ, the first is truly golden. The rest, the farther they are removed from
the first, are the more worthless and degenerate. Therefore when choice was to
be made, I chose the golden age."—*Murdock.*

profitable are there condemned unto. No doubt, the Authors of those *Ecclesiastical Impositions* and *Severities,* which drove the *English* Christians into the *Dark Regions* of *America,* esteemed those *Christians* to be a very *unprofitable* sort of Creatures. But behold, ye *European* Churches, There are *Golden Candlesticks* [more than *twice Seven times Seven!*] in the midst of this *Outer Darkness;* Unto the *upright* Children of *Abraham,* here hath arisen *Light in Darkness.* And let us humbly speak it, it shall be *Profitable* for you to consider the *Light,* which from the midst of this *Outer Darkness,* is now to be Darted over unto the other side of the *Atlantick Ocean.* But we must therewithal ask your Prayers, that these *Golden Candlesticks* may not *quickly* be *Removed out of their place!*

§ 4. But whether *New-England* may *Live* any where else or no, it must *Live* in our *History!*

HISTORY, in general, hath had so many and mighty Commendations from the Pens of those Numberless Authors, who, from *Herodotus* to *Howel,*[11] have been the professed Writers of it, that a tenth part of them Transcribed, would be a Furniture for a *Polyanthea in Folio.*[12] We, that have neither liberty, nor occasion, to quote those Commendations of *History,* will content our selves with the Opinion of one who was not much of a *profess'd Historian,* expressed in that passage, whereto all Mankind subscribe, *Historia est Testis temporum, Nuntia vetustatis, Lux veritatis, vita memoriæ, magistra vitæ.*[13] But of all *History* it must be confessed, that the *Palm* is to be given unto *Church History;* wherein the *Dignity,* the *Suavity,* and the *Utility* of the *Subject* is transcendent. I observe, that for the Description of the *whole World* in the Book of *Genesis,* that *First-born of all Historians,*

---

[11] James Howell, 1594?-1666, famous for his familiar letters, the *Epistolæ Ho-Elianæ,* was somewhat of a historian. . . . —*Murdock.*

[12] *I.e.,* a large collection of select quotations, an anthology.—*Murdock.*

[13] "History is the witness of periods of time, the messenger of antiquity, the light of truth, the life of memory, the instructress of life." Cotton Mather here quotes Cicero (*De Oratore,* II, 9) but fails to preserve the original order. . . . —*Murdock.*

the great *Moses,* employes but *one* or *two* Chapters, whereas he
implies,[14] it may be *seven times* as many Chapters, in describing
that one little *Pavilion, The Tabernacle.* And when I am thinking, what may be the Reason of this *Difference,* methinks it in-
timates unto us, That the *Church* wherein the Service of God is
performed, is much more Precious than the *World,* which was
indeed created for the Sake and Use of the *Church.* 'Tis very certain, that the greatest Entertainments must needs occur in the
History of the *People,* whom the *Son* of God hath *Redeemed* and
Purified unto himself, as a *Peculiar People,* and whom the *Spirit*
of God, by *Supernatural Operations* upon their Minds, does cause
to live like *Strangers* in *this World,* conforming themselves unto
the *Truths* and *Rules* of his Holy Word, in Expectation of a
Kingdom, whereto they shall be in another and a better *World*
advanced. Such a *People* our Lord Jesus Christ hath procured and
preserved in all Ages *visible;* and the Dispensations of his *won-
derous Providence* towards this People (for, *O Lord, thou do'st
lift them up, and cast them down!*) their Calamities, their De-
liverances, the Dispositions which they have still discovered, and
the considerable *Persons* and *Actions* found among them, cannot
but afford Matters of *Admiration* and *Admonition,* above what
any other Story can pretend unto: 'Tis nothing but *Atheism* in
the Hearts of Men, that can perswade them otherwise. Let any
Person of good Sense peruse the History of *Herodotus,* which,
like a River taking Rise, where the *Sacred Records* of the *Old
Testament* leave off, runs along smoothly and sweetly, with Relations that sometimes perhaps want an *Apology,* down until the
Grecians drive the *Persians* before them. Let him then peruse
Thucydides, who from *Acting* betook himself to *Writing,* and
carries the ancient State of the *Grecians,* down to the twenty first
Year of the *Peloponnesian Wars* in a manner, which *Casaubon*
judges to be *Mirandum potius quam imitandum.*[15] Let him next
Revolve *Xenophon,* that *Bee* of *Athens,* who continues a Narrative of the *Greek Affairs,* from the *Peloponnesian Wars,* to the

[14] Employes?—*Murdock.*
[15] "To be admired rather than imitated."—*Murdock.*

Battle of *Mantinea,* and gives us a *Cyrus* into the bargain, at such a rate, that *Lipsius* reckons the Character of a *Suavi, Fidus & Circumspectus Scriptor,*[16] to belong unto him. Let him from hence proceed unto *Diodorus Siculus,* who, besides a rich Treasure of *Egyptian, Assyrian, Lybian* and *Grecian,* and other *Antiquities,* in a Phrase, which according to *Photius's* Judgment, is ἱστορία μάλιστα πρεπούσῃ, *of all most becoming an Historian,*[17] carries on the Thread begun by his Predecessors, until the End of the Hundred and nineteenth *Olympiad;* and where he is defective, let it be supplied from *Arianus,* from *Justin,* and from *Curtius,* who in the relish of *Colerus* is, *Quovis melle dulcior.*[18] Let him hereupon consult *Polybius,* and acquaint himself with the Birth and Growth of the *Roman Empire,* as far as 'tis described, in *Five* of the *Forty* Books composed by an Author, who with a Learned *Professor of History* is, *Prudens Scriptor, si quis alius.*[19] Let him now run over the Table of the *Roman* Affairs, compendiously given by *Lucius Florus,* and then let him consider the Transactions of above three hundred Years reported by *Dionysius Halicarnassæus,* who, if the Censure of *Bodin* may be taken, *Græcos omnes & Latinos superasse videatur.*[20] Let him from hence pass to *Livy,* of whom the famous Critick says, *Hoc solum ingenium (de Historicis Loquor) populus Romanus par Imperio suo habuit,*[21] and supply those of his *Decads* that are lost, from the best Fragments of Antiquity, in others (and especially *Dion* and *Salust*) that lead us on still further in our way. Let him then proceed unto the Writers of the *Cesarean* times, and first revolve *Suetonius,* then *Tacitus,* then *Herodian,* then a whole Army more of *Historians,* which now crowd into our *Library;* and unto all the

---

[16] "An agreeable, faithful and careful writer." Justus Lipsius, 1547-1606, was a learned critic, and editor of classical texts.—*Murdock.*

[17] Photius, patriarch of Constantinople in the second half of the ninth century.—*Murdock.*

[18] "More sweet than honey." Colerus is probably Johann Coler, a German theological writer of the sixteenth century.—*Murdock.*

[19] "A discreet writer, if there ever was one."—*Murdock.*

[20] "Seems to have surpassed all the Greeks and Latins."—*Murdock.*

[21] "As for historians, the Romans had this one genius worthy of their empire."—*Murdock.*

rest, let him not fail of adding the Incomparable *Plutarch,* whose Books they say, *Theodore Gaza* preferred above any in the World, next unto the Inspired Oracles of the *Bible:* But if the Number be still too little to satisfie an *Historical Appetite,* let him add *Polyhistor* unto the number, and all the *Chronicles* of the following Ages. After all, he must sensibly acknowledge, that the two short Books of *Ecclesiastical History,* written by the Evangelist *Luke,* hath given us more *glorious Entertainments,* than all these voluminous Historians if they were put all together. The *Atchievements* of one *Paul* particularly, which that Evangelist hath *Emblazon'd,* have more *True Glory* in them, than all the Acts of those Execrable *Plunderers* and *Murderers,* and irresistible *Banditti* of the World, which have been dignified wtih the Name of *Conquerors.* *Tacitus* counted *Ingentia bella, Expugnationes urbium, fusos captosque Reges,*[22] the Ravages of *War,* and the glorious *Violences,* whereof great Warriors make a wretched Ostentation, to be the *Noblest Matter* for an *Historian.* But there is a *Nobler,* I humbly conceive, in the planting and forming of *Evangelical Churches,* and the *Temptations,* the *Corruptions,* the *Afflictions,* which assault them, and their *Salvations* from those Assaults, and the Exemplary *Lives* of those that Heaven employs to be Patterns of *Holiness* and *Usefulness* upon Earth: And unto such it is, that I now invite my Readers; Things, in comparison whereof, the Subjects of many other Histories, are of as little weight, as the Questions about Z, the last Letter of our Alphabet, and whether H is to be pronounced with an Aspiration, where about whole Volumes have been written, and of no more Account, than the Composure of *Didymus.*[23] But for the *manner* of my treating this *Matter,* I must now give some account unto him.

§ 5. *Reader!* I have done the part of an *Impartial Historian,* albeit not without all occasion perhaps, for the Rule which a worthy Writer, in his *Historica,* gives to every Reader, *Historici Legantur cum Moderatione & venia, & cogitetur fieri non posse*

---

[22] "Vast wars, captures of cities, kings captured or in flight."—*Murdock.*
[23] Alexandrian grammarian of the time of Cicero. . . . —*Murdock.*

ut in omnibus circumstantiis sint Lyncei.[24] *Polybius* complains
of those *Historians,* who always made either the *Carthagenians*
brave, and the *Romans* base, or è *contra,* in all their Actions, as
their Affection for their own *Party* led them. I have endeavoured,
with all *good Conscience,* to decline this writing meerly for a
Party, or doing like the Dealer in History, whom *Lucian* derides,
for always calling the Captain of his own Party an *Achilles,* but
of the adverse Party a *Thersites:* Nor have I added unto the just
Provocations for the Complaint made by the Baron *Maurier,*[25]
That the *greatest part of Histories* are but so many *Panegyricks*
composed by *Interested Hands,* which *elevate Iniquity to the
Heavens, like Paterculus,* and like *Machiavel,* who propose
Tiberius Cesar, and *Cesar Borgia,* as Examples fit for *Imitation,*
whereas *True History* would have Exhibited them as Horrid
Monsters as very *Devils.* 'Tis true, I am not of the Opinion, that
one cannot merit the Name of an *Impartial Historian,* except he
write bare *Matters of Fact,* without all *Reflection;* for I can tell
where to find this given as the Definition of *History, Historia est
rerum gestarum, cum laude aut vituperatione, Narratio.*[26] And if
I am not altogether a *Tacitus,* when *Vertues* or *Vices* occur to be
matters of *Reflection,* as well as of *Relation,* I will, for my Vindication, appeal to *Tacitus* himself, whom *Lipsius* calls one of the
Prudentest (tho' *Tertullian,* long before, counts him the *Lyingest*)
of them who have Inriched the World with *History:* He says,
*Præcipuum munus Annalium reor, ne virtutes sileantur, utque
pravis Dictis, Factisque ex posteritate & Infamia metus sit.*[27] I
have not *Commended* any Person, but when I have really judg'd,
not only *That* he *Deserved* it, but also that it would be a Benefit

---

[24] "Historians are to be read with moderation and indulgence, and it is to be
remembered that they cannot in everything be as keen-sighted as Lynceus."—
Murdock.
[25] Probably Louis Aubery, Seigneur du Maury, d. 1687, writer of several historical works.—*Murdock.*
[26] "History is the story of events, with praise or blame."—*Murdock.*
[27] "I regard it as history's highest function not to let virtues be uncelebrated,
and to hold up as a terror the censure of posterity for bad words and deeds."
(Tacitus, *Annals,* iii, 65.)—*Murdock.*

unto Posterity to know, Wherein he deserved it: And my Judgment of *Desert,* hath not been *Biassed,* by Persons being of my own particular Judgment in matters of *Disputation,* among the Churches of God. I have been as willing to wear the Name of *Simplicius Verinus,*[28] throughout my whole undertaking, as he that, before me, hath assumed it: Nor am I like Pope *Zachary,* impatient so much as to hear of any *Antipodes.*[29] The Spirit of a *Schlusselbergius,*[30] who falls foul with Fury and Reproach on all who differ from him; The Spirit of an *Heylin,* who seems to count no Obloquy too hard for a *Reformer;* and the Spirit of those (*Folio-writers* there are, some of them, in the English Nation!) whom a Noble Historian Stigmatizes, as, *Those Hotheaded, Passionate Bigots, from whom, 'tis enough, if you be of a Religion contrary unto theirs, to be defamed, condemned and pursued with a thousand Calumnies.* I thank Heaven I Hate it with all my Heart. But how can the *Lives* of the *Commendable* be written without *Commending* them? Or, is that Law of *History* given in one of the eminentest pieces of *Antiquity* we now have in our hands, wholly antiquated, *Maxime proprium est Historiæ, Laudem rerum egregie gestarum persequi?* [31] Nor have I, on the other side, forbore to mention many *Censurable* things, even in the Best of my Friends, when the things, in my opinion, were *not Good;* or so bore away for *Placentia,* in the course of our Story, as to pass by *Verona;* but been mindful of the Direction which *Polybius* gives to the Historian, *It becomes him that writes an History, sometimes to extol Enemies in his Praises, when their praise-worthy Actions bespeak it, and at the same time to reprove the best Friends, when their Deeds appear worthy of a reproof;*

---

[28] Simplicius Verinus was the name assumed at times by Claude Saumaise (Salmasius), 1588-1653, a French classical scholar, famous for his controversy with Milton.—*Murdock.*

[29] Pope Zacharias, bishop of Rome from 741 to 752, directed that there be expelled from the church one Virgilius who held that there was another world below the earth.—*Murdock.*

[30] Konrad Schlüsselburg, 1543-1619, Lutheran writer and controversialist.—*Murdock.*

[31] "It is in the highest degree the property of history to record praise of good deeds."—*Murdock.*

in-as much as History is good for nothing, if Truth (which is the very Eye of the Animal) be not in it. Indeed I have thought it my duty upon all accounts, (and if it have proceeded unto the degree of a *Fault,* there is, it may be, something in my *Temper* and *Nature,* that has betray'd me therein) to be more sparing and easie, in thus mentioning of *Censurable* things, than in my *other Liberty:* A writer of *Church-History,* should, I know, be like the *builder of the Temple,* one of the *Tribe of Naphthali;* and for this I will also plead my *Polybius* in my Excuse; *It is not the Work of an Historian, to commemorate the Vices and Villanies of Men, so much as their just, their fair, their honest Actions: And the Readers of History get more good by the Objects of their Emulation, than of their Indignation.* Nor do I deny, that tho' I cannot approve the Conduct of *Josephus,* (whom *Jerom* not unjustly nor ineptly calls, *The Greek Livy*) when he left out of his *Antiquities,* the Story of the *Golden Calf,* and I don't wonder to find *Chamier,* and *Rivet,*[32] and others, taxing him for his *Partiality* towards his Country-men; yet I have left unmentioned some *Censurable Occurrences* in the *Story* of our *Colonies,* as things no less *Unuseful* than *Improper* to be raised out of the Grave, wherein *Oblivion* hath now buried them; lest I should have incurred the *Pasquil* bestowed upon Pope *Urban,* who employing a *Committee* to Rip up the *Old Errors* of his Predecessors, one clap'd a pair of Spurs upon the heels of the Statue of *St. Peter;* and a Label from the Statue of St. *Paul* opposite thereunto, upon the Bridge, ask'd him, *Whither he was bound?* St. *Peter* answered, *I apprehend some Danger in staying here; I fear they'll call me in Question for denying my Master.* And St. *Paul* replied, *Nay, then I had best be gone too, for they'll question me also, for Persecuting the Christians before my Conversion.* Briefly, My Pen shall Reproach none, that can give a Good Word unto any Good Man that is not of their *own Faction,* and shall *Fall out* with none, but those that can *Agree* with no body else, except those of their own *Schism.* If I draw any sort of Men with *Charcoal,* it shall be, because I

---

[32] Daniel Chamier, 1570?-1621, French Protestant writer, and André Rivet, 1573-1651, French Calvinist theologian.—*Murdock.*

remember a notable passage of the *Best Queen* that ever was in
the World, our late *Queen Mary*. Monsieur *Jurieu,* that he might
Justifie the Reformation in *Scotland,* made a very black Representation of their old Queen *Mary;* for which, a certain *Syco-
phant* would have incensed our Queen *Mary* against that Reverend Person, saying, *Is it not a Shame that this Man, without
any Consideration for your Royal Person, should dare to throw
such Infamous Calumnies upon a Queen, from whom your Royal
Highness is descended?* But that Excellent Princess replied, *No,
not at all; Is it not enough that by fulsome Praises great Persons
be lull'd asleep all their Lives; But must Flattery accompany them
to their very Graves? How should they fear the Judgment of
Posterity, if Historians be not allowed to speak the Truth after
their Death?* But whether I do my self *Commend,* or whether
I give my Reader an opportunity to *Censure,* I am careful above
all things to do it with *Truth;* and as I have considered the words
of *Plato, Deum indigne & graviter ferre, cum quis ei similem hoc
est, virtute præstantem, vituperet, aut laudet contrarium.*[33] So I
have had the *Ninth Commandment* of a greater *Law-giver* than
Plato, to preserve my care of *Truth* from first to last. If any Mistake have been any where committed, it will be found meerly *Circumstantial,* and wholly *Involuntary;* and let it be remembred,
that tho' no *Historian* ever merited better than the Incomparable
Thuanus,[34] yet learned Men have said of *his* Work, what they
never shall truly say of *ours,* that it contains *multa falsissima &
indigna.*[35] I find *Erasmus* himself mistaking *One* Man for *Two,*
when writing of the Ancients. And even our own English Writers too are often mistaken, and in Matters of a very late Importance, as *Baker,* and *Heylin,* and *Fuller,* (professed Historians)
tell us, that *Richard Sutton,* a single Man, founded the *Charter-
House;* whereas his Name was *Thomas,* and he was a married
Man. I think I can Recite such Mistakes, it may be *Sans* Number

---

[33] "It is to act unworthily and offensively toward God, to abuse anyone who is
like him excelling in virtue, or to praise the opposite of such a one."—*Murdock*.

[34] Jacques Auguste de Thou, French historian and poet, 1553-1617.—*Murdock*.

[35] "Much that is most false and unworthy."—*Murdock*.

occurring in the most credible Writers; yet I hope I shall *commit* none such. But altho' I thus challenge, as my due, the Character of an *Impartial,* I doubt I may not challenge *That* of an *Elegant Historian.* I cannot say, whether the *Style,* wherein this *Church-History* is written, will please the Modern *Cricks:* But if I seem to have used ἀπλουστάτη συντάξει γραφῆς,[36] a Simple, Submiss, Humble *Style,* 'tis the same that *Eusebius* affirms to have been used by *Hegesippus,* who, as far as we understand, was the first Author (after *Luke*) that ever composed an entire Body of *Ecclesiastical History,* which he divided into *Five Books,* and Entitled, ὑπομνήματα τῶν ἐκκλησιαστικῶν πράξεων.[37] Whereas *others,* it may be, will reckon the *Style* Embellished with too much of *Ornament,* by the multiplied References to other and former Concerns, closely couch'd, for the Observation of the *Attentive,* in almost every Paragraph; but I must confess, that I am of his mind who said, *Sicuti sal modice cibis aspersus Condit, & gratiam saporis addit, ita si paulum Antiquitatis admiscueris, Oratio fit venustior.*[38] And I have seldom seen that Way of Writing faulted, but by those, who, for a certain odd Reason, sometimes find fault, *That the Grapes are not ripe.* These *Embellishments* (of which yet I only—*Veniam pro laude peto*)[39] are not the puerile Spoils of *Polyanthea's;* but I should have asserted them to be as choice *Flowers* as most that occur in Ancient or Modern Writings, almost unavoidably putting themselves into the Authors Hand, while about his Work, if those words of *Ambrose* had not a little frightened me, as well as they did *Baronius, Unumquemque Fallunt sua scripta.*[40] I observe that Learned Men have been so terrified by the Reproaches of *Pedantry,* which little Smatterers at Reading and Learning have, by their *Quoting Humours* brought upon themselves, that, for to avoid all Approaches towards that which those Feeble Creatures have gone to imitate,

---

[36] "The most simple style of writing."—*Murdock.*

[37] "Memorials of ecclesiastical transactions."—*Murdock.*

[38] "Just as salt discreetly spread on food seasons it, and increases its flavor, so to mix in a little of antiquity makes style more pleasing."—*Murdock.*

[39] "I ask pardon for this praise."—*Murdock.*

[40] "Everyone errs about his own writings."—*Murdock.*

the best way of Writing has been most injuriously deserted. But what shall we say? The Best way of Writing, under Heaven, shall be the Worst, when *Erasmus* his Monosyllable Tyrant[41] will have it so! And if I should have resign'd my self wholly to the Judgment of *others,* What way of Writing to have taken, the Story of the two Statues made by *Policletus* tells me, what may have been the Issue:[42] He contrived one of them according to the Rules that best pleased himself, and the other according to the Fancy of every one that look'd upon his Work: The former was afterwards Applauded by all, and the latter Derided by those very Persons who had given their Directions for it. As for such *Unaccuracies* as the *Critical* may discover, *Opere in longo,*[43] I appeal to the *Courteous,* for a favourable Construction of them; and certainly they will be favourably Judged of, when there is considered the *Variety* of my *other Employments,* which have kept me in continual Hurries, I had almost said, like those of the *Ninth Sphere,*[44] for the few Months in which this Work has been *Digesting.* It was a thing well thought, by the wise Designers of *Chelsey-Colledge,* wherein able *Historians* were one sort of Persons to be maintained;[45] That the Romanists do in one Point condemn the Protestants; for among the Romanists, they don't burden their *Professors* with any *Parochial Incumbrances;* but among the *Protestants,* the very same *Individual* Man must *Preach, Catechize,* Administer the *Sacraments,* Visit the Afflicted, and manage all the parts of *Church-Discipline;* and if any *Books* for the Service of Religion, be written, Persons thus *extreamly incumbred* must be the Writers. Now, of all the Churches under Heaven, there are none that expect so much *Variety* of Service from their

---

[41] "Our speech at this day (for the most part) consisteth of words of one sillable. Which thing Erasmus observing, merily in his Ecclesiast, compareth the English toong to a Dogs barking, that soundeth nothing els, but Baw, waw, waw, in Monosillable." William Lambarde, *Perambulation of Kent,* p. 233 (ed. 1826). This was written in 1570.—*Murdock*.

[42] The story which follows occurs in Ælian, and, doubtless, elsewhere.—*Murdock*.

[43] "In a long work."—*Murdock*.

[44] The ninth or "Crystalline Sphere" in the Ptolemaic system of astronomy.—*Murdock*.

[45] King James' College, Chelsea, founded 1609.—*Murdock*.

Pastors, as those of *New-England;* and of all the Churches in *New-England,* there are none that require more, than those in *Boston,* the Metropolis of the English *America;* whereof *one* is, by the Lord Jesus Christ, committed unto the Care of the unworthy Hand, by which this *History* is compiled. Reader, Give me leave humbly to mention, with him in *Tully, Antequam de Re, Pauca de Me!* [46] Constant *Sermons,* usually more than once, and perhaps three or four times, in a Week, and all the other Duties of a *Pastoral Watchfulness,* a very *large Flock* has all this while demanded of me; wherein, if I had been furnished with as many *Heads* as a *Typheus,* as many *Eyes* as an *Argos,* and as many *Hands* as a *Briareus,* I might have had Work enough to have employ'd them all; nor hath my *Station* left me free from Obligations to spend very much time in the *Evangelical Service* of *others* also. It would have been a great *Sin* in me, to have *Omitted,* or *Abated,* my Just Cares, to *fulfil my Ministry in these things,* and in a manner *Give my self wholly to them.* All the time I have had for my *Church-History,* hath been perhaps only, or chiefly, that, which I might have taken else for less profitable Recreations; and it hath all been done by *Snatches.* My Reader will not find me the Person intended in his *Littany,* when he says, *Libera me ab homine unius Negotis:* [47] Nor have I spent *Thirty Years* in shaping this my *History,* as *Diodorus Siculus* did for his, [and yet both *Bodinus* and *Sigonius* [48] complain of the Σφαλματα [49] attending it.] But I wish I could have enjoy'd entirely for this Work, one quarter of the little more than *Two Years* which have roll'd away since I began it; whereas I have been forced sometimes wholly to throw by the Work whole Months together, and then resume it, but by a stolen hour or two in a day, not without some hazard of incurring the *Title* which *Coryat* put upon his History of his Travels, *Crudities hastily gobbled up in*

---

[46] "Before coming to the subject, a little about myself."—*Murdock.*

[47] "Deliver me from a man of but one interest."—*Murdock.*

[48] Charles Sigonius (Carlo Sigonio), 1524-1585, Italian writer and philologist.—*Murdock.*

[49] "Errors."—*Murdock.*

five Months. Protogenes being seven Years in drawing a Picture, *Apelles* upon the sight of it, said, *The Grace of the Work was much allay'd by the length of the Time*. Whatever else there may have been to take off the *Grace of the Work,* now in the Readers hands, (whereof the *Pictures* of Great and Good Men make a considerable part) I am sure there hath not been the *length of the Time* to do it. Our English Martyrologer, counted it a sufficient *Apology,* for what Meanness might be found in the first Edition of his *Acts and Monuments,* that it was *hastily rashed up in about fourteen Months:* And I may Apologize for this Collection of our *Acts and Monuments,* that I should have been glad, in the little more than *Two Years* which have ran out, since I enter'd upon it, if I could have had one half of *About fourteen Months* to have entirely devoted thereunto. But besides the *Time,* which the *Daily Services* of *my own* first, and then many *other* Churches, have necessarily call'd for, I have lost abundance of precious *Time,* thro' the feeble and broken State of my *Health,* which hath un-fitted me for *Hard Study;* I can do nothing to purpose at *Lucubrations.* And yet, in this *Time* also of the two or three Years last past, I have not been excused from the further Diversion of *Publishing* (tho' not so many as they say *Mercurius Trismegistus* did, yet) more than a *Score* of other Books, upon a copious Variety of other Subjects, besides the composing of several more, that are not yet published. Nor is this neither all the *Task* that I have in this while had lying upon me; for (tho' I am very sensible of what *Jerom* said, *Non bene fit, quod occupato Animo fit;*[50] and of *Quintilian's* Remark, *Non simul in multa intendere Animus totum potest,*)[51] when I applied my mind unto this way of serving the Lord JESUS CHRIST in my Generation, I set upon another and a greater, which has had, I suppose, more of my *Thought* and *Hope* than this, and wherein there hath passed me, for the most part, *Nulla dies sine linea.*[52] I considered, That all

---

[50] "What is done with an occupied mind, is not well done."—*Murdock.*

[51] "One cannot put his whole mind on many things at the same time."—*Murdock.*

[52] "No day without a line."—*Murdock.*

sort of *Learning* might be made gloriously Subservient unto the *Illustration* of the *Sacred Scripture;* and that no *professed Commentaries* had hitherto given a thousandth part of so much *Illustration* unto it, as might be given. I considered, that Multitudes of *particular Texts,* had, especially of later Years, been more notably *Illustrated* in the *Scattered Books* of Learned Men, than in any of the *Ordinary Commentators.* And I consider'd, That the *Treasures* of *Illustration* for the Bible, dispersed in many hundred Volumes, might be fetch'd all together by a Labour that would resolve to *Conquer all things;* and that all the *Improvements* which the *Later-ages* have made in the *Sciences,* might be also, with an inexpressible Pleasure, call'd in, to Assist the *Illustration* of the *Holy Oracles,* at a Rate that hath not been attempted in the vulgar *Annotations;* and that a common degree of *Sense,* would help a Person, who should converse much with these things, to attempt sometimes also an *Illustration* of his own, which might expect some Attention. Certainly, it will not be ungrateful unto good Men, to have innumerable *Antiquities, Jewish, Chaldee, Arabian, Grecian* and *Roman,* brought home unto us, with a *Sweet Light* Reflected from them on the *Word,* which is our *Light:* Or, To have all the *Typical* Men and things in our *Book of Mysteries,* accommodated with their *Antitypes:* Or, To have many Hundreds of References to our dearest *Lord Messiah,* discovered in the Writings which *Testifie of Him,* oftner than the most of Mankind have hitherto imagined: Or, To have the *Histories* of all Ages, coming in with punctual and surprising *Fulfillments* of the Divine *Prophecies,* as far as they have been hitherto fulfilled; and not meer *Conjectures,* but even Mathematical and Incontestable *Demonstrations,* given of *Expositions* offered upon the *Prophecies,* that yet remain to be accomplished: Or, To have in *One Heap,* Thousands of those *Remarkable Discoveries of the deep things of the Spirit of God,* whereof *one* or *two,* or a few, sometimes, have been, with good Success accounted Materials enough to advance a Person into *Authorism;* or to have the delicious *Curiosities* of *Grotius,* and *Bochart,* and *Mede,* and *Lightfoot,* and *Selden,* and *Spencer*[53] (carefully selected and corrected) and many more Giants in Knowledge, all set upon one Table. Travellers tell us, That at *Florence* there is a rich Table, worth a thousand Crowns, made of Precious Stones neatly inlaid; a Table that was fifteen Years in making, with no less than Thirty Men daily at work upon it; even such a Table could not afford so rich Entertainments, as one that should have the Soul-feasting Thoughts of those Learned Men together set upon it. Only 'tis pitty, that instead of one poor feeble *American,* overwhelm'd with a thousand other Cares, and capable of touching this Work no otherwise than in a Digression, there be not more than Thirty Men daily employ'd about it. For, when the excellent Mr. *Pool* [54] had finished his Laborious and Immortal Task, it was noted by some considerable Persons, *That wanting Assistance to Collect for him many miscellaneous Criticisms, occasionally scattered in other Authors, he left many better Things behind him than he found.* At more than all this, our *Essay* is levell'd, if it be not anticipated with that Epitaph, *magnis tamen excidit ausis.* [55] Designing accordingly, to give the Church of God such displays of his blessed Word, as may be more Entertaining for the Rarity and Novelty of them, than any that have hitherto been seen together in any *Exposition;* and yet such as may be acceptable unto the most Judicious, for the Demonstrative Truth of them, and unto the most Orthodox, for the regard had unto the *Analogy of Faith* in all, I have now, in a few Months, got ready an huge number of *Golden Keys* to open the *Pandects* of Heaven, and some thousands of charming and curious and singular Notes, by the *New Help* whereof, the *Word of* CHRIST *may run and be glorified.* If the *God of my Life,* will please to spare my Life [my

---

[53] Grotius, 1583-1645, the great Dutch lawyer and theologian; Samuel Bochart, 1599-1667, French Protestant scholar; Joseph Mede, 1586-1638, English theologian; John Lightfoot, 1602-1675, learned English divine; John Selden, 1584-1654, statesman, political writer and archæologist; and John Spencer, 1630-1695, theologian and Hebraist, were all men whose works Cotton Mather knew well.—*Murdock.*

[54] Matthew Poole, 1624-1709, compiled a famous *Synopsis* of the various biblical commentators.—*Murdock.*

[55] "Yet he fell short of what he had ventured to attempt."—*Murdock.*

yet Sinful, and Slothful, and thereby Fofeited Life!] as many years longer as the *Barren Fig-tree* had in the Parable, I may make unto the Church of God, an humble Tender of our BIBLIA AMERICANA, a Volumn enrich'd with better things than all the Plate of the *Indies;* YET NOT I, BUT THE GRACE OF CHRIST WITH ME. My Reader sees, why I commit the Fault of a περιαυτία,[56] which appears in the mention of these Minute-passages; 'tis to excuse whatever other Fault of Inaccuracy, or Inadvertency, may be discovered in an History, which hath been a sort of Rapsody made up (like the Paper whereon 'tis written!) with many little Rags, torn from an Employment, multifarious enough to overwhelm one of my small Capacities.

Magna dabit, qui magna potest; mihi parva potenti,
Parvaque poscenti, parva dedisse sat est.[57]

§ 6. But shall I prognosticate thy Fate, now that,

Parve (sed invideo) ne me, Liber, ibis in Urbem.[58]

Luther, who was himself owner of such an Heart, advised every Historian to get the *Heart of a Lion;* and the more I consider of the Provocation, which this our *Church-History* must needs give to that Roaring Lion, who has, through all Ages hitherto, been tearing the Church to pieces, the more occasion I see to wish my self a *Cœur de Lion.* But had not my Heart been Trebly Oak'd and Brass'd for such Encounters as this our History may meet withal, I would have worn the Silk-worms Motto, *Operitur dum Operatur,*[59] and have chosen to have written *Anonymously;* or, as *Claudius Salmasius* calls himself *Walo Messalinus,* as *Ludovicus Molinæus* calls himself *Ludiomæus Colvinus,* as *Carolus*

---

[56] "Discussion about myself."—*Murdock.*
[57] "He will give great things, who is able; for me, who am able to do little, and who ask for little, it is enough to have given a little."—*Murdock.*
[58] "O little book, though I envy, you, not I, shall go forth to the world."—*Murdock.*
[59] "It is hidden while it works."—*Murdock.*

Scribanius calls himself *Clarus Bonarscius,* (and no less Men than *Peter du Moulin,* and Dr. *Henry More,* stile themselves, the one *Hippolytus Fronto,* the other *Franciscus Paleopolitanus.*)[60] Thus I would have tried, whether I could not have Anagrammatized my Name into some Concealment; or I would have referr'd it to be found in the second Chapter of the second Syntagm of *Selden de Diis Syris.*[61] Whereas now I freely confess, 'tis COTTON MATHER that has written all these things;

Me, me, ad sum qui scripsi; in me convertite Ferrum.[62]

I hope 'tis a right Work that I have done; but we are not yet arrived unto the *Day, wherein God will bring every Work into Judgment* (the Day of the *Kingdom* that was promised unto *David*) and a Son of *David* hath as Truly as Wisely told us, that until the arrival of that Happy Day, this is one of the *Vanities* attending Humane Affairs; *For a right Work a Man shall be envied of His Neighbour.* It will not be so much a surprise unto me, if I should live to see our *Church-History* vexed with *Aniemad-versions* of Calumnious Writers, as it would have been unto *Virgil,* to read his *Bucolicks* reproached by the *Antibucolica* of a *Nameless Scribbler,* and his *Æneids* travestied by the *Æneido-mastix* of *Carbilius:* Or *Herennius* taking pains to make a Collection of the *Faults,* and *Faustinus* of the *Thefts,* in his incomparable Composures: Yea, *Pliny,* and *Seneca* themselves, and our *Jerom,* reproaching him, as a Man of no Judgment, nor Skill in Sciences; while *Pædianus* affirms of him, that he was himself, *Usque adeo invidiæ Expers, ut si quid erudite dictum*

---

[60] Louis Molinæus, or Moulin, was an English physician, born about 1603; Charles Scribani, or Scribanius, was a Jesuit historian, living 1561-1629; Peter du Moulin was an English theologian, and Henry More was one of the English "Cambridge Platonists."—*Murdock*.

[61] The name Mather occurs in the book of John Selden referred to (p. 165 of the London 1617 edition).—*Murdock*.

[62] "It is I who have written; turn the sword against me." This is an alteration of the *Æneid*, ix, 427.—*Murdock*.

inspiceret alterius, non minus gauderet ac si suum esset.[63] How should a Book, no better laboured than this of ours, escape *Zoilian*[64] Outrages, when in all Ages, the most exquisite Works have been as much vilified, as *Plato's* by *Scaliger,* and *Aristotle's* by *Lactantius?* In the time of our *K. Edward* VI. there was an Order to bring in all the Teeth of St. *Apollonia,* which the People of his one Kingdom carried about them for the Cure of the *Tooth ach;* and they were so many, that they almost fill'd a Tun. Truly *Envy* hath as many *Teeth* as Madam *Apollonia* would have had, if all those pretended Reliques had been really hers. And must all these *Teeth* be fastned on thee, *O my Book?* It may be so! And yet the *Book,* when ground between these *Teeth,* will prove like *Ignatius* in the *Teeth* of the furious Tygers, *The whiter Manchet for the Churches of God.* The greatest and fiercest Rage of *Envy,* is that which I expect from those IDUMÆANS, whose Religion is all Ceremony, and whose Charity is more for them who deny the most Essential things in the Articles and Homilies of the Church of *England,* than for the most Conscientious Men in the World, who manifest their being so, by their Dissent in some little Ceremony: Or those Persons whose Hearts are notably expressed in those words used by one of them ['tis *Howel* in his *Familiar Letters,* Vol. 1. Sect. 6. Lett. 32.] *I rather pitty, than hate, Turk or Infidel, for they are of the same Metal, and bear the same Stamp, as I do, tho' the Inscriptions differ; If I hate any, 'tis those Schismaticks that puzzle the sweet Peace of our Church; so that I could be content to see an Anabaptist go to Hell on a Brownists Back.*[65] The Writer whom I last quoted, hath given us a Story of a young Man in *High-Holbourn,* who being after his death Dissected, there was a Serpent with divers

---

[63] "Ever so very free of envy, that when he examined anything learnedly written by another, he was not less delighted than as if it were his own."—*Murdock*.

[64] Zoilus, a fourth century Greek rhetorician, so severely criticized Homer as to be known as the "Scourge of Homer."—*Murdock*.

[65] The Brownists were those who followed the beliefs of Robert Brown—in general, they were the more extreme Independents among the English Puritans. . . . —*Murdock*.

tails, found in the left Ventricle of his Heart. I make no question,
that our Church-History will find some Reader disposed like
that Writer, with an Heart as full of Serpent and Venom as ever
it can hold: Nor indeed will they be able to hold, but the Tongues
and Pens of those angry Folks, will scourge me as with Scorpions,
and cause me to feel (if I will feel) as many Lashes as *Cornelius
Agrippa* expected from their Brethren, for the Book in which
he exposed their Vanities.[66] A Scholar of the great JUELS, made
once about fourscore Verses, for which the Censor of *Corpus
Christi* Colledge in the beginning of Queen *Maries* Reign, publickly and cruelly scourged him, with one Lash for every Verse.[67]
Now in those Verses, the young Man's Prayers to the Lord
JESUS CHRIST, have this for part of the answer given to them.

Respondet Dominus, spectans de sedibus altis,
  Ne dubites recte credere, parve puer.
Olim sum passus mortem, nunc occupo dextram
  Patris, nunc summi sunt mea regna poli.
Sed tu, crede mihi, vires Scriptura resumet,
  Tolleturque suo tempore missa nequam.

In English.

The Lord beholding from his Throne, reply'd,
Doubt not, *O Youth,* firmly in me confide.
I dy'd long since, now sit at the Right Hand
Of my bless'd Father, and the World command.
Believe me, *Scripture* shall regain her sway,
And wicked *Mass* in due time fade away.

Reader, I also expect nothing but *Scourges* from that Generation, to whom the *Mass book* is dearer than the Bible. But I have
now likewise confessed another Expectation, that shall be my

---

[66] Heinrich Cornelius Agrippa, 1487-1535, published in 1531 his *De Vanitate et
Incertitude Scientiarum,* which brought him into difficulties with the Inquisition.—
Murdock.
[67] Bishop John Jewel of Salisbury, 1522-1571. . . .—*Murdock.*

Consolation under all. They tell us, That on the highest of the *Caspian* Mountains in *Spain,* there is a Lake, whereinto if you throw a Stone, there presently ascends a Smoke, which forms a dense Cloud, from whence issues a Tempest of Rain, Hail, and horrid Thunder-claps, for a good quarter of an hour. Our Church-History will be like a Stone cast into that Lake, for the furious Tempest which it will raise among some, whose Ecclesiastical Dignities have set them, as on the top of Spanish Mountains. The Catholick Spirit of Communion wherewith 'tis written, and the Liberty which I have taken, to tax the Schismatical Impositions and Persecutions of a Party, who have always been as real Enemies to the English Nation, as to the Christian and Protestant Interest, will certainly bring upon the whole Composure, the quick Censures of that Party, at the first cast of their look upon it. In the Duke of *Alva's* Council of twelve Judges, there was one *Hessels* a *Flemming,* who slept always at the Trial of Criminals, and when they wak'd him to deliver his Opinion, he rub'd his Eyes, and cry'd between sleeping and waking, *Ad patibulum! ad Patibulum!* To the Gallows with 'em! [And, by the way, this Blade was himself, at the last, condemned unto the Gallows, without an Hearing!] As quick Censures must this our Labour expect from those who will not bestow waking thoughts upon the Representations of Christianity here made unto the World; but have a Sentence of Death always to pass, or at least, Wish, upon these Generous Principles, without which, 'tis impossible to maintain the Reformation: And I confess, I am very well content, that this our Labour takes the Fate of those Principles: Nor do I dissent from the words of the Excellent *Whitaker* upon *Luther, Fœlix ille, quem Dominus eo Honore dignatus est, ut Homines nequissimos suos haberet inimicos.*[68] But if the old Epigrammatist, when he saw Guilty Folks raving Mad at his Lines, could say——

Hoc volo; nunc nobis carmina nostra placent:[69]

---

[68] "Happy is he, whom God has deemed worthy of the honor that he may have the worst of men for his enemies."—*Murdock*.

[69] "This is what I wish; now my songs please me."—*Murdock*.

Certainly an Historian should not be displeased at it, if the Enemies of Truth discover their Madness at the true and free Communications of his History: and therefore the more Stones they
throw at this Book, there will not only be the more Proofs, that
it is a Tree which hath good Fruits growing upon it, but I will
build my self a Monument with them, whereon shall be inscribed,
that Clause in the Epitaph of the Martyr *Stephen:*

Excepit Lapides, cui petra Christus erat:[76]

Albeit perhaps the *Epitaph,* which the old *Monks* bestow'd
upon *Wickliff,* will be rather endeavour'd for me, (*If I am
thought worth one!*) by the Men, who will, with all possible
Monkery, strive to stave off the approaching *Reformation.*

But since an Undertaking of this Nature, must thus encounter
so much Envy, from those who are under the Power of the
Spirit that works in the Children of Unperswadeableness, methinks I might perswade my self, that it will find another sort
of Entertainment from those Good Men who have a better Spirit
in them: For, as the Apostle *James* hath noted, (so with Monsieur *Claude* I read it) *The Spirit that is in us, lusteth against
Envy;* and yet even in *us* also, there will be the *Flesh,* among
whose Works, one is *Envy,* which will be *Lusting* against the
Spirit. All Good Men will not be satisfied with every thing that
is here set before them. In my own Country, besides a considerable number of loose and vain Inhabitants risen up, to whom
the Congregational Church-Discipline, which cannot Live well,
where the Power of Godliness dyes, is become distasteful for
the Purity of it; there is also a number of eminently Godly Persons, who are for a Larger way, and unto these my Church-
History will give distast, by the things which it may happen to
utter, in favour of that Church-Discipline on some few occasions;
and the Discoveries which I may happen to make of my Apprehensions, that *Scripture,* and *Reason,* and *Antiquity* is for it;
and that it is not far from a glorious Resurrection. But that, as

---

[76] . . . "He died by *stoning,* but his *Rock* was Christ."—*Murdock.*

the Famous Mr. *Baxter,* after Thirty or Forty Years hard Study, about the true Instituted Church-Discipline, at last, not only own'd, but also invincibly prov'd, That it is *The Congregational;* so, The further that the *Unprejudiced Studies* of Learned Men proceed in this Matter, the more generally the *Congregational Church-Discipline* will be pronounced for. On the other side, There are some among us, who very strictly profess the *Congregational Church-Discipline,* but at the same time they have an unhappy Narrowness of Soul, by which they confine their value and Kindness too much unto their own Party; and unto those my *Church History* will be offensive, because my Regard unto our own declared Principles, does not hinder me from giving the Right-hand of Fellowship unto the valuable Servants of the Lord Jesus Christ, who find not our Church-Discipline as yet agreeable unto their present Understandings and Illuminations. If it be thus in my own Country, it cannot be other wise in That whereto I send this account of my own. Briefly, as it hath been said, That if all *Episcopal* Men were like Archbishop *Usher,* and all *Presbyterians* like *Stephen Marshal,* and all *Independents* like *Jeremiah Burroughs,* the Wounds of the Church would soon be healed;[71] my Essay to carry that Spirit through this whole Church-History, will bespeak Wounds for it, from those that are of another Spirit. And there will also be in every Country those Good Men, who yet have not had the Grace of Christ so far prevailing in them, as utterly to divest them of that piece of Ill Nature which the Comedian resents, *In homine Imperito, quo nil quicquam Injustius, quia nisi quod ipse facit, nil recte factum putat.*[72]

However, All these things, and an hundred more such things which I think of, are very small Discouragements for such a Service as I have here endeavoured. I foresee a Recompence, which

---

[71] James Ussher, Archbishop of Armagh, an Anglican, liberal toward Puritanism, 1581-1656; Marshall, 1594?-1655, and Burroughs, 1599-1646, were men of breadth of view and wide influence.—*Murdock.*

[72] "Nothing is more unjust than an inexperienced man, who thinks nothing is right except what he has done himself." (Terence, *Adelphi,* ll. 98-99.)—*Murdock.*

will abundantly swallow up all Discouragements! It may be
Strato the Philosopher counted himself well recompensed for
his Labours, when *Ptolemy* bestow'd fourscore Talents on him.
It may be Archimelus the Poet counted himself well recompensed, when Hiero sent him a thousand Bushels of Wheat for
one little Epigram: And *Saleius* the Poet might count himself
well recompensed, when Vespasian sent him twelve thousand
and five hundred *Philippicks;* and *Oppian* the Poet might count
himself well recompensed, when Caracalla sent him a piece of
Gold for every Line that he had inscribed unto him. As I live
in a Country where such Recompences never were in fashion;
it hath no Preferments for me, and I shall count that I am well
Rewarded in it, if I can escape without being heavily Reproached,
Censured and Condemned, for what I have done: So I thank the
Lord, I should exceedingly Scorn all such mean Considerations,
I seek not out for Benefactors, to whom these Labours may be
Dedicated: There is ONE to whom all is due! From Him I shall
have a Recompence: And what Recompence? The Recompence,
whereof I do, with inexpressible Joy, assure my self, is this, *That
these my poor Labours will certainly serve the Churches and
Interests of the Lord Jesus Christ*. And I think I may say, That
I ask to live no longer, than I count a Service unto the Lord
Jesus Christ, and his Churches, to be it self a glorious Recompence for the doing of it. When *David* was contriving to build
the House of God, there was that order given from Heaven concerning him, *Go tell* David, *my Servant*. The adding of *that* more
than *Royal Title* unto the Name of David, was a sufficient Recompence for all his Contrivance about the House of God. In
our whole *Church-History,* we have been at work for the House
of the Lord Jesus Christ, [Even that *Man* who is the *Lord God,*
and whose *Form* seems on that occasion represented unto His
David] And herein 'tis Recompence enough, that I have been a
Servant unto that heavenly Lord. The greatest *Honour,* and the
sweetest *Pleasure,* out of *Heaven,* is to Serve our Illustrious Lord
JESUS CHRIST, who hath *loved us, and given himself for us;*
and unto whom it is infinitely reasonable that we should *give*

our selves, and all that we *have* and *Are:* And it may be the *Angels* in *Heaven* too, aspire not after an higher *Felicity.*

Unto thee, therefore, O thou Son of God, and King of Heaven, and Lord of all things, whom all the Glorious Angels of Light, unspeakably love to Glorifie; I humbly offer up a poor History of Churches, which own thee alone for their Head, and Prince, and Law-giver; Churches which thou hast purchas'd with thy own Blood, and with wonderful Dispensations of thy Providence hitherto protected and preserved; and of a People which thou didst Form for thy self, to shew forth thy Praises. I bless thy great Name, for thy inclining of me to, and carrying of me through, the Work of this History: I pray thee to sprinkle the Book of this History with thy Blood, and make it acceptable and profitable unto thy Churches, and serve thy Truths and ways among thy People, by that which thou hast here prepared; for 'tis THOU that hast prepar'd it for them. Amen.

Quid sum? Nil. Quis sum? Nullus. Sed Gratia CHRISTI, Quod sum, quod Vivo, quodque Laboro, facit.[73]

---

[73] "What am I? Nothing. Who am I? No one. But the Grace of Christ makes what I am, my life, and what I do."—*Murdock.*

BOOK II, CHAPTER I. THE LIFE OF
WILLIAM BRADFORD

*Omnium Somnos, illius vigilantia defendit, omnium otium illius
Labor, omnium Delitias illius Industria, omnium vacationem
illius occupatio.*[1]

§ 1. It has been a Matter of some Observation, that although
Yorkshire be one of the largest Shires in *England,* yet, for all the
Fires of Martyrdom which were kindled in the Days of Queen
Mary, it afforded no more *Fuel* than one poor *Leaf;* namely,
John Leaf, an Apprentice, who suffered for the *Doctrine* of the
Reformation at the same Time and Stake with the Famous *John
Bradford.* But when the Reign of Queen *Elizabeth* would not
admit the *Reformation* of *Worship* to proceed unto those De-
grees, which were proposed and pursued by no small number of
the Faithful in those Days, *Yorkshire* was not the least of the
Shires in *England* that afforded Suffering *Witnesses* thereunto.
The *Churches* there *gathered* were quickly molested with such a
raging *Persecution,* that if the Spirit of *Separation* in them did
carry them unto a further *Extream* than it should have done,
one blameable Cause thereof will be found in the *Extremity* of
that *Persecution.* Their *Troubles* made that *Cold* Country too
Hot for them, so that they were under a necessity to *seek* a Retreat in the *Low Countries;* and yet the watchful Malice and
Fury of their Adversaries rendred it almost impossible for them
to *find* what they sought. For them to leave their *Native Soil,*
their *Lands* and their *Friends,* and go into a *Strange Place,* where
they must hear *Forreign Language,* and live *meanly* and *hardly,*
and in other Imployments than that of *Husbandry,* wherein they
had been Educated, *these* must needs have been such *Discouragements* as could have been Conquered by none, save those who
sought first the Kingdom of God, and the Righteousness thereof.

---

[1] "His vigilance defends the sleep of all; his labor, their rest; his industry, their
pleasures; and his diligence, their leisure."—*Murdock.*

But that which would have made these Discouragements the more Unconquerable unto an ordinary Faith, was the terrible Zeal of their Enemies to Guard all *Ports,* and Search all *Ships,* that none of them should be carried off. I will not relate the *sad things* of this kind, then *seen* and *felt* by this People of God; but only exemplifie those *Trials* with one short Story. Divers of this People having Hired a *Dutchman* then lying at *Hull,* to carry them over to *Holland,* he promised faithfully to take them in between *Grimsly* and *Hull;*[2] but *they* coming to the Place a Day or Two too soon, the appearance of such a Multitude alarmed the *Officers* of the Town adjoining, who came with a great Body of *Soldiers* to seize upon them. Now it happened that one Boat full of *Men* had been carried Aboard, while the *Women* were yet in a *Bark* that lay Aground in a Creek at Low-Water. The *Dutchman* perceiving the *Storm* that was thus beginning *Ashore,* swore by the *Sacrament* that he would stay no longer for any of them; and so taking the Advantage of a Fair Wind then Blowing, he put out to *Sea* for *Zealand.* The Women thus left near *Grimsly-Common,* bereaved of their Husbands, who had been hurried from them, and forsaken of their Neighbours, of whom none durst in this Fright stay with them, were a very rueful Spectacle; some crying for *Fear,* some shaking for *Cold,* all dragg'd by Troops of *Armed* and *Angry* Men from one Justice to another, till not knowing what to do with them, they e'en dismiss'd them to shift as well as they could for themselves. But by their singular *Afflictions,* and by their Christian *Behaviours,* the *Cause* for which they exposed themselves did gain considerably. In the mean time, the Men at Sea found Reason to be glad that their Families were not with them, for they were surprized with an *horrible Tempest,* which held them for Fourteen Days together, in Seven whereof they saw not *Sun, Moon,* or *Star,* but were driven upon the Coast of *Norway.* The *Mariners* often despaired of Life, and once with doleful shrieks gave over all, as thinking the Vessel was Foundred: But the Vessel rose again, and when The *Mariners* with

---

[2] *I.e.,* Grimsby.—*Murdock.*

sunk Hearts often cried out, *We Sink! We Sink!* The Passengers without such Distraction of Mind, even while the Water was running into their Mouths and Ears, would chearfully Shout, *Yet Lord, thou canst save! Yet Lord, thou canst save!* And the Lord accordingly brought them at last safe unto their *Desired Haven:* And not long after helped their Distressed Relations thither after them, where indeed they found upon almost all Accounts *a new World,* but a World in which they found that they must live like *Strangers* and *Pilgrims.*

§ 2. Among those Devout People was our *William Bradford,* who was Born *Anno* 1588. in an obscure Village call'd *Ansterfield,* where the People were as unacquainted with the *Bible,* as the *Jews* do seem to have been with *part* of it in the Days of *Josiah;* a most Ignorant and Licentious *People,* and *like unto their Priest.* Here, and in some other Places, he had a Comfortable *Inheritance* left him of his Honest Parents, who died while he was yet a Child, and cast him on the Education, first of his *Grand Parents,* and then of his *Uncles,* who devoted him, like his Ancestors, unto the Affairs of *Husbandry.* Soon and long Sickness kept him, as he would afterwards thankfully say, from the *Vanities of Youth,* and made him the fitter for what he was afterwards to undergo. When he was about a Dozen Years Old, the Reading of the *Scriptures* began to cause great Impressions upon him; and those Impressions were much assisted and improved, when he came to enjoy Mr. *Richard Clifton's*[3] Illuminating Ministry, not far from his Abode; he was then also further befriended, by being brought into the Company and Fellowship of such as were then called *Professors;*[4] though the Young Man that brought him into it, did after become a Prophane and Wicked *Apostate.* Nor could the *Wrath* of his *Uncles,* nor the *Scoff* of his *Neighbours* now turn'd upon him, as one of the *Puritans,* divert him from his Pious Inclinations.

§ 3. At last beholding how fearfully the Evangelical and Apos-

---

[3] Richard Clifton, a Puritan, minister at Scrooby and later in Amsterdam. He died in 1610.—*Murdock.*

[4] *I.e.,* those who professed to have religious faith.—*Murdock.*

tolical *Church-Form,* whereinto the Churches of the *Primitive Times* were cast by the good Spirit of God, had been *Deformed* by the *Apostacy* of the *Succeeding Times;* and what little Progress the *Reformation* had yet made in many Parts of *Christendom* towards its Recovery, he set himself by Reading, by Discourse, by Prayer, to learn whether it was not his Duty to *withdraw* from the Communion of the *Parish-Assemblies,* and *engage* with some *Society* of the Faithful, that should keep close unto the *Written Word* of God, as the *Rule* of their *Worship.* And after many Distresses of Mind concerning it, he took up a very Deliberate and Understanding *Resolution* of doing so; which *Resolution* he chearfully Prosecuted, although the provoked *Rage* of his Friends tried all the ways imaginable to reclaim him from it, unto all whom his Answer was, *Were I like to endanger my Life, or consume my Estate by any ungodly Courses, your Counsels to me were very seasonable: But you know that I have been Diligent and Provident in my Calling, and not only desirous to augment what I have, but also to enjoy it in your Company; to part from which will be as great a Cross as can befal me. Nevertheless, to keep a good Conscience, and walk in such a Way as God has prescribed in his Word, is a thing which I must prefer before you all, and above Life it self. Wherefore, since 'tis for a good Cause that I am like to suffer the Disasters which you lay before me, you have no Cause to be either angry with me, or sorry for me; yea, I am not only willing to part with every thing that is dear to me in this World for this Cause, but I am also thankful that God has given me an Heart so to do, and will accept me so to suffer for him. Some* lamented him, *some* derided him, *all* disswaded him: Nevertheless the more they did it, the more fixed he was in his Purpose to seek the Ordinances of the Gospel, where they should be dispensed with most of the *Commanded Purity;* and the *sudden Deaths* of the chief Relations which thus lay at him, quickly after convinced him what a Folly it had been to have quitted his *Profession,* in Expectation of any Satisfaction from them. So to *Holland* he attempted a removal.

§ 4. Having with a great Company of Christians Hired a Ship

to Transport them for *Holland*, the Master perfidiously betrayed them into the Hands of those *Persecutors*, who Rifled and Ransack'd their Goods, and clapp'd their Persons into Prison at *Boston*, where they lay for a Month together. But Mr. *Bradford* being a Young Man of about *Eighteen*, was dismissed sooner than the rest, so that within a while he had Opportunity with some others to get over to *Zealand*, through *Perils* both by *Land* and *Sea* not inconsiderable; where he was not long Ashore e're a *Viper* seized on his Hand, that is, an Officer, who carried him unto the Magistrates, unto whom an envious Passenger had accused him as having *fled* out of *England*. When the Magistrates understood the True Cause of his coming thither, they were well satisfied with him; and so he repaired joyfully unto his Brethren at *Amsterdam*, where the Difficulties to which he afterwards stooped in Learning and Serving of a *Frenchman* at the Working of *Silks*, were abundantly Compensated by the *Delight* wherewith he sat under the *Shadow* of our Lord in his purely dispensed Ordinances. At the end of Two Years, he did, being of Age to do it, convert his Estate in *England* into Money; but Setting up for himself, he found some of his Designs by the *Providence* of God frowned upon, which he judged a *Correction* bestowed by God upon him for certain Decays of *Internal Piety*, whereinto he had fallen; the *Consumption* of his *Estate* he thought came to prevent a *Consumption* in his *Virtue*. But after he had resided in *Holland* about half a Score Years, he was one of those who bore a part in that Hazardous and Generous Enterprize of removing into *New-England*, with part of the *English* Church at *Leyden*, where at their first Landing, his dearest Consort accidentally falling Overboard, was drowned in the *Harbour*; and the rest of his Days were spent in the Services, and the Temptations, of that *American Wilderness*.

§ 5. Here was Mr. *Bradford* in the Year 1621. Unanimously chosen the *Governour* of the Plantation: The Difficulties whereof were such, that if he had not been a Person of more than Ordinary Piety, Wisdom and Courage, he must have sunk under them. He had with a Laudable Industry been laying up a Treasure of *Ex-*

periences, and he had now occasion to use it: Indeed nothing but an *Experienced* Man could have been suitable to the Necessities of the People. The Potent Nations of the *Indians,* into whose Country they were come, would have cut them off, if the Blessing of God upon *his* Conduct had not quell'd them; and if his Prudence, Justice and Moderation had not overruled them, they had been ruined by their own *Distempers.* One *Specimen* of his Demeanour is to this Day particularly spoken of. A Company of Young Fellows that were newly arrived, were very unwilling to comply with the Governour's Order for *Working* abroad on the Publick Account; and therefore on *Christmass-Day,* when he had called upon them, they excused themselves, with a pretence that it was against their *Conscience* to *Work* such a Day. The Governour gave them no Answer, only that he would spare them till they were better informed; but by and by he found them all at *Play* in the Street, sporting themselves with various Diversions; whereupon Commanding the Instruments of their Games to be taken from them, he effectually gave them to understand, *That it was against his Conscience that they should play whilst others were at Work; and that if they had any Devotion to the Day, they should show it at Home in the Exercises of Religion, and not in the Streets with Pastime and Frolicks;* and this gentle Reproof put a final stop to all such Disorders for the future.

§ 6. For Two Years together after the beginning of the Colony, whereof he was now Governour, the poor People had a great Experiment of *Man's not living by Bread alone;* for when they were left all together without one Morsel of *Bread* for many Months one after another, still the good Providence of God relieved them, and supplied them, and this for the most part out of the *Sea.* In this low Condition of Affairs, there was no little Exercise for the *Prudence* and *Patience* of the Governour, who chearfully bore his part in all: And that *Industry* might not flag, he quickly set himself to settle *Propriety*[5] among the New-Planters; foreseeing that while the whole Country labour'd upon a *Common Stock,* the *Husbandry* and *Business* of the Plantation could not *flourish,*

---

[5] *I.e.,* property.—*Murdock.*

as *Plato* and others long since dream'd that it would, if a *Community* were established. Certainly, if the Spirit which dwelt in the *Old Puritans,* had not inspired these *New-Planters,* they had sunk under the Burden of these Difficulties; but our *Bradford* had a *double Portion* of that Spirit.

§ 7. The Plantation was quickly thrown into a *Storm* that almost overwhelmed it, by the unhappy Actions of a Minister sent over from *England* by the *Adventurers* concerned for the Plantation; but by the Blessing of Heaven on the Conduct of the Governour, they Weathered out that *Storm*. Only the *Adventurers* hereupon breaking to pieces, threw up all their Concernments with the *Infant Colony;* whereof they gave this as one Reason, *That the Planters dissembled with His Majesty, and their Friends in their Petition, wherein they declared for a Church-Discipline, agreeing with the* French *and others of the Reforming Churches in* Europe. Whereas 'twas now urged, that they had admitted into their Communion a Person, who at his Admission utterly *renounced* the Churches of *England,* (which Person by the way, was *that* very Man who had made the Complaints against them) and therefore though they denied the *Name* of *Brownists* yet they were the *Thing*. In Answer hereunto, the very Words written by the Governour were these; *Whereas you Tax us with dissembling about the* French Discipline, *you do us wrong, for we both hold and practice the* Discipline *of the* French *and other* Reformed *Churches* (*as they have published the same in the* Harmony *of Confessions*) *according to our Means, in Effect and Substance. But whereas you would tie us up to the* French Discipline *in every Circumstance, you derogate from the* Liberty *we have in Christ Jesus. The Apostle* Paul *would have none* to follow him *in any thing, but wherein he* follows Christ; *much less ought any Christian or Church in the World to do it. The* French *may err, we may err, and other Churches may err, and doubtless do in many* Circumstances. *That Honour therefore belongs only to the* Infallible Word of God, *and* pure Testament of Christ, *to be propounded and followed as the* only *Rule and Pattern for Direction herein to all Churches and Christians. And*

*it is too great Arrogancy for any Men or Church to think, that
he or they have so sounded the Word of God unto the bottom,
as precisely to set down the Churches Discipline without Error in
Substance or Circumstance, that no other without blame may di-
gress or differ in any thing from the same. And it is not difficult to
shew that the* Reformed Churches *differ in many* Circumstances
among themselves. By which Words it appears how far he was
free from that *Rigid Spirit* of *Separation,* which broke to pieces
the *Separatists* themselves in the *Low Countries,* unto the great
Scandal of the *Reforming Churches.* He was indeed a Person of a
well-temper'd Spirit, or else it had been scarce possible for him to
have kept the Affairs of *Plymouth* in so good a *Temper* for *Thirty
Seven* Years together; in every one of which he was chosen their
Governour, except the *Three Years,* wherein Mr. *Winslow,* and
the *Two Years,* wherein Mr. *Prince,* at the choice of the People,
took a *turn* with him.

§ 8. The *Leader* of a People in a *Wilderness* had need be a
Moses; and if a *Moses* had not led the People of *Plymouth-Colony,*
when this Worthy Person was their Governour, the People had
never with so much Unanimity and Importunity still called *him*
to lead them. Among many Instances thereof, let this one piece
of *Self denial be told for a Memorial of him, wheresoever this
History shall be considered.* The Patent of the Colony was taken
in *his* Name, running in these Terms, *To* William Bradford, *his
Heirs, Associates and Assigns:* But when the number of the *Freemen* was much Increased, and many New *Townships* Erected,
the *General Court* there desired of Mr. *Bradford,* that he would
make a Surrender of the same into *their Hands,* which *he* willingly and presently assented unto, and confirmed it according to
their Desire by his *Hand* and *Seal,* reserving no more for himself
than was his *Proportion,* with others, by *Agreement.* But as he
found the Providence of Heaven many ways *Recompencing* his
many Acts of *Self-denial,* so he gave this Testimony to the Faithfulness of the Divine Promises; *That he had forsaken Friends,
Houses and Lands for the sake of the Gospel, and the Lord gave
them him again. Here* he prospered in his *Estate;* and besides a

Worthy *Son* which he had by a former Wife, he had also Two Sons and a Daughter by another, whom he Married in this Land.

§ 9. He was a Person for *Study* as well as *Action;* and hence, notwithstanding the Difficulties through which he passed in his Youth, he attained unto a notable Skill in *Languages;* the *Dutch* Tongue was become almost as Vernacular to him as the *English;* the *French* Tongue he could also manage; the *Latin* and the *Greek* he had Mastered; but the *Hebrew* he most of all studied, *because,* he said, *he would see with his own Eyes the Ancient Oracles of God in their Native Beauty.* He was also well skill'd in *History,* in *Antiquity,* and in *Philosophy;* and for *Theology* he became so versed in it, that he was an *Irrefragable Disputant* against the *Errors,* especially those of *Anabaptism,* which with Trouble he saw rising in his Colony; wherefore he wrote some Significant things for the Confutation of those Errors. But the *Crown* of all was his Holy, Prayerful, Watchful and Fruitful *Walk with God,* wherein he was very Exemplary.

§ 10. At length he fell into an Indisposition of Body, which rendred him unhealthy for a whole *Winter;* and as the *Spring* advanced, his Health yet more declined; yet he felt himself not what he counted *Sick,* till one *Day;* in the *Night* after which, the God of Heaven so fill'd his Mind with *Ineffable Consolations,* that he seemed little short of *Paul,* rapt up unto the *Unutterable* Entertainments of *Paradise.* The next Morning he told his Friends, *That the good Spirit of God had given him a Pledge of his Happiness in another World, and the First-fruits of his Eternal Glory:* And on the Day following he died, *May* 9. 1657. in the 69th Year of his Age. Lamented by all the Colonies of *New-England,* as a Common Blessing and Father to them all.

O mihi si Similis Contingat Clausula Vitæ![5a]

Plato's brief Description of a *Governour,* is all that I will now leave as his Character, in an

---

[5a] "Oh, may a similar ending of life come to me."—*Murdock.*

EPITAPH.

Νομεὺς Τροφός ἀγέλης ἀνθρωπίνης.[6]

MEN are but FLOCKS: BRADFORD beheld their Need,
And long did them at once both Rule *and* Feed.

---

[6] "Shepherd and feeder of the human herd."—*Murdock*.

BOOK II, CHAPTER IV. THE LIFE OF
JOHN WINTHROP

Quicunq; Venti erunt, Ars nostra certe non aberit. Cicer.[6a]

§ 1. Let *Greece* boast of her patient *Lycurgus*, the *Lawgiver*, by whom *Diligence*, *Temperance*, *Fortitude* and *Wit* were made the *Fashions* of a therefore Long-lasting and Renowned Commonwealth: Let *Rome* tell of her Devout *Numa*, the *Lawgiver*, by whom the most Famous Commonwealth saw *Peace* Triumphing over extinguished *War*, and cruel *Plunders*, and *Murders* giving place to the more mollifying Exercises of his *Religion*. Our *New-England* shall tell and boast of her WINTHROP, a *Lawgiver*, as patient as *Lycurgus*, but not admitting any of *his* Criminal Disorders; as Devout as *Numa*, but not liable to any of *his* Heathenish Madnesses; a *Governour* in whom the Excellencies of *Christianity* made a most improving Addition unto the *Virtues*, wherein even without *those* he would have made a *Parallel* for the Great Men of *Greece*, or of *Rome*, which the Pen of a *Plutarch* has Eternized.

§ 2. A stock of *Heroes* by right should afford nothing but what is *Heroical;* and nothing but an extream Degeneracy would make any thing less to be expected from a Stock of *Winthrops*. Mr. *Adam Winthrop*, the Son of a Worthy Gentleman wearing the same Name, was himself a Worthy, a Discreet, and a Learned Gentleman, particularly Eminent for *Skill* in the *Law*, nor without Remark for *Love* to the *Gospel*, under the Reign of King *Henry* VIII. And Brother to a Memorable *Favourer* of the *Reformed Religion* in the Days of Queen *Mary*, into whose Hands the Famous Martyr *Philpot* committed his *Papers*, which afterwards made no Inconsiderable part of our *Martyr-Books*. This Mr. *Adam Winthrop* had a Son of the same Name also, and of the same Endowments and Imployments with his Father; and this Third *Adam Winthrop* was the Father of that Renowned *John Winthrop*, who was the Father of *New-England*, and the Founder of a Colony, which upon many Accounts, like *him* that Founded

---

[6a] "Whatever winds shall blow, our art surely shall not die."—*Murdock*.

it, may challenge the *First Place* among the *English* Glories of *America*. Our JOHN WINTHROP thus Born at the Mansion-House of his Ancestors, at *Groton* in *Suffolk*, on *June* 12. 1587. enjoyed afterwards an agreeable Education. But though he would rather have Devoted himself unto the Study of Mr. *John Calvin*, than of Sir *Edward Cook*; nevertheless, the Accomplishments of a *Lawyer*, were those wherewith Heaven made his chief Opportunities to be Serviceable.

§ 3. Being made, at the unusually early Age of *Eighteen*, a *Justice of Peace*, his Virtues began to fall under a more general Observation; and he not only so *Bound himself to the Behaviour* of a *Christian*, as to become Exemplary for a Conformity to the *Laws* of *Christianity* in his own Conversation, but also discovered a more than ordinary Measure of those Qualities, which adorn an *Officer of Humane Society*. His *Justice* was Impartial, and used the *Ballance* to weigh not the *Cash*, but the *Case* of those who were before him: *Prosopolatria*, he reckoned as bad as *Idololatria*:[7] His *Wisdom* did exquisitely Temper things according to the *Art of Governing*, which is a Business of more Contrivance than the *Seven Arts* of the *Schools: Oyer* still went before *Terminer* in all his Administrations:[8] His *Courage* made him *Dare to do right*, and fitted him to stand among the *Lions*, that have sometimes been the *Supporters* of the Throne: All which Virtues he rendred the more Illustrious, by *Emblazoning* them with the Constant *Liberality* and *Hospitality* of a *Gentleman*. This made him the *Terror* of the Wicked, and the *Delight* of the Sober, the *Envy* of the many, but the *Hope* of those who had any *Hopeful Design* in Hand for the Common Good of the Nation, and the Interests of Religion.

§ 4. Accordingly when the *Noble Design* of carrying a Colony of *Chosen People* into an *American* Wilderness, was by *some* Eminent Persons undertaken, *This* Eminent Person was, by the Consent of all, *Chosen* for the *Moses*, who must be the Leader of so great an Undertaking: And indeed nothing but a *Mosaic Spirit*

---

[7] "Worship of persons" as bad as "worship of idols."—*Murdock*.

[8] "Hearing" before "judging."—*Murdock*.

could have carried him through the *Temptations,* to which either
his *Farewel* to his *own Land,* or his *Travel* in a *Strange Land,*
must needs expose a Gentleman of his *Education.* Wherefore
having Sold a fair Estate of Six or Seven Hundred a Year, he
Transported himself with the Effects of it into *New-England* in
the Year 1630. where he spent it upon the Service of a famous
Plantation founded and formed for the Seat of the most *Reformed
Christianity:* And continued there, conflicting with *Temptations*
of all sorts, as many Years as the *Nodes* of the *Moon* take to dispatch a Revolution.[9] Those Persons were never concerned in a
New-Plantation, who know not that the unavoidable Difficulties
of such a thing, will call for all the *Prudence* and *Patience* of a
Mortal Man to Encounter therewithal; and they must be very insensible of the Influence, which the *Just Wrath* of Heaven has
permitted the *Devils* to have upon *this World,* if they do not think
that the Difficulties of a *New-Plantation,* devoted unto the *Evangelical Worship* of our Lord Jesus Christ, must be yet more than
Ordinary. How *Prudently,* how *Patiently,* and with how much
Resignation to our Lord Jesus Christ, our brave *Winthrop* waded
through these *Difficulties,* let Posterity Consider with Admiration. And know, that as the *Picture* of this their *Governour,* was,
after his *Death,* hung up with Honour in the *State-House* of his
Country, so the *Wisdom, Courage,* and Holy *Zeal* of his *Life,*
were an Example well-worthy to be Copied by all that shall succeed in *Government.*

§ 5. Were he now to be consider'd only as a *Christian,* we
might therein propose him as greatly Imitable. He was a very
Religious Man; and as he strictly kept his *Heart,* so he kept his
House, under the Laws of *Piety; there* he was every Day constant
in Holy Duties, both Morning and Evening, and on the *Lord's
Days,* and *Lectures;* though he *wrote* not after the Preacher, yet
such was his *Attention,* and such his *Retention* in *Hearing,* that
he repeated unto his *Family* the *Sermons* which he had heard in
the Congregation. But it is chiefly as a *Governour* that he is now

---

[9] The time required for a revolution of the nodes of the moon is 18.6 years.—
Murdock.

to be consider'd. Being the *Governour* over the considerablest Part of *New-England,* he maintain'd the Figure and Honour of his Place with the Spirit of a true *Gentleman;* but yet with such obliging *Condescention* to the Circumstances of the Colony, that when a certain troublesome and malicious Calumniator, well known in those Times, printed his Libellous *Nick-Names* upon the chief Persons here, the worst *Nich-Name* [*sic*] he could find for the Governour, was *John Temper-well;* and when the Calumnies of that ill Man caused the Arch-Bishop to Summon one Mr. *Cleaves* before the King, in hopes to get some Accusation from him against the Country, Mr. *Cleaves* gave such an Account of the Governour's laudable Carriage in all Respects, and the serious Devotion wherewith Prayers were both publickly and privately made for His Majesty, that the King expressed himself most highly *Pleased* therewithal, only *Sorry* that so Worthy a Person should be no better Accommodated than with the Hardships of *America.* He was, indeed, a *Governour,* who had most exactly studied that Book, which pretending to Teach *Politicks,* did only contain *Three Leaves,* and but *One Word* in each of those Leaves, which Word was, MODERATION. Hence, though he were a Zealous Enemy to all *Vice,* yet his *Practice* was according to his *Judgment* thus expressed; *In the Infancy of Plantations, Justice should be administred with more Lenity than in a settled State; because People are more apt then to Transgress; partly out of Ignorance of new Laws and Orders, partly out of Oppression of Business, and other Straits.* [*LENTO GRADU*[10]] *was the old Rule; and if the Strings of a new Instrument be wound up unto their heighth, they will quickly crack.* But when some Leading and Learned Men took Offence at his Conduct in this Matter, and upon a *Conference* gave it in as their Opinion, *That a stricter Discipline was to be used in the beginning of a Plantation, than after its being with more Age established and confirmed,* the Governour being readier to see *his own* Errors than *other Mens,* professed his Purpose to endeavour their Satisfaction with less of

---

[10] "By slow degrees."—*Murdock.*

Lenity in his Administrations. At that *Conference* there were drawn up several other *Articles* to be observed between the Governour and the rest of the Magistrates, which were of this Import: *That* the *Magistrates,* as far as might be, should aforehand ripen their *Consultations,* to produce that *Unanimity* in their *Publick Votes,* which might make them liker to the *Voice of God; that* if *Differences* fell out among them in their Publick Meetings, they should speak only to the *Case,* without any Reflection, with all due *Modesty,* and but by way of *Question;* or Desire the deferring of the *Cause* to further time; and after *Sentence* to intimate privately no *Dislike; that* they should be more *Familiar,* Friendly and Open unto each other, and more frequent in their *Visitations,* and not any way expose each other's *Infirmities,* but seek the *Honour* of each other, and all the Court; *that* One Magistrate shall not *cross* the Proceedings of another, without first advising with him; and *that* they should in all their Appearances abroad, be so circumstanced as to prevent all Contempt of Authority; and *that* they should Support and Strengthen all *Under Officers.* All of which *Articles* were observed by no Man more than by the *Governour* himself.

§ 6. But whilst he thus did as our *New-English Nehemiah,* the part of a *Ruler* in Managing the Public Affairs of our *American Jerusalem,* when there were *Tobijahs* and *Sanballats* enough to vex him, and give him the Experiment of *Luther's* Observation, *Omnis qui regit, est tanquam signum, in quod omnia Jacula, Satan & Mundus dirigunt;*[11] he made himself still an exacter *Parallel* unto that Governour of *Israel,* by doing the part of a *Neighbour* among the distressed People of the *New-Plantation.* To teach them the *Frugality* necessary for those times, he abridged himself of a Thousand comfortable things, which he had allow'd himself elsewhere: His *Habit* was not that *soft Raiment,* which would have been disagreeable to a *Wilderness;* his *Table* was not covered with the *Superfluities* that would have invited unto *Sensualities: Water* was commonly his *own Drink,* though he gave

---

[11] "Everyone who rules is like a target against which Satan and the World aim all their darts."—*Murdock.*

Wine to *others*. But at the same time his *Liberality* unto the Needy was even beyond measure Generous; and therein he was continually causing *The Blessing of him that was ready to Perish to come upon him, and the Heart of the Widow and the Orphan to sing for Joy:* But none more than those of Deceas'd *Ministers,* whom he always treated with a very singular Compassion; among the Instances whereof we still enjoy with us the Worthy and now Aged Son of that Reverend *Higginson,* whose Death left his Family in a wide World soon after his arrival here, publickly acknowledging the Charitable *Winthrop* for his *Foster-Father.* It was oftentimes no small Trial unto his *Faith,* to think, *How a Table for the People should be furnished when they first came into the Wilderness!* And for very many of the People, his *own good Works* were needful, and accordingly employed for the answering of his *Faith.* Indeed, for a while the Governour was the *Joseph,* unto whom the whole Body of the People repaired when their *Corn* failed them: And he continued Relieving of them with his *open-handed Bounties,* as long as he had any Stock to do it with; and a lively *Faith* to *see* the return of the *Bread after many Days,* and not *Starve* in the Days that were to pass till that *return* should be *seen,* carried him chearfully through those Expences. Once it was observable, that on *Feb.* 5. 1630. when he was distributing the last Handful of *the Meal in the Barrel* unto a Poor Man distressed by the Wolf *at the Door,* at that Instant they spied a Ship arrived at the Harbour's Mouth Laden with *Provisions* for them all. Yea, the Governour sometimes made his own *private Purse* to be the *Publick;* not by *sucking* into it, but by *squeezing* out of it; for when the *Publick Treasure* had nothing in it, he did himself defray the Charges of the *Publick.* And having learned that Lesson of our Lord, *That it is better to Give, than to Receive,* he did, at the General Court when he was a Third time chosen Governour, make a Speech unto this purpose, *That he had received Gratuties from divers Towns, which he accepted with much Comfort and Content; and he had likewise received Civilities from particular Persons, which he could not refuse without Incivility in himself: Nevertheless, he took them with a trembling*

Heart, in regard of God's Word, and the Conscience of his own Infirmities; and therefore he desired them that they would not hereafter take it Ill if he refused such Presents for the time to come. 'Twas his Custom also to send some of his Family upon Errands, unto the Houses of the Poor about their *Mealtime,* on purpose to *spy* whether they *wanted;* and if it were found that they *wanted,* he would make *that* the Opportunity of sending Supplies unto them. And there was one Passage of his *Charity* that was perhaps a little *unusual:* In an hard and long Winter, when *Wood* was very scarce at *Boston,* a Man gave him a private *Information,* that a needy Person in the Neighbourhood stole *Wood* sometimes from *his* Pile; whereupon the Governour in a seeming Anger did reply, *Does he so? I'll take a Course with him; go, call that Man to me, I'll warrant you I'll cure him of Stealing!* When the Man came, the Governour considering that if he had *Stoln,* it was more out of *Necessity* than *Disposition,* said unto him, *Friend, It is a severe Winter, and I doubt you are but meanly provided for Wood; wherefore I would have you supply your self at my Wood-Pile till this cold Season be over.* And he then Merrily asked his Friends, *Whether he had not effectually cured this Man of Stealing his Wood?*

§ 7. One would have imagined that so *good* a Man could have had no *Enemies;* if we had not had a daily and woful Experience to Convince us, that *Goodness* it self will *make* Enemies. It is a wonderful Speech of *Plato,* (in one of his Books, *De Republica*) *For the trial of true Vertue, 'tis necessary that a good Man* μηδὲν ἀδικῶν, δόξαν ἔχει την μεγίστην ἀδικιας. *Tho' he do no unjust thing, should suffer the Infamy of the greatest Injustice.* The Governour had by his unspotted *Integrity,* procured himself a great Repntation [*sic*] among the *People;* and then the Crime of *Popularity* was laid unto his Charge by such, who were willing to deliver him from the Danger of having *all Men speak well of him.* Yea, there were Persons eminent both for Figure and for Number, unto whom it was almost *Essential* to *dislike* every thing that came from *him;* and yet *he* always maintained an Amicable Correspondence with them; as believing that they acted according to their Judgment and Conscience, or that their Eyes were held by some *Temptation* in the worst of all their Oppositions. Indeed, his *right Works* were so many, that they exposed him unto the *Envy* of his Neighbours; and of such *Power* was that *Envy,* that sometimes he could not *stand before it;* but it was by *not standing* that he most effectually *withstood* it all. Great Attempts were sometimes made among the *Freemen,* to get him left out from his Place in the *Government* upon little Pretences, lest by the too *frequent Choice* of One Man, the *Government* should cease to be by *Choice;* and with a particular aim at *him,* Sermons were Preached at the Anniversary Court of *Election,* to disswade the *Freemen* from chusing *One Man* Twice together. This was the Reward of his *extraordinary Serviceableness!* But when these Attempts *did* succeed, as they sometimes *did,* his Profound *Humility* appeared in that *Equality of Mind,* wherewith he applied himself cheerfully to serve the Country in whatever Station their *Votes* had allotted for him. And one Year when the *Votes* came to be Numbered, there were found Six less for Mr. *Winthrop,* than for another Gentleman who then stood in Competition: But several other Persons regularly Tendring their *Votes* before the *Election* was published, were, upon a very frivolous Objection, refused by some of the Magistrates, that were afraid lest the *Election* should at last fall upon Mr. *Winthrop:* Which though it was well perceived, yet such was the *Self-denial,* of this *Patriot,* that he would not permit any Notice to be taken of the Injury. But these *Trials* were nothing in Comparison of those harsher and harder *Treats,* which he sometimes had from the *Frowardness* of not a few in the Days of their *Paroxisms;* and from the *Faction* of some against him, not much unlike that of the *Piazzi* in *Florence* against the Family of the *Medices:* All of which he at last Conquered by Conforming to the Famous *Judges* Motto, *Prudens qui Patiens.*[12] The Oracles of God have said, *Envy is rottenness to the Bones;* and *Gulielmus Parisiensis,*[13] applies it unto Rulers, who are as it were the *Bones* of the So-

---

[12] "He is prudent who is patient."—*Murdock.*

[13] William, who became Bishop at Paris, in 1228.—*Murdock.*

cieties which they belong unto: *Envy*, says he, *is often found among them, and it is rottenness unto them*. Our *Winthrop* Encountred this *Envy* from others, but Conquered it, by being free from it himself.

§ 8. Were it not for the sake of introducing the Exemplary Skill of this Wise Man, *at giving soft Answers*, one would not chuse to Relate those Instances of *Wrath*, which he had sometimes to Encounter with; but he was for his *Gentleness*, his *Forbearance*, and his *Longanimity*, a Pattern so worthy to be Written *after*, that something must here be Written *of* it. He seemed indeed never to speak any other Language than that of *Theodosius*, *If any Man speak evil of the Governour, if it be thro' Lightness, 'tis to be contemned; if it be thro' Madness, 'tis to be pitied; if it be thro' Injury, 'tis to be remitted*. Behold, Reader, the *Meekness of Wisdom* notably exemplified! There was a time when he received a very sharp Letter from a Gentleman, who was a Member of the Court, but he delivered back the Letter unto the Messengers that brought it with such a Christian Speech as this, *I am not willing to keep such a matter of Provocation by me!* Afterwards the same Gentleman was compelled by the scarcity of Provisions to send unto him that he would Sell him some of his Cattel; whereupon the Governour prayed him to accept what he had sent for as a *Token* of his Good Will; but the Gentleman returned him this Answer, *Sir, your overcoming of your self hath overcome me;* and afterwards gave Demonstration of it. The *French* have a saying, That *Un Honeste Homme, est un Homme mesle!* A *good* Man is a *mixt Man;* and there hardly ever was a more sensible *Mixture* of those Two things, *Resolution* and *Condescention*, than in this good Man. There was a time when the Court of *Election*, being for fear of Tumult, held at *Cambridge*, May 17. 1637. The Sectarian part of the Country, who had the Year before gotten a *Governour* more unto their Mind, had a Project now to have confounded the *Election*, by demanding that the *Court* would consider a *Petition* then tendered before their Proceeding thereunto. Mr. *Winthrop* saw that this was only a Trick to throw all into Confusion, by putting off the *Choice* of the *Governour* and

Assistents until the *Day* should be over; and therefore he did, with a strenuous *Resolution,* procure a disappointment unto that mischievous and ruinous Contrivance. Nevertheless, Mr. *Winthrop* himself being by the Voice of the Freemen in this Exigence chosen the *Governour,* and all of the other Party left out, that ill-affected Party discovered the *Dirt* and *Mire,* which remained with them, after the *Storm* was over; particularly the *Serjeants,* whose Office 'twas to attend the *Governour,* laid down their *Halberts;* but such was the *Condescention* of this Governour, as to take no present Notice of this Anger and Contempt, but only Order some of his own Servants to take the *Halberts:* And when the Country manifested their deep Resentments of the Affront thus offered him, *he* prayed them to *overlook* it. But it was not long before a Compensation was made for these things by the *doubled Respects* which were from all Parts paid unto him. Again, there was a time when the Suppression of an *Antinomian* and *Familistical* Faction, which extreamly threatned the Ruin of the Country, was generally thought much owing unto this Renowned Man;[14] and therefore when the Friends of that Faction could not wreak their Displeasure on him with any *Politick* Vexations, they set themselves to do it by *Ecclesiastical* ones. Accordingly when a Sentence of *Banishment* was passed on the Ringleaders of those Disturbances, who

> —*Maria & Terras, Cælumq; profundum,*
> *Quippe ferant, Rapidi, secum, vertantq; per Auras;*[15]

many at the Church of *Boston,* who were then that way too much inclined, most earnestly solicited the Elders of that Church, whereof the Governour was a *Member,* to call him forth as an *Offender* for passing of that Sentence. The *Elders* were unwilling to do any such thing; but the Governour understanding the *Fer-*

---

[14] This refers to the "persecution" of Anne Hutchinson for her nonconformity to Puritan ideas . . . —*Murdock.*

[15] "Swift bear with them sea and earth and the lofty sky, and drive them through the air."—*Murdock.*

ment among the *people,* took that occasion to make a Speech in
the Congregation to this Effect. *'Brethren,* Understanding that
'some of you have desired that I should Answer for an *Offence*
'lately taken among you; had I been called upon so to do, I would,
'First, Have advised with the Ministers of the Country, whether
'the *Church* had Power to call in Question the *Civil Court;*
'and I would, *Secondly,* Have advised with the rest of the *Court,*
'whether I might discover their Counsels unto the *Church.* But
'though I know that the Reverend *Elders* of this Church, and
'some others, do very well apprehend that the *Church* cannot
'enquire into the Proceedings of the *Court;* yet for the Satisfac-
'tion of the weaker who do not apprehend it, I will declare my
'Mind concerning it. If the *Church* have any such Power, they
'have it from the Lord Jesus Christ; but the Lord Jesus Christ
'hath disclaimed it, not only by *Practice,* but also by *Precept,*
'which we have in his Gospel, *Mat.* 20. 25, 26. It is true indeed,
'that *Magistrates,* as they are *Church-Members,* are accountable
'unto the *Church* for their Failings; but that is when they are out
'of their Calling. When *Uzziah* would go offer Incense in the
'Temple, the Officers of the *Church* called him to an account, and
'withstood him; but when *Asa* put the Prophet in Prison, the
'Officers of the *Church* did not call *him* to an account for *that.* If
'the *Magistrate* shall in a *private way* wrong any Man, the *Church*
'may call him to an Account for it; but if he be in Pursuance of a
'Course of *Justice,* though the thing that he does be *unjust,* yet
'he is not accountable for it before the *Church.* As for my self I
'did nothing in the Causes of any of the *Brethren,* but by the
'Advice of the *Elders* of the *Church.* Moreover, in the *Oath* which
'I have taken there is this Clause, *In all Causes wherein you are*
'to give your Vote, you shall do as in your Judgment and Con-
'science you shall see to be Just, and for the publick Good. And
'I am satisfied, it is most for the Glory of God, and the *publick*
'Good, that there has been such a *Sentence* passed; yea, those
'Brethren are so divided from the *rest* of the Country in their
'Opinions and Practices, that it cannot stand with the *publick*
'Peace for them to continue with us; *Abraham* saw that *Hagar*

'and *Ishmael* must be sent away. By such a Speech he marvellously convinced, satisfied and mollified the *uneasie Brethren* of the Church; *Sic cunctus Pelagi cecidit Fragor*—.[16] And after a little patient waiting, the *differences* all so wore away, that the Church, meerly as a Token of Respect unto the Governour, when he had newly met with some *Losses* in his Estate, sent him a Present of several *Hundreds* of Pounds. Once more there was a time, when some active Spirits among the *Deputies* of the Colony, by their endeavours not only to make themselves a *Court of Judicature,* but also to take away the *Negative* by which the *Magistrates* might check their *Votes,* had like by over-driving to have run the whole Government into something too *Democratical.* And if there were a Town in *Spain* undermined by *Coneys,* another Town in *Thrace* destroyed by *Moles,* a Third in *Greece* ranversed by *Frogs,* a Fourth in *Germany* subverted by *Rats;* I must on this Occasion add, that there was a Country in *America* like to be confounded by a *Swine.* A certain *stray Sow* being found, was claimed by Two several Persons with a Claim so equally maintained on both sides, that after Six or Seven Years *Hunting* the Business, from one Court unto another, it was brought at last into the *General Court,* where the final Determination was, *that it was impossible to proceed unto any Judgment in the Case.* However in the debate of this Matter, the *Negative* of the *Upper-House* upon the *Lower* in that Court was brought upon the Stage; and agitated with so hot a Zeal, that a *little more and all had been in the Fire.* In these Agitations the Governour was informed that an offence had been taken by some eminent Persons, at certain Passages in a Discourse by him written thereabouts; whereupon with his usual *Condescendency,* when he next came into the General Court, he made a Speech of this Import. 'I understand, that some 'have *taken* Offence at something that I have lately written; 'which *Offence* I desire to remove now, and begin this Year in a 'reconciled State with you all. As for the *Matter* of my Writing, I 'had the Concurrence of my *Brethren;* it is a Point of *Judgment*

---

[16] "So all the din of the sea subsided."—*Murdock.*

'which is not at my own disposing. I have examined it over and
'over again, by such *Light* as God has given me, from the Rules
'of *Religion, Reason,* and *Custom;* and I see no cause to Retract
'any thing of it: Wherefore I must enjoy my *Liberty* in *that,* as
'*you* do your selves. But for the *Manner, this,* and all that was
'blame-worthy in it, was wholly *my own;* and whatsoever I might
'alledge for my own Justification therein before *Men,* I wave it,
'as now setting my self before another *Judgment-Seat.* However,
'what I wrote was upon *great Provocation,* and to vindicate my
'self and others from great Aspersion; yet that was no sufficient
'Warrant for me to allow any *Distemper of Spirit* in my self; and
'I doubt I have been too prodigal of my *Brethren's Reputation;* I
'might have maintained my Cause without casting any Blemish
'upon others, when I made that my Conclusion, *And now, let*
'*Religion and sound Reason give Judgment in the Case;* it look'd
'as if I arrogated too much unto *my self,* and too little to *others.*
'And when I made that Profession, *That I would maintain what*
'*I wrote before all the World,* though such Words might modestly
'be spoken, yet I perceive an unbeseeming *Pride* of my own Heart
'breathing in them. For these Failings I ask Pardon both of God
'and Man.

> *Sic ait, & dicto citius Tumida Æquora placat,*
> *Collectasq; fugat Nubes, Solemq; reducit.*[17]

This *acknowledging Disposition* in the Governour, made them
all *acknowledge,* that he was truly *a Man of an excellent Spirit.*
In fine, the *Victories* of an *Alexander,* an *Hannibal,* or a *Cæsar*
over *other Men,* were not so Glorious, as the *Victories* of this
great Man over *himself,* which also at last prov'd *Victories* over
other Men.

§ 9. But the stormiest of all the *Trials* that ever befel this
Gentleman, was in the Year 1645. when he was in *Title* no more
than *Deputy-Governour* of the Colony. If the famous *Cato* were

---

[17] "So he spoke, and thus quickly calmed the swelling sea, put to rout the
gathered clouds, and brought back the sun."—*Murdock.*

Forty-four times call'd into Judgment, but as often acquitted; let it not be wondred, and if our Famous *Winthrop* were one time so. There hapning certain Seditious and Mutinous Practices in the Town of *Hingham,* the *Deputy-Governour* as legally as prudently interposed his *Authority* for the checking of them: Whereupon there followed such an *Enchantment* upon the minds of the *Deputies* in the General Court, that upon a scandalous Petition of the Delinquents unto *them,* wherein a pretended Invasion made upon the *Liberties* of the *People* was complained of the *Deputy-Governour,* was most Irregularly call'd forth unto an Ignominous *Hearing* before them in a vast Assembly; whereto with a *Sagacious Humility* he *consented,* although he shew'd them how he might have *Refused* it. The result of that *Hearing* was, That notwithstanding the touchy *Jealousie* of the *People* about their *Liberties* lay at the bottom of all this Prosecution, yet Mr. *Winthrop* was publickly Acquitted, and the Offenders were severally Fined and Censured. But Mr. *Winthrop* then resuming the Place of *Deputy-Governour* on the Bench, saw cause to speak unto the *Root of the Matter* after this manner. 'I shall not now 'speak any thing about the past *Proceedings* of this Court, or the '*Persons* therein concerned. Only I bless God that I see an Issue 'of this troublesome Affair. I am well satisfied that I was publickly '*Accused,* and that I am now publickly *Acquitted.* But though I 'am justified before *Men,* yet it may be the *Lord* hath seen so 'much amiss in my Administrations, as calls me to be *humbled;* 'and indeed for me to have been thus charged by *Men,* is it self 'a Matter of *Humiliation,* whereof I desire to make a right use 'before the *Lord.* If *Miriam's* Father spit in her Face, she is to be '*Ashamed.* But give me leave before you go, to say something that 'may rectifie the *Opinions* of many *People,* from whence the *Dis-* '*tempers* have risen that have lately prevailed upon the *Body* of '*this* People. The Questions that have troubled the Country have 'been about the *Authority of the Magistracy,* and the *Liberty of* '*the People.* It is *You* who have called *us* unto this Office; but 'being thus *called,* we have our *Authority* from *God;* it is the '*Ordinance* of *God,* and it hath the *Image* of *God* stamped upon

'it; and the contempt of it has been vindicated by *God* with ter-
'rible Examples of his Vengeance. I intreat you to consider, That
'when you chuse *Magistrates,* you take them from among your
'selves, *Men subject unto like Passions with your selves.* If you
'see *our* Infirmities, reflect on *your own,* and you will not be so
'severe Censurers of *Ours.* We count him a *good Servant* who
'*breaks not his Covenant:* The *Covenant* between *Us* and *You,*
'is the *Oath* you have taken of *us,* which is to this Purpose, *That
'we shall govern you, and judge your Causes, according to God's
'Laws, and our own, according to our best Skill.* As for our *Skill,*
'you must run the hazard of it; and if there be an Error, not in the
'*Will,* but only in the *Skill,* it becomes *you* to bear it. Nor would
'I have you to mistake in the Point of your own *Liberty.* There
'is a *Liberty* of corrupt Nature, which is affected both by *Men*
'and *Beasts,* to do what they list; and this *Liberty* is inconsistent
'with *Authority,* impatient of all Restraint; by this *Liberty, Sumus*
'*Omnes Deteriores;*[18] 'Tis the Grand Enemy of *Truth* and *Peace,*
'and all the *Ordinances* of God are bent against it. But there is a
'Civil, a Moral, a Federal *Liberty,* which is the proper End and
'Object of *Authority;* it is a *Liberty* for that only which is *just*
'and *good;* for this *Liberty* you are to stand with the hazard of
'your very *Lives;* and whatsoever Crosses it, is not *Authority,* but
'a *Distemper* thereof. This *Liberty* is maintained in a way of
'*Subjection* to *Authority;* and the *Authority* set over you, will in
'all Administrations for your good be quietly submitted unto, by
'all but such as have a Disposition to *shake off the Yoke,* and lose
'their true *Liberty,* by their murmuring at the Honour and Power
'of *Authority.*'

The *Spell* that was upon the Eyes of the People being thus dissolved, their *distorted* and *enraged* notions of things all vanished;
and the People would not afterwards entrust the Helm of the
Weather-beaten Bark in any other Hands, but Mr. *Winthrop's,*
until he Died.

§ 10. Indeed such was the *Mixture* of *distant Qualities* in him,

---

[18] "We are all the worse."—*Murdock.*

as to make a most admirable *Temper;* and his having a certain *Greatness of Soul,* which rendered him Grave, Generous, Courageous, Resolved, Well-applied, and every way a *Gentleman* in his Deameanour, did not hinder him from taking sometimes the old *Romans* way to avoid Confusions, namely, *Cedendo;*[19] or from discouraging some things which are agreeable enough to most that wear the Name of *Gentlemen.* Hereof I will give no Instances, but only *oppose* two Passages of his Life.

In the Year 1632. the Governour, with his Pastor Mr. *Wilson,* and some other Gentlemen, to settle a good understanding between the Two Colonies, travelled as far as *Plymouth,* more than Forty Miles, through an Howling Wilderness, no better accommodated in those early Days, than the *Princes* that in *Solomon's* time saw *Servants on Horseback,* or than *Genus* and *Species* in the old Epigram, *going on Foot.* The difficulty of the *Walk,* was abundantly compensated by the Honourable, *first* Reception, and *then* Dismission, which they found from the Rulers of *Plymouth;* and by the good Correspondence thus established between the New Colonies, who were like the floating Bottels wearing this Motto, *Si Collidimur, Frangimur.*[20] But there were at this time in *Plymouth* two Ministers, leavened so far with the Humours of the *Rigid Separation,* that they insisted vehemently upon the Unlawfulness of calling any *unregenerate* Man by the Name of *Good-man such an One,* until by their indiscreet urging of this Whimsey, the place began to be disquieted. The wiser People being troubled at these Trifles, they took the opportunity of Governour *Winthrop's* being *there,* to have the thing publickly propounded in the Congregation; who in answer thereunto, distinguished between a *Theological* and a *Moral Goodness;* adding, that when *Juries* were first used in *England,* it was usual for the *Crier,* after the Names of Persons fit for that Service were called over, to bid them all, *Attend, Good Men, and True;* whence it grew to be a *Civil Custom* in the *English Nation,* for Neighbours living by one another, to call one another *Good-man such*

---

[19] "By yielding."—*Murdock.*
[20] "If we collide, we break."—*Murdock.*

an One: And it was pity now to make a stir about a *Civil Custom,* so innocently introduced. And that Speech of Mr. *Winthrop's* put a lasting stop to the Little, Idle, Whimsical *Conceits,* then beginning to grow Obstreperous. Nevertheless there was one *Civil Custom* used *in* (and in few *but*) the *English Nation,* which this Gentleman did endeavour to abolish in *this Country;* and that was, *The usage of Drinking to one another.* For although by *Drinking to one another,* no more is meant than an act of *Courtesie,* when one going to *Drink,* does Invite another to do so too, for the same Ends with himself; nevertheless the Governour (not altogether unlike *to Cleomenes,* of whom 'tis reported by *Plutarch,* ἄηοντι οὐδεὶς ποτήριον προσέφερε, *Nolenti poculum nunquam præbuit,*[21]) considered the *Impertinency* and *Insignificancy* of this Usage, as to any of *those Ends* that are usually pretended for it; and that indeed it ordinarily served for *no Ends* at all, but only to provoke Persons unto *unseasonable,* and perhaps *unreasonable* Drinking, and at last produce that abominable *Health-Drinking,* which the *Fathers* of old so severely rebuked in the *Pagans,* and which the *Papists* themselves do Condemn, when their Casuists pronounce it, *Peccatum mortale, provocare ad Æquales Calices, & Nefas Respondere.*[22] Wherefore in his own most Hospitable House he left it off, not out of any silly or stingy *Fancy,* but meerly that by his *Example* a greater *Temperance,* with *Liberty* of *Drinking,* might be Recommended, and sundry *Inconveniences* in Drinking avoided; and his *Example* accordingly began to be much followed by the sober People in *this Country,* as it now also begins to be among Persons of the *Highest* Rank in the *English Nation* it self; until an *Order of Court* came to be made against that *Ceremony* in Drinking, and then the *old Wont* violently returned, with a *Nitimur in Vetitum.*[23]

§ 11. *Many were the Afflictions of this Righteous Man!* He lost

---

[21] "Never offered drink to one who was unwilling."—*Murdock.*

[22] "It is a mortal sin to challenge anyone to a drinking match, and wrong to accept such a challenge."—*Murdock.*

[23] "We strive for what is forbidden."—*Murdock.*

much of his Estate in a Ship, and in an *House,* quickly after his coming to *New-England,* besides the Prodigious Expence of it in the Difficulties of his first coming hither. Afterwards his assiduous Application unto the Publick *Affairs,* (wherein *Ipse se non habuit, postquam Respublica eum Gubernatorem habere capit*)[24] made him so much to neglect his own *private Interests,* that an *unjust Steward* ran him 2500 *l.* in Debt before he was aware; for the Payment whereof he was forced, many Years before his Decease, to sell the most of what he had left unto him in the Country. Albeit, by the observable Blessing of God upon the *Posterity* of this *Liberal Man,* his Children all of them came to fair Estates, and lived in good Fashion and Credit. Moreover, he successively Buried Three *Wives;* the First of which was the Daughter and Heiress of Mr. *Forth, of Much Stambridge* in *Essex,* by whom he had *Wisdom with an Inheritance;* and an excellent Son. The Second was the Daughter of Mr. *William Clopton,* of *London,* who Died with her Child, within a very little while. The Third was the Daughter of the truly Worshipful Sir *John Tyndal,* who made it her whole Care to please, First *God,* and then her *Husband;* and by whom he had Four Sons, which Survived and Honoured their Father. And unto all these, the Addition of the *Distempers,* ever now and then raised in the *Country,* procured unto him a very singular share of Trouble; yea, so hard was the Measure which he found even among Pious Men, in the Temptations of a *Wilderness,* that when the *Thunder* and *Lightning* had smitten a *Wind-mill,* whereof he was Owner, some had *such things in their Heads,* as publickly to Reproach this *Charitablest* of Men, as if the *Voice of the Almighty* had rebuked, I know not what *Oppression,* which they *judged* him Guilty of: Which things I would not have mentioned, but that the Instances may fortifie the Expectations of my *best Readers* for such Afflictions.

§ 12. He that had been for his Attainments, as they said of the blessed *Macarius,* a Παιδαριογερων *An old Man, while a young One,* and that had in his *young Days* met with many of those

---

[24] "He did not possess himself after the state began to possess him as governor." —*Murdock.*

Ill Days, whereof he could say, he had *little Pleasure in them;* now found *old Age* in its Infirmities advancing *Earlier* upon him, than it came upon his much longer lived Progenitors. While he was yet Seven Years off of that which we call *the grand Climacterical,*[25] he felt the Approaches of his *Dissolution;* and finding he could say,

> *Non Habitus, non ipse Color non Gressus Euntis,*
> *Non Species Eadem, quæ fuit ante, manet.*[26]

he then wrote this account of himself, *Age now comes upon me, and Infirmities therewithal, which makes me apprehend that the time of my departure out of this World is not far off. However our times are all in the Lord's Hand, so as we need not trouble our Thoughts how long or short they may be, but how we may be found Faithful when we are called for.* But at last when *that* Year came, he took a *Cold* which turned into a *Feaver,* whereof he lay *Sick* about a Month, and in that *Sickness,* as it hath been observed, that there was allowed unto the *Serpent* the *bruising of the Heel;* and accordingly at the *Heel* or the *Close* of our Lives the *old Serpent* will be *Nibbling* more than ever in our Lives before; and when the Devil sees that we shall shortly be, *where the wicked cease from troubling,* that *wicked One* will *trouble* us more than ever; so this eminent Saint now underwent sharp Conflicts with the *Tempter,* whose *Wrath* grew *Great,* as the *Time* to exert it grew *Short;* and he was Buffetted with the Disconsolate Thoughts of Black and Sore *Desertions,* wherein he could use that sad Representation of his own Condition.

> *Nuper Eram Judex; Jam Judicor; Ante Tribunat,*
> *Subsistens paveo, Judicor ipse modo.*[27]

---

[25] The sixty-third year of life.—*Murdock.*

[26] "There remains not the appearance, not even the color, nor the way of life, and not the same aspect, of that which was before."—*Murdock.*

[27] "Once I was a judge, now I am judged. I stand trembling before the tribunal, now I myself am judged."—*Murdock.*

But it was not long before those *Clouds* were Dispelled, and he enjoyed in his Holy Soul the *Great Consolations of God!* While he thus lay *Ripening* for Heaven, he did out of Obedience unto the *Ordinance* of our Lord, send for the *Elders of the Church* to *Pray* with him; yea, they and the whole Church *Fasted* as well as *Prayed* for him; and in that *Fast* the venerable *Cotton*[28] Preached on *Psal.* 35. 13, 14. *When they were Sick, I humbled my self with Fasting; I behaved my self as though he had been my Friend or Brother; I bowed down heavily, as one that Mourned for his Mother:* From whence I find him raising that Observation, *The Sickness of one that is to us as a Friend, a Brother, a Mother, is a just occasion of deep humbling our Souls with Fasting and Prayer;* and making this Application, 'Upon this Occasion we are 'now to attend this Duty for a *Governour,* who has been to us as 'a *Friend* in his *Counsel* for all things, and *Help* for our *Bodies* 'by *Physick,* for our *Estates* by *Law,* and of whom there was no 'fear of his becoming an *Enemy,* like the *Friends* of *David:* A '*Governour* who has been unto us as a *Brother;* not usurping '*Authority* over the Church; often speaking his *Advice,* and often 'contradicted, even by Young Men, and some of low degree; yet 'not replying, but offering Satisfaction also when any supposed 'Offences have arisen; a *Governour* who has been unto us as a '*Mother,* Parent-like distributing his *Goods* to Brethren and 'Neighbours at his first coming: and *gently* bearing our *Infirm-* '*ities* without taking notice of them.'

Such a *Governour* after he had been more than *Ten* several times by the People chosen their *Governour,* was *New-England* now to lose; who having, like *Jacob,* first left his *Council* and *Blessing* with his Children gathered about his Bed-sides; and, like *David, served his Generation by the Will of God,* he *gave up the Ghost* and *fell asleep* on March 26. 1649. Having, like the dying Emperour *Valentinian,* this above all his other *Victories* for his Triumphs, *His overcoming of himself.*

The Words of *Josephus* about *Nehemiah,* the Governour of

---

[28] Rev. John Cotton, grandfather of Cotton Mather.—*Murdock.*

Israel, we will now use upon this Governour of *New-England,* as his

EPITAPH.

Ἀνὴρ ἐγένετο χρηστὸς τὴν φύσιν, καὶ δίκαιος,
Καὶ περὶ τοὺς ὁμοεθνεῖς φιλοτιμότατος:
Μνημεῖον αἰώνιον αὐτω καταλιπὼν τὰ τῶν
Ἱεροσολύμων τείχη[29]

VIR FUIT INDOLE BONUS, AC JUSTUS:
ET POPULARIUM GLORIÆ AMANTISSIMUS:
QUIBUS ETERNUM RELIQUIT MONUMENTUM,
Novanglorum MOENIA.

from THE CHRISTIAN PHILOSOPHER (1721)

THE PREFACE

RELIGIO PHILOSOPHICA;[1]

OR, THE

Christian Philosopher:

BEING

A Commentary, of the more Modern and Certain PHILOSOPHY,[2] upon that Instruction,

JOB. xxxvi. 24.

Remember that thou magnify His Work which Men behold.

The Works of the Glorious GOD in the *Creation* of the World, are what I now propose to exhibit; in brief *Essays* to enumerate

---

[29] "He was a man by nature good and just, and most zealous for honor for his countrymen, leaving for them an eternal memorial—the walls of Jerusalem." The Latin paraphrase which follows substitutes New England for Jerusalem.—*Murdock.*

[1] "Philosophic (or Scientific) Religion."—*Murdock.*

[2] Philosophy in the sense of science in general.—*Murdock.*

some of them, that He may be glorified in them: And indeed my *Essays* may pretend unto no more than *some of them;* for, *Theophilus*[3] writing, *of the Creation,* to his Friend *Antolycus,* might very justly say, That if he should have a *Thousand Tongues,* and live a *Thousand Years,* yet he were not able to describe the admirable Order of the Creation, διὰ τὸ ὑπερβάλλον μεγεθὸς καὶ τὸν πλοῦτον σοφίας τοῦ Θεοῦ. *Such a Transcendent Greatness of God, and the Riches of his Wisdom appearing in it!*

Chrysostom, I remember, mentions a *Twofold Book* of GOD; the Book of the *Creatures,* and the Book of the *Scriptures:* GOD having taught first of all us διὰ πραγμάτων, by his *Works,* did it afterwards διὰ γραμμάτων, by his *Words.* We will now for a while read the *Former* of these *Books,* 'twill help us in reading the *Latter:* They will admirably assist one another. The Philosopher being asked, What his *Books* were; answered, *Totius Entis Naturalis Universitas.*[4] All Men are accommodated with that *Publick Library. Reader,* walk with me into it, and see what we shall find so legible there, *that he that runs may read it.* Behold, a Book, whereof we may agreeably enough use the words of honest *Ægardus; Lectu hic omnibus facilis, etsi nunquam legere didicerint, & communis est omnibus, omniumque oculis expositus.*[5]

THE
INTRODUCTION

The Essays now before us will demonstrate, that *Philosophy* is no *Enemy,* but a mighty and wondrous *Incentive* to *Religion;* and they will exhibit that PHILOSOPHICAL RELIGION, which will carry with it a most sensible *Character,* and victorious *Evidence* of a *reasonable Service. GLORY TO GOD IN THE HIGHEST,* and *GOOD-WILL TOWARDS MEN,* animated and exercised; and a Spirit of *Devotion* and of *Charity* inflamed, in such

---

[3] Theophilus of Antioch, died 190 A.D.—*Murdock.*

[4] "The natural university of all the existing universe."—*Murdock.*

[5] "Here is reading easy for everyone even though they have not learned to read, and it is open to all, and set out before everyone's eyes."—*Murdock.*

Methods as are offered in these *Essays,* cannot but be attended with more Benefits, than any *Pen* of ours can declare, or any *Mind* conceive.

In the *Dispositions* and *Resolutions* of PIETY thus enkindled, a *Man* most effectually *shews himself a* MAN, and with unutterable Satisfaction answers the grand END of his Being, which is, *To glorify GOD.* He discharges also the Office of a *Priest* for the *Creation,* under the Influences of an admirable *Saviour,* and therein asserts and assures his Title unto that *Priesthood,* which the Blessedness of the *future State* will very much consist in being advanced to. The whole *World* is indeed a *Temple* of GOD, *built* and *filled* by that Almighty *Architect;* and in this *Temple,* every such one, affecting himself with the Occasions for it, will *speak of His Glory.* He will also rise into that *Superior Way* of *Thinking* and of *Living,* which the *Wisest* of Men will chuse to take; which the more *Polite Part* of Mankind, and the *Honourable of the Earth,* will esteem it no Dishonour for them to be acquainted with. Upon that Passage occurring in the best of Books, *Ye Sons of the Mighty, ascribe unto the Lord Glory and Strength;* it is a Gloss and an Hint of *Munster,* which carries with it a Cogency: *Nihil est tam sublime, tamque magnificum, quod non teneatur laudare & magnificare Deum Creatorem suum.*[6] Behold, a *Religion,* which will be found *without Controversy;* a *Religion,* which will challenge all possible Regards from the *High,* as well as the *Low,* among the People; I will resume the Term, a PHILO-SOPHICAL RELIGION: And yet how *Evangelical!*

In prosecuting this *Intention,* and in introducing almost every *Article* of it, the Reader will continually find some *Author* or other *quoted.* This constant Method of *Quoting,* 'tis to be hoped, will not be censured, as proceeding from an *Ambition to intimate and boast a Learning,* which the *Messieurs du Port-Royal*[7] have rebuked; and that the Humour for which *Austin* reproached

---

[6] "Nothing is so sublime or magnificent as not to be bound to magnify and praise the Lord, its creator."—*Murdock.*

[7] Port-Royal, a famous community in France, including among its members some of the most learned men of the 17th century.—*Murdock.*

Julian, will not be found in it: *Quis hæc audiat, & non ipso nomi-
num strepitu terreatur, si est ineruditus, qualis est hominum
multitudo, & existimet te aliquem magnum qui hæc scire potue-
ris?* [8] Nor will there be discernible any Spice of the impertinent
Vanity, which *La Bruyere* hath so well satirized: 'Herillus will
'always *cite,* whether he speaks or writes. He makes the *Prince of
'Philosophers* to say, *That Wine inebriates;* and the *Roman
'Orator, That Water temperates it.* If he talks of *Morality,* it is not
'he, but the Divine *Plato,* who affirms, *That Virtue is amiable,
'and Vice odious.* The most common and trivial things, which he
'himself is able to think of, are ascribed by him to *Latin* and
'*Greek* Authors.' But in these *Quotations,* there has been proposed, first, a due *Gratitude* unto those, who have been my *In-
structors;* and indeed, *something within me* would have led me
to it, if *Pliny,* who is one of them, had not given me a Rule;
Ingenuum est profiteri per quos profeceris.[9] It appears also but
a piece of *Justice,* that the *Names* of those whom the Great GOD
has distinguished, by employing them to make those *Discoveries*
which are here collected, should live and shine in every such Collection. Among these, let it be known, that there are especially
Two, unto whom I have been more indebted, than unto many
others; the Industrious Mr. RAY, and the Inquisitive Mr. DER-
HAM; *Fratrum dulce par:*[10] upon whom, in divers Paragraphs of
this *Rhapsody,*[11] I have had very much of my Subsistence; (I
hope without doing the part of a *Fidentinus* upon them) and I
give thanks to Heaven for them.

'Tis true, some Scores of other *Philosophers* have been consulted on this Occasion; but an *Industry* so applied, has in it very
little to bespeak any *Praises* for him that has used it: He earnestly
renounces them, and sollicits, that not only *he,* but the *Greater
Men,* who have been his *Teachers,* may disappear before the

---

[8] "Who can hear this and not be frightened by the very sound of the names—
provided he is not learned, as most men are not—and who but will consider you
great because you know so much?"—*Murdock.*

[9] "It is noble to acknowledge by whom you have profited."—*Murdock.*

[10] "A sweet pair of brothers." . . . —*Murdock.*

[11] A collection, a literary work without definite form.—*Murdock.*

Glorious GOD, whom these *Essays* are all written to represent as *worthy to be praised,* and by whose *Grace we are what we are;* nor have we *any thing but what we have received* from Him.

A considerable Body of Men (if the *Jansenists*[12] may now be thought so) in *France,* have learnt of Monsieur *Pascal,* to denote themselves by the *French* Impersonal Particle *On;* and it was his opinion, that an honest Man should not be found of *naming himself,* or using the word I, and ME; that *Christian Piety* will annihilate our I, and ME, and *Human Civility* will suppress it, and conceal it.

Most certainly there can be very little Pretence to an I, or ME, for what is done in these *Essays.* 'Tis done, and entirely, *by the Help of God:* This is all that can be pretended to.

There is very little, that may be said, really to be performed by the Hand that is now writing; but only the *Devotionary Part* of these *Essays,* tho they are not altogether destitute of *American* Communications: And if the *Virtuoso's,* and all the *Genuine Philosophers* of our Age, have approved the Design of the devout RAY and DERHAM, and others, in their Treatises; it cannot be distasteful unto them, to see what was more *generally hinted at* by those Excellent Persons, here more *particularly carried on,* and the more *special Flights* of the true PHILOSOPHICAL RELIGION exemplified. Nor will they that value the Essays of the memorable Antients, *Theodoret,* and *Nazianzen,* and *Ambrose,* upon *the Works of the six Days,* count it a Fault, if among lesser Men in our Days, there be found those who say, *Let me run after them.* I remember, when we read, *Praise is comely for the Upright,* it is urged by *Kimchi,* that the Word which we render *comely,* signifies *desirable,* and *acceptable;* and the Sense of that Sentence is, that *Qui recti sunt, aliud nihil desiderant quam Laudem & Gloriam Dei.*[13] Sure I am, such *Essays* as these, to observe, and proclaim, and publish the *Praises* of the Glorious GOD, will be *desirable* and *acceptable* to all that have a *right Spirit* in them;

---

[12] A school of Roman Catholic theologians, whose views dominated Port-Royal. —*Murdock.*

[13] "The righteous desire nothing but the praise and glory of God."—*Murdock.*

the rest, who are *blinded,* are Fools, and unregardable: As little to be regarded as a *Monster* flourishing a *Broomstick! Vix illis optari quidquam pejus potest, quam ut fatuitate sua fruantur.*[14] For such *Centaurs* to be found in the Tents of professed *Christianity!—Good God, unto what Times hast thou reserved us!* If the *self-taught Philosopher* will not, yet *Abubeker,* a *Mahometan* Writer, by whom such an one was exhibited more than five hundred Years ago, will *rise up in the Judgment with this Generation, and condemn it.* Reader, even a *Mahometan* will shew thee one, without any *Teacher,* but *Reason* in a serious View of *Nature,* led on to the Acknowledgment of a Glorious GOD. Of a Man, supposed as but using his *Rational Faculties* in viewing the Works of GOD, even the *Mahometan* will tell thee; 'There ap-
'peared unto him those Fooststeps of Wisdom and Wonders in
'the *Works of Creation,* which affected his Mind with an exces-
'sive Admiration; and he became hereby assured, that all these
'things must proceed from such a *Voluntary Agent* as was *infi-*
'*nitely perfect,* yea, above all Perfection: such an one to whom
'the Weight of the least Atom was not unknown, whether in
'Heaven or Earth. Upon his viewing of the *Creatures,* whatever
'*Excellency* he found of any kind, he concluded, it must needs
'proceed from the Influence of that *Voluntary Agent,* so illustri-
'ously glorious, the *Fountain* of *Being,* and of *Working.* He
'knew therefore, that whatsoever Excellencies were by Nature in
'*Him,* were by so much the greater, the more perfect, and the
'more lasting; and that there was no proportion between those
'*Excellencies* which were in *Him,* and those which were found
'in the *Creatures.* He discerned also, by the virtue of that more
'Noble Part of his, whereby he knew the *necessarily existent*
'*Being,* that there was in him a certain Resemblance thereof: And
'he saw, that it was his Duty to labour by all manner of Means,
'how he might obtain the Properties of that *Being,* put on *His*
'*Qualities,* and imitate *His Actions;* to be diligent and careful also
'in promoting *His Will;* to commit all his Affairs unto *Him,* and

---

[14] "Hardly anything worse can be hoped for them, than that they may have the fruit of their folly."—*Murdock.*

'heartily to acquiesce in all those *Decrees* of *His* which concerned 'him, either from within, or from without: so that he pleased him-'self in *Him*, tho he should *afflict* him, and even *destroy* him.' I was going to say, *O Mentis aureæ Verba bracteata!* [15] But the Great *Alsted* instructs me, that we *Christians*, in our valuable Citations from them that are Strangers to *Christianity*, should seize upon the Sentences as containing *our Truths*, detained in the hands of *Unjust Possessors;* and he allows me to say, *Audite Ciceronem, quem Natura docuit.*[16] However, this I may say, *God has thus far taught a* Mahometan! And this I will say, *Christian,* beware lest a *Mahometan* be called in for thy *Condemnation!*

Let us conclude with a Remark of *Minutius Fælix:*[17] 'If so 'much Wisdom and Penetration be requisite to *observe* the won-'derful Order and Design in the Structure of the World, how 'much more were necessary to *form* it!' If Men so much admire Philosophers, because they *discover* a small Part of the *Wisdom* that made all things; they must be stark blind, who do not admire that *Wisdom* itself!

ESSAY XXIII. OF THE EARTH.

The Lord by Wisdom has founded the Earth. A poor Sojourner on the *Earth* now thinks it his Duty to behold and admire the *Wisdom* of his glorious Maker there.

The *Earth*, which is the Basis and Support of so many Vege-tables and Animals, and yields the alimentary Particles, whereof *Water* is the Vehicle, for their Nourishment: *Quorum omnium* (as *Tully* saith well) *incredibilis Multitudo, insatiabili Varietate distinguitur.*[18]

The various Moulds and Soils of the Earth declare the admi-

---

[15] "O golden words of a golden mind."—*Murdock*.
[16] "Hear Cicero, whom Nature taught."—*Murdock*.
[17] Marcus Minucius Felix, Latin apologist for Christanity, in the third century.—*Murdock*.
[18] "Of all these an incredible number, divided with inexhaustible variety."—*Murdock*.

rable Wisdom of the Creator, in making such a provision for a vast variety of Intentions. *God said, Let the Earth bring forth!*

And yet,

> *Nec vero Terræ ferre omnes omnia possunt.*[19]

It is pretty odd; they who have written *de Arte Combinatoria,* reckon of no fewer than one hundred and seventy-nine Millions, one thousand and sixty different sorts of Earth: But we may content ourselves with Sir *John Evelyn's* Enumeration, which is very short of *that.*[20]

However, the *Vegetables* owe not so much of their Life and Growth to the *Earth* itself, as to some agreeable Juices or Salts lodg'd in it. Both Mr. *Boyle* and *Van Helmont,* by Experiments, found the Earth scarce at all diminished when *Plants,* even *Trees,* had been for divers Years growing in it.

The *Strata* of the Earth, its *Lays* and *Beds,* afford surprizing Matters of Observation: the *Objects* lodged in them; the *Uses* made of them; and particularly the *Passage* they give to *sweet Waters,* as being the *Calanders*[21] wherein they are sweetned. It is asserted that these are found all to lie very much according to the Laws of *Gravity.* Mr. *Derham* went far to demonstrate this Assertion.

The *vain Colts of Asses,* that *fain would be wise,* have cavill'd at the *unequal Surface of the Earth,* have open'd against the *Mountains,* as if they were *superfluous Excrescences;* but *Warts* deforming the Face of the Earth, and Proofs the *Earth* is but an Heap of Rubbish and Ruins. *Pliny* had more of Religion in him.

The sagacious Dr. *Halley* has observed, That the Ridges of *Mountains* being placed thro the midst of their Continents, do serve as *Alembicks,* to distil fresh Waters in vast Quantities for

---

[19] "Not all lands can bear all things."—*Murdock.*

[20] Mather here draws on Evelyn's *Terra,* whence he takes his reference to the *De Arte Combinatoria.*—*Murdock.*

[21] *I.e.,* colanders, strainers.—*Murdock.*

the Use of the World: And their *Heights* give a Descent unto
the *Streams,* to run gently, like so many Veins of the *Macrocosm,*
to be the more beneficial to the Creation. The generation of
Clouds, and the distribution of *Rains,* accommodated and accomplished by the *Mountains,* is indeed so observable, that the learned
Scheuchzer and *Creitlovius* can't forbear breaking out upon it
with a *Mirati summam Creatoris Sapientiam!* [22]

What *Rivers* could there be without those admirable *Tools of
Nature!*

Vapours being raised by the *Sun,* acting on the Surface of the
Sea, as a *Fire* under an Alembick, by rarefying of it, makes the
lightest and freshest Portions thereof to rise first; which *Rarefac-
tion* is made (as Dr. *Cheyne* observes) [23] by the insinuation of its
active Particles among the porous Parts thereof, whereby they are
put into a violent Motion many different ways, and so are expanded into little Bubbles of larger Dimensions than formerly
they had; and so they become specifically lighter, and the weight-
ier *Atmosphere* buoys them up. The Streams of these *Vapours*
rest in places where the Air is of equal *Gravity* with them, and
are carried up and down the *Atmosphere* by the course of that
Air, till they hit at last against the sides of the *Mountains,* and
by this Concussion are condensed, and thus become heavier than
the Air they swum in, and so gleet down the rocky Caverns of
these *Mountains,* the inner parts whereof being hollow and stony,
afford them a *Bason,* until they are accumulated in sufficient
Quantities, to break out at the first *Crany:* whence they descend
into Plains, and several of them uniting, form Rivulets; and many
of those uniting, do grow into *Rivers.* This is the Story of them;
this their *Pedigree!*

Minerals are dug out of *Mountains;* which, if they were sought
only in level Countries, the Delfs would be so flown with Waters,
that it would be impossible to make *Addits* or *Soughs* to drein

---

[22] "Wonderful is the lofty wisdom of the Creator." The quotation and the
names of the two authorities, are taken direct from Derham.—*Murdock.*

[23] Mather refers to Dr. George Cheyne's *Philosophical Principles of Religion,
Natural and Revealed.—Murdock.*

them.[24] Here is, as *Olaus Magnus* expresses it, *Inexhausta pretiosorum Metallorum ubertas.*[25]

A *German* Writer, got upon the *Mountains,* gives this Account of them: *Sunt ceu tot naturales Fornaces Chymicæ, in quibus Deus varia Metalla & Mineralia excoquit & maturat.*[26]

The *Habitations* and *Situations* of Mankind are made vastly the more comfortable for the *Mountains.* There is a vast Variety of *Plants* proper to the *Mountains:* and many Animals find the *Mountains* their most proper places to breed and feed in. *The highest Hills a Refuge to the wild Goats!* A Point Mr. *Ray* has well spoken to.

They report that *Hippocrates* did usually repair to the *Mountains* for the *Plants,* by which he wrought the chief of his Cures.

Mountains also are the most convenient Boundaries to Territories, and afford a Defence unto them. One calls them *the Bulwarks of Nature, cast up at the Charges of the Almighty; the Scorns of the most victorious Armies.* The *Barbarians* in *Curtius*[27] were confidently sensible of this!

Yea, we may appeal to the Senses of all Men, whether the grateful Variety of *Hills* and *Dales* be not more pleasing than the largest continued *Plains.*

'Tis also a *salutary Conformation* of the Earth; some Constitutions are best suited *above,* and others *below.*

Truly these massy and lofty Piles can by no means be spared.

Galen, thou shalt chastize the *Pseudo-Christians,* who reproach the Works of God. Say! —— *Accusandi sanè meâ Sententiâ hic sunt Sophistæ, qui cùm nondum invenire neque exponere Opera Naturæ queant, eam tamen inertia atque inscitia condemnant.*[28]

Say now, O *Man,* say, under the sweet Constraints of Demonstration, *Great GOD, the Earth is full of thy Goodness!*

---

[24] Delf = a ditch; addits and soughs = drains, gutters.—*Murdock.*

[25] "Inexhaustible plenty of precious minerals."—*Murdock.*

[26] "They are like so many natural chemical furnaces in which God tempers and ripens various metals and minerals."—*Murdock.*

[27] Quintus Curtius, historian.—*Murdock.*

[28] "Those sophists are blameable, who, since they cannot discover or make clear the works of nature, condemn it from laziness and ignorance."—*Murdock.*

And Dr. *Grew* shall carry on the more general Observation for us. 'How little is the Mischief which the *Air, Fire,* or *Water* some-'times doth, compared with the innumerable *Uses* to which they 'daily serve? Besides the *Seas* and *Rivers,* how many *wholesome* 'Springs* are there for one that is *poisonous?* Are the Northern 'Countries subject to *Cold?* They have a greater plenty of *Furs* 'to keep the People warm. Would those under or near the Line 'be subject to *Heat?* They have a constant *Easterly Breeze,* which 'blows strongest in the Heat of the Day, to refresh them: And 'with this Refreshment *without,* they have a variety of excellent 'Fruits* to comfort and cool them *within.* How admirably are the 'Clouds* fed with Vapours, and carried about with the *Winds,* 'for the gradual, equal, and seasonable watering of most Coun-'tries? And in those which have less *Rain,* how abundantly is the 'want of that supplied with noble *Rivers?*'

Even the subterraneous *Caverns* have their Uses. And so have the *Ignivomous Mountains:* Those terrible things are *Spiracles,* to vent the *Vapours,* which else might make a dismal Havock. Dr. *Woodward* observes, That tho Places which are very subject unto *Earthquakes* usually have these *Volcano's,* yet without these fiery *Vents* their *Earthquakes* would bring more tremendous Desolations upon them.

Those two flammivomous Mountains, *Vesuvius* and *Ætna,* have sometimes terrified the whole World with their tremendous Eruptions. *Vesuvius* transmitted its frightful Cinders as far as *Constantinople,* which obliged the Emperor to leave the City; and Historians tell us there was kept an Anniversary Commemoration of it. *Kircher* has given us a Chronicle of what furious things have by done by *Ætna;* the melted Matter which one time it poured forth, spreading in breadth six Miles, ran down as far as *Catanea,*[29] and forced a Passage into the Sea.

Asia abounds in these *Volcano's. Africa* is known to have eight at least. In *America* 'tis affirmed that there are not less than fif-teen, among that vast Chain of Mountains called the *Andes.* One

---

[29] Catania.—*Murdock.*

says, 'Nature seems here to keep house under ground, and the 'Hollows of the *Mountains* to be the *Funnels* or *Chimneys,* by 'which the fuliginous Matter of those everlasting Fires ascends.'

The *North* too, that seems doom'd unto *eternal Cold,* has its famous *Hecla.* And *Bartholomew Zenet* [30] found one in *Greenland,* yet nearer to the Pole; the Effects whereof are very surprizing.

A reasonable and religious Mind cannot behold these formidable *Mountains,* without some Reflections of this importance: *Great GOD, who knows the Power of thine Anger? Or what can stand before the powerful Indignation of that God, who can kindle a Fire in his Anger that shall burn to the lowest Hell, and set on fire the Foundations of the Mountains!*

The *Volcano's* would lead us to consider the *Earthquakes,* wherein the *Earth* often suffers violent, and sometimes very destructive Concussions.

The History of Earthquakes would be a large, as well as a sad Volume. Whether a *Colluctation*[31] *of Minerals* in the Bowels of the *Earth* is the cause of those direful Convulsions, may be considered: As we know a Composition of Gold which *Aqua Regia* has dissolved; *Sal Armoniack,* and *Salt of Tartar,* set on fire, will with an horrible crack break thro all that is in the way. But Mankind ought herein to tremble before the Justice of God. Particular *Cities* and *Countries,* what fearful Desolations have been by Earthquakes brought upon them!

The old sinking of *Helice* and *Buris,* absorbed by *Earthquakes* into the Sea, mention'd by *Ovid,* or the twelve Cities that were so swallow'd up in the Days of *Tiberius,* are small things to what *Earthquakes* are to do on our Globe; yea, have already done. I know not what we shall think of the huge *Atlantis,* mentioned by *Plato,* now at the bottom of the *Atlantick* Ocean: But I know *Varenius* thinks it probable, that the Northern Part of *America*

---

[30] Possibly a reference to Nicolo Zeno, who, in the 14th century is said to have gone to Greenland, and to have discovered a volcano there.—*Murdock.*

[31] Conflict.—*Murdock.*

was joined unto *Ireland*, till Earthquakes made the vast and amazing Separation. Others have thought so of *England* and *France;*
of *Spain* and *Africa;* of *Italy* and *Sicily*.

Ah, *Sicily!* Art thou come to be spoken of? No longer ago than
t'other day what a rueful Spectacle was there exhibited in the
Island of *Sicily* by an *Earthquake*,[31] in which there perished the
best part of two hundred thousand Souls!

Yea, *Ammianus Marcellinus* tells us, in the Year 365, *Horrendi
Tremores per omnem Orbis Ambitum grassati sunt.*[32]

O Inhabitants of the Earth, how much ought you to fear the
things that will bring you into ill Terms with the Glorious GOD!
Fear, lest the *Pit* and the *Snare* be upon you! Against all other
Strokes there may some Defence or other be thought on: There is
none against an *Earthquake!* It says, *Tho they hide in the top of*
Carmel, *I will find them there!*

But surely the *Earthquakes* I have met with will effectually
instruct me to avoid the Folly of setting my Heart inordinately
on any *Earthly* Possessions or Enjoyments. Methinks I hear
Heaven saying *Surely he will receive this Instruction!*

A modern Philosopher speaks at this rate, 'We do not know
'when and where we stand upon *good Ground:* It would amaze
'the stoutest Heart, and make him ready to die with Fear, if he
'could see into the *subterraneous World,* and view the dark Re-
'cesses of Nature under ground; and behold, that even the strong-
'est of our Piles of Building, whose Foundation we think is laid
'firm and fast, yet are set upon an Arch or Bridge, made by the
'bending Parts of the Earth one upon another, over a prodigious
'Vault, at the bottom of which there lies an unfathomable Sea,
'but its upper Hollows are filled with stagnating Air, and with
'Expirations of sulphureous and bituminous Matter. Upon such
'a *dreadful Abyss* we walk, and ride, and sleep; and are sustained
'only by an *arched Roof,* which also is not in all places of an equal
'Thickness.'

Give me leave to say, I take *Earthquakes* to be very *moving*

---

[31] Probably the earthquakes in January, 1693.—*Murdock.*
[32] "Fearful shakings went through all the surface of the earth."—*Murdock.*

Preachers unto *worldly-minded Men:* Their Address may be very agreeably put into the Terms of the Prophet; *O Earth, Earth, Earth, hear the Word of the Lord!*

'Chrysostom did well, among his other Epithets, to call the 'Earth *our Table;* but it shall *teach* me as well as *feed* me: May 'I be a *Deipnosophist*[33] upon it.

'Indeed, what is the Earth but a *Theatre,* as has been long since 'observed? *In quo Infinita & Illustria, Providentiæ, Bonitatis, Po-'tentiæ ac Sapientiæ Divinæ Spectacula contemplanda!* [34] But I must not forget 'that this *Earth* is very shortly to be my *sleeping-'place;* it has a *Grave* waiting for me: *I will not fear to go down, 'for thou has promised, O my Saviour, to bring me up again.'*

APPENDIX

§. Having arrived thus far, I will here make a Pause, and ac-knowledge the shine of Heaven on *our Parts of the Earth,* in the Improvements of our *modern Philosophy.*

To render us the more sensible hereof, we will propose a few Points of the *Mahometan Philosophy,* or Secrets reveal'd unto *Mahomet,* which none of his Followers, who cover so much of the Earth at this Day, may dare to question.

The *Winds;* 'tis an *Angel* moving his *Wings* that raises them.

The *Flux* and *Reflux* of the *Sea,* is caused by an *Angel's* put-ting his Foot on the middle of the *Ocean,* which compressing the Waves, the Waters run to the Shores; but being removed, they retire into their proper Station.

Falling Stars are the *Firebrands* with which the *good Angels* drive away the *bad,* when they are too saucily inquisitive, and approach too near the Verge of the Heavens, to eves-drop the Secrets there.

Thunder is nothing else but the cracking of an *Angel's Whip,* while he slashes the dull Clouds into such and such places, when they want *Rains* to fertilize the Earth.

---

[33] "A master of the art of dining."—*Murdock.*
[34] "In which are to be contemplated infinite and glorious spectacles of the Divine providence, goodness, power, and wisdom."—*Murdock.*

Eclipses are made thus: The *Sun* and *Moon* are shut in a *Pipe,* which is turned up and down; from each Pipe is a Window, by which they enlighten the World; but when God is angry at the Inhabitants of it for their Transgressions, He bids an *Angel* clap to the Window, and so turn the Light towards Heaven from the Earth: for this Occasion *Forms of Prayer* are left, that the Almighty would avert his Judgments, and restore Light unto the World.

The thick-skull'd Prophet sets another *Angel* at work for *Earthquakes;* he is to hold so many *Ropes* tied unto every Quarter of the Globe, and when he is commanded, he is to pull; so he shakes that part of the Globe: and if a City, or Mountain, or Tower, is to be overturned, then he tugs harder at the Pulley, till the Rivers dance, and the Valleys are filled with Rubbish, and the Waters are swallowed up in the Precipices.

May our Devotion exceed the Mahometan *as much as our Philosophy!*

. . . . .

ESSAY XXXII. OF MAN

¶. *Hear now the Conclusion of the Matter.* To enkindle the *Dispositions* and the *Resolutions* of PIETY in my Brethren, is the *Intention* of all my ESSAYS, and must be the *Conclusion* of them.

Atheism is now for ever chased and hissed out of the World, every thing in the World concurs to a Sentence of *Banishment* upon it. *Fly, thou Monster, and hide, and let not the darkest Recesses of* Africa *itself be able to cherish thee; never dare to shew thyself in a World where every thing stands ready to overwhelm thee!* A BEING that must be *superior* to *Matter,* even the *Creator* and *Governor* of all *Matter,* is every where so conspicuous, that there can be nothing more *monstrous* than *to deny the God that is above.* No *System* of *Atheism* has ever yet been offered among the Children of Men, but what may presently be convinced of such *Inconsistences,* that a Man must ridiculously believe *nothing certain* before he can imagine them; it must be a

System of *Things which cannot stand together!* A Bundle of *Contradictions* to themselves, and to all *common Sense*. I doubt it has been an *inconsiderate* thing to pay so much of a Compliment to *Atheism,* as to bestow solemn *Treatises* full of learned *Arguments* for the Refutation of a *delirious Phrenzy,* which ought rather to be put out of countenance with the most *contemptuous Indignation*. And I fear such Writers as have been at the pains to put the *Objections* of *Atheism* into the most plausible Terms, that they may have the honour of *laying a Devil when they have raised him,* have therein done too *unadvisedly*. However, to so much notice of the raving *Atheist* we may condescend while we go along, as to tell him, that for a Man to question the *Being of a* GOD, who requires from us an *Homage* of *Affection,* and *Wonderment,* and Obedience to Himself, and a perpetual Concern for the Welfare of the *Human Society,* for which He has in our *Formation* evidently *suited* us, would be an *exalted Folly,* which undergoes especially two Condemnations; it is first condemned by this, that every Part of the *Universe* is continually *pouring in* something for the *confuting* of it; there is not a Corner of the whole World but what supplies a *Stone* towards the Infliction of such a *Death* upon the *Blasphemy* as justly belongs to it: and it has also this condemning of it, that Men would soon become *Canibals* to one another by embracing it; Men being utterly destitute of any Principle to keep them *honest in the Dark,* there would be no *Integrity* left in the World, but they would be as the *Fishes of the Sea to one another,* and worse than *the creeping Things, that have no Ruler over them*. Indeed from every thing in the World there is this Voice more audible than the loudest Thunder to us; *God hath spoken, and these two things have I heard!* First, *Believe and adore a glorious GOD, who has made all these Things, and know thou that He will bring thee into Judgment!* And then *be careful to do nothing but what shall be for the Good of the Community which the glorious GOD has made thee a Member of*. Were what God *hath spoken* duly regarded, and were these *two things* duly complied with, the World would be soon revived into a desirable *Garden of God,* and Mankind would be fetch'd up into very comfortable Circumstances; till *then* the World continues in a wretched Condition, *full of doleful Creatures,* with *wild Beasts crying* in its *desolate Houses, Dragons* in its most *pleasant Palaces.* And now declare, *O every thing that is reasonable,* declare and pronounce upon it whether it be possible that *Maxims* absolutely *necessary* to the *Subsistence* and *Happiness* of Mankind, can be *Falsities?* There is no possibility for this, that *Cheats* and *Lyes* must be so *necessary,* that the *Ends* which alone are worthy of a glorious GOD, cannot be attain'd without having *them* imposed upon us!

Having dispatch'd the *Atheist,* with bestowing on him *not many* Thoughts, yet *more* than could be deserved by such an *Idiot;* I will proceed now to propose two general Strokes of *Piety,* which will appear to a *Christian Philosopher* as unexceptionable as any Proposals that ever were made to him.

First, the Works of the glorious God exhibited to our View, 'tis most certain they do *bespeak,* and they should *excite* our *Acknowledgments of His Glories* appearing in them: the Great GOD is infinitely *gratified* in beholding the Displays of His own infinite *Power,* and *Wisdom,* and *Goodness,* in the Works which He has made; but it is also a most acceptable Gratification to Him, when such of His Works as are the *rational Beholders* of themselves, and of the rest, shall with devout Minds *acknowledge* His Perfections, which they see shining there. Never does one endued with *Reason* do anything more evidently *reasonable,* than when he makes every thing that occurs to him in the vast Fabrick of the World, an *Incentive* to some agreeable Efforts and Salleys of *Religion.* What can any Man living object against the *Piety* of a Mind awaken'd by the sight of God in His Works, to such Thoughts as these: *Verily, there is a glorious GOD! Verily, the GOD who does these things is worthy to be feared, worthy to be loved, worthy to be relied on! Verily, all possible Obedience is due to such a GOD; and most abominable, most inexcusable is the Wickedness of all Rebellion against Him!* A Mind kept under the Impression of such Thoughts as these, is an *holy* and a *noble* Mind, a *Temple* of God, a *Temple filled with the Glory of God.*

There is nothing but what will afford an *Occasion* for the *Thoughts;* the oftner a Man improves the *Occasion,* the more does he *glorify GOD,* and answer the *chief End of Man;* and why should he not *seek occasion* for it, by visiting for this purpose the several *Classes* of the Creatures (for *Discipulus in hâc Scholâ erit Peripateticus*)[35] as he may have opportunity for so generous an Exercise! But since the horrid Evil of all *Sin* is to be inferred from this; *it is a Rebellion against the Laws of the glorious GOD, who is the Maker and the Ruler of all Worlds;* and *it is a disturbance of the good Order wherein the glorious Maker and Ruler of all Things has placed them all;* how much ought a quickned *Horror of Sin* to accompany this Contemplation, and produce this most agreeable Resolution, *My God, I will for ever fear to offend thy glorious Majesty!* Nor is this all the *Improvement* which we are to make of what we see in the *Works of God;* in our *improving* of them, we are to accept of the *Rebuke* which they give to our *Presumption,* in pretending to criticize upon the *dark things* which occur in the Dispensations of His *Providence;* there is not any one of all the *Creatures* but what has those *fine things* in the *Texture* of it, which have never yet been reached by our *Searches,* and we are as much at a loss about the *Intent* as about the *Texture* of them; *as yet* we know not what the glorious God *intends* in His forming of those *Creatures,* nor what *He has to do* in them, and with them; He therein proclaims this Expectation, *Surely they will fear me, and receive Instruction.* And the Point wherein we are now instructed is this: 'What! Shall I be 'so vain as to be *dissatisfied* because I do not *understand* what is 'done by the glorious GOD in the Works of His *Providence!*' *O my Soul, hast thou not known, hast thou not heard concerning the everlasting God, the Lord, the Creator of the Ends of the Earth, that there is no searching of His Understanding?*

And then, secondly, the CHRIST of God must not be forgotten, who is *the Lord of all. I am not ashamed of the Gospel of CHRIST,* of which I will *affirm constantly,* that if the *Philoso-*

---

[35] "A disciple of this school must be a Peripatetic."—*Murdock.*

pher do not call it in, he *paganizes,* and leaves the finest and brightest Part of his Work unfinished. Let *Colerus*[36] persuade us if he can, that in the Time of *John Frederick* the Elector of *Saxony* there was dug up a *Stone,* on which there was a Representation of our *crucified Saviour;* but I cannot forbear saying, there is not a *Stone* any where which would not look *black* upon me, and *speak* my Condemnation, if my *Philosophy* should be so *vain* as to make me lay aside my Thoughts of my *enthroned Saviour.* Let *Lambecius,*[37] if he please, employ his Learning upon the Name of our Saviour CHRIST, found in Letters naturally engraven at the bottom of a large *Agate-Cup,* which is to be seen among the Emperor's Curiosities; I have never drank in that *Cup,* however I can more easily believe it than I can the *Crucifixus ex Radice Crambres enatus,*[38] or the *Imago Virginis cum Filiolo, in Minerâ Ferri expressa,*[39] and several more such things, which the Publishers of the *German Ephemerides*[40] have mingled with their better Entertainments: but I will assert, that a glorious CHRIST is more to be considered in the *Works of Nature* than the *Philosopher* is generally aware of; and my *CHRISTIAN Philosopher* has not fully done his Part, till He who is *the First-born of every Creature* be come into Consideration with him. *Alsted* mentions a *Siclus Judæo-Christianus,*[41] which had on one side the Name *JESUS,* with the Face of our *Saviour,* and on the other the Words that signify *the King Messiah comes with Peace, and God becomes a Man;* and *Leusden*[42] says he had a couple of these *Coins* in his possession. I have nothing to say on the behalf of the *Zeal* in those *Christianized Jews,* who probably were the Authors of these *Coins,* a *Zeal* that *boil'd* into so needless an Expression of an

---

[36] Johann Jacob Coler, 16th century German theologian and writer.—*Murdock.*

[37] Peter Lambeck, 1628-80, German historian.—*Murdock.*

[38] "The crucifix springing from a cabbage root." Mather misprints "crambres" for "crambes."—*Murdock.*

[39] "Image of the Virgin and Child moulded in iron ore."—*Murdock.*

[40] The "German Ephemerides" was a scientific periodical in Germany, *Miscellanea Curiosa sive Ephemeridum Medico-Physicarum Germanicarum,* etc. Cotton Mather refers to articles in the volume for 1670.—*Murdock.*

[41] "A Jewish-Christian shekel (coin)."—*Murdock.*

[42] Johann Leusden, 1624-1699, Dutch scholar, and friend of Cotton Mather's father.—*Murdock.*

Homage, that indeed cannot be too much expressed in the *instituted ways* of it to a Redeemer, whose *Kingdom is not of this World*: but this I will say, *all the Creatures in this World are part of His Kingdom;* there are no *Creatures* but what are His *Medals,* on every one of them the Name of JESUS is to be found inscribed. Celebrate, O *Danhaver,*[43] thy *Granatilla,* the *Peruvian Plant,* on which a strong Imagination finds a Representation of the *Instruments* employed in the *Sufferings* of our Saviour, and especially the *bloody Sweat* of His Agonies; were the Representation as really and lively made as has been imagined, I would subscribe to the Epigram upon it, which concludes:

Flos hic ità formâ vincit omnes Flosculos,
Ut totus optet esse Spectator Oculus.[44]

But I will, with the Exercise of the most *solid Reason,* by every part of the World, as well as the *Vegetables,* be led to my Saviour.

A *View of the Creation* is to be taken, with suitable Acknowledgments of the glorious CHRIST, in whom the *eternal Son of God* has personally united Himself to ONE of His *Creatures,* and becomes on *his* account propitious to *all the rest;* our *Piety* indeed will not be *Christianity* if HE be left unthought upon.

This is HE, of whom we are instructed, *Col.* 1. 16, 17. *All things were created by Him, and for Him; and He is before all things, and by Him all things consist.* It is no contemptible Thought wherewith *De Sabunde* has entertained us: *Productio Mundi à Deo facta de Nihilo, arguit aliam productionem, summam, occultam, & æternam in Deo, quæ est de sua propria Natura, in qua producitur Deus de Deo, & per quam ostenditur summa Trinitas in Deo.*[45] And certainly he that as a *Father* does produce a *Son,*

---

[43] Johann Conrad Danhawer, 1603-1666, German theologian.—*Murdock.*

[44] "This flower so surpasses all others in its form that every eye may wish to see it."—*Murdock.*

[45] "The creation of the world, made by God from nothing, shows that there is another creation, high, secret, and eternal, in God, which is of His own nature, in which God is created from God, and by which is made plain the Trinity in God." Raymond de Sebonde, d. 1432, was a Spanish physician, author of *Theologia Naturalis.—Murdock.*

but as an *Artist* only produce an *House,* has a Value for the *Son*
which he has not for the *House;* yea, we may say, if GOD had
not first, and from Eternity, been a *Father* to our *Saviour,* He
would never have exerted Himself as an *Artist* in that *Fabrick,*
which He has built *by the Might of His Power, and for the
Honour of His Majesty!*

The Great Sir *Francis Bacon* has a notable Passage in his *Con-
fession of Faith: I believe that God is so holy, as that it is impossible for Him to be pleased in any Creature, tho the Work of his
own Hands, without beholding of the same in the Face of a Mediator; —— without which it was impossible for Him to have descended to any Work of Creation, but He should have enjoyed the
blessed and individual Society of three Persons in the Godhead for
ever; but out of His eternal and infinite Goodness and Love pur-
posing to become a Creature, and communicate with His Creatures, He ordained in His eternal Counsel that one Person of the
Godhead should be united to one Nature, and to one particular of
His Creatures; that so in the Person of the Mediator the true Ladder might be fixed, whereby God might descend to His Creatures,
and His Creatures ascend to Him.*

It was an high Flight of *Origen,*[46] who urges, that our *High-
Priest's* having *tasted of Death,* ὑπὲρ παντος, FOR ALL, is to be
extended even to the very *Stars,* which would otherwise have
been *impure* in the sight of God; and thus are ALL THINGS
restored to the *Kingdom* of the Father. Our Apostle *Paul* in a
famous Passage to the *Colossians* [i. 19, 20.] may seem highly to
favour this Flight. One says upon it, 'If this be so, we need not
'break the Glasses of *Galilæo,* the *Spots* may be washed out of
'the *Sun,* and *total Nature* sanctified to God that made it.'

Yea, the sacred Scriptures plainly and often invite us to a Conception, which Dr. *Goodwin* has chosen to deliver in such Terms
as these: 'The *Son of God* personally and actually existing as the
'Son of God with God, afore the World or any Creature was
'made, *He* undertaking and covenanting with God to become a

---

[46] Alexandrian Christian writer of the 2d and 3d centuries.—*Murdock.*

'Man, yea, *that Man* which He hath now taken up into one Person
'with Himself, as well for *this End,* as for *other Ends* more glori-
'ous; God did in the Foreknowledge of *that,* and in the Assurance
'of that *Covennant* of His, proceed to the *creating* of all things
'which He hath made; and without the Intuition of *this,* or hav-
'ing *this* in His Eye, He would not have made any thing which
'He hath made.'

O CHRISTIAN, *lift up now thine Eyes, and look from the
place where thou art* to all Points of the Compass, and concerning *whatever thou seest,* allow that all these things were formed
for the Sake of that Glorious-One, who is now *God manifest in
the Flesh* of our JESUS; 'tis on *His* Account that the eternal
Godhead has the *Delight* in all these things, which preserves
them in their Being, and grants them the *Help,* in the *obtaining*
whereof they *continue to this day.*

But were they not all made *by the hand,* as well as *for the Sake*
of that Glorious-ONE? They were verily so. *O my JESUS, it was
that Son of God who now dwells in thee, in and by whom the
Godhead exerted the Power, which could be exerted by none but
an all-powerful GOD, in the creating of the World!* He is that
Word of GOD *by whom all things were made, and without
whom was not any thing made that was made.*

This is not all that we have to think upon; we see an incomparable *Wisdom* of GOD in His *Creatures;* one cannot but presently infer, *What an incomprehensible Wisdom then in the
Methods and Affairs of that Redemption, whereof the glorious
GOD has laid the Plan in our JESUS!* Things which the *Angels
desire to look into.* But, O *evangelized Mind,* go on, mount up,
soar higher, think at this rate; *the infinite Wisdom which formed
all these things is peculiarly seated in the Son of God;* He is that
reflexive Wisdom of the eternal *Father,* and that *Image of the
invisible God, by whom all things were created;* in *Him* there is
after a peculiar manner the original *Idea* and *Archetype* of every
thing that offers the infinite *Wisdom* of God to our Admiration.
Wherever we see the *Wisdom* of God admirably shining before us,
we are invited to such a Thought as this; *this Glory is originally*

to be found in thee, O our Immanuel! 'Tis in Him *transcendently.*
But then 'tis impossible to stop without adding, *How glorious,
how wondrous, how lovely art thou, O our Saviour!*

Nor may we lay aside a grateful Sense of this, that as the *Son*
of God is *the Upholder of all Things in all Worlds,* thus, that it
is owing to his potent *Intercession* that the *Sin of Man* has made
no more havock on this *our World.* This *our World* has been by
the *Sin of Man* so perverted from the *true Ends* of it, and rendred
full of such loathsome and hateful Regions, and such *Scelerata
Castra,*[47] that the Revenges of God would have long since rendred
it as a *fiery Oven,* if our blessed JESUS had not *interceded* for it:
*O my Saviour, what would have become of me, and of all that
comforts me, if thy Interposition had not preserved us!*

We will add one thing more: Tho the one GOD in His *three
Subsistences* be the *Governor* as well as the *Creator* of the World,
and so the *Son* of God ever had what we call the *natural Government* of the World, yet upon the *Fall* of Mankind there is a *mediatory Kingdom* that becomes expedient, that so *guilty Man,* and
that which was *lost,* may be brought to God; and the singular
Honour of this *mediatory Kingdom* is more *immediately* and most
agreeably assign'd to the *Son of God,* who assumes the Man
JESUS into His own Person, and has *all Power in Heaven and
Earth given to Him;* all things are now commanded and ordered
by the *Son of God* in the *Man upon the Throne,* and this *to the
Glory of the Father,* by whom the *mediatory Kingdom* is erected,
and so conferred. This *peculiar Kingdom* thus managed by the
Son of God in our JESUS, will cease when the illustrious Ends of
it are all accomplished, and *then* the *Son of God* no longer having
such a *distinct Kingdom* of His own, shall return to those eternal
Circumstances, wherein He shall reign with the *Father* and the
Holy Spirit, one God, blessed for ever. In the mean time, what
Creatures can we behold without being obliged to some such
Doxology as this; *O Son of God, incarnate and enthroned in my
JESUS, this is part of thy Dominion! What a great King art
thou, and what a Name hast thou above every Name, and how*

---

[47] "Wicked settlements."—*Murdock.*

vastly extended is thy Dominion! Dominion and Fear is with thee, and there is no Number of thine Armies! All the Inhabitants of the Earth, and their most puissant Emperors, are to be reputed as nothing before thee!

But then at last I am losing myself in such Thoughts as these: *Who can tell* what *Uses* our Saviour will put all these *Creatures* to at the *Restitution of all things,* when He comes to rescue them from the *Vanity* which as yet captivates them and incumbers them; and His raised People in the *new Heavens* will make their Visits to a *new Earth,* which they shall find flourishing in *Paradisaick* Regularities? *Lord, what thou meanest in them, I know not now, but I shall know hereafter!* I go on, *Who can tell* how sweetly our Saviour may *feast* His *chosen People* in the *Future State,* with Exhibitions of all these *Creatures,* in their various *Natures,* and their curious *Beauties* to them? *Lord, I hope for an eternally progressive Knowledge, from the Lamb of God successively leading me to the Fountains of it!*

I recover out of my more *conjectural Prognostications,* with resolving what may *at present* yield to a serious Mind a *Satisfaction,* to which this World knows none superior: When in a way of *occasional Reflection* I employ the *Creatures* as my *Teachers,* I will by the *Truths* wherein those ready *Monitors* instruct me, be led to my glorious JESUS; I will consider the *Truths as they are in JESUS,* and count my *Asceticks* deficient, till I have some Thoughts of HIM and of His *Glories* awakened in me. To conclude, It is a good Passage which a little Treatise entitled, *Theologia Ruris,* or, *The Book of Nature,* breaks off withal, and I might make it my Conclusion: 'If we mind *Heaven* whilst we 'live here upon *Earth,* this *Earth* will serve to conduct us to 'Heaven, thro the Merits and Mediation of the *Son of God,* who 'was made the *Son of Man,* and came thence on purpose into this 'lower World to convey us up thither.'

I will finish with a Speculation, which my most valuable Dr. *Cheyne* has a little more largely prosecuted and cultivated.

All *intelligent compound Beings* have their whole Entertainment in these three Principles, the DESIRE, the OBJECT, and the SENSATION arising from the *Congruity* between them; this *Analogy* is preserved full and clear thro the *Spiritual World,* yea, and thro the *material* also; so *universal* and *perpetual* an *Analogy* can arise from nothing but its *Pattern* and *Archetype* in the infinite God or Maker; and could we carry it up to the Source of it, we should find the TRINITY of Persons in the eternal GODHEAD admirably exhibited to us. In the GODHEAD we may first apprehend a *Desire,* an infinitely active, ardent, powerful *Thought,* proposing of *Satisfaction;* let this represent GOD the FATHER: but it is not possible for any Object but God Himself to *satisfy Himself,* and fill His *Desire* of Happiness; therefore HE Himself *reflected* in upon Himself, and contemplating His own infinite Perfections, even the *Brightness of His Glory,* and the *express Image of His Person,* must answer this glorious Intention; and this may represent to us GOD the SON. Upon this Contemplation, wherein GOD Himself does behold, and possess, and enjoy Himself, there cannot but arise a *Love,* a *Joy,* an *Acquiescence* of God Himself within Himself, and worthy of a God; this may shadow out to us the third and the last of the Principles in this *mysterious Ternary,* that is to say, the Holy SPIRIT. Tho these *three Relations* of the Godhead in itself, when derived analogically down to Creatures, may appear but *Modifications* of a *real Subsistence,* yet in the supreme Infinitude of the Divine Nature, they must be infinitely *real* and *living* Principles. Those which are but *Relations* when transferred to *created Beings,* are glorious REALITIES in the infinite God. And in this View of the Holy Trinity, low as it is, it is impossible the SON should be without the FATHER, or the FATHER without the SON, or both without the Holy SPIRIT; it is impossible the SON should not be necessarily and eternally begotten of the FATHER, or that the Holy SPIRIT should not necessarily and eternally proceed both from Him and from the SON. Thus from what occurs throughout the whole Creation, *Reason* forms an imperfect Idea of this incomprehensible Mystery.

But it is time to stop here, and indeed how can we go any further!

PURITAN POETRY

Bibliographical Note. The best general study of Puritan poetry is that in K. B. Murdock, *Literature and Theology in Colonial New England* (Cambridge, 1949), pp. 137-172. Invaluable for newly discovered texts and for bibliographies is H. S. Jantz, *The First Century of New England Verse* (Worcester, 1944). For special studies see, on Anne Bradstreet: S. E. Morison, *Builders of the Bay Colony* (Boston, 1930), pp. 320-336; on Michael Wigglesworth: F. O. Matthiessen, "Michael Wigglesworth: A Puritan Artist," *New England Quarterly,* I (1928), 491-504; on Edward Taylor: Austin Warren, "Edward Taylor's Poetry: Colonial Baroque," *Kenyon Review,* III (1941), 355-371; R. H. Pearce, "Edward Taylor: The Poet as Puritan," *New England Quarterly,* XXIII (1950), 31-46; Herbert Blau, "Heaven's Sugar Cake: Theology and Imagery in the Poetry of Edward Taylor," *New England Quarterly,* XXVI (1953), 337-360. Sources for texts here printed are given in a headnote to each poem.

(ANONYMOUS)

"ANAGRAM ON THOMAS DUDLEY" *

(1645 ?)

Text: H. S. Jantz, ed., *The First Century of New England Verse* (Worcester, 1944), p. 34.

> Thomas Dudley
> ah! old, must dye
> A deaths head on your hand you neede not weare
> a dying hand you on your shoulders beare
> you need not one to minde you, you must dye
> you in your name may spell mortalitye
> younge men may dye, but old men these dye must
> t'will not be long before you turne to dust.
> before you turne to dust! ah! must; old! dye!
> what shall younge doe, when old in dust doe lye?
> when old in dust lye, what N. England doe?
> when old in dust doe lye, it's best dye too.

---

* Reprinted by courtesy of the American Antiquarian Society.

SAMUEL DANFORTH
(d. 1674)

from AN ALMANACK FOR THE YEAR OF
OUR LORD 1647 *

Text: K. B. Murdock, ed., *Handkerchiefs for Paul* (Cambridge, 1927), pp. 101-104.

[March]

A Coal-white Bird appeares this spring
That neither cares to sigh or sing.
This when the merry Birds espy,
They take her for some enemy.
Why so, when as she humbly stands
Only to shake you by your hands?

[April]

That which hath neither tongue nor wings
This month how merrily it sings:
To see such, out for dead who lay
To cast their winding sheets away?
Friends! would you live? some pils then take
When head and stomack both doe ake.

[June]

Who dig'd this spring of Gardens here,
Whose mudded streames at last run cleare?
But why should we such water drink?
Give loosers what they list to think,
Yet know, one God, one Faith profest
To be New-Englands interest.

---

* Reprinted from *Handkerchiefs for Paul*, edited by K. B. Murdock and used with permission of the Harvard University Press.

[July]

The wooden Birds are now in sight,
Whose voices roare, whose wings are white,
Whose mawes are fill'd with hose and shooes,
With wine, cloth, sugar, salt and newes,
When they have eas'd their stomacks here
They cry, farewell untill next yeare.

[August]

Many this month I doe fore-see
Together by the eares will bee:
Indian and English in the field
To one another will not yeild.
Some weeks continue will this fray,
Till they be carted all away.

[September]

Four heads should meet and counsell have,
The chickens from the kite to save,
The idle drones away to drive,
The little Bees to keep i'th hive.
How hony m[a]y be brought to these
By making fish to dance on trees.

[October]

If discontented Bellyes shall
Wish that the highest now might fall:
Their wish fulfilled they shall see,
Whenas within the woods they bee.
Poor Tinker think'st our shrubs will sing:
The Bramble here shall be our King.

[November]

None of the wisest now will crave
To know what winter we shall have.

If shall be milde, let such be told.
If that it be not over cold.
Nor over cold shall they it see,
If very temperate it bee

[December]

It maybe now some enemy—
Not see, but felt, will make you fly.
Where is it best then to abide:
I think close by the fier side.
If you must fight it out i'th field,
Your hearts let woollen breast-plates shield.

[January]

Great bridges shall be made alone
Without ax, timber, earth or stone,
Of chrystall metall, like to glasse;
Such wondrous works soon come to passe,
If you may then have such a way,
The Ferry-man you need not pay.

[February]

Our Lillyes which refus'd to spin
All winter past, shall now begin
To feel the lash of such a Dame,
Whom some call Idleness by name.
Excepting such who all this time
Had reason good against my rime.

ANNE BRADSTREET
(*1612-1672*)

"CONTEMPLATIONS"
(*1678*)

Text: *The Poems of Mrs. Anne Bradstreet* (Boston, 1897), pp. 249-258.

Some time now past in the autumnal tide,
   When Phoebus wanted but one hour to bed,
The trees all richly clad, yet void of pride,
   Were gilded o'er by his rich golden head;
Their leaves and fruits seemed painted, but were true
Of green, of red, of yellow, mixed hue.
Rapt were my senses at this delectable view.

I wist not what to wish, yet sure, thought I
   If so much excellence abide below
How excellent is He that dwells on high,
   Whose power and beauty by his works we know!
Sure He is goodness, wisdom, glory, light,
That hath this under world so richly dight.
More heaven than earth was here, no winter and no night.

Then on a stately oak I cast mine eye,
   Whose ruffling top the clouds seemed to aspire.
How long since thou wast in thine infancy?
   Thy strength and stature more thy years admire.
Hath hundred winters passed since thou wast born,
Or thousand since thou break'st at thy shell of horn?
If so, all these as naught eternity doth scorn.

Then higher on the glistering sun I gazed,
   Whose beams were shaded by the leafy tree;
The more I looked the more I grew amazed,
   And softly said, What glory's like to thee?

Soul of this world, this universe's eye,
No wonder some made thee a deity.
Had I not better known, alas, the same had I.

Thou as a bridegroom from thy chamber rushes,
    And as a strong man joys to run a race;
The morn doth usher thee with smiles and blushes,
    The earth reflects her glances in thy face.
Birds, insects, animals, with vegetive,
Thy heart from death and dulness doth revive,
And in the darksome womb of fruitful nature dive.

Thy swift annual and diurnal course,
    Thy daily straight and yearly oblique path,
Thy pleasing fevor, and thy scorching force
    All mortals here the feeling knowledge hath.
Thy presence makes it day, thy absence night.
Quarternal seasons caused by thy might.
Hail, creature full of sweetness, beauty, and delight!

Art thou so full of glory that no eye
    Hath strength thy shining rays once to behold?
And is thy splendid throne erect so high
    As to approach it can no earthly mould?
How full of glory then must thy Creator be
Who gave this bright light luster unto thee?
Admired, adored, forever be that Majesty.

Silent, alone, where none or saw or heard,
    In pathless paths I led my wandering feet;
My humble eyes to lofty skies I reared,
    To sing some song my amazed muse thought meet.
My great Creator I would magnify
That nature had thus decked liberally.
But ah, and ah again, my imbecility!

I heard the merry grasshopper then sing,
   The black-clad cricket bear a second part;
They kept one tune and played on the same string,
   Seeming to glory in their little art.
Shall creatures abject thus their voices raise,
And in their kind resound their maker's praise,
Whilst I as mute can warble forth no higher lays?

When present times look back to ages past,
   And men in being fancy those are dead,
It makes things gone perpetually to last,
   And calls back months and years that long since fled;
It makes a man more aged in conceit
Than was Methuselah or his grandsire great
While of their persons and their acts his mind doth treat.

Sometimes in Eden fair he seems to be,
   Sees glorious Adam there made lord of all,
Fancies the apple dangle on the tree
   That turned his sovereign to a naked thrall,
Who like a miscreant was driven from that place
To get his bread with pain and sweat of face—
A penalty imposed on his backsliding race.

Here sits our grandam in retired place,
   And in her lap her bloody Cain new born;
The weeping imp oft looks her in the face,
   Bewails his unknown hap and fate forlorn.
His mother sighs to think of paradise,
And how she lost her bliss to be more wise,
Believing him that was and is father of lies.

Here Cain and Abel come to sacrifice;
   Fruits of the earth and fatlings each doth bring.
On Abel's gift the fire descends from skies,
   But no such sign on false Cain's offering.

With sullen hateful looks he goes his ways,
Hath thousand thoughts to end his brother's days,
Upon whose blood his future good he hopes to raise.

There Abel keeps his sheep, no ill he thinks;
  His brother comes, then acts his fratricide;
The virgin earth of blood her first draught drinks,
  But since that time she often hath been cloyed.
The wretch with ghastly face and dreadful mind
Thinks each he sees will serve him in his kind,
Though none on earth but kindred near then could he find.

Who fancies not his looks now at the bar,
  His face like death, his heart with horror fraught,
Nor malefactor ever felt like war
  When deep despair with wish of life hath sought.
Branded with guilt, and crushed with treble woes,
A vagabond to land of Nod he goes,
A city builds, that walls might him secure from foes.

Who thinks not oft upon the fathers' ages,
  Their long descent, how nephews' sons they saw,
The starry observations of those sages,
  And how their precepts to their sons were law;
How Adam sighed to see his progeny
Clothed all in his black sinful livery,
Who neither guilt nor yet the punishment could fly?

Our life compare we with their length of days,
  Who to the tenth of theirs doth now arrive?
And though thus short, we shorten many ways,
  Living so little while we are alive—
In eating, drinking, sleeping, vain delight;
So unawares comes on perpetual night,
And puts all pleasures vain unto eternal flight.

When I behold the heavens as in their prime,
  And then the earth, though old, still clad in green,
The stones and trees insensible of time,
  Nor age nor wrinkle on their front are seen;
If winter come, and greenness then doth fade,
A spring returns, and they're more youthful made.
But man grows old, lies down, remains where once he's laid.

By birth more noble than those creatures all,
  Yet seems by nature and by custom cursed—
No sooner born but grief and care make fall
  That state obliterate he had at first;
Nor youth, nor strength, nor wisdom spring again,
Nor habitations long their names retain,
But in oblivion to the final day remain.

Shall I then praise the heavens, the trees, the earth,
  Because their beauty and their strength last longer?
Shall I wish there or never to had birth,
  Because they're bigger and their bodies stronger?
Nay, they shall darken, perish, fade, and die,
And when unmade so ever shall they lie;
But man was made for endless immortality.

Under the cooling shadow of a stately elm
  Close sat I by a goodly river's side
Where gliding streams the rocks did overwhelm;
  A lonely place, with pleasure dignified.
I once that loved the shady woods so well
Now thought the rivers did the trees excel,
And if the sun would ever shine there would I dwell.

While on the stealing stream I fixed mine eye
  Which to the longed-for ocean held its course,
I marked nor crooks nor rubs that there did lie

Could hinder aught, but still augment its force.
O happy flood, quoth I, that holds thy race
Till thou arrive at thy beloved place,
Nor is it rocks or shoals that can obstruct thy pace.

Nor is it enough that thou alone mayst slide,
    But hundred brooks in thy clear waves do meet;
So hand in hand along with thee they glide
    To Thetis' house, where all embrace and greet.
Thou emblem true of what I count the best,
Oh, could I lead my rivulets to rest!
So may we press to that vast mansion ever blest!

Ye fish which in this liquid region abide,
    That for each season have your habitation,
Now salt, now fresh, where you think best to glide,
    To unknown coasts to give a visitation,
In lakes and ponds you leave your numerous fry;
So nature taught, and yet you know not why,
You watery folk that know not your felicity.

Look how the wantons frisk to taste the air,
    Then to the colder bottom straight they drive;
Eftsoon to Neptune's glassy hall repair
    To see what trade the great ones there do drive;
Who forage o'er the spacious sea-green field,
And take the trembling prey before it yield;
Whose armor is their scales, their spreading fins their shield.

While musing thus with contemplation fed,
    And thousand fancies buzzing in my brain,
The sweet-tongued philomel perched o'er my head,
    And chanted forth a most melodious strain,
Which rapt me so with wonder and delight
I judged my hearing better than my sight,
And wished me wings with her awhile to take my flight.

O merry bird, said I, that fears no snares,
That neither toils nor hoards up in thy barn,
Feels no sad thoughts, nor cruciating cares
To gain more good or shun what might thee harm,
Thy clothes ne'er wear, thy meat is everywhere,
Thy bed a bough, thy drink the water clear,
Reminds not what is past, nor what's to come dost fear!

The dawning morn with songs thou dost prevent,
Settest hundred notes unto thy feathered crew;
So each one tunes his pretty instrument,
And, warbling out the old, begins anew.
And thus they pass their youth in summer season,
Then follow thee into a better region
Where winter's never felt by that sweet airy legion.

Man, at the best a creature frail and vain,
In knowledge ignorant, in strength but weak,
Subject to sorrows, losses, sickness, pain,
Each storm his state, his mind, his body, break,
From some of these he never finds cessation,
But day or night, within, without, vexation,
Troubles from foes, from friends, from dearest, nearest relation.

And yet this sinful creature, frail and vain,
This lump of wretchedness, of sin and sorrow,
This weather-beaten vessel racked with pain,
Joys not in hope of an eternal morrow;
Nor all his losses, crosses, and vexation,
In weight, in frequency, and long duration,
Can make him deeply groan for that divine translation.

The mariner that on smooth waves doth glide
Sings merrily, and steers his bark with ease,
As if he had command of wind and tide,
And now become great master of the seas;

But suddenly a storm spoils all the sport,
And makes him long for a more quiet port,
Which 'gainst all adverse winds may serve for fort.

So he that faileth in this world of pleasure,
    Feeding on sweets, that never bit of the sour,
That's full of friends, of honor, and of treasure,
    Fond fool, he takes this earth e'en for heaven's bower.
But sad affliction comes, and makes him see
Here's neither honor, wealth, nor safety;
Only above is found all with security.

O time, the fatal wreck of mortal things,
That draws oblivion's curtains over kings!
Their sumptuous monuments men know them not,
Their names without a record are forgot,
Their parts, their ports, their pomps, all laid in the dust,
Nor wit, nor gold, nor buildings 'scape time's rust.
But he whose name is graved in the white stone
Shall last and shine when all of these are gone.

"THE FLESH AND THE SPIRIT"
(1678)

Text: *The Poems*, pp. 259-262.

In secret place where once I stood,
Close by the banks of lacrym flood,
I heard two sisters reason on
Things that are past and things to come.
One Flesh was called, who had her eye
On worldly wealth and vanity;
The other Spirit, who did rear
Her thoughts unto a higher sphere.
"Sister," quoth Flesh, "what livest thou on—
Nothing but meditation?
Doth contemplation feed thee, so

Regardlessly to let earth go?
Can speculation satisfy
Notion without reality?
Dost dream of things beyond the moon,
And dost thou hope to dwell there soon?
Hast treasures there laid up in store
That all in the world thou countest poor?
Art fancy sick, or turned a sot,
To catch at shadows which are not?
Come, come, I'll show unto thy sense
Industry hath its recompense.
What canst desire but thou mayst see
True substance in variety?
Dost honor like? Acquire the same,
As some to their immortal fame,
And trophies to thy name erect
Which wearing time shall ne'er deject.
For riches dost thou long full sore?
Behold enough of precious store;
Earth hath more silver, pearls and gold
Than eyes can see or hands can hold.
Affectest thou pleasure? Take thy fill;
Earth hath enough of what you will.
Then let not go what thou mayst find
For things unknown, only in mind."

Spirit. "Be still, thou unregenerate part;
Disturb no more my settled heart,
For I have vowed, and so will do,
Thee as a foe still to pursue,
And combat with thee will and must
Until I see thee laid in the dust.
Sisters we are, yea, twins we be,
Yet deadly feud 'twist thee and me;
For from one father are we not.
Thou by old Adam wast begot,
But my arise is from above,

Whence my dear Father I do love.
Thou speakest me fair, but hatest me sore;
Thy flattering shows I'll trust no more.
How oft thy slave hast thou me made
When I believed what thou hast said,
And never had more cause of woe
Than when I did what thou bad'st do.
I'll stop mine ears at these thy charms,
And count them for my deadly harms.
Thy sinful pleasure I do hate,
Thy riches are to me no bait,
Thine honors do nor will I love,
For my ambition lies above.
My greatest honor it shall be
When I am victor over thee,
And triumph shall, with laurel head,
When thou my captive shalt be led.
How I do live thou needst not scoff,
For I have meat thou knowest not of:
The hidden manna I do eat,
The word of life it is my meat.
My thoughts do yield me more content
Than can thy hours in pleasure spent.
Nor are they shadows which I catch,
Nor fancies vain at which I snatch,
But reach at things that are so high
Beyond thy dull capacity.
Eternal substance I do see,
With which enrichéd I would be;
Mine eye doth pierce the heavens, and see
What is invisible to thee.
My garments are not silk or gold,
Nor such like trash which earth doth hold,
But royal robes I shall have on,
More glorious than the glistering sun.
My crown not diamonds, pearls, and gold,

But such as angels' heads enfold.
The city where I hope to dwell
There's none on earth can parallel:
The stately walls, both high and strong,
Are made of precious jasper stone;
The gates of pearl both rich and clear,
And angels are for porters there;
The streets thereof transparent gold,
Such as no eye did e'er behold;
A crystal river there doth run,
Which doth proceed from the Lamb's throne;
Of life there are the waters sure,
Which shall remain for ever pure;
Of sun or moon they have no need,
For glory doth from God proceed—
No candle there, nor yet torch-light,
For there shall be no darksome night.
From sickness and infirmity
For evermore they shall be free,
Nor withering age shall e'er come there,
But beauty shall be bright and clear.
This city pure is not for thee,
For things unclean there shall not be.
If I of Heaven may have my fill,
Take thou the world, and all that will.

"TO MY DEAR AND LOVING HUSBAND"
(*1678*)

Text: *The Poems,* p. 270.

If ever two were one, then surely we;
If ever man were loved by wife, then thee;
If ever wife was happy in a man,
Compare with me, ye women, if you can.
I prize thy love more than whole mines of gold,
Or all the riches that the East doth hold.

My love is such that rivers cannot quench,
Nor aught but love from thee give recompense.
Thy love is such I can no way repay;
The heavens reward thee manifold, I pray.
Then while we live in love let's so persevere
That when we live no more we may live ever.

"BEFORE THE BIRTH OF ONE OF HER CHILDREN"

(1678)

Text: *The Poems,* pp. 269-270.

All things within this fading world have end.
Adversity doth still our joys attend;
No ties so strong, no friends so dear and sweet,
But with death's parting blow are sure to meet.
The sentence passed is most irrevocable,
A common thing, yet, oh, inevitable.
How soon, my dear, death may my steps attend,
How soon it may be thy lot to lose thy friend,
We both are ignorant; yet love bids me
These farewell lines to recommend to thee,
That when that knot's untied that made us one
I may seem thine who in effect am none.
And if I see not half my days that are due,
What nature would God grant to yours and you.
The many faults that well you know I have
Let be interred in my oblivion's grave;
If any worth or virtue were in me,
Let that live freshly in thy memory,
And when thou feelest no grief, as I no harms,
Yet love thy dead, who long lay in thine arms;
And when thy loss shall be repaid with gains
Look to my little babes, my dear remains,
And if thou love thyself, or lovedst me,
These oh protect from stepdam's injury.
And if chance to thine eyes shall bring this verse,

With some sad sighs honor my absent hearse;
And kiss this paper for thy love's dear sake,
Who with salt tears this last farewell did take.

MICHAEL WIGGLESWORTH
(*1631-1705*)

THE DAY OF DOOM
(*1662*)

Text: *The Day of Doom,* ed. K. B. Murdock (New York, 1929),
pp. 9-65.

I

Still was the night, Serene and Bright,
    when all Men sleeping lay;
Calm was the season, and carnal reason
    thought so 'twould last for ay.
Soul, take thine ease, let sorrow cease,
    much good thou hast in store:
This was their Song, their Cups among,
    the Evening before.

> The security
> of the World
> before Christs
> coming to
> judgment.
> Luke 12:19

2

Wallowing in all kind of sin,
    vile wretches lay secure:
The best of men had scarcely then
    their Lamps kept in good ure.
Virgins unwise, who through disguise
    amongst the best were number'd,
Had clos'd their eyes; yea, and the wise
    through sloth and frailty slumber'd.

> Mat. 25:5

3

Like as of old, when Men grow bold
    Gods' threatnings to contemn,
Who stopt their Ear, and would not hear,

> Mat. 24:37,
> 38

when Mercy warned them:
But took their course, without remorse,
  till God began to powre
Destruction the World upon
  in a tempestuous showre.

4

They put away the evil day,
  And drown'd their care and fears,
Till drown'd were they, and swept away
  by vengeance unawares:

1 Thes. 5:3　So at the last, whilst Men sleep fast
  in their security,
Surpriz'd they are in such a snare
  as cometh suddenly.

5

The sudden-
ness, Majesty,
& Terror of
Christ's ap-
pearing.
Mat. 25:6
2 Pet. 3:10

For at midnight brake forth a Light,
  which turn'd the night to day,
And speedily an hideous cry
  did all the world dismay.
Sinners awake, their hearts do ake,
  trembling their loynes surprizeth;
Amaz'd with fear, by what they hear,
  each one of them ariseth.

6

They rush from Beds with giddy heads,
  and to their windows run,
Viewing this light, which shines more bright
  then doth the Noon-day Sun.

Mat. 24:29,
30

Straightway appears (they see't with tears)
  the Son of God most dread;
Who with his Train comes on amain
  To Judge both Quick and Dead.

7

Before his face the Heav'ns gave place,
  and Skies are rent asunder,   2 Pet. 3:10
With mighty voice, and hideous noise,
  more terrible than Thunder.
His brightness damps heav'ns glorious lamps
  and makes them hide their heads,
As if afraid and quite dismay'd,
  they quit their wonted steads.

8

Ye sons of men that durst contemn
  the Threatnings of Gods Word,
How cheer you now? your hearts, I trow,
  are thrill'd as with a sword.
Now Atheist blind, whose brutish mind
  a God could never see,
Dost thou perceive, dost now believe,
  that Christ thy Judge shall be?

9

Stout Courages, (whose hardiness
  could Death and Hell out-face)
Are you as bold now you behold
  your Judge draw near apace?
They cry, no, no: Alas! and wo!
  our Courage all is gone:
Our hardiness (fool hardiness)
  hath us undone, undone.

10

No heart so bold, but now grows cold
  and almost dead with fear:
No eye so dry, but now can cry,   Rev. 6:16
  and pour out many a tear.

Earths Potentates and pow'rful States,
    Captains and Men of Might
Are quite abasht, their courage dasht
    at this most dreadful sight.

11

Mean men lament, great men do rent
    their Robes, and tear their hair:
Mat. 24:30   They do not spare their flesh to tear
    through horrible despair.
All Kindreds wail: all hearts do fail:
    horror the world doth fill
With weeping eyes, and loud out-cries,
    yet knows not how to kill.

12

Rev. 6:15, 16   Some hide themselves in Caves and Delves,
    in places under ground:
Some rashly leap into the Deap,
    to scape by being drown'd:
Some to the Rocks (O sensless blocks!)
    and woody Mountains run,
That there they might this fearful sight,
    and dreaded Presence shun.

13

In vain do they to Mountains say,
    Fall on us, and us hide
From Judges ire, more hot than fire,
    for who may it abide?
No hiding place can from his Face,
    sinners at all conceal,
Whose flaming Eyes hid things doth 'spy,
    and darkest things reveal.

14

The Judge draws nigh, exalted high
   upon a lofty Throne,
Amidst the throng of Angels strong,
   lo, Israel's Holy One!
The excellence of whose presence
   and awful Majesty,
Amazeth Nature, and every Creature,
   doth more than terrify.

Mat. 25:31

15

The Mountains smoak, the Hills are shook,
   the Earth is rent and torn,
As if she should be clean dissolv'd,
   or from the Center born.
The Sea doth roar, forsakes the shore,
   and shrinks away for fear;
The wild Beasts flee into the Sea,
   so soon as he draws near.

Rev. 6:14

16

Whose Glory bright, whose wondrous might,
   whose Power Imperial,
So far surpass whatever was
   in Realms Terrestrial;
That tongues of men (nor Angels pen)
   cannot the same express,
And therefore I must pass it by,
   lest speaking should transgress.

17

Before his Throne a Trump is blown,
   Proclaiming th' Day of Doom:
Forthwith he cries, *Ye Dead arise,
   and unto Judgment come.*

1 Thes. 4:16
Resurrection
of the Dead.
John 5:28, 29

No sooner said, but 'tis obey'd;
   Sepulchers open'd are:
Dead Bodies all rise at his call,
   and's mighty power declare.

18

Both Sea and Land, at his Command,
   their Dead at once surrender:
The Fire and Air constrained are
   also their dead to tender.
The mighty word of this great Lord
   links Body and Soul together
Both of the Just, and the unjust,
   to part no more for ever.

19

The living
Changed.

The same translates, from Mortal states
   to Immortality,
All that survive, and be alive,
   i' th' twinkling of an eye:

Luk. 20:36
1 Cor. 15:52

That so they may abide for ay
   to endless weal or woe;
Both the Renate and Reprobate
   are made to dy no more.

20

All brought
to Judgment.
Mat. 24:31

His winged Hosts flie through all Coasts,
   together gathering
Both good and bad, both quick and dead,
   and all to Judgment bring.
Out of their holes those creeping Moles,
   that hid themselves for fear,
By force they take, and quickly make
   before the Judge appear.

21

Thus every one before the Throne
   of Christ the Judge is brought,
Both righteous and impious
   that good or ill had wrought.
A separation, and diff'ring station
   by Christ appointed is
(To sinners sad) 'twixt good and bad,
   'twixt Heirs of woe and bliss.

*2 Cor. 5:10
The Sheep
separated
from the
Goats.
Mat. 25*

22

At Christ's right hand the Sheep do stand,
   his holy Martyrs, who
For his dear Name suffering shame,
   calamity and woe,
Like Champions stood, and with their Blood
   their testimony sealed;
Whose innocence without offence,
   to Christ their Judge appealed.

*Who are
Christ's
Sheep.
Mat. 5:10, 11*

23

Next unto whom there find a room
   all Christ's afflicted ones,
Who being chastised, neither despised
   nor sank amidst their groans:
Who by the Rod were turn'd to God,
   and loved him the more,
Not murmuring nor quarrelling
   when they were chast'ned sore.

*Heb. 12:5, 6,
7*

24

Moreover, such as loved much,
   that had not such a tryal,
As might constrain to so great pain,

Luke 7:41, 47

and such deep self denyal:
Yet ready were the Cross to bear,
    when Christ them call'd thereto,
And did rejoyce to hear his voice,
    they're counted Sheep also.

25

Joh. 21:15
Mat. 19:14
Joh. 3:3

Christ's Flock of Lambs there also stands,
    whose Faith was weak, yet true;
All sound Believers (Gospel receivers)
    whose Grace was small, but grew:
And then among an Infant throng
    of Babes, for whom Christ dy'd;
Whom for his own, by wayes unknown
    to men, he sanctify'd.

26

Rev. 6:11
Phil. 3:21

All stand before their Saviour
    in long white Robes yclad,
Their countenance full of pleasance,
    appearing wondrous glad.
O glorious sight! Behold how bright
    dust heaps are made to shine,
Conformed so their Lord unto,
    whose Glory is Divine.

27

The Goats
described or
the several
sorts of Rep-
robates on
the left hand.
Mat. 24:51

At Christ's left hand the Goats do stand,
    all whining hypocrites,
Who for self-ends did seem Christ's friends,
    but foster'd guileful sprites;
Who Sheep resembled, but they dissembled
    (their hearts were not sincere);
Who once did throng Christ's Lambs among,
    but now must not come near.

28

Apostates and Run-awayes,
  such as have Christ forsaken,
Of whom the Devil, with seven more evil,
  hath fresh possession taken:
Sinners in grain, reserv'd to pain
  and torments most severe:
Because 'gainst light they sinn'd with spight,
  are also placed there.

Luk. 11:24, 26
Heb. 6:4, 5, 6
Heb. 10:29

29

There also stand a num'rous band,
  that no Profession made
Of Godliness, nor to redress
  their wayes at all essay'd:
Who better knew, but (sinful Crew)
  Gospel and Law despised;
Who all Christ's knocks withstood like blocks
  and would not be advised.

Luk. 12:47
Prov. 1:24, 26
Joh. 3:19

30

Moreover, there with them appear
  a number, numberless
Of great and small, vile wretches all,
  that did Gods Law transgress:
Idolaters, false worshippers,
  Prophaners of Gods Name,
Who not at all thereon did call,
  or took in vain the same.

Gal. 3:10
1 Cor. 6:9
Rev. 21:8

31

Blasphemers lewd, and Swearers shrewd,
  Scoffers at Purity,
That hated God, contemn'd his Rod,
  and lov'd Security;

Exed. 20:7, & 8

Sabbath-polluters, Saints persecuters,
    Presumptuous men and Proud,

2 Thes. 1:6,
8, 9

Who never lov'd those that reprov'd;
    all stand amongst this Crowd.

32

Heb. 13:4
1 Cor. 6:10

Adulterers and Whoremongers
    were there, with all unchast:
There Covetous, and Ravenous,
    that Riches got too fast:
Who us'd vile ways themselves to raise
    t'Estates and worldly wealth,
Oppression by, or Knavery,
    by force, or fraud, or stealth.

33

Moreover, there together were
    Children flagitious,

Zach, 5:3, 4
Gal. 5:19, 20,
21

And Parents who did them undo
    by Nurture vicious.
False-witness-bearers, and self-forswearers,
    Murd'rers, and Men of blood,
Witches, Inchanters, and Ale-house-haunters,
    beyond account there stood.

34

Their place there find all Heathen blind,
    that Natures light abused,

Rom. 2:13

Although they had no tydings glad,
    of Gospel-grace refused.
There stands all Nations and Generations
    of *Adam's* Progeny,
Whom Christ redeem'd not, who Christ esteem'd
    not,
    through Infidelity.

35

Who no Peace-maker, no Undertaker,
    to shrow'd them from Gods ire,
Ever obtain'd; they must be pained
    with everlasting fire.
These num'rous bands, wringing their hands
    and weeping, all stand there,
Filled with anguish, whose hearts do languish
    through self-tormenting fear.

Act. 4:12

36

Fast by them stand at Christ's left hand
    the Lion fierce and fell,
The Dragon bold, that Serpent old,
    that hurried Souls to Hell.
There also stand, under command,
    Legions of Sprights unclean,
And hellish Fiends, that are no friends
    to God, nor unto Men.

1 Cor. 6:3

37

With dismal chains, and strongest reins,
    like Prisoners of Hell,
They're held in place before Christ's face,
    till He their Doom shall tell.
These void of tears, but fill'd with fears,
    and dreadful expectation
Of endless pains, and scalding flames,
    stand waiting for Damnation.

Jude 6

38

All silence keep, both Goats and Sheep,
    before the Judge's Throne;
With mild aspect to his Elect
    then spake the Holy One:
My Sheep draw near, your Sentence hear,

The Saints
cleared &
justified.

which is to you no dread,
Who clearly now discern, and know
    your sins are pardoned.

39

2 Cor. 5:10
Eccles. 3:17
Joh. 3:18

'Twas meet that ye should judged be,
    that so the world may spy
No cause of grudge, when as I Judge
    and deal impartially.
Know therefore all, both great and small,
    the ground and reason why
These Men do stand at my right hand,
    and look so chearfully.

40

Joh. 17:6
Eph. 1:4

These Men be those my Father chose
    before the worlds foundation,
And to me gave, that I should save
    from Death and Condemnation.
For whose dear sake I flesh did take,
    was of a Woman born,
And did inure my self t' indure,
    unjust reproach and scorn.

41

For them it was that I did pass
    through sorrows many one:
That I drank up that bitter Cup,
Rev. 1:5   which made me sigh and groan.
The Cross his pain I did sustain;
    yea more, my Fathers ire
I underwent, my Blood I spent
    to save them from Hell fire.

42

Thus I esteem'd, thus I redeem'd
  all these from every Nation,
That they may be (as now you see)
  a chosen Generation.
What if ere-while they were as vile,
  and bad as any be,   Eph. 2:1, 3
And yet from all their guilt and thrall
  at once I set them free?

43

My grace to one is wrong to none: Mat. 20:13,
  none can Election claim,   15
Amongst all those their souls that lose, Rom. 9:20,
  none can Rejection blame.   21
He that may chuse, or else refuse,
  all men to save or spill,
May this Man chuse, and that refuse,
  redeeming whom he will.

44

But as for those whom I have chose   Isa. 53:4, 5,
  Salvations heirs to be,   11
I underwent their punishment,
  and therefore set them free;
I bore their grief, and their relief
  by suffering procur'd,
That they of bliss and happiness
  might firmly be assur'd.

45

And this my grace they did imbrace,   Acts. 13:48
  believing on my Name;   Jam. 2:18
Which Faith was true, the fruits do shew Heb. 12:7
  proceeding from the same: Mat. 19:29

Their Pentinence, their Patience,
   their Love and Self-denial
In suffering losses, and bearing Crosses,
   when put upon the tryal.

46

Their sin forsaking, their chearful taking
   my yoke, their Charity
Unto the Saints in all their wants,
   and in them unto me,
These things do clear, and make appear
   their Faith to be unfaigned,
And that a part in my desert
   and purchase they have gained.

1 Joh. 3:3
Mat. 25:39,
40

47

Their debts are paid, their peace is made,
   their sins remitted are;
Therefore at once I do pronounce,
   and openly declare
That Heav'n is theirs, that they be Heirs
   of Life and of Salvation!
Nor ever shall they come at all
   to Death or to Damnation.

Isa. 53:11, 12
Rom. 8:16,
17, 33, 34
John 3:18

48

Come, Blessed Ones, and sit on Thrones,
   Judging the World with me:
Come, and possess your happiness,
   and bought felicitie.
Henceforth no fears, no care, no tears,
   no sin shall you annoy,
Nor any thing that grief doth bring:
   Eternal Rest enjoy.

Luk. 22:29,
30
Mat. 19:28

49

You bore the Cross, you suffered loss
   of all for my Names sake:
Receive the Crown that's now your own;
   come, and a Kingdom take.
Thus spake the Judge; the wicked grudge,
   and grind their teeth in vain;
They see with groans these plac't on Thrones
   which addeth to their pain:

Mat. 25:34
They are
placed on
Thrones to
joyn with
Christ in
judging the
wicked.

50

That those whom they did wrong and slay,
   must now their judgment see!
Such whom they slighted, and once despighted,
   must now their Judges be!
Thus 'tis decreed, such is their meed,
   and guerdon glorious!
With Christ they sit, Judging is fit
   to plague the Impious.

1 Cor. 6:2

51

The wicked are brought to the Bar,
   like guilty Malefactors,
That oftentimes of bloody Crimes
   and Treasons have been Actors.
Of wicked Men, none are so mean
   as there to be neglected:
Nor none so high in dignity,
   as there to be respected.

The wicked
brought to
the Bar.
Rom. 2:3, 6,
11

52

The glorious Judge will priviledge
   nor Emperour, nor King:
But every one that hath mis-done
   doth into Judgment bring.

Rev. 6:15, 16
Isa. 30:33

And every one that hath mis-done,
  the Judge impartially
Condemneth to eternal wo,
  and endless misery.

53

Thus one and all, thus great and small,
  the Rich as well as Poor,
And those of place as the most base,
  do stand the Judge before.
They are arraign'd, and there detain'd,
  before Christ's Judgment-seat
With trembling fear, their Doom to hear,
  and feel his angers heat.

54

Eccles. 11:9 &
12:14

There Christ demands at all their hands
  a strict and strait account
Of all things done under the Sun,
  whose number far surmount
Man's wit and thought: yet all are brought
  unto this solemn Tryal;
And each offence with evidence,
  so that there's no denial.

55

There's no excuses for their abuses,
  since their own Consciences
More proof give in of each Man's sin,
  than thousand Witnesses,
Though formerly this faculty
  had grosly been abused,
Men could it stifle, or with it trifle,
  when as it them accused.

56

Now it comes in, and every sin
   unto Mens charge doth lay:
It judgeth them, and doth condemn,
   though all the world say nay.
It so stingeth and tortureth,
   it worketh such distress,
That each Man's self against himself,
   is forced to confess.

57

It's vain, moreover, for Men to cover
   the least iniquity:
The Judge hath seen, and privy been
   to all their villany.
He unto light, and open sight
   the works of darkness brings:
He doth unfold both new and old,
   both known and hidden things.

Secret sins
and works of
darkness
brought to
light.
Psal. 139:2, 4,
12
Rom. 2:16

58

All filthy facts, and secret acts,
   however closly done,
And long conceal'd, are there reveal'd
   before the mid-day Sun.
Deeds of the night shunning the light,
   which darkest corners sought,
To fearful blame, and endless shame,
   are there most justly brought.

Eccles. 12:14

59

And as all facts and grosser acts,
   so every word and thought,
Erroneous notion, and lustful motion,
   are unto judgment brought,

Mat. 12:36
Rom. 7:7

No sin so small and trivial
   but hither it must come:
Nor so long past, but now at last
   it must receive a doom.

60

An account
demanded of
all their ac-
tions.
Joh. 5:40 &
3:19
Mat. 25:19,
27

At this sad season, Christ asks a Reason
   (with just Austerity)
Of Grace refused, of light abus'd
   so oft, so wilfully:
Of Talents lent by them mispent,
   and on their Lust bestown;
Which if improv'd, as it behov'd,
   Heav'n might have been their own!

61

Of times neglected, of means rejected,
   of God's long-suffering,

Rom. 2:4, 5

And Patience, to Penitence
   that sought hard hearts to bring.
Why Cords of love did nothing move
   to shame or to remorse?
Why warnings grave, and counsels, have
   nought chang'd their sinful course?

62

Why chastenings, and evil things,
   why judgments so severe

Isa. 1:5

Prevailed not with them a jot,
   nor wrought an awful fear?

Jer. 2:20

Why Promises of Holiness,
   and new Obedience,
They oft did make, but always brake
   the same, to God's offence?

63

Why still Hell-ward, without regard,
    they boldly ventured,
And chose Damnation before Salvation,
    when it was offered:
Why sinful pleasures, and earthly treasures,
    like fools, they prized more
Than heav'nly wealth, Eternal health,
    and all Christ's Royal store.

John 3:19, 20
Prov. 8:36
Luk. 12:20,
21

64

Why, when he stood off'ring his Blood
    to wash them from their sin,
They would embrace no saving Grace,
    but liv'd and dy'd therein?
Such aggravations, where no evasions,
    nor false pretences hold,
Exaggerate and cumulate
    guilt more than can be told.

Luk. 13:34
Joh. 5:40 &
15:22

65

They multiply and magnify
    mens gross iniquities,
They draw down wrath (as Scripture saith)
    out of Gods treasuries.
Thus all their ways Christ open lays
    to men and Angels view,
And, as they were, makes them appear
    in their own proper hew.

66

Thus he doth find of all Mankind,
    that stand at his left hand,
No Mothers Son, but hath mis-done,
    and broken God's Command.

Rom. 3:10,
12

All have transgrest, even the best,
   and merited God's wrath
Unto their own perdition,
   and everlasting scath.

67

Rom. 6:23

Earths dwellers all, both great and small,
   have wrought iniquity,
And suffer must, for it is just,
   Eternal misery.
Amongst the many there come not any,
   before the Judge's face,
That able are themselves to clear,
   of all this cursed race.

68

Nevertheless, they all express,
   Christ granting liberty,
What for their way they have to say,
   how they have liv'd, and why.

Hypocrites
plead for
themselves

They all draw near, and seek to clear
   themselves by making pleas;
There Hypocrites, false hearted wights,
   do make such pleas as these:

69

Lord, in thy Name, and by the same,
   we Devils dispossest,

Mat. 7:21, 22, 23

We rais'd the dead, and ministred
   succour to the distrest.
Our painful teaching, and pow'rful preaching
   by thine own wondrous might,
Did throughly win to God from sin
   many a wretched wight.

70

All this, quoth he, may granted be,
    and your case little better'd,
Who still remain under a chain,
    and many irons fetter'd.
You that the dead have quickened,
    and rescu'd from the grave,
Your selves were dead, yet never ned,
    a Christ your Souls to save.

The judge
replyeth. Joh.
6:70
1 Cor. 9:27

71

You that could preach, and others teach
    what way to life doth lead;
Why were you slack to find that track,
    and in that way to tread?
How could you bear to see or hear
    of others freed at last,
From Satan's pawes, whilst in his jawes
    your selves were held more fast?

Rom. 2:19:
21, 22, 23

72

Who though you knew Repentance true,
    and Faith in my great Name,
The only mean to quit you clean,
    from punishment and blame,
Yet took no pain true Faith to gain,
    such as might not deceive,
Nor would repent, with true intent,
    your evil deeds to leave.

Joh. 9:41

Rev. 2:21, 22

73

His Masters will how to fulfill
    the servant that well knew,
Yet left undone his duty known,
    more plagues to him are due.

Luk. 12:47
Mat. 11:21,
22, 24

You against light perverted right;
    wherefore it shall be now
For *Sidon* and for *Sodoms* Land
    more easie than for you.

74

*Another plea
of hypocrites.
Luk. 13:26*

But we have in thy presence been,
    say some, and eaten there.
Did we not eat thy Flesh for meat,
    and feed on heavenly Cheer?
Whereon who feed shall never need,
    as thou thy self dost say,
Nor shall they dy eternally,
    but live with Christ for ay.

75

We may alledge, thou gav'st a pledge
    of thy dear love to us
In Wine and Bread, which figured
    thy Grace bestowed thus.
Of strengthning Seals, of sweetest Meals,
    have we so oft partaken;
And shall we be cast off by thee,
    and utterly forsaken?

76

*Is Answered.
Luk. 13:27
Mat. 22:12*

To whom the Lord thus in a word
    returns a short reply,
I never knew any of you
    that wrought iniquity.
You say y'have been my Presence in;
    but friends, how came you there
With Raiment vile that did defile
    and quite disgrace my Cheer?

77

Durst you draw near without due fear
   unto my holy Table?
Durst you prophane, and render vain
   so far as you were able,
Those Mysteries? which whoso prize
   and carefully improve
Shall saved be undoubtedly,
   and nothing shall them move.

78

How durst you venture, bold guests, to enter
   in such a sordid hew,
Amongst my guests, unto those Feasts   1 Cor. 11:27, 29
   that were not made for you?
How durst you eat for spiritual meat
   your bane, and drink damnation,
Whilst by your guide you rendred vile
   so rare and great Salvation?

79

Your fancies fed on heav'nly Bread,
   your hearts fed on some Lust:
You lov'd the Creature more than th' Creator,
   your Souls clave to the dust.   Mat. 6:21, 24
And think you by Hypocrisie,   Rom. 1:25
   and cloaked Wickedness,
To enter in, laden with sin,
   to lasting happiness?

80

This your excuse shews your abuse   1 Cor. 11:27, 29
   of things ordain'd for good;
And doth declare you guilty are
   of my dear Flesh and Blood.

Wherefore those Seals and precious Meals
   you put so much upon
As things divine, they seal and sign
   you to Perdition.

81

Then forth issue another Crew
   (those being silenced)

*Another sort
of hypocrites
make their
pleas.*

Who drawing nigh to the most High
   adventure thus to plead:
We sinners were, say they, it's clear,
   deserving Condemnation:
But did not we rely on thee,
   O Christ, for whole Salvation?

82

We did believe and oft receive
   thy gracious promises:

*Act. 8:13
Isa. 58:2, 3
Heb. 64:5*

We took great care to get a share
   in endless happiness.
We pray'd and wept, we Fast-dayes kept,
   lewd ways we did eschew:
We joyful were thy Word to hear;
   we form'd our lives anew.

83

We thought our sin had pard'ned been;
   that our Estate was good,
Our debts all paid, our peace well made,
   our Souls wash'd with thy Blood.

2 Pet. 2:20

Lord, why dost thou reject us now,
   who have not thee rejected,
Nor utterly true sanctity
   and holy life neglected.

84

The Judge incensed at their pretenced
  self-vanting Piety,
With such a look as trembling strook
  into them, made reply;
O impudent, impenitent,
  and guileful generation!
Think you that I cannot descry
  your hearts abomination?

The Judge
uncaseth
them.

John. 2:24,
25

85

You nor receiv'd, nor yet believ'd
  my Promises of Grace;
Nor were you wise enough to prize
  my reconciled Face:
But did presume that to assume
  which was not yours to take,
And challenged the Childrens bread,
  yet would not sin forsake.

Joh. 6:64

Psal. 50:16
Mat. 15:26

86

Being too bold you laid fast hold,
  where int'rest you had none,
Your selves deceiving by your believing,
  all which you might have known,
You ran away, but ran astray,
  with Gospel-promises,
And perished; being still dead
  in sins and trespasses.

Rev. 3:17

Mat. 13:20

87

How oft did I Hypocrisie
  and Hearts deceit unmask
Before your sight, giving you light
  to know a Christians task?
But you held fast unto the last

Mat. 6:2, 4,
24
Jer. 8:5, 6, 7,
8

your own Conceits so vain;
   No warning could prevail, you would
     your own Deceits retain.

88

As for your care to get a share
     in bliss; the fear of Hell,
Psal. 78:34,   And of a part in endless smart,
35, 36, 37   did thereunto compel.
Your holiness and ways redress,
     such as it was, did spring
From no true love to things above,
     but from some other thing.

89

Zach. 7:5, 6   You pray'd and wept, you Fast-days kept;
Isa. 58:3, 4   but did you this to me?
1 Sam. 15:13,   No, but for sin, you sought to win,
21   the greater libertie.
Isaiah 1:11,   For all your vaunts, you had vile haunts,
15   for which your Consciences
Did you alarm, whose voice to charm
     you us'd these practices.

90

Your Penitence, your diligence
     to Read, to Pray, to Hear,
Mat. 6:2, 5   Were but to drown'd the clamorous sound
John 5:44   of Conscience in your ear.
If light you lov'd, vain glory mov'd
     your selves therewith to store,
That seeming wise, men might you prize,
     and honour you the more.

91

Thus from your selves unto your selves,
   your duties all do tend:
And as self-love the wheels doth move,
   so in self-love they end.
Thus Christ detects their vain projects,
   and close Impiety,
And plainly shews that all their shows
   were but Hypocrisy.

Zach. 7:15, 6
Hos. 10:1

92

Then were brought nigh a Company
   of Civil honest Men,
That lov'd true dealing, and hated stealing,
   ne'r wrong'd their Bretheren;
Who pleaded thus, Thou knowest us
   that we were blameless livers;
No Whoremongers, no Murderers,
   no quarrellers nor strivers.

Civil honest
mens pleas.
Luk. 18:11

93

Idolaters, Adulterers,
   Church-robbers we were none,
Nor false-dealers, no couzeners,
   but paid each man his own.
Our way was fair, our dealing square,
   we were no wastful spenders,
No lewd toss-pots, no drunken sots,
   no scandalous offenders.

94

We hated vice, and set great price,
   by vertuous conversation:
And by the same we got a name,
   and no small commendation.

1 Sam. 15:22
Gods Laws express that righteousness,
    is that which he doth prize;
And to obey, as he doth say,
    is more than sacrifice.

95

Thus to obey, hath been our way;
    let our good deeds, we pray,
Find some regard and some reward
    with thee, O Lord, this day.

Eccles. 7:20
And whereas we transgressors be,
    of *Adam's* Race were none,
No not the best, but have confest
    themselves to have mis-done.

96

Are taken off
& rendered
invalid.
Deut. 10:12
Tit. 2:12
Jam. 2:10
Then answered unto their dread,
    the Judge: True Piety
God doth desire and eke require
    no less than honesty.
Justice demands at all your hands
    perfect Obedience:
If but in part you have come short,
    that is a just offence.

97

On Earth below, where men did ow
    a thousand pounds and more,
Could twenty pence it recompence?
    could that have clear'd the score?
Think you to buy felicity
    with part of what's due debt?
Or for desert of one small part,
    the whole should off be set?

98

And yet that part, whose great desert
  you think to reach so far
For your excuse, doth you accuse,
  and will your boasting mar.
However fair, however square,
  your way and work hath been,
Before mens eyes, yet God espies
  iniquity therein.

Luk. 18:11,
14

99

God looks upon th' affection
  and temper of the heart;
Not only on the action,
  and the external part.
Whatever end vain men pretend,
  God knows the verity;
And by the end which they intend
  their words and deeds doth try.

1 Sam. 16:7
2 Chron. 25:2

100

Without true Faith, the Scripture saith
  God cannot take delight
In any deed, that doth proceed
  from any sinful wight.
And without love all actions prove
  but barren empty things.
Dead works they be, and vanitie,
  the which vexation brings.

Heb. 11:6

1 Cor. 13:1,
2, 3

101

Nor from true faith, which quencheth wrath,
  hath your obedience flown:
Nor from true love, which wont to move
  Believers, hath it grown.

Your argument shews your intent,
    in all that you have done:
You thought to scale Heav'ns lofty Wall
    by Ladders of your own.

102

Rom. 10:3

Your blinded spirit, hoping to merit
    by your own Righteousness,
Needed no Saviour, but your behaviour,
    and blameless carriages;
You trusted to what you could do,
    and in no need you stood:
Your haughty pride laid me aside,
    and trampled on my Blood.

103

All men have gone astray, and done,
    that which Gods Laws condemn:
But my Purchase and offered Grace

Rom. 9:30,
32
Mat. 11:23,
24 & 12:41

    all men did not contemn.
The *Ninevites,* and *Sodomites,*
    had no such sin as this:
Yet as if all your sins were small,
    you say, All did amiss.

104

Mat. 6:5

Again you thought and mainly sought
    a name with men t' acquire;
Pride bare the Bell, that made you swell,
    and your own selves admire.
Mean fruit it is, and vile, I wiss,
    that springs from such a root:
Vertue divine and genuine
    wonts not from pride to shoot.

105

Such deeds as your are worse than poor;
   they are but sins guilt over
With silver dross, whose glistering gloss   Prov. 26:23
   can them no longer cover.   Mat. 23:27
The best of them would you condemn,
   and ruine you alone,
Although you were from faults so clear,
   that other you had none.

106

Your Gold is brass, your silver dross,   Prov. 15:8
   your righteousness is sin: Rom. 3:20
And think you by such honesty
   eternal life to win?
You much mistake, if for its sake
   you dream of acceptation;
Whereas the same deserveth shame,
   and meriteth Damnation.

107

A wond'rous Crowd then 'gan aloud,   Those that
   thus for themselves to say,   pretend want
We did intend, Lord to amend,   of opportu-
   and to reform our way: nity to repent.
Our true intent was to repent,   Prov. 27:1
   and make our peace with thee;   Jam. 4:13
But sudden death stopping our breath,
   left us no libertie.

108

Short was our time, for in his prime
   our youthful flow'r was cropt:
We dy'd in youth, before full growth,
   so was our purpose stopt.

Let our good will to turn from ill,
   and sin to have forsaken,
Accepted be, O Lord, by thee,
   and in good part be taken.

109

Are confuted
and Con-
vinced.
Eccles. 12:1
Rev. 2:21

To whom the Judge: where you alledge
   the shortness of the space,
That from your birth you liv'd on earth,
   to compass saving Grace:
It was Free grace that any space
   was given you at all
To turn from evil, defie the Devil,
   and upon God to call.

110

Luk. 13:24
2 Cor. 6:2
Heb. 3:7, 8, 9

One day, one week, wherein to seek
   God's face with all your hearts,
A favour was that far did pass
   the best of your deserts.
You had a season, what was your reason
   such precious hours to waste?
What could you find, what could you mind
   that was of greater haste?

111

Could you find time for vain pastime,
   for loose licentious mirth?

Eccles. 11:9
Luk. 14:18,
19, 20

For fruitless toyes, and fading joyes
   that perish in the birth?
Had you good leasure for carnal Pleasure,
   in dayes of health and youth?
And yet no space to seek God's face,
   and turn to him in truth?

112

In younger years, beyond your fears,
    what if you were surprised?
You put away the evil day,
    and of long life devised.
You oft were told, and might behold,
    that Death no Age doth spare;
Why then did you your time foreslow,
    and slight your Souls welfare?

Amos 6:3 to 6

Eph. 5:16
Luk. 19:42

113

Had your intent been to repent,
    and had you it desir'd,
There would have been endeavours seen,
    before your time expir'd.
God makes no treasure, nor hath he pleasure,
    in idle purposes:
Such fair pretences are foul offences,
    and cloaks for wickedness.

Luk. 13:24,
25 &c.
Phil. 2:12

114

Then were brought in, and charg'd with sin,
    another Company,
Who by Petition obtain'd permission,
    to make Apology:
They argued, We were misled,
    as is well known to thee,
By their Example, that had more ample
    abilities than we:

Some plead
Examples of
their betters.
Mat. 18:7

115

Such as profest they did detest,
    and hate each wicked way:
Whose seeming grace whilst we did trace,
    our Souls were led astray.

John 7:48

When men of Parts, Learning and Arts,
    Professing Piety,
Did thus and thus, it seem'd to us
    we might take liberty.

116

*Who are told
that Exam-
ples are no
Rules.
Psal. 19:8, 11
Exo. 23:2
Psal. 50:17,
18*

The Judge replies, I gave you eyes,
    and light to see your way,
Which had you lov'd, and well improv'd
    you had not gone astray.
My Word was pure, the Rule was sure,
    why did you it forsake,
Or thereon trample, and mens example
    your Directory make?

117

2 Tim. 3:5

This you well knew, that God is true
    and that most men are liars,
In word professing holiness,
    in deed thereof deniers.
O simple fools! that having Rules
    your lives to regulate,
Would then refuse, and rather chuse
    vile men to imitate.

118

*They urge
that they
were misled
by godly
mens Exam-
ples.
But all their
shifts turn to
their greater
shame.
1 Cor. 11*

But Lord, say they, we went astray,
    and did more wickedlie,
By means of those whom thou hast chose
    Salvation heirs to be.
To whom the Judge: What you alledge,
    doth nothing help the case;
But makes appear how vile you were,
    and rend'reth you more base.

119

You understood that what was good,
　　was to be followed,
And that you ought that which was naught
　　to have relinquished.
Contrariwayes, it was your guise,　　　　　Phil. 4:8
　　only to imitate
Good mens defects, and their neglects
　　that were regenerate.

120

But to express their holiness,
　　or imitate their grace,
You little car'd, nor once prepar'd　　　　Psal. 32:5
　　your hearts to seek my face.　　　　　2 Chro. 32:26
They did repent, and truly rent　　　　　Mat. 26:75
　　their hearts for all known sin:　　　　Prov. 1:24,
You did offend, but not amend,　　　　　25
　　to follow them therein.

121

We had thy Word, say some, O Lord,　　Some plead
　　but wiser men than we　　　　　　　the Scriptures
Could never yet interpret it,　　　　　　darkness.
　　but alway disagree.　　　　　　　　And differ-
How could we fools be led by Rules,　　ence amongst
　　so far beyond our ken,　　　　　　　Interpreters.
Which to explain did so much pain,　　　2 Pet. 3:16
　　and puzzle wisest men?

122

Was all my word abstruse and hard?
　　the Judge then answered:　　　　　　They are con-
It did contain much truth so plain,　　　futed.
　　you might have run and read,　　　　Pro. 14:6
But what was hard you never car'd　　　Isa. 35:8
　　　　　　　　　　　　　　　　　　Hos. 8:12

to know nor studied,
And things that were most plain and clear
  you never practised.

123

Mat. 11:25
The Mystery of Pietie
  God unto Babes reveals,
When to the wise he it denies,
  and from the world conceals.

Prov. 2:3, 4, 5
If to fulfil Gods holy will
  had seemed good to you,
You would have sought light as you ought,
  and done the good you knew.

124

Others the fear of Persecution.
Acts 28:22
Then came in view another Crew,
  and 'gan to make their pleas.
Amongst the rest, some of the best
  had such poor shifts as these:
Thou know'st right well, who all canst tell
  we liv'd amongst thy foes,
Who the Renate did sorely hate,
  and goodness much oppose.

125

We holiness durst not profess,
  fearing to be forlorn
John 12:42, 43
Of all our friends, and for amends
  to be the wickeds scorn.
We knew their anger would much endanger
  our lives, and our estates:
Therefore for fear we durst appear
  no better than our mates.

126

To whom the Lord returns this word:
 O wonderful deceits!
To cast off aw of Gods strict Law,
 and fear mens wrath and threats.
To fear hell-fire and Gods fierce ire
 less than the rage of men,
As if Gods wrath, could do less scath
 than wrath of bretheren.

They are
answered.
Luk. 12:4, 5
Isa. 51:12, 13

127

To use such strife, a temporal life,
 to rescue and secure,
And be so blind as not to mind
 that life that will endure:
This was your case, who carnal peace
 more than true joyes did favour;
Who fed on dust, clave to your lust,
 and spurned at my favour.

128

To please your kin, mens love to win,
 to flow in wordly wealth,
To save your skin, these things have bin
 more than Eternal health.
You had your choice, wherein rejoyce,
 it was your portion,
For which you chose your Souls t'expose
 unto perdition.

Luk. 9:23,
24, 25
Chap. 16:25

129

Who did not hate friends, life, and state,
 with all things else for me,
And all forsake, and's Cross up-take,
 shall never happy be.

Luk. 9:26
Prov. 8:36
John 3:19, 20

Well worthy they to dye for ay,
　　who death then life had rather:
Death is their due, that so value
　　the friendship of my Father.

130

Others plead
for Pardon
both from
Gods mercy
and justice.
Psal. 78:38

Others Argue, and not a few,
　　is not God gracious?
His Equity and Clemency
　　are they not marvellous?
Thus we believ'd; are we deceiv'd?
　　cannot his mercy great,
(As hath been told to us of old)
　　asswage his angers heat?

131

2 Kings
14:26

How can it be that God should see
　　his Creatures endless pain,
Or hear the groans and rueful moans,
　　and still his wrath retain?
Can it agree with Equitie?
　　can mercy have the heart
To recompence few years offence
　　with Everlasting smart?

132

Can God delight in such a sight
　　as sinners misery?
Or what great good can this our blood
　　bring unto the most High?
Psal. 30:9
Mic. 7:18
Oh, thou that dost thy Glory most
　　in pard'ning sin display!
Lord, might it please thee to release,
　　and pardon us this day?

133

Unto thy Name more glorious fame
  would not such mercy bring?
Would not it raise thine endless praise,
  more than our suffering?
With that they cease, holding their peace,
  but cease not still to weep;
Grief ministers a flood of tears,
  in which their words do steep.

134

But all too late, grief's out of date,
  when life is at an end.
The glorious King thus answering,
  all to his voice attend:
God gracious is, quoth he, like his
  no mercy can be found;
His Equity and Clemency
  to sinners do abound.

They an-
swered.

135

As may appear by those that here
  are plac'd at my right hand;
Whose stripes I bore, and clear'd the score,
  that they might quitted stand.
For surely none, but God alone,
  whose Grace transcends mens thought,
For such as those that were his foes
  like wonders would have wrought.

Mercy that
now shines
forth in the
vessels of
Mercy.
Mic. 7:18
Rom. 9:23

136

And none but he such lenitee
  and patience would have shown
To you so long, who did him wrong,
  and pull'd his judgments down.
How long a space (O stiff neck'd race)

Did also long
wait upon
such as
abused it.
Rom. 2:4
Hos. 11:4

did patience you afford?
How oft did love you gently move,
   to turn unto the Lord?

137

Luk. 13:34
The day of
Grace now
past.

With Cords of love God often strove
   your stubborn hearts to tame:
Nevertheless your wickedness,
   did still resist the same.
If now at last Mercy be past
   from you for evermore,
And Justice come in Mercies room,
   yet grudge you not therefore.

138

If into wrath God turned hath
   his long long suffering,

Luk. 19:42,
43
Jude 4

And now for love you vengeance prove,
   it is an equal thing.
Your waxing worse, hath stopt the course
   of wonted Clemency:
Mercy refus'd and Grace misus'd,
   call for severity.

139

Rom. 2:5, 6
Isa. 1:24
Amos 2:13
Gen. 18:25

It's now high time that ev'ry Crime
   be brought to punishment:
Wrath long contain'd, and oft restrain'd,
   at last must have a vent:
Justice severe cannot forbear
   to plague sin any longer,
But must inflict with hand most strict
   mischief upon the wronger.

140

In vain do they for Mercy pray.
   the season being past,
Who had no care to get a share
   therein, while time did last.
The man whose ear refus'd to hear
   the voice of Wisdoms cry,
Earn'd this reward, that none regard
   him in his misery.

Mat. 25:3, 11, 12
Prov. 1:28, 29, 30

141

It doth agree with equity,
   and with Gods holy Law,
That those should dye eternally
   that death upon them draw.
The Soul that sins damnation wins,
   for so the Law ordains;
Which Law is just, and therefore must
   such suffer endless pain.

Isa. 5:18, 19
Gen. 2:17
Rom. 2:8, 9

142

Eternal smart is the desert,
   ev'n of the least offence;
Then wonder not if I allot
   to you this Recompence:
But wonder more, that since so sore
   and lasting plagues are due
To every sin, you liv'd therein,
   who well the danger knew.

Rom. 6:23
2 Thess. 1:8, 9

143

God hath no joy to crush or 'stroy,
   and ruine wretched wights,
But to display the glorious Ray
   of Justice he delights.

Ezek. 33:11
Exod. 34:7
& 14:17
Rom. 9, 22

To manifest he doth detest,
   and throughly hate all sin,
By plaguing it as is most fit,
   this shall him glory win.

144

Then at the Bar arraigned are
   an impudenter sort,

Some pretend
they were
shut out
from Heaven
by Gods
Decree.
Rom. 9:18,
19

Who to evade the guilt that's laid
   upon them, thus retort;
How could we cease thus to transgress?
   how could we Hell avoid,
Whom Gods Decree shut out from thee,
   and sign'd to be destroy'd?

145

Whom God ordains to endless pains,
   by Law unalterable,
Repentance true, Obedience new,
   to save such are unable:

Heb. 22:17
Rom. 11:7, 8

Sorrow for sin, no good can win,
   to such as are rejected;
Ne can they grieve, nor yet believe,
   that never were elected.

146

Of Man's fall'n Race, who can true Grace,
   or Holiness obtain?
Who can convert or change his heart,
   if God withhold the same?
Had we apply'd our selves, and try'd
   as much as who did most
God's love to gain, our busie pain
   and labour had been lost.

147

Christ readily makes this Reply,
    I damn you not because
You are rejected, or not elected,
    but you have broke my Laws:
It is but vain your wits to strain,
    the end and means to sever:
Men fondly seek to part or break
    what God hath link'd together.

Their pleas taken off.
Luk. 13:27
2 Pet. 1:9, 10
compared
with
Mat. 19:6

148

Whom God will save, such he will have,
    the means of life to use:
Whom he'll pass by, shall chuse to dy,
    and ways of life refuse.
He that fore-sees, and foredecrees,
    in wisdom order'd has,
That man's free-will electing ill,
    shall bring his will to pass.

Acts 3:19 &
16:31
* 1 Sam. 2:15
John 3:19
Joh. 5:40
2 Thes. 2:11,
12

149

High God's Decree, as it is free,
    so doth it none compel
Against their will to good or ill,
    it forceth none to Hell.
They have their wish whose Souls perish
    with Torments in Hell-fire,
Who rather chose their Souls to lose,
    than leave a loose desire.

Ezek. 33:11,
12, 13
Luk. 13:34
Prov. 8:33,
36

150

God did ordain sinners to pain
    and I to Hell send none,
But such as swerv'd, and have deserv'd
    destruction as their own,

Gen. 2:17
Mat. 25:41,
42
Ezek. 18:20

His pleasure is, that none from bliss
    and endless happiness
Be barr'd, but such as wrong'd him much
    by wilful wickedness.

151

You, sinful Crew, no other knew
    but you might be elect;
Why did you then your selves condemn?
    why did you me reject?
Where was your strife to gain that life
    which lasteth evermore?
You never knock'd, yet say God lock'd
    against you Heav'ns door.

2 Pet. 1:10
Acts 13:46
Luk. 13:24

152

'Twas no vain task to knock, to ask,
    whilst life continued.
Whoever sought heav'n as he ought,
    and seeking perished?
The lowly meek who truly seek
    for Christ, and for Salvation,
There's no Decree whereby such be
    ordain'd to Condemnation.

Mat. 7:7, 8
Gal. 5:22, 23

153

You argue then: But abject men,
    whom God resolves to spill,
Cannot repent, nor their hearts rent;
    ne can they change their will.
Not for his *Can* is any man
    adjudged unto Hell:
But for his *Will* to do what's ill,
    and nilling to do well.

John 3:19

154

I often stood tend'ring my Blood
  to wash away your guilt:
And eke my Spright to frame you right,
  lest your Souls should be spilt.
But you vile Race, rejected Grace,   John 5:40
  when Grace was freely proffer'd:
No changed heart, no heav'nly part
  would you, when it was offer'd.

155

Who wilfully the Remedy,
  and means of life contemned,
Cause have the same themselves to blame,
  if now they be condemned.   John 15:22,
You have your selves, you and none else,   24
  your selves have done to dy.   Heb. 2:3
You chose the way to your decay,   Isa. 66:3, 4
  and perisht wilfully.

156

These words appall and daunt them all;
  dismai'd, and all amort,
Like stocks they stand at Christ's left-hand,
  and dare no more retort.
Then were brought near with trembling fear,
  a number numberless
Of blind Heathen, and brutish men,
  that did Gods Laws transgress.

157

Whose wicked ways Christ open layes,   Heathen men
  and makes their sins appear,   plead want of
They making pleas their case to ease,   the written
  if not themselves to clear.   Word.

Thy written Word (say they) good Lord,
   we never did enjoy:
We nor refus'd, nor it abus'd;
   Oh, do not us destroy!

158

Mat. 11:22
Luk. 12:48

You ne'r abus'd, nor yet refus'd
   my written Word, you plead,
That's true (quoth he) therefore shall ye
   the less be punished.
You shall not smart for any part
   of other mens offence,
But for your own transgression
   receive due recompence.

159

1 Cor. 1:21
And insuffi-
ciency of the
Light of
Nature.

But we were blind, say they, in mind,
   too dim was Natures Light,
Our only guide, as hath been try'd
   to bring us to the sight
Of our estate degenerate,
   and curst by *Adam's* Fall;
How we were born and lay forlorn
   in bondage and in thrall.

160

We did not know a Christ till now,
   nor how faln man be saved,
Else would we not, right well we wot,
   have so our selves behaved.
Mat. 11:21
We should have mourn'd, we should have turn'd
   from sin at thy Reproof,
And been more wise through thy advice,
   for our own Souls behoof.

161

But Natures Light shin'd not so bright
   to teach us the right way:
We might have lov'd it, and well improv'd   They are
   and yet have gone astray.   answered.
The Judge most High makes this Reply,
   you ignorance pretend,
Dimness of sight, and want of light
   your course Heav'nward to bend.

162

How came your mind to be so blind?   Gen. 1:27
   I once you knowledge gave,   Eccles. 7:29
Clearness of sight, and judgment right;   Hos. 13:9
   who did the same deprave?
If to your cost you have it lost.
   and quite defac'd the same;
Your own desert hath caus'd the smart,
   you ought not me to blame.

163

Your selves into a pit of woe,   Mat. 11:25
   your own transgression led: compared
If I to none my Grace had shown,   with 20 & 15
   who had been injured?
If to a few, and not to you,
   I shew'd a way of life,
My Grace so free, you clearly see,
   gives you no ground of strife.

164

'Tis vain to tell, you wot full well,
   if you in time had known
Your Misery and Remedy,
   your actions had it shown.

Rom. 1:20,
21, 22

You, sinful Crew, have not been true
    unto the Light of Nature,
Nor done the good you understood,
    nor owned your Creator.

165

He that the Light, because 'tis Light,
    hath used to despize,

Rom. 2:12,
15 & 1:32
Mat. 12:41
Reprobate In-
fants plead
for them-
selves.
Rev. 20:12,
15
Compared
with Rom.
5:12, 14 &
9:11, 13

Would not the Light shining more bright,
    be likely for to prize.
If you had lov'd, and well improv'd
    your knowledge and dim sight,
Herein your pain had not been vain,
    your plagues had been more light.

166

Then to the Bar, all they drew near
    who dy'd in Infancy,
And never had or good or bad
    effected pers'nally,
But from the womb unto the tomb
    were straightway carried,
(Or at the last e're they transgrest)
    who thus began to plead:

167

Ezek. 18:2

If for our own transgression,
    or disobedience,
We here did stand at thy left-hand
    just were the Recompence:
But *Adam's* guilt our souls hath spilt,
    his fault is charg'd on us;
And that alone hath overthrown,
    and utterly undone us.

168

Not we, but he, ate of the Tree,
  whose fruit was interdicted:
Yet on us all of his sad Fall,
  the punishment's inflicted.
How could we sin that had not been,
  or how is his sin our,
Without consent, which to prevent,
  we never had a pow'r?

169

O great Creator, why was our Nature
  depraved and forlorn?
Why so defil'd, and made so vild
  whilst we were yet unborn?
If it be just, and needs we must
  transgressors reck'ned be,
Thy Mercy, Lord, to us afford,   Psal. 51:5
  which sinners hath set free.

170

Behold we see *Adam* set free,
  and sav'd from his trespass,
Whose sinful Fall hath split us all,
  and brought us to this pass.
Canst thou deny us once to try,
  or Grace to us to tender,
When he finds grace before thy face,
  that was the chief offender?

171

Then answered the Judge most dread,   Their Argu-
  God doth such doom forbid,   ment taken
That men should dye eternally   off.
  for what they never did.   Ezek. 18:20
But what you call old *Adam's* Fall,   Rom. 5:12,
                                        19

and only his Trespass,
You call amiss to call it his,
    both his and yours it was.

172

He was design'd of all Mankind
    to be a publick Head,
A common Root, whence all should shoot,
    and stood in all their stead.

1 Cor. 15:48, 49

He stood and fell, did ill or well,
    not for himself alone,
But for you all, who now his Fall,
    and trespass would disown.

173

If he had stood, then all his brood
    had been established
In Gods true love, never to move,
    nor once awry to tread:
Then all his Race, my Father's Grace,
    should have enjoy'd for ever,
And wicked Sprights by subtile sleights
    could them have harmed never.

174

Would you have griev'd to have receiv'd
    through *Adam* so much good,
As had been your for evermore,
    if he at first had stood?
Would you have said, we ne'r obey'd,
    nor did thy Laws regard;
It ill befits with benefits,
    us, Lord, so to reward?

175

Since then to share in his welfare,
   you could have been content,
You may with reason share in his treason,
   and in the punishment.
Hence you were born in state forlorn,   Rom. 5:12
   with Natures so depraved: Psa. 51:5
Death was your due, because that you   Gen. 5:3
   had thus your selves behaved.

176

You think if we had been as he,   Mat. 23:30,
   whom God did so betrust,   31
We to our cost would ne're have lost
   all for a paltry Lust.
Had you been made in *Adam's* stead,
   you would like things have wrought,
And so into the self-same wo,
   your selves and yours have brought.

177

I may deny you once to try,   Rom. 9:15,
   or Grace to you to tender,   18
Though he finds Grace before my face, The free gift.
   who was the chief offender: Rom. 5:15
Else should my Grace cease to be Grace;
   for it should not be free,
If to release whom I should please,
   I have no libertee.

178

If upon one what's due to none
   I frankly shall bestow,
And on the rest shall not think best,
   compassions skirts to throw,

Whom injure I? will you envy,
    and grudge at others weal?
Or me accuse, who do refuse
    your selves to help and heal?

179

Mat. 20:15

Am I alone of what's my own,
    no Master or no Lord?
Or if I am, how can you claim
    what I to some afford?
Will you demand Grace at my hand,
    and challenge what is mine?
Will you teach me whom to set free,
    and thus my Grace confine?

180

Psa. 58:3
Ro. 6:23
Gal. 3:10
Rom. 8:29,
30 & 11:7
Rev. 21:27
Luk. 12:48

You sinners are, and such a share
    as sinners may expect,
Such you shall have; for I do save
    none but mine own Elect.
Yet to compare your sin with their,
    who liv'd a longer time,
I do confess yours is much less,
    though every sin's a crime.

181

Mat. 11:22
The wicked
all convinced
and put to
silence.
Ro. 3:19
Mat. 22:12

A crime it is, therefore in bliss
    you may not hope to dwell;
But unto you I shall allow
    the easiest room in Hell.
The glorious King thus answering,
    they cease, and plead no longer:
Their Consciences must needs confess
    his Reasons are the stronger.

182

Thus all mens Pleas the Judge with ease
  doth answer and confute,
Until that all, both great and small,
  are silenced and mute.
Vain hopes are cropt, all mouths are stopt,
  sinners have nought to say,
But that 'tis just, and equal most
  they should be damn'd for ay.

Behold the formidable estate of all the ungodly, as they stand hopeless & helpless before an impartial Judge, expecting their final Sentence.
Rev. 6:16, 17

183

Now what remains, but that to pains
  and everlasting smart,
Christ should condemn the Sons of men,
  which is their just desert;
Oh, rueful plights of sinful wights!
  Oh wretches all forlorn:
'T had happy been they ne're had seen
  the Sun, or not been born.

184

Yea, now it would be good they could
  themselves annihilate,
And cease to be, themselves to free
  from such a fearful state.
Oh happy Dogs, and Swine, and Frogs:
  yea Serpents generation,
Who do not fear this doom to hear,
  and sentence of Damnation!

185

This is their state so desperate:
  their sins are fully known;
Their vanities and villanies
  before the world are shown.

Psa. 139:2, 3, 4
Eccl. 12:14

As they are gross and impious,
   so are their numbers more
Than motes i'th' Air, or then their hair,
   or sands upon the shore.

186

Divine Justice offended is
   and Satisfaction claimeth:
God's wrathful ire kindled like fire,
   against them fiercely flameth.
Their Judge severe doth quite cashier
   and all their Pleas off take,
That never a man, or dare, or can
   a further Answer make.

Mat. 25:45

187

Mat. 22:12
Rom. 2:5, 6
Luk. 19:42

Their mouths are shut, each man is put
   to silence and to shame:
Nor have they ought within their thought,
   Christ's Justice for to blame.
The Judge is just, and plague them must,
   nor will he mercy shew
(For Mercies day is past away)
   to any of this Crew.

188

Mat. 28:18
Psal. 139:7

The Judge is strong, doers of wrong
   cannot his power withstand:
None can by flight run out of sight,
   nor scape out of his hand.
Sad is their state: for Advocate
   to plead their Cause there's none:
None to prevent their punishment,
   or misery bemone.

189

O dismal day! whither shall they
   for help and succour flee?
To God above, with hopes to move
   their greatest Enemee:
His wrath is great, whose burning heat
   no floods of tears can slake: Isa. 33:14
His word stands fast, that they be cast   Psal. 11:6
   into the burning Lake.   Numb. 23:19

190

To Christ their Judge, he doth adjudge
   them to the Pit of Sorrow;
Nor will he hear, or cry, or tear,   Matt. 25:41
   nor respite them one morrow.
To Heav'n alas, they cannot pass,   Matt. 25:10,
   it is against them shut;   11, 12
To enter there (O heavy cheer)
   they out of hopes are put.

191

Unto their Treasures, or to their Pleasures, Luk. 12:20
   all these have them forsaken: Psal. 49:7, 17
Had they full Coffers to make large offers,
   their Gold would not be taken
Unto the place where whilome was
   their Birth and Education?   Deut. 32:2
Lo! Christ begins for their great sins
   to fire the Earths Foundation:

192

And by and by the flaming Sky   2 Pet. 3:10
   shall drop like molten Lead
About their ears, t'increase their fears,
   and aggravate their dread.

To Angels good that ever stood
   in their integrity,
Should they betake themselves, and make
   their sute incessantly?

193

Mat. 13:41,
42

They neither skill, nor do they will
   to work them any ease:
They will not mourn to see them burn,
   nor beg for their release.
To wicked men, their bretheren
   in sin and wickedness,
Should they make mone? their case is one,

Rev. 20:13,
15

   they're in the same distress.

194

Ah, cold comfort, and mean support
   from such like Comforters!
Ah, little joy of Company,
   and fellow-sufferers!

Luk. 16:28

Such shall increase their hearts disease,
   and add unto their woe,
Because that they brought to decay
   themselves and many moe.

195

Unto the Saints with sad complaints
   should they themselves apply?

Rev. 21:4

They're not dejected, nor ought affected
   with all their misery.
Friends stand aloof, and make no proof
   what Prayers or Tears can do:

Psal. 58:10

Your godly friends are now more friends
   to Christ than unto you.

196

Where tender love mens hearts did move
    unto a sympathy,
And bearing part of others smart
    in their anxiety;
Now such compassion is out of fashion,   1 Cor. 6:2
    and wholly laid aside:
No Friends so near, but Saints to hear
    their Sentence can abide.

197

One natural Brother beholds another
    in this astonied fit,
Yet sorrows not thereat a jot,   Compare
    nor pitties him a whit.   Prov. 1:26
The godly wife conceives no grief,   with 1 Joh.
    nor can she shed a tear   3:2 & 2 C:
For the sad state of her dear Mate,   5:16
    when she his doom doth hear.

198

He that was erst a Husband pierc't
    with sense of Wives distress,
Whose tender heart did bear a part
    of all her grievances,
Shall mourn no more as heretofore
    because of her ill plight;
Although he see her now to be
    a damn'd forsaken wight.

199

The tender Mother will own no other
    of all her numerous brood,
But such as stand at Christ's right hand
    acquitted through his Blood.

Luk. 16:25

The pious Father had now much rather
    his graceless Son should ly
In Hell with Devils, for all his evils
    burning eternally,

200

Then God most high should injury,
Psal. 58:10
    by sparing him sustain;
And doth rejoyce to hear Christ's voice
    adjudging him to pain;
Who having all, both great and small,
    convinc'd and silenced,
Did then proceed their Doom to read,
    and thus it uttered:

201

The Judge
pronounceth
the Sentence
of condemna-
tion.
Mat. 25:41

Ye sinful wights, and cursed sprights,
    that work Iniquity,
Depart together from me for ever
    to endless Misery;
Your portion take in yonder Lake,
    where Fire and Brimstone flameth:
Suffer the smart, which your desert
    as it's due wages claimeth.

202

Oh piercing words more sharp than swords!
    what, to depart from *Thee,*
The terrour
of it.
Whose face before for evermore
    the best of Pleasures be!
What? to depart (unto our smart)
    from thee *Eternally:*
To be for aye banish'd away,
    with *Devils* company!

203

What? to be sent to *Punishment,*
    and flames of *Burning Fire,*
To be surrounded, and eke confounded
    with Gods *Revengful ire.*
What? to abide, not for a tide
    these Torments, but for *Ever:*
To be released, or to be eased,
    not after years, but *Never.*

204

Oh, *fearful Doom!* now there's no room
    for hope or help at all:
Sentence is past which aye shall last,
    Christ will not it recall.
There might you hear them rent and tear
    the Air with their out-cries:
The hideous noise of their sad voice
    ascendeth to the Skies.

205

They wring their hands, their caitiff-hands   Luk. 13:28
    and gnash their teeth for terrour;
They cry, they roar for anguish sore,
    and gnaw their tongues for horrour.
But get away without delay,
    Christ pitties not your cry:
Depart to Hell, there may you yell,
    and roar Eternally.   Prov. 1:26

206

That word, *Depart,* maugre their heart,   It is put in
    drives every wicked one,   Execution.
With mighty pow'r, the self-same hour,
    far from the Judge's Throne.

Mat. 25:46

> Away they're chaste by the strong blast
>   of his Death-threatning mouth:
> They flee full fast, as if in haste,
>   although they be full loath.

207

> As chaff that's dry, and dust doth fly
>   before the Northern wind:
> Right so are they chased away,
>   and can no Refuge find.
> They hasten to the Pit of Wo,
>   guarded by Angels stout;
> Who to fulfil Christ's holy will,
>   attend this wicked Rout.

Matt. 13:41,
42

208

HELL
Mat. 25:30
Mark. 9:43
Isa. 30:33
Rev. 21:8

> Whom having brought, as they are taught,
>   unto the brink of Hell,
> (That dismal place far from Christ's face,
>   where Death and Darkness dwell:
> Where Gods fierce Ire kindleth the fire,
>   and vengeance feeds the flame
> With piles of Wood, and Brimstone Flood,
>   that none can quench the same,)

209

Wicked Men
and Devils
cast into it for
ever.
Mat. 22:13 &
25:46

> With Iron bands they bind their hands,
>   and cursed feet together,
> And cast them all, both great and small,
>   into that Lake for ever.
> Where day and night, without respite,
>   they wail, and cry, and howl
> For tort'ring pain, which they sustain
>   in Body and in Soul.

210

For day and night, in their despight,
  their torments smoak ascendeth.
Their pain and grief have no relief,
  their anguish never endeth.
There must they ly, and never dy,
  though dying every day:
There must they dying ever ly,
  and not consume away.

Rev. 14:10, 11

211

Dy fain they would, if dy they could,
  but Death will not be had;
God's direful wrath their bodies hath
  for ev'r Immortal made.
They live to ly in misery,
  and bear eternal wo;
And live they must whilst God is just,
  that he may plague them so.

212

But who can tell the plagues of Hell,
  and torments exquisite?
Who can relate their dismal state,
  and terrours infinite?
Who fare the best, and feel the least,
  yet feel that punishment
Whereby to nought they should be brought,
  if God did not prevent.

The unsufferable torments of the damned.
Luk. 16:24
Jude 7

213

The least degree of miserie
  there felt's incomparable,
The lightest pain they there sustain

more than intolerable.
But God's great pow'r from hour to hour
   upholds them in the fire,
That they shall not consume a jot,
   nor by it's force expire.

214

But ah, the wo they undergo
   (they more than all besides)
Who had the light, and knew the right,

   yet would not it abide.
The sev'n-fold smart, which to their part,
   and portion doth fall,
Who Christ his Grace would not imbrace,
   nor hearken to his call.

215

The *Amorites* and *Sodomites*

   although their plagues be sore,
Yet find some ease, compar'd to these,
   who feel a great deal more.
Almighty God, whose Iron Rod,
   to smite them never lins,
Doth most declare his Justice rare
   in plaguing these mens sins.

216

The pain of loss their Souls doth toss,
   and wond'rously distress,
To think what they have cast away
   by wilful wickedness.
We might have been redeem'd from sin,
   think they, and liv'd above,
Being possest of heav'nly rest,
   and joying in God's love.

217

But wo, wo, wo our Souls unto!   Luk. 13:34
  we would not happy be;
And therefore bear Gods Vengeance here
  to all Eternitee.
Experience and woful sense
  must be our painful teachers
Who n'ould believe, nor credit give,
  unto our faithful Preachers.

218

Thus shall they ly, and wail, and cry,   Mark. 9:44
  tormented, and tormenting   Rom. 2:15
Their galled hearts with pois'ned darts
  but now too late repenting.
There let them dwell i'th' Flames of Hell;
  there leave we them to burn,
And back agen unto the men
  whom Christ acquits, return.

219

The Saints behold with courage bold,   The Saints re-
  and thankful wonderment,   joyce to see
To see all those that were their foes   Judgment
  thus sent to punishment: executed
Then do they sing unto their King   upon the
  a Song of endless Praise: wicked
They praise his Name, and do proclaim   World.
  that just are all his ways.   Ps. 58:10
                                    Rev. 19:1, 2,
                                    3

220

Thus with great joy and melody   They ascend
  to Heav'n they all ascend,   with Christ
Him there to praise with sweetest layes,   into Heaven
                                      triumphing.

Mat. 25:46
1 Joh. 3:2
1 Cor. 13:12
and Hymns that never end,
Where with long Rest they shall be blest,
    and nought shall them annoy:
Where they shall see as seen they be,
    and whom they love enjoy.

221

Their Eternal
happiness and
incomparable
Glory there.
O glorious Place! where face to face
    Jehovah may be seen,
By such as were sinners whilere
    and no dark vail between.
Where the Sun shine, and light Divine,
    of Gods bright Countenance,
Doth rest upon them every one,
    with sweetest influence.

222

O blessed state of the Renate!
    O wondrous Happiness,
To which they're brought, beyond what thought
    can reach, or words express!
Rev. 21:4
Griefs water-course, and sorrows sourse,
    are turn'd to joyful streams.
Their old distress and heaviness
    are vanished like dreams.

223

For God above in arms of love
    doth dearly them embrace,
Psal. 16:11
And fills their sprights with such delights,
    and pleasures in his grace;
As shall not fail, nor yet grow stale
    through frequency of use:
Nor do they fear Gods favour there,
    to forfeit by abuse.

224

For there the Saints are perfect Saints,   Heb. 12:23
   and holy ones indeed,
From all the sin that dwelt within
   their mortal bodies freed:
Made Kings and Priests to God through Christs
   dear loves transcendency,   Rev. 1:6 &
There to remain, and there to reign   22:5
   with him Eternally.

JOHN FISKE
(1608-1677)
"UPON THE DECEASE OF THE REVEREND MR THO: HOOKER &C" *
(1647)

Text: Jantz, *The First Century*, p. 123.

Thomas Hooker
Anagr.
A Rest; oh com'! oh

A Rest's at hand after thy weary dayes
After thy Tossings heere in wilderness:

A rest is it? oh com'! oh, no delayes
let bee! of this life end the wretchednes.

---

* Reprinted by courtesy of the American Antiquarian Society and the Brown University Library.

COTTON MATHER
(*1663-1728*)

EPITAPH ON SHUBAEL DUMMER,
KILLED BY INDIANS, 1691
(*1702*)

Text: *Magnalia Christi Americana* (Hartford, 1820), II, 531.

DUMMER the shepherd sacrific'd
By wolves, because the sheep he priz'd.
The orphans father, churches light,
The love of heav'n, of hell the spight.
The countries gapman, and the face
That shone, but knew it not, with grace.
Hunted by devils, but reliev'd
By Angels, and on high receiv'd
The martyr'd Pelican, who bled
Rather than leave his charge unfed.
A proper bird of paradise,
Shot, and flown thither in a trice.

Lord, hear the cry of righteous DUMMER'S wounds,
Ascending still against the salvage hounds,
That worry thy dear flocks, and let the cry
Add force to theirs that at thine altar lye.

EDWARD TAYLOR
(1642-1729)

"HUSWIFERY" *

Text: *The Poetical Works of Edward Taylor,* ed. T. H. Johnson
(Princeton, 1943), p. 116.

Make me, O Lord, thy Spin[n]ing Wheele compleat;
   Thy Holy Worde my Distaff make for mee.
Make mine Affections thy Swift Flyers neate,
   And make my Soule thy holy Spoole to bee.
   My Conversation make to be thy Reele,
   And reele the yarn thereon spun of thy Wheele.

Make me thy Loome then, knit therein this Twine:
   And make thy Holy Spirit, Lord, winde quills:
Then weave the Web thyselfe. The yarn is fine.
   Thine Ordinances make my Fulling Mills.
   Then dy the same in Heavenly Colours Choice,
   All pinkt with Varnish't Flowers of Paradise.

Then cloath therewith mine Understanding, Will,
   Affections, Judgment, Conscience, Memory;
My Words and Actions, that their shine may fill
   My wayes with glory and thee glorify.
   Then mine apparell shall display before yee
   That I am Cloathd in Holy robes for glory.

MEDITATION SIX

CANTICLES II: I: I AM . . . THE LILY OF THE VALLEYS.

Am I thy gold? Or Purse, Lord, for thy Wealth;
   Whether in mine or mint refinde for thee?

---

* This and the four poems following are reprinted, with permission, from *The
Poetical Works of Edward Taylor,* edited by Thomas H. Johnson. Copyright 1939.
Rockland Editions. Copyright 1943. Princeton University Press.

Ime counted so, but count me o're thyselfe,
    Lest gold washt face, and brass in Heart I bee.
I Feare my Touchstone touches when I try
    Mee, and my Counted Gold too overly.

Am I new minted by thy Stamp indeed?
    Mine Eyes are dim; I cannot clearly see.
Be thou my Spectacles that I may read
    Thine Image and Inscription stampt on mee.
    If thy bright Image do upon me stand.
    I am a Golden Angell in thy hand.

Lord, make my Soule thy Plate: thine Image bright
    Within the Circle of the same enfoile.
And on its brims in golden Letters write
    Thy Superscription in an Holy style.
    Then I shall be thy Money, thou my Hord:
    Let me thy Angell bee, bee thou my Lord.

MEDITATION EIGHT

(*written 1684*)

JOHN VI:51: I AM THE LIVING BREAD.

Text: *Poetical Works*, pp. 129-130.

I ken[n]ing through Astronomy Divine
    The Worlds bright Battlement, wherein I spy
A Golden Path my Pensill cannot line
    From that bright Throne unto my Threshold ly.
    And while my puzzled thoughts about it pore,
    I find the Bread of Life in't at my doore.

When that this Bird of Paradise put in
    This Wicker Cage (my Corps) to tweedle praise
Had peckt the Fruite forbid: and so did fling
    Away its Food, and lost its golden dayes,

It fell into Celestiall Famine sore,
And never could attain a morsell more.

Alas! alas! Poore Bird, what wilt thou doe?
  This Creatures field no food for Souls e're gave:
And if thou knock at Angells dores, they show
  An Empty Barrell: they no soul bread have.
  Alas! Poore Bird, the Worlds White Loafe is done,
  And cannot yield thee here the smallest Crumb.

In this sad state, Gods Tender Bowells run
  Out streams of Grace: And he to end all strife,
The Purest Wheate in Heaven, his deare-dear Son
  Grinds, and kneads up into this Bread of Life:
  Which Bread of Life from Heaven down came and stands
  Disht in thy Table up by Angells Hands.

Did God mould up this Bread in Heaven, and bake,
  Which from his Table came, and to thine goeth?
Doth he bespeake thee thus: This Soule Bread take;
  Come, Eate thy fill of this, thy Gods White Loafe?
  Its Food too fine for Angells; yet come, take
  And Eate thy fill! Its Heavens Sugar Cake.

What Grace is this knead in this Loafe? This thing
  Souls are but petty things it to admire.
Yee Angells, help: This fill would to the brim
  Heav'ns whelm'd-down Chrystall meele Bowle, yea and higher.
  This Bread of Life dropt in thy mouth doth Cry:
  Eate, Eate me, Soul, and thou shalt never dy.

MEDITATION FIFTY-SIX
(*written 1703*)

JOHN XV: 24: IF I HAD NOT DONE AMONG THEM THE WORKS WHICH
NONE OTHER MAN DID, THEY HAD NOT HAD SIN: BUT NOW HAVE THEY
BOTH SEEN AND HATED BOTH ME AND MY FATHER.

Text: *Poetical Works,* pp. 165-166.

Should I with silver tooles delve through the Hill
　　Of Cordilera for rich thoughts, that I
My Lord, might weave with an angelick skill
　　A Damask Web of Velvet Verse, thereby
　　To deck thy Works up, all my Web would run
　　To rags and jags: so snick-snarld to the thrum.

Thine are so rich: within, without refin'd:
　　No worke like thine. No Fruits so sweete that grow
On th' trees of righteousness of Angell kinde,
　　And Saints, whose limbs reev'd with them bow down low.
　　Should I search ore the Nutmeg Gardens shine,
　　Its fruits in flourish are but skegs to thine.

The Clove, when in its White-green'd blossoms shoots,
　　Some Call the pleasantst s[c]ent the World doth show,
None Eye e're saw, nor nose e're smelt such Fruits,
　　My Lord, as thine, Thou Tree of Life in 'ts blow.
　　Thou Rose of Sharon, Vallies Lilly true,
　　Thy Fruits most sweet and glorious ever grew.

Thou art a Tree of Perfect nature trim,
　　Whose golden lining is of perfect Grace,
Perfum'de with Deity unto the brim,
　　Whose fruits, of the perfection, grow, of Grace.
　　Thy Buds, thy Blossoms, and thy fruits adorne
　　Thyselfe and Works, more shining than the morn.

Art, natures Ape, hath many brave things done:
  As th' Pyramids, the Lake of Meris vast,
The Pensile Orchards built in Babylon,
  Psammitich's Labyrinth, (arts Cramping task)
  Archimedes his Engins made for war,
  Romes Golden House, Titus his Theater.

The Clock of Strasburgh, Dresdens Table-sight,
  Regsamonts Fly of Steele about that flew,
Turrian's Wooden Sparrows in a flight,
  And th' Artificiall man Aquinas slew,
  Mark Scaliota's Lock and Key and Chain
  Drawn by a Flea, in our Queen Betties reign.

Might but my pen in natures Inventory
  Its progress make, 't might make such things to jump,
All which are but Inventions Vents or glory:
  Wits Wantonings, and Fancies frollicks plump:
  Within whose maws lies buried Times, and Treasures,
  Embalmed up in thick dawbd sinfull pleasures.

Nature doth better work than Art, yet thine
  Out vie both works of nature and of Art.
Natures Perfection and the perfect shine
  Of Grace attend thy deed in ev'ry part.
  A Thought, a Word, and Worke of thine, will kill
  Sin, Satan, and the Curse: and Law fulfill.

Thou art the Tree of Life in Paradise,
  Whose lively branches are with Clusters hung
Of Lovely fruits, and Flowers more sweet than spice.
  Bende down to us, and doe outshine the sun.
  Delightfull unto God, doe man rejoyce
  The pleasant'st fruits in all Gods Paradise.

Lord, feed mine eyes then with thy Doings rare,
  And fat my heart with these ripe fruites thou bear'st;

Adorn my Life well with thy works; make faire
My Person with apparrell thou prepar'st.
My Boughs shall loaded bee with fruits that spring
Up from thy Works, while to thy praise I sing.

"PREFACE" TO GODS DETERMINATIONS
TOUCHING HIS ELECT [2]

Text: *Poetical Works,* pp. 31-32.

Infinity, when all things it beheld,
In Nothing, and of Nothing all did build,
Upon what Base was fixt the Lath, wherein
He turn'd this Globe, and riggalld it so trim?
Who blew the Bellows of his Furnace Vast?
Or held the Mould wherein the world was Cast?
Who laid its Corner Stone? Or whose Command?
Where stand the Pillars upon which it stands?
Who Lac'de and Fillitted the earth so fine,
With Rivers like green Ribbons Smaragdine?
Who made the Sea's its Selvedge, and it locks
Like a Quilt Ball within a Silver Box?
Who Spread its Canopy? Or Curtains Spun?
Who in this Bowling Alley bowld the Sun?
Who made it always when it rises set:
To go at once both down, and up to get?
Who th' Curtain rods made for this Tapistry?
Who hung the twinckling Lanthorns in the Sky?
Who? who did this? or who is he? Why, know
It's Onely Might Almighty this did doe.
His hand hath made this noble worke which Stands
His Glorious Handywork not made by hands.
Who spake all things from nothing; and with ease
Can speake all things to nothing, if he please.
Whose Little finger at his pleasure Can

---

[2] *Gods Determinations* is Taylor's longest poem, in which, in the manner of a morality play, he dramatizes the structure of Puritan Theology.

Out mete ten thousand worlds with halfe a Span:
Whose Might Almighty can by half a looks
Root up the rocks and rock the hills by th' roots.
Can take this mighty World up in his hande,
And shake it like a Squitchen or a Wand.
Whose single Frown will make the Heavens shake
Like as an aspen leafe the Winde makes quake.
Oh! what amight is this! Whose single frown
Doth shake the world as it would shake it down?
Which All from Nothing fet, from Nothing, All:
Hath All on Nothing set, lets Nothing fall.
Gave All to nothing Man indeed, whereby
Through nothing man all might him Glorify.
In Nothing is imbosst the brightest Gem
More pretious than all pretiousness in them.
But Nothing man did throw down all by sin:
And darkened that lightsom Gem in him,
    That now his Brightest Diamond is grown
    Darker by far than any Coalpit Stone.

"UPON THE SWEEPING FLOOD: AUGUST 13 AND 14, 1683" *

Text: T. H. Johnson, ed., "Some Edward Taylor Gleanings," *New England Quarterly,* XVI (1943), 284.

O! that I'd had a tear to've quencht that flame
    Which did dissolve the Heavens above
    Into those liquid drops that came
      To drown our carnal love.
Our cheeks were dry and eyes refusde to weep.
    Tears bursting out ran down the skies darke cheek.

Were th' Heavens sick? must wee their Doctors bee
    And physick them with pills, our sin?

---

* Reprinted with the permission of the editor of the *New England Quarterly* and Thomas H. Johnson.

To make them purge and vomit; see:
　　And Excrements out fling?
We've griev'd them by such Physick that they shed
Their Excrements upon our lofty heads.

URIAN OAKES
(1631-1681)

"AN ELEGY UPON THE DEATH OF THE REVEREND MR. THOMAS SHEPARD" *
(1677)

Text: Perry Miller and T. H. Johnson, eds., *The Puritans* (New York, 1938), pp. 641-650.

[1]

Oh! that I were a Poet now in grain!
How would I invoke the Muses all
To deign their presence, lend their flowing Vein,
And help to grace dear *Shepard's* Funeral!
　　How would I paint our griefs, and succours borrow
　　From Art and Fancy, to limn out our sorrow!

[2]

Now could I wish (if wishing would obtain)
The sprightli'est Efforts of Poetick Rage,
To vent my Griefs, make others feel my pain,
For this loss of the Glory of our Age.
　　Here is a subject for the loftiest Verse
　　That ever waited on the bravest Hearse.

[3]

And could my Pen ingeniously distill
The purest Spirits of a sparkling wit
In rare conceits, the quintessence of skill

---

* Reprinted from *The Puritans,* edited by Perry Miller and T. H. Johnson and used with permission of the American Book Company.

In *Elegiack Strains;* none like to it:
  I should think all too little to condole
  The fatal loss (to us) of such a Soul.

[4]

Could I take highest Flights of Fancy, soar
Aloft; If Wits Monopoly were mine:
All would be much too low, too light, too poor,
To pay due tribute to this great Divine.
  Ah! Wit avails not, when th'Heart's like to break,
  Great griefs are Tongue-ti'ed, when the lesser speak.

[5]

Away loose rein'd Careers of Poetry,
The celebrated Sisters may be gone;
We need no *Mourning Womens* Elegy,
No forc'd, affected, artificial Tone.
  Great and good *Shepard's* Dead! Ah! this alone
  Will set our eyes abroach, dissolve a stone.

[6]

Poetick Raptures are of no esteem,
Daring *Hyperboles* have here no place,
Luxuriant Wits on such a copious Theme,
Would shame themselves, and blush to shew their face
  Here's worth enough to overmatch the skill
  Of the most stately Poet *Laureat's Quill.*

[7]

Exube'rant Fancies useless here I deem,
Transcendent vertue scorns feign'd Elogies:
He that gives *Shepard* half his due, may seem,
If Strangers hear it, to Hyperbolize.
  Let him that can, tell what his vertues were,
  And say, this Star mov'd in no common Sphere.

[8]

Here need no Spices, Odours, curious Arts,
No skill of *Egypt,* to embalm the Name
Of such a Worthy: let men speak their hearts,
They'l say, He merits an Immortal Fame.
    When *Shepard* is forgot, all must conclude,
    This is prodigious ingratitude.

[9]

But live he shall in many a gratefull Breast,
VVhere he hath rear'd himself a Monument,
A Monument more stately than the best,
On which Immensest Treasures have been spent.
    Could you but into th'Hearts of thousands peep,
    There would you read his Name engraven deep.

[10]

Oh! that my head were Waters, and mine Eyes
A flowing Spring of Tears, still issuing forth
In streams of bitterness, to solemnize
    The *Obits* of this Man of matchless worth!
    Next to the Tears our sins do need and crave,
    I would bestow my Tears on *Shepards* Grave.

[11]

Not that he needs our Tears: for he hath dropt
His measure full; not one Tear more shall fall
Into God's Bottle from his eyes; *Death* stopt
That water-course, his sorrows ending all.
    He Fears, he Cares, he Sighs, he Weeps no more:
    Hee's past all storms, Arriv'd at th'wished Shoar.

[12]

Dear *Shepard* could we reach so high a strain
Of pure Seraphick love, as to devest
Our selves, and love, of self-respects, thy gain

Would joy us, though it cross our interest.
 Then would we silence all compaints with this,
 Our Dearest Friend is doubtless gone to Bliss.

[13]

Ah! but the Lesson's hard, thus to deny
Our own dear selves, to part with such a Loan
Of Heaven (in time of such necessity)
And love thy comforts better than our own.
 Then let us moan our loss, adjourn our glee,
 Till we come thither to rejoice with thee.

[14]

As when some formidable Comets blaze,
As when Portentous Prodigies appear,
Poor Mortals with amazement stand and gaze,
With hearts affrighted, and with trembling fear:
 So are we all amazed at this blow,
 Sadly portending some approaching woe.

[15]

We shall not summon bold Astrologers,
To tell us what the Stars say in the case,
(Those Cousin-Germans to black Conjurers)
We have a sacred Oracle that says,
 When th'Righteous perish, men of mercy go,
 It is a sure presage of coming wo.

[16]

He was (ah woful word! to say he was)
Our wrestling *Israel,* second unto none,
The man that stood i'th'gap, to keep the pass,
To stop the Troops of Judgments rushing on.
 This Man the honour had to hold the hand
 Of an incensed God against our Land.

[17]

When such a Pillar's faln (Oh such an one!)
When such a glorious, shining Light's put out,
When Chariot and Horsemen thus are gone;
Well may we fear some Downfal, Darkness, Rout.
   When such a Bank's broke down, there's sad occasion
   To wail, and dread some grievous Inundation.

[18]

What! must we with our God, and Glory part?
Lord! Is thy Treaty with *New-England* come
Thus to an end? And is War in thy Heart?
That this Ambassadour is called home.
   So Earthly Gods (Kings) when they War intend,
   Call home their Ministers, and Treaties end.

[19]

Oh for the Raptures, Transports, Inspirations
Of *Israel's Singers* when his *Jon'athan's* Fall
So tun'd his mourning Harp! what Lamentations
Then would I make for *Shepards* Funerall
   How truly can I say, as well as He?
   My *Dearest Brother I'am distress'd for thee*.

[20]

How Lovely, Worthy, Peerless, in my view?
How Precious, Pleasant hast thou been to me?
How Learned, Prudent, Pious, Grave, and True?
And what a Faithful Friend? who like to thee?
   Mine Eye's desire is vanish'd: who can tell
   Where lives my dearest *Shepard's* Parallel?

[21]

'Tis strange to think: but we may well believe,
That not a few of different Perswasions
From this great Worthy, do now truly grieve

I'th'Mourning croud, and joyn their Lamentations.
  Such Powers Magnetick had He to draw to Him
  The very Hearts, and Souls, of all that knew Him!

[22]

Art, Nature, Grace, in Him were all combin'd
To shew the World a matchless *Paragon:*
In whom of Radiant Virtues no less shin'd,
Than a whole Constellation: but hee's gone!
  Hee's gone alas! Down in the Dust must ly
  As much of this rare Person as could dy.

[23]

If to have solid Judgement, Pregnant Parts,
A piercing Wit, and comprehensive Brain;
If to have gone the *Round* of all the Arts,
Immunity from Deaths Arrest would gain,
  Shepard would have been Death-proof, and secure
  From that All conquering Hand, I'm very sure.

[24]

If Holy Life, and Deeds of Charity,
If Grace illustrious, and Virtue tri'ed,
If modest Carriage, rare Humility,
Could have brib'd Death, good *Shepard* had not di'ed.
  Oh! but inexorable Death attacks
  The best Men, and promiscu'ous havock makes.

[25]

Come tell me, Criticks, have you ever known
Such Zeal, so temper'd well with moderation?
Such Prudence, and such Inno'cence met in one?
Such Parts, so little Pride and Ostentation?
  Let *Momus* carp, and *Envy* do her worst,
  And swell with *Spleen* and *Rancour* till she burst.

[26]

To be descended well, doth *that* commend?
Can Sons their Fathers Glory call their own?
Our *Shepard* justly might to this pretend,
(His Blessed Father was of high Renown,
    Both *Englands* speak him great, admire his Name)
    But his own pers'onal worth's a better claim.

[27]

Great was the Father, once a glorious Light
Among us, Famous to an high Degree:
Great was this Son: indeed (to do him right)
As Great and Good (to say no more) as He.
    A double portion of his Fathers Spirit
    Did this (his Eldest) Son, through Grace, inherit.

[28]

His Look commanded Reverence and Awe,
Though Mild and Amiable, not Austere:
Well Humour'd was He (as I ever saw)
And rul'd by Love and Wisdome, more than Fear.
    The Muses, and the Graces too, conspir'd
    To set forth this Rare Piece, to be admir'd.

[29]

He govern'd well the Tongue (that busie thing,
Unruly, Lawless and Pragmatical)
Gravely Reserv'd, in Speech not lavishing,
Neither too sparing, nor too liberal.
    His Words were few, well season'd, wisely weigh'd,
    And in his Tongue the Law of kindness sway'd.

[30]

Learned he was beyond the common Size,
Befriended much by Nature in his Wit,
And Temper, (Sweet, Sedate, Ingenious, Wise)

And (which crown'd all) he was Heav'ens Favourite:
  On whom the God of all Grace did command,
  And show'r down Blessings with a lib'eral hand.

[31]

Wise He, not wily, was; Grave, not Morose;
Not stiffe, but steady; Seri'ous, but not Sowre;
Concern'd for all, as if he had no Foes;
(Strange if he had!) and would not wast an Hour.
  Thoughtful and Active for the common good:
  And yet his own place wisely understood.

[32]

Nothing could make him stray from Duty; Death
Was not so frightful to him, as Omission
Of Ministerial work; he fear'd no breath
Infecti'ous, i'th'discharge of his Commission.
  Rather than run from's work, he chose to dy,
  Boldly to run on Death, than duty fly.

[33]

(Cruel Disease! that didst (like *High-way-men*)
Assault the honest Trav'eller in his way,
And rob dear *Shepard* of his life (Ah!) then,
When he was on the Road, where Duty lay.
  Forbear, bold Pen! 'twas God that took him thus,
  To give him great Reward, and punish us.)

[34]

Zealous in God's cause, but meek in his own;
Modest of Nature, bold as any Lion,
Where Consc'ience was concern'd: and there were none
More constant Mourners for afflicted Sion:
  So gene'ral was his care for th'Churches all,
  His Spirit seemed Apostolical.

[35]

Large was his Heart, to spend without regret,
Rejoycing to do good: not like those *Moles*
That root i'th'Earth, or roam abroad, to get
All for themselves (those sorry, narrow Souls!)
   But He, like th'Sun (i'th'Center, as some say)
   Diffus'd his Rayes of Goodness every way.

[36]

He breath'd Love, and pursu'd Peace in his day,
As if his Soul were made of Harmony:
Scarce ever more of Goodness crouded lay
In such a piece of frail Mortality.
   Sure Father *Wilsons* genuine Son was he,
   New-England's Paul had such a *Timothy*.

[37]

No slave to th' Worlds grand *Idols;* but he flew
At *Fairer Quarries,* without stooping down
To Sublunary prey: his great Soul knew
Ambition none, but of the Heave'nly Crown.
   Now he hath won it, and shall wear't with Honour,
   Adoring Grace, and God in Christ, the Donour.

[38]

A Friend to Truth, a constant Foe to Errour,
Pow'erful i'th'*Pulpit,* and sweet in converse,
To weak ones gentle, to th'Profane a Terrour.
Who can his vertues, and good works rehearse?
   The Scripture-Bishops-Character read o'er,
   Say this was *Shepards:* what need I say more?

[39]

I say no more: let them that can declare
His rich and rare endowments, paint this Sun,
With all its dazling Rayes: But I despair,

Hopeless by any hand to see it done.
    They that can *Shepards* goodness well display,
    Must be as good as he: But who are they?

[40]

See where our Sister *Charlstown* sits and Moans!
Poor Widowed *Charlstown!* all in Dust, in Tears!
Mark how she wrings her hands! hear how she groans!
See how she weeps! what sorrow like to hers!
    Charlstown, that might for joy compare of late
    With all about her, now looks desolate.

[41]

As you have seen some Pale, Wan, Ghastly look,
When grisly Death, that will not be said nay,
Hath seiz'd all for it self, Possession took,
And turn'd the Soul out of its house of Clay:
    So Visag'd is poor *Charlstown* at this day;
    Shepard, her very Soul, is torn away.

[42]

Cambridge groans under this so heavy cross,
And Sympathizes with her Sister dear;
Renews her Griefs afresh for her old loss
Of her own *Shepard,* and drops many a Tear.
    Cambridge and *Charlstown* now joint Mourners are,
    And this tremendous loss between them share.

[43]

Must Learnings Friend (Ah! worth us all) go thus?
That Great Support to *Harvards* Nursery!
Our *Fellow* (that no Fellow had with us)
Is gone to Heave'ns great University.
    Our's now indeed's a lifeless *Corporation,*
    The Soul is fled, that gave it *Animation!*

[44]

Poor *Harvard's* Sons are in their Mourning Dress:
Their sure Friend's gone! their Hearts have *put on Mourning;*
Within their Walls are Sighs, Tears, Pensiveness;
Their new Foundations dread an overturning.
 Harvard! where's such a fast Friend left to thee!
 Unless thy great Friend, *Leveret,* it be.

[45]

We must not with our greatest Soveraign strive,
Who dare find fault with him that is most High?
That hath an absolute Prerogative,
And doth his pleasure: none may ask him, why?
 We're Clay-lumps, Dust-heaps, nothings in his sight:
 The Judge of all the Earth doth always right.

[46]

Ah! could not Prayers and Tears prevail with God!
Was there no warding off that dreadful Blow!
And was there no averting of that Rod!
Must *Shepard* dy! and that good Angel go!
 Alas! Our heinous sins (more than our haits)
 It seems, were louder, and out-crie'd our Prayers.

[47]

See what our sins have done! what Ruines wrought
And how they have pluck'd out our very eyes!
Our sins have slain our *Shepard!* we have bought,
And dearly paid for, our Enormities.
 Ah Cursed sins! that strike at God, and kill
 His *Servants,* and the Blood of *Prophets* spill.

[48]

As you would loath the Sword that's warm and red,
As you would hate the hands that are embru'd
I'th'Hearts-blood of your dearest Friends: so dread,

And hate your sins; Oh! let them be pursu'd:
  Revenges take on bloody sins: for there's
  No Refuge-City for these Murtherers.

[49]

In vain we build the Prophets Sepulchers,
In vain bedew their Tombs with Tears, when Dead;
In vain bewail the Deaths of Ministers,
Whilst Prophet-killing sins are harboured.
  Those that these Murth'erous Traitors favour, hide;
  Are with the blood of Prophets deeply di'ed.

[50]

New-England! know thy Heart-plague: feel this blow;
A blow that sorely wounds both Head and Heart,
A blow that reaches All, both high and low,
A blow that may be felt in every part.
  Mourn that this *Great Man's* faln in *Israel:*
  Lest it be said, *with him New-England fell!*

[51]

Farewel, Dear *Shepard!* Thou art gone before,
Made free of *Heaven,* where thou shalt sing loud *Hymns*
Of *High triumphant Praises* evermore,
In the sweet Quire of *Saints* and *Seraphims.*
  Lord! look on us here, clogg'd with sin and clay,
  And we, through Grace, shall be as happy as they.

[52]

My Dearest, Inmost, Bosome-Friend, is Gone!
Gone is my sweet Companion, Soul's delight!
Now in an Huddling Croud I'm all alone,
And almost could bid all the World *Goodnight:*
  Blest be my Rock! God lives: Oh let him be,
  As He is, so All in All to me.

The Bereaved, Sorrowful

URIAN OAKES

JOHN WISE

(1652-1725)

Bibliographical Note. There is no modern edition of Wise's writings. The selection here printed follows the text of *A Vindication of the Government of New England Churches* (Boston, 1772), pp. 21-48; this was the text used as an anti-British, democratic tract. There is no large general study of Wise. The most satisfactory essay is C. L. Rossiter, "John Wise: Colonial Democrat," *New England Quarterly,* XII (1949), 3-32.

from A VINDICATION OF THE GOVERNMENT OF NEW ENGLAND CHURCHES
(*1717*)

[ON NATURAL LAW AND THE GOVERNMENT OF MEN AND CHURCHES]

CHAP. I

The divine establishment in providence of the [New England] churches, in their order is apparently the royal assent of the supream monarch of the churches, to the grave decisions of reason in favour of mans natural state of being, and original freedom. For if we should make a new *survey* of the institution before named under the brightest light of nature, there is no greater example of natural wisdom in any settlement on earth; for the present and future security of human beings in all that is most valuable and grand, than in this. That it seems to me as though wise and provident nature by the dictates of right reason excited by the moving suggestions of humanity; and awed with the just demands of natural liberty, equity, equality, and principles of self-preservation, originally drew up the scheme, and then obtained the royal approbation. And certainly it is agreeable that we attribute it to God whether we receive it nextly from reason or revelation, for that each is equally an emanation of his wisdom, *Prov.* 20. 27. The spirit of man is the candle of the Lord, searching all the inward parts of the belly. There be many larger volumes in this dark recess called the belly to be read by that candle God has lighted up. And I am very well assured the forenamed constitution is a transcript out of some of their pages, John I. 4, 9. *And the life was the light of men, which lighteth every man which cometh into the world.* This admirable effect of Christ's creating power in hanging out so many lights to guide man through a dark world, is as applicable to the light of reason, as to that of revelation. For that the light of reason as a law and rule of right, is an effect of Christ's goodness, care and creating power, as well as of revelation; though revelation is natures law in a fairer and brighter edition. This is granted by the *London* ministers, *p. 8. C.* 3. 'That, that which is evident by, and consonant to the true light of nature, or natural reason, is to be accounted, *Jure Divino,* in matters of religion.' But in the further and more distinct management of this plea; I shall,

1. Lay before the reader several principles [of] natural knowledge.

2. Apply or improve them in ecclesiastical affairs.

3. Infer from the premises, a demonstration that these churches, if not properly formed; yet are fairly established in their present order by the law of nature.

CHAP. II

1. I shall disclose several principles of natural knowledge; plainly discovering the law of nature; or the true sentiments of natural reason, with respect to mans being and government. And in this essay I shall peculiarly confine the discourse to two heads, *viz.*

1. Of the natural (in distinction to the civil) and then,

2. Of the civil being of man. And I shall principally take baron *Puffendorff* for my chief guide and spokes-man.

1. I shall consider man in a state of natural being, as a free-born subject under the crown of heaven, and owing homage to none but God himself. It is certain civil government in general,

is a very admirable result of providence, and an incomparable benefit to mankind, yet must needs be acknowledged to be the effect of human free-compacts and not of divine institution; it is the produce of mans reason, of human and rational combinations, and not from any direct orders of infinite wisdom, in any positive law wherein is drawn up this or that scheme of civil government. Government (says the Lord *Warrington*)[1] is necessary—in that no society of men can subsist without it; and that particular form of government is necessary which best suits the temper and inclination of a people. Nothing can be God's ordinance, but what he has particularly declared to be such; there is no particular form of civil government described in God's word, neither does nature prompt it. The government of the *Jews* was changed five times. Government is not formed by nature, as other births or productions; if it were, it would be the same in all countries; because nature keeps the same method, in the same thing, in all climates. If a common-wealth be changed into a monarchy, is it nature that forms, and brings forth the monarch? Or if a royal family be wholly extinct (as in *Noah's* case, being not heir apparent from descent from *Adam*) is it nature that must go to work (with the kings bees, who themselves alone preserve the royal race in that empire) to breed a monarch before the people can have a king, or a government sent over them? And thus we must leave kings to resolve which is their best title to their crowns, whether natural right, or the constitution of government settled by human compacts, under the direction and conduct of reason. But to proceed under the head of a state of natural being, I shall more distinctly explain the state of human nature in its original capacity, as man is placed on earth by his maker, and cloathed with many investitures, and immunities which properly belong to man separately considered. As,

   1. The prime immunity in mans state, is that he is most prop-

---

[1] Henry Booth, Earl of Warrington (1652 1694), known for his defense of civil and religious liberty against royal prerogative. His *Works,* principally political speeches and pamphlets, were published in 1694.

erly the subject of the law of nature. He is the favourite animal on earth; in that this part of God's image, *viz.* reason is congenate with his nature, wherein by a law immutable, instampt upon his frame, God has provided a rule for men in all their actions, obliging each one to the performance of that which is right, not only as to justice, but likewise as to all other moral virtues, the which is nothing but the dictate of right reason founded in the soul of man. *Molloy, De Mao, Præf.*[2] That which is to be drawn from mans reason, flowing from the true current of that faculty, when unperverted, may be said to be the law of nature, on which account, the holy scriptures declare it written on mens hearts. For being endowed with a soul, you may know from yourself, how, and what you ought to act, Rom. 2. 14. *These having not a law, are a law to themselves.* So that the meaning is, when we acknowledge the law of nature to be the dictate of right reason, we must mean that the understanding of man is endowed with such a power, as to be able, from the contemplation of human condition to discover a necessity of living agreably with this law: And likewise to find out some principle, by which the precepts of it, may be clearly and solidly demonstrated. The way to discover the law of nature in our own state, is by a narrow watch, and accurate contemplation of our natural condition, and propensions. Others say this is the way to find out the law of nature. *scil.* If a man any ways doubts, whether what he is going to do to another man be agreable to the law of nature, then let him suppose himself to be in that other mans room; and by this rule effectually executed. A man must be a very dull scholar to nature not to make proficiency in the knowledge of her laws. But more particularly in pursuing our condition for the discovery of the law of nature, this is very obvious to view, *viz.*

1. A principal of self love, and self preservation, is very predominant in every mans being.

2. A sociable disposition.

3. An affection or love to mankind in general. And to give such

---

[2] A reference to the discussion of natural law in Charles Molloy, *De Jure Maritimo* (1676), a standard legal treatise often reprinted in Wise's lifetime.

sentiments the force of a law, we must suppose a God who takes care of all mankind, and has thus obliged each one, as a subject of higher principles of being, than meer instincts. For that all law properly considered, supposes a capable subject, and a superiour power, and the law of God which is binding, is published by the dictates of right reason as other ways: Therefore says *Plutarch, to follow God and obey reason is the same thing.* But moreover that God has established the law of nature, as the general rule of government, is further illustrable from the many sanctions in providence, and from the peace and guilt of conscience in them that either obey, or violate the law of nature. But moreover, the foundation of the law of nature with relation to government, may be thus discovered. *scil.* Man is a creature extreamly desirous of his own preservation; of himself he is plainly exposed to many wants, unable to secure his own safety, and maintenance without assistance of his fellows; and he is also able of returning kindness by the furtherance of mutual good; but yet man is often found to be malicious; insolent, and easily provoked, and as powerful in effecting mischief, as he is ready in designing it. Now that such a creature may be preserved, it is necessary that he be sociable; that is, that he be capable and disposed to unite himself to those of his own species, and to regulate himself towards them, that they may have no fair reason to do him harm; but rather incline to promote his interests, and secure his rights and concerns. This then is a fundamental law of nature, that every man as far as in him lies, do maintain a sociableness with others, agreable with the main end and disposition of human nature in general. For this is very apparent, that reason and society render man the most potent of all creatures. And finally, from the principles of sociableness it follows as a fundamental law of nature, that man is not so wedded to his own interest, but that he can make the common good the mark of his aim: And hence he becomes capacitated to enter into a civil state by the law of nature; for without this property in nature, *viz.* Sociableness, which is for cementing of parts, every government would soon moulder and dissolve.

2. The second great immunity of man is an original liberty

instampt upon his rational nature. He that intrudes upon this liberty, violates the law of nature. In this discourse I shall wave the consideration of mans moral turpitude, but shall view him physically as a creature which God has made and furnished essentially with many enobling immunities, which render him the most august animal in the world, and still, whatever has happened since his creation, he remains at the upper-end of nature, and as such is a creature of a very noble character. For as to his dominion, the whole frame of the lower part of the universe is devoted to his use, and at his command; and his liberty under the conduct of right reason, is equal with his trust. Which liberty many be briefly considered, internally as to his mind, and externally as to his person.

1. The native liberty of man's nature implies, a faculty of doing or omitting things according to the direction of his judgment. But in a more special meaning, this liberty does not consist in a loose and ungovernable freedom, or in an unbounded license of acting. Such licence is disagreeing with the condition and dignity of man, and would make man of a lower and meaner constitution than bruit creatures; who in all their liberties are kept under a better and more rational government, by their instincts. Therefore as *Plutarch* says, *Those persons only who live in obedience to reason, are worthy to be accounted free: They alone live as they will, who have learnt what they ought to will.* So that the true natural liberty of man, such as really and truely agrees to him, must be understood, as he is guided and restrained by the tyes of reason, and laws of nature; all the rest is brutal, if not worse.

2. Mans external personal, natural liberty, antecedent to all human parts, or alliances must also be considered. And so every man must be conceived to be perfectly in his own power and disposal, and not to be controuled by the authority of any other. And thus every man, must be acknowleded equal to every man, since all subjection and all command are equally banished on both sides; and considering all men thus at liberty, every man, has a prerogative to judge for himself, *viz.* What shall be most for his behoof, happiness and well-being.

3. The third capital immunity belonging to mans nature, is an
equality amongst men; which is not to be denied by the law of
nature, till man has resigned himself with all his rights for the
sake of a civil state; and then his personal liberty and equality is
to be cherished, and preserved to the highest degree, as will consist with all just distinctions amongst men of honor, and shall
be agreable with the public good. For man has a high valuation
of himself, and the passion seems to lay its first foundation (not
in pride, but) really in the high and admirable frame and constitution of human nature. The word man, says my author, is
thought to carry somewhat of dignity in its sound; and we commonly make use of this as the most proper and prevailing argument against a rude insulter, *viz. I am not a beast or a dog. But
am a man as well as yourself.* Since then human nature agrees
equally with all persons; and since no one can live a sociable life
with another that does not own or respect him as a man; It follows as a command of the law of nature, that every man esteem
and treat another as one who is naturally his equal, or who is a
man as well as he. There be many popular, or plausible reasons
that greatly illustrate this equality, *viz.* that we all derive our
being from one stock, the same common father of human race.
On this consideration *Bœthius* checks the pride of the insulting
nobility.

> *Quid Genus et Proavos Strepitis?*
> *Si Primordia Vestra,*
> *Auteremque Deum Spectas,*
> *Nullus Degener Extat*
> *Nisi vitiis Pejora fovens,*
> *Proprium Deserat Orturn.*

> *Fondly our first descent we boast;*
> *If whence at first our breath we draw,*
> *The common springs of life we view,*
> *The airy Notion soon is lost.*
> *The almighty made us equal all:*

But he that slavishly complys
To do the drudgery of vice,
Denyes his high original.

And also that our bodies are composed of matter, frail, brittle, and lyable to be destroyed by thousand accidents; we all owe our existence to the same method of propagation. The noblest mortal in his entrance on the stage of life, is not distinguished by any pomp or of passage from the lowest of mankind; and our life hastens to the same general mark: Death observes no ceremony, but knocks as loud at the barriers of the court, as at the door of the cottage. This equality being admitted, bears a very great force in maintaining peace and friendship amongst men. For that he who would use the assistance of others, in promoting his own advantage, ought as freely to be at their service, when they want his help on the like occasions. *One good turn requires another,* is the common proverb; for otherwise he must need esteem others unequal to himself, who constantly demands their aid, and as constantly denies his own. And whoever is of this insolent temper, cannot but highly displease those about him, and soon give occasion of the breach of the common peace. It was a manly reproof which *Charactacus* gave the *Romans. Num Si vos Omnibus &c.* What! because you desire to be masters of all men, does it follow therefore that all men should desire to be your slaves, for that it is a command of natures law, that no man that has not obtained a particular and special right, shall arrogate to himself a larger share than his fellows, but shall admit others to equal priviledges with himself. So that the principle of equality in a natural state, is peculiarly transgressed by pride, which is when a man without sufficient reason prefers himself to others. And though as *Hensius,* paraphrases upon *Aristotle's* politicks to this purpose. *viz. Nothing is more suitable to nature, then that those who excel in understanding and prudence, should rule and controul those who are less happy in those advantages, &c.* Yes we must note, that there is room for an answer, *scil.* That it would be the greatest absurdity to believe, that nature actually invests the wise with a sovereignity over the weak; or with a right of forcing them against their wills; for that no sovereignity can be established, unless some human deed, or covenant precede: Nor does natural fitness for government make a man presently governor over another; for that as *Ulpian* says, *by a natural right all men are born free;* and nature having set all men upon a level and made them equals, no servitude or subjection can be conceived without inequality; and this cannot be made without usurpation or force in others, or voluntary compliance in those who resign their freedom, and give away their degree of natural being. And thus we come,

2. To consider man in a civil state of being; wherein we shall observe the great difference between a natural, and political state; for in the latter state many great disproportions appear, or at least many obvious distinctions are soon made amongst men; which doctrine is to be laid open under a few heads.

1. Every man considered in a natural state, must be allowed to be free, and at his own dispose; yet to suit mans inclinations to society; and in a peculiar manner to gratify the necessity he is in of public rule and order, he is impelled to enter into a civil community; and divests himself of his natural freedom, and puts himself under government; which amongst other things comprehends the power of life and death over him; together with authority to anjoyn him some things to which he has an utter aversion, and to prohibit him other things, for which he may have as strong an inclination; so that he may be often under this authority, obliged to sacrifice his private, for the public good. So that though man is inclined to society, yet he is driven to a combination by great necessity. For that the true and leading cause of forming governments, and yielding up natural liberty, and throwing mans equality into a common pile to be new cast by the rules of fellowship; was really and truly to guard themselves against the injuries men were lyable to interchangeably; for none so good to man, as man, and yet none a greater enemy. So that,

2. The first human subject and original of civil power is the people. For as they have a power every man over himself in a natural state, so upon a combination they can and do bequeath

this power unto others; and settle it according as their united discretion shall determine. For that this is very plain, that when the subject of sovereign power is quite extinct, that power returns to the people again. And when they are free, they may set up what species of government they please; or if they rather incline to it, they may subside into a state of natural being, if it be plainly for the best. In the *Eastern* country of the *Mogul,* we have some resemblance of the case; for upon the death of an absolute monarch, they live so many days without a civil head; but in that *Interregnum,* those who survive the vacancy, are glad to get into a civil state again; and usually they are in a very bloody condition when they return under the covert of a new monarch; this project is to indear the people to a tyranny, from the experience they have so lately had of an anarchy.

3. The formal reason of government is the will of a community, yielded up and surrendered to some other subject, either of one particular person, or more, conveyed in the following manner.

Let us conceive in our mind a multitude of men, all naturally free and equal; going about voluntarily, to erect themselves into a new common-wealth. Now their condition being such, to bring themselves into a politick body, they must needs enter into divers covenants.

1. They must interchangeably each man covenant to joyn in one lasting society, that they may be capable to concert the measures of their safety, by a publick vote.

2. A vote or decree must then nextly pass to set up some particular species of government over them. And if they are joyned in their first compact upon absolute terms to stand to the decision of the first vote concerning the species of government: Then all are bound by the majority to acquiesce in that particular form thereby settled, though their own private opinion, incline them to some other model.

3. After a decree has specified the particular form of government, then there will be need of new covenant, whereby those on whom sovereignty is conferred, engage to take care of the common peace, and welfare. And the subjects on the other head,

to yield them faithful obedience. In which covenant is included that submission and union of wills, by which a state may be conceived to be but one person. So that the most proper definition of a civil state, is this, *viz.* A civil state is a compound moral person. Whose will (united by those covenants before passed) is the will of all; to the end it may use, and apply the strength and riches of private persons towards maintaining the common peace, security, and well-being of all, which may be conceived as tho' the whole state was now become but one man; in which the aforesaid covenants may be supposed under God's providence, to be the divine *Fiat,* pronounced by God, let us make man. And by way of resemblance the aforesaid being may be thus anatomized.

1. The sovereign power is the soul infused, giving life and motion to the whole body.

2. Subordinate officers are the joynts by which the body moves.

3. Wealth and riches are the strength.

4. Equity and laws are the reason.

5. Councellors the memory.

6. *Salus Populi,* or the happiness of the people, is the end of its beings: or main business to be attended and done.

7. Concord amongst the members, and all estates, is the health.

8. Sedition is sickness, and civil war death.

9. The parts of sovereignty may be considered: So,

1. As it prescribes the rule of action: It is rightly termed legislative power.

2. As it determines the controversies of subjects by the standard of those rules. So is it justly termed judiciary power.

3. As it arms the subjects against foreigners, or forbids hostility, so its called the power of peace and war.

4. As it takes in ministers for the discharge of business, so it is called the right of appointing magistrates. So that all great officers and public servants, must needs owe their original to the creating power of sovereignty. So that those whose right it is to create, may dissolve the being of those who are created, unless they cast them into an immortal frame. And yet must needs be dissoluble if they justly forfeit their being to their creators.

5. The chief end of civil communities, is, that men thus conjoyned, may be secured against the injuries, they are liable to from their own kind. For if every man could secure himself singly; it would be great folly for him, to renounce his natural liberty, in which every man is his own king and protector.

6. The sovereign authority besides, that it inheres in every state as in a common and general subject. So farther according as it resides in some one person, or in a council (consisting of some select persons, or of all the members of a community) as in a proper and particular subject, so it produceth different forms of common-wealths, *viz.* Such as are either simple and regular, or mixt.

1. The forms of a regular state are three only, which forms arise from the proper and particular subject, in which the supream power resides. As,

1. A democracy, which is when the sovereign power is lodged in a council consisting of all the members, an where every member has the privilege of a vote. This form of government, appears in the greatest part of the world to have been the most ancient. For that reason seems to shew it to be most probable, that when men (being originally in a condition of natural freedom and equality) had thoughts of joyning in a civil body, would without question be inclined to administer their common affairs, by their common judgment, and so must necessarily to gratify that inclination established a democracy; neither can it be rationally imagined, that fathers of families being yet free and independent, should in a moment, or little time take off their long delight in governing their own affairs, and devolve all upon some single sovereign commander; for that it seems to have been thought more equitable, that what belonged to all should be managed by all, when all had entered by compact into one community. The original of our government, says *Plato,* (speaking of the *Athenian* common-wealth) was taken from the equality of our race. Other states there are composed of different blood, and of unequal lines, the consequence of which are disproportionable soveraignty, tyranical or oligarchycal sway; under which men live in such a

manner, as to esteem themselves partly lords, and partly slaves to each other. But we and our countrymen, being all born brethren of the same mother, do not look upon ourselves, to stand under so hard a relation, as that of lords and slaves; but the parity of our descent incline us to keep up the like parity of our laws, and to yield the precedency to nothing but to superior virtue and wisdom. And moreover it seems very manifest that most civil communities arose at first from the union of families, that were nearly allyed in race and blood. And though ancient story make frequent mention of kings, yet it appears that most of them were such that had an influence rather in perswading, then in any power of commanding. So *Justin* discribes that kind of government, as the most primitive, which *Aristotle* stiles an heroical kingdom. *viz*. Such as is no ways inconsistent with a democratical state. *De princip. Reru.* 1. *L.* 1. *C.*

A democracy is then erected, when a number of free persons, do assemble together, in order to enter into a covenant for uniting themselves in a body: And such a preparative assembly hath some appearance already of a democracy; it is a democracy in *embrio,* properly in this respect, that every man hath the priviledge freely to deliver his opinion concerning the common affairs. Yet he who dissents from the vote of the majority, is not in the least obliged by what they determine, till by a second covenant, a popular form be actually established; for not before then can we call it a democratical government, *viz*. Till the right of determining all matters relating to the public safety, is actually placed in a general assembly of the whole people; or by their own compact and mutual agreement, determine themselves the proper subject for the exercise of sovereign power. And to compleat this state, and render it capable to exert its power to answer the end of a civil state: These conditions are necessary.

1. That a certain time and place be assigned for assembling.

2. That when the assembly be orderly met, as to time and place, that then the vote of the majority must pass for the vote of the whole body.

3. That magistrates be appointed to exercise the authority of the

whole for the better dispatch of business, of every days occurence; who also may with more mature diligence, search into more important affairs; and if in case any thing happens of greater consequence, may report it to the assembly; and be peculiarly serviceable in putting all public decrees into execution. Because a large body of people is almost useless in respect of the last service, and of many others as to the more particular application and exercise of power. Therefore it is most agreable with the law of nature, that they institute their officers to act in their name, and stead.

2. The second species of regular government, is an aristocracy; and this is said then to be constituted when the people, or assembly united by a first covenant, and having thereby cast themselves into the first rudiments of a state; do then by common decree, devolve the sovereign power, on a council consisting of some select members; and these having accepted of the designation, are then properly invested with sovereign command; and then an aristocracy is formed.

3. The third species of a regular government, is a monarchy which is settled when the sovereign power is conferred on some one worthy person. It differs from the former, because a monarch who is but one person in natural, as well as in moral account, and so is furnished with an immediate power of excercising sovereign command in all instances of government; but the forenamed must needs have particular time and place assigned; but the power and authority is equal in each.

2. Mixt governments, which are various and of divers kinds (not now to be enumerated) yet possibly the fairest in the world is that which has a regular monarchy; settled upon a noble democracy as its basis. And each part of the government is so adjusted by pacts and laws that renders the whole constitution an *elisium*. It is said of the British empire, that it is such a monarchy, as that by the necessary subordinate concurrence of the lords and commons, in the making and repealing all statutes or acts of parliament; it hath the main advantages of an aristocracy, and of a democracy, and yet free from the disadvantages and evils of either. It is such a monarchy, as by most admirable tempera-

ment affords very much to the industry, liberty, and happiness of the subject, and reserves enough for the majesty and prerogative of any king, who will own his people as subjects, not as slaves. It is a kingdom, that of all the kingdoms of the world, is most like to the kingdom of Jesus Christ, whose yoke is easy, and burden light. Present state of England 1st part 64 *p.* Thus having drawn up this brief scheme concerning man, and the nature of civil government, he is become sole subject of. I shall nextly proceed to make improvements of the premises, to accommodate the main subject under our consideration.

2. I shall now make some improvement of the foregoing principles of civil knowledge, fairly deduced from the law of nature. And I shall peculiarly refer to ecclesiastical affairs, whereby we may in probability discover more clearly the kind, and something of the nature of that government, which Christ has placed in and over his church. The learned debates of men, and divine writ sometimes seems to cast such a grandure on the church and its officers, as tho' they stood in peerage with civil empire. *Rev.* 1. 6, 9. 1, *Pet.* 2. 9. 1 *Cor.* 4. 8. 1 *Cor.* 12. 28. 2. *Cor.* 10. 8. But all such expressions must needs be otherways interpreted. God is the highest cause that acts by council; and it must needs be altogether repugnant, to think he should fore-cast the state of this world by no better a scheme, than to order two sovereign powers, in the same grand community, which would be like placing two suns in the firmament, which would be to set the universe into a flame: That should such an error happen, one must needs be forthwith extinguished, to bring the frame of nature into a just temper and keep it out of harms way. But to proceed with my purpose I shall go back upon the civil scheme, and inquire after two things: First of rebellion against government in general, and then in special; whether any of the aforesaid species of regular government can be predicable of the church of God on earth.

1. In general concerning rebellion against government for particular subjects to break in upon regular communities duly established, is from the premises to violate the law of nature; and is a high usurpation upon the first grand immunities of mankind.

Such rebels in states, and usurpers in churches affront the world, with a presumption that the best of the brotherhood are a company of fools, and that themselves have fairly monopolized all the reason of human nature. Yea, they take upon them the boldness to assume a prerogative of trampling under foot the natural original equality and liberty of their fellows; for to push the proprietors of settlements out of possession of their old, and impose new schemes upon them, is vertually to declare them in a state of vassalage, or that they were born so; and therefore will the usurper be so gracious as to insure them they shall not be sold at the next market: They must esteem it a favour, for by this time all the original prerogatives of mans nature are intentionally a victim, smoaking to satiate the usurpers ambition. It is a very tart observation on an *English* monarch, and where is may by proportion be applied to a subject must needs sink very deep, and serve for evidence under this head. It is in the secret history of K. *C.* 2. and K. *J.* 2. *p.* 2. says my author, Where the constitution of a nation is such, that the laws of the land are the measures both of the sovereigns commands, and the obedience of the subjects, whereby it is provided; that as the one are not to invade what by concessions and stipulations is granted to the ruler; so the other is not to deprive them of their lawful and determined rights and liberties; then the prince who strives to subvert the fundamental laws of the society, is the traytor and the rebel, and not the people, who endeavour to preserve and defend their own. It's very applicable to particular men in their rebellions or usurpations in church or state.

2. In special I shall now proceed to enquire, whether any of the aforesaid species of regular, unmixt governments can with any good shew of reason be predicable of the church of Christ on earth. If the churches of Christ, as churches, are either the object or subject of a sovereign power intrusted in the hands of men, then most certainly one of the fore-cited schemes of a perfect government will be applicable to it.

Before I pursue the enquiry, it may not be improper to pause, and make some caution here, by distinguishing between that which may have some resemblance of civil power, and the thing itself; and so the power of churches is but a faint resemblance of civil power; it comes in reality nothing near to the thing itself; for the one is truly coercive, the other persuasive; the one is sovereign power, the other is delegated and ministerial: But not to delay, I shall proceed with my enquiry, and therein shall endeavour to humour the several great claimers of government in the church of Christ. And,

1. I shall begin with a monarchy. It's certain, his holiness, either by reasonable pleas, or powerful cheats, has assumed an absolute and universal sovereignty; this fills his cathedral chair, and is adorned with a triple crown, and in defence thereof does protect, The Almighty has made him both key-keeper of heaven and hell, with the adjacent territories of purgatory, and vested in him an absolute sovereignty over the christian world. And his right has so far prevailed, that princes and civil monarchs hold their crowns and donations as his dutiful sons, and loyal subjects; he therefore decks himself with the spoils of the divine attributes, stiling himself, our Lord God, *optimum, maximum et supremum numen in Terris;* a God on earth, a visible deity, and that his power is absolute, and his wisdom infallible. And many of the great potentates of the earth have paid their fealty, as though it was really so. One of them clad in canvas, going bare-foot in the depth of winter, (in obedience to the decree, stinting the penance in proportion to the wickedness of princes) has waited many days for absolution at his pious gates. Another has thrown himself down prostrate a humble penitent before him: He has placed his holy foot on the monarchs profane neck as crushing a vermine, crawling out of the stable of his sovereignty; and others frequently kiss his toes with very profound devotion. These and such like triumphant signals of his sovereign power does he wear. And indeed if he is the universal monarch of the catholic church, princes that are members of it must needs knock under; for that in one world there cannot possibly be two *Most High's,* any more than two *Infinites.* Thus you see the clergy, or gospel ministry of the chris-

tian world have so wisely, handled business, and managed the
gospel, that they have fairly (as they avouch) found a sovereign
power bequeathed in it to the ministry of Christ, and romaging
more warily and nicely, at last found a spiritual monarch, very
compleatly furnished with the keys of all sorts of power hanging
at his girdle; an may we not pronounce the wiser they! seeing the
world growing weary of religion, was willing to loll itself down
to sleep, and leave them in sole trust with the whole interest of
God's kingdom. But the sad enquiry is, whether this sort of government has not plainly subverted the design of the gospel, and
the end for which Christ's government was ordained, *viz*. the
moral, spiritual, and eternal happiness of men?

But I have no occasion to pursue this remark with tedious
demonstrations: It's very plain, it's written with blood in capital
letters, to be read at midnight by the flames of *Smithfield,* and
other such like consecrated fires. That the government of this
ecclesiastical monarch has instead of sanctifying, absolutely de-
bauched the world, and subverted all good christianity in it. So
that without the least shew of any vain presumption we may
infer, that God and wise nature were never propitious to the birth
of this monster.

An aristocracy which places the supream power in a select company of choice persons. Here I freely acknowledge were the gospel ministry established the subject of this power, *viz*. To will and
do, in all church affairs without controul, &c. This government
might do to support the church in its most valuable rights, &c.
If we could be assured they would make the scripture, and not
their private will the rule of their personal and ministerial actions:
and indeed upon these terms any species of government, might
serve the great design of redemption; but considering how great
an interest is embarked, and how frail a bottom we trust, though
we should rely upon the best of men, especially if we remember
what is in the hearts of good men, (*viz*. much ignorance, abundance of small ends, many times cloked with a high pretence in
religion; pride skulking and often breeding revenge upon a small

affront; and blown up by a pretended zeal; yet really and truly by
nothing more divine than interest, or ill nature) and also considering how very uncertain we are of the real goodness of those we
esteem good men; and also how impossible it is to secure the
intail of it to successors: and also if we remind how christianity by
the foresaid principle has been peel'd, rob'd and spoiled already;
it cannot consist with the light of nature to venture again upon such
perils, especially if we can find a safer way home. More distinctly.

It is very plain (allowing me to speak emblematically) the
primitive constitution of the churches was a democracy, as appears
by the foregoing parallel. But after the christian churches were
received into the favour of the imperial court, under the dominion
of *Constantine* the great; there being many præliminaries which
had furnished the ministers with a disposition thereunto, they
quickly deprived the fraternities of their rights in the government
of the churches, when they were once provided of a plentiful
maintenance through the liberality of *Constantine,* that when
christianity was so luxuriantly treated, as by his great bounty, and
noble settlement, it is said there was a voice heard from heaven,
saying, Now is poyson poured into the church. But the subver-
sion of the constitution, is a story too long now to tell. Take
therefore part of it, out of a late author well versed in antiquity,
which may give some brief image of the whole.

*Nun multa secula jus Plebis Illasum Mansit, neque Aliter
Evenire Potuit, Quin Illud, vel amittatur, vel saltem diminuatur,
&c. De Ordina; Diss. Hystorica. P.* 36. 40. 41.

The right of the people did not remain unhurt through many
ages; neither could it well be otherways, but that it must be lost,
or much diminished. *Zonaras*[3] does confess that heretofore bishops were chosen by the suffrage of the people. But many seditions
happening among them; it was decreed that every bishop should
hereafter be chosen by the authority of the bishops of every province. The cause seemed to be so very specious, that nothing could

---

[3] John Zonaras, from whom Wise has just quoted and translated, a twelfth-
century Byzantine historian.

be more decent, or more conducive to the safety of the common-wealth.

Yet (says my author) if you do well weigh the business, you must needs acknowledge nothing could have happened more pernicious or destructive to the church of God. For soon after these things came to pass, it is very obvious, that tyranny over the consciences of the faithful; and an intolerable pride every where grew rampant among the guides of the church. Yet there was one thing still very needful to be done; and that was to establish or confirm the power which the metropolitans, and bishops had acquired to themselves. Therefore they fell to it tooth and nail to drive away the fraternity from all interest in elections: And alas poor hearts! They began to sleep with both ears; that then was scarce any enemy left to interrupt, or controul the conquerors. This was the manner of the clergy till they had made themselves the subjects of all power and then acted arbitrarily, and did what they pleased in the church of God.

But let the learned, knowing world, consider, what the issue of all this was, *scil.* what a wretched capacity the drowsiness and cowardise of the people; and the usurpation and ambition of the ministry brought the professing world into. If those who were truely godly on both sides had in a few ages lookt down from heaven, and had eyed the following centuries, they might have beheld a world of matter for sorrowful impressions; to think that they themselves had occasioned the ruin of millions, by their remis and passive temper in one sort; and too much humouring, and nourishing pride, and high conceits of themselves and others, in the other; when as if they had stood firm to the government as left settled by the apostles; they had certainly prevented an apostacy that has damned, and confounded a great part of about thirty generations of men, women, and children. That for my own part I can upon experience, in some measure truly say (to the history of the primitive churches in the loss of their government; and the consequents which followed, when I am impelled to repeat it to myself) as one *Eneas* said to queen *Dido,*

Infandum Regina Jubes Renovare Dolorem
——— Quis tulia fando
Temperet e Lacrimis! ———

So doleful a contemplation is it to think the world should be destroyed by those men, who by God were ordained to save it!

In a word, an aristocracy is a dangerous constitution in the church of Christ, as it possesses the presbytery of all church power: What has been observed sufficiently evinces it. And not only so but from the nature of the constitution, for it has no more barrier to it, against the ambition, insults, and arbitrary measures of men, then an obsolute monarchy. But to abbreviate; it seems most agreable with the light of nature, that if there be any of the regular government settled in the church of God it must needs be,

3. A democracy. This is a form of government, which the light of nature does highly value, and often directs to as most agreable to the just and natural prerogatives of human beings. This was of great account, in the early times of the world. And not only so, but upon the experience of several thousand years, after the world had been tumbled, and tost from one species of government to another, at a great expence of blood and treasure, many of the wise nations of the world have sheltered themselves under it again; or at least have blendished, and balanced their governments with it.

It is certainly a great truth, *scil*. That mans original liberty after it is resigned, (yet under due restrictions) ought to be cherished in all wise governments; or otherwise a man in making himself a subject, he alters himself from a freeman, into a slave, which to do is repugnant to the law of nature. Also the natural equality of men amongst men must be duly favored; in that government was never established by God or nature, to give one man a prerogative to insult over another; therefore in a civil, as well as in a natural state of being, a just equality is to be indulged so far as that every man, is bound to honor every man, which is agreable both with nature and religion, 1. Pet. 2.17. *Honor all men.*—The end of all good government is to cultivate humanity, and promote the happiness of all, and the good of every man in all his rights, his life, liberty, estate, honor, &c. without injury or abuse done to any. Then certainly it cannot easily be thought, that a company of men, that shall enter into a voluntary compact, to hold all power in their own hands, thereby to use and improve their united force, wisdom, riches and strength for the common and particular good of every member, as is the nature of a democracy; I say it cannot be that this sort of constitution, will so readily furnish those in government with an appetite, or disposition to prey upon each other, or imbezle the common stock; as some particular persons may be apt to do when set off, and intrusted with the same power. And moreover this appears very natural, that when the aforesaid government or power, settled in all, when they have elected certain capable persons to minister in their affairs, and the said ministers remain accountable to the assembly; these officers must needs be under the influence of many wise cautions from their own thoughts (as well as under confinement by their commission) in their whole administration: And from thence it must needs follow that they will be more apt, and inclined to steer right for the main point, *viz.* The peculiar good, and benefit of the whole, and every particular member fairly and sincerely. And why may not these stand for very rational pleas in church order?

For certainly if Christ has settled any form of power in his church he has done it for his churches safety, and for the benefit of every member: Then he must needs be presumed to have made choice of that government as should least expose his people to hazard, either from the fraud, or arbitrary measures of particular men. And it is as plain as day light, there is no species of government like a democracy to attain this end. There is but about two steps from an aristocracy, to a monarchy, and from thence but one to a tyranny; an able standing force, and an ill-nature, *Ipso facto,* turns an absolute monarch into a tyrant; this is obvious among the Roman *Cæsars,* and through the world. And all these direful transmutations are easier in church affairs (from the different qualities of things) then in civil states. For what is it that cunning and learned men can't make the world swallow as an article of their creed, if they are once invested with an uncontroulable power, and are to be the standing orators to mankind in matters of faith and obedience? indeed some very wise and learned men are pleased to inveigh, and reproach the notion of a democracy in the church, which makes the *Cetu fidelium* or community of the faithful the first subject of the power of government. This they say tends to *Brownism,* and abhorred anarchy, and then they say they upon such præmises, it must needs follow that every member of the body must be an officer; and then every one must preach and dispence the sacraments, *&c.*

Reply. Certainly such gentlemen, either designs to pose and baffle their reader with falacy; or they themselves never took up, or understood the true ideas of the several species of government; in that a democracy is as regular a form, and as particular as any other.

For,

1. An absolute or limited monarch can't manage the power or government devolved upon him, without the great officers of the crown, or a large sett of ministers; though possible he may with the quicker dispatch issue out his degrees, yet he must execute all by his ministry. And why may not a democracy be indulged the same liberty? And this will prevent all anarchy or confusion most apparently. But,

2. The bitter pill to swallow in this doctrine of a democracy in the church, is the terrible power of life and death; or the accountableness of particular members to the assembly, and especially those in the ministry; but yet this is agreable with the nature of the constitution, and easily managed without anarchy, or popular confusion also, which would be made very evident, if we should but run the parallel in all points between the democracy of the state and church. But nextly from the premises, I shall

3. Infer, That if these churches are not properly formed, yet are fairly established in their present order by the law of nature. And will they be advised, I would exhort them to try who will be

so bold as to dare to disseize them. A monarchy has been tryed in the church with a witness, but it has absolutely failed us. An aristocracy in a deep calm threw the democracy overboard, and took not only the helm in hand, but seized ship and cargo as their right and title; but after some time brought all to shipwreck, and that in a good harbour too.

A democracy was the noble government which beat out in all the bad weather of ten bloody persecutions under the management of antiquity. And this is our constitution, and what can't we be pleased? This constitution is as agreable with the light and laws of nature as any other whatsoever, as has been fairly laid down and fully evinced, and more accommodated to the concerns of religion than any other. Therefore I shall now conclude my demonstration with this brief appeal to the common reason of mankind, *viz.*

How can it consist with the honourable terms man holds upon here on earth; that the best sort of men that we can find in the world; such men are as adorned with a double sett of enobling immunities, the first from nature, the other from grace; that these men when they enter into charter-party to manage a trade for heaven, must *ipso facto* be clapt under a government, that is arbitrary and dispotick; yea that carries the plain symptoms of a tyranny in it, when the light of nature knows of a better species, and frequently has made use of it? It wants no farther demonstration, for it's most apparent, that nature is so much mistress of herself, that man in a natural state of being, is under God the first subject of all power, and therefore can make his own choice, and by deliberate compacts settles his own conditions for the government of himself in a civil state of being: And when a government so settled shall throw itself from its foundations, or the subjects of sovereign power shall subvert or confound the constitution, they then degrade themselves; and so all power returns again to the people, who are the first owners. And what! Is man become so unfortunate, degraded and debased, as to be without all power in settling a government over himself, relating to the matters of his eternal well-being? Or when he comes back to a fathers house, must he fall into the capacity of a meer passive being, and be put under such tutors, as can easily turn tyrants over him, and no relief left for him in his own hands; this is certainly most repugnant to the light of nature, and very disagreable with the liberty and free genius of a gospel state. Nay, in a word, if the government of the churches be settled by God, either in the hands of a church monarch, or aristocracy, and the people are no ways the subject of church-power: Nay, if they are not under Christ, the fountain of power; then the reformation so called, is but a meer cheat, a schism, and notorious rebellion; neither is there room left for the least paliation, or shadow of excuse, for the reformers in renouncing their obedience to their publick governors. And the Martyrologies which pretend to immortalize the fame of eminent heroes, must be changed into chronicles, handling along an account of the just and deserved fate of a crew of rebels against God and government; for what business had such a company of illeterate crack brain'd fellows to meddle with their rulers, or examine into their administrations? For if they have no right of power in government, they stand absolutely bound to yield a passive obedience and non-resistance; and if they are so hardy and daring as to oppose their lawful rulers, the sharpest penality in this world, is too easy for them; the inquisition is but dallying and playing with them; hell is their desert. But how it comes about that a state of grace, when in want of a suitable government, it become such a vassil, and wise and cunning nature is by her creator intrusted, and adorned with more enobling prerogatives, I must leave, and resign unto those learned men to solve, who plead for an aristocracy in the churches of Christ.

But to wind up the whole discourse in a few words, I acknowledge many objections may be here made, and several questions of moment might here fall under debate; but having obtained what I have principally sought for, in traversing the paths of nature, in the three following particulars; therefore with them, and with one objection answered; and also with some brief improvement of the grand hypothesis in this demonstration, I shall finish the argument.

1. Three particulars; or so many golden maxims, securing the honor of congregational churches.

Particular 1. That the people or fraternity under the gospel, are the first subject of power; or else religion sinks the dignity of human nature into a baser capacity with relation to ecclesiasitical, then it is in, in a natural state of being with relation to civil government.

Particular 2. That a democracy in church or state, is a very honorable and regular government according to the dictates of right reason. And therefore,

Particular 3. That these churches of *New-England,* in their ancient constitution of church order; it being a democracy, are manifestly justified and defended by the law and light of nature.

2. The objection. The plea from the law of nature for a democracy in the church, is as forceable for any other species of government; because nature is furnished with such a variety of schemes as has been pleaded to: And why may not the wise christian nations take which likes them best?

Answ. We must distinguish between man left solely to the direction of the law of nature, and as the subject of revelation, wherein divine wisdom may interpose; and determine on some particular species, without hurting or crossing the law of nature. Therefore,

1. I readily grant and acknowledge, a christian people may settle what species of government they please, when they are solely left to determine by the law of nature, what government in the church they will have. But then we must remember, that by the argument or concession, the power is originally in the people; and then our own case is secure and safe enough; both on the account of the reversion of power, and especially, for that the people the first subjects of power, have been pleased to settle a democracy for their government, in the churches of this country. And if after the peaceable possession of about an hundred years, any persons can persuade them to alter their government into any other species, this will be less worthy of blame, than craftily, or unfairly to force it out of their hands.

2. It's granted, that according to the light of nature, there be various regular models of government; but if divine wisdom is pleased to interpose and over-rule natures agitations, and cast the scales for this or that particular form, nature will be but fair manuered to submit to its author and rector. So that if we find that God has disclosed his mind by revelation, that his churches be the subjects of a democracy, than all stand obliged to comply under a double bond. And so we come under a proper crisis to enquire in the next place for scripture-evidence in the justification of these churches.

But before I proceed to it, I shall

3. Make some brief improvement of the main *Hypothesis* in the demonstration; that is to say, if the government of the gospel churches, be a democracy, these consequences must necessarily follow, *scil.*

1. *Cons.* That the right of convoking councils ecclesiastical, is in the churches.

2. *Cons.* That such a council has only consultative not a juridical power in it. A juridical power comitted to such a representative body is both needless, and also dangerous to the distinct and perfect states they derive from. Compleat states settled upon a body of immutiable and imperial laws as its basis, may want council; but to create a new subject of juridical power, is some way to endanger the being of the creators.

3. *Cons.* That all the members of an ecclesiastical council, deriving from a democracy are subjects of equal power. Whatever the power is, the several delegates must from the nature of the government they derive from, be equal sharers in it. Democratical states, in their representative body can make but one house, because they have but one subject of supream power in their nature, and therefore their delegates, let them be who or what they may be, are under equal trust; so that none can justly claim superiority over their fellows, or pretend to a higher power in their suffrage. Indeed in such kingdoms, where the sovereign power is distributed and settled in divers subjects, that the ballance of power may be more even, for the safety of the whole, and of all parts

under all acts of sovereign power: From such a settlement of power, there arises several distinct states in the same government, which when convened as one subject of sovereign power, they make different houses in their grand sessions; and so one house or state can negative another. But in every distinct house of these states, the members are equal in their vote; the most ayes makes the affirmative vote, and most no's the negative: They don't weigh the intellectual furniture, or other distinguishing qualifications of the several voters in the scales of the golden rule of fellowship; they only add up the ayes, and the no's, and so determine the suffrage of the house.

JONATHAN EDWARDS
(1703-1758)

Bibliographical Note. The best edition of Edwards' writings is Samuel Austin, ed., *The Works of President Edwards* (Worcester, 1808-1809). An excellent selection, the only extensive scholarly editing Edwards has had, is C. H. Faust and T. H. Johnson, *Jonathan Edwards: Representative Selections* (New York, 1935); this edition contains a careful critical bibliography. Perry Miller has recently edited from manuscript Edwards' important *Images or Shadows of Divine Things* (New Haven, 1948). The selections printed below follow the texts of Faust and Johnson's *Representative Selections,* pp. 52-72, 155-172, and 349-357 and of Miller's edition of the *Images,* pp. 43-44, 48-49, 69-70, 79, 94-95, 97, 102, 104-105, 109, 135-137. For Edwards' life see Ola E. Winslow, *Jonathan Edwards* (New York, 1940); on his mind, see the introduction to the Faust and Johnson *Representative Selections* and, most important, Perry Miller, *Jonathan Edwards* (New York, 1949).

PERSONAL NARRATIVE *
(WRITTEN AFTER 1739)

I had a variety of concerns and exercises about my soul from my childhood; but had two more remarkable seasons of awakening, before I met with that change by which I was brought to those new dispositions, and that new sense of things, that I have since had. The first time was when I was a boy, some years before I went to college, at a time of remarkable awakening in my father's congregation, I was then very much affected for many months, and concerned about the things of religion, and my soul's salvation; and was abundant in duties. I used to pray five times a day in secret, and to spend much time in religious talk with other boys; and used to meet with them to pray together. I experienced I know not what kind of delight in religion. My mind was much engaged in it, and had much selfrighteous pleasure; and it was my delight to abound in religious duties. I with some of my schoolmates joined together, and built a booth in a swamp, in a very retired spot, for a place of prayer. And besides,

---

* Reprinted from *Jonathan Edwards: Representative Selections,* edited by C. H. Faust and T. H. Johnson and used with permission of the American Book Company.

I had particular secret places of my own in the woods, where I used to retire by myself; and was from time to time much affected. My affections seemed to be lively and easily moved, and I seemed to be in my element when engaged in religious duties. And I am ready to think, many are deceived with such affections, and such a kind of delight as I then had in religion, and mistake it for grace.

But in process of time, my convictions and affections were off; and I entirely lost all those affections and delights and left off secret prayer, at least as to any constant performance of it; and returned like a dog to his vomit, and went on in the ways of sin. Indeed I was at times very uneasy, especially towards the latter part of my time at college; when it pleased God, to seize me with a pleurisy; in which he brought me nigh to the grave, and shook me over the pit of hell. And yet, it was not long after my recovery, before I fell again into my old ways of sin. But God would not suffer me to go on with any quietness; I had great and violent inward struggles, till, after many conflicts with wicked inclinations, repeated resolutions, and bonds that I laid myself under by a kind of vows to God, I was brought wholly to break off all former wicked ways, and all ways of known outward sin; and to apply myself to seek salvation, and practise many religious duties; but without that kind of affection and delight which I had formerly experienced. My concern now wrought more by inward struggles and conflicts, and selfreflections. I made seeking my salvation the main business of my life. But yet, it seems to me, I sought after a miserable manner; which has made me sometimes since to question, whether ever it issued in that which was saving; being ready to doubt, whether such miserable seeking ever succeeded. I was indeed brought to seek salvation in a manner that I never was before; I felt a spirit to part with all things in the world, for an interest in Christ. My concern continued and prevailed, with many exercising thoughts and inward struggles; but yet it never seemed to be proper to express that concern by the name of terror.

From my childhood up, my mind had been full of objections

against the doctrine of God's sovereignty, in choosing whom he
would to eternal life, and rejecting whom he pleased; leaving
them eternally to perish, and be everlastingly tormented in hell.
It used to appear like a horrible doctrine to me. But I remember
the time very well, when I seemed to be convinced, and fully satisfied, as to this sovereignty of God, and his justice in thus eternally disposing of men, according to his sovereign pleasure. But
never could give an account, how, or by what means, I was thus
convinced, not in the least imagining at the time, nor a long time
after, that there was any extraordinary influence of God's Spirit
in it; but only that now I saw further, and my reason apprehended the justice and reasonableness of it. However, my mind
rested in it; and it put an end to all those cavils and objections.
And there has been a wonderful alteration in my mind, in respect
to the doctrine of God's sovereignty, from that day to this; so that
I scarce ever have found so much as the rising of an objection
against it, in the most absolute sense, in God's shewing mercy to
whom he will shew mercy, and hardening whom he will. God's
absolute sovereignty and justice, with respect to salvation and
damnation, is what my mind seems to rest assured of, as much
as of any thing that I see with my eyes; at least it is so at times.
But I have often, since that first conviction, had quite another
kind of sense of God's sovereignty than I had then. I have often
since had not only a conviction, but a delightful conviction. The
doctrine has very often appeared exceeding pleasant, bright, and
sweet. Absolute sovereignty is what I love to ascribe to God. But
my first conviction was not so.

The first instance that I remember of that sort of inward,
sweet delight in God and divine things that I have lived much
in since, was on reading those words, I Tim. i. 17. *Now unto
the King eternal, immortal, invisible, the only wise God, be honor
and glory for ever and ever, Amen.* As I read the words, there
came into my soul, and was as it were diffused through it, a
sense of the glory of the Divine Being; a new sense, quite different from any thing I ever experienced before. Never any words
of scripture seemed to me as these words did. I thought with my-

self, how excellent a Being that was, and how happy I should be, if I might enjoy that God, and be rapt up to him in heaven, and be as it were swallowed up in him for ever! I kept saying, and as it were singing over these words of scripture to myself; and went to pray to God that I might enjoy him, and prayed in a manner quite different from what I used to do; with a new sort of affection. But it never came into my thought, that there was any thing spiritual, or of a saving nature in this.

From about that time, I began to have a new kind of apprehensions and ideas of Christ, and the work of redemption, and the glorious way of salvation by him. An inward, sweet sense of these things, at times, came into my heart; and my soul was led away in pleasant views and contemplations of them. And my mind was greatly engaged to spend my time in reading and meditating on Christ, on the beauty and excellency of his person, and the lovely way of salvation by free grace in him. I found no books so delightful to me, as those that treated of these sub-jects. Those words Cant. ii. 1, used to be abundantly with me, *I am the Rose of Sharon, and the Lilly of the valleys.* The words seemed to me, sweetly to represent the loveliness and beauty of Jesus Christ. The whole book of Canticles used to be pleasant to me, and I used to be much in reading it, about that time; and found, from time to time, an inward sweetness, that would carry me away, in my contemplations. This I know not how to express otherwise, than by a calm, sweet abstraction of soul from all the concerns of this world; and sometimes a kind of vision, or fixed ideas and imaginations, of being alone in the mountains, or some solitary wilderness, far from all mankind, sweetly conversing with Christ, and wrapt and swallowed up in God. The sense I had of divine things, would often of a sudden kindle up, as it were, a sweet burning in my heart; an ardor of soul, that I know not how to express.

Not long after I first began to experience these things, I gave an account to my father of some things that had passed in my mind. I was pretty much affected by the discourse we had together; and when the discourse was ended, I walked abroad alone, in a solitary place in my father's pasture, for contemplation. And as I was walking there, and looking up on the sky and clouds, there came into my mind so sweet a sense of the glorious *majesty* and *grace* of God, that I know not how to express. I seemed to see them both in a sweet conjunction; majesty and meekness joined together; it was a sweet, and gentle, and holy majesty; and also a majestic meekness; an awful sweetness; a high, and great, and holy gentleness.

After this my sense of divine things gradually increased, and became more and more lively, and had more of that inward sweetness. The appearance of every thing was altered; there seemed to be, as it were, a calm, sweet cast, or appearance of divine glory, in almost every thing. God's excellency, his wisdom, his purity and love, seemed to appear in every thing; in the sun, moon, and stars; in the clouds, and blue sky; in the grass, flowers, trees; in the water, and all nature; which used greatly to fix my mind. I often used to sit and view the moon for continuance; and in the day, spent much time in viewing the clouds and sky, to behold the sweet glory of God in these things; in the mean time, singing forth, with a low voice my contemplations of the Creator and Redeemer. And scarce any thing, among all the works of nature, was so sweet to me as thunder and lightning; formerly, nothing had been so terrible to me. Before, I used to be uncommonly terrified with thunder, and to be struck with terror when I saw a thunder storm rising; but now, on the contrary, it rejoiced me. I felt God, so to speak, at the first appearance of a thunder storm; and used to take the opportunity, at such times, to fix myself in order to view the clouds, and see the lightnings play, and hear the majestic and awful voice of God's thunder, which oftentimes was exceedingly entertaining, leading me to sweet contemplations of my great and glorious God. While thus engaged, it always seemed natural to me to sing, or chant for my meditations; or, to speak my thoughts in soliloquies with a singing voice.

I felt then great satisfaction, as to my good state; but that did not content me. I had vehement longings of soul after God and

Christ, and after more holiness, wherewith my heart seemed to be full, and ready to break; which often brought to my mind the words of the Psalmist, Psal. cxix. 28. *My soul breaketh for the longing it hath.* I often felt a mourning and lamenting in my heart, that I had not turned to God sooner, that I might have had more time to grow in grace. My mind was greatly fixed on divine things; almost perpetually in the contemplation of them. I spent most of my time in thinking of divine things, year after year; often walking alone in the woods, and solitary places, for meditation, soliloquy, and prayer, and converse with God; and it was always my manner, at such times, to sing forth my contemplations. I was almost constantly in ejaculatory prayer, wherever I was. Prayer seemed to be natural to me, as the breath by which the inward burnings of my heart had vent. The delights which I now felt in the things of religion, were of an exceeding different kind from those before mentioned, that I had when a boy; and what I then had no more notion of, than one born blind has of pleasant and beautiful colors. They were of a more inward, pure, soul animating and refreshing nature. Those former delights never reached the heart; and did not arise from any sight of the divine excellency of the things of God; or any taste of the soul satisfying and life-giving good there is in them.

My sense of divine things seemed gradually to increase, until I went to preach at Newyork, which was about a year and a half after they began; and while I was there, I felt them, very sensibly, in a much higher degree than I had done before. My longings after God and holiness, were much increased. Pure and humble, holy and heavenly Christianity, appeared exceeding amiable to me. I felt a burning desire to be in every thing a complete Christian; and conformed to the blessed image of Christ; and that I might live, in all things, according to the pure, sweet and blessed rules of the gospel. I had an eager thirsting after progress in these things; which put me upon pursuing and pressing after them. It was my continual strife day and night, and constant inquiry, how I should *be* more holy, and *live* more holily, and more becoming a child of God, and a disciple of Christ. I now sought an increase of grace and holiness, and a holy life, with much more earnestness, than ever I sought grace before I had it. I used to be continually examining myself, and studying and contriving for likely ways and means, how I should live holily, with far greater diligence and earnestness, than ever I pursued any thing in my life; but yet with too great a dependence on my own strength; which afterwards proved a great damage to me. My experience had not then taught me, as it has done since, my extreme feebleness and impotence, every manner of way; and the bottomless depths of secret corruption and deceit there was in my heart. However, I went on with my eager pursuit after more holiness, and conformity to Christ.

The heaven I desired was a heaven of holiness; to be with God, and to spend my eternity in divine love, and holy communion with Christ. My mind was very much taken up with contemplations on heaven, and the enjoyments there; and living there in perfect holiness, humility and love: And it used at that time to appear a great part of the happiness of heaven, that there the saints could express their love to Christ. It appeared to me a great clog and burden, that what I felt within, I could not express as I desired. The inward ardor of my soul, seemed to be hindered and pent up, and could not freely flame out as it would. I used often to think, how in heaven this principle should freely and fully vent and express itself. Heaven appeared exceedingly delightful, as a world of love; and that all happiness consisted in living in pure, humble, heavenly, divine love.

I remember the thoughts I used then to have of holiness; and said sometimes to myself, "I do certainly know that I love holiness, such as the gospel prescribes." It appeared to me, that there was nothing in it but what was ravishingly lovely; the highest beauty and amiableness . . . a *divine* beauty; far purer than any thing here upon earth; and that every thing else was like mire and defilement, in comparison of it.

Holiness, as I then wrote down some of my contemplations on it, appeared to me to be of a sweet, pleasant, charming, serene, calm nature; which brought an inexpressible purity, brightness, peacefulness and ravishment to the soul. In other words, that it made the soul like a field or garden of God, with all manner of pleasant flowers; all pleasant, delightful, and undisturbed; enjoying a sweet calm, and the gently vivifying beams of the sun. The soul of a true Christian, as I then wrote my meditations, appeared like such a little white flower as we see in the spring of the year; low and humble on the ground, opening its bosom to receive the pleasant beams of the sun's glory; rejoicing as it were in a calm rapture; diffusing around a sweet fragrancy; standing peacefully and lovingly, in the midst of other flowers round about; all in like manner opening their bosoms, to drink in the light of the sun. There was no part of creature holiness, that I had so great a sense of its loveliness, as humility, brokenness of heart and poverty of spirit; and there was nothing that I so earnestly longed for. My heart panted after this, to lie low before God, as in the dust; that I might be nothing, and that God might be ALL, that I might become as a little child.

While at Newyork, I was sometimes much affected with reflections of my past life, considering how late it was before I began to be truly religious; and how wickedly I had lived till then; and once so as to weep abundantly, and for a considerable time together.

On *January* 12, 1723. I made a solemn dedication of myself to God, and wrote it down; giving up myself, and all that I had to God; to be for the future, in no respect, my own; to act as one that had no right to himself, in any respect. And solemnly vowed, to take God for my whole portion and felicity; looking on nothing else, as any part of my happiness, nor acting as if it were; and his law for the constant rule of my obedience: engaging to fight, with all my might, against the world, the flesh, and the devil, to the end of my life. But I have reason to be infinitely humbled, when I consider, how much I have failed, of answering my obligation.

I had, then, abundance of sweet, religious conversation, in the family where I lived, with Mr. John Smith, and his pious mother. My heart was knit in affection, to those, in whom were appearances of true piety; and I could bear the thoughts of no other companions, but such as were holy, and the disciples of the blessed Jesus. I had great longings, for the advancement of Christ's kingdom in the world; and my secret prayer used to be, in great part, taken up in praying for it. If I heard the least hint, of any thing that happened, in any part of the world, that appeared, in some respect or other, to have a favourable aspect, on the interests of Christ's kingdom, my soul eagerly catched at it; and it would much animate and refresh me. I used to be eager to read public news-letters, mainly for that end; to see if I could not find some news, favourable to the interest of religion in the world.

I very frequently used to retire into a solitary place, on the banks of Hudson's River, at some distance from the city, for contemplation on divine things and secret converse with God: and had many sweet hours there. Sometimes Mr. Smith and I walked there together, to converse on the things of God; and our conversation used to turn much on the advancement of Christ's kingdom in the world, and the glorious things that God would accomplish for his church in the latter days. I had then, and at other times, the greatest delight in the holy scriptures, of any book whatsoever. Oftentimes in reading it, every word seemed to touch my heart. I felt a harmony between something in my heart, and those sweet and powerful words. I seemed often to see so much light exhibited by every sentence, and such a refreshing food communicated, that I could not get along in reading; often dwelling long on one sentence, to see the wonders contained in it; and yet almost every sentence seemed to be full of wonders.

I came away from Newyork in the month of April, 1723, and had a most bitter parting with Madam Smith and her son. My heart seemed to sink within me, at leaving the family and city, where I had enjoyed so many sweet and pleasant days. I went from New York to Wethersfield, by water; and as I sailed away, I kept sight of the city as long as I could. However, that night after this sorrowful parting, I was greatly comforted in God at Westchester, where we went ashore to lodge: and had a pleasant time of it all the voyage to Saybrook. It was sweet to me to think of meeting dear christians in heaven, where we should never part more. At Saybrook we went ashore to lodge on Saturday, and there kept the Sabbath; where I had a sweet and refreshing season, walking alone in the fields.

After I came home to Windsor, I remained much in a like frame of mind, as when at Newyork; only sometimes I felt my heart ready to sink, with the thoughts of my friends at Newyork. My support was in contemplations on the heavenly state; as I find in my Diary of May 1, 1723. It was a comfort to think of that state, where there is fulness of joy; where reigns heavenly, calm, and delightful love, without alloy; where there are continually the dearest expressions of this love; where is the enjoyment of the persons loved, without ever parting; where those persons who appear so lovely in this world, will really be inexpressibly more lovely, and full of love to us. And how sweetly will the mutual lovers join together, to sing the praises of God and the Lamb! How will it fill us with joy to think, that this enjoyment, these sweet exercises, will never cease, but will last to all eternity. . . . I continued much in the same frame, in the general, as when at Newyork, till I went to Newhaven, as Tutor of the College: particularly, once at Bolton, on a journey from Boston, while walking out alone in the fields. After I went to Newhaven, I sunk in religion; my mind being diverted from my eager pursuits after holiness, by some affairs, that greatly perplexed and distracted my thoughts.

In September, 1725, I was taken ill at Newhaven, and while endeavouring to go home to Windsor, was so ill at the North Village, that I could go no farther; where I lay sick, for about a quarter of a year. In this sickness, God was pleased to visit me again, with the sweet influences of his Spirit. My mind was greatly engaged there, on divine and pleasant contemplations, and longings of soul. I observed, that those who watched with me, would often be looking out wishfully for the morning; which brought to my mind those words of the Psalmist, and which my soul with delight made its own language, *My soul waiteth for the Lord, more than they that watch for the morning; I say, more than they that watch for the morning;* and when the light of day came in at the window, it refreshed my soul, from one morning to another. It seemed to be some image of the light of God's glory.

I remember, about that time, I used greatly to long for the conversion of some, that I was concerned with; I could gladly honour them, and with delight be a servant to them, and lie at their feet, if they were but truly holy. But some time after this, I was again greatly diverted with some temporal concerns, that exceedingly took up my thoughts, greatly to the wounding of my soul; and went on, through various exercises, that it would be tedious to relate, which gave me much more experience of my own heart, than I ever had before.

Since I came to this town, I have often had sweet complacency in God, in views of his glorious perfections and the excellency of Jesus Christ. God has appeared to me a glorious and lovely Being, chiefly on account of his holiness. The holiness of God has always appeared to me the most lovely of all his attributes. The doctrines of God's absolute sovereignty, and free grace, in shewing mercy to whom he would shew mercy; and man's absolute dependence on the operations of God's Holy Spirit, have very often appeared to me as sweet and glorious doctrines. These doctrines have been much my delight. God's sovereignty has ever appeared to me, great part of his glory. It has often been my delight to approach God, and adore him as a sovereign God, and ask sovereign mercy of him.

I have loved the doctrines of the gospel; they have been to my soul like green pastures. The gospel has seemed to me the richest treasure; the treasure that I have most desired, and longed that it might dwell richly in me. The way of salvation by Christ has appeared, in a general way, glorious and excellent, most pleasant and most beautiful. It has often seemed to me, that it would in a great measure spoil heaven, to receive it in any other way. That text has often been affecting and delightful to me, Isa. xxxii. 2. *A man shall be an hiding place from the wind, and a covert from the tempest, &c.*

It has often appeared to me delightful, to be united to Christ; to have him for my head, and to be a member of his body; also to have Christ for my teacher and prophet. I very often think with sweetness, and longings, and pantings of soul, of being a little child, taking hold of Christ, to be led by him through the wilderness of this world. That text, Math. xviii. 3, has often been sweet to me, *except ye be converted and become as little children, &c.* I love to think of coming to Christ, to receive salvation of him, poor in spirit, and quite empty of self, humbly exalting him alone; cut off entirely from my own root, in order to grow into, and out of Christ; to have God in Christ to be all in all; and to live by faith in the son of God, a life of humble, unfeigned confidence in him. That scripture has often been sweet to me, Psal. cxv. 1. *Not unto us, O Lord, not unto us, but unto thy name give glory, for thy mercy, and for thy truth's sake.* And those words of Christ, Luke x. 21. *In that hour Jesus rejoiced in spirit, and said, I thank thee, O Father, Lord of heaven and earth, that thou hast hid these things from the wise and prudent, and hast revealed them unto babes: Even so, Father, for so it seemed good in thy sight.* That sovereignty of God which Christ rejoiced in, seemed to me worthy of such joy; and that rejoicing seemed to shew the excellency of Christ, and of what spirit he was.

Sometimes, only mentioning a single word caused my heart to burn within me; or only seeing the name of Christ, or the name of some attribute of God. And God has appeared glorious to me, on account of the Trinity. It has made me have exalting thoughts of God, that he subsists in three persons; Father, Son and Holy Ghost. The sweetest joys and delights I have experienced, have not been those that have arisen from a hope of my own good estate; but in a direct view of the glorious things of the gospel. When I enjoy this sweetness, it seems to carry me above the thoughts of my own estate; it seems at such times a loss that I cannot bear, to take off my eye from the glorious, pleasant object I behold without me, to turn my eye in upon myself, and my own good estate.

My heart has been much on the advancement of Christ's kingdom in the world. The histories of the past advancement of Christ's kingdom have been sweet to me. When I have read histories of past ages, the pleasantest thing in all my reading has been, to read of the kingdom of Christ being promoted. And when I have expected, in my reading, to come to any such thing, I have rejoiced in the prospect, all the way as I read. And my mind has been much entertained and delighted with the scripture promises and prophecies, which relate to the future glorious advancement of Christ's kingdom upon earth.

I have sometimes had a sense of the excellent fulness of Christ, and his meetness and suitableness as a Saviour; whereby he has appeared to me, far above all, the chief of ten thousands. His blood and atonement have appeared sweet, and his righteousness sweet; which was always accompanied with ardency of spirit; and inward strugglings and breathings, and groanings that cannot be uttered, to be emptied of myself, and swallowed up in Christ.

Once, as I rode out into the woods for my health, in 1737, having alighted from my horse in a retired place, as my manner commonly has been, to walk for divine contemplation and prayer, I had a view that for me was extraordinary, of the glory of the Son of God, as Mediator between God and man, and his wonderful, great, full, pure and sweet grace and love, and meek and gentle condescension. This grace that appeared so calm and sweet, appeared also great above the heavens. The person of Christ appeared ineffably excellent with an excellency great enough to swallow up all thought and conception . . . which continued as near as I can judge, about an hour; which kept me the greater part of the time in a flood of tears, and weeping aloud. I felt an ardency of soul to be, what I know not otherwise how to express, emptied and annihilated; to lie in the dust, and to be full of Christ alone; to love him with a holy and pure love; to trust in him; to live upon him; to serve and follow him; and to be perfectly sanctified and made pure, with a divine and heavenly purity. I have, several other times, had views very much of the same nature, and which have had the same effects.

I have many times had a sense of the glory of the third person in the Trinity, in his office of Sanctifier; in his holy operations, communicating divine light and life to the soul. God, in the communications of his Holy Spirit, has appeared as an infinite fountain of divine glory and sweetness; being full, and sufficient to fill and satisfy the soul; pouring forth itself in sweet communications; like the sun in its glory, sweetly and pleasantly diffusing light and life. And I have sometimes had an affecting sense of the exelency of the word of God, as a word of life; as the light of life; a sweet, excellent lifegiving word; accompanied with a thirsting after that word, that it might dwell richly in my heart.

Often, since I lived in this town, I have had very affecting views of my own sinfulness and vileness; very frequently to such a degree as to hold me in a kind of loud weeping, sometimes for a considerable time together; so that I have often been forced to shut myself up. I have had a vastly greater sense of my own wickedness, and the badness of my heart, than ever I had before my conversion. It has often appeared to me, that if God should mark iniquity against me, I should appear the very worst of all mankind; of all that have been, since the beginning of the world to this time; and that I should have by far the lowest place in hell. When others, that have come to talk with me about their soul concerns, have expressed the sense they have had of their own wickedness, by saying that it seemed to them, that they were as bad as the devil himself; I thought their expressions seemed exceeding faint and feeble, to represent my wickedness.

My wickedness, as I am in myself, has long appeared to me perfectly ineffable, and swallowing up all thought and imagination; like an infinite deluge, or mountain over my head. I know not how to express better what my sins appear to me to be, than by heaping infinite upon infinite, and multiplying infinite by infinite. Very often, for these many years, these expressions are in my mind, and in my mouth, "Infinite upon infinite . . . Infinite upon infinite!" When I look into my heart, and take a view of my wickedness, it looks like an abyss infinitely deeper than hell. And it appears to me, that were it not for free grace, exalted and raised up to the infinite height of all the fulness and glory

of the great Jehovah, and the arm of his power and grace stretched
forth in all the majesty of his power, and in all the glory of his
sovereignty, I should appear sunk down in my sins below hell
itself; far beyond the sight of every thing, but the eye of sovereign
grace, that can pierce even down to such a depth. And yet it seems
to me, that my conviction of sin is exceeding small, and faint; it
is enough to amaze me, that I have no more sense of my sin. I
know certainly, that I have very little sense of my sinfulness.
When I have had turns of weeping and crying for my sins I
thought I knew at the time, that my repentance was nothing to
my sin.

I have greatly longed of late, for a broken heart, and to lie low
before God; and, when I ask for humility, I cannot bear the
thoughts of being no more humble than other Christians. It seems
to me, that though their degrees of humility may be suitable for
them, yet it would be a vile selfexaltation in me, not to be the
lowest in humility of all mankind. Others speak of their longing
to be "humbled to the dust;" that may be a proper expression for
them, but I always think of myself, that I ought, and it is an
expression that has long been natural for me to use in prayer, "to
lie infinitely low before God." And it is affecting to think, how
ignorant I was, when a young Christian, of the bottomless, infinite depths of wickedness, pride, hypocrisy and deceit, left in
my heart.

I have a much greater sense of my universal, exceeding dependence on God's grace and strength, and mere good pleasure,
of late, than I used formerly to have; and have experienced more
of an abhorrence of my own righteousness. The very thought of
any joy arising in me, on any consideration of my own amiableness, performances, or experiences, or any goodness of heart or
life, is nauseous and detestable to me. And yet I am greatly
afflicted with a proud and selfrighteous spirit, much more sensibly
than I used to be formerly. I see that serpent rising and putting
forth its head continually, every where, all around me.

Though it seems to me, that, in some respects, I was a far better Christian, for two or three years after my first conversion,

than I am now; and lived in a more constant delight and pleasure; yet, of late years, I have had a more full and constant sense of the absolute sovereignty of God, and a delight in that sovereignty; and have had more of a sense of the glory of Christ, as a Mediator revealed in the gospel. On one Saturday night, in particular, I had such a discovery of the excellency of the gospel above all other doctrines, that I could not but say to myself, "This is my chosen light, my chosen doctrine;" and of Christ, "This is my chosen Prophet." It appeared sweet, beyond all expression, to follow Christ, and to be taught, and enlightened, and instructed by him; to learn of him, and live to him. Another Saturday night, (*January* 1739) I had such a sense, how sweet and blessed a thing it was to walk in the way of duty; to do that which was right and meet to be done, and agreeable to the holy mind of God; that it caused me to break forth into a kind of loud weeping, which held me some time, so that I was forced to shut myself up, and fasten the doors. I could not but, as it were, cry out, "How happy are they which do that which is right in the sight of God! They are blessed indeed, they are the happy ones!" I had, at the same time, a very affecting sense, how meet and suitable it was that God should govern the world, and order all things according to his own pleasure; and I rejoiced in it, that God reigned, and that his will was done.

SINNERS IN THE HANDS OF AN ANGRY GOD *

(PREACHED 1741)

DEUT. XXXII. 35

—Their foot shall slide in due time.—

In this verse is threatened the vengeance of God on the wicked unbelieving Israelites, who were God's visible people, and who lived under the means of grace; but who, notwithstanding all God's wonderful works towards them, remained (as ver. 28.) void of counsel, having no understanding in them. Under all the cultivations of heaven, they brought forth bitter and poisonous fruit; as in the two verses next preceding the text.—The expression I have chosen for my text, *Their foot shall slide in due time,* seems to imply the following things, relating to the punishment and destruction to which these wicked Israelites were exposed.

1. That they were always exposed to *destruction;* as one that stands or walks in slippery places is always exposed to fall. This is implied in the manner of their destruction coming upon them, being represented by their foot sliding. The same is expressed, Psalm lxxiii. 18. "Surely thou didst set them in slippery places; thou castedst them down into destruction."

2. It implies, that they were always exposed to sudden unexpected destruction. As he that walks in slippery places is every moment liable to fall, he cannot foresee one moment whether he shall stand or fall the next; and when he does fall, he falls at once without warning: Which is also expressed in Psalm lxxiii. 18, 19. "Surely thou didst set them in slippery places; thou castedst them down into destruction: How are they brought into desolation as in a moment!"

3. Another thing implied is, that they are liable to fall *of themselves,* without being thrown down by the hand of another; as he that stands or walks on slippery ground needs nothing but his own weight to throw him down.

4. That the reason why they are not fallen already, and do not

---

* Reprinted from *Jonathan Edwards: Representative Selections,* edited by C. H. Faust and T. H. Johnson and used with permission of the American Book Company.

fall now, is only that God's appointed time is not come. For it is said, that when that due time, or appointed times comes, *their foot shall slide*. Then they shall be left to fall, as they are inclined by their own weight. God will not hold them up in these slippery places any longer, but will let them go; and then, at that very instant, they shall fall into destruction; as he that stands on such slippery declining ground, on the edge of a pit, he cannot stand alone, when he is let go he immediately falls and is lost.

The observation from the words that I would now insist upon is this.—"There is nothing that keeps wicked men at any one moment out of hell, but the mere pleasure of God"—By the *mere* pleasure of God, I mean his *sovereign* pleasure, his arbitrary will, restrained by no obligation, hindered by no manner of difficulty, any more than if nothing else but God's mere will had in the least degree, or in any respect whatsoever, any hand in the preservation of wicked men one moment.—The truth of this observation may appear by the following considerations.

1. There is no want of *power* in God to cast wicked men into hell at any moment. Men's hands cannot be strong when God rises up. The strongest have no power to resist him, nor can any deliver out of his hands.—He is not only able to cast wicked men into hell, but he can most easily do it. Sometimes an earthly prince meets with a great deal of difficulty to subdue a rebel, who has found means to fortify himself, and has made himself strong by the numbers of his followers. But it is not so with God. There is no fortress that is any defence from the power of God. Though hand join in hand, and vast multitudes of God's enemies combine and associate themselves, they are easily broken in pieces. They are as great heaps of light chaff before the whirlwind; or large quantities of dry stubble before devouring flames. We find it easy to tread on and crush a worm that we see crawling on the earth; so it is easy for us to cut or singe a slender thread that any thing hangs by: thus easy is it for God, when he pleases, to cast his enemies down to hell. What are we, that we should think to stand before him, at whose rebuke the earth trembles, and before whom the rocks are thrown down?

2. They *deserve* to be cast into hell; so that divine justice never

stands in the way, it makes no objection against God's using his power at any moment to destroy them. Yea, on the contrary, justice calls aloud for an infinite punishment of their sins. Divine justice says of the tree that brings forth such grapes of Sodom, "Cut it down, why cumbereth it the ground?" Luke xiii. 7. The sword of divine justice is every moment brandished over their heads, and it is nothing but the hand of arbitrary mercy, and God's mere will, that holds it back.

3. They are already under a sentence of *condemnation* to hell. They do not only justly deserve to be cast down thither, but the sentence of the law of God, that eternal and immutable rule of righteousness that God has fixed between him and mankind, is gone out against them, and stands against them; so that they are bound over already to hell. John iii. 18. "He that believeth not is condemned already." So that every unconverted man properly belongs to hell; that is his place; from thence he is, John viii. 23. "Ye are from beneath:" And thither he is bound; it is the place that justice, and God's word, and the sentence of his unchangeable law assign to him.

4. They are now the objects of that very same *anger* and wrath of God, that is expressed in the torments of hell. And the reason why they do not go down to hell at each moment, is not because God, in whose power they are, is not then very angry with them; as he is with many miserable creatures now tormented in hell, who there feel and bear the fierceness of his wrath. Yea, God is a great deal more angry with great numbers that are now on earth: yea, doubtless, with many that are now in this congregation, who it may be are at ease, than he is with many of those who are now in the flames of hell.

So that it is not because God is unmindful of their wickedness, and does not resent it, that he does not let loose his hand and cut them off. God is not altogether such an one as themselves, though they may imagine him to be so. The wrath of God burns against them, their damnation does not slumber; the pit is prepared, the fire is made ready, the furnace is now hot, ready to receive them; the flames do now rage and glow. The glittering sword is whet, and held over them, and the pit hath opened its mouth under them.

5. The *devil* stands ready to fall upon them, and seize them as his own, at what moment God shall permit him. They belong to him; he has their souls in his possession, and under his dominion. The scripture represents them as his goods, Luke xi. 12. The devils watch them; they are ever by them at their right hand; they stand waiting for them, like greedy hungry lions that see their prey, and expect to have it, but are for the present kept back. If God should withdraw his hand, by which they are restrained, they would in one moment fly upon their poor souls. The old serpent is gaping for them; hell opens its mouth wide to receive them; and if God should permit it, they would be hastily swallowed up and lost.

6. There are in the souls of wicked men those hellish *principles* reigning, that would presently kindle and flame out into hell fire, if it were not for God's restraints. There is laid in the very nature of carnal men, a foundation for the torments of hell. There are those corrupt principles, in reigning power in them, and in full possession of them, that are seeds of hell fire. These principles are active and powerful, exceeding violent in their nature, and if it were not for the restraining hand of God upon them, they would soon break out, they would flame out after the same manner as the same corruptions, the same enmity does in the hearts of damned souls, and would beget the same torments as they do in them. The souls of the wicked are in scripture compared to the troubled sea, Isa, lvii. 20. For the present, God restrains their wickedness by his mighty power, as he does the raging waves of the troubled sea, saying, "Hitherto shalt thou come, but no further;" but if God should withdraw that restraining power, it would soon carry all before it. Sin is the ruin and misery of the soul; it is destructive in its nature; and if God should leave it without restraint, there would need nothing else to make the soul perfectly miserable. The corruption of the heart of man is immoderate and boundless in its fury; and while wicked men live here, it is like fire pent up by God's restraints, whereas

if it were let loose, it would set on fire the course of nature; and as the heart is now a sink of sin, so if sin was not restrained, it would immediately turn the soul into a fiery oven, or a furnace of fire and brimstone.

7. It is no security to wicked men for one moment, that there are no visible means of death at hand. It is no security to a natural man, that he is now in health, and that he does not see which way he should now immediately go out of the world by any accident, and that there is no visible danger in any respect in his circumstances. The manifold and continual experience of the world in all ages, shows this is no evidence, that a man is not on the very brink of eternity, and that the next step will not be into another world. The unseen, unthought-of ways and means of persons going suddenly out of the world are innumerable and inconceivable. Unconverted men walk over the pit of hell on a rotten covering, and there are innumerable places in this covering so weak that they will not bear their weight, and these places are not seen. The arrows of death fly unseen at noon-day; the sharpest sight cannot discern them. God has so many different unsearchable ways of taking wicked men out of the world and sending them to hell, that there is nothing to make it appear, that God had need to be at the expence of a miracle, or go out of the ordinary course of his providence, to destroy any wicked man, at any moment. All the means that there are of sinners going out of the world, are so in God's hands, and so universally and absolutely subject to his power and determination, that it does not depend at all the less on the mere will of God, whether sinners shall at any moment go to hell, than if means were never made use of, or at all concerned in the case.

8. Natural men's prudence and care to preserve their own lives, or the care of others to preserve them, do not secure them a moment. To this, divine providence and universal experience do also bear testimony. There is this clear evidence that men's own wisdom is no security to them from death; that if it were otherwise we should see some difference between the wise and politic men of the world, and others, with regard to their liableness to

early and unexpected death: but how is it in fact? Eccles. ii. 16. "How dieth the wise man? even as the fool."

9. All wicked men's pains and *contrivance* which they use to escape hell, while they continue to reject Christ, and so remain wicked men, do not secure them from hell one moment. Almost every natural man that hears of hell, flatters himself that he shall escape it; he depends upon himself for his own security; he flatters himself in what he has done, in what he is now doing, or what he intends to do. Every one lays out matters in his own mind how he shall avoid damnation, and flatters himself that he contrives well for himself, and that his schemes will not fail. They hear indeed that there are but few saved, and that the greater part of men that have died heretofore are gone to hell; but each one imagines that he lays out matters better for his own escape than others have done. He does not intend to come to that place of torment; he says within himself, that he intends to take effectual care, and to order matters so for himself as not to fail.

But the foolish children of men miserably delude themselves in their own schemes, and in confidence in their own strength and wisdom; they trust to nothing but a shadow. The greater part of those who heretofore have lived under the same means of grace, and are now dead, are undoubtedly gone to hell; and it was not because they were not as wise as those who are now alive: it was not because they did not lay out matters as well for themselves to secure their own escape. If we could speak with them, and inquire of them, one by one, whether they expected, when alive, and when they used to hear about hell, ever to be the subjects of that misery: we doubtless, should hear one and another reply, "No, I never intended to come here: I had laid out matters otherwise in my mind; I thought I should contrive well for myself: I thought my scheme good. I intended to take effectual care; but it came upon me unexpected; I did not look for it at that time, and in that manner; it came as a thief: Death outwitted me: God's wrath was too quick for me. Oh, my cursed foolishness! I was flattering myself, and pleasing myself with vain dreams of what I would do hereafter; and when I was say-in, Peace and safety, then suddenly destruction came upon me."

10. God has laid himself under *no obligation,* by any promise
to keep any natural man out of hell one moment. God certainly
has made no promises either of eternal life, or of any deliverance
or preservation from eternal death, but what are contained in
the covenant of grace, the promises that are given in Christ, in
whom all the promises are yea and amen. But surely they have
no interest in the promises of the covenant of grace who are not
the children of the covenant, who do not believe in any of the
promises, and have no interest in the Mediator of the covenant.

So that, whatever some have imagined and pretended about
promises made to natural men's earnest seeking and knocking,
it is plain and manifest, that whatever pains a natural man takes
in religion, whatever prayers he makes, till he believes in Christ,
God is under no manner of obligation to keep him a moment
from eternal destruction.

So that, thus it is that natural men are held in the hand of
God, over the pit of hell; they have deserved the fiery pit, and
are already sentenced to it; and God is dreadfully provoked, his
anger is as great towards them as to those that are actually suffering the executions of the fierceness of his wrath in hell, and they
have done nothing in the least to appease or abate that anger,
neither is God in the least bound by any promise to hold them
up one moment; the devil is waiting for them, hell is gaping for
them, the flames gather and flash about them, and would fain lay
hold on them, and swallow them up; the fire pent up in their
own hearts is struggling to break out: and they have no interest
in any Mediator, there are no means within reach that can be
any security to them. In short, they have no refuge, nothing to
take hold of; all that preserves them every moment is the mere
arbitrary will, and uncovenanted, unobliged forbearance of an
incensed God.

APPLICATION

The use of this awful subject may be for awakening unconverted persons in this congregation. This that you have heard

is the case of every one of you that are out of Christ.—That world of misery, that lake of burning brimstone, is extended abroad under you. There is the dreadful pit of the glowing flames of the wrath of God; there is hell's wide gaping mouth open; and you have nothing to stand upon, nor any thing to take hold of; there is nothing between you and hell but the air; it is only the power and mere pleasure of God that holds you up.

You probably are not sensible of this; you find you are kept out of hell, but do not see the hand of God in it; but look at other things, as the good state of your bodily constitution, your care of your own life, and the means you use for your own preservation. But indeed these things are nothing; if God should withdraw his hand, they would avail no more to keep you from falling, than the thin air to hold up a person that is suspended in it.

Your wickedness makes you as it were heavy as lead, and to tend downwards with great weight and pressure towards hell; and if God should let you go, you would immediately sink and swiftly descend and plunge into the bottomless gulf, and your healthy constitution, and your own care and prudence, and best contrivance, and all your righteousness, would have no more influence to uphold you and keep you out of hell, than a spider's web would have to stop a fallen rock. Were it not for the sovereign pleasure of God, the earth would not bear you one moment; for you are a burden to it; the creation groans with you; the creature is made subject to the bondage of your corruption, not willingly; the sun does not willingly shine upon you to give you light to serve sin and Satan; the earth does not willingly yield her increase to satisfy your lusts; nor is it willingly a stage for your wickedness to be acted upon; the air does not willingly serve you for breath to maintain the flame of life in your vitals, while you spend your life in the service of God's enemies. God's creatures are good, and were made for men to serve God with, and do not willingly subserve to any other purpose, and groan when they are abused to purposes so directly contrary to their nature and end. And the world would spew you out, were it not for the sovereign hand of him who hath subjected it in hope. There are black clouds of God's wrath now hanging directly over your heads, full of the dreadful storm, and big with thunder; and were it not for the restraining hand of God, it would immediately burst forth upon you. The sovereign pleasure of God, for the present, stays his rough wind; otherwise it would come with fury, and your destruction would come like a whirlwind, and you would be like the chaff of the summer threshing floor.

The wrath of God is like great waters that are damned for the present; they increase more and more, and rise higher and higher, till an outlet is given; and the longer the stream is stopped, the more rapid and mighty is its course, when once it is let loose. It is true, that judgment against your evil works has not been executed hitherto; the floods of God's vengeance have been withheld; but your guilt in the mean time is constantly increasing, and you are every day treasuring up more wrath; the waters are constantly rising, and waxing more and more mighty; and there is nothing but the mere pleasure of God, that holds the waters back, that are unwilling to be stopped, and press hard to go forward. If God should only withdraw his hand from the flood-gate, it would immediately fly open, and the fiery floods of the fierceness and wrath of God, would rush forth with inconceivable fury, and would come upon you with omnipotent power; and if your strength were ten thousand times greater than it is, yea, ten thousand times greater than the strength of the stoutest, sturdiest devil in hell, it would be nothing to withstand or endure it.

The bow of God's wrath is bent, and the arrow made ready on the string, and justice bends the arrow at your heart, and strains the bow, and it is nothing but the mere pleasure of God, and that of an angry God, without any promise or obligation at all, that keeps the arrow one moment from being made drunk with your blood. Thus all you that never passed under a great change of heart, by the mighty power of the Spirit of God upon your souls; all you that were never born again, and made new creatures, and raised from being dead in sin, to a state of new, and before altogether unexperienced light and life, are in the hands of an angry God. However you may have reformed your life in many things, and may have had religious affections, and may keep up a form of religion in your families and closets, and in the house of God, it is nothing but his mere pleasure that keeps you from being this moment swallowed up in everlasting destruction. However unconvinced you may now be of the truth of what you hear, by and by you will be fully convinced of it. Those that are gone from being in the like circumstances with you, see that it was so with them; for destruction came suddenly upon most of them; when they expected nothing of it, and while they were saying, Peace and safety: now they see, that those things on which they depended for peace and safety, were nothing but thin air and empty shadows.

The God that holds you over the pit of hell, much as one holds a spider, or some loathsome insect over the fire, abhors you, and is dreadfully provoked: his wrath towards you burns like fire; he looks upon you as worthy of nothing else, but to be cast into the fire; he is of purer eyes than to bear to have you in his sight; you are ten thousand times more abominable in his eyes, than the most hateful venomous serpent is in ours. You have offended him infinitely more than ever a stubborn rebel did his prince; and yet it is nothing but his hand that holds you from falling into the fire every moment. It is to be ascribed to nothing else, that you did not go to hell the last night; that you was suffered to awake again in this world, after you closed your eyes to sleep. And there is no other reason to be given, why you have not dropped into hell since you arose in the morning, but that God's hand has held you up. There is no other reason to be given why you have not gone to hell, since you have sat here in the house of God, provoking his pure eyes by your sinful wicked manner of attending his solemn worship. Yea, there is nothing else that is to be given as a reason why you do not this very moment drop down into hell.

O sinner! Consider the fearful danger you are in: it is a great furnace of wrath, a wide and bottomless pit, full of the fire of wrath, that you are held over in the hand of that God, whose wrath is provoked and incensed as much against you, as against many of the damned in hell. You hang by a slender thread, with the flames of divine wrath flashing about it, and ready every moment to singe it, and burn it asunder; and you have no interest in any Mediator, and nothing to lay hold of to save yourself, nothing to keep off the flames of wrath, nothing of your own, nothing that you ever have done, nothing that you can do, to induce God to spare you one moment.—And consider here more particularly,

1. *Whose* wrath it is: it is the wrath of the infinite God. If it were only the wrath of man, though it were of the most potent prince, it would be comparatively little to be regarded. The wrath of kings is very much dreaded, especially of absolute monarchs, who have the possessions and lives of their subjects wholly in their power, to be disposed of at their mere will. Prov. xx. 2. "The fear of a king is as the roaring of a lion: Whoso provoketh him to anger, sinneth against his own soul." The subject that very much enrages an arbitrary prince, is liable to suffer the most extreme torments that human art can invent, or human power can inflict. But the greatest earthly potentates in their greatest majesty and strength, and when clothed in their greatest terrors, are but feeble, despicable worms of the dust, in comparison of the great and almighty Creator and King of heaven and earth. It is but little that they can do, when most enraged, and when they have exerted the utmost of their fury. All the kings of the earth, before God, are as grasshoppers; they are nothing, and less than nothing: both their love and their hatred is to be despised. The wrath of the great King of kings, is as much more terrible than theirs, as his majesty is greater. Luke xii. 4, 5. "And I say unto you, my friends, Be not afraid of them that kill the body, and after that, have no more that they can do. But I will forewarn you whom you shall fear: fear him, which after he hath killed, hath power to cast into hell: yea, I say unto you, Fear him."

2. It is the *fierceness* of his wrath that you are exposed to. We often read of the fury of God; as in Isaiah lix. 18. "According to their deeds, accordingly he will repay fury to his adversaries." So Isaiah lxvi. 15. "For behold, the Lord will come with fire, and with his chariots like a whirlwind, to render his anger with fury,

and his rebuke with flames of fire." And in many other places. So, Rev. xix. 15. we read of "the wine press of the fierceness and wrath of Almighty God." The words are exceeding terrible. If it had only been said, "the wrath of God," the words would have implied that which is infinitely dreadful: but it is "the fierceness and wrath of God." The fury of God! the fierceness of Jehovah! Oh, how dreadful must that be! Who can utter or conceive what such expressions carry in them! But it is also "the fierceness and wrath of *Almighty* God." As though there would be a very great manifestation of his almighty power in what the fierceness of his wrath should inflict, as though omnipotence should be as it were enraged, and exerted, as men are wont to exert their strength in the fierceness of their wrath. Oh! then, what will be the consequence! What will become of the poor worms that shall suffer it! Whose hands can be strong? And whose heart can endure? To what a dreadful, inexpressible, inconceivable depth of misery must the poor creature be sunk who shall be the subject of this!

Consider this, you that are here present, that yet remain in an unregenerate state. That God will execute the fierceness of his anger, implies, that he will inflict wrath without any pity. When God beholds the ineffable extremity of your case, and sees your torment to be so vastly disproportioned to your strength, and sees how your poor soul is crushed, and sinks down, as it were, into an infinite gloom; he will have no compassion upon you, he will not forbear the executions of his wrath, or in the least lighten his hand; there shall be no moderation or mercy, nor will God then at all stay his rough wind; he will have no regard to your welfare, nor be at all careful lest you should suffer too much in any other sense, than only that you shall *not suffer beyond what strict justice requires*. Nothing shall be withheld, because it is so hard for you to bear. Ezek. viii. 18. "Therefore will I also deal in fury: mine eye shall not spare, neither will I have pity; and though they cry in mine ears with a loud voice, yet I will not hear them." Now God stands ready to pity you; this is a day of mercy; you may cry now with some encouragement of obtaining mercy. But when once the day of mercy is past, your most lamentable and dolorous cries and shrieks will be in vain; you will be wholly lost and thrown away of God, as to any regard to your welfare. God will have no other use to put you to, but to suffer misery; you shall be continued in being to no other end; for you will be a vessel of wrath fitted to destruction; and there will be no other use of this vessel, but to be filled full of wrath. God will be so far from pitying you when you cry to him, that it is said he will only "laugh and mock," Prov. i. 25, 26, &c.

How awful are those words, Isa. lxiii. 3, which are the words of the great God. "I will tread them in mine anger, and will trample them in my fury, and their blood shall be sprinkled upon my garments, and I will stain all my raiment." It is perhaps impossible to conceive of words that carry in them greater manifestations of these three things, *viz.* contempt, and hatred, and fierceness of indignation. If you cry to God to pity you, he will be so far from pitying you in your doleful case, or showing you the least regard or favour, that instead of that, he will only tread you under foot. And though he will know that you cannot bear the weight of omnipotence treading upon you, yet he will not regard that, but he will crush you under his feet without mercy; he will crush out your blood, and make it fly, and it shall be sprinkled on his garments, so as to stain all his raiment. He will not only hate you, but he will have you, in the utmost contempt: no place shall be thought fit for you, but under his feet to be trodden down as the mire of the streets.

3. The *misery* you are exposed to is that which God will inflict to that end, that he might show what that wrath of Jehovah is. God hath had it on his heart to show to angels and men, both how excellent his love is, and also how terrible his wrath is. Sometimes earthly kings have a mind to show how terrible their wrath is, by the extreme punishments they would execute on those that would provoke them. Nebuchadnezzar, that mighty and haughty monarch of the Chaldean empire, was willing to show his wrath when enraged with Shadrach, Meshech, and Abednego; and accordingly gave orders that the burning fiery furnace should be heated seven times hotter than it was before; doubtless, it was

raised to the utmost degree of fierceness that human art could raise it. But the great God is also willing to show his wrath, and magnify his awful majesty and mighty power in the extreme sufferings of his enemies. Rom. ix. 22. "What if God, willing to show his wrath, and to make his power known, endure with much long-suffering the vessels of wrath fitted to destruction?" And seeing this is his design, and what he has determined, even to show how terrible the unrestrained wrath, the fury and fierceness of Jehovah is, he will do it to effect. There will be something accomplished and brought to pass that will be dreadful with a witness. When the great and angry God hath risen up and executed his awful vengeance on the poor sinner, and the wretch is actually suffering the infinite weight and power of his indignation, then will God call upon the whole universe to behold that awful majesty and mighty power that is to be seen in it. Isa. xxxiii. 12-14. "And the people shall be as the burnings of lime, as thorns cut up shall they be burnt in the fire. Hear ye that are far off, what I have done; and ye that are near, acknowledge my might. The sinners in Zion are afraid; fearfulness hath surprised the hypocrites," &c.

Thus it will be with you that are in an unconverted state, if you continue in it; the infinite might, and majesty, and terribleness of the omnipotent God shall be magnified upon you, in the ineffable strength of your torments. You shall be tormented in the presence of the holy angels, and in the presence of the Lamb; and when you shall be in this state of suffering, the glorious inhabitants of heaven shall go forth and look on the awful spectacle, that they may see what the wrath and fierceness of the Almighty is; and when they have seen it, they will fall down and adore that great power and majesty. Isa. lxvi. 23, 24. "And it shall come to pass, that from one new moon to another, and from one sabbath to another, shall all flesh come to worship before me, saith the Lord. And they shall go forth and look upon the carcasses of the men that have transgressed against me; for their worm shall not die, neither shall their fire be quenched, and they shall be an abhorring unto all flesh."

4. It is *everlasting* wrath. It would be dreadful to suffer this fierceness and wrath of Almighty God one moment; but you must suffer it to all eternity. There will be no end to this exquisite horrible misery. When you look forward, you shall see a long for ever, a boundless duration before you, which will swallow up your thoughts, and amaze your soul; and you will absolutely despair of ever having any deliverance, any end, any mitigation, any rest at all. You will know certainly that you must wear out long ages, millions of millions of ages, in wrestling and conflicting with this almighty merciless vengeance; and then when you have so done, when so many ages have actually been spent by you in this manner, you will know that all is but a point to what remains. So that your punishment will indeed be infinite. Oh, who can express what the state of a soul in such circumstances is! All that we can possibly say about it, gives but a very feeble, faint representation of it; it is inexpressible and inconceivable: For "who knows the power of God's anger?"

How dreadful is the state of those that are daily and hourly in the danger of this great wrath and infinite misery! But this is the dismal case of every soul in this congregation that has not been born again, however moral and strict, sober and religious, they may otherwise be. Oh that you would consider it, whether you be young or old! There is reason to think, that there are many in this congregation now hearing this discourse, that will actually be the subjects of this very misery to all eternity. We know not who they are, or in what seats they sit, or what thoughts they now have. It may be they are now at ease, and hear all these things without much disturbance, and are now flattering themselves that they are not the persons, promising themselves that they shall escape. If we knew that there was one person, and but one, in the whole congregation, that was to be the subject of this misery, what an awful thing would it be to think of! If we knew who it was, what an awful sight would it be to see such a person! How might all the rest of the congregation lift up a lamentable and bitter cry over him! But, alas! instead of one, how many is it likely will remember this discourse in hell? And it would be a wonder, if some that are now present should not be in hell in a very short time, even before this year is out. And it would be no wonder if some persons, that now sit here, in some seats of this meeting-house, in health, quiet and secure, should be there before to-morrow morning. Those of you that finally continue in a natural condition, that shall keep out of hell longest will be there in a little time! your damnation does not slumber; it will come swiftly, and, in all probability, very suddenly upon many of you. You have reason to wonder that you are not already in hell. It is doubtless the case of some whom you have seen and known, that never deserved hell more than you, and that heretofore appeared as likely to have been now alive as you. Their case is past all hope; they are crying in extreme misery and perfect despair; but here you are in the land of the living and in the house of God, and have an opportunity to obtain salvation. What would not those poor damned hopeless souls give for one day's opportunity such as you now enjoy!

And now you have an extraordinary opportunity, a day wherein Christ has thrown the door of mercy wide open, and stands in calling and crying with a loud voice to poor sinners; a day wherein many are flocking to him, and pressing into the kingdom of God. Many are daily coming from the east, west, north and south; many that were very lately in the same miserable condition that you are in, are now in a happy state, with their hearts filled with love to him who has loved them, and washed them from their sins in his own blood, and rejoicing in hope of the glory of God. How awful is it to be left behind at such a day! To see so many others feasting, while you are pining and perishing! To see so many rejoicing and singing for joy of heart, while you have cause to mourn for sorrow of heart, and howl for vexation of spirit! How can you rest one moment in such a condition? Are not your souls as precious as the souls of the people at Suffield,* where they are flocking from day to day to Christ?

Are there not many here who have lived long in the world, and are not to this day born again? and so are aliens from the

---

* A town in the neighbourhood. [Edwards's note.]

commonwealth of Israel, and have done nothing ever since they have lived, but treasure up wrath against the day of wrath? Oh, sirs, your case, in an especial manner, is extremely dangerous. Your guilt and hardness of heart is extremely great. Do you not see how generally persons of your years are passed over and left, in the present remarkable and wonderful dispensation of God's mercy? You had need to consider yourselves, and awake thoroughly out of sleep. You cannot bear the fierceness and wrath of the infinite God.—And you, young men, and young women, will you neglect this precious season which you now enjoy, when so many others of your age are renouncing all youthful vanities, and flocking to Christ? You especially have now an extraordinary opportunity; but if you neglect it, it will soon be with you as with those persons who spent all the precious days of youth in sin, and are now come to such a dreadful pass in blindness and hardness. —And you, children, who are unconverted, do not you know that you are going down to hell, to bear the dreadful wrath of that God, who is now angry with you every day and every night? Will you be content to be the children of the devil, when so many other children in the land are converted, and are become the holy and happy children of the King of kings?

And let every one that is yet of Christ, and hanging over the pit of hell, whether they be old men and women, or middle aged, or young people, or little children, now hearken to the loud calls of God's word and providence. This acceptable year of the Lord, a day of such great favours to some, will doubtless be a day of as remarkable vengeance to others. Men's hearts harden, and their guilt increases apace at such a day as this, if they neglect their souls; and never was there so great danger of such persons being given up to hardness of heart and blindness of mind. God seems now to be hastily gathering in his elect in all parts of the land; and probably the greater part of adult persons that ever shall be saved, will be brought in now in a little time, and that it will be as it was on the great out-pouring of the Spirit upon the Jews in the apostles' days: the election will obtain, and the rest will be blinded. If this should be the case with you, you will eternally curse this day, and will curse the day that ever you was born, to see such a season of the pouring out of God's Spirit, and will wish that you had died and gone to hell before you had seen it. Now undoubtedly it is, as it was in the days of John the Baptist, the axe is in an extraordinary manner laid at the root of the trees, that every tree which brings not forth good fruit, may be hewn down and cast into the fire.

Therefore, let every one that is out of Christ, now awake and fly from the wrath to come. The wrath of Almighty God is now undoubtedly hanging over a great part of this congregation: Let every one fly out of Sodom: "Haste and escape for your lives, look not behind you, escape to the mountain, lest you be consumed."

from IMAGES OR SHADOWS OF DIVINE THINGS *

[ON THE NATURE OF IMAGES]

25. There are many things in the constitution of the world that are not properly shadows and images of divine things that yet are significations of them, as children's being born crying is a signification of their being born to sorrow. A man's coming into the world after the same manner as the beasts is a signification of the ignorance and brutishness of man, and his agreement in many things with the beasts.

· · · · ·

70. If we look on these shadows of divine things as the voice of God purposely by them teaching us these and those spiritual and divine things, to show of what excellent advantage it will be, how agreeably and clearly it will tend to convey instruction to our minds, and to impress things on the mind and to affect the mind, by that we may, as it were, have God speaking to us. Wherever we are, and whatever we are about, we may see divine things ex-

---

* Reprinted from *Images or Shadows of Divine Things* by Jonathan Edwards. Edited by Perry Miller and used with permission of the Yale University Press.

cellently represented and held forth. And it will abundantly tend to confirm the Scriptures, for there is an excellent agreement between these things and the holy Scripture.

. . .

118. Images of divine things. It is with many of these images as it was with the sacrifices of old: they are often repeated, whereas the antitype is continual and never comes to pass but once. Thus sleep is an image of death that is repeated every night; so the morning is the image of the resurrection; so the spring of the year is the image of the resurrection which is repeated every year. And so of many other things that might be mentioned, they are repeated often, but the antitype is but once. The shadows are often repeated to show t[w]o things, viz., [1.] that the thing shadowed is not yet fulfilled, and 2. to signify the great importance of the antitype that we need to be so renewedly and continually put in mind of it.

. . . . . .

156. The book of Scripture is interpreter of the book of nature two ways, viz., by declaring to us those spiritual mysteries that are indeed signified and typified in the constitution of the natural world; and secondly, in actually making application of the signs and types in the book of nature as representations of those spiritual mysteries in many instances.

[ON THE MEANING OF SOME IMAGES]

4. The heavens' being filled with glorious, luminous bodies is to signify the glory and happiness of the heavenly inhabitants, and amongst these the sun signifies Christ and the moon the church.

. . . . .

26. Christ often makes use of representations of spiritual things in the constitution of the [world] for argument, as thus: the tree is known by its fruit. These things are not merely mentioned as illustrations of his meaning, but as illustrations and evidences of the truth of what he says.

. . . . .

79. The whole material universe is preserved by gravity or attraction, or the mutual tendency of all bodies to each other. One part of the universe is hereby made beneficial to another; the beauty, harmony, and order, regular progress, life, and motion, and in short all the well-being of the whole frame depends on it. This is a type of love or charity in the spiritual world.

. . . . .

129. That a child needs correction, and the benefit of correcting children is a type of what is true with respect to God's children.

. . . . .

146. The late invention of telescopes, whereby heavenly objects are brought so much nearer and made so much plainer to sight and such wonderfull discoveries have been made in the heavens, is a type and forerunner of the great increase in the knowledge of heavenly things that shall be in the approaching glorious times of the Christian church.

. . . . .

152. The changes that pass on the face of the earth by the gradual approach of the sun is a remarkeable type of what will come to pass in the visible church of God and world of mankind in the approach of the church's latter day glory. The latter will be gradual, as the former is. The light and warmth of the sun in the former is often interrupted by return of clouds and cold, and the fruits of the earth kept back from a too sudden growth and a too quick transition from the dead state in winter to their summer's glory, which in the end would be hurtfull to them and would kill them. So it is in the spiritual world: if there should be such warm

weather constantly without interruption as we have sometimes in Feb., March, and April, the fruits of the earth would flourish mightily for a little while, but would not be prepared for the summer's heat, but that would kill them. This is typical of what is true concerning the church of God and particular souls. The earth being stripped of its white winter garments in which all looked clean, but all was dead, and the making of it so dirty as it is early in the spring in order to fit it for more beautifull clothing in a living state in summer, is also typical of what passes in the spiritual change of the world and also a particular soul. The surface of the earth is, as it were, dissolved in the spring; the ground is loosened and broke up and soften[ed] with moisture, and its filthiness never so much appears as then, and then is the most windy, turbulent season of all.

. . . . .

[THE BEAUTY OF THE WORLD]

The beauty of the world consists wholly of sweet mutual consents, either within itself or with the supreme being. As to the corporeal world, though there are many other sorts of consents, yet the sweetest and most charming beauty of it is its resemblance of spiritual beauties. The reason is that spiritual beauties are infinitely the greatest, and bodies being but the shadows of beings, they must be so much the more charming as they shadow forth spiritual beauties. This beauty is peculiar to natural things, it surpassing the art of man.

Thus there is the resemblance of a decent trust, dependence and acknowledgment in the planets continually moving round the sun, receiving his influences by which they are made happy, bright and beautiful: a decent attendance in the secondary planets, an image of majesty, power, glory, and beneficence in the sun in the midst of all, and so in terrestrial things, as I have shown in another place.

It is very probable that that wonderful suitableness of green for the grass and plants, the blues of the skie, the white of the clouds, the colours of flowers, consists in a complicated proportion that these colours make one with another, either in their magnitude of the rays, the number of vibrations that are caused in the atmosphere, or some other way. So there is a great suitableness between the objects of different senses, as between sounds, colours, and smells; as between colours of the woods and flowers and the smells and the singing of birds, which it is probable consist in a certain proportion of the vibrations that are made in the different organs. So there are innumerable other agreeablenesses of motions, figures, etc. The gentle motions of waves, of [the] lily, etc., as it is agreeable to other things that represent calmness, gentleness, and benevolence, etc. the fields and woods seem to rejoice, and how joyfull do the birds seem to be in it. How much a resemblance is there of every grace in the field covered with plants and flowers when the sun shines serenely and undisturbedly upon them, how a resemblance, I say, of every grace and beautifull disposition of mind, of an inferiour towards a superiour cause, preserver, benevolent benefactor, and a fountain of happiness.

How great a resemblance of a holy and virtuous soul is a calm, serene day. What an infinite number of such like beauties is there in that one thing, the light, and how complicated an harmony and proportion is it probable belongs to it.

There are beauties that are more palpable and explicable, and there are hidden and secret beauties. The former pleases, and we can tell why; we can explain the particular point for the agreement that renders the thing pleasing. Such are all artificial regularities; we can tell wherein the regularity lies that affects us. [The] latter sort are those beauties that delight us and we cannot tell why. Thus, we find ourselves pleased in beholding the colour of the violets, but we know not what secret regularity or harmony it is that creates that pleasure in our minds. These hidden beauties are commonly by far the greatest, because the more complex a beauty is, the more hidden is it. In this latter fact consists principally the beauty of the world, and very much in light and colours. Thus mere light is pleasing to the mind. If it be to the degree of effulgence, it is very sensible, and mankind have agreed in it: they all represent glory and extraordinary beauty by brightness. The reason of it is either that light or our organ of seeing is so contrived that an harmonious motion is excited in the animal spirits and propagated to the brain. That mixture we call white is a proportionate mixture that is harmonious, as Sir Isaac Newton has shown, to each particular simple colour, and contains in it some harmony or other that is delightfull. And each sort of rays play a distinct tune to the soul, besides those lovely mixtures that are found in nature. Those beauties, how lovely is the green of the face of the earth in all manner of colours, in flowers, the colour of the skies, and lovely tinctures of the morning and evening.

Corollary: Hence the reason why almost all men, and those that seem to be very miserable, love life, because they cannot bear to lose sight of such a beautiful and lovely world. The ideas, that every moment whilst we live have a beauty that we take not distinct notice of, brings a pleasure that, when we come to the trial, we had rather live in much pain and misery than lose.

THE NATURE OF TRUE VIRTUE
(1756)

FROM CHAPTER I

SHOWING WHEREIN THE ESSENCE OF TRUE VIRTUE CONSISTS

Whatever controversies and variety of opinions there are about the nature of virtue, yet all (excepting some skeptics, who deny any real difference between virtue and vice) mean by it, something *beautiful,* or rather some kind of *beauty,* or excellency. —It is not *all* beauty, that is called virtue; for instance, not the beauty of a building, of a flower, or of the rainbow: but some beauty belonging to Beings that have *perception* and *will.*—It is not all beauty of *mankind,* that is called virtue; for instance, not the external beauty of the countenance, or shape, gracefulness of motion, or harmony of voice: but it is a beauty that has its original seat in the mind.—But yet perhaps not *every* thing that may be called a beauty of mind, is properly called virtue. There is a beauty of understanding and speculation. There is something in the ideas and conceptions of great philosophers and statesmen, that may be called beautiful; which is a different thing from what is most commonly meant by virtue. But virtue is the beauty of those qualities and acts of the mind, that are of a *moral* nature, i. e., such as are attended with desert or worthiness of *praise,* or *blame*. Things of this sort, it is generally agreed, so far as I know, are not any thing belonging merely to speculation; but to the *disposition* and *will,* or (to use a general word, I suppose commonly well understood) the *heart*. Therefore I suppose, I shall not depart from the common opinion, when I say, that virtue is the beauty of the qualities and exercises of the heart, or those actions which proceed from them. So that when it is inquired, What is the nature of true *virtue?*—this is the same as to inquire, what that is which renders any habit, disposition, or exercise of the heart truly *beautiful*. I use the phrase *true* virtue, and speak of things *truly* beautiful, because I suppose it will generally be allowed, that there is a distinction to be made between some things which are truly virtuous, and others which only seem to be virtuous, through a partial and imperfect view of things: that some actions and dispositions appear beautiful, if considered partially and superficially, or with regard to some things belonging to them, and in some of their circumstances and tendencies, which would appear otherwise in a more extensive and comprehensive view, wherein they are seen clearly in their whole nature and the extent of their connections in the universality of things.—There is a general and a particular beauty. By a *particular* beauty, I mean that by which a thing appears beautiful when considered only with regard to its connection with, and tendency to some particular things within a limited, and, as it were, a private sphere. And a *general* beauty is that by which a thing appears beautiful when viewed most perfectly, comprehensively and universally, with regard to all its tendencies, and its connections with every thing it stands related to. The former may be without and against the latter. As, a few notes in a tune, taken only by themselves, and in their relation to one another, may be harmonious; which when considered with respect to all the notes in the tune, or the entire series of sounds they are connected with, may be very discordant and disagreeable.— (Of which more afterwards.)—*That only,* therefore, is what I mean by true virtue, which is *that,* belonging to the *heart* of an intelligent Being, that is beautiful by a *general* beauty, or beautiful in a comprehensive view as it is in itself, and as related to every thing that it stands in connection with. And therefore when we are inquiring concerning the nature of true virtue, viz., wherein this true and general beauty of the heart does most essentially consist—this is my answer to the inquiry:

True virtue most essentially consists in benevolence to Being in general. Or perhaps to speak more accurately, it is that consent, propensity and union of heart to Being in general, that is immediately exercised in a general good will.

The things which were before observed of the nature of true virtue, naturally lead us to such a notion of it. If it has its seat in the heart, and is the general goodness and beauty of the disposition and exercise of that, in the most comprehensive view, considered with regard to its universal tendency, and as related to every thing that it stands in connection with; what can it consist in, but a consent and good will to Being in general?— Beauty does not consist in discord and dissent, but in consent and agreement. And if every intelligent Being is some way related to Being in general, and is a part of the universal system of existence; and so stands in connection with the whole; what can its general and true beauty be, but its union and consent with the great whole?

If any such thing can be supposed as a union of heart to some particular Being, or number of Beings, disposing it to benevolence to a private circle or system of Beings, which are but a small part of the whole; not implying a tendency to a union with the great system, and not at all inconsistent with enmity towards Being in general; this I suppose not to be of the nature of true virtue: although it may in some respects be good, and may appear beautiful in a confined and contracted view of things.—But of this more afterwards.

It is abundantly plain by the holy Scriptures, and generally allowed, not only by Christian divines, but by the more considerable deists, that virtue most essentially consists in love. And I suppose, it is owned by the most considerable writers, to consist in general love of benevolence, or kind affection: though it seems to me, the meaning of some in this affair is not sufficiently explained, which perhaps occasions some error or confusion in discourses on this subject.

When I say, true virtue consists in love to Being in general, I shall not be likely to be understood, that no one act of the mind or exercise of love is of the nature of true virtue, but what has Being in general, or the great system of universal existence, for its direct and immediate object: so that no exercise of love or kind affection to any one particular Being, that is but a small part of this whole, has any thing of the nature of true virtue. But, that the nature of true virtue consists in a disposition to benevolence towards Being in general. Though, from such a disposition may arise exercises of love to particular Beings, as objects are presented and occasions arise. No wonder, that he who is of a generally benevolent disposition, should be more disposed than another to have his heart moved with benevolent affection to particular persons, whom he is acquainted and conversant with, and from whom arise the greatest and most frequent occasions for exciting his benevolent temper. But my meaning is, that no affections towards particular persons or Beings are of the nature of true virtue, but such as arise from a generally benevolent temper, or from that habit or frame of mind, wherein consists a disposition to love Being in general.

And perhaps it is needless for me to give notice to my readers, that when I speak of an intelligent Being's having a heart united and benevolently disposed to Being in general, I thereby mean *intelligent* Being in general. Not inanimate things, or Beings that have no perception or will, which are not properly capable objects of benevolence.

Love is commonly distinguished into love of benevolence and love of complacence. Love of *benevolence* is that affection or propensity of the heart to any Being, which causes it to incline to its well being, or disposes it to desire and take pleasure in its happiness. And if I mistake not, it is agreeable to the common opinion, that beauty in the object is not always the ground of this propensity: but that there may be such a thing as benevolence, or a disposition to the welfare of those that are not considered as beautiful; unless mere existence be accounted a beauty. And benevolence or goodness in the Divine Being is generally supposed, not only to be prior to the beauty of many of its objects, but to their existence: so as to be the ground both of their existence and their beauty, rather than they the foundation of God's benevolence; as it is supposed that it is God's goodness which moved him to give them both Being and beauty. So that if all virtue primarily consists in that affection of heart to Being, which is exercised in benevolence, or an inclination to its good, then God's virtue is so extended as to include a propensity, not only to Being actually existing, and actually beautiful, but to possible Being, so as to incline him to give Being, beauty and happiness. But not now to insist particularly on this. What I would have observed at present, is, that it must be allowed, benevolence doth not necessarily presuppose beauty in its object.

What is commonly called love of *complacence,* presupposes beauty. For is no other than delight in beauty; or complacence in the person or Being beloved for his beauty.

If virtue be the beauty of an intelligent Being, and virtue consists in love, then it is a plain inconsistence, to suppose that virtue primarily consists in any love to its object *for its beauty;* either in a love of complacence, which is delight in a Being for his beauty, or in a love of benevolence, that has the beauty of its object for its foundation. For that would be to suppose, that the beauty of intelligent beings primarily consists in love to beauty; or, that their virtue first of all consists in their love to virtue. Which is an inconsistence, and going in a circle. Because it makes virtue, or beauty of mind, the foundation or first motive of that love wherein virtue originally consists, or wherein the very first virtue consists; or, it supposes the first virtue to be the consequence and effect of virtue. So that virtue is originally the foundation and exciting cause of the very beginning or first Being of virtue. Which makes the first virtue, both the ground, and the consequence, both cause and effect of itself. Doubtless virtue primarily consists in something else besides any effect or consequence of virtue. If virtue consists primarily in love to virtue, then virtue, the thing loved, is the love of virtue: so that virtue must consist in the love of the love of virtue. And if it be inquired, what that virtue is, which virtue consists in the love of the love of, it must be answered, it is the love of virtue. So that there must be the love of the love of the love of virtue, and so on *in infinitum*. For there is no end of going back in a circle. We never come to any beginning, or foundation. For it is without beginning and hangs on nothing.

Therefore if the essence of virtue or beauty of mind lies in love, or a disposition to love, it must primarily consist in something *different* both from complacence, which is a delight in beauty, and also from any benevolence that has the beauty of its object for its foundation. Because it is absurd, to say that virtue is primarily and first of all the consequence of itself. For this makes virtue primarily prior to itself.

Nor can virtue primarily consist in *gratitude;* or one Being's benevolence to another for his benevolence to him. Because this implies the same inconsistence. For it supposes a benevolence prior to gratitude, that is the cause of gratitude. Therefore the first benevolence, or that benevolence which has none prior to it, cannot be gratitude.

Therefore there is room left for no other conclusion than that the primary object of virtuous love is Being, simply considered; or, that true virtue primarily consists, not in love to any particular Beings, because of their virtue or beauty, nor in gratitude, because they love us; but in a propensity and union of heart to Being simply considered; exciting absolute benevolence (if I may so call it) to Being in general.—I say, true virtue *primarily* consists in this. For I am far from asserting that there is no true virtue in any other love than this absolute benevolence. But I would express what appears to me to be the truth on this subject, in the following particulars.

The *first* object of a virtuous benevolence is *Being,* simply considered: and if Being, *simply* considered, be its object, then Being *in general* is its object; and the thing it has an ultimate propensity to, is the *highest good* of Being in general. And it will seek the good of every *individual* Being unless it be conceived as not consistent with the highest good of Being in general. In which case the good of a particular Being, or some Beings, may be given up for the sake of the highest good of Being in general. And particularly if there be any Being that is looked upon as statedly and irreclaimably opposite and an enemy to Being in general, then consent and adherence to Being in general will induce the truly virtuous heart to forsake that Being, and to oppose it.

And further, if Being, simply considered, be the first object of a truly virtuous benevolence, then that Being who has *most* of Being, or has the greatest share of existence, other things being equal, so far as such a Being is exhibited to our faculties or set in our view, will have the *greatest* share of the propensity and benevolent affection of the heart. I say, *other things being equal,* especially because there is a *secondary* object of virtuous benevolence, that I shall take notice of presently. Which is one thing that must be considered as the ground or motive to a purely virtuous benevolence. Pure benevolence in its first exercise is nothing else but Being's uniting consent, or propensity to Being; appearing true and pure by its extending to Being in general, and inclining to the general highest good, and to each Being, whose welfare is consistent with the highest general good, in proportion to the degree of *existence*[1] understood, other things being equal.

---

[1] I say, in proportion to the degree of *existence,* because one Being may have more *existence* than another, as he may be *greater* than another. That which is *great,* has more existence, and is further from nothing, than that which is *little.* One Being may have every thing positive belonging to it, or every thing which goes to its positive existence (in opposition to defect) in a higher degree than

The *second* object of a virtuous propensity of heart is *benevolent* Being. A secondary ground of pure benevolence is virtuous benevolence itself in its object. When any one under the influence of general benevolence, sees another Being possessed of the like general benevolence, this attaches his heart to him, and draws forth greater love to him, than merely his having existence: because so far as the Being beloved has love to Being in general, so far his own Being is, as it were, enlarged, extends to, and in some sort comprehends, Being in general: and therefore he that is governed by love to Being in general must of necessity have complacence in him, and the greater degree of benevolence to him, as it were out of gratitude to him for his love to general existence, that his own heart is extended and united to, and so looks on its interest as its own. It is because his heart is thus united to Being in general, that he looks on a benevolent propensity to Being in general, wherever he sees it, as the beauty of the Being in whom it is; an excellency, that renders him worthy of esteem, complacence, and the greater good will.

But several things may be noted more particularly concerning this secondary ground of a truly virtuous love.

1. That loving a Being on *this ground* necessarily arises from pure benevolence to Being *in general,* and comes to the same thing. For he that has a simple and pure good will to general entity or existence, must love that temper in others, that agrees and conspires with itself. A spirit of consent to Being must agree with consent to Being. That which truly and sincerely seeks the good of others, must approve of, and love, that which joins with him in seeking the good of others.

2. This which has been now mentioned as a secondary ground of virtuous love, is the thing wherein true moral or spiritual *beauty* primarily consists. Yea, spiritual beauty consists wholly in this, and the various qualities and exercises of mind which pro-

---

another; or a greater capacity and power, greater understanding, every faculty and every positive quality in a higher degree. An *archangel* must be supposed to have more existence, and to be every way further removed from *nonenity,* than a *worm,* or a *flea.*—Edwards.

ceed from it, and the external actions which proceed from these internal qualities and exercises. And in these things consists all true *virtue,* viz., in this love of Being, and the qualities and acts which arise from it.

3. As all spiritual beauty lies in these virtuous principles and acts, so it is primarily *on this account* they are beautiful, *viz.,* that they imply *consent* and *union* with Being *in general.* This is the primary and most essential Beauty of every thing that can justly be called by the name of virtue, or is any moral excellency in the eye of one that has a perfect view of things. I say, the *primary* and *most essential* beauty—because there is a secondary and inferior sort of beauty; which I shall take notice of afterwards.

4. This spiritual beauty, that is but a *secondary* ground of a virtuous benevolence, is the ground, not only of benevolence, but *complacence,* and is the *primary* ground of the latter; that is, when the complacence is truly virtuous. Love to us in particular, and kindness received, may be a secondary ground. But this is the primary objective foundation of it.

5. It must be noted, that the *degree* of the *amiableness* or *valuableness* of true virtue, primarily consisting in consent and a benevolent propensity of heart to Being in general, in the eyes of one that is influenced by such a spirit, is not in the *simple* proportion of the degree of benevolent affection seen, but in a proportion *compounded* of the greatness of the benevolent Being or the degree of *Being* and the degree of *benevolence.* One that loves Being in general, will necessarily value good will to Being in general, wherever he sees it. But if he sees the same benevolence in *two* Beings, he will value it *more* in two, than in one only. Because it is a greater thing, more favorable to Being in general, to have two Beings to favor it, than only one of them. For there is more Being that favors Being: both together having more Being than one alone. So, if one Being be as great as two, has as much existence as both together, and has the same degree of general benevolence, it is more favorable to Being in general than if there were general benevolence in a Being that had but half that share of existence. As a large quantity of gold, with the same degree of

preciousness, i. e. with the same excellent quality of matter, is more valuable than a small quantity of the same metal.

6. It is impossible that any one should truly *relish* this beauty, consisting in general benevolence, who has *not* that temper himself. I have observed, that if any Being is possessed of such a temper, he will unavoidably be pleased with the same temper in another. And it may in like manner be demonstrated, that it is such a spirit, and nothing else, which will relish such a spirit. For if a Being, destitute of benevolence, should love benevolence to Being in general, it would prize and seek that which it had no value for. Because to love an inclination to the good of Being in general, would imply a loving and prizing the good of Being in general. For how should one love and value a *disposition* to a thing, or a *tendency to promote* a thing, and for that very reason, because it tends to promote it—when the *thing* itself is what he is regardless of, and has no value for, nor desires to have promoted.

. . . .

THE VIRGINIA GENTLEMAN

Although the planting of Virginia was primarily an enterprise in financial speculation and empire building, we must not forget that for the seventeenth-century Englishman, the idea of empire was only a reflection of a larger, more inclusive idea—that of a divine mission to give order to the new world and to make it like the old. The shape of Virginia society and its notion of the gentleman who was to be at its center—both these must be understood as products at once of socioeconomic and intellectual history.

Gentlemen, yeomen-freeman, and indentured servants who came to Virginia intended to work the land according to the patterns of British farming. If gentlemen were being established on large estates, still there would be great opportunity for yeomen to operate small farms and even for indentured servants to work their way up to the status of small farmers. But Virginia society did not pattern itself thus. Conditions of soil, availability of land, the cheap labor of indentured servants, and ease of cultivation soon led to a one-crop economy. Tobacco was king. As it was discovered that it was impossible (and undesirable) to establish the diversified kind of farming that was known in England, the gentlemen took over more and more land. Yeomen on their small farms, finding it increasingly difficult to handle and ship their tobacco, discovering, moreover, that the single crop soon exhausted the small amounts of land they owned, could only give up and sell out to the gentlemen. Then, towards the end of the seventeenth century, with the discovery of an apparently limitless source of cheaper labor in Negro slaves, the need for indentured servants began to decrease. By the beginning of the eighteenth century, the gentlemen were almost completely in control.

Such a society—unified in its economy, controlled by the landed few—was bound to have the gentleman as its ideal. The gentleman had organized the society; the society, as it took shape around him, had made his existence not only possible but necessary. He was a kind of feudal lord with responsibilities above and below. Generally speaking, his blood was good but not aristocratic, upper-middle-class English. He was determined to establish in a kind of upper-middle-class country squirearchy, patterned after its British equivalent but adjusted to American social and economic conditions. He would realize, in his fashion, the Renaissance idea of the gentleman as the well-rounded man, in whom the religious and the secular—expressed in piety, learning, and conduct—were fused. Yet he did not have to be born the complete gentleman: he could make himself into such. Indeed, his ideal was the Renaissance ideal of *virtú* accommodated to his time and to his place. So he raised his crops and sold them; looked after his family, relatives, friends, and slaves; participated in politics; studied to make himself a good and useful man; and worshipped a God merciful and bounteous enough to give him Virginia. He might well be at once farmer, doctor, veterinarian, hunter, surveyor, political leader, and handyman. *Virtú* was the *virtú* of living fully and wisely and responsibly in his world.

The Virginia gentleman (and his Maryland and South Carolina counterpart) everywhere set the pattern for the southern gentleman. In the later eighteenth and early nineteenth centuries, yeomen and ex-indentured servants, frontiersmen and small farmers, moving to the south and to the west, would try to establish themselves in his image. As often as not, they became something else—even as he, feeling economic and ideological pressures, was eventually to romanticize and sectionalize himself into something else. What is important is that we understand his image as it existed before 1750 and look not only to its immediate influence but also to its development into the Jeffersons and Madisons in whom it found its fullest embodiment.

The selections here printed reveal that image variously. First, there are two views, both more or less antagonistic, of Nathaniel Bacon, who tried in the 1670's to assert the independence and right of self-determination and self-protection of Virginia gentlemen pioneering on the frontier; here in "Bacon's Epitaph" above all, there is the noble tribute to the Virginia ideal—in whom "Mars and Minerva concurred." Second, there are a Virginia gentleman's views of his America in the pieces from Byrd's *History of the Dividing Line* and the matter of fact self-portraiture in four weeks from his secret diary; in the case of the latter, it is rewarding to compare Byrd as diarist with Samuel Sewall, so to see the difference between the New England and the Virginia gentleman. And third, there is, in the chapters from Beverly's *History,* the Virginia gentleman's view of his own society. What is disclosed, in all, is a mind and an imagination which are secular, expansive, devout but not devoted, centered on the ideal of the best and most responsible life for the best and most responsible gentlemen. We are on our way to Jefferson's idea of the natural aristocrat.

Bibliographical Note. The best general study of the historical background is the section on Virginia in Wesley F. Craven's *The Southern Colonies in the Seventeenth Century* (Baton Rouge, 1949); the detailed critical bibliographies are especially valuable. A more specialized study of value is Thomas J. Wertenbaker's *The Old South* (New York, 1942). Most important for the understanding of the Virginia gentleman is L. B. Wright's *First Gentlemen of Virginia* (San Marino, 1940). For the later history and influence of this Virginia gentleman see W. J. Cash, *The Mind of the South* (New York, 1941) and R. J. Osterweis, *Romanticism and Rationalism in the Old South* (New Haven, 1949). A careful survey of the earliest Virginia writing is H. M. Jones, *The Literature of Virginia in the Seventeenth Century* (Boston, 1946). The most detailed bibliographical and historical survey, probably definitive, is in the relevant sections of Jay Hubbell's magisterial *The South in American Literature, 1607-1900* (Durham, N. C., 1954).

TWO VIEWS OF NATHANIEL BACON

Bibliographical Note. The most important texts concerning Bacon and his Rebellion are collected in C. M. Andrews, ed. *Narratives of the Insurrections, 1675-1690* (New York, 1915); the selections here printed follow this edition, pp. 108-120, 74-77. On Bacon's Rebellion, see T. J. Wertenbaker, *Torchbearer of the Revolution* (Princeton, 1940).

from SIR JOHN BERRY (1635-1690), COLONEL
HERBERT JEFFREYS (d. 1678), AND FRANCIS
MORYSON (fl. 1649-1677), *A TRUE NARRATIVE
OF THE LATE REBELLION IN VIRGINIA,
BY THE ROYAL COMMISSIONERS*
(written 1677)*

[BACON'S CHARACTER AND RISE TO POWER]

The Murders, Rapines and outrages of the Indians became soe much the more Barbarous, fierce and frequent, by how much the more they perceived the Public Preparations of the English against them, Prosecuting their mischiefs upon the extreem Plantations thereby forcing many to dessert them to their Ruines, and destroying those that adventur'd to stay behind.

The unsatisfied People finding themselves still lyable to the Indian Crueltyes,[1] and the cryes of their wives and children growing grievous and intollerable to them, gave out in Speeches that they were resolved to Plant tobacco rather than pay the Tax for maintaining of Forts, and that the erecting of them was a great Grievance, Juggle and cheat, and of no more use or service to them than another Plantation with men at it, and that it was

---

* Reprinted from *Narratives of the Insurrections, 1675-1690,* edited by C. M. Andrews and used with permission of Barnes & Noble, Inc.

[1] Nathaniel Bacon (1647-1676), a planter on the Virginia frontier led other Virginians ostensibly against such "Indian Crueltyes." Because Governor Berkeley of Virginia would not give them enough support, Bacon's followers gradually followed him in a revolt against governmental authority. This selection, and the following, are from official reports on the Rebellion and its leader, who died by fever at the height of his success. His Rebellion virtually died with him.

merely a Designe of the Grandees to engrosse all their Tobacco into their owne hands.

Thus the sense of this oppression and the dread of a comon approaching calamity made the giddy-headed multitude madd, and precipitated them upon that rash overture of Running out upon the Indians themselves, at their owne voluntary charge and hazard of their Lives and Fortunes, onely they first by Petition humbly craved leave or comission to be ledd by any comander or comanders as the Governor should please to appoint over them to be their Chieftaine or Generall. But instead of Granting this Petition the Governor by Proclamation under great Penalty forbad the like Petitioning for the future.

This made the People jealous that the Governor for the lucre of the Beaver and otter trade etc. with the Indians, rather sought to protect the Indians than them, Since after publick Proclamation prohibiting all trade with the Indians (they complaine) hee privately gave commission to some of his Friendes to truck with them, and that those persons furnished the Indians with Powder, Shott etc. soe that they were better provided than his Majestye's Subjects.

The People of Charles City County (neer Merchants Hope) being denyed a Commission by the Governor although he was truly informed (as by a Letter of his to his Ma'tie he confesseth) of Several formidable Bodies of Indians coming downe on the heads of James River within 50 or 60 miles of the English Plantations, and knew not where the Storme would light, they begin to beat up drums for Volunteers to goe out against the Indians and soe continued Sundry dayes drawing into armes, the Magistrates being either soe remise or of the Same faction, that they suffered this disaster without contradiction or endeavouring to prevent soe dangerous a beginning and going on.

The Rout being got together now wanted nor waited for nothing but one to head and lead them out on their design. It soe happen'd that one Nathaniel Bacon Junr, a person whose lost and desperate fortunes had thrown him into that remote part of the world about 14 months before, and fram'd him fitt for such a purpose, as by the Sequel will appeare, which may make a short character of him no impertinent Digression.

Hee was a person whose erratique fortune had carryed and shewne him many Forraigne Parts, and of no obscure Family. Upon his first comming into Virginia hee was made one of the Councill, the reason of that advancement (all on a suddain) being best known to the Governour, which honor made him the more considerable in the eye of the Vulgar, and gave some advantage to his pernicious designes. Hee was said to be about four or five and thirty yeares of age, indifferent tall but slender, black-hair'd and of an ominous, pensive, melancholly Aspect, of a pestilent and prevalent Logical discourse tending to atheisme in most companyes, not given to much talke, or to make suddain replyes, of a most imperious and dangerous hidden Pride of heart, despising the wisest of his neighbours for their Ignorance, and very ambitious and arrogant. But all these things lay hidd in him till after hee was a councillor, and untill he became powerfull and popular.

Now this man being in Company with one Crews, Isham and Bird,[2] who growing to a highth of Drinking and making the Sadnesse of the times their discourse, and the Fear they all lived in, because of the Susquahanocks who had settled a little above the Falls of James River, and comitted many murders upon them, among whom Bacon's overseer happen'd to be one, Crews and the rest persuaded Mr. Bacon to goe over and see the Soldiers on the other Side James river and to take a quantity of Rum with them to give the men to drinke, which they did, and (as Crews etc. had before laid the Plot with the Soldiers) they all at once in field shouted and cry'd out, a Bacon! a Bacon! a Bacon! w'ch taking Fire with his ambition and Spirit of Faction and Popularity, easily prevail'd on him to Resolve to head them, His Friends endeavouring to fix him the Faster to his Resolves by telling him that they would also goe along with him to take Revenge upon the Indians, and drink Damnation to their Soules to be true to

---

[2] Father of William Byrd II.—*Andrews.*

him, and if hee could not obtain a Comission they would assist him as well and as much as if he had one; to which Bacon agreed.

This Forwardnesse of Bacons greatly cheer'd and animated the People, who looked upon him as the onely Patron of the Country and preserver of their Lives and Fortunes.

For he pretended and bosted what great Service hee would doe for the country, in destroying the Comon Enemy, securing their Lives and Estates, Libertyes, and such like fair frauds hee subtily and Secretly insinuated by his owne Instruments over all the country, which he seduced the Vulgar and most ignorant People to believe (two thirds of each county being of that Sort) Soe that theire whole hearts and hopes were set now upon Bacon. Next he charges the Governour as negligent and wicked, treacherous and incapable, the Lawes and Taxes as unjust and oppressive and cryes up absolute necessity of redress.

Thus Bacon encouraged the Tumult and as the unquiet crowd follow and adhere to him, he listeth them as they come in upon a large paper, writing their name circular wise, that their Ring-Leaders might not be found out.

Having conjur'd them into this circle, given them Brandy to wind up the charme, and enjoyn'd them by an oth to stick fast together and to him, and the othe being administered, he went and infected New Kent County ripe for Rebellion.

Bacon having gott about 300 men together in armes prepared to goe out against the Indians, the Governour and his Friends endeavour to divert his designes, but cannot.

Hee Proclames Bacon and his Followers Rebells and Mutineers for going forth against the Indians without a Commission, and (getting a company of Gentlemen together) the Governor marcheth up to the Falls of James River to pursue and take Bacon, or to Seize him at his Returne; but all in vaine, For Bacon had gott over the River with his Forces and hastning away into the woods, went directly and fell upon the Indians and killed some of them who were our best Friends of Indians and had fought ag't the Susquahanocks enemyes to the English.

The Governour having issued forth a Proclamation importing

noe commerce with the reputed Indian Enemyes, Besides the
cloggs and conditions w'ch were put on the Garrisons placed or
to be Placed in the new erected Forts, enjoying them not to make
any attempt upon the Indians untill they should first give the
Governor an account thereof, and receive orders from him
therein, Put many to a stand, made the People expostulate and
say how shall wee know our enemyes from our Friends, are not
the Indians all of a colour, and if wee must not defend ourselves
before they oppose us, they may take their usual advantage of
surprize, and soe destroy us ere wee are capable of making any
resistance; Soe that after all that charge in erecting of Forts, after
all the Troubles of the Congresse[3] of our forces, after all their
toyle and diligence used in discovering the enemy (who are sel-
dome to bee dealt with but in their owne way of surprize) the
very point of Execution was to be determined of by a person re-
siding in all likelihood at least a 100 miles distant from the Place
of action, to the losse of opportunityes and utter discouragement
of the soldiers and ourselves. Besides of what Security were these
Forts like to be, when the Indians cutt off and destroy'd divers
people within a small distance of the Forts and some of the very
Soldiers in them, and they not daring to stir out to relieve any
that were in danger and distresse, themselves being scarce secure
upon the Place they were Posted on. Nor would the people understand any distinction of Friendly Indians and Indian Enemyes,
for at that tyme it was impossible to distinguish one nation from
another, they being deformed with Paint of many colors, and at
best (say they) who is hee that can doe it, for there was never
any open or free Trade among us that we might know them, But
the whole Trade monopolized by the Governour and Grandees.

Soe the common cry and vogue of the Vulgar was, away with
these Forts, away with these distinctions, wee will have warr with
all Indians which come not in with their armes, and give Hostages
for their Fidelity and to ayd against all others; we will spare none.
and wee must bee hang'd for Rebells for killing those that will

---

[3] Bringing together.—*Andrews.*

destroy us, let them hang us, wee will venture that rather than lye at the mercy of a Barbarous Enemy, and be murdered as we are etc. Thus went the ruder sort raging and exclaiming agt. the Indians, expressing the calamity that befell New England by them.[4] While the Governour was in the Upper Parts to wait Bacon's returne the people below began to draw into armes, and to declare against the Forts. Hee to appease the comotions of the People leaves off that designe and comes immediately back to his own house, and caused at his returne the Surry and other Forts to be forthwith dismantled, and dissolving the assembly that enacted them, gave the country a free new election, which new assembly were to be for the Settlement of the then distracted condition of Virginia.

At this new election (such was the Prevalency of Bacon's Party) that they chose instead of Freeholders, Free men that had but lately crept out of the condition of Servants (which were never before Eligible) for their Burgesses and such as were eminent abettors to Bacon, and for faction and ignorance fitt Representatives of those that chose them.

At the Same time Bacon being come back from his Indian march with a thousand braging lyes to the credulous Silly People of what feats he had perform'd, was by the Inhabitants of the county of Henrico chosen a Burgess, as was also Crews for the Same county.

The assembly being mett Bacon comes down in a sloope to James Towne. But the People being very Fond of him, would not trust his person without a Guard, fearing some violence should be offered him by the Governour for what hee had already acted against his will, and Soe sent Forty armed men along in the Sloope with Bacon, coming somewhat neerer to Towne than Swanns Point dropt anchor and sent (as tis said) on Shore to the Governour to know if he might in safety come on shore, and sett as a Member etc. What answer was return'd we have not heard, onely what the Governor caused to be given him from the great

---

[4] King Philip's War, 1675-1676.—*Andrews.*

guns that fired at the Sloope from the Towne Fort, soe that having gott his Sloope out of Gunshott, he lay higher up the River, and in the night tyme with a party of his men ventured on shore, and having had some conference (at Laurances house) with Laurance and Drumond came off again undiscovered. Several Propositions were made and some boats sent off to apprehend him but could effect nothing. Bacon endeavours to make his Escape up the River. In this Juncture Capt. Thomas Gardner Master of the Ship *Adam and Eve* being at Towne, having an order from the Governor to pursue and seize him, immediately got on Board his ship, and as Bacon returned up the River comanded his Sloope in by Firing at him from on Board, and soe tooke him and all his men Prisoners and brought them away to the Governor at Towne.

Bacon being delivered up Prisoner to the Governor by Capt. Gardner, the Governor lifting up his hands and eyes said in the hearing of many people, "Now I behold the greatest Rebell that ever was in Virginia," who (with a dejected look) made noe Reply, till after a short pause the Governour ask'd Bacon these words: "Sir, doe you continue to be a Gentleman, and may I take your word? if soe you are at Liberty upon your owne parrol."

Bacon feignes a most deep sense of shame and sorrow for his Guilt, and expresses the greatest kind of obligacion to Gratitude towards the Governour imaginable. And to make it looke the more reall and sincere drew up an humble Submission for and acknowledgem't of his soe late crimes and disobedience, imploring thereby the Governor's Pardon and Favor, which Bacon being in readyness to Present on his coming before the Governor hee told the Councill then Sitting, "Now you shall see a Penitent Sinner."

Whereupon Bacon in very humble manner and with many low bowings of his Body approacht the Governor and on his knee gave up his Parasiticall Paper into the Governor's hands, and soe withdrew himself.

After a short while hee was sent for in againe and had his pardon confirmed to him, Is restor'd into favor and readmitted into the councell, to the wonder of all men.

Now Capt. Gardner instead of a Reward for the Service hee performed in taking and bringing away Bacon Prisoner was suffered to be fined 70 *lb*. damage for seizing him and the Sloope, although Capt. Gardner had discharged himself of her, the sd sloope being afterwards by a storme drove on shore and lost.[5]

However soe powerfull (it seems) was Bacon's interest in this new assembly that he procured a Public order to passe ag't Gardner for the payment of the 70 *lb*. where upon he threw Gardner into goale till he found Security for his Enlargement. But when they understand that the Governor had not onely sett him free, but readmitted him into the Councill, with Promise also of a commission to be given him to goe out against the Indians, the People were so well pacified for the present as that every man with great gladnesse return'd to his owne home.

Bacon attending at Towne for a Comission (w'ch the Governor is said to have promised him) and being delayed or putt off, was secretly whispered to by some of his Friends that those delayes would endanger his Life, and that if speedily he endeavour'd not to prevent it, there was a conspiracy to murder him on such a night; upon w'ch hee privately leaves the Towne. Now whether this was onely a rais'd rumor of Bacon's, or a reall truth wee cannot determine, but being rais'd after Bacon was gone we suppose it false.

Hee no sooner was come to the upper Parts of James River, but the impatient people run to him to ask how affairs Stood, exclaiming still more and more against the Indians, and desired to know if he had yet a comission, and understanding he had or could not obtaine any, they began to sett up their throats in one common kry of othes and curses and cry'd out aloud that they would either have a comission for Bacon that they might serve under his conduct or else they would pull downe the Towne or doe worse to some if they had it not, and if Bacon would go but with them they would gett him a commission. Thus the Raging

---

[5] It is a wonder Sir Wm. Berkeley (being then in Towne) did not protect or preserve a Person he had imploy'd in so signal a Service.—*Marginal note in original*.

Tumult came downe to Towne (Sitting the assembly) and Bacon at the head of them, having entred the Towne, hee Seises and secures the Principal Places and avenues, setts Sentinells and sends forth scouts, so that noe Place could bee more Securely guarded.

Having soe done, hee drawes up all his men in armes against the State house where the Governour councell and Burgesses were then assembled and Sitting, and sends in to the Assembly to know if now they would grant him a commission, which Sr. Wm. Berkeley utterly refused, and rising from his chair of judica-ture came downe to Bacon, and told him to his Face and before all his men that hee was a Rebell and a Traytor etc. and should have noe commission, and uncovering his naked Bosome before him, required that some of his men might shoot him, before ever he would be drawne to signe or consent to a commission for such a Rebell as Bacon, "Noe" (said the Governor) "lett us first try and end the difference singly between ourselves," and offer'd to meas-ure swords with him; all the answer Bacon gave the Governor was, "Sir, I came not, nor intend to hurt a haire of your honor's head, and for your sword your Honor may please to putt it up, it shall rust in the scabbard before ever I shall desire you to drawe it. I come for a commission against the Heathen who dayly in-humanely murder us and spill our Brethrens Blood, and noe care is taken to prevent it," adding, "God damne my Blood, I came for a commission, and a commission I will have before I goe," and turning to his soldiers, said "Make ready and Present," which they all did. Some of the Burgesses looking out at the windows and seeing the soldiers in that posture of Firing cry'd out to them, "For God's sake hold your handes and forebear a little, and you shall have what you please." Much hurrying, solicitation and im-portunity is used on all sides to the Governor to grant Bacon a commission. At last the Governor consents, a commission is drawne up and sent him, he dislikes it, they pray him to draw or direct one himself and the Governour should signe it. Whereupon Bacon drawes up the contents of a commission according to his owne mind, and returnes it to the Clerke, to prepare one by, which is done, liked of and received.

After the Governor had signed the Principall Commission to Bacon, hee is also pleas'd to signe 30 commissions more [Blanke] for officers that were to serve under him.

But Bacon finding occasion for more, sent to Sir William Berkley to signe others also, who said hee had signed enough already, and bid him signe the rest himself if hee would.

The assembly also passe orders to raise or presse 1000 men, and to raise Provisions etc. for this intended service ag't the Indians wherein severell of the councell and assembly-members were concern'd and acted in the promoting this designe, encouraging others to list themselves into Bacon's service, and particularly one Ballard who endeavoure'd to perswade some (who scrupled the Legality of Bacon's commission) that it was fairly and freely granted by Governor, Councill and Burgesses, this Ballard being one of the councill, and of those that both tooke and administer'd Bacon's Oath.

There was also an act of Indempnity pass'd to Bacon and his party who committed the offence on the assembly, and a Publick Letter of applause and approbation of Bacon's actions and Loyalty writ to the King and signed by the Governor and assembly. Which upon the Breaking up of this Session were sent abroad and read among the Ignorant People who believ'd thereby that all was well and nothing coming forth of a long time to quash, contradict or disowne this Commission, Indempnity, Lre etc. granted to Bacon, But on the contrary other comissions of the Governors own signing and seal'd with the Publick seal of the Colony coming to them, they were the more easily inclined to swallow down so fair a bait not seeing Rebellion at the end of it, and most men grew ambitious of the service as thinking it both safe and for the Publick good as having the approbation of the Governor and assembly, at least there yet appeared nothing to the contrary nor of a good while after.

Severall Volunteers and Reformadoes come in to list themselves under Bacon, and many were press'd into this service, till at last having his complement of men, and all things else being in readynesse according as the Assembly had provided for this expedition, A general Rendezvous is appointed by Bacon at the Falls of James River, where all things being well appointed for the march, Bacon makes a speech to his men, Assuring them all of his Loyalty to his Prince, declaring to them that his designe was no other than merely to serve his King and country and to cleere all suspicion of the contrary (if any were amongst them) by what had bin by him already acted or Proclamed against him, as also of what he said about the procuring his comission; hee urges to them the reasons that induced it, the necessity of that tyme that compell'd him, the negligence and coldnesse of others that hated him and the cryes of his Brethrens blood that alarm'd and waken'd him to this Publique revenge, using what motives hee could to raise up the spirits of his men. And finally before them all tooke the oath of allegiance and supremacy, willing his soldiers also to doe the like, which having freely comply'd with Hee drew up an oath of Fidelity to himselfe, which hee (as their head and Generall) required them to take; it comprehended the following contents or heads:

That they should not conceale any Plot or conspiracy of hurt against his Person, but immediately reveale the same to him or such others by whome he might come to the knowledge of it.

That if any harme or damage was intended towards any of his men, whether by surprizal or otherwise, or any conference used, or councell kept about the Same, to discover it.

That noe commerce or correspondence should be had with the Heathen, and if any knowne, to discover it.

That no news or information should be sent out least himself or army by such intelligence should be endanger'd either in Repute or otherwise.

All Councells, Plotts and conspiracyes known of the Heathen, to discover them, etc.

Just now (even on the very night before their going out on the intended march ag't the Indians) a messenger comes Post from Gloster Countyes bringing Intelligence to Bacon, that the Governor was there endeavouring to raise Forces to come and surprize him and his men and that hee was resolved by Force to take his extorted commission away from him, For that the whole county had Petitioned ag't him as a Rebell and a Traytor etc.

This amusing message was noe sooner brought to Bacon, but immediately he causes the Drums to Beat and Trumpett to Sound for calling his men together to whome he spake after this manner:

Gentlemen and Fellow Soldiers: The Newes just now brought mee may not a little startle you as well as myselfe. But seeing it is not altogether unexpected, wee may the better beare it and provide our remedies. The Governour is now in Gloster County endeavouring to raise Forces against us, having Declared us Rebells and Traytors: if true, crimes indeed too great for Pardon; our consciences herein are our best witnesses, and theres soe conscious, as like cowards therefore they will not have the courage to face us. It is Revenge that hurryes them on without regard to the Peoples Safety, and had rather wee should be murder'd and our ghosts sent to our Slaughter'd country-men by their actings, than wee live to hinder them of their Interest with the heathen, and preserve the remaining part of our Fellow Subjects from their crueltyes. Now then wee must bee forced to turne our swords to our owne defence, or expose ourselves to their Mercyes, or Fortune of the woodes, whilest his majestyes country here lyes in Bloode and Wasting (like a candle) at both ends. How Incapable wee may be made (if wee should proceede) through Sicknesse, want of Provisions, Slaughter, wounds lesse or more, none of us is void of the Sense hereof.

Therefore while wee are sound at heart, unwearied and not receiving damage by the fate of Warr, lett us descend to know the reasons why such Proceedings are used against us, That those whome they have raised for their Defence, to Preserve them against the Fury of the Heathen, they should thus seeke to Destroy, and to Betray our Lives whome they raised to Preserve theirs. If ever such Treachery was heard of, such wickednesse and inhumanity (and call all the former ages to Witnesse) and if any, that they suffered in like nature as wee are like by the sword and Ruines of warr.

But they are all damn'd Cowards, and you shall see they will not dare to meete us in the Field to try the Justnesse of our cause and soe wee will downe to them etc.

To which they all cry'd "Amen, amen, wee are all ready and will rather die in the Field than be hang'd like Roges, or Perish in the woods, expos'd to the Favours of the mercylesse Indians."

How unhappy, unsuccessfull and how fatale this avocation prov'd the consequence will but too Plainly Shewe. For Bacon (then the hopes of the People) was just upon the Point of marching out, and nothing could have call'd him back, or turn'd the sword of a civil warr into the heart and bowels of the country but soe ill-tymed a Project as this Prov'd.

from THE BURWELL PAPERS (WRITTEN 1676)

[BACON'S DEATH AND HIS MEMORY]

Bacon haveing for som time bin beseiged by sickness, and now not able to hould out any longer, all his strength, and provissions being spent, surrendred up that Fort he was no longer able to keepe, into the hands of that grim and all conquering Captaine, Death; after that he had implor'd the assistance of the above mentioned Minester, for the well makeing his Artickles of Rendition. The onely Religious duty (as they say) he was observ'd to perform dureing these Intregues of affaires, in which he was so considerable an actor, and soe much consearn'd, that rather then he would decline the cause, he became so deeply ingaged in, in the first rise there of, though much urged by arguments of dehortations, by his nearest Relations and best friends, that he subjected him selfe to all those inconvenences that, singly, might bring a Man of a more Robust frame to his last hom. After he was dead he was bemoned in these following lines (drawne by the Man that waited upon his person, as it is said) and who attended his Corps to there Buriall place: But where depossited till the Generall day, not knowne, onely to those who are ressalutly silent in that particuler. There was many coppes of Verces made after his

departure, calculated to the Lattitude of there affections who composed them; as a relish taken from both appetites I have here sent
you a cuple.

Bacons Epitaph, made by his Man.

Death why soe crewill! what, no other way
To manifest thy splleene, but thus to slay
Our hopes of safety; liberty, our all
Which, through thy tyrany, with him must fall
To its late Caoss? Had thy riged force
Bin delt by retale, and not thus in gross
Griefe had bin silent: Now wee must complaine
Since thou, in him, hast more then thousand slane
Whose lives and safetys did so much depend
On him there lif, with him there lives must end.

If't be a sin to thinke Death brib'd can bee
Wee must be guilty; say twas bribery
Guided the fatall shaft. Verginias foes,
To whom for secrit crimes just vengance owes
Disarved plagues, dreding their just disart
Corrupted Death by Parasscellcian[6] art
Him to destroy; whose well tride curage such,
There heartless harts, nor arms, nor strength could touch.

Who now must heale those wounds, or stop that blood
The Heathen made, and drew into a flood?
Who i'st must pleade our Cause? nor Trump nor Drum
Nor Deputations; these alass are dumb,
And Cannot speake. Our Arms (though nere so strong)
Will want the aide of his Commanding tongue,
Which Conquer'd more than Ceaser: He orethrew
Onely the outward frame; this Could subdue
The ruged workes of nature. Soules repleate
With dull Child could,[7] he'd annemate with heate

---

[6] Medical or alchemical; from Paracelsus, the celebrated physician (1493-1541).
—*Andrews.*

[7] Chilled cold. In the next line, Lymbick for alembic.—*Andrews.*

Drawne forth of reasons Lymbick. In a word
Marss and Minerva both in him Concurd
For arts, for arms, whose pen and sword alike,
As Catos did, may admireation strike
In to his foes; while they confess withall
It was there guilt stil'd him a Criminall.
Onely this differance doth from truth proceed:
They in the guilt, he in the name must bleed,
While none shall dare his Obseques to sing
In disarv'd measures, untill time shall bring
Truth Crown'd with freedom, and from danger free,
To sound his praises to posterity.
   Here let him rest; while wee this truth report,
Hee's gon from hence unto a higher Court
To pleade his Cause: where he by this doth know
Whether to Ceaser hee was friend, or foe.

Upon the Death of G: B.

   Whether to Ceaser he was Friend or Foe?
Pox take such Ignorance, do you not know?
Can he be Friend to Ceaser, that shall bring
The Arms of Hell, to fight againt the King?
(Treason, Rebellion) then what reason have
Wee for to waite upon him to his Grave,
There to express our passions? Wilt not bee
Worss then his Crimes, to sing his Ellegie
In well tun'd numbers; where each Ella beares
(To his Flagitious name) a flood of teares?
A name that hath more soules with sorrow fed,
Then reched [8] Niobe single teares ere shed;
A name that fil'd all hearts, all eares, with paine,
Untill blest fate proclamed, Death had him slane.
Then how can it be counted for a sin
Though Death (nay though my selfe) had bribed bin,

---

[8] Wretched.—*Andrews.*

To guide the fatall shaft? we honour all
That lends a hand unto a T[r]ators fall.
What though the well paide Rochit soundly ply
And box the Pulpitt in to flatterey;
Urging his Rethorick, and straind elloquence,
T' adorne incoffin'd filth and excrements;
Though the Defunct (like ours) nere tride
A well intended deed untill he dide?
'Twill be nor sin, nor shame, for us, to say
A two fould Passion checker-workes this day
Of Joy and Sorow; yet the last doth move
On feete impotent, wanting strength to prove
(Nor can the art of Logick yeild releife)
How Joy should be surmounted, by our greife.
Yet that wee Grieve it cannot be denide,
But 'tis because he was, not cause he dide.
So wep the poore destresed Ilyum Dames[1]
Hereing those nam'd, there Citty put in flames,
And Country ruing'd; If wee thus lament
It is against our present Joyes consent.
For if the rule, in Phisick, trew doth prove,
Remove the cause, th' effects will after move,
We have outliv'd our sorows, since we see
The Causes shifting, of our miserey.

Nor is't a single cause, that's slipt away,
That made us warble out a well-a-day.
The Braines to plot, the hands to execute
Projected ills, Death Joyntly did nonsute
At his black Bar. And what no Baile could save
He hath commited Prissoner to the Grave;
From whence there's no repreive. Death keep him close
We have too many Divells still goe loose.

WILLIAM BYRD II
(1674-1744)

Bibliographical Note. Byrd's published writings are collected in J. S. Bassett, ed., *The Writings of "Colonel William Byrd, of Westover in Virginia, Esqr"* (New York, 1901). Writings edited from manuscript are published in: W. K. Boyd, ed. *William Byrd's Histories of the Dividing Line Betwixt Virginia and North Carolina* (Raleigh, 1929); L. B. Wright and Marion Tinling, eds., *The Secret Diary of William Byrd of Westover, 1709-1712* (Richmond, 1941); Maude Woodfin, ed., *Another Secret Diary of William Byrd of Westover, 1739-1741, with Letters and Literary Exercises, 1696-1726* (Richmond, 1942). The text of the following selections follows Bassett's edition of *The Writings,* pp. 3-21, 44-47, 94-103, and the *Wright-Tinling* edition of *The Secret Diary,* pp. 457-469. The best biography of Byrd is R. C. Beatty, *William Byrd of Westover* (Boston, 1932); but it was written without knowledge of Byrd's *Secret History of the Dividing Line* (first published by Boyd) and of the Byrd diaries. The best sketch of Byrd as diarist is L. B. Wright and Marion Tinling, "William Byrd of Westover, an American Pepys," *South Atlantic Quarterly,* XXXIX (1940), 259-274.

from THE HISTORY OF THE DIVIDING LINE: RUN IN THE YEAR 1728 (written 1729?)

[ON THE FIRST SETTLERS OF AMERICA]

Before I enter upon the Journal of the Line between Virginia and North Carolina, it will be necessary to clear the way to it, by shewing how the other British Colonies on the Main have, one after the other, been carved out of Virginia, by Grants from his Majesty's Royal Predecessors. All that part of the Northern American Continent now under the Dominion of the King of Great Britain, and Stretching quite as far as the Cape of Florida, went *at first under the General Name of Virginia.*

The only Distinction, in those early Days, was, that all the Coast to the Southward of Chesapeake Bay was called South Virginia, and all to the Northward of it, North Virginia.

The first Settlement of this fine Country was owing to that

great Ornament of the British Nation, Sir Walter Raleigh, who obtained a Grant thereof from Queen Elizabeth of ever-glorious Memory, by Letters Patent, dated March the 25th, 1584.

But whether that Gentleman ever made a Voyage thither himself is uncertain; because those who have favour'd the Public with an Account of His Life mention nothing of it. However, thus much may be depended on, that Sir Walter invited sundry persons of Distinction to Share in his Charter, and join their Purses with his in the laudable project of fitting out a Colony to Virginia.

Accordingly, 2 Ships were Sent away that very Year, under the Command of his good Friends Amidas and Barlow, to take possession of the Country in the Name of his Roial Mistress, the Queen of England.

These worthy Commanders, for the advantage of the Trade Winds, shaped their Course first to the Charibbe Islands, thence stretching away by the Gulph of Florida, dropt Anchor not far from Roanoak Inlet. They ventured ashoar near that place upon an Island now called Colleton island, where they set up the Arms of England, and Claimed the Adjacent Country in Right of their Sovereign Lady, the Queen; and this Ceremony being duly performed, they kindly invited the neighbouring Indians to traffick with them.

These poor people at first approacht the English with great Caution, having heard much of the Treachery of the Spaniards, and not knowing but these Strangers might be as treacherous as they. But, at length, discovering a kind of good nature in their looks, they ventured to draw near, and barter their Skins and Furs, for the Bawbles and Trinkets of the English.

These first Adventurers made a very profitable Voyage, raising at least a Thousand per cent. upon their Cargo. Amongst other Indian Commodities, they brought over Some of that bewitching Vegetable, Tobacco. And this being the first that ever came to England Sir Walter thought he could do no less than make a present of Some of the brightest of it to His Roial Mistress, for her own Smoaking.

The Queen graciously accepted of it, but finding her Stomach sicken after two or three Whiffs, it was presently whispered by the earl of Leicester's Faction, that Sir Walter had certainly Poison'd Her. But Her Majesty soon recovering her Disorder, obliged the Countess of Nottingham and all her Maids to Smoak a whole Pipe out amongst them.

As it happen'd some Ages before to be the fashion to Santer to the Holy Land, and go upon other Quixot Adventures, so it was now grown the Humour to take a Trip to America. The Spaniards had lately discovered Rich Mines in their Part of the West Indies, which made their Maritime Neighbours eager to do so too. This Modish Frenzy being still more Inflam'd by the Charming Account given of Virginia, by the first Adventurers, made many fond of removeing to such a Paradise.

Happy was he, and still happier She, that cou'd get themselves transported, fondly expecting their Coarsest Utensils, in that happy place, would be of Massy Silver.

This made it easy for the Company to procure as many Volunteers as they wanted for their new Colony; but, like most other Undertakers who have no Assistance from the Public, they Starved the Design by too much Frugality; for, unwilling to Launch out at first into too much Expense, they Ship't off but few People at a Time, and Those but Scantily provided. The Adventurers were, besides, Idle and extravagant, and expected they might live without work in so plentiful a Country.

These Wretches were set Ashoar not far from Roanoak Inlet, but by some fatal disagreement, or Laziness, were either Starved or cut to Pieces by the Indians.

Several repeated Misadventures of this kind did, for some time, allay the Itch of Sailing to this New World; but the Distemper broke out again about the Year 1606. Then it happened that the Earl of Southampton and several other Persons, eminent for their Quality and Estates, were invited into the Company, who apply'd themselves once more to People the then almost abandon'd Colony. For this purpose they embarkt about an Hundred men, most of them Riprobates of good Familys, and related to some of the company, who were men of Quality and Fortune.

The Ships that carried them made a Shift to find a more direct way to Virginia, and ventured thro the Capes into the Bay of Chesapeak. The same Night they came to an Anchor at the Mouth of Powatan, the same as James River, where they built a Small Fort at a Place call'd Point Comfort.

This Settlement stood its ground from that time forward in spite of all the Blunders and Disagreement of the first Adventurers, and the many Calamitys that befel the Colony afterwards.

The six gentlemen who were first named of the company by the crown, and who were empowered to choose an annual President from among themselves, were always engaged in Factions and Quartels, while the rest detested Work more than Famine. At this rate the Colony must have come to nothing, had it not been for the vigilance and Bravery of Capt. Smith, who struck a Terrour into all the Indians round about. This Gentleman took some pains to perswade the men to plant Indian corn, but they lookt upon all Labor as a Curse. They chose rather to depend upon the Musty Provisions that were sent from England: and when they fail'd they were forct to take more pains to Seek for Wild Fruits in the Woods, than they would have taken in tilling the Ground. Besides, this Exposd them to be knockt on the head by the Indians, and gave them Fluxes into the Bargain, which thind the Plantation very much. To Supply this mortality, they were reinforct the year following with a greater number of People, amongst which were fewer Gentlemen and more Labourers, who, however, took care not to kill themselves with Work.

These found the First Adventurers in a very starving condition, but relievd their wants with the fresh Supply they brought with them. From Kiquotan they extended themselves as far as James-Town, where like true Englishmen, they built a Church that cost no more than Fifty Pounds, and a Tavern that cost Five hundred.

They had now made peace with the Indians, but there was one thing wanting to make that peace lasting. The Natives coud, by no means, perswade themselves that the English were heartily their Friends, so long as they disdained to intermarry with them.

And, in earnest, had the English consulted their own Security and the good of the Colony—Had they intended either to Civilize or Convert these Gentiles, they would have brought their Stomachs to embrace this prudent Alliance.

The Indians are generally tall and well-proportion'd, which may make full Amends for the Darkness of their Complexions. Add to this, that they are healthy & Strong, with Constitutions untainted by Lewdness, and not enfeebled by Luxury. Besides, Morals and all considered, I cant think the Indians were much greater Heathens than the first Adventurers, who, had they been good Christians, would have had the Charity to take this only method of converting the Natives to Christianity. For, after all that can be said, a sprightly Lover is the most prevailing Missionary that can be sent amongst these, or any other Infidels.

Besides, the poor Indians would have had less reason to Complain that the English took away their Land, if they had received it by way of Portion with their Daughters. Had such Affinities been contracted in the Beginning, how much Bloodshed had been prevented, and how populous would the Country have been, and, consequently, how considerable? Nor wou'd the Shade of the Skin have been any reproach at this day; for if a Moor may be washt white in 3 Generations, Surely an Indian might have been blancht in two.

The French, for their Parts, have not been so Squeamish in Canada, who upon Trial find abundance of Attraction in the Indians. Their late Grand Monarch thought it not below even the Dignity of a Frenchman to become one flesh with this People, and therefore Ordered 100 Livres for any of his Subjects, Man or Woman, that would intermarry with a Native.

By this piece of Policy we find the French Interest very much Strengthen'd amongst the Savages, and their Religion, such as it is, propagated just as far as their Love. And I heartily wish this well-concerted Scheme don't hereafter give the French an Advantage over his Majesty's good Subjects on the Northern Continent of America.

About the same time New England was pared off from Vir-

ginia by Letters Patent, bearing date April the 10th, 1608.[1]
Several Gentlemen of the Town and Neighborhood of Plymouth
obtain'd this Grant, with the Ld Chief Justice Popham at their
Head.

Their Bounds were Specified to extend from 38 to 45 Degrees
of Northern Latitude, with a Breadth of one Hundred Miles
from the Sea Shore. The first 14 Years, this Company encounter'd many Difficulties, and lost many men, tho' far from being
discouraged, they sent over Numerous Recruits of Presbyterians,
every year, who for all that, had much ado to stand their Ground,
with all their Fighting and Praying.

But about the year 1620, a Large Swarm of Dissenters fled
thither from the Severities of their Stepmother, the Church.
These Saints conceiving the same Aversion to the Copper Complexion of the Natives, with that of the first Adventurers to Virginia, would, on no Terms, contract Alliances with them, afraid
perhaps, like the Jews of Old, lest they might be drawn into
Idolatry by those Strange Women.

Whatever disgusted them I can't say, but this false delicacy
creating in the Indians a Jealousy that the English were ill
affected towards them, was the Cause that many of them were
cut off, and the rest Exposed to various Distresses.

This Reinforcement was landed not far from Cape Codd,
where, for their greater Security they built a Fort, and near it a
Small Town, which in Honour of the Proprietors, was call'd
New Plymouth. But they Still had many discouragements to
Struggle with, tho' by being well Supported from Home, they
by Degrees Triumph't over them all.

Their Brethren, after this, flockt over so fast, that in a few
Years they extended the Settlement one hundred Miles along
the Coast, including Rhode Island and Martha's Vineyard.

Thus the Colony throve apace, and was throng'd with large
Detachments of Independents and Presbyterians, who thought
themselves persecuted at home.

---

[1] The charters of the London and the Plymouth companies were both dated
April 10, 1606.—*Bassett.*

Tho' these People may be ridiculd for some Pharisaical Particularitys in their Worship and Behaviour, yet they were very useful Subjects, as being Frugal and Industrious, giving no Scandal or bad Example, at least by any Open and Public Vices. By which excellent Qualities they had much the Advantage of the Southern Colony, who thought their being Members of the Establish't Church sufficient to Sanctifie very loose and Profligate Morals. For this Reason New England improved much faster than Virginia, and in Seven or Eight Years New Plimouth, like Switzerland, seemd too Narrow a Territory for its Inhabitants.

For this Reason, several Gentlemen of Fortune purchas'd of the Company that Canton of New England now called Massachuset colony. And King James confirm'd the Purchase by his Royal Charter, dated March the 4th, 1628. In less than 2 years after, above 1000 of the Puritanical Sect removed thither with considerable Effects, and these were followed by such Crowds, that a Proclamation was issued in England, forbidding any more of his Majesty's Subjects to be Shipt off. But this had the usual Effect of things forbidden, and serv'd only to make the Wilful Independents flock over the faster. And about this time it was that Messrs. Hampden and Pym, and (some say) Oliver Cromwell, to show how little they valued the King's Authority, took a Trip to New England.

In the Year 1630, the famous City of Boston was built, in a Commodious Situation for Trade and Navigation, the same being on a Peninsula at the Bottom of Massachuset Bay.

This Town is now the most considerable of any on the British Continent, containing at least 8,000 houses and 40,000 Inhabitants. The Trade it drives, is very great to Europe, and to every Part of the West Indies, having near 1,000 Ships and lesser Vessels belonging to it.

Altho the Extent of the Massachuset Colony reach't near one Hundred and Ten Miles in Length, and half as much in Breadth, yet many of its Inhabitants, thinking they wanted Elbow-room, quitted their Old Seats in the Year 1636, and formed 2 New

Colonies: that of Connecticut and New Haven. These King Charles the 2d erected into one Government in 1664,[2] and gave them many Valuable Privileges, and among the rest, that of chusing their own Governors. The Extent of these united Colonies may be about Seventy Miles long and fifty broad.

Besides these several Settlements, there Sprang up still another, a little more Northerly, called New Hampshire. But that consisting of no more than two Counties, and not being in condition to Support the Charge of a Distinct Government, was glad to be incorporated with that of Massachuset, but upon Condition, however, of being Named in all Public Acts, for fear of being quite lost and forgot in the Coalition.

In like manner New Plymouth joyn'd itself to Massachuset, except only Rhode Island, which, tho' of small Extent, got itself erected into a Separate government by a Charter from King Charles the 2d, soon after the Restoration, and continues so to this day.

These Governments all continued in Possession of their Respective Rights and Privileges till the Year 1683, when that of Massachuset was made Void in England by a Quo Warranto.

In Consequence of which the King was pleased to name Sir Edmund Andros His first Governor of that Colony. This Gentleman, it seems, ruled them with a Rod of Iron till the Revolution, when they laid unhallowed Hands upon Him, and sent him Prisoner to England.

This undutiful proceeding met with an easy forgiveness at that happy Juncture. King William and his Royal Consort were not only pleasd to overlook this Indignity offered to their Governor, but being made sensible how unfairly their Charter had been taken away, most graciously granted them a new one.

By this some new Franchises were given them, as an Equivalent for those of Coining Money and Electing a governour, which were taken away. However, the other Colonies of Connecticut

---

[2] 1662.—*Bassett.*

and Rhode Island had the luck to remain in Possession of their
Original Charters, which to this Day have never been calld in
Question.

The next Country dismembered from Virginia was New Scotland, claimd by the Crown of England in Virtue of the first
Discovery by Sebastian Cabot. By Colour of this Title, King
James the first granted it to Sir William Alexander by Patent,
dated September the 10th, 1621.

But this Patentee never sending any Colony thither, and the
French believing it very Convenient for them, obtained a Surrender of it from their good Friend and Ally, king Charles the
2d, by the Treaty of Breda. And, to show their gratitude, they
stirred up the Indians soon after to annoy their Neighbours of
New England. Murders happend continually to his Majesty's
Subjects by their Means, till Sr William Phipps took their Town
of Port Royal, in the year 1690. But as the English are better at
taking than keeping Strong Places, the French retook it soon, and
remaind Masters of it till 1710, when General Nicholson wrested
it, once more, out of their Hands.

Afterwards the Queen of Great Britain's Right to it was recog-
nized and confirmed by the treaty of Utrecht.

Another Limb lopt off from Virginia was New York, which
the Dutch seized very unfairly, on pretence of having Purchasd
it from Captain Hudson, the first Discoverer. Nor was their way
of taking Possession of it a whit more justifiable than their pretended Title.

Their West India Company tamperd with some worthy English Skippers (who had contracted with a Swarm of English
Dissenters to transport them to Hudson river) by no means to
land them there, but to carry 'em some leagues more northerly.

This Dutch Finesse took Exactly, and gave the Company time
soon after to seize the Hudson River for themselves. But Sr Samuel Argall, then governor of Virginia, understanding how the
King's Subjects had been abused by these Republicans, marcht
thither with a good Force, and obligd them to renounce all pretensions to that Country. The worst of it was, the Knight de-

pended on their Parole to Ship themselves to Brasile, but took no measures to make this Slippery People as good as their Word.

No sooner was the good Governor retired, but the honest Dutch began to build Forts and strengthen themselves in their ill-gotten Possessions; nor did any of the King's Liege People take the trouble to drive these Intruders thence. The Civil War in England, And the Confusions it brought forth, allowed no Leisure to such distant Considerations. Tho tis strange that the Protector, who negleced no Occasion to mortify the Dutch, did not afterwards call them to Account for this breach of Faith. However, after the Restoration, the King sent a Squadron of his Ships of War, under the Command of Sir Robert Carr, and reduced that Province to his Obedience.

Some time after, His Majesty was Pleasd to grant that Country to his Royal Highness, the Duke of York, by Letters Patent, dated March the 12th, 1664. But to shew the Modesty of the Dutch to the Life, tho they had no Shaddow of Right to New York, yet they demanded Surinam, a more valuable Country, as an Equivalent for it, and our able Ministers at that time had the Generosity to give it them.

But what wounded Virginia deepest was the cutting off MARY-LAND from it, by Charter from King Charles the 1st, to sir George Calvert, afterwards Ld Baltimore, bearing date the 20th of June, 1632. The Truth of it is, it begat much Speculation in those days, how it came about that a good Protestant King should bestow so bountiful a Grant upon a Zealous Roman catholic. But 'tis probable it was one fatal Instance amongst many other of his Majesty's complaisance to the Queen.

However that happened, 'tis certain this Province afterwards provd a Commodious Retreat for Persons of that Communion. The Memory of the Gun-Powder-Treason-Plot was Still fresh in every body's mind, and made England too hot for Papists to live in, without danger of being burnt with the Pope, every 5th of November; for which reason Legions of them transplanted themselves to Maryland in Order to be Safe, as well from the Insolence of the Populace as the Rigour of the Government.

Not only the Gun-Powder-Treason, but every other Plot, both pretended and real, that has been trump't up in England ever Since, has helpt to People his Lordship's Propriety.

But what has provd most Serviceable to it was the Grand Rebellion against King Charles the 1st, when every thing that bore the least tokens of Popery was sure to be demolisht, and every man that Profest it was in Jeopardy of Suffering the same kind of Martyrdom the Romish Priests do in Sweden.

Soon after the Reduction of New York, the Duke was pleasd to grant out of it all that Tract of Land included between Hudson and Delaware Rivers, to the Lord Berkley and Sir George Carteret, by deed dated June the 24th, 1664. And when these Grantees came to make Partition of this Territory, His Lordp's Moiety was calld West Jersey, and that to Sir George, East Jersey.

But before the Date of this Grant, the Swedes began to gain Footing in part of that Country; tho, after they saw the Fate of New York, they were glad to Submit to the King of England, on the easy Terms of remaining in their Possessions, and rendering a Moderate Quit-rent. Their Posterity continue there to this Day, and think their Lot cast in a much fairer Land than Dalicarlia.[3]

The Proprietors of New Jersey, finding more Trouble than Profit in their new Dominions, made over their Right to several other Persons, who obtain a fresh Grant from his Royal Highness, dated March 14th, 1682.

Several of the Grantees, being Quakers and Anababtists, faild not to encourage many of their own Perswasion to remove to this Peaceful Region. Amongst them were a Swarm of Scots Quakers, who were not tolerated to exercise the Gifts of the Spirit in their own Country.

Besides the hopes of being Safe from Persecution in this Retreat, the New Proprietors inveigled many over by this tempting Account of the Country: that it was a Place free from those 3 great Scourges of Mankind, Priests, Lawyers, and Physicians.

---

[3] Name of a former province of Sweden.—*Bassett.*

Nor did they tell a Word of a Lye, for the People were yet too poor to maintain these Learned Gentlemen, who, every where, love to be paid well for what they do; and, like the Jews, cant breathe in a Climate where nothing is to be got.

The Jerseys continued under the Government of these Propri-etors till the Year 1702, when they made a formal Surrender of the Dominion to the Queen, reserving however the Property of the Soil to themselves. So soon as the Bounds of New Jersey came to be distinctly laid off, it appeared that there was still a Narrow Slipe of Land, lying betwixt that Colony and Maryland. Of this, William Penn, a Man of much Worldly Wisdom, and some Eminence among the Quakers, got early Notice, and, by the Credit he had with the Duke of York, obtain a Patent for it, Dated March the 4th, 1680.

It was a little Surprising to some People how a Quaker should be so much in the good Graces of a Popish Prince; tho, after all, it may be pretty well Accounted for. This Ingenious Person had not been bred a Quaker; but, in his Earlier days, had been a Man of Pleasure about the Town. He had a beautiful form and very taking Address, which made him Successful with the Ladies, and Particularly with a Mistress of the Duke of Monmouth. By this Gentlewoman he had a Daughter, who had Beauty enough to raise her to be a Dutchess, and continued to be a Toast full 30 Years.[4]

But this Amour had like to have brought our Fine Gentleman in Danger of a Duell, had he not discreetly shelterd himself under this peaceable Perswasion. Besides, his Father having been a Flag-Officer in the Navy, while the Duke of York was Lord High Admiral, might recommend the Son to his Favour. This piece of secret History I thought proper to mention, to wipe off the Suspicion of his having been Popishly inclind.

This Gentleman's first Grant confind Him within pretty Nar-row Bounds, giving him only that Portion of Land which con-tains Buckingham, Philadelphia and Chester Counties. But to get

---

[4] This piece of London gossip seems not to have been recorded by any other contemporary.—*Bassett.*

these Bounds a little extended, He pusht His Interest still further with His Royal Highness, and obtain a fresh Grant of the three Lower Counties, called New-Castle, Kent and Sussex, which still remaind within the New York Patent, and had been luckily left out of the Grant of New Jersey.

The Six Counties being thus incorporated, the Proprietor dignifyd the whole with the Name of Pensilvania.

The Quakers flockt over to this Country in Shoals, being averse to go to Heaven the same way with the Bishops. Amongst them were not a few of good Substance, who went Vigorously upon every kind of Improvement; and thus much I may truly say in their Praise, that by Diligence and Frugality, For which this Harmless Sect is remarkable, and by haveing no Vices but such as are Private, they have in a few Years made Pensilvania a very fine Country.

The Truth is, they have observed exact Justice with all the Natives that border upon them; they have purchasd all their Lands from the Indians; and tho they paid but a Trifle for them, it has procured them the Credit of being more righteous than their Neighbours. They have likewise had the Prudence to treat them kindly upon all Occasions, which has savd them from many Wars and Massacres wherein the other Colonies have been indiscreetly involved. The Truth of it is, a People whose Principles forbid them to draw the Carnal Sword, were in the Right to give no Provocation.

[ON THE PEOPLE OF THE NORTH CAROLINA FRONTIER]

[March 10.] The Sabbath happen'd very opportunely to give some ease to our jaded People, who rested religiously from every work, but that of cooking the Kettle. We observed very few cornfields in our Walks, and those very small, which seem'd the Stranger to us, because we could see no other Tokens of Husbandry or Improvement. But, upon further Inquiry, we were given to understand People only made Corn for themselves and not for their Stocks, which know very well how to get their own Living.

Both Cattle and Hogs ramble in the Neighbouring Marshes and Swamps, where they maintain themselves the whole Winter long, and are not fetch'd home till the Spring. Thus these Indolent Wretches, during one half of the Year, lose the Advantage of the Milk of their cattle, as well as their Dung, and many of the poor Creatures perish in the Mire, into the Bargain, by this ill Management.

Some, who pique themselves more upon Industry than their Neighbours, will, now and then, in compliment to their Cattle, cut down a Tree whose Limbs are loaden with the Moss aforemention'd. The trouble wou'd be too great to Climb the Tree in order to gather this Provender, but the Shortest way (which in this Country is always counted the best) is to fell it, just like the Lazy Indians, who do the same by such Trees as bear fruit, and so make one Harvest for all. By this bad Husbandry Milk is so Scarce, in the Winter Season, that were a Big-belly'd Woman to long for it, She would lose her Longing. And, in truth, I believe this is often the Case, and at the same time a very good reason why so many People in this Province are markt with a Custard Complexion.

The only Business here is raising of Hogs, which is manag'd with the least Trouble, and affords the Diet they are most fond of. The Truth of it is, the Inhabitants of N Carolina devour so much Swine's flesh, that it fills them full of gross Humours. For want too of a constant Supply of Salt, they are commonly obliged to eat it Fresh, and that begets the highest taint of Scurvy. Thus, whenever a Severe Cold happens to Constitutions thus Vitiated, tis apt to improve into the Yaws, called there very justly the country-Distemper. This has all the Symptoms of the Pox, with this Aggravation, that no Preparation of Mercury will touch it. First it seizes the Throat, next the Palate, and lastly shews its spite to the poor Nose, of which tis apt in a small time treacherously to undermine the Foundation.

This Calamity is so common and familiar here, that it ceases to be a Scandal, and in the disputes that happen about Beauty, the Noses have in some Companies much ado to carry it. Nay, tis said that once, after three good Pork years, a Motion had like to have been made in the House of Burgesses, that a Man with a Nose shou'd be incapable of holding any Place of Profit in the Province; which Extraordinary Motion could never have been intended without Some Hopes of a Majority.

Thus, considering the foul and pernicious Effects of Eating Swine's Flesh in a hot Country, it was wisely forbidden and made an Abomination to the Jews, who liv'd much in the same Latitude with Carolina.

11. We ordered the Surveyors early to their Business, who were blesst with pretty dry Grounds for three Miles together. But they paid dear for it in the next two, consisting of one continued frightfull Pocoson, which no Creatures but those of the amphibious kind ever had ventur'd into before.

This filthy Quagmire did in earnest put the Men's Courage to a Tryal, and tho' I can't say it made them lose their Patience, yet they lost their Humour for Joking. They kept their Gravity like so many Spaniards, so that a Man might then have taken his Opportunity to plunge up to the Chin, without Danger of being laught at. However, this unusual composure of countenance could not fairly be call'd complaining.

Their Day's-Work ended at the Mouth of Northern's Creek, which empties itself into N W River; tho' we chose to Quarter a little higher up the River, near Mossy Point. This we did for the Convenience of an Old house to Shelter our Persons and Baggage from the rain, which threaten'd us hard. We judg'd the thing right, for there fell an heavy shower in the Night, that drove the most hardy of us into the House. Tho' indeed, our case was not much mended by retreating thither, because that Tenement having not long before been us'd as a Pork-Store, the Moisture of the Air dissolv'd the Salt that lay Scatter'd on the Floor, and made it as wet within Doors as without. However, the Swamps and Marshes we were lately accustom'd to had made such Beavers and Otters of us that Nobody caught the least cold.

We had encamp so early, that we found time in the Evening to walk near half a Mile into the Woods. There we came upon a Family of Mulattoes, that call'd themselvs free, tho' by the

Shyness of the Master of the House, who took care to keep least
in Sight, their Freedom seem'd a little Doubtful. It is certain
many Slaves Shelter themselves in this Obscure Part of the
World, nor will any of their righteous Neighbours discover them.
On the Contrary, they find their Account in Settling such Fugitives on some out-of-the-way-corner of their Land, to raise Stocks
for a mean and inconsiderable Share, well knowing their Condition makes it necessary for them to Submit to any Terms.

Nor were these worthy Borderers content to Shelter Runaway
Slaves, but Debtors and Criminals have often met with the like
Indulgence. But if the Government of North Carolina has encourag'd this unneighbourly Policy in order to increase their
People, it is no more than what Ancient Rome did before them,
which was made a City of Refuge for all Debtors and Fugitives,
and from that wretched Beginning grew up in time to be Mistress
of a great Part of the World. And, considering how Fortune delights in bringing great things out of Small, who knows but
Carolina may, one time or other, come to be the Seat of some
other great Empire?

[ON THE INDIANS AND RELATIONS WITH THEM]

[April 7.] The Next day being Sunday, we order'd Notice to
be sent to all the Neighbourhood that there wou'd be a Sermon
at this Place, and an Opportunity of Christening their Children.
But the Likelihood of Rain got the better of their Devotion, and
what perhaps, Might Still be a Stronger motive of their Curiosity.
In the Morning we dispacht a runner to the Nottoway Town, to
let the Indians know we intended them a Visit that Evening, and
our honest Landlord was so kind as to be our Pilot thither, being
about 4 Miles from his House.

Accordingly in the Afternoon we marcht in good Order to the
Town, where the Female Scouts, station'd on an Eminence for
that purpose, had no sooner spy'd us, but they gave Notice of our
Approach to their Fellow-Citizens by continual Whoops and
Cries, which cou'd not possibly have been more dismal at the
Sight of their most implacable Enemys.

This Signal Assembled all their Great Men, who receiv'd us in a Body, and conducted us into the Fort. This Fort was a Square Piece of Ground, inclos'd with Substantial Puncheons, or Strong Palisades, about ten feet high, and leaning a little outwards, to make a Scalade more difficult.

Each side of the Square might be about 100 Yards long, with Loop-holes at proper Distances, through which they may fire upon the Enemy.

Within this Inclosure we found Bark Cabanes Sufficient to lodge all their people, in Case they should be obliged to retire thither. These Cabanes are no other but Close Arbours made of Saplings, arched at the top, and cover'd so well with Bark as to be proof against all Weather. The fire is made in the Middle, according to the Hibernian Fashion, the Smoak whereof finds no other Vent but at the Door, and so keeps the whole family Warm, at the Expense both of their Eyes and Complexion.

The Indians have no standing Furniture in their Cabanes but Hurdles to repose their Persons upon, which they cover with Mats or Deer-skins. We were conducted to the best Appartments in the Fort, which just before had been made ready for our Reception, and adorn'd with new Mats, that were sweet and clean.

The Young Men had Painted themselves in a Hideous Manner, not so much for Ornament as Terror. In that frightful Equipage they entertain'd us with Sundry War-Dances, wherein they endeavour'd to look as formidable as possible. The Instrument they danct to was an Indian-drum, that is, a large Gourd with a Skin bract tort over the Mouth of it. The Dancers all Sang to this Musick, keeping exact Time with their feet, while their Heads and Arms were screw'd into a thousand Menacing Postures.

Upon this occasion the Ladies had array'd themselves in all their finery. They were Wrapt in their Red and Blue Match-Coats, thrown so Negligently about them, that their Mehogony Skins appear'd in Several Parts, like the Lacedaemonian Damsels of Old. Their Hair was breeded with white and Blue Peak, and hung gracefully in a large Roll upon their Shoulders.

This peak Consists of Small Cylinders cut out of a Conque-Shell, drill'd through and Strung like Beads. It serves them both for Money and Jewels, the Blue being of much greater Value than the White, for the same reason that Ethiopian Mistresses in France are dearer than French, because they are more Scarce. The Women wear Necklaces and Bracelets of these precious Materials, when they have a mind to appear lovely. Tho' their complexions be a little Sad-Colour'd, yet their Shapes are very Strait and well proportion'd. Their Faces are Seldom handsome, yet they have an Air of Innocence and Bashfulness, that with a little less dirt wou'd not fail to make them desirable. Such Charms might have had their full Effect upon Men who had been so long deprived of female conversation, but that the whole Winter's Soil was so crusted on the Skins of those dark Angels, that it re-quir'd a very strong Appetite to approach them. The Bear's oyl, with which they anoint their Persons all over, makes their skins Soft, and at the Same time protects them from every Species of Vermin that use to be troublesome to other uncleanly People.

We were unluckily so many, that they cou'd not well make us the Complement of Bed-fellows, according to the Indian Rules of Hospitality, tho' a grave Matron whisper'd one of the Commissioners very civily in the Ear, that if her Daughter had been but one year Older, she should have been at his Devotion.

It is by no means a loss of Reputation among the Indians, for Damsels that are Single to have Intrigues with the Men; on the contrary, they count it an Argument of Superior Merit to be liked by a great Number of Gallants. However, like the Ladys that Game they are a little Mercenary in their Amours, and sel-dom bestow their Favours out of Stark Love and Kindness. But after these Women have once appropriated their Charms by Marriage, they are from thenceforth faithful to their Vows, and will hardly ever be tempted by an Agreeable Gallant, or be provokt by a Brutal or even by a fumbling Husband to go astray.

The little Work that is done among the Indians is done by the poor Women, while the men are quite idle, or at most employ'd only in the Gentlemanly Diversions of Hunting and Fishing.

In this, as well as in their Wars, they now use nothing but Fire-Arms, which they purchase of the English for Skins. Bows and Arrows are grown into disuse, except only amongst their Boys. Nor is it ill Policy, but on the contrary very prudent, thus to furnish the Indians with Fire-Arms, because it makes them depend entirely upon the English, not only for their Trade, but even for their subsistence. Besides, they were really able to do more mischief, while they made use of Arrows, of which they wou'd let Silently fly Several in a Minute with Wonderful Dexterity, whereas now they hardly ever discharge their Fire-locks more than once, which they insidiously do from behind a Tree, and then retire as nimbly as the Dutch Horse us'd to do now and then formerly in Flanders.

We put the Indians to no expense, but only of a little Corn for our Horses, for which in Gratitude we cheer'd their hearts with what Rum we had left, which they love better than they do their Wives and Children.

Tho' these Indians dwell among the English, and see in what Plenty a little Industry enables them to live, yet they chuse to continue in their Stupid Idleness, and to Suffer all the Inconveniences of Dirt, Cold, and Want, rather than to disturb their heads With care, or defile their Hands with labour.

The whole Number of People belonging to the Notoway Town, if you include Women and Children, amount to about 200. These are the only Indians of any consequence now remaining within the Limits of Virginia. The rest are either removed, or dwindled to a very inconsiderable Number, either by destroying one another, or else by the Small-Pox and other Diseases. Tho' nothing has been so fatal to them as their ungovernable Passion for Rum, with which, I am sorry to say it, they have been but too liberally supply'd by the English that live near them.

And here I must lament the bad Success Mr. Boyle's Charity[5]

---

[5] Money left by the scientist Robert Boyle was used to support a foundation in Indian education at the College of William and Mary.

has hitherto had towards converting any of these poor Heathens to Christianity. Many children of our Neighbouring Indians have been brought up in the College of William and Mary. They have been taught to read and write, and have been carefully Instructed in the Principles of the Christian Religion, till they came to be men. Yet after they return'd home, instead of civilizeing and converting the rest, they have immediately Relapt into Infidelity and Barbarism themselves.

And some of them too have made the worst use of the Knowledge they acquir'd among the English, by employing it against their Benefactors. Besides, as they unhappily forget all the good they learn, and remember the Ill, they are apt to be more vicious and disorderly than the rest of their Countrymen.

I ought not to quit this Subject without doing Justice to the great Prudence of Colo Spotswood in this Affair. That Gentleman was lieut Governor of Virginia when Carolina was engaged in a bloody War with the Indians. At that critical Time it was thought expedient to keep a Watchful Eye upon our Tributary Savages, who we knew had nothing to keep them to their Duty but their Fears.

Then it was that he demanded of each Nation a Competent Number of their great Men's Children to be sent to the College, where they serv'd as so many Hostages for the good Behaviour of the Rest, and at the same time were themselves principled in the Christian Religion. He also Plac'd a School-Master among the Saponi Indians, at the salary of Fifty Pounds P Annum, to instruct their Children. The Person that undertook that Charitable work was Mr. Charles Griffin, a Man of good Family, who by the Innocence of his Life, and the Sweetness of his Temper, was perfectly well qualify'd for that pious undertaking. Besides, he had so much the Secret of mixing Pleasure with instruction, that he had not a Scholar, who did not love him affectionately.

Such Talents must needs have been blest with a Proportionable Success, had he not been unluckily remov'd to the College, by which he left the good work he had begun unfinisht. In short, all the Pains he had undertaken among the Infidels had no other Effect but to make them something cleanlier than other Indians are.

The Care Colo Spotswood took to tincture the Indian Children with Christianity produc'd the following Epigram, which was not publisht during his Administration, for fear it might then have lookt like flattery.

> Long has the Furious Priest assay'd in Vain,
> With Sword and Faggot, Infidels to gain,
> But now the Milder Soldier wisely tryes
> By Gentler Methods to unveil their Eyes.
> Wonders apart, he knew 'twere vain t'engage
> The fix'd Preventions of Misguided Age.
> With fairer Hopes he forms the Indian Youth
> To early Manners, Probity and Truth.
> The Lyon's whelp thus on the Lybian Shore ⎫
> Is tam'd and Gentled by the Artful Moor, ⎬
> Not the Grim Sire, inured to Blood before. ⎭

I am sorry I can't give a Better Account of the State of the Poor Indians with respect to Christianity, altho' a great deal of Pains has been and still continues to be taken with them. For my Part, I must be of Opinion, as I hinted before, that there is but one way of Converting these poor Infidels, and reclaiming them from Barbarity, and that is, Charitably to intermarry with them, according to the Modern Policy of the most Christian King in Canada and Louisiana.

Had the English done this at the first Settlement of the Colony, the Infidelity of the Indians had been worn out at this Day, with their Dark Complexions, and the Country had swarm'd with People more than it does with Insects.

It was certainly an unreasonable Nicety, that prevented their entering into so good-Natur'd an Alliance. All Nations of men have the same Natural Dignity, and we all know that very bright Talents may be lodg'd under a very dark Skin. The principal

Difference between one People and another proceeds only from the Different Opportunities of Improvement.

The Indians by no means want understanding, and are in their Figure tall and well-proportion'd. Even their Copper-colour'd Complexion wou'd admit of Blanching, if not in the first, at the farthest in the Second Generation.

I may safely venture to say, the Indian Women would have made altogether as Honest Wives for the first Planters, as the Damsels they us'd to purchase from aboard the Ships. It is Strange, therefore, that any good Christian Shou'd have refused a wholesome, Straight Bed-fellow, when he might have had so fair a Portion with her, as the Merit of saving her Soul.

8. We rested on our clean Mats very comfortably, tho' alone, and the next Morning went to the Toilet of some of the Indian Ladys, where, what with the Charms of their Persons and the Smoak of their Apartments, we were almost blinded. They offer'd to give us Silk-Grass Baskets of their own making, which we Modestly refused, knowing that an Indian present, like that of a Nun, is a Liberality put out to Interest, and a Bribe plac'd to the greatest Advantage.

Our Chaplain observ'd with concern, that the Ruffles of Some of our Fellow Travellers were a little discolour'd with pochoon, wherewith the good Man had been told those Ladies us'd to improve their invisible charms.

About 10 a Clock we marched out of Town in good order, & the War Captains saluted us with a Volley of Small-Arms. From thence we proceeded over Black-water Bridge to colo' Henry Harrisons, where we congratulated each other upon our Return into Christendom.

from THE SECRET DIARY OF WILLIAM BYRD
OF WESTOVER, 1709-1712 *

[FOUR WEEKS IN THE LIFE OF A VIRGINIA GENTLEMAN]

[December 23, 1711]. I rose about 7 o'clock and read a chapter in Hebrew and some Greek in Homer. I said my prayers and ate boiled milk for breakfast. I wrote out a chronology of the Bible which the Governor lent me and did not go to church, God forgive me. About 12 o'clock Dr. Cocke came to me in order to go to Queen's Creek and we got on horseback about one and rode there and [found] them pretty well. The weather was cold and had hindered them from going to church likewise. We waited till 3 o'clock for dinner and then I ate some turkey and chine and after dinner we sat by a fire and chatted and were merry, without much scandal to our [talk]. The Doctor was very pleasant company, as he commonly is. We had some roast apples and wine, with which we diverted ourselves till about 10 o'clock and then we retired to our lodgings where I said my prayers and had good health, good thoughts, and good humor, thank God Almighty.

24. I rose about 7 o'clock but read nothing because all the company was up. However, I said my prayers and ate boiled milk for breakfast. It was very cold and had frozen very hard. However, about 10 we took leave and rode to Williamsburg. Mr. Bland came to my lodging and told me he had bought Mr. Brodnax's land for me that lay near the Falls and was to give him £165 for it. Then I went to the coffeehouse, where I met all my brtohers of the Council that were in town. About 12 o'clock Colonel Ludwell and I went to the Governor's to learn from himself how long he intended to keep us and to persuade him to give leave to the House of Burgesses to adjourn for a month without their asking, which he at last consented to. He asked us to dine but we [. . .] ⁶ to the rest of the Council and dined with

---

* Copyright 1941 by Louis B. Wright and Marion Tinling, and used with their permission.

⁶ The diary is transcribed from Byrd's shorthand. Hiatuses such as these, like ᴖccasional unexpanded abbreviations, represent problems of translation.

them at the coffeehouse and I ate some beef for dinner. I paid all my debts and about 3 o'clock we went to the capitol to expect the coming of the Governor, who adjourned the assembly till the 24th of January and then we all took leave and went away and I went to Queen's Creek and surprised a good company there. I ate some toast and cider and roast apples and sat and chatted till 10 o'clock and then I recommended the company to the divine protection and said a short prayer and had good thoughts and good health and good humor, thank God Almighty.

25. I rose about 7 o'clock and read nothing because I prepared for my journey to Colonel Duke's. However I said my prayers and ate boiled milk for breakfast. The weather threatened snow but it did not frighten me from taking my leave about 11 o'clock, but before that I wrote a letter to Mr. C-s and enclosed to Mr. Graeme who was to go soon in the man-of-war. About 2 o'clock I got to Colonel Duke's and found both him and his old woman in good health, only the last was grown very deaf. We sat and talked till about 4 and then we went to dinner and I ate some wild duck. In the meantime the Colonel sent a negro man to see whether the river was open at my brother Duke's and he brought word it was, and therefore I took leave of the Colonel and his old countess and rode away to the river and with some difficulty got over as soon as it was dark. I found all well there and we drank a bottle of wine. About 9 o'clock I went to bed. I said my prayers and had good health, good thoughts, and good humor, thank God Almighty.

26. I rose about 7 o'clock and read nothing because I prepared for my journey. However I said my prayers and ate boiled milk for breakfast. It was cold and threatened rain or snow. About 9 I took leave and rode towards home and between Captain Stith's and home I met my wife and Mrs. Dunn going to Williamsburg to see what was become of me, but they turned back with me home where I found all well, thank God Almighty, except old Jane who was very ill of a fever. About 3 o'clock we went to dinner and I ate some wild goose. In the afternoon I looked about and found all things in good order. Mr. Anderson dined with

me and after dinner gave old Jane the Sacrament. He stayed with me till the evening and then returned home. I inquired of my people how everything was and they told me well. Then I gave them some rum and cider to be merry with and afterwards read some Italian and wrote two letters to my overseers. I said my prayers and had good health, and good thoughts, and good humor, thank God Almighty. I rogered my wife [lustily].

27. I rose about 7 o'clock and read nothing because I put my things in order, but I wrote in my journal. I should have said my prayers but as soon as I had eaten boiled milk for breakfast Colonel Hill and Mrs. Anderson came to see us. My wife had [c-s] some of her [f-x]. The Colonel inquired how matters went below and I acquainted him with everything I knew concerning it. The weather was more moderate than it had been lately. Mr. Anderson would have come likewise but he was obliged to go to marry a couple of his parishioners. About 1 o'clock we went to dinner and I ate some roast beef. The company stayed with me till 4 o'clock and then went away. Then I danced my dance and said my prayers devoutly and then walked in my library because the ground was wet. In the evening I wrote in my journal and caused several of my people to be let blood by way of prevention. Then I read some Latin in Terence till 10 o'clock. I said my prayers and had good health, good thoughts, and good humor, thank God Almighty. I rogered my wife [lustily].

28. I rose about 7 o'clock and read two chapters in Hebrew and some Greek in Lucian. I said my prayers and ate boiled milk for breakfast. The weather was warm but cloudy. I danced my dance. I wrote some accounts and put several matters in order. Poor old Jane was very ill. We had several of the people let blood by way of prevention and Jenny for a sore throat. I ate boiled beef for dinner. In the afternoon settled several accounts till the evening and then I took a walk about the plantation and found matters pretty well, thank God. At night I wrote in my journal and read some Latin in Terence till 10 o'clock. It snowed a little this evening. I said my prayers and had good health, good thoughts, and good humor, thank God Almighty. About 8 o'clock

came Mr. G-r-l and George Smith by whom I learned that all was well at Falling Creek and the coal-pit.

29. I rose about 7 o'clock and read two chapters in Hebrew and some Greek in Lucian. I said my prayers and ate boiled milk for breakfast. I had abundance of talk with Mr. G-r-l about the affairs of Falling Creek and he told me some of his wants and so did George Smith, which I endeavored to supply as well as I could. I gave John G-r-l leave to go visit his mother. Poor old Jane died this morning about 9 o'clock and I caused her to be buried as soon as possible because she stank very much. It was not very cold today. I danced my dance. Mr. G-r-l and George Smith went away about 12 o'clock. I ate some broiled goose for dinner. In the afternoon I set my razor, and then went out to shoot with bow and arrow till the evening and then I ran to breathe myself and looked over everything. At night I read some Latin in Terence till about 10 o'clock. I said my prayers and had good health, good thoughts, and good humor, thank God Almighty.

30. I rose about 7 o'clock and read a chapter in Hebrew and three chapters in the Greek Testament. I said my prayers very devoutly and ate boiled milk for breakfast. The weather was very clear and warm so that my wife walked out with Mrs. Dunn and forgot dinner, for which I had a little quarrel with her and another afterwards because I was not willing to let her have a book out of the library. About 12 o'clock came Mr. Bland from Williamsburg but brought no news. He stayed to dinner and I ate some roast beef. In the afternoon we sat and talked till about 4 o'clock and then I caused my people to set him over the river and then I walked with the women about the plantation till they were very weary. At night we ate some eggs and drank some Virginia beer and talked very gravely without reading anything. However I said my prayers and spoke with all my people. I had good health, good thoughts, and good humor, thank God Almighty. I danced my dance in the morning.

31. I rose about 7 o'clock and read a chapter in Hebrew and six leaves in Lucian. I said my prayers and ate boiled milk for breakfast. The weather continued warm and clear. I settled my

accounts and wrote several things till dinner. I danced my dance. I ate some turkey and chine for dinner. In the afternoon I weighed some money and then read some Latin in Terence and then Mr. Mumford came and told me my man Tony had been very sick but he was recovered again, thank God. He told me Robin Bolling had been like to die and that he denied that he was the first to mention the imposition on skins which he certainly did. Then he and I took a walk about the plantation. When I returned I was out of humor to find the negroes all at work in our chambers. At night I ate some broiled turkey with Mr. Mumford and we talked and were merry all the evening. I said my prayers and had good health, good thoughts, and good humor, thank God Almighty. My wife and I had a terrible quarrel about whipping Eugene while Mr. Mumford was there but she had a mind to show her authority before company but I would not suffer it, which she took very ill; however for peace sake I made the first advance towards a reconciliation which I obtained with some difficulty and after abundance of crying. However it spoiled the mirth of the evening, but I was not conscious that I was to blame in that quarrel.

JANUARY, 1712

1. I lay abed till 9 o'clock this morning to bring my wife into temper again and rogered her by way of reconciliation. I read nothing because Mr. Mumford was here, nor did I say my prayers, for the same reason. However I ate boiled milk for breakfast, and after my wife tempted me to eat some pancakes with her. Mr. Mumford and I went to shoot with our bows and arrows but shot nothing, and afterwards we played at billiards till dinner, and when we came we found Ben Harrison there, who dined with us. I ate some partridge for dinner. In the afternoon we played at billiards again and I won two bits. I had a letter from Colonel Duke by H-e the bricklayer who came to offer his services to work for me. Mr. Mumford went away in the evening and John Bannister with him to see his mother. I took a walk about the plantation and at night we drank some mead

of my wife's making which was very good. I gave the people some cider and a dram to the negroes. I read some Latin in Terence and had good health, good thoughts, and good humor, thank God Almighty. I said my prayers.

2. I rose about 7 o'clock and read two chapters in Hebrew and some Greek in Lucian. I said my prayers and ate boiled milk for breakfast. I danced my dance. It rained pretty much in the night and was cloudy this morning. I settled several accounts and wrote a letter to Colonel Duke. About 12 o'clock came Colonel Eppes but could not stay because he was obliged to go to court. A little before dinner came Ben Harrison in his best clothes, because he happened to come yesterday in his worst. He dined with us and I ate roast beef and before we had done Colonel Hill and Mrs. Harrison came and the Colonel ate some pudding with us, but Mrs. Harrison ate nothing. They went away about 4 o'clock and then my wife and I went to walk about the plantation and saw some young trees that Tom had planted this day. At night I read some Terence till almost 10 o'clock. I said my prayers and had good health, good thoughts, and good humor, thank God Almighty. My mulatto Jacky came from Falling Creek with a very sore arm and told me all was well there, thank God.

3. I rose about 7 o'clock and read two chapters in Hebrew and some Greek in Lucian. I said my prayers and ate boiled milk for breakfast. I danced my dance and then settled several accounts. The weather was very clear and cold. Mr. Bland's sloop brought two hogsheads of cider and 66 hides from Williamsburg which were put ashore. I read some Latin till dinner and then I ate some roast pork. I gave Anaka a good scolding for letting Billy Brayne have a hole in his stocking. In the afternoon I set my razor and then went to prune the trees in the young orchard and then I took a walk about the plantation and my wife and Mrs. Dunn came to walk with me. At night I read some Latin in Terence and then we drank some cider. I said my prayers and had good health, good thoughts, and good humor, thank God Almighty.

4. I rose about 7 o'clock and read two chapters in Hebrew and some Greek in Homer. I said my prayers and ate boiled milk for breakfast. I danced my dance and then settled several accounts. The weather was clear and warm. My wife was indisposed with the colic but recovered pretty soon again, thank God, by the help of good drams of caraway water. I took a walk in the garden till dinner. I ate no meat this day but only fruit. In the afternoon I weighed some money and then went into the new orchard to trim some trees and stayed there till it was dark almost and then took a little walk about the plantation. In the evening Tom Turpin brought 30 hogs from the Falls and told me all was well, thank God. At night I read some Latin in Terence and said my prayers and had good health, good thoughts, and good humor, thank God Almighty. I ate some broiled turkey for supper.

5. I rose about 7 o'clock and read nothing because Tom Turpin was here. He came with 30 hogs from the Falls. He told me all was well above. I said my prayers and ate boiled milk for breakfast. I danced my dance. About 9 o'clock came Major Harrison and the captain of the "Pelican". I gave them a bottle of sack. Then we played at billiards and I won 7 shillings, and sixpence. About one o'clock we went to dinner and I ate some boiled beef. In the afternoon we were merry and made the Quaker captain drink the Queen's health on his knees. About 2 o'clock came my brother and sister Custis and sat down to dinner. They brought no news. My sister was much tired. In the evening the captain and Major Harrison went away to Mrs. Harrison's where I understood that Mr. Clayton was come. We drank a bottle of wine at night. This day a negro of mine at Falling Creek had a tree fall on his head and had his brains beat out. I neglected to say my prayers and had good health, good thoughts, and good humor, thank God Almighty.

6. I rose about 8 o'clock because my wife made me lie in bed and I rogered her. I read nothing and neglected to say my prayers but had boiled milk for breakfast. About 10 o'clock came Mr. Clayton and brought me two English letters without any news because they were of an old date. I gave him a dram and about 11

o'clock we walked to church where we heard a good sermon from Mr. Anderson. I invited Colonel Hill to dine with me and ate wild goose for dinner. In the afternoon it rained so that Colonel Hill agreed to stay all night. In the evening we drank a supper bottle and were merry with nonsense but Colonel Hill's head ached a little. However it did not mar the supper or conversation. The Colonel is a man of good sense and good principles notwithstanding what has been said of him. I neglected to say my prayers but had good health, good thoughts, and good humor, thank God Almighty.

7. I rose about 7 o'clock and read nothing because we prepared to go to Colonel Hill's. I ate chocolate for breakfast. I said a short prayer. About 10 o'clock our ladies made a shift to get dressed, when we got on horseback and my horse was very frolicsome. The weather was cold and very clear. We called at Captain Llewellyn's and took Lew Eppes and his wife with us to Colonel Hill's, where we found all well. We were as merry as we could be, considering there was but little [w—]. About 2 o'clock we went to dinner and I ate some boiled pork for dinner. In the afternoon we went to see the ship and found them far advanced. Then we returned and saw my sloop bringing to at the Hundred, where my people left behind 50 bushels of wheat from G-r-l. In the evening we were very merry and the women offered violence to me because I would not dance and my wife quarrelled with her sister because she would not dance. About 10 o'clock we went to bed. I recommended myself and my family to the protection of Almighty God, and had good health, good thoughts, and good humor, thank God Almighty.

8. I rose about 7 o'clock and read a little in Horace. I neglected to say my prayers because the women came in with a dram of strong water of which I [drank] two drams. Then I left the women and went to the men and talked with them. About 9 o'clock came Colonel Frank Eppes to discourse with me concerning the rangers in the upper county and he told me nobody would accept of that place because the pay was too little. I ate some roast beef for breakfast contrary to my custom. About 10

o'clock we went away home and found all well, thank God. We expected Mr. Clayton and Major Harrison from Prince George court and therefore we ordered dinner late. About 3 o'clock came Dr. Cocke and brought me some English letters, by which I learned there were plenipotentiaries appointed to agree about a peace, which God prosper. About 5 o'clock came Mr. Clayton, Major Harrison, and his brother Harry. We went to supper and I ate some boiled beef. We were very merry and I gave them some of my best wine. We played at cards and I won 15 shillings. I neglected to say my prayers because the company kept me up late but I had good health, good thoughts, and good humor, thank God Almighty. Parson Finney dined with us also and stayed all night.

9. I rose about 7 o'clock and found the weather exceedingly cold. I neglected to say my prayers because of the company. However I drank chocolate for breakfast and ate some cake. After breakfast we went to [p-l-y] and I won £10 at cards. About 10 o'clock Major Harrison and his brother Harry went away but the rest of the company was persuaded to stay a day longer, only Parson Finney, who went away likewise. Mr. Clayton and I took a walk till dinner and then I ate some roast mutton which was very good. My sloop went away this morning to Falling Creek. In the afternoon we were merry without drinking but did not venture out because of the [. . .] cold weather. In the evening Peter came from the Falls and told me all was well, thank God. We drank some of my best wine and were merry but would not let the women part from us. About 10 we ate some bread and cheese and drank a bottle on it, and about 11 we went to bed. My wife had got some cold and was disordered in her hip. I neglected to say my prayers but had good health, good thoughts, and good humor, thank God Almighty, only I was a little displeased at a story somebody had told the Governor that I had said that no Governor ought to be trusted with £20,000.[7] Little Peter brought a wild goose with him and two ducks.

---

[7] In order to carry on the war against the Tuscaroras, the Burgesses attempted to raise £20,000 by extraordinary taxes. . . .—*Wright-Tinling*.

10. I rose about 7 o'clock and found it terribly cold. My wife was a little better. I neglected my prayers and ate boiled milk for breakfast but the company ate some chicken pie. About 11 o'clock my company took leave and went away and then I could do everything which too much company had hindered me from. I read this day no Hebrew nor Greek in Lucian but read my English letters and settled some accounts. Mr. Chamberlayne came from Appomattox and told me all was well there, thank God. He would dine with me whether I asked him or not and I ate roast beef. In the afternoon I weighed some money and settled some accounts till the evening and then took a walk about the plantation. Redskin Peter pretended he fell and hurt himself but it was dissimulation. I had a cow die this day. At night I read some Latin in Terence. Then I said my prayers and had good health, good thoughts, and good humor, thank God Almighty.

11. I rose about 7 o'clock and read two chapters in Hebrew and some Greek in Lucian. I said my prayers and ate boiled milk for breakfast. I danced my dance. It was not so cold as it has been because the wind came to south. My wife was a little indisposed with a cold. I settled several accounts and put many things in order till dinner. I ate some raspberries for dinner. In the afternoon I set my razor and then went into the new orchard and trimmed the trees till the evening and then I took a walk about the plantation. Redskin Peter was very well again after he had worn the bit 24 hours and went to work very actively. Before I came in I took a run for my health. At night I read some Latin in Terence. I said my prayers and had thoughts [sic], good health, and good humor, thank God Almighty.

12. I rose about 8 o'clock and read two chapters in Hebrew and some Greek in Lucian. I said my prayers devoutly and ate boiled milk for breakfast. I danced my dance. Jacky's arm was almost well, thank God. The weather was warm but the wind was northeast. My wife was well again, thank God, and went about again as usual. I read some Latin in Terence till dinner and then I ate some roast pork. In the afternoon I went into the orchard and trimmed the young trees till I was called away by

one of the girls who told me that Mr. Peter Butts would speak with me. His business was to desire me to get a sheriff's place for his brother and in order to persuade me to it told me several things of Ned [Goodrich] and how he had once hindered my man Tony from paying £30 for lying with an Indian wife. A man came from New Kent concerning a protested bill and he stayed here all night. In the evening I took a walk and at night read some Latin in Terence. I said my prayers and had good health, good thoughts, and good humor, thank God Almighty.

ROBERT BEVERLY

(c. 1673-1722)

Bibliographical Note. Beverly's *History and Present State of Virginia* has been edited by L. B. Wright (Chapel Hill, 1947); the selections here printed follow this text, pp. 8-11, 271-274, 286-288, 308-319. The Introduction to Wright's edition furnishes a fine brief account of Beverly and his *History.*

from THE HISTORY AND PRESENT STATE OF VIRGINIA* (1705)

THE PREFACE

'Tis agreed, that Travellers are of all Men, the most suspected of Insincerity. This does not only hold, in their private Conversations; but likewise in the *Grand Tours,* and Travels, with which they pester the Publick, and break the Bookseller. There are no Books, (the Legends of Saints always excepted,) so stuff'd with Poetical Stories, as Voyages; and the more distant the Countries lie, which they pretend to describe, the greater License those priviledg'd Authors take, in imposing upon the World. The *French* Travels are commonly more infamous on this Account, than any other, which must be imputed to the strong Genius of that Nation to *Hyperbole,* and *Romance.* They are fond of dressing up every thing in their gay Fashion, from a happy Opinion, that their own *Fopperies* make any Subject more entertaining. The *English,* it must be granted, invent more within the Compass of Probability, and are contented to be less Ornamental, while they are more Sincere.

I make no Question, but the following Account will come in for its Share of this Imputation. I shall be reputed as arrant a Traveller as the rest, and my Credit, (like that of Women,) will be condemn'd for the Sins of my Company. However, I intreat the gentle Reader to be so just, as not to convict me upon bare Suspicion; let the Evidence be plain, or at least amount

* Reprinted from *History and Present State of Virginia* edited by L. B. Wright and published by the University of North Carolina Press.

to a violent Presumption, and then I don't fear being acquitted. If an honest Author might be believ'd in his own Case, I wou'd solemnly declare, that I have not knowingly asserted any untrue Thing in the whole Book. On the contrary, I fear, I shall rather be accused of saying too much Truth, than too little. If I have had the Misfortune to have err'd in any Particular this Way, which yet I have used all imaginable Care to avoid, I hope the World, with all its Uncharitableness, will vouchsafe to forgive my Understanding.

If I might be so happy, as to settle my Credit with the Reader, the next Favour I wou'd ask of him, shou'd be, not to Criticize too unmercifully upon my Stile. I am an *Indian,* and don't pretend to be exact in my Language: But I hope the Plainness of my Dress, will give him the kinder Impressions of my Honesty, which is what I pretend to. Truth desires only to be understood, and never affects the Reputation of being finely equipp'd. It depends upon its own intrinsick Value, and, like Beauty, is rather conceal'd, than set off, by Ornament.

I wonder no Body has ever presented the World, with a tolerable Account of our *Plantations.* Nothing of that kind has yet appear'd, except some few General Descriptions, that have been calculated more for the Benefit of the Bookseller, than for the Information of Mankind. If I may judge of the rest, by what has been publish'd concerning *Virginia,* I will take the Liberty to say, that there's none of 'em either true, or so much as well invented. Such Accounts are as impertinent as ill Pictures, that resemble any Body, as much as the Persons they are drawn for. For my part, I have endeavour'd to hit the *Likeness;* though, perhaps, my *Colouring* may not have all the Life and Beauty I cou'd wish.

The Method I have taken in this Performance, is as follows. I have divided the Whole into Four distinct Parts. The first contains, a Chronological History, of the most remarkable Things that have happen'd in *Virginia,* ever since it was first seated by the *English.* It shows all the Wars with the *Indians,* and their Causes, all the Massacres, and other Disasters, occasion'd by the Resentment of the Natives. It likewise gives a faithful Account, of all the successive Governours of that Country, and their Administration, together with the principal Laws, that have been enacted in the Time of Each. In the doing of which, I have been cartful to mention nothing, but what I can make good by very Authentique Testimony. So that if I have taken the Freedom, to represent the Mismanagements of several Gentlemen, it is their Fault, that acted such Irregularities, and not mine, that report them to the World. If Men will please to be unjust, run counter to the *Royal Instructions,* oppress the People, and offer Violence to all the *Laws* of a Country, they ought to be known, and abhorr'd by Mankind.

The Second Part treats of the Spontaneous Productions of that Country, and the Original State, wherein the *English* found it at their first Arrival. This is a very copious Subject, but I have handled it with more Brevity than it deserves, because I am conscious of my want of Skill in the *Works of Nature.* However I flatter my self, that what I have said, will be sufficient, to give a Handle to a more compleat Undertaking. The World had some Years ago an unhappy Loss, by the Death of Mr. *Banister,* who was making curious Collections for a *Natural History of* Virginia: But the sudden Death of that Gentleman, put an End to that excellent Design. He had great Talents that Way, and if he had liv'd a few Years longer, he wou'd have done Justice to so fine a Country, by describing it in all its Native Perfections.

The Third Part gives a true Account of the *Indians,* together with their Religion, Customs, and Government. There I have added Fourteen Copper Plates, to illustrate the Dress, and Way of Living of the Natives, the Draughts of which were taken exactly from the Life. Herein, as well as throughout the whole Book, I have been very scrupulous, not to insert any thing, but what I can justifie, either by my own Knowledge, or by credible Information.

In the Fourth Part, I have represented the *English* Form of Government in that Country, with all the Publick Officers, their

Business, and Salary. There I have mention'd many of their most material Laws, and Methods of proceeding. I have likewise shown the small Improvements, that the *English* have made, since they have been in Possession, and pointed at several great Advantages, which they might secure to themselves, by a due Spirit of Industry, and Management. I have everywhere made it my chief Business, to avoid *Partiality*; and therefore have fairly expos'd the Inconveniences, as well as proclaim'd the Excellencies of my Country.

This is the *Bill of Fare*, of what the Reader may expect to meet with in the following Discourse; and I shou'd be very happy, if he wou'd have the Goodness, to think it a tolerable Entertainment.

from BOOK IV, "THE PRESENT STATE OF THE COUNTRY, AS TO THE POLICY OF THE GOVERNMENT, AND THE IMPROVEMENTS OF THE LAND."

CHAPTER X.

OF THE SERVANTS AND SLAVES IN VIRGINIA.

Their Servants, they distinguish by the Names of Slaves for Life, and Servants for a time.

Slaves are the Negroes, and their Posterity, following the condition of the Mother, according to the Maxim, *partus sequitur ventrem*. They are call'd Slaves, in respect of the time of their Servitude, because it is for Life.

Servants, are those which serve only for a few years, according to the time of their Indenture, or the Custom of the Country. The Custom of the Country takes place upon such as have no Indentures. The Law in this case is, that if such Servants be under Nineteen years of Age, they must be brought into Court, to have their Age adjudged; and from the Age they are judg'd to be of, they must serve until they reach four and twenty: But if they be adjudged upwards of Nineteen, they are then only to be Servants for the term of five Years.

The Male-Servants, and Slaves of both Sexes, are imployed together in Tilling and Manuring the Ground, in Sowing and Planting Tobacco, Corn, &c. Some Distinction indeed is made between them in their Cloaths, and Food; but the Work of both, is no other than what the Overseers, the Freemen, and the Planters themselves do.

Sufficient Distinction is also made between the Female-Servants, and Slaves; for a White Woman is rarely or never put to work in the Ground, if she be good for any thing else: And to Discourage all Planters from using any Women so, their Law imposes the heaviest Taxes upon Female-Servants working in the Ground, while it suffers all other white Women to be absolutely exempted: Whereas on the other hand, it is a common thing to work a Woman Slave out of Doors; nor does the Law make any Distinction in her Taxes, whether her Work be Abroad, or at Home.

Because I have heard how strangely cruel, and severe, the Service of this Country is represented in some parts of *England;* I can't forbear affirming, that the work of their Servants, and Slaves, is no other than what every common Freeman do's. Neither is any Servant requir'd to do more in a Day, than his Overseer. And I can assure you with a great deal of Truth, that generally their Slaves are not worked near so hard, nor so many Hours in a Day, as the Husbandmen, and Day-Labourers in *England.* An Overseer is a Man, that having served his time, has acquired the Skill and Character of an experienced Planter, and is therefore intrusted with the Direction of the Servants and Slaves.

But to compleat this account of Servants, I shall give you a short Relation of the care their Laws take, that they be used as tenderly as possible.

BY THE LAWS OF THEIR COUNTRY.

1. All Servants whatsoever, have their Complaints heard without Fee, or Reward; but if the Master be found Faulty, the charge

of the Complaint is cast upon him, otherwise the business is done *ex Officio*.

2. Any Justice of Peace may receive the Complaint of a Servant, and order every thing relating thereto, till the next County-Court, where it will be finally determin'd.

3. All Masters are under the Correction, and Censure of the County-Courts, to provide for their Servants, good and wholsome Diet, Clothing, and Lodging.

4. They are always to appear, upon the first Notice given of the Complaint of their Servants, otherwise to forfeit the Service of them, until they do appear.

5. All Servants Complaints are to be receiv'd at any time in Court, without Process, and shall not be delay'd for want of Form; but the Merits of the Complaint must be immediately inquir'd into by the Justices; and if the Master cause any delay therein, the Court may remove such Servants, if they see Cause, until the Master will come to Tryal.

6. If a Master shall at any time disobey an Order of Court, made upon any Complaint of a Servant; the Court is impower'd to remove such Servant forthwith to another Master, who will be kinder; Giving to the former Master the produce only, (after Fees deducted) of what such Servants shall be sold for by Publick Outcry.

7. If a Master should be so cruel, as to use his Servant ill, that is faln Sick, or Lame in his Service, and thereby render'd unfit for Labour, he must be remov'd by the Church-Wardens out of the way of such Cruelty, and boarded in some good Planters House, till the time of his Freedom, the charge of which must be laid before the next County-Court, which has power to levy the same from time to time, upon the Goods and Chattels of the Master; After which, the charge of such Boarding is to come upon the Parish in General.

8. All hired Servants are intituled to these Priviledges.

9. No Master of a Servant, can make a new Bargain for Service, or other Matter with his Servant, without the privity and consent of a Justice of Peace, to prevent the Master's Over-reach-

ing, or scareing such Servant into an unreasonable Complyance.

10. The property of all Money and Goods sent over thither to Servants, or carry'd in with them; is reserv'd to themselves, and remain intirely at their disposal.

11. Each Servant at his Freedom, receives of his Master fifteen Bushels of Corn, (which is sufficient for a whole year) and two new Suits of Cloaths, both Linnen and Woollen; and then becomes as free in all respects, and as much entituled to the Liberties, and Priviledges of the Country, as any other of the Inhabitants or Natives are.

12. Each Servant has then also a Right to take up fifty Acres of Land, where he can find any unpatented: But that is no great Privilege, for any one may have as good a right for a piece of Eight.

This is what the Laws prescribe in favour of Servants, by which you may find, that the Cruelties and Severities imputed to that Country, are an unjust Reflection. For no People more abhor the thoughts of such Usage, than the *Virginians,* nor take more precaution to prevent it.

CHAPTER XV.

OF THE PEOPLE, INHABITANTS OF VIRGINIA.

I can easily imagin with Sir *Josiah Child,* that this, as well as all the rest of the Plantations, was for the most part at first peopled by Persons of low Circumstances, and by such as were willing to seek their Fortunes in a Foreign Country. Nor was it hardly possible it should be otherwise; for 'tis not likely that any Man of a plentiful Estate, should voluntarily abandon a happy Certainty, to roam after imaginary Advantages, in a New World. Besides which incertainty, he must have propos'd to himself, to encounter the infinite Difficulties and Dangers, that attend a New Settlement. These Discouragements were sufficient to terrifie any Man, that cou'd live easy in *England,* from going to provoke his Fortune in a strange Land.

Those that went over to that Country first, were chiefly single

Men, who had not the Incumbrance of Wives and Children in *England;* and if they had, they did not expose them to the fatigue and hazard of so long a Voyage, until they saw how it should fare with themselves. From hence it came to pass, that when they were setled there in a comfortable way of Subsisting a Family, they grew sensible of the Misfortune of wanting Wives, and such as had left Wives in *England,* sent for them; but the single Men were put to their Shifts. They excepted against the *Indian* Women, on account of their being *Pagans,* and for fear they shou'd conspire with those of their own Nation, to destroy their Husbands. Under this Difficulty they had no hopes, but that the Plenty in which they liv'd, might invite Modest Women of small Fortunes, to go over thither from *England*. However, they wou'd not receive any, but such as cou'd carry sufficient Certificate of their Modesty, and good Behaviour. Those if they were but moderately qualified in all other Respects, might depend upon Marrying very well in those Days, without any Fortune. Nay, the first Planters were so far from expecting Money with a Woman, that 'twas a common thing for them to buy a deserving Wife, at the price of 100 Pound, and make themselves believe, they had a hopeful bargain.

But this way of Peopling the Colony was only at first; for after the advantages of the Climate, and the fruitfulness of the Soil were well known, and all the dangers incident to Infant Settlements were over, People of better Condition retir'd thither with their Families, either to increase the Estates they had before, or else to avoid being persecuted for their Principles of Religion, or Government.

Thus in the time of the Rebellion in *England,* several good Cavalier Families went thither with their Effects, to escape the Tyranny of the Usurper. And so again, upon the Restoration, many People of the opposite Party took Refuge there, to shelter themselves from the King's Resentment. But they had not many of these last, because that Country was famous, for holding out the longest for the Royal Family, of any of the *English* Dominions; for which reason, the Roundheads went for the most part to *New-England,* as did most of those, that in the Reign of King *Charles* II. were molested on the account of their Religion, though some of these fell likewise to the share of *Virginia.* As for Malefactors condemn'd to Transportation, they have always receiv'd very few, and for many years last past, their Laws have been severe against them.

CHAPTER XXI.

OF THE RECREATIONS, AND PASTIMES USED IN VIRGINIA.

For their Recreation, the Plantations, Orchards, and Gardens constantly afford 'em fragrant and delightful Walks. In their Woods and Fields, they have an unknown variety of Vegetables, and other rarities of Nature to discover and observe. They have Hunting, Fishing, and Fowling, with which they entertain themselves an hundred ways. Here is the most Good-nature, and Hospitality practis'd in the World, both towards Friends and Strangers: but the worst of it is, this Generosity is attended now and then, with a little too much Intemperance. The Neighbourhood is at much the same distance, as in the Country in *England:* but with this Advantage, that all the better sort of People have been abroad, and seen the World, by which means they are free from that stiffness and formality, which discover more Civility, than Kindness: And besides, the goodness of the Roads, and the fairness of the Weather, bring People oftener together.

The *Indians,* as I have already observ'd, had in their Hunting, a way of concealing themselves, and coming up to the Deer, under the blind of a Stalking-Head, in imitation of which, many People have taught their Horses to stalk it, that is, to walk gently by the Huntsman's side, to cover him from the sight of the Deer. Others cut down Trees for the Deer to browze upon, and lie in wait behind them. Others again set Stakes, at a certain distance within their Fences, where the Deer have been used to leap over into a Field of Peas, which they love extreamly; these Stakes they so place, as to run into the Body of the Deer, when he Pitches, by which means they Impale him.

They Hunt their Hares, (which are very numerous) a Foot, with Mungrils or swift Dogs, which either catch them quickly, or force them to hole in a hollow Tree, whither all their Hares generally tend, when they are closely pursued. As soon as they are thus hoed, and have crawl'd up into the Body of the Tree, the business is to kindle a Fire, and smother them with Smoak, till they let go their hold, and fall to the bottom stifled; from whence they take them. If they have a mind to spare their Lives, upon turning them loose, they will be as fit as ever to hunt at another time; for the mischief done them by the Smoak, immediately wears off again.

They have another sort of Hunting, which is very diverting, and that they call Vermine Hunting; It is perform'd a Foot, with small Dogs in the Night, by the Light of the Moon or Stars. Thus in Summertime they find abundance of Racoons, Opossums, and Foxes in the Corn-Fields, and about their Plantations: but at other times, they must go into the Woods for them. The Method is to go out with three or four Dogs, and as soon as they come to the place, they bid the Dogs seek out, and all the Company follow immediately. Where-ever a Dog barks, you may depend upon finding the Game; and this Alarm, draws both Men and Dogs that way. If this Sport be in the Woods, the Game by that time you come near it, is perhaps mounted to the top of an high Tree, and then they detach a nimble Fellow up after it, who must have a scuffle with the Beast, before he can throw it down to the Dogs; and then the Sport increases, to see the Vermine encounter those little Currs. In this sort of Hunting, they also carry their great Dogs out with them, because Wolves, Bears, Panthers, Wild-Cats, and all other Beasts of Prey, are abroad in the Night.

For Wolves they make Traps, and set Guns bated in the Woods, so that when he offers to seize the Bate, he pulls the Trigger, and the Gun discharges upon him. What *Elian* and *Pliny* write, of the Horses being benummed in their Legs, if they tread in the

Track of a Wolf, does not hold good here; for I my self, and many others, have rid full Speed after Wolves in the Woods, and have seen live ones taken out of a Trap, and drag'd at a Horse's Tail; and yet those that follow'd on Horseback, have not perceived any of their Horses to falter in their pace.

They have many pretty devices besides the Gun, to take wild Turkeys; And among others, a Friend of mine invented a great Trap, wherein he at times caught many Turkeys, and particularly seventeen at one time, but he could not contrive it so, as to let others in after he had entrapped the first flock, until they were taken out.

The *Indian* Invention of Weirs in Fishing, is mightily improved by the English besides which, they make use of Seins, Trolls, Casting-Netts, Setting-Netts, Hand-fishing, and Angling, and in each find abundance of Diversion. I have set in the shade, at the Heads of the Rivers Angling, and spent as much time in taking the Fish off the Hook, as in waiting for their taking it. Like those of the *Euxine Sea,* they also Fish with Spilyards, which is a long Line staked out in the River, and hung with a great many Hooks on short strings, fasten'd to the main Line, about three or four Foot asunder. The only difference is, our Line is supported by Stakes, and theirs is buoyed up with Gourds.

Their Fowling is answerable to their Fishing for plenty of Game, in its proper Season, no Plantation being so ill stored, as to be without a great deal. They have a vast variety of it, several sorts of which, I have not yet mention'd, as Beaver, Otter, Squirrels, Partridges, Pigeons, and an infinite number of small Birds, &c.

The admirable Oeconomy of the Beavers, deserves to be particularly remember'd. They cohabit in one House, are incorporated in a regular Form of Government, something like Monarchy, and have over them a Superintendent, which the *Indians* call *Pericu.* He leads them out to their several Imployments, which consist in Felling of Trees, biting off the Branches, and cutting them into certain lengths, suitable to the business they design them for, all which they perform with their Teeth. When this is done, the Governor orders several of his Subjects to joyn together, and take up one of those Logs, which they must carry to their House or Damm, as occasion requires. He walks in State by them all the while, and sees that every one bear his equal share of the burden; while he bites with his Teeth, and lashes with his Tail, those that lag behind, and do not lend all their Strength. They commonly build their Houses in Swamps, and then to raise the Water to a convenient height, they make a Damm with Logs, and a binding sort of Clay, so firm, that though the Water runs continually over, it cannot wash it away. Within these Damms, they'l inclose Water enough to make a Pool, like a Mill-pond; and if a Mill happen to be built upon the same Stream, below their Damm, the Miller in a dry Season, finds it worth his while to cut it, to supply his Mill with Water. Upon which Disaster, the Beavers are so expert at their Work, that in one or two Nights time, they will repair the breach, and make it perfectly whole again. Sometimes they build their Houses in a broad Marsh, where the Tide ebbs and flows, and then they make no Damm at all. The Doors into their Houses are under Water. I have been at the Demolishing one of these Houses, that was found in a Marsh, and was surpriz'd to find it fortify'd with Logs, that were six Foot long, and ten Inches through, and had been carried at least one hundred and fifty yards. This House was three Stories high, and contain'd five Rooms, that is to say, two in the lower, and middle Stories, and but one at the top. These Creatures have a great deal of Policy, and know how to defeat all the Subtilty and Strategems of the Hunter, who seldom can meet with them, tho' they are in great numbers all over the Country.

There is yet another kind of Sport, which the young People take great Delight in, and that is, the Hunting of wild Horses; which they pursue sometimes with Dogs, and sometimes without. You must know they have many Horses foaled in the Woods of the Uplands, that never were in hand, and are as shy as any Savage Creature. These having no mark upon them, belong to him, that first takes them. However, the Captor commonly purchases these Horses very dear, by spoiling better in the pursuit; in which case, he has little to make himself amends, besides the pleasure of the Chace. And very often this is all he has for it, for the wild Horses are so swift, that 'tis difficult to catch them; and when they are taken, tis odds but their Grease is melted, or else being old, they are so sullen, that they can't be tam'd.

The Inhabitants are very Courteous to Travellers, who need no other Recommendation, but the being Human Creatures. A Stranger has no more to do, but to inquire upon the Road, where any Gentleman, or good House-keeper Lives, and there he may depend upon being received with Hospitality. This good Nature is so general among their People, that the Gentry when they go abroad, order their Principal Servant to entertain all Visitors, with every thing the Plantation affords. And the poor Planters, who have but one Bed, will very often sit up, or lie upon a Form or Couch all Night, to make room for a weary Traveller, to repose himself after his Journey.

If there happen to be a Churl, that either out of Covetousness, or Ill-nature, won't comply with this generous Custom, he has a mark of Infamy set upon him, and is abhorr'd by all. But I must confess, (and am heartily sorry for the occasion) that this good Neighbourhood has of late been much depraved by the present Governor, who practices, the detestable Politicks of governing by Parties; by which, Feuds and Heart-burnings have been kindled in the Minds of the People; and Friendship, Hospitality, and Good-Neighbourhood, have been extreamly discouraged.

CHAPTER XXII.

OF THE NATURAL PRODUCT OF VIRGINIA, AND THE ADVANTAGES OF THEIR HUSBANDRY.

The extream fruitfulness of that Country, has been sufficiently shewn in the Second Book, and I think we may justly add, that in that particularly it is not exceeded by any other. No Seed is Sowed there, but it thrives, and most Plants are improved, by being Transplanted thither. And yet there's very little Improvement made among them, nor any thing us'd in Traffique, but Tobacco.

Besides all the natural Productions mention'd in the Second Book, you may take notice, that Apples from the Seed, never degenerate into Crabs, or Wildings there, but produce the same, or better Fruit than the Mother-Tree, (which is not so in *England,*) and are wonderfully improved by Grafting and Managing; yet there are very few Planters that graft at all, and much fewer that take any care to get choice Fruits.

The Fruit-Trees are wonderfully quick of growth, so that in six or seven years time from the Planting, a Man may bring an Orchard to bear in great plenty, from which he may make store of good Cyder, or distill great quantities of Brandy; for the Cyder is very strong, and yields abundance of in Spirit. Yet they have very few, that take any care at all for an Orchard; nay, many that have good Orchards, are so negligent of them, as to let them go to ruine, and expose the Trees to be torn, and barked by the Catle.

Peaches, Nectarines, and Apricocks, as well as Plums and Cherries, grow there upon Standard Trees. They commonly bear in three years from the Stone, and thrive so exceedingly, that they seem to have no need of Grafting or Inoculating, if any Body would be so good a Husband; and truly I never heard of any that did Graft either Plum, Nectarine, Peach or Apricock in that Country.

Peaches and Nectarines I believe to be Spontaneous somewhere or other on that Continent; for the *Indians* have, and ever had greater variety, and finer sorts of them than the *English*. The best sort of these cling to the Stone, and will not come off clear, which they call Plum-Nectarines, and Plum-Peaches, or Cling-Stones. Some of these are 12 or 13 Inches in the Girt. These sorts of Fruits are raised so easily there, that some good Husbands plant great Orchards of them, purposely for their Hogs; and others make a Drink of them, which they call Mobby, and either drink it as Cyder, or Distill it off for Brandy. This makes the best Spirit next to Grapes.

Grape-Vines of the *English* Stock, as well as those of their own Production, bear most abundantly, if they are suffered to run near the Ground, and increase very kindly by Slipping; yet very few have them at all in their Gardens, much less indeavour to improve them by cutting or laying. Indeed my Curiosity the last year, caused me to lay some of the white Muscadine, which came of a Stock removed thither from *England,* and they increased by this method to Admiration: I likewise set several Slips of the cuttings of the same Vine, and the Major part of the Sets bore Grapes in perfection the first year, I remember I had seven full Bunches from one of them.

When a single Tree happens in clearing the Ground, to be left standing with a Vine upon it, open to the Sun and Air; that Vine generally produces as much as 4 or five others, that remain in the Woods. I have seen in this case, more Grapes upon one single Vine, than wou'd load a *London* Cart. And for all this, the People never remove any of them into their Gardens, but content themselves throughout the whole Country, with the Grapes they find thus wild; much less can they be expected to attempt the making of Wine or Brandy from the Grape.

The Almond, Pomgranate and Fig, ripen there very well, and yet there are not ten People in the Country, that have any of them in their Gardens, much less endeavour to preserve any of them for future spending, or to propagate them to make a Trade.

A Garden is no where sooner made than there, either for Fruits, or Flowers. Tulips from the Seed-flower the second year at farthest. All sorts of Herbs have there a perfection in their flavour, beyond what I ever tasted in a more *Northern* Climate. And yet they han't many Gardens in the Country, fit to bear that name.

All sorts of *English* Grain thrive, and increase there, as well as in any other part of the World as for Example, Wheat, Barley, Oats, Rye, Peas, Rape, &c. And yet they don't make a Trade of any of them. Their Peas indeed, are troubled with Wivels, which eat a Hole in them: But this Hole does neither dammage the Seed, nor make the Peas unfit for Boiling. And such as are sow'd late, and gather'd after *August,* are clear of that Inconvenience.

It is thought too much for the same Man, to make the Wheat, and grind it, bolt it, and bake it himself. And it is too great a charge for every Planter, who is willing to sow Barley, to build a Malt-House, and Brew-House too, or else to have no benefit of his Barley; nor will it answer, if he wou'd be at the Charge. These things can never be expected from a single Family: But if they had cohabitations, it might be thought worth attempting. Neither as they are now settled, can they find any certain Market for their other Grain, which if they had Towns, would be quite otherwise.

Rice has been tried there, and is found to grow as well, as in *Carolina,* or in any other part of the Earth: But it labours under the same inconvenience, the want of a Community, to husk and clean it; and after all, to take it off the Planters Hands.

I have related at large in the first Book, how Flax, Hemp, Cotton, and the Silk-Worms have thriven there, in the several essays made upon them; how formerly there was Incouragement given for making of Linnen, Silk, &c. and how all Persons not performing several things towards produceing of them were put under a Fine: But now all Incouragement of such things is taken away, and People are not only suffer'd to neglect them, but such as do go about them, are discouraged by their Governor, according to the Maxim laid down in the Memorials before recited.

Silk-grass is there spontaneous in many places, and may be cut several times in a Year. I need not mention what Advantage may be made of so useful a Plant, whose Fibres are as fine as Flax, and much stronger than Hemp. Mr. *Purchas* tells us, in his *Fourth Pilgrim,* Page 1786, That in the first Discovery of this part of the World, they presented Q. *Elizabeth* with a Piece of Grogram that had been made of it. And yet to this Day they make no manner of use of this Plant, no, not so much as the *Indians* did, before the *English* came among them, who then made their Baskets, Fishing Nets, and Lines, of it.

The Sheep increase well, and bear good Fleeces, but they generally are suffer'd to be torn off their Backs by Briers, and Bushes, instead of being shorn, or else are left rotting upon the Dunghil with their Skins.

Bees thrive there abundantly, and will very easily yield to the careful Huswife, two Crops of Honey in a Year, and besides lay up a Winter-store sufficient to preserve their Stocks.

The Beeves, when any Care is taken of them in the Winter, come to great Perfection. They have noble Marshes there, which, with the Charge of draining only, would make as fine Pastures as any in the World; and yet there is not an hundred Acres of Marsh drained throughout the whole Country.

Hogs swarm like Vermine upon the Earth, and are often accounted such, insomuch that when an Inventory of any considerable Man's Estate is taken by the Executors, the Hogs are left out, and not listed in the Appraisement. The Hogs run where they list, and find their own Support in the Woods, without any Care of the Owner; and in many Plantations it is well, if the Proprietor can find and catch the Pigs, or any part of a Farrow, when they are young, to mark them; for if there be any markt in a Gang of Hogs, they determine the Property of the rest, because they seldom miss their Gangs; but as they are bred in Company, so they continue to the End.

The Woods produce great Variety of Incense and sweet Gums, which distil from several Trees; as also Trees bearing Honey, and Sugar, as before was mention'd: Yet there's no use made of any of them, either for Profit or Refreshment.

All sorts of Naval Stores may be produced there, as Pitch, Tar, Rosin, Turpentine, Plank, Timber, and all sorts of Masts, and Yards, besides Sails, Cordage, and Iron, and all these may be transported, by an easy Water-Carriage.

These and a Thousand other Advantages that Country naturally affords, which its Inhabitants make no manner of use of. They can see their Naval Stores daily benefit other People, who send thither to build Ships; while they, instead of promoting such Undertakings among themselves, and easing such as are willing to go upon them, allow them no manner of Encouragement, but rather the contrary. They receive no Benefit nor Refreshment from the Sweets, and precious things they have growing amongst them, but make use of the Industry of *England* for all such things.

What Advantages do they see the Neighbouring Plantations make of their Grain and Provisions, while they, who can produce them infinitely better, not only neglect the making a Trade thereof, but even a necessary Provision against an accidental Scarcity, contenting themselves with a supply of Food from hand to mouth, so that if it should please God, to send them an unseasonable Year, there wou'd not be found in the Country, Provision sufficient to support the People for three Months extraordinary.

By reason of the unfortunate Method of the Settlement, and want of Cohabitation, they cannot make a beneficial use of their Flax, Hemp, Cotten, Silk, Silkgrass, and Wool, which might otherwise supply their Necessities, and leave the Produce of Tobacco to enrich them, when a gainful Market can be found for it.

Thus they depend altogether upon the Liberality of Nature, without endeavouring to improve its Gifts, by Art or Industry. They spunge upon the Blessings of a warm Sun, and a fruitful Soil, and almost grutch the Pains of gathering in the Bounties of the Earth. I should be asham'd to publish this slothful Indolence of my Countrymen, but that I hope it will rouse them out of their Lethargy, and excite them to make the most of all those happy Advantages which Nature has given them; and if it does this, I am sure they will have the Goodness to forgive me.

THE QUAKER

For us, as also for most colonial Americans, the prime significance of the Quaker movement lies in its radically individualistic protestantism. Quakers were willing to realize the fullest implications of protestant thinking; they found the very source of order in society in the sacred inviolability of the individual. That inviolability was literal, a divine categorical imperative which meant that man could live only by knowing himself in others and others in himself. He could not be an empire-builder; he could only show men the possibilities of empire within themselves. Everyman was his brother, as Everyman was somehow himself. So he preached; so he lived; so he died. And his way came to represent to those to whom he preached, those whom he often as not annoyed into toleration and love, the way of the radically-minded, simply-minded peacemaker—literally, as he called himself, the Friend of man.

The background of the Quaker movement, however, is wider than that of English protestantism. Behind English and American Quakerism there is also German pietism of the sixteenth and seventeenth centuries—that of Jacob Boehme in particular—and the neo-platonic revival of the seventeenth century. In pietism and neo-platonism emphasis was on the individual contact with divinity and on the faculty which was the means of that contact. The Quakers came to call this faculty the "Inner Light." Seeing by this Light, the first Friend, George Fox (1624-1691) travelled and preached anywhere and everywhere, "convincing" all those he could. He "convinced" William Penn in 1677; and in 1681-1682 Penn moved to found a colony in America for others who had come to believe as he had. Meantime Quakers had been at work in the colonies. In 1656 and 1657 they came to Massachusetts and were barbarously mistreated; for they represented to proper Puritans all the dangers of antinomianism, democracy, and surrender to the corrupt self. But the Quakers survived, even thrived, elsewhere in America. Pennsylvania was a success; while Quakers were in control of the colony, frontier relations with the Indians were more peaceful than anywhere in the colonies; Philadelphia became the center of American life. Yet in practical terms, the Quaker way was too simple. Gradually losing political power in the eighteenth century, the Quakers took on their permanent role as protesters, gadflies, and peacemakers. Trying to protect Indians and to end slavery, they became for Enlightened Americans and Europeans the symbol of all that was free, intelligent, and rational. But their belief remained in something beyond the reason, something which was from God, something, however, which led inevitably to freedom, intelligence, and reason.

Records of the Quaker enterprise in America are voluminous. For Quakers felt it part of their duty to record lives which were at all points spiritualized. Thus we have myriad Quaker journals of experiences. Indubitably the greatest of these is that of John Woolman. Woolman's journal not only records a Quaker life but captures in its informal, sensitive, quietly ordered style a Quaker sensibility. Here—as in the essay of William Penn which precedes it in this collection—is a Quaker conscience. In many ways, it is an American conscience; for the destiny of the Quaker has been to be an American conscience.

Bibliographical Note. Elbert Russel, *A History of Quakerism* (New York, 1943) is a general introduction to the subject. Rufus Jones, *The Quakers in the American Colonies* (London, 1911) is an extended and inclusive study; F. B. Tolles, *Meeting House and Counting House* (Chapel Hill, 1948) is an important and valuable special study of Philadelphia Quaker attempts to mediate between the claims of work and worship and to live fully in the world. Luella Wright, *The Literary Life of the Early Friends,* 1650-1725 (New York, 1932) furnishes the best available introduction to Quaker writings.

WILLIAM PENN
(*1644-1718*)

Bibliographical Note. The best, but not complete, collection of Penn's writings is in 2 vols., *A Collection of the Works of William Penn* (London, 1726). There is no modern edition. The text of the selection which follows is from *Narratives of Early Pennsylvania, West Jersey, and Delaware, 1630-1707,* ed. A. C. Myers (New York, 1912), pp. 225-242. For Penn's life, see William Hull, *William Penn* (New York, 1937); for his social ideas, see E. C. O. Beatty, *William Penn as a Social Philosopher* (New York, 1939).

LETTER FROM WILLIAM PENN TO THE COMMITTEE OF THE FREE SOCIETY OF TRADERS (1683)*

My Kind Friends;

The Kindness of yours by the Ship *Thomas and Anne,* doth much oblige me; for by it I perceive the Interest you take in my Health and Reputation, and the prosperous Beginnings of this Province, which you are so kind as to think may much depend upon them. In return of which, I have sent you a long Letter, and yet containing as brief an Account of My self, and the Affairs of this Province, as I have been able to make.

In the first place, I take notice of the News you sent me, whereby I find some Persons have had so little Wit, and so much Malice, as to report my Death, and to mend the matter, dead a Jesuit too. One might have reasonably hop'd, that this Distance, like Death, would have been a protection against Spite and Envy; and indeed, Absence being a kind of Death, ought alike to secure the Name of the Absent as the Dead; because they are equally unable as such to defend themselves: But they that intend Mischief, do not use to follow good Rules to effect it. However, to the great Sorrow and Shame of the Inventors, I am still Alive, and No Jesuit, and I thank God, very well: And without Injustice to

---

* Reprinted from *Narratives of Early Pennsylvania, West Jersey, and Delaware, 1630-1707,* edited by A. C. Myers and used with permission of Barnes & Noble, Inc.

the Authors of this, I may venture to infer, That they that wilfully and falsly Report, would have been glad it had been So. But I perceive, many frivolous and Idle Stories have been Invented since my Departure from England, which perhaps at this time are no more Alive, than I am Dead.

But if I have been Unkindly used by some I left behind me, I found Love and Respect enough where I came; an universal kind Welcome, every sort in their way. For here are some of several Nations, as well as divers Judgments: Nor were the Natives wanting in this, for their Kings, Queens and Great Men both visited and presented me; to whom I made suitable Returns, etc.

For the Province, the general Condition of it take as followeth.

I. The Country it self in its Soyl, Air, Water, Seasons and Produce both Natural and Artificial is not to be despised. The Land containeth divers sorts of Earth, as Sand Yellow and Black, Poor and Rich: also Gravel both Loomy and Dusty; and in some places a fast fat Earth, like to our best Vales in England, especially by Inland Brooks and Rivers, God in his Wisdom having ordered it so, that the Advantages of the Country are divided, the Back-Lands being generally three to one Richer than those that lie by Navigable Waters. We have much of another Soyl, and that is a black Hasel Mould, upon a Stony or Rocky bottom.

II. The Air is sweet and clear, the Heavens serene, like the South-parts of France, rarely Overcast; and as the Woods come by numbers of People to be more clear'd, that it self will Refine.

III. The Waters are generally good, for the Rivers and Brooks have mostly Gravel and Stony Bottoms, and in Number hardly credible. We have also Mineral Waters, that operate in the same manner with Barnet and North-hall, not two Miles from Philadelphia.

IV. For the Seasons of the Year, having by God's goodness now lived over the Coldest and Hottest, that the Oldest Liver in the Province can remember, I can say something to an English Understanding.

1st, Of the Fall, for then I came in: I found it from the 24th of October, to the beginning of December, as we have it usually in

England in September, or rather like an English mild Spring. From December to the beginning of the Moneth called March, we had sharp Frosty Weather; not foul, thick, black Weather, as our North-East Winds bring with them in England; but a Skie as clear as in Summer, and the Air dry, cold, piercing and hungry; yet I remember not, that I wore more Clothes than in England. The reason of this Cold is given from the great Lakes that are fed by the Fountains of Canada. The Winter before was as mild, scarce any Ice at all; while this for a few dayes Froze up our great River Delaware. From that Moneth to the Moneth called June, we enjoy'd a sweet Spring, no Gusts, but gentle Showers, and a fine Skie. Yet this I observe, that the Winds here as there, are more Inconstant Spring and Fall, upon that turn of Nature, than in Summer or Winter. From thence to this present Moneth, which endeth the Summer (commonly speaking) we have had extraordinary Heats, yet mitigated sometimes by Cool Breezese. The Wind that ruleth the Summer-season, is the South-West; but Spring, Fall and Winter, 'tis rare to want the wholesome North Wester seven dayes together: And whatever Mists, Fogs or Vapours foul the Heavens by Easterly or Southerly Winds, in two Hours time are blown away; the one is alwayes followed by the other: A Remedy that seems to have a peculiar Providence in it to the Inhabitants; the multitude of Trees, yet standing, being liable to retain Mists and Vapours, and yet not one quarter so thick as I expected.

V. The Natural Produce of the Country, of Vegetables, is Trees, Fruits, Plants, Flowers. The Trees of most note are, the black Walnut, Cedar, Cyprus, Chestnut, Poplar, Gumwood, Hickery, Sassafrax, Ash, Beech and Oak of divers sorts, as Red, White and Black; Spanish Chestnut and Swamp, the most durable of all: of All which there is plenty for the use of man.

The Fruits that I find in the Woods, are the White and Black Mulbery, Chestnut, Wallnut, Plumbs, Strawberries, Cranberries, Hurtleberries and Grapes of divers sorts. The great Red Grape (now ripe) called by Ignorance, the Fox-Grape (because of the Relish it hath with unskilful Palates) is in it self an extraordinary

Grape, and by Art doubtless may be Cultivated to an excellent Wine, if not so sweet, yet little inferior to the Frontimack, as it is not much unlike in taste, Ruddiness set aside, which in such things, as well as Mankind, differs the case much. There is a white kind of Muskedel, and a little black Grape, like the cluster-Grape of England, not yet so ripe as the other; but they tell me, when Ripe, sweeter, and that they only want skilful Vinerons to make good use of them: I intend to venture on it with my French man this season, who shews some knowledge in those things. Here are also Peaches, and very good, and in great quantities, not an Indian Plantation without them; but whether naturally here at first, I know not, however one may have them by Bushels for little; they make a pleasant Drink and I think not inferior to any Peach you have in England, except the true Newington. 'Tis disputable with me, whether it be best to fall to Fining the Fruits of the Country, especially the Grape, by the care and skill of Art, or send for forreign Stems and Sets, already good and approved. It seems most reasonable to believe, that not only a thing groweth best, where it naturally grows; but will hardly be equalled by another Species of the same kind, that doth not naturally grow there. But to solve the doubt, I intend, if God give me Life, to try both, and hope the consequence will be as good Wine as any European Countries of the same Latitude do yield.

VI. The Artificial Produce of the Country, is Wheat, Barley, Oats, Rye, Pease, Beans, Squashes, Pumkins, Water-Melons, Mus-Melons, and all Herbs and Roots that our Gardens in England usually bring forth.

VII. Of living Creatures; Fish, Fowl, and the Beasts of the Woods, here are divers sorts, some for Food and Profit, and some for Profit only: For Food as well as Profit, the Elk, as big as a small Ox, Deer bigger than ours, Beaver, Racoon, Rabbits, Squirrels, and some eat young Bear, and commend it. Of Fowl of the Land, there is the Turkey (Forty and Fifty Pound weight) which is very great; Phesants, Heath-Birds, Pidgeons and Partridges in abundance. Of the Water, the Swan, Goose, white and gray, Brands, Ducks, Teal, also the Snipe and Curloe, and that in great

Numbers; but the Duck and Teal excel, nor so good have I ever eat in other Countries. Of Fish, there is the Sturgeon, Herring, Rock, Shad, Catshead, Sheepshead, Ele, Smelt, Pearch, Roach; and in Inland Rivers, Trout, some say Salmon, above the Falls. Of Shelfish, we have Oysters, Crabbs, Cockles, Concks, and Mushels; some Oysters six Inches long, and one sort of Cockles as big as the Stewing Oysters, they make a rich Broth. The Creatures for Profit only by Skin or Fur, and that are natural to these parts, are the Wild Cat, Panther, Otter, Wolf, Fox, Fisher, Minx, Musk-Rat; and of the Water, the Whale for Oyl, of which we have good store, and two Companies of Whalers, whose Boats are built, will soon begin their Work, which hath the appearance of a considerable Improvement. To say nothing of our reasonable Hopes of good Cod in the Bay.

VIII. We have no want of Horses, and some are very good and shapely enough; two Ships have been freighted to Barbadoes with Horses and Pipe-Staves, since my coming in. Here is also Plenty of Cow-Cattle, and some Sheep; the People Plow mostly with Oxen.

IX. There are divers Plants that not only the Indians tell us, but we have had occasion to prove by Swellings, Burnings, Cuts, etc., that they are of great Virtue, suddenly curing the Patient: and for smell, I have observed several, especially one, the wild Mirtle; the other I know not what to call, but are most fragrant.

X. The Woods are adorned with lovely Flowers, for colour, greatness, figure, and variety: I have seen the Gardens of London best stored with that sort of Beauty, but think they may be improved by our Woods: I have sent a few to a Person of Quality this Year for a tryal.

Thus much of the Country, next of the Natives or Aborigines.

XI. The *Natives* I shall consider in their Persons, Language, Manners, Religion and Government, with my sence of their Original. For their Persons, they are generally tall, streight, well-built, and of singular Proportion; they tread strong and clever, and mostly walk with a lofty Chin: Of Complexion, Black, but by design, as the Gypsies in England: They grease themselves with

Bears-fat clarified, and using no defence against Sun or Weather, their skins must needs be swarthy; Their Eye is little and black, not unlike a straight-look't Jew: The thick Lip and flat Nose, so frequent with East-Indians and Blacks, are not common to them; for I have seen as comely European-like faces among them of both, as on your side the Sea; and truly an Italian Complexion hath not much more of the White, and the Noses of several of them have as much of the Roman.

XII. Their Language is lofty, yet narrow, but like the Hebrew; in Signification full, like Short-hand in writing; one word serveth in the place of three, and the rest are supplied by the Understanding of the Hearer: Imperfect in their Tenses, wanting in their Moods, Participles, Adverbs, Conjunctions, Interjections: I have made it my business to understand it, that I might not want an Interpreter on any occasion: And I must say, that I know not a Language spoken in Europe, that hath words of more sweetness or greatness, in Accent and Emphasis, than theirs; for Instance, *Octorockon, Rancocas, Ozicton, Shakamacon, Poquerim,* all of which are names of Places, and have Grandeur in them: Of words of Sweetness, *Anna,* is Mother, *Issimus,* a Brother, *Netap,* Friend, *usque ozet,* very good; *pone,* Bread, *metse,* eat, *matta,* no, *hatta,* to have, *payo,* to come; *Sepassen, Passijon,* the Names of Places; *Tamane, Secane, Menanse, Secatereus,* are the names of Persons. If one ask them for anything they have not, they will answer, *mattá ne hattá,* which to translate is, not I have, instead of I have not.

XIII. Of their Customs and Manners there is much to be said; I will begin with Children. So soon as they are born, they wash them in Water, and while very young, and in cold Weather to chuse, they Plunge them in the Rivers to harden and embolden them. Having wrapt them in a Clout, they lay them on a straight thin Board, a little more than the length and breadth of the Child, and swadle it fast upon the Board to make it straight; wherefore all Indians have flat Heads; and thus they carry them at their Backs. The Children will go very young, at nine Moneths commonly; they wear only a small Clout round their Waste, till they are big; if Boys, they go a Fishing till ripe for the Woods, which is about Fifteen; then they Hunt, and after having given some Proofs of their Manhood, by a good return of Skins, they may Marry, else it is a shame to think of a Wife. The Girls stay with their Mothers, and help to hoe the Ground, plant Corn and carry Burthens; and they do well to use them to that Young, they must do when they are Old; for the Wives are the true Servants of their Husbands: otherwise the Men are very affectionate to them.

XIV. When the Young Women are fit for Marriage, they wear something upon their Heads for an Advertisement, but so as their Faces are hardly to be seen, but when they please: The Age they Marry at, if Women, is about thirteen and fourteen; if Men, seventeen and eighteen; they are rarely elder.

XV. Their Houses are Mats, or Barks of Trees set on Poles, in the fashion of an English Barn, but out of the power of the Winds, for they are hardly higher than a Man; they lie on Reeds or Grass. In Travel they lodge in the Woods about a great Fire, with the Mantle of Duffills they wear by day, wrapt about them, and a few Boughs stuck round them.

XVI. Their Diet is Maze, or Indian Corn, divers ways pre-pared: sometimes Roasted in the Ashes, sometimes beaten and Boyled with Water, which they call *Homine;* they also make Cakes, not unpleasant to eat: They have likewise several sorts of Beans and Pease that are good Nourishment; and the Woods and Rivers are their Larder.

XVII. If an European comes to see them, or calls for Lodging at their House or *Wigwam* they give him the best place and first cut. If they come to visit us, they salute us with an *Itah* which is as much as to say, Good be to you, and set them down, which is mostly on the Ground close to their Heels, their Legs upright; may be they speak not a word more, but observe all Passages: If you give them any thing to eat or drink, well, for they will not ask; and be it little or much, if it be with Kindness, they are well pleased, else they go away sullen, but say nothing.

XVIII. They are great Concealers of their own Resentments, brought to it, I believe, by the Revenge that hath been practised among them; in either of these, they are not exceeded by the Italians. A Tragical Instance fell out since I came into the Country; A King's Daughter thinking her self slighted by her Husband, in suffering another Woman to lie down between them, rose up, went out, pluck't a Root out of the Ground, and ate it, upon which she immediately dyed; and for which, last Week he made an Offering to her Kindred for Attonement and liberty of Marriage; as two others did to the Kindred of their Wives, that dyed a natural Death: For till Widdowers have done so, they must not marry again. Some of the young Women are said to take undue liberty before Marriage for a Portion; but when marryed, chaste; when with Child, they know their Husbands no more, till delivered; and during their Moneth, they touch no Meat, they eat, but with a Stick, least they should defile it; nor do their Husbands frequent them, till that time be expired.

XIX. But in Liberality they excell, nothing is too good for their friend; give them a fine Gun, Coat, or other thing, it may pass twenty hands, before it sticks; light of Heart, strong Affections, but soon spent; the most merry Creatures that live, Feast and Dance perpetually; they never have much, nor want much: Wealth circulateth like the Blood, all parts partake; and though none shall want what another hath, yet exact Observers of Property. Some Kings have sold, others presented me with several parcels of Land; the Pay or Presents I made them, were not hoarded by the particular Owners, but the neighbouring Kings and their Clans being present when the Goods were brought out, the Parties chiefly concerned consulted, what and to whom they should give them? To every King then, by the hands of a Person for that work appointed, is a proportion sent, so sorted and folded, and with that Gravity, that is admirable. Then that King subdivideth it in like manner among his Dependents, they hardly leaving themselves an Equal share with one of their Subjects: and be it on such occasions, at Festivals, or at their common Meals, the Kings distribute, and to themselves last. They care for little, because they want but little; and the Reason is, a little contents them: In this they are sufficiently revenged on us; if they are ignorant of our Pleasures, they are also free from our Pains. They are not disquieted with Bills of Lading and Exchange, nor perplexed with Chancery-Suits and Exchequer-Reckonings. We sweat and toil to live; their pleasure feeds them, I mean, their Hunting, Fishing and Fowling, and this Table is spread every where; they eat twice a day, Morning and Evening; their Seats and Table are the Ground. Since the European came into these parts, they are grown great lovers of strong Liquors, Rum especially, and for it exchange the richest of their Skins and Furs: If they are heated with Liquors, they are restless till they have enough to sleep; that is their cry, Some more, and I will go to sleep; but when Drunk, one of the most wretchedst Spectacles in the world.

XX. In sickness impatient to be cured, and for it give any thing, especially for their Children, to whom they are extreamly natural; they drink at those times a *Teran* or Decoction of some Roots in spring Water; and if they eat any flesh, it must be of the Female of any Creature; If they dye, they bury them with their Apparel, be they Men or Women, and the nearest of Kin fling in something precious with them, as a token of their Love: Their Mourning is blacking of their faces, which they continue for a year; They are choice of the Graves of their Dead; for least they should be lost by time, and fall to common use, they pick off the Grass that grows upon them, and heap up the fallen Earth with great care and exactness.

XXI. These poor People are under a dark Night in things relating to Religion, to be sure, the Tradition of it; yet they believe a God and Immortality, without the help of Metaphysicks; for they say, There is a great King that made them, who dwells in a glorious Country to the Southward of them, and that the Souls of the good shall go thither, where they shall live again. Their Worship consists of two parts, Sacrifice and *Cantico*. Their Sacrifice is their first Fruits; the first and fattest Buck they kill, goeth to the fire, where he is all burnt with a Mournful Ditty of him that performeth the Ceremony, but with such marvellous Fervency and Labour of Body, that he will even sweat to a foam.

The other part is their *Cantico,* performed by round-Dances, sometimes Songs, then Shouts, two being in the middle that begin, and by Singing and Drumming on a Board direct the Chorus: Their Postures in the Dance are very Antick and differing, but all keep measure. This is done with equal Earnestness and Labour, but great appearance of Joy. In the Fall, when the Corn cometh in, they begin to feast one another; there have been two great Festivals already, to which all come that will: I was at one my self; their Entertainment was a green Seat by a Spring, under some shady Trees, and twenty Bucks, with hot Cakes of new Corn, both Wheat and Beans, which they make up in a square form, in the leaves of the Stem, and bake them in the Ashes: And after that they fell to Dance, But they that go, must carry a small Present in their Money, it may be six Pence, which is made of the Bone of a Fish; the black is with them as Gold, the white, Silver; they call it all *Wampum.*

XXII. Their Government is by Kings, which they call *Sachema,* and those by Succession, but always of the Mothers side; for Instance, the Children of him that is now King, will not succeed, but his Brother by the Mother, or the Children of his Sister, whose Sons (and after them the Children of her Daughters) will reign; for no Woman inherits; the Reason they render for this way of Descent, is, that their Issue may not be spurious.

XXIII. Every King hath his Council, and that consists of all the Old and Wise men of his Nation, which perhaps is two hundred People: nothing of Moment is undertaken, be it War, Peace, Selling of Land or Traffick, without advising with them; and which is more, with the Young Men too. 'Tis admirable to consider, how Powerful the Kings are, and yet how they move by the Breath of their People. I have had occasion to be in Council with them upon Treaties for Land, and to adjust the terms of Trade; their Order is thus: The King sits in the middle of an half Moon, and hath his Council, the Old and Wise on each hand; behind them, or at a little distance, sit the younger Fry, in the same figure. Having consulted and resolved their business, the King ordered one of them to speak to me; he stood up, came to me, and in the Name of his King saluted me, then took me by the hand, and told me, That he was ordered by his King to speak to me, and that now it was not he, but the King that spoke, because what he should say, was the King's mind. He first pray'd me, To excuse them that they had not complyed with me the last time; he feared, there might be some fault in the Interpreter, being neither Indian nor English; besides, it was the Indian Custom to deliberate, and take up much time in Council, before they resolve; and that if the Young People and Owners of the Land had been as ready as he, I had not met with so much delay. Having thus introduced his matter, he fell to the Bounds of the Land they had agreed to dispose of, and the Price, (which now is little and dear, that which would have bought twenty Miles, not buying now two.) During the time that this Person spoke, not a man of them was observed to whisper or smile; the Old, Grave, the Young, Reverend in their Deportment; they do speak little, but fervently, and with Elegancy: I have never seen more natural Sagacity, considering them without the help, (I was agoing to say, the spoil) of Tradition; and he will deserve the Name of Wise, that Outwits them in any Treaty about a thing they understand. When the Purchase was agreed, great Promises past between us of Kindness and good Neighbourhood, and that the Indians and English must live in Love, as long as the Sun gave light. Which done, another made a Speech to the Indians, in the Name of all the *Sachamakers* or Kings, first to tell them what was done; next, to charge and command them, To Love the Christians, and particularly live in Peace with me, and the People under my Government: That many Governours had been in the River, but that no Governour had come himself to live and stay here before; and having now such a one that had treated them well, they should never do him or his any wrong. At every sentence of which they shouted, and said, Amen, in their way.

XXIV. The Justice they have is Pecuniary: In case of any Wrong or evil Fact, be it Murther it self, they Attone by Feasts and Presents of their *Wampon,* which is proportioned to the quality of the Offence or Person injured, or of the Sex they are of: for in case they kill a Woman, they pay double, and the Reason they render, is, That she breedeth Children, which Men cannot do. 'Tis rare that they fall out, if Sober; and if Drunk, they forgive it, saying, It was the Drink, and not the Man, that abused them.

XXV. We have agreed, that in all Differences between us, Six of each side shall end the matter: Don't abuse them, but let them have Justice, and you win them: The worst is, that they are the worse for the Christians, who have propagated their Vices, and yielded them Tradition for ill, and not for good things. But as low an Ebb as they are at, and as glorious as their Condition looks, the Christians have not out-liv'd their sight with all their Pretensions to an higher Manifestation: What good then might not a good People graft, where there is so distinct a Knowledge left between Good and Evil? I beseech God to incline the Hearts of all that come into these parts, to out-live the Knowledge of the Natives, by a fixt Obedience to their greater Knowledge of the Will of God, for it were miserable indeed for us to fall under the just censure of the poor Indian Conscience, while we make profession of things so far transcending.

XXVI. For their Original, I am ready to believe them of the Jewish Race, I mean, of the stock of the Ten Tribes, and that for the following Reasons; first, They were to go to a Land not planted or known, which to be sure Asia and Africa were, if not Europe; and he that intended that extraordinary Judgment upon them, might make the Passage not uneasie to them, as it is not impossible in it self, from the Easter-most parts of Asia, to the Wester-most of America. In the next place, I find them of like Countenance and their Children of so lively Resemblance, that a man would think himself in Dukes-place[1] or Berry-street[1] in London, when he seeth them. But this is not all, they agree in Rites, they reckon by Moons: they offer their first Fruits, they have a kind of Feast of Tabernacles; they are said to lay their Alter upon twelve Stones; their Mourning a year, Customs of Women, with many things that do not now occur.

---

[1] . . . Jewish quarter.—*Myers.*

So much for the Natives, next the Old Planters will be considered in this Relation, before I come to our Colony, and the Concerns of it.

XXVII. The first Planters in these parts were the Dutch, and soon after them the Sweeds and Finns. The Dutch applied themselves to Traffick, the Sweeds and Finns to Husbandry. There were some Disputes between them some years, the Dutch looking upon them as Intruders upon their Purchase and Possession, which was finally ended in the Surrender made by John Rizeing, the Sweeds Governour, to Peter Styvesant, Governour for the States of Holland, *Anno* 1655.

XXVIII. The Dutch inhabit mostly those parts of the Province, that lie upon or near to the Bay, and the Sweeds the Freshes of the River Delaware. There is no need of giving any Description of them, who are better known there then here; but they are a plain, strong, industrious People, yet have made no great progress in Culture or propagation of fruit-Trees, as if they desired rather to have enough, than Plenty or Traffick. But I presume, the Indians made them the more careless, by furnishing them with the means of Profit, to wit, Skins and Furs, for Rum, and such strong Liquors. They kindly received me, as well as the English, who were few, before the People concerned with me came among them; I must needs commend their Respect to Authority, and kind Behaviour to the English; they do not degenerate from the Old friendship between both Kingdoms. As they are People proper and strong of Body, so they have fine Children, and almost every house full; rare to find one of them without three or four Boys, and as many Girls; some six, seven and eight Sons: And I must do them that right, I see few Young men more sober and laborious.

XXIX. The Dutch have a Meeting-place for Religious Worship at New Castle, and the Sweedes three, one at Christina, one at Tenecum, and one at Wicoco, within half a Mile of this Town.

XXX. There rests, that I speak of the Condition we are in, and what Settlement we have made, in which I will be as short as I can; for I fear, and not without reason, that I have tryed your Patience with this long Story. The Country lieth bounded on the East, by the River and Bay of Delaware, and Eastern Sea; it hath the Advantage of many Creeks or Rivers rather, that run into the main River or Bay; some Navigable for great Ships, some for small Craft: Those of most Eminency are Christina, Brandywine, Skilpot, and Skulkill; any one of which have room to lay up the Royal Navy of England, there being from four to eight Fathom Water.

XXXI. The lesser Creeks or Rivers, yet convenient for Sloops and Ketches of good Burthen, are Lewis, Mespilion, Cedar, Dover, Cranbrook, Feversham, and Georges, below, and Chichester, Chester, Toacawny, Pemmapecka, Portquessin, Neshimenck and Pennberry in the Freshes; many lesser that admit Boats and Shallops. Our People are mostly settled upon the upper Rivers, which are pleasant and sweet, and generally bounded with good Land. The Planted part of the Province and Territories is cast into six Counties, Philadelphia, Buckingham, Chester, New Castle, Kent and Sussex, containing about Four Thousand Souls. Two General assemblies have been held, and with such Concord and Dispatch, that they sate but three Weeks, and at least seventy Laws were past without one Dissent in any material thing. But of this more hereafter, being yet Raw and New in our Geer: However, I cannot forget their singular Respect to me in this Infancy of things, who by their own private Expenses so early consider'd Mine for the Publick, as to present me with an Impost upon certain Goods Imported and Exported: Which after my Acknowledgements of their Affection, I did as freely Remit to the Province and the Traders to it. And for the well Government of the said Counties, Courts of Justice are establisht in every County, with proper Officers, as Justices, Sheriffs, Clarks, Constables, etc., which Courts are held every two Moneths: But to prevent Law-Suits, there are three Peace-makers chosen by every County-Court, in the nature of common Arbitrators, to hear and end Differences betwixt man and man; and Spring and Fall there is an Orphan's Court in each County, to inspect, and regulate the Affairs of Orphans and Widdows.

XXXII. Philadelphia, the Expectation of those that are concern'd in this Province, is at last laid out to the great Content of those here, that are any wayes Interested therein; The Scituation is a Neck of Land, and lieth between two Navigable Rivers, Delaware and Skulkill, whereby it hath two Fronts upon the Water, each a Mile, and two from River to River. Delaware is a glorious River, but the Skulkill being an hundred Miles Boatable above the Falls, and its Course North-East toward the Fountain of Susquahannah (that tends to the Heart of the Province, and both sides our own) it is like to be a great part of the Settlement of this Age. I say little of the Town it self, because a *Plat-form* will be shewn you by my Agent, in which those who are Purchasers of me, will find their Names and Interests: But this I will say for the good Providence of God, that of all the many Places I have seen in the World, I remember not one better seated; so that it seems to me to have been appointed for a Town, whether we regard the Rivers, or the conveniency of the Coves, Docks, Springs, the loftiness and soundness of the Land and the Air, held by the People of these parts to be very good. It is advanced within less than a Year to about four Score Houses and Cottages, such as they are, where Merchants and Handicrafts, are following their Vocations as fast as they can, while the Country-men are close at their Farms; Some of them got a little Winter-Corn in the Ground last Season, and the generality have had a handsom Summer-Crop, and are preparing for their Winter-Corn. They reaped their Barley this Year in the Moneth called May; the Wheat in the Moneth following; so that there is time in these parts for another Crop of divers Things before the Winter-Season. We are daily in hopes of Shipping to add to our Number; for blessed be God, here is both Room and Accommodation for them; the Stories of our Necessity being either the Fear of our Friends, or the Scare-Crows of our Enemies; for the greatest hardship we have suffered, hath been Salt-Meat, which by Fowl in Winter, and Fish in Summer, together with some Poultery, Lamb, Mutton, Veal, and plenty of Venison the best part of the year, hath been made very passable. I bless God, I am fully satisfied with

the Country and Entertainment I can get in it; for I find that
particular Content which hath alwayes attended me, where God
in his Providence hath made it my place and service to reside.
You cannot imagin, my Station can be at present free of more
than ordinary business, and as such, I may say, It is a trouble-
som Work; but the Method things are putting in, will facilitate
the Charge, and give an easier Motion to the Administration of
Affairs. However, as it is some mens Duty to plow, some to sow,
some to water, and some to reap; so it is the Wisdom as well as
Duty of a man, to yield to the mind of Providence, and chearfully,
as well as carefully imbrace and follow the Guidance of it.

XXXIII. For your particular Concern, I might entirely refer
you to the Letters of the President of the Society; but this I will
venture to say, Your Provincial Settlements both within and
without the Town, for Scituation and Soil, are without Excep-
tion; Your City-Lot is an whole Street, and one side of a Street,
from River to River, containing near one hundred Acers, not
easily valued, which is besides your four hundred Acers in the
City Liberties, part of your twenty thousand Acers in the Coun-
tery. Your Tannery hath such plenty of Bark, the Saw-Mill for
Timber, the place of the Glass-house so conveniently posted for
Water-carriage, the City-Lot for a Dock, and the Whalery for a
sound and fruitful Bank, and the Town Lewis by it to help
your People, that by Gods blessing the Affairs of the Society will
naturally grow in their Reputation and Profit. I am sure I have
not turned my back upon any Offer that tended to its Prosperity;
and though I am ill at Projects, I have sometimes put in for a
Share with her Officers, to countenance and advance her Interest.
You are already informed what is fit for you further to do, whatsoever tends to the Promotion of Wine, and to the Manufacture
of Linnen in these parts, I cannot but wish you to promote it;
and the French People are most likely in both respects to answer
that design: To that end, I would advise you to send for some
Thousands of Plants out of France, with some able Vinerons,
and People of the other Vocation: But because I believe you have
been entertained with this and some other profitable Subjects by

your President, I shall add no more, but to assure you, that I am
heartily inclined to advance your just Interest, and that you will
always find me

Your Kind Cordial Friend,

WILLIAM PENN

Philadelphia, the 16th of the
6th Moneth, call'd August,
1683.

JOHN WOOLMAN
(1720-1772)

The most complete edition of Woolman's *Journal* is that edited from the original manuscripts by Amelia Gummere, *The Journal and Essays of John Woolman* (New York, 1922). The text of the selection which follows, however, is from the edition edited by Vida D. Scudder in Everyman's Library (London, 1910), pp. 99-110; this latter text in turn derives from the 1871 edition of John Greenleaf Whittier, that best known in America. The best account of Woolman's life, aside from his own interpretation of it in the *Journal,* is in the introduction to the Gummere edition of *The Journal and Essays*.

from THE JOURNAL (1774)

[EARLY DAYS]

I have often felt a Motion of Love to leave some Hints in Writing of my Experience of the Goodness of God; and now, in the thirty-sixth Year of my Age, I begin this Work.

I was born in *Northampton,* in *Burlington* County, *West-Jersey,* in the Year 1720; and before I was seven Years old I began to be acquainted with the Operations of divine Love. Through the Care of my Parents, I was taught to read nearly as soon as I was capable of it; and, as I went from School one seventh Day, I remember, while my Companions went to play by the Way, I went forward out of Sight, and, sitting down, I read the 22d Chapter of the *Revelations:* "He shewed me a pure River of Water of Life, clear as Chrystal, proceeding out of the Throne of God and of the Lamb, *etc.*" and, in reading it, my Mind was drawn to seek after that pure Habitation, which, I then believed, God had prepared for his Servants. The Place where I sat, and the Sweetness that attended my Mind, remain fresh in my Memory.

This, and the like gracious Visitations, had that Effect upon me, that when Boys used ill Language it troubled me; and, through the continued Mercies of God, I was preserved from it.

The pious Instructions of my Parents were often fresh in my Mind when I happened to be among wicked Children, and were of Use to me. My Parents, having a large Family of Children, used frequently, on first Days after Meeting, to put us to read in the holy Scriptures, or some religious Books, one after another, the rest sitting by without much Conversation; which, I have since often thought, was a good Practice. From what I had read and heard, I believed there had been, in past Ages, People who walked in Uprightness before God, in a Degree exceeding any that I knew, or heard of, now living: And the Apprehension of there being less Steadiness and Firmness, amongst People in this Age than in past Ages, often troubled me while I was a Child.

A Thing remarkable in my Childhood was, that once, going to a Neighbour's House, I saw, on the Way, a *Robin* sitting on her Nest, and as I came near she went off, but, having young ones, flew about, and with many Cries expressed her Concern for them; I stood and threw Stones at her, till, one striking her, she fell down dead: At first I was pleased with the Exploit, but after a few Minutes was seized with Horror, as having, in a sportive Way, killed an innocent Creature while she was careful for her Young: I beheld her lying dead, and thought these young ones, for which she was so careful, must now perish for want of their Dam to nourish them; and, after some painful Considerations on the Subject, I climbed up the Tree, took all the young Birds, and killed them; supposing that better than to leave them to pine away and die miserably: And believed, in this Case, that Scripture-proverb was fulfilled, "The tender Mercies of the Wicked are cruel." I then went on my Errand, but, for some Hours, could think of little else but the Cruelties I had committed, and was much troubled. Thus he, whose tender Mercies are over all his Works, hath placed a Principle in the human Mind, which incites to exercise Goodness towards every living Creature; and this being singly attended to, People become tender hearted and sympathising; but being frequently and totally rejected, the Mind becomes shut up in a contrary Disposition.

About the twelfth Year of my Age, my Father being abroad, my Mother reproved me for some Misconduct, to which I made an undutiful Reply; and, the next first Day, as I was with my

Father returning from Meeting, he told me he understood I had behaved amiss to my Mother, and advised me to be more careful in future. I knew myself blameable, and in Shame and Confusion remained silent. Being thus awakened to a Sense of my Wickedness, I felt Remorse in my Mind, and, getting home, I retired and prayed to the Lord to forgive me; and do not remember that I ever, after that, spoke unhandsomely to either of my Parents, however foolish in some other Things.

Having attained the Age of sixteen Years, I began to love wanton Company; and though I was preserved from prophane Language, or scandalous Conduct, still I perceived a Plant in me which produced much wild Grapes; yet my merciful Father forsook me not utterly, but, at Times, through his Grace, I was brought seriously to consider my Ways; and the Sight of my Backslidings affected me with Sorrow; but, for want of rightly attending to the Reproofs of Instruction, Vanity was added to Vanity, and Repentance to Repentance: Upon the whole, my Mind was more and more alienated from the Truth, and I hastened toward Destruction. While I meditate on the Gulph towards which I travelled, and reflect on my youthful Disobedience, for these Things I weep, mine Eyes run down with Water.

Advancing in Age, the Number of my Acquaintances increased, and thereby my Way grew more difficult; though I had found Comfort in reading the holy Scriptures, and thinking on heavenly Things, I was now estranged therefrom: I knew I was going from the Flock of Christ, and had no Resolution to return; hence serious Reflections were uneasy to me, and youthful Vanities and Diversions my greatest Pleasure. Running in this Road I found many like myself; and we associated in that which is the reverse of true Friendship.

But in this swift Race it pleased God to visit me with Sickness, so that I doubted of recovering; and then did Darkness, Horror, and Amazement, with full Force, seize me, even when my Pain and Distress of Body was very great. I thought it would have been better for me never to have had a Being, than to see the Day which I now saw. I was filled with Confusion; and in great

Affliction, both of Mind and Body, I lay and bewailed myself. I had not Confidence to lift up my Cries to God, whom I had thus offended; but, in a deep Sense of my great Folly, I was humbled before him; and, at length, that Word which is as a Fire and a Hammer, broke and dissolved my rebellious Heart, and then my Cries were put up in Contrition; and in the multitude of his Mercies I found inward Relief, and felt a close Engagement, that, if he was pleased to restore my Health, I might walk humbly before him.

After my Recovery, this Exercise remained with me a considerable Time; but, by Degrees, giving Way to youthful Vanities, they gained Strength, and, getting with wanton young People, I lost Ground. The Lord had been very gracious, and spoke Peace to me in the Time of my Distress; and I now most ungratefully turned again to Folly; on which Account, at Times, I felt sharp Reproof. I was not so hardy as to commit Things scandalous; but to exceed in Vanity, and promote Mirth, was my chief Study. Still I retained a Love for pious People, and their Company brought an Awe upon me. My dear Parents, several Times, admonished me in the Fear of the Lord, and their Admonition entered into my Heart, and had a good Effect for a Season; but, not getting deep enough to pray rightly, the Tempter, when he came, found Entrance. I remember once, having spent a Part of the Day in Wantonness, as I went to Bed at Night, there lay in a Window, near my Bed, a Bible, which I opened, and first cast my Eye on this Text, "We lie down in our Shame, and our Confusion covers us:" This I knew to be my Case; and, meeting with so unexpected a Reproof, I was somewhat affected with it, and went to Bed under Remorse of Conscience; which I soon cast off again.

Thus Time passed on: My Heart was replenished with Mirth and Wantonness, and pleasing Scenes of Vanity were presented to my Imagination, till I attained the Age of eighteen Years; near which Time I felt the Judgments of God, in my Soul, like a consuming Fire; and, looking over my past Life, the Prospect was moving.—I was often sad, and longed to be delivered from those Vanities; then again, my Heart was strongly inclined to them, and there was in me a sore Conflict: At Times I turned to Folly, and then again, Sorrow and Confusion took hold of me. In a while, I resolved totally to leave off some of my Vanities; but there was a secret Reserve, in my Heart, of the more refined Part of them, and I was not low enough to find true Peace. Thus, for some Months, I had great Troubles; there remaining in me an unsubjected Will, which rendered my Labours fruitless, till at length, through the merciful Continuance of heavenly Visitations, I was made to bow down in Spirit before the Lord. I remember one Evening I had spent some Time in reading a pious Author; and walking out alone, I humbly prayed to the Lord for his Help, that I might be delivered from all those Vanities which so ensnared me. Thus, being brought low, he helped me; and, as I learned to bear the Cross, I felt Refreshment to come from his Presence; but, not keeping in that Strength which gave Victory, I lost Ground again; the Sense of which greatly affected me; and I sought Deserts and lonely Places, and there, with Tears, did confess my Sins to God, and humbly craved Help of him. And I may say with Reverence, he was near to me in my Troubles, and in those Times of Humiliation opened my Ear to Discipline. I was now led to look seriously at the Means by which I was drawn from the pure Truth, and learned this, that, if I would live in the Life which the faithful Servants of God lived in, I must not go into Company as heretofore in my own Will; but all the Cravings of Sense must be governed by a divine Principle. In Times of Sorrow and Abasement these Instructions were sealed upon me, and I felt the Power of Christ prevail over selfish Desires, so that I was preserved in a good degree of Steadiness; and, being young, and believing at that Time that a single Life was best for me, I was strengthened to keep from such Company as had often been a Snare to me.

I kept steadily to Meetings; spent First-day Afternoons chiefly in reading the Scriptures and other good Books; and was early convinced in Mind, that true Religion consisted in an inward Life, wherein the Heart doth love and reverence God the Creator, and learns to exercise true Justice and Goodness, not only toward all Men, but also toward the brute Creatures.—That as the Mind was moved, by an inward Principle, to love God as an invisible incomprehensible Being, by the same Principle it was moved to love him in all his Manifestations in the visible World.—That, as by his Breath the Flame of Life was kindled in all animal sensible Creatures, to say we love God, and, at the same Time exercise Cruelty toward the least Creature, is a Contradiction in itself.

I found no Narrowness respecting Sects and Opinions; but believed, that sincere upright-hearted People, in every Society, who truly love God, were accepted of him.

As I lived under the Cross, and simply followed the Openings of Truth, my Mind, from Day to Day, was more enlightened; my former Acquaintance were left to judge of me as they would, for I found it safest for me to live in private, and keep these Things sealed up in my own Breast. While I silently ponder on that Change wrought in me, I find no Language equal to it, nor any Means to convey to another a clear Idea of it. I looked on the Works of God in this visible Creation, and an Awfulness covered me; my Heart was tender and often contrite, and universal Love to my Fellow-creatures increased in me: This will be understood by such as have trodden the same Path. Some Glances of real Beauty may be seen in their Faces, who dwell in true Meekness. There is a Harmony in the Sound of that Voice to which divine Love gives Utterance, and some Appearance of right Order in their Temper and Conduct, whose Passions are regulated; yet all these do not fully shew forth that inward Life to such as have not felt it: But this white Stone and new Name is known rightly to such only as have it.

. . . . .

[WHITE MEN AND INDIANS]

In my Youth I was used to hard Labour; and, though I was middling healthy, yet my Nature was not fitted to endure so much as many others: So that, being often weary, I was prepared to sympathize with those whose Circumstances in Life, as free Men,

required constant Labour to answer the Demands of their Cred-
itors, and with others under Oppression. In the Uneasiness of
Body, which I have many Times felt by too much Labour, not
as a forced but as a voluntary Oppression, I have often been excited to think on the original Cause of that Oppression, which
is imposed on many in the World: And, the latter Part of the
Time wherein I laboured on our Plantation, my Heart, through
the fresh Visitations of heavenly Love, being often tender, and
my leisure Time frequently spent in reading the Life and Doctrines of our blessed Redeemer, the Account of the Sufferings
of Martyrs, and the History of the first Rise of our Society, a Belief was gradually settled in my Mind, that if such, as had great
Estates, generally lived in that Humility and Plainness which
belongs to a *Christian* Life, and laid much easier Rents and Interests on their Lands and Monies, and thus led the Way to a right
Use of Things, so great a Number of People might be employed
in Things useful, that Labour, both for Men and other Creatures,
would need to be no more than an agreeable Employ; and divers
Branches of Business, which serve chiefly to please the natural
Inclinations of our Minds, and which, at present, seem necessary
to circulate that Wealth which some gather, might, in this Way
of pure Wisdom, be discontinued. And, as I have thus considered
these Things, a Query, at Times, hath arisen: Do I, in all my
Proceedings, keep to that Use of Things which is agreeable to
universal Righteousness? And then there hath some Degree of
Sadness, at Times, come over me, for that I accustomed myself to
some Things, which occasioned more Labour than I believe divine Wisdom intends for us.

From my early Acquaintance with Truth I have often felt an
inward Distress, occasioned by the striving of a Spirit in me
against the Operation of the heavenly Principle; and in this
Circumstance have been affected with a Sense of my own Wretchedness, and in a mourning Condition felt earnest Longing for that
divine Help, which brings the Soul into true Liberty; and sometimes, in this State, retiring into private Places, the Spirit of
Supplication hath been given me; and, under a heavenly Cover-

ing, I have asked my gracious Father to give me a Heart in all Things resigned to the Direction of his Wisdom.

In visiting People of Note in the Society who had Slaves, and labouring with them in brotherly Love on that Account, I have seen, and the Sight hath affected me, that a Conformity to some Customs, distinguishable from pure Wisdom, has entangled many; and the Desire of Gain, to support these Customs, greatly opposed the Work of Truth: And sometimes, when the Prospect of the Work before me has been such, that in Bowedness of Spirit, I have been drawn into retired Places, and besought the Lord with Tears that he would take me wholly under his Direction, and shew me the Way in which I ought to walk, it hath revived, with Strength of Conviction, that, if I would be his faithful Servant, I must, in all Things, attend to his Wisdom, and be teachable; and so cease from all Customs contrary thereto, however used amongst religious People.

As he is the Perfection of Power, of Wisdom, and of Goodness, so, I believe, he hath provided, that so much Labour shall be necessary for Men's Support, in this World, as would, being rightly divided, be a suitable Employment of their Time; and that we cannot go into Superfluities, or grasp after Wealth in a Way contrary to his Wisdom, without having Connection with some Degree of Oppression, and with that Spirit which leads to Self-exaltation and Strife, and which frequently brings Calamities on Countries, by Parties contending about their Claims.

In the eleventh Month of the Year 1762, feeling an Engagement of Mind to visit some Families in *Mansfield,* I joined my beloved Friend, BENJAMIN JONES, and we spent a few Days together in that Service. In the second Month, 1763, I joined in Company with ELIZABETH SMITH and MARY NOBLE on a Visit to the Families of Friends at *Ancocas;* in both which Visits, through the baptizing Power of Truth, the sincere Labourers were often comforted, and the Hearts of Friends opened to receive us. And, in the fourth Month following, I accompanied some Friends in a Visit to the Families of Friends in *Mount-Holly,* in which my Mind was often drawn into an inward Awfulness, wherein strong

Desires were raised for the everlasting Welfare of my Fellow-creatures; and, through the Kindness of our heavenly Father, our Hearts were, at Times, enlarged, and Friends invited, in the Flowings of divine Love, to attend to that which would settle them on the sure Foundation.

Having many Years felt Love in my Heart towards the Natives of this Land, who dwell far back in the Wilderness, whose Ancestors were the Owners and Possessors of the Land where we dwell; and who, for a very small Consideration, assigned their Inheritance to us; and, being at *Philadelphia,* in the eighth Month, 1761, in a Visit to some Friends who had Slaves, I fell in Company with some of those Natives who lived on the East Branch of the River *Susquehannah,* at an *Indian* Town called *Wehaloosing,* two hundred Miles from *Philadelphia,* and, in Conversation with them by an Interpreter, as also by Observations on their Countenances and Conduct, I believed some of them were measurably acquainted with that divine Power which subjects the rough and forward Will of the Creature: And, at Times, I felt inward Drawings toward a Visit to that Place, of which I told none except my dear Wife, until it came to some Ripeness; and, then, in the Winter, 1762, I laid it before Friends at our Monthly and Quarterly, and afterwards at our general Spring-meeting; and, having the Unity of Friends, and being thoughtful about an *Indian* Pilot, there came a Man and three Women from a little beyond that Town to *Philadelphia* on Business: And I, being informed thereof by Letter, met them in Town in the fifth Month, 1763; and, after some Conversation, finding they were sober People, I, by the Concurrence of Friends in that Place, agreed to join with them as Companions in their Return; and, on the seventh Day of the sixth Month following, we appointed to meet at SAMUEL FOULK's, at *Richland* in *Bucks* County. Now, as this Visit felt weighty, and was performed at a Time when Travelling appeared perilous, so the Dispensations of divine Providence, in preparing my Mind for it, have been memorable; and I believe it good for me to give some Hints thereof.

After I had given up to go, the Thoughts of the Journey were often attended with unusual Sadness; in which Times my Heart was frequently turned to the Lord with inward Breathings for his heavenly Support, that I might not fail to follow him wheresoever he might lead me: And, being at our Youths Meeting at *Chester-field,* about a Week before the Time I expected to set off, I was there led to speak on that Prayer of our Redeemer to his Father: "I pray not that thou shouldest take them out of the World, but that thou shouldest keep them from the Evil." And, in attending to the pure Openings of Truth, I had to mention what he else-where said to his Father; "I know that thou hearest me at all Times:" So that, as some of his Followers kept their Places, and as his Prayer was granted, it followed necessarily that they were kept from Evil: And, as some of those met with great Hardships and Afflictions in this World, and at last suffered Death by cruel Men, it appears, that whatsoever befalls Men while they live in pure Obedience to God, as it certainly works for their Good, so it may not be considered an Evil as it relates to them. As I spake on this Subject, my Heart was much tendered, and great Awful-ness came over me; and then, on the first Day of the next Week, being at our own Afternoon-meeting, and my Heart being en-larged in Love, I was led to speak on the Care and Protection of the Lord over his People, and to make mention of that Passage, where a Band of *Assyrians* endeavouring to take captive the Prophet, were disappointed; and how the Psalmist said, "The Angel of the Lord encampeth round about them that fear him." And thus, in true Love and Tenderness, I parted from Friends, expecting the next Morning, to proceed on my Journey, and, being weary, went early to Bed; and, after I had been asleep a short Time, I was awaked by a Man calling at my Door; and, arising, was invited to meet some Friends at a Publick-house in our Town, who came from *Philadelphia* so late, that Friends were generally gone to Bed: These Friends informed me, that an Express arrived the last Morning from *Pittsburgh,* and brought News that the *Indians* had taken a Fort from the *English* West-ward, and slain and scalped *English* People in divers Places, some near the said *Pittsburgh;* and that some elderly Friends in *Phila-*

delphia, knowing the Time of my expecting to set off, had conferred together, and thought good to inform me of these Things,
before I left Home, that I might consider them, and proceed as
I believed best; so I, going again to Bed, told not my Wife till
Morning. My Heart was turned to the Lord for his heavenly
Instruction; and it was an humbling Time to me. When I told
my dear Wife, she appeared to be deeply concerned about it; but,
in a few Hours Time, my Mind became settled in a Belief, that
it was my Duty to proceed on my Journey; and she bore it with
a good Degree of Resignation. In this Conflict of Spirit, there
were great Searchings of Heart, and strong Cries to the Lord,
that no Motion might be, in the least Degree, attended to, but
that of the pure Spirit of Truth.

The Subjects before-mentioned, on which I had so lately spoken
in publick, were now very fresh before me; and I was brought
inwardly to commit myself to the Lord, to be disposed of as he
saw best. So I took Leave of my Family and Neighbours, in much
Bowedness of Spirit, and went to our Monthly-meeting at *Burlington;* and, after taking Leave of Friends there, I crossed the
River, accompanied by my Friends, ISRAEL and JOHN PEMBERTON;
and, parting the next Morning with ISRAEL, JOHN bore me Company to SAMUEL FOULK's, where I met the before-mentioned
Indians, and we were glad to see each other: Here my Friend,
BENJAMIN PARVIN, met me, and proposed joining as a Companion, we having passed some Letters before on the Subject; and
now, on his Account, I had a sharp Trial; for, as the Journey appeared perilous, I thought, if he went chiefly to bear me Company, and we should be taken Captive, my having been the Means
of drawing him into these Difficulties would add to my own
Afflictions: So I told him my Mind freely, and let him know that
I was resigned to go alone; but, after all, if he really believed it
to be his Duty to go on, I believed his Company would be very
comfortable to me: It was indeed a Time of deep Exercise, and
BENJAMIN appeared to be so fastened to the Visit, that he could
not be easy to leave me; so we went on, accompanied by our
Friends, JOHN PEMBERTON, and WILLIAM LIGHTFOOT of *Pikeland,*

and lodged at *Bethlehem;* and there, parting with JOHN, WILLIAM and we went forward on the ninth Day of the sixth Month, and got Lodging on the Floor of a House, about five Miles from *Fort-Allen:* Here we parted with WILLIAM; and at this Place we met with an *Indian* Trader, lately come from *Wioming;* and, in Conversation with him, I perceived that many white People do often sell Rum to the *Indians,* which, I believe, is a great Evil; first, they being thereby deprived of the Use of their Reason, and their Spirits violently agitated, Quarrels often arise, which end in Mischief; and the Bitterness and Resentments, occasioned hereby, are frequently of long Continuance; Again, their Skins and Furs, gotten through much Fatigue and hard Travels in Hunting, with which they intended to buy Clothing, when they become intoxicated, they often sell at a low Rate for more Rum; and afterward, when they suffer for want of the Necessaries of Life, are angry with those who, for the Sake of Gain, took the Advantage of their Weakness: Of this their Chiefs have often complained, at their Treaties with the *English.* Where cunning People pass Counterfeits, and impose that on others which is good for nothing, it is considered as a Wickedness; but, to sell that to People which we know does them Harm, and which often works their Ruin, for the Sake of Gain, manifests a hardened and corrupt Heart, and is an Evil, which demands the Care of all true Lovers of Virtue to suppress: And while my Mind, this Evening, was thus employed, I also remembered, that the People on the Frontiers, among whom this Evil is too common, are often poor; who venture to the Outside of a Colony, that they may live more independent on such as are wealthy, who often set high Rents on their Land: Being renewedly confirmed in a Belief, that, if all our Inhabitants lived according to sound Wisdom, labouring to promote universal Love and Righteousness, and ceased from every inordinate Desire after Wealth, and from all Customs which are tinctured with Luxury, the Way would be easy for our Inhabitants, though much more numerous than at present, to live comfortably on honest Employments, without having that Temptation they are often under of being drawn into Schemes to make Settlements on Lands which have not been purchased of the *Indians,* or of applying to that wicked Practice of selling Rum to them.

On the tenth Day of the Month we set out early in the Morning, and crossed the Western Branch of *Delaware,* called the *Great Lehie,* near *Fort-Allen;* the Water being high, we went over in a Canoe: Here we met an *Indian,* and had some friendly Conversation with him, and gave him some Biscuit; and he having killed a Deer, gave the *Indians* with us some of it: Then, after travelling some Miles, we met several *Indian* Men and Women with a Cow and Horse, and some Household Goods, who were lately come from their Dwelling at *Wioming,* and going to settle at another Place; we made them some small Presents, and, some of them understanding *English,* I told them my Motive in coming into their Country, with which they appeared satisfied: And, one of our Guides talking a While with an ancient Woman concerning us, the poor old Woman came to my Companion and me, and took her Leave of us with an Appearance of sincere Affection. So, going on, we pitched our Tent near the Banks of the same River, having laboured hard in crossing some of those Mountains called the Blue-Ridge; and, by the Roughness of the Stones, and the Cavities between them, and the Steepness of the Hills, it appeared dangerous; but we were preserved in Safety, through the Kindness of him, whose Works in those mountainous Desarts appeared awful: Toward whom my Heart was turned during this Day's Travel.

Near our Tent, on the Sides of large Trees peeled for that Purpose, were various Representations of Men going to, and returning from the Wars, and of some killed in Battle; this being a Path heretofore used by Warriours: And, as I walked about viewing those *Indian* Histories, which were painted mostly in red, but some in black; and thinking on the innumerable Afflictions which the proud, fierce, Spirit produceth in the World; thinking on the Toils and Fatigues of Warriours, travelling over Mountains and Desarts; thinking on their Miseries and Distresses when wounded far from Home by their Enemies; and of their Bruises and great

Weariness in chasing one another over the Rocks and Mountains; and of their restless, unquiet, State of Mind, who live in this Spirit; and of the Hatred which mutually grows up in the Minds of the Children of those Nations engaged in War with each other: During these Meditations, the Desire to cherish the Spirit of Love and Peace amongst these People arose very fresh in me. This was the first Night that we lodged in the Woods; and, being wet with travelling in the Rain, the Ground, our Tent, and the Bushes, which we proposed to lay under our Blankets, being also wet, all looked discouraging; but I believed, that it was the Lord who had thus far brought me forward, and that he would dispose of me as he saw good; and therein I felt easy: So we kindled a Fire, with our Tent open to it; and, with some Bushes next the Ground, and then our Blankets, we made our Bed, and, lying down, got some Sleep; and, in the Morning, feeling a little un-well, I went into the River; the Water was cold, but soon after I felt fresh and well.

The eleventh Day of the sixth Month, the Bushes being wet, we tarried in our Tent till about eight o'Clock; when, going on, we crossed a high Mountain supposed to be upwards of four Miles over; the Steepness on the North Side exceeding all the others. We also crossed two Swamps, and, it raining near Night, we pitched our Tent and lodged.

About Noon, on our Way, we were overtaken by one of the *Moravian* Brethren, going to *Wehaloosing,* and an *Indian* Man with him, who could talk *English;* and we, being together while our Horses ate Grass, had some friendly Conversation; but they, travelling faster than we, soon left us. This *Moravian,* I under-stood, had spent some Time this Spring at *Wehaloosing,* and was, by some of the *Indians,* invited to come again.

The twelfth Day of the sixth Month, and first of the Week, it being a rainy Day, we continued in our Tent; and here I was led to think on the Nature of the Exercise which hath attended me: Love was the first Motion, and thence a Concern arose to spend some Time with the *Indians,* that I might feel and under-stand their Life, and the Spirit they live in, if haply I might receive some Instruction from them, or they be in any Degree helped forward by my following the Leadings of Truth amongst them: And, as it pleased the Lord to make Way for my going at a Time when the Troubles of War were increasing, and when, by Reason of much wet Weather, Travelling was more difficult than usual at that Season, I looked upon it as a more favourable Opportunity to season my Mind, and bring me into a nearer Sympathy with them: And, as mine Eye was to the great Father of Mercies, humbly desiring to learn what his Will was concerning me, I was made quiet and content.

Our Guide's Horse, though hoppled, went away in the Night; after finding our own, and searching some Time for him, his Footsteps were discovered in the Path going back again, whereupon my kind Companion went off in the Rain, and, about seven Hours after, returned with him: And here we lodged again; tying up our Horses before we went to Bed, and loosing them to feed about Break of Day.

On the thirteenth Day of the sixth month, the Sun appearing, we set forward; and, as I rode over the barren Hills, my Meditations were on the Alterations of the Circumstances of the Natives of this Land since the Coming in of the *English*. The Lands near the Sea are conveniently situated for fishing; the Lands near the Rivers, where the Tides flow, and some above, are in many Places fertile, and not mountainous; while the Running of the Tides makes passing up and down easy with any Kind of Traffic. Those Natives have, in some Places, for trifling Considerations, sold their Inheritance so favourably situated; and, in other Places, been driven back by superior Forces: So that in many Places, as their Way of clothing themselves is now altered from what it was, and they, far remote from us, have to pass over Mountains, Swamps, and barren Desarts, Travelling is very troublesome, in bringing their Skins and furs to trade with us.

By the extending of *English* Settlements, and partly by *English* Hunters, the wild Beasts, they chiefly depend on for a Subsistance, are not so plenty as they were; and People too often, for the Sake of Gain, open a Door for them to waste their Skins and Furs, in purchasing a Liquor which tends to the Ruin of them and their Families.

My own Will and Desires were now very much broken, and my Heart, with much Earnestness, turned to the Lord, to whom alone I looked for Help in the Dangers before me. I had a Prospect of the *English* along the Coast, for upwards of nine hundred Miles, where I had travelled; and the favourable Situation of the *English,* and the Difficulties attending the Natives in many Places, and the Negroes, were open before me; and a weighty and heavenly Care came over my Mind, and Love filled my Heart toward all Mankind, in which I felt a strong Engagement, that we might be obedient to the Lord, while, in tender Mercies, he is yet calling to us; and so attend to pure universal Righteousness, as to give no just Cause of Offence to the *Gentiles,* who do not profess *Christianity,* whether the Blacks from *Africa,* or the native Inhabitants of this Continent: And here I was led into a close laborious Enquiry, whether I, as an Individual, kept clear from all Things which tended to stir up, or were connected with Wars, either in this Land or *Africa;* and my Heart was deeply concerned, that, in future, I might in all Things keep steadily to the pure Truth, and live and walk in the Plainness and Simplicity of a sincere Follower of Christ. And, in this lonely Journey, I did, this Day, greatly bewail the Spreading of a wrong Spirit, believing, that the prosperous, convenient, Situation of the *English,* requires a constant Attention to divine Love and Wisdom to guide and support us in a Way answerable to the Will of that good, gracious, and almighty Being, who hath an equal Regard to all Mankind: And, here, Luxury and Covetousness, with the numerous Oppressions, and other Evils attending them, appeared very afflicting to me; and I felt in that which is immutable, that the Seeds of great Calamity and Desolation are sown and growing fast on this Continent: Nor have I Words sufficient to set forth that Longing I then felt, that we, who are placed along the Coast, and have tasted the Love and Goodness of God, might arise in his Strength; and, like faithful Messengers, labour to check the Growth of these Seeds, that they may not ripen to the Ruin of our Posterity.

.　.　.　.　.

THE AMERICAN AS AUGUSTAN POET

If, in the first half of the eighteenth century, colonial Americans could not produce a distinguished belles lettres, still they felt the need for one. Edward Taylor, it is true, was writing early in the century; yet his affinities in poetry as well as in religion were with the century before; and, like other Puritan poetry, his work derived its strength from a religious attitude alien to most Americans in his time. A Virginia gentleman such as William Byrd is more characteristic of his time than is Taylor. Byrd often indulged himself in flights of poetic fancy—but only briefly and with no high seriousness; for him esthetic experience was that which adorned a gentleman's leisure. His way, indeed, points to the way of most other colonial poets of the first half of the eighteenth century. They wrote poems enough, even devout poems; they were, however, poems *à la mode,* to be taken only as seriously as the time spent on them would allow. Literature represented high culture. High culture, the culture of learned, imaginative leisure, came from England. Americans who wanted to be highly cultured aspired to be cultured Englishmen. Thus the American, if he was to be a poet, was an Augustan poet, or none. Literary nationalism was still in the very dim future.

The poetry is not distinguished, certainly; and we should not take it very seriously. Still, we cannot afford to neglect it if we are to understand the nature of our colonial culture. It is a poetry of the kind which anonymous or pseudonymous Englishmen contributed to their *Gentleman's Magazine.* It represents all the proper modes—songs, satires, Miltonic imitations, and the like—in all the proper forms. It covers all the proper subject-matters—the foibles of colonial society, love for the classically named maiden, worship of the sublime deity, and celebration of neoclassical contentment. Yet we must read it not only for its imitativeness but for its significance to colonial Americans becoming conscious of their own need for imaginative maturity, happy to do in America what was done in England, determined, even in their leisure, to establish a civilization.

Bibliographical Note. There are no general studies of this period of American poetry except those in Tyler's *History* and the first volume of the *Literary History of the United States;* highly specialized studies are listed in the bibliographies in the third volume of the latter.

EBENEZER COOK

(fl. 1694-1729)

"THE SOTWEED FACTOR"

(1731)

Text: *The Maryland Muse,* ed. L. C. Wroth, *Proceedings of the American Antiquarian Society,* XLIV (1934), 327-335. "The Sotweed Factor" was first printed in a different version from that which follows, in 1708.

CONDEMN'D by Fate, to wayward Curse,
Of Friends unkind, and empty Purse,
Plagues worse than fill'd *Pandora's Box,*
I took my Leave of *Albion's Rocks,*
With heavy Heart, concern'd that I
Was forc'd my native Soil to fly,
And the old World must bid Good-b'ye:
But Heav'n ordain'd it shou'd be so,
And to repine is vain, we know.

FREIGHTED with Fools, from *Plimouth* Sound,
To *MARYLAND* our Ship was bound;
Where we arriv'd, in dreadul Pain,
Shock'd by the Terrors of the Main;
For full Three Months our wav'ring Boat
Did thro' the surly Ocean float,
And furious Storms and threatning Blasts,
Both split our Sails, and sprung our Masts:
Weary'd, yet pleas'd we did escape
Such Ills, we achor'd at the *Cape;*
But weighing soon, we plow'd the *Bay,*
To cove it in *Piscataway.*

INTENDING there to open Store,
I put myself and Goods on Shore,
Where soon repair'd a numerous Crew,

In Shirts and Draw'rs, of *Scotch*-cloth blew,
With neither Stocking, Hat, nor Shoe:
These *Sotweed* Planters crowd the Shore,
In Hew as tawny as a *Moor;*
Figures, so strange, no G O D design'd
To be a Part of Human-kind:
But wanton Nature, void of Rest,
Moulded the brittle Clay in Jest.

AT last, a Fancy very odd,
Took me, This was *The Land of Nod,*
Planted at first when Vagrant *Cain*
His Brother had unjustly slain;
Then, conscious of the Crime he'd done,
From Vengeance dire hither run,
And in a Hut supinely dwelt,
The first in *Furrs* and *Sotweed* dealt:
And ever since that Time, this Place
Has harbour'd a detested Race,
Who, when they could not thrive at Home;
For Refuse to these Worlds did roam,
In Hopes by Flight they might prevent
The Devil, and his fell Intent,
Obtain from Tripple-Tree Reprieve,
And Heav'n and Hell alike deceive:
But e're their Manners I display,
I think it fit I open lay
My Entertainment by the Way,
That Strangers well may be aware on
What homely Diet they must fare on;
To see that Shore where no good sense is found,
But Conversation's lost, and Manners drown'd.
I cross'd unto the other Side
A River, whose impetuous Tide,
Those *Salvage* Borders do divide,
In such a swimming odd Invension,

I scarce can give it's due Dimension,
The *Indians* call this watry Waggon,
Canoe, a Vessel none can brag on,
Cut from a Poplar Tree, or Pine,
And fashion'd like a Trough for Swine:
In this most noble Fishing-boat,
I boldly put my self afloat,
Standing erect, with Legs stretch'd wide,
We paddled to the other Side;
Where being landed safe by Hap,
(As *Sol* fell into *Thetis'* Lap)
A ravenous Gang, bent on the Strowl,
Of Wolves for Prey, began to howl:
This put me in a pannick Fright,
Lest I shou'd be devour'd quite:
But as I there a Musing stood,
And quite benighted in the Wood,
A Female Voice pierc'd thro' my Ears,
Crying, You Rogue drive home the Steers:
I listen'd that attractive Sound,
And streight A Herd of Cattle found,
Drove by a Youth, and homeward bound.
Cheer'd with the Sight, I streight thought fit
To ask, Where I a Bed might get?
The surly Peasant bid me stay,
And ask'd, From whom I'd run away?
Surpris'd at such a sawcy Word,
I instantly lugg'd out my Sword,
Swearing I was no Fugitive,
But from *Great Britain* did arrive,
In hopes I here might better thrive.
To which he mildly made Reply,
I beg your Pardon, Sir, that I
Shou'd talk to you unmannerly:
But if you please to go with me,
To yonder House you'll welcome be.

ENCOUNTRING soon the smoaky Seat,
The Planter old did thus me greet,
Whether You're come from Gaol, or College,
You're Welcome, to my certain Knowledge,
And if You'll please all Night to stay,
My Son shall put You in the Way:
Which Offer I most kindly took,
And for a Seat did round me look,
When presently among the rest
He plac'd his unknown *English* Guest,
Who found 'em drinking, for a Whet,
A Cask of Sider on the Fret:
'Till Supper came upon the Table,
On which I fed whilst I was able;
So after hearty Entertainment,
Of Drink and Victuals, without Payment,
For Planters Tables, you must know
Are free for all that come and go,
Whilst Pone, with Milk and Mush well stor'd,
In wooden Dishes grac'd the Board,
With Hominy and Sider-Pap,
Which scarce an *English* Dog would lap,
Well stuff'd with Fat from Bacon fry'd,
And with Melasses dulcify'd.
Than out our Landlord pulls his Pouch,
As greasy as the Leather Couch
On which he sat, and streight begun
To load with Weed his *Indian* Gun,
In Length scarce longer than one's Finger,
Or that for which the Ladies linger.
His Pipe smoak'd out, with awful Grace,
With Aspect grave and solemn Pace,
The Reverend Sir, walks to a Chest,
Of all his Furniture the best,
Closely confin'd within a Room,
Which seldom felt the Weight of Broom:

From thence he lugs a Cagg of Rum,
And nodding to me, thus begun:
I find, says he, *you don't much care*
For this our Indian *Country Fare;*
But let me tell you, Friend of mine,
You may be glad of it in Time,
Tho' now you're Stomach is so fine;
And if within this Land you stay,
You'll find it true what I do say:
This said, the Rundlet up he threw,
And bending backwards strongly drew;
I pluck'd as stoutly, for my Part,
Altho' it made me sick at Heart,
And got so soon into my Head,
I scarce could find my Way to Bed;
Where I was instantly convey'd,
By one that pass'd for Chamber-Maid,
Tho' by her loose and sluttish Dress,
She rather seem'd a *Bedlam-Bess.*
Curious to know from whence she came,
I press'd her to declare her Name?
She blushing, seem'd to hide her Eyes,
And thus in civil Terms replies:
In better Times, o'er to this Land
I was unhappily trepann'd,
Perchance as well I did appear,
As any Gentlewoman here,
Not then a Slave for Twice Two Year;
My Cloaths were fashionably new,
Nor were my Shifts of Scotch *Cloth blew:*
But Things are chang'd: Now at the Hoe
I daily work, and barefoot go,
In weeding Corn, and feeding Swine,
I spend my melancholly Time;
Kidnapp'd and fool'd, I hither fled,
To shun a hated Nuptial Bed;

And, to my Grief, already find
Worse Plagues than those I left behind.

WHATE'ER the Wand'rer did profess,
Good faith I cou'd not chuse but guess
The Cause which brought her to this Place,
Was Supping e're the Priest said Grace:
Quick as my Thoughts the Slave was fled,
Her Candle left to shew my Bed,
Which, made of Feathers soft and good,
Close in the Chimney-corner stood:
I laid me down, expecting Rest,
To be in Golden Slumbers blest;
But soon a Noise disturb'd my Quiet,
And plagu'd me with Nocturnal Riot:
A Puss, which in the Ashes lay,
With grunting Pig, began a Fray,
And prudent Dog, that Feuds might cease,
Most sharply bark'd, to keep the Peace:
This Quarrel scarcely was decided
By Stick, that ready lay provided,
But *Reynard,* arch and cunning Loon,
Crept into my Apartment soon,
In hot Pursuit of Ducks and Geese,
With full Intent the same to seize;
Their cackling Plaints with strange Surprise
Chac'd Sleep's thick Vapours from my Eyes;
Raging, I jump'd upon the Floor,
And like a drunken Sailor swore,
With Sword I fiercely laid about,
And soon dispers'd the feather'd Rout,
The Poultry out of Window flew,
And *Reynard* cautiously withdrew;
The Dogs who this Encounter heard,
Fiercely themselves to aid me rear'd,
And to the Place of Combat run,

Exactly as the Field was won,
Fretting and hot as roasted Capon,
And Greasy as a Flitch of Bacon.

I to the Orchard did repair,
To breathe the cool and open Air,
Impatient waiting for bright Day,
Extended on a Bank I lay;
But Fortune here, that sawcy Whore,
Disturb'd me worse, and plagu'd me more
Than she had done the Night before;
Hoarse croaking Frogs did round me ring,
Such Peals the Dead to Life wou'd bring,
A Noise might move their Wooden King:
I stuff'd my Ears with Cotton white,
And curs'd the melancholly Night,
For fear of being deaf outright:
But soon my Vows I did recant,
And *Hearing* as a Blessing grant,
When a confounded *Rattle-Snake*
With Hissing made my Heart to ach,
Not knowing how to fly the Foe,
Or whither in the dark to go,
By strange good Luck I took a Tree,
Prepar'd by Fate to set me free,
Where, riding on a Limb astride,
Night and the Branches did me hide,
And I the De'el and Snake defy'd.
Not yet from Plagues exempted quite,
The curs'd *Muschetoes* did me bite;
'Til rising Morn, and blushing Day,
Drove both my Fears and Ills away,
And from Night's Terrors set me free,
Discharg'd from hospitable Tree.
I did to Planter's Booth repair,
And there at Breakfast nobly fare,

On Rasher broil'd, of infant Bear;
I thought the Cubb delicious Meat,
Which ne'er did ought but Chesnuts eat,
Nor was young *Orson's* Flesh the worse,
Because he suck'd a *Pagan* Nurse:
Our Breakfast done, the Planter stout,
Handed a Glass of Rum about.

PLEAS'D with the Treatment I did find,
I took my Leave of Host so kind,
Who, to oblige me, did provide
His eldest Son to be my Guide;
And let me Horses of his own,
A skittish Colt and aged Roan,
The four legg'd Prop of his Wife Joan.
Steering our Course in Trott or Pace,
We sail'd directly for a Place,
In *MARYLAND* of high Renown;
Known by the Name of *Battle-Town:*
To view the Crowds did there resort,
Which Justice made, and Law, their Sport,
In their Sagacious Country Court:
Scarce had we enter'd on the Way,
Which thro' the Woods and Marshes lay,
But *Indian* strange did soon appear
In hot Pursuit of wounded Deer;
No moral Creature can express
His wild fantastick Air and Dress;
His painted Skin, in Colours dy'd,
His sable Hair, in Satchel ty'd,
Show'd *Salvages* not free from Pride:
His tawny Thighs and Bosom bare,
Disdain'd an useless Coat to wear,
Scorn'd Summers Heat and Winters Air;
His manly Shoulders, such as please
Widows and Wives, were bath'd with Grease,

Of Cub and Bear, whose supple Oil,
Prepar'd his Limbs in Heat and Toil.

THUS naked Picts in Battle fought,
Or undisguid'd his Mistress sought;
And knowing well his Ware was good,
Refus'd to skreen it with a Hood:
His Visage Dun, and Chin that near
Did Razor feel, nor Scissars bear,
Or know the Ornament of Hair,
Look'd sternly grim; surpriz'd with Fear,
I spurr'd my Horse as he drew near;
But Roan, who better knew than I,
The little Cause I had to fly,
Seem'd by his solemn Step and Pace,
Resolv'd I shou'd the Spector face,
Nor faster mov'd, tho' spurr'd and prick'd,
Than *Balam's* Ass by Prophet kick'd;
Kekicnatop, the *Heathen* cry'd,
How is it *Tom,* my Friend reply'd;
Judging from thence, the Brute was civil,
I boldly fac'd the courteous Devil,
And lugging out a Dram of Rum,
I gave his tawny Worship some;
Who in his Language as I guess,
My Guide informing me no less,
Implor'd the Devil me to bless:
I thank'd him for his good Intent,
And forward on my Journey went;
Discoursing as along I rode,
Whether this Race was fram'd of G O D,
Or whether some malignant Power,
Had fram'd them in an evil Hour,
And from his own infernal Look,
Their dusky Form and Image took.

FROM hence we fell to Argument
Whence peopl'd was this Continent?
My Friend suppos'd *Tartarians* wild,
Or *Chinese*, from their home exil'd,
Wandring thro' Mountains hid with Snow,
And Rills that in the Valleys flow,
Far to the *South* of *Mexico*,
Broke thro' the Bars which Nature cast,
And wide unbeaten Regions past;
'Till near those Streams the human Deluge roll'd,
Which sparkling shin'd with glittering Sands of Gold;
And fetch'd *Pisarro* from the *Iberian* Shore
To rob the *Indians* of their native Store.

I smil'd to hear my young Logician,
Thus reason like a Polititian;
Who ne'r by Father's Pains and Earning,
Had got, at Mother, *Cambridge* Learning;
Where lubber Youth just free from Birch,
Most stoutly drink to prop the Church;
Nor with grey Coat had taken Pains
To purge his Head, and cleanse his Reins;
And in Obedience to the College,
Had pleas'd himself with carnal Knowledge;
And tho' I lik'd the Youngster's Wit,
I judg'd the Truth he had not hit;
And could not chuse but smile to think,
What they cou'd do for Meat and Drink,
Who o'er so many Desarts ran,
With Brats and Wives in Carravan;
Unless perchance they'd got a Trick,
To eat no more than Porker sick,
Or could with well-contented Maws,
Quarter like Bears upon their Paws:
Thinking his Reason to confute,

I gravely thus commenc'd Dispute;
And urg'd, that tho' a *Chinese* Host
Might penetrate this *Indian* Coast,
Yet this was certainly most true,
They never could the Isles subdue;
For knowing not to steer a Boat,
They could not on the Ocean float,
Or plant their Sun-burnt Colonies,
In Regions parted by the Seas:
I thence inferr'd, *Phoenicians* old
Discover'd first, with Vessels bold,
These *Western* Shores, and planted here,
Returning once or twice a Year,
With Naval Stores, and Lasses kind,
To comfort those were left behind;
'Till by the Winds and Tempests tore,
From their intended golden Shore,
They suffer'd Shipwreck, or were drown'd,
And lost the World so newly found:
But after long and learn'd Contention,
We could not finish our Dissention;
And when that both had talk'd their Fill,
We had the self same Notion still.

THUS Parson Grave well read, and Sage,
Does in Dispute with Priest engage,
The one protests they are not wise,
Who judge by Sense, and trust their Eyes,
And vows he'd burn for it at Stake,
That Man may GOD his Maker make;
The other smiles at his Religion,
And vows he's but a learned Widgeon,
And when they've emptied all their Store,
From Books and Fathers, are not more
Convinc'd, or wiser than before.

SCARCE had we finish'd serious Story,
But I espy'd the Town before me;
And roaring Planters on the Ground,
Drinking of Healths, in Circle round:
Dismounting Steed with friendly Guide,
Our Horses to a Tree we ty'd,
And forward pass'd amongst the Rout,
To chuse convenient Quarters out;
But being none were to be found,
We sat like others on the Ground,
Carousing Punch in open Air,
'Till Cryer did the Court declare:
The planting Rabble being met,
Their drunken Worships like wise sat,
Cryer proclaims the Noise shou'd cease,
And streight the Lawyers broke the Peace,
Wrangling for Plantiff and Defendant,
I thought they ne'r wou'd make an End on't,
With Nonsense, Stuff, and false Quotations,
With brazen Lies, and Allegations;
And in the Splitting of the Cause,
Us'd such strange Motions with their Paws,
As shew'd their Zeal was rather bent
In Blows to end the Argument.
A Reverend Judge, who to the Shame,
Of all the Bench, cou'd write his Name,
At Petty-Fogger took Offence,
And wonder'd at his Impudence:
My Neighbour *Dash,* with Scorn replies,
And in the Face of Justice flies;
And Scribles take on Judge's Side;
The Jury, Lawyers, and their Clients,
Contending, fight, like Earth-born Giants,
'Till Sh'riff that slily lay perdue,
Hoping Indictments would ensue;
And when—

A Hat or Wig fell in the Way,
He seiz'd 'em for the Queen, as Stray;
The Court adjourn'd in usual Manner,
In Battle, Blood and fractious Clamour.

   I thought it proper to provide,
A Lodging for my self and Guide,
So to our Inn we march'd away,
Which at a little Distance lay;
Where all Things were in such Confusion,
I thought the World at its Conclusion;
A Heard of Planters on the Ground,
O'rewhelm'd with Punch, dead Drunk we found;
Others were fighting and contending,
Some burn'd their Cloaths, to save the mending;
A few whose Heads, by frequent Use,
Could better bear the potent Juice,
Gravely debated State Affairs,
Whilst I most nimbly tripp'd up Stairs,
Leaving my Friend discoursing oddly,
And mixing Things Prophane and Godly;
Just then beginning to be drunk,
As from the Company I slunk:
To every Room and Nook I crept,
In hopes I might have somewhere slept;
But all the Beding was possest,
By one or other drunken Guest;
But after looking long about,
I found an antient Corn-loft out;
Glad that I might in Quiet sleep,
And there my Bones unfractur'd keep:
I laid me down secur'd from Fray,
And soundly snor'd 'till break o'Day;
When waking fresh, I sat upright,
And found my Shoes were vanish'd quite,
Hat, Wig, and Stockings, all were fled,

From this extended *Indian* Bed:
Vex'd at the Loss of Goods and Chattle,
I swore I'd give the Rascal Battle,
Who had abus'd me in this Sort,
And Merchant-Stranger made his Sport:
I furiously descended Ladder,
No Hare in *March* was ever madder,
And did with Host and Servants quarrel,
But all in vain, for my Apparel;
For one whose Mind did much aspire
To Mischief, threw them in the Fire.
Equipp'd with neither Hat nor Shoe,
I did my coming hither rue,
And doubtful thoughts what I should do:
When looking round I saw my Friend,
Lye naked on a Table's End,
A Sight so dismal to behold,
One would have thought him dead and cold,
There ready laid, to be next Day
On Shoulders Four convey'd away:
'Till wringing of his bloody Nose,
By fighting got, we may suppose,
I found him not so fast asleep,
Might give his Friends some cause to weep:
Rise *Oronoko,* rise, said I,
And from this *Hell* and *Bedlam* fly:
My Guide starts up, and in a Maze,
With Bloodshot Eyes did round him gaze,
At Length with many Sigh and Groan,
He went in search of aged Roan;
But Roan who seldom us'd to falter,
Had fairly this Time slipt his Halter,
And not content all Night to stay,
Ty'd up from Fodder, run away;
After my Guide to catch him ran,
And so I lost both Horse and Man;

Which Disappointment tho' so great,
Did only Jest and Mirth create:
'Till one more civil than the rest,
In Conversation far the best,
Observing that for want of Roan,
I shou'd be left to walk alone,
Most readily did me intreat,
To take a Bottle at his Seat,
A Favour at that Time so great,
I blest my kind propitious Fate;
And finding soon a fresh Supply
Of Cloaths, from Store-House kept hard by,
I mounted streight on such a Steed,
Did rather Curb than Whipping need;
And Straining at the usual Rate,
With Spur of Punch which lies in Pate,
E'er long we lighted at the Gate;
Where in an antient Cedar-House,
Dwelt my new Friend, a *Cockerouse,*
Whose Fabrick, tho' 'twas built of Wood,
Had many Springs and Winters stood:
When sturdy Oaks and lofty Pines,
Were levell'd with Musk-Melon-Vines,
And Plants eradicated were,
By Hurricans drove in the Air:
There with good Punch and Apple Juice,
We spent our Time without Abuse,
'Till Midnight in her sable Vest,
Persuaded Gods and Men to rest;
And with a pleasing kind Surprize,
Indulg'd soft Slumber to my Eyes.

FIERCE Æthon, Courser of the Sun,
Had half his Race exactly Run,
And breath'd on me a furious Ray,
Darting hot Beams the following Day,

When Rug in Blanket white, I lay;
But Heat and Chinces rais'd the Sinner,
Most opportunely to his Dinner;
Wild Fowl and Fish delicious Meats,
As good as *Neptune's* Doxy eats,
Began our hospitable Chear,
Fat Venison follow'd in the Rear,
And Turkeys-wild, luxurious Fare:
But what the Feast did most commend,
Was hearty Welcome from my Friend.

    THUS having made a noble Feast,
I eat as well as pamper'd Priest;
Madera strong in flowing Bowles,
Fill'd with extreme Delight our Souls;
'Till wearied with a purple Flood,
Of gen'rous Wine, the Giants Blood,
As Poets feign, away I made
For some refreshing verdant Shade;
Where musing on my Rambles strange,
And Fortune, which so oft did change,
In midst of various Contemplations,
Of Fancies odd and Meditations,
I slumber'd long,—
'Till airy Night and noxious Dews,
Did Sleep's unwholsome Fetters loose,
With Vapours cold and misty Air,
To Fire-side I did repair;
Near which a jolly Female Crew,
Were deep engag'd at *Lanterloo*,
In Nightrails white, with dirty Mien,
Such Sights are scarce in *England* seen:
I thought them first some Witches, bent
On black Designs, in dire Convent;
'Till one who with affected Air,
Had nicely learn'd to Curse and Swear,

Cry'd, *Dealing's lost, 'tis but a Flam,*
And vow'd by G— *she'd have her Pam:*
When Dealing thro' the Board had run,
They ask'd me kindly, *to make one:*
Not staying often to be bid,
I sate me down as others did;
We scarce had play'd a Round about,
But that those *Indian* Frows fell out:
D-m you, says one, *tho' now so Brave,*
I knew you late a Four Years Slave,
What, if for Planter's Wife you go,
Nature design'd you for the Hoe:
Rot you, replies the other streight,
The Captain kiss'd you for his Freight;
And if the Truth was known aright,
And how you walk'd the Streets by Night,
You'd blush, if one could blush for Shame,
Who from Bridewell *and* Newgate *came.*
From Words they fairly fell to Blows,
And being loth to interpose,
Or meddle in the Wars of Punk,
Away to Bed in Haste I slunk:
Waking next Day with aking Head,
And Thirst that made me quit the Bed,
I rigg'd my self and soon got up,
To cool my Liver with a Cup
Of *Succahanah* fresh and clear,
Not half so good as *English* Beer,
Which ready stood in Kitchin Pail,
And was, in Fact, but *Adam's* Ale.

FOR Planters Cellars, you must know,
Seldom with good *October* flow,
But Perry, Quince, and Apple Juice,
Spout from the Tap, like any Sluice,
Until the Cask grows low and stale,

They're forc'd again to Goard and Pail,
The soothing Draught scarce down my Throat,
Enough to set a Ship on float,
With *Cockerouse* as I was sitting
I felt a Fever intermitting,
A fiery Pulse beat in my Veins,
From cold I felt resembling Pains;
This cursed Seasoning I remember,
Lasted from *March* 'till cold *December;*
Nor could it then its Quarter shift,
Until by *Carduus* turn'd adrift:
And had my Doct'ress wanted Skill,
Or Kitchin-Phisick at her Will
My Father's Son has lost his Lands,
And never seen the *Goodwin Sands:*
But Thanks to *Fortune,* and a *Nurse,*
Whose Care depended on my Purse,
I saw my self in good Condition,
Without the Help of a Phisician:
At length the shivering Ill reliev'd
My Heart and Head, which long had griev'd.

I then began to think with Care,
How I might sell my *British* Ware;
That with my Freight I might comply,
Did on my Charter-Party lye:
To this Intent, with Guide before,
I tript it to the *Eastern* Shore;
Where riding near a Sandy Bay,
I met a Planter in my Way,
A pious, consciencious Rogue,
As e're wore Bonnet, Hat, or Brogue,
Who neither swore, nor kept his Word,
But cheated in the Fear o' th'Lord;
And when his Debts he could not pay,
From trusting Fools he'd run away.

WITH this sly Zealot, soon I struck
A Bargain, for my *English* Truck,
Agreeing for Ten Thousand Weight
Of *Sotweed* good, and fit for Freight:
Broad *Oronoko,* bright and sound,
The Growth and Product of his Ground;
In Cask, that shou'd contain compleat
Five Hundred of Tobacco neat.

THE Contract thus betwixt us made,
Not well acquainted with the Trade,
My Goods I trusted to the Cheat,
Whose Crop was then o'board the Fleet;
And going to receive my own,
I found the Bird was newly flown:
Cursing this execrable Slave
This damn'd pretended Godly Knave,
On due Revenge and Justice bent,
I instantly to Council went;
Unto an ambodexter Quack,
Who learnedly had got the Knack
Of giving Clysters, making Pills,
Of filling Bonds, and forging Wills;
And with a Stock of Impudence,
Supply'd his want of Wit and Sence,
With Looks demure, amazing People,
No wiser than a Daw on Steeple:
My Anger flushing in my Face,
I stated the preceeding Case,
And of my Money was so free
That he'd have poison'd you or me,
And hang'd his Father on a Tree,
For such another tempting Fee.

SMILING, said he, the Cause is clear,
I'll manage him, you need not fear,

The Case is judg'd, good Sir, but look
In *Galen,* no, in my Lord Cook,
I vow to G-d, I was mistook:
I'll take out a Provincial Writ,
And trownce him for his knavish Wit,
Upon my Life, I'll win the Cause,
With as much Ease I cure the Yaws:
Resolv'd to plague the Holy Brother,
I set one Rogue to catch another.

TO try the Cause then fully bent,
Up to *Annapolis* I went,
A City situate on a Plain,
[1] Where scarce a House will keep out Rain;
The Buildings fram'd with *Cypress* rare,
Resembles much our *Southwark-Fair;*
But Strangers there will scarcely meet,
With Market Place, Exchange, or Street;
And if the Truth I may report,
It's not so large as *Tottenham-Court.*
St. Mary's once was in Repute,
Now Here the Judges try the Suit,
And Lawyers twice a Year dispute.
As oft the Bench most gravely meet,
Some to get drink, and some to eat
A swinging Share of Country Treat:
But as for Justice write or wrong,
Not one amongst the numerous Throng
Knows what it means, or has the Heart,
To vindicate a Stronger's Part.

NOW, Court being call'd by beat of Drum,
The Judges left their Punch and Rum;
When Pettifogging Doctor draws

---

[1] This Account of Annapolis was given Twenty Years ago, and does not resemble its present State.—*Cook, referring to the edition of 1708.*

His Papers forth, and opens Cause;
And lest I should the Better get,
Brib'd Quack suppress'd his knavish Wit:
So Maid upon the downy Field,
Pretends a Rape, and fights to yield:
The byass'd Court without Delay,
Adjudg'd my Debt in Country Pay,
In Pipe Staves, Corn, or Flesh of Boar,
Rare Cargo for the *English* Shore.
Raging with Grief, full Speed I ran,
To join the Fleet at *Kickatan*:
And while I waited for a Wind,
This Wish proceeded from my Mind,

   IF any Youngster cross the Ocean,
To sell his Wares—may he with Caution
Before he pays, receive each Hogshead,
Lest he be cheated by some Dogshead,
Both of his Goods and his Tobacco;
And then like me, he shall not lack-woe.
   AND may that Land where Hospitality
Is every Planter's darling Quality,
Be by each Trader kindly us'd,
And may no Trader be abus'd;
Then each of them shall deal with Pleasure,
And each encrease the other's Treasure.

WILLIAM DAWSON
(1704-1752)

"HYMN TO THE MORNING" *
(1736)

Text: *Poems on Several Occasions,* ed. R. L. Rusk (New York, 1930), pp. 5-8.

Awake, my Soul, and with the constant Morn,
Carol th' ALMIGHTY's Praise; awake and tune
The vocal Shell to sympathetic Sounds,
And heav'nly Consort. See! the radiant Sun
Stains with etherial Gold the varied *East,*
And vast Expanse; behold! with Giant stride
He' advances ruddy, and with him returns
The sweet Vicissitude of Day, and all
The' obsequious Train of filial Colours. Now
The vivid Green extends her welcome Sway
O'er the sequester'd Lawns, and smiling Meads:
And now the purpled *Violet* resumes
Its costly Dye; and all th' extended Plains
Confess th' ALMIGHTY's Hand, of Ornament
Profuse. Behold! with fleshy *Pink* they smile
Enamel'd, and the *Daisy's* dwarfy Bloom
Of pallid Hue, and gorgeous *Marygold.*

ON ev'ry grassy Sprig a pearly Drop
Hangs wav'ring, and with varied Ray proclaims
Its great Progenitor. The liquid Gem,
Pendent and tremulous, with rival Gleam
Mimicks the Lustre of its Parent Orb.
Vain Man's best Emblem! who with BORROW'D LIGHT
Which EV'RY TOUCH DESTROYS, against his GOD
Dares wage an impious and gigantic War.

---

* Reprinted by courtesy of the Columbia University Press.

FROM downy Nest of artificial Weft
The sedulous Airlings rise, and to their Task
Hye joious. Or with gamesome Wing they cut
The yielding Fluent, and with transient Touch
Skim the moist Element in sportive Whirl:
Or else to studious Wand'rer's curious View
Delightful, they collect their grainy Food
And masticative Stones. But heark! the Grove,
Respondent to the tuneful Choir, resound
Celestial Symphony. The speckled *Thrush*
Of various Note, and *Blackbirds* piercing Sound,
Conjoin'd to *Philomela's* parting Lay,
Mournfully sweet, conspire to usher in
The pompous Morn. Nor shall my only Voice
Be wanting in the general Hymn: Of Song
Unskilful, yet with grateful Hand I'll touch
The trembling String, and chant th' ALMIGHTY'S Praise.
Vagrant, like the industrious Bee, I'll cull
Nature's choice Sweets, and still with prying Ken
Descry the Wonders of her fruitful Womb.

BUT see! the great Exemplar of my Verse,
The Lab'rer Bee, assiduous rise! Behold!
From waxen Cell and more inglorious Ease,
Active he hastens, and with hov'ring Buzz
Extracts mellific Juice. From Bloom to Bloom
He wanders dainty, and with nice Discern
Rejects each vulgar Sweet. Hail, mighty Chief!
Hyblaan Wand'rer, hail! Still may'st thou sip
The pure and elemental Dews; whilst I,
With daring Song, and more advent'rous Foot,
Attempt the steepy Heights, where MILTON first,
Great Chieftain, solitary trod; and taught
The list'ning World, what MICHAEL's potent Arm
In Fight could do, and human Wit atchieve.

"SONG"

(*1736*)

Text: *Poems on Several Occasions*, pp. 21-22.

YOUNG Poets, in Love,
Will call from above
Cytherea, drest all in her Graces and Airs;
And will tell their fond Dreams of *Ida's* soft Grove,
Of Cupids, of Doves, and of Carrs.

SOME *Cloe* beside,
Or *Sylvia* must hide
The Name of the Fair that possesses their Heart.
Thus fighting in Pomp of Poetical Pride,
They vainly make Shew of their Art.

NO Poet am I,
And no Dame of the Sky,
No Fiction shall ever disgrace my bright Flame;
That the Truth is most beautiful, none will deny,
When I tell them, that —————— is her Name.

THEN fill up my Glass;
Here's a Health to the Lass:
As for *Venus,* I fairly now bid you Adieu;
Since on her you can never reflect any Praise,
I'll not labour to compliment you.

MATHER BYLES

(*1707-1788*)

"WRITTEN IN MILTON'S *PARADISE LOST*" *

(*1744*)

Text: *Poems on Several Occasions,* ed. C. L. Carlson (New York, 1940), pp. 25-34.

Had I, O had I all the tuneful Arts
Of lofty Verse; did ev'ry Muse inspire
My flowing Numbers, and adorn my Song!
Did Milton's Fire flash furious in my Soul;
Could I command the Harmony, the Force,
The glitt'ring Language, and the true Sublime
Whose mingled Beauties grace his glowing Lays,
Then should my Lines glide languishingly slow,
Or thundring roar, and rattle as they fleet,
Or, lovely-smiling, bud immortal Bloom,
As various as the Subjects they describe,
And imitate the Beauties which they mark.
Thus with ambitious Hand, I'd boldly snatch
A spreading Branch from his immortal Laurels.

But, O my Muse, where shall thy Song begin?
Or where conclude? ten thousand Glories charm
My ravish'd Heart, and dance before my Sight.
O Milton! I'm transported at thy Name!
My Soul takes Wing at once; or shoots away,
Born eager by a Tyde of Thought along

Sometimes big Fury swells thy awful Verse,
And rolling Thunder bursts along thy Lines.
Now Hell is open'd, and I see the Flames
Wide-waving, blazing high, and flutt'ring dance:
Now clanking Chains amaze my list'ning Ears,

* Reprinted by courtesy of the Columbia University Press.

And hideous Spectres skim before my Sight.
Or in my wild Imagination stare.

Here *Satan* rears his mighty Bulk on high,
And tow'rs amid th' infernal Legions; fill'd
With Pride, and dire Revenge; daring his Looks;
Rage heaves his lab'ring Breast, and all around
His fiery Eye-balls formidably roll,
And dart destructive Flames; with dreadful Blaze
The ruddy Ligh'ning rapid runs along,
And guilds the gloomy Regions of Despair,
With Streaks tremendous. Here assaults my Sight
The gressly Monster *Death,* He onward stalks
With horrid Strides, Hell trembles as he treads;
On his fierce Front a bold defiance low'rs;
Bent is his Brow, in his right Hand he shakes
His quiv'ring Lance. How fell the Fiend appears
In ev'ry Prospect, wrathful or serene?
Pleas'd, *horrible he grins a gastly Smile;*
And *Erebus* grows blacker as he Frowns.

But tell, immortal Muse, O Goddess! tell
The joyful Dread, the terrible Delight,
Which fill my Mind, when I behold the Ranks,
Th' embatt'led Ranks of mighty Cherubim,
In dreadful Quadrate croud the Plains of Heav'n.
I hear, I hear the Trumpets loud Alarms;
The keen Vibration cuts the yielding Air,
And the shril Clangors ring around the Sky.
I see the bold intrepid Cohorts move;
From ev'ry Scabbard flies a flaming Sword,
Wav'd by the mighty Combatants on high,
So flashing radiant from a gloomy Cloud,
Long Lightnings flourish with a livid Glare.
Now on at once th' immortal Hero's rush,
And with a sudden Onset shake the Field.

Hark! how confus'd Sounds thicken in the Air,
Mingling, tumultous, and perplex'd, and rough,
Of Shouts, and Groans, and grating Clang of Arms,
The twanging Bow, the Lav'lins deadly Hiss,
Loud-clashing Swords, and Spears encountring Spears.
Helms found on Helms, on Bucklers Bucklers ring.
Vast waving Wings high in the Air are heard,
Whilst loud-resounding Feet beat thick the Ground,
And all the jarring Sounds of War unite,
In direful Discord, and outragious Roar.
    Behold, my Muse, where Michael bends his Course,
Starts his swift Car, and bounds impetuous on,
With rapid Rage it rattles thro' the Ranks,
Smokes o'er the Field, and drives the War along.

    But who can tell the Raptures which I feel,
When fix'd in deep Astonishment, my Eyes
Behold Messiah, dread Messiah! arm'd
With all the dire Artillery of God?
Unnumber'd Seraphim around him throng,
Clap their expanded Wings, and shout aloud;
Heav'ns mighty Concave echo's to their Voice,
The everlasting Hills return the Sound.
Oh! how I feel the noble Ardor warm
My beating Breast, and thrill along my Veins!
My charging Spirits pour around my Heart;
My Eyes bright-sparkling with immortal Fires.
His flying Chariot shakes the tott'ring Sky,
Swift all the vast Expanse behind him rolls,
Resistless Thunders rattle from his Hand,
Devouring Lightnings shoot beneath his Feet,
Ten thousand Terrors thicken where he bends.
What Havock! What Confusion spreads the Plain!
What Myriads fall by his descending Bolts,
Dash'd to the Ground, and crush'd beneath his Wheels?
Tumult and Ruin, Horror, Rage and Death,

Play round his Sword, and shake their shaggy Wings:
Hell flames before him, wild Despair stalks on,
And Purple Vict'ry hovers o'er his Head.
Great GOD! what Vengeance kindled in thy Eyes!
What Thunders bellow'd! and what Lightnings blaz'd!
When *Satan,* daring Chief of all thy Foes!
Was seiz'd, as trembling and agast he stood,
Seiz'd by thy mighty Hand, and rais'd aloft,
Then headlong hurl'd down the high Steep of Heav'n?
At the dire Sight his bold compeers amaz'd,
Confounded, shiver ev'n amidst the Flames,
Forget to Fight, drop all their idle Arms,
Swift from thy Fury fly away, and down
Down from the tow'ring Battlements they rush
Precipitant, into the Dark profound,
Whilst *Chaos* loud rebellows to the Fall.

No more—my fainting Muse folds up her Wings,
Unable to sustain so strong a Flight—
The Battle only Raphael should relate,
Or Milton in such Strains as Raphael sings.

Let softer Subjects now command my Muse,
Let softer Numbers smoothly flow along,
And bloom, and blossom as the Ever-greens,
That deck the flow'ry Face of Paradise.
O Milton, *Eden* opens by thy Art,
And with redoubl'd Beauty wanton smiles.
I'm charm'd, I'm ravish'd, all my Soul dissolves,
I loose my Life amid the heav'nly Scenes;
That in gay Order from thy Pencil flow.
O beauteous Garden! O delightful Walks!
In you forever, ever will I stray,
Glide o'er thy flow'ry Vales, clumb thy fair Hills,
And thro' thy fragrant Lawns transported tread
I'd trace the mazy Windings of thy Bow'rs,
And in the Gloom of thy surrounding Groves

Ask the cool Shadow, and the fanning Breeze.
Here rising Perfume should regale my Smell,
And heav'nly Harmony transport my Ears;
While all the Trees around, to court a look,
Flourish luxuriant with unfading Charms.
Roses, and Violets, and Daffodils,
And gaudy Tulips of a thousand Dyes,
Shall spring profusely round; the Lilly too,
Ambitious, offer its unsullied White,
To grace a Garland for fair Innocence.
Ye feather'd Songsters of the Spring, arise,
Display your spangled Plumes, where twinkling Gems,
With blended Beauties, cast a doubtful Blaze,
And, keenly-flashing, strike the Gazer's Sight.
Let your sweet Voices warble thro' the Grove,
While in concording Harmony I hear
The purling Murmurs of the bubbling Brooks
Mean time the embroider'd Banks on either Hand
Shall open all their everlasting Sweets,
Their verdant Honours, and their flow'ry Pride,
As the pure floating Volumes wind along.
Here the first Pair, divinely reign'd supream,
And sunk reclining on the flow'ry Turff.
Hail, happy *Adam,* Heav'n adorns thy Soul,
Full bless'd. And thou, immortal Mother, Hail!
O heav'nly-fair, divinely-beauteous *Eve!*
Thee to adorn what endless Charms conspire?
Caelestial Coral blushes on thy Lips,
No op'ning Rose glows with so bright a Bloom.
Thy Breath abroad diffusive Odor spreads,
A gay Carnation purple o'er thy Cheeks,
While thy fair Eyes roll around their radiant Orbs,
With winning Majesty, and nat'ral Art.
Thy waving Tresses on thy Shoulders play,
Flow loosely down, and wanton in the Wind.
You, am'rous *Zephires,* kiss her snowy Breast,

Flit softly by, and gently lift her Locks.
Forgive, fair Mother, O forgive thy Son,
Forgive his vain Redundance of Expression.
Fir'd by thy Beauty, and by Milton's Song.
Here could the ravish'd Fancy rove perpetual,
Amid the Raptures, the transporting Bliss,
That in soft Measures move for ever round.—

But, O my Muse, shake off these idle Dreams,
Imaginary Trances! vain Illusions!
Count the gay Stars, and number all the Sands,
And ev'ry Drop that in the Ocean floats:
But never hope to sum th' unnumber'd Charms,
That swim before thy ever-ravish'd Eyes,
When they on thee, O Milton, give a glance.
In vain thou striv'st to lisp his lofty Praise;
Imperfect Accents flutter round thy Tongue,
And on thy Lips Unfinish'd, Milton dies.
His mighty Numbers tow'r above thy Sight,
Mock thy low Musick, and elude thy Strains.

"TO PICTORIO, *ON THE SIGHT OF HIS PICTURES*"

(*1744*)

Text: *Poems on Several Occasions,* 89-93.

Ages our Land a barbarous Desart stood,
And savage Nations howl'd in ev'ry Wood;
No laurel'd Art o'er the rude Region smil'd,
Nor bless'd Religion dawn'd admidst the Wild;
Dulness and Tyranny confederate reign'd,
And Ignorance her gloomy State maintain'd.
An hundred Journies now the Earth has run,
In annual Circles, round the central Sun,
Since the first ship the unpolish'd Letters bore
Thro' the wide Ocean to the barb'rous Shore.

Then Infant-Science made it's early Proof,
Honest, sincere, tho' unadorn'd, and rough;
Still thro' a Cloud the rugged Stranger shone,
Politeness, and the softer Arts unknown:
No heavenly Pencil the free Stroke could give,
Nor the warm Canvass felt its Colours live.
No moving Rhet'rick rais'd the ravish'd Soul,
Flourish'd in Flames, or heard it's Thunder roll;
Rough horrid Verse, harsh, grated thro' the Ear,
And jarring Discords tore the tortur'd Air;
Solid, and grave, and plain the Country stood,
Inelegant, and rigorously good.

Each Year, succeeding, the rude Rust devours,
And softer Arts lead on the following Hours;
The Tuneful Nine begin to touch the Lyre,
And flowing Pencils light the living Fire;
In the fair Page new Beauties learn to shine,
The Thoughts to brighten, and the Style refine,
Till the great Year the finish'd Period brought;
Pictorio painted, and Maecenas wrote.

Thy Fame, Pictorio, shall the Muse rehearse,
And sing her Sister-Art in softer Verse:
'Tis your's, great Master, in just Lines to trace
The rising Prospect, or the lovely Face.
In the fair Round to swell the glowing Cheek,
Give Thought to Shades, and teach the Paints to speak.
Touch'd by thy Hand, how *Sylvia's* Charms engage!
And *Flavia's* Features smile thro' ev'ry Age.
In *Clio's* Face, th' attentive Gazer spies
Minerva's reasoning Brow, and azure Eyes,
Thy Blush, *Belinda,* future Hearts shall warm,
And *Celia* shine in *Citberea's* Form.
In hoary Majesty, see Cato here;
Fix'd strong in Thought, there Newton's Lines appear;
Here in full Beauty blooms the charming Maid;

Here *Roman* Ruins nod their awful Head;
Here gloting Monks their am'rous Rights debate,
The *Italian* Master sits in easy State,
Vandike and Rubens show their rival Forms,
And Caesar flashes in the Blaze of Arms.

But cease, fond Muse, nor the rude Lays prolong,
A thousand Wonders must remain unsung;
Crowds of new Beings lift their wond'ring Heads,
In conscious Forms, and animated Shades.
What Sounds can speak, to ev'ry Figure just,
The breathing Statue, and the living Bust?
Landskips how gay! arise in ev'ry Light,
And fresh Creations rush upon the Sight;
Thro' fairy Scenes the roving Fancy strays,
Lost in the endless, visionary Maze.

Still, wondrous Artist, let thy Pencil flow,
Still, warm with Life, thy blended Colours glow,
Raise the ripe Blush, bid the quick Eye-balls roll
And call forth every Passion of the Soul.
Let thy soft Shades in mimick Figures play,
Steal on the Heart, and catch the Mind away.
Yet *Painter,* on the kindred Muse attend,
The Poet ever proves the Painter's Friend.
In the same Studies Nature we pursue,
I the description touch, the Picture you;
The same gay Scenes our beauteous Works adorn,
The purple Ev'ning, or the flamy Morn:
Now, with bold Hand, we strike the strong Design;
Mature in Thought, now soften every Line;
Now, unrestrain'd in freer Airs suprize,
And sudden, at our Word, new World's arise,
In gen'rous Passion let our Breasts conspire,
As is the Fancy's, be the Friendship's Fire;
Alike our Labour, and alike our Flame:
'Tis thine to raise the Shape; 'tis mine to fix the Name.

BENJAMIN CHURCH

(*1734-1776*)

"THE CHOICE"

(*1757*)

Text: *The Choice, A Poem After the Manner of M. Pomfret* (Boston, 1757).

IF youthful Fancy might it's Choice pursue,
And act as natural Reason prompts it to;
If Inclination could dispose our State,
And human Will might govern future Fate;
Remote From Grandeur, I'd be humbly wise,
And all the Glitter of a Court despise:
Unskill'd the Proud, or Vicious to commend,
To cringe to Insolence, or Fools attend;
Within myself contended and secure,
Above what mean Ambition can endure;
Nor yet so anxious to obtain a Name,
To bleed for Honor, in the Fields of Fame;
Empty Parade, is all that Heroes know,
Unless fair Vertue hover in the Show.

BUT in these Walls, where Heav'n has fix'd my stay,
One half of Life, I'd wish to breath away:
The Fall and Winter of each future Year,
I'd humbly hope to spend contented here;
'Mid the fierce Ravage of a wintry Storm,
Kind Friends to cheer me, moderate Wine to warm;
Securely happy we'd delude the Day,
And smile the Seasons chearfully away.

NO needless Show my modest Dome should claim,
Neat and genteel without, within the same;
Decently furnish'd to content and please,
Sufficient for Necessity and Ease;

Vain is the Pomp of Prodigal Expence,
Frugality denotes the Man of sense;
My Doors the needy Stranger should befriend,
And Hospitality my Board attend;
With frugal Plenty be my Table spread,
Those, and those only whom I love be fed:
The Meek and Indigent my Banquet share,
Who love the Master, and approve the Fare;
Thy mellow Vintage *Lisbon!* should abound,
Pouring a mirthful Inspiration 'round;
While laughing *Bacchus* baths within the Bowl,
Love, Mirth and Friendship swallow up the Soul.

I'D have few Friends, and those by Nature true,
Sacred to Friendship, and to Vertue too;
Tho' but to few an Intimate profest,
I'd be no Foe, nor useless to the Rest:
Each Friend belov'd requires a friendly Care,
Each Grief, Dejections, and his Fate to share;
For this my Choice should be to Bounds confin'd,
Nor with a Burst of Passion flood Mankind.
Above the Rest, one dear selected Friend,
Kind to advise and cautious to offend;
To Malice, Envy, and to Pride unknown,
Nor apt to censure Foibles, but his own;
Firm in Religion, in his Morals just,
Wise in discerning, and advising best;
Learn'd without Pedantry, in Temper kind,
Soft in his Manners, happy in his Mind;
Is there in whom, these social Virtues blend,
The Muse lisps Pollio, and she calls him Friend:
To him, when flush'd with Transport I'd repair,
His faithful Bosom should my Solace share;
To him I'd fly when Sorrows prove too great,
To him discover all the Stings of Fate:

His social Soul, should all my Pangs allay,
Tune every Nerve, and charm my Griefs away.

O, How I wish to join the friendly Throng,
Elude the Hours, and harmonize the Song;
Each generous Soul still sedulous to please,
With calm good Temper, and with mutual Ease;
Glad to receive and give, the keen Reply,
Nor Approbation to the Jest deny.

BUT at a decent hour with social Heart,
In Love, and Humor should my Friends depart:
Then to my Study, eager I'd repair,
And feast my Mind with new Refreshment there;
There plung'd in Tho't my active Mind should tread,
Through all the Labours of the learned Dead;
Homer, great Parent of Heroick Strains,
Virgil, whose Genius was improv'd with Pains;
Horace, in whom the Wit and Courtier join'd,
Ovid, the tender, amorous and refin'd;
Keen *Juvenal,* whose all-correcting Page
Lash'd daring Vice, and sham'd an unproud Age;
Expressive *Lucan,* who politely sung
With hum'rous *Martial* tickling as he stung;
Elaborate *Terence,* studious where he smil'd,
Familiar *Plautus,* regularly wild;
With frequest Visit these I would survey,
And read, and mediate the Hours away.

NOR these alone, should on my Shelves recline,
But awful *Pope!* majestically shine,
Unequall'd Bard! Who durst thy Praise engage?
Nor yet grown reverend with the Rust of Age;
Sure Heav'n alone thy Art unrival'd taught,
To think so well, so well express the Tought;
What Villain hears thee, but regrets the Smart?

But tears the lurking Demon from his Heart?
Virtue attends thee, with the best Applause,
Conscious Desert! great Victor in her Cause,
She faithful to thy Worth, thy Name shall grace
Beyond all Period and beyond all Space:
Go, shine a Seraph and thy Notes prolong
For Angels only merit such a Song!

AIL Briton's Genuis, *Milton!* deathless Name!
Blest with a full Satiety of Fame:
Who durst attempt Impertinence of Praise!
Or sap insidious thy eternal Bays?
For greater Song, or more exalted Fame,
Exceeds Humanity to make, or claim.
These to peruse, I'd oft forget to dine,
And suck Refection from each migty Line,
Next Addison's great Labours should be join'd,
Prais'd by all Tongues and known to all Mankind:
With *Littleton* the tender, and correct,
And copious *Dryden,* glorious in Defect;
Now would I leave the great and pious *Young,*
Divinely fir'd, and sublime in Song.
Next would I add the unaffect'd *Gay,*
And gentle *Waller,* with his flowing Lay;
Last Nature-Lirnning Thompson should appear,
Who link'd Eternity within his Year.
These for Diverson, with the Comic Throng,
Should raise my Fancy, and improve my Song;
Extend my View, 'till op'ning Visions roll,
And all Piaeria bursts upon my Soul.

BUT to inform the Mind, and mend the Heart,
Great *Tillotson* and *Butler,* light impart;
Sagacious *Newton,* with all Science blest,
And *Lock,* who always tho't and reason'd best.

BUT LO! for real Worth, and true Desert,
Exhaustless Science, and extensive Art,
Boerhaave superior stands; in whom we find
The other Saviour of diseas'd Mankind;
Whose skilful Hand could almost Life create,
And make us leap the very Bounds of Fate;
Death, Tyrant Death, beholding his decline,
That *Boerhaave* would his Kingdom undermine,
Arm'd with his surest Shafts attack'd his Foe,
Who long eluded the repeated Throw,
At Length fatigu'd with Life, he bravely fell,
And Health with *Boerhaave* bad the World farewell.

THUS 'till the Year recedes I'd be employ'd,
Ease, Health and Friendship happily enjoy'd;
But when the Vernal Sun revolves it's Ray,
Melting hoar Winter with her Rage away,
When vocal Groves a gay perspective yield,
And a new Verdure springs from Field to Field;
With the first Larks I'd to the Plains retire,
For rural Pleasures are my chief Desire.

AH doubly blest! on native Verdure laid,
Whose Fields support him, and whose arbours Shade;
In his own Hermitage in Peace resides,
Fann'd by his Breeze, and slumbering by his Tides;
Who drinks a Fragrance from paternal Groves,
Nor lives ungrateful for the Life he loves.

I'D have a handsome Seat not far from Town,
The Prospect beautous, and the Taste my own;
The Fabrick modern, faultless the Design,
Not large, nor yet imoderately fine;
But neat Oeconomy my Mansion boast,

Nor should Convenience be in Beauty lost;
Each Part should speak superior Skill and Care,
And all the Artist be distinquish'd there.

ON some small Elevation should it stand,
And a free Prospect to the South command;
Where safe from Damps I'd snuff the wholesome Gale,
And Life and Vigour thro' the Lungs inhald;
Eastward my moderate Fields should wave with Grain,
Southward the Verdure of a broad Champaign;
Where gamesome Flocks and rampart Herds might play,
To the warm Sun-shine of the Vernal Day;
Northward, a Garden on a Slope should lye,
Finely adjusted to the nicest Eye;
In midst of This should stand a Cherry Grove,
A breezy, blooming Canopy of Love!
Whose blossom'd Boughs the timeful Choir should chear,
And pour Regalement on the Eye and Ear:
A gay Parterre the vivid Box should bound,
To waft a Fragrance thro' the Fields around;
Where blushing Fruits might tempt another *Eve,*
Without another Serpent to deceive.
Westward, I'd have a thick-set Forest grow,
Thro' which the bounded Sight should scarcely go;
Confus'dly rude, the Scen'ry should impart
A view of Nature unimprov'd by Art—

RAPT in the soft retreat my anxious Breast,
Pants eager still for something unpossess'd;
Whence Springs this sudden Hope, this warm Desire?
To what Enjoyment would my Soul aspire?
'Tis Love! extends my Wishes, and my Care,
Eden was tasteless 'til an *Eve* was there:
Almightly Love! I own thy powerful Sway,
Resign my Soul, and willingly obey.

GRANT me kind Heav'n! the Nymph still form'd to please,
Impassionate as Infants when at Ease;
Fair as the op'ning Rose; her Person small,
Artless as Parent *Eve* before her Fall;
Courteous as Angels, unreserv'dly kind,
Of modest Carriage, and the chastest Mind;
Her Temper sweet, her Conversation keen,
Not wildly gay, but soberly serene;
Not Talkative, nor apt to take Offence,
With Female Softness form'd to Manly Sense;
Her Dress and Language elegantly plain,
Not sluttish, forward, prodigal or vain;
Not proud of Beauty, nor elate with Praise,
Not fond to govern, but by *Choice* obeys;
True to my Arms in Body and in Soul,
As the touch'd Needle to the attractive Pole.
Caution, oppos'd to Charms like these were vain,
And Man would glory in the silken Chain;
Unlike the sensual Wish that burns and Stains,
But where the purest Admiration reigns;
Give me, O give me! such superior Love,
Before the Nectar of the God's above;
Then Time on downy Wings would steal away,
And Love still be the Business of the Day.

WHILE sporting Flocks in fond Rotations court
And to the Thicket Pair by Pair resort;
While toneful Birds in tender Murmurings plead,
Chanting their amorous Carolls through the Mead;
Link'd Arm in Arm we'd search the Twilight Grove,
Where all inspires with Harmony and Love:
Ye Boughs, your friendly Umbrage wide extend!
Guard from rude Eyes, and from the Sun defend:
Ye wanton Gales! pant gently on my Fair,
Thou Love-inspiring Goddess meet us there!

While soft-invited, and with Joy obey'd,
We press the Herbage, and improve the Shade.

BUT is th' Almighty ever bound to please?
Rul'd by my Wish, or studious of my Ease?
Shall I determine where his Frowns shall fall?
And fence my Grotto from the Lot of all!
Prostrate, his sovereign Wisdom I adore,
Intreat his Mercy, but I dare no more:
No constant Joys Mortality attend,
But Sorrows violate, and Cares offend;
Heav'n wisely mixt our Pleasures with Alloy,
And gilds our Sorrows, with a Ray of Joy;
Life without Storms a stagnant Pool appears,
And grows offensive with unruffled Years;
An active State, is Vertue's proper Sphere,
To do, and suffer is our duty here:
Foes to encounter, Vices to disdain,
Pleasures to shun, and Passions to restrain;
To fly Temptation's open, flowery Road,
And labour to be obstinately good.

THEN, blest is he who takes a calm Survey,
Of all th' Events that paint the checquer'd Day;
Content, that Blessing makes the Balance even,
And poizes Fortune, by the Scale of Heav'n.

I'LL let no future Ill my Peace destroy,
Or cloud the Aspect of a present Joy;
He who directed and dispenc'd the past,
O'er-rules the present, and shall guide the last:
If Providence a present Good has giv'n,
I clasp the Boon in Gratitude to Heav'n:
May Resignation fortify my Mind,
He cannot be unhappy that's resign'd.

GUARD my Repose thou Lord of all within!
An equal Temper, and a Soul serene;
O! teach me Patience when oppos'd to Wrong,
Restrain the mad'ning Heart, and curb the Tongue;
May Prudence govern, Piety controul,
All Slander, Rage and Bitterness of Soul;
Peace, Plenty, Health and Innocence be made,
The blissful Tenants of my tranquil Shade.

O LET me not maliciously comply,
To that curst Action that shall raise a Sigh;
Or cause the wretched Orphan to complain,
Or see the Widow's Tears, and see in vain;
From a remorseless Soul O set me free,
And prompt a Pang for every Wretch I see.

WHATEVER Station be for me design'd,
May Virtue be the Mistress of my Mind;
May I despise th' Abandon'd and the Base,
Tho' Opulent, or dignified with Place;
And spurn the Wretch who meanly lost to Shame,
Thinks Wealth or Place, a Substitute for Fame:
If Wisdom, Wealth or Honor, Heav'n lend,
Teach me those Talents happily to spend;
Nor make so blest, as I would wish to live,
Beyond those Moments Heav'n is pleas'd to give;
Then when Life trembles on the Verge of Rest,
And brings expended Minutes to the Test;
Absolve me Conscience, thou imperial Power!
O bless me with a self-approving Hour.

THE FRONTIERSMAN

The existence of a series of frontiers, as Frederick Jackson Turner and his followers have taught us, is one of the facts of American life. Indeed, the natural riches of the west, a land going unused, even the savage Indian—all these have seemed to cry out to eastern Americans for settlement and order, for "civilization," as believers in Manifest Destiny termed it. Pioneering has been one of the deepest of American drives. Yet movement to the west has always meant more than imposing eastern "civilization" on an "uncivilized" frontier; it has meant the creation of a new kind of life, new and overpowering awareness of the need for and the possibilities of freedom, independence, abundance, and economic, spiritual, and legal elbow-room. It has meant the creation of the frontier character.

We must view this character as the product of the meeting of the east and the west. Americans moving onto the frontier at once made their environment and were made by it. The Puritan Mrs. Rowlandson interpreted violence of her captivity by Indians as the sort of message that she, as a sinner, had been taught to expect from God; William Byrd interpreted the lubber-land North Carolinians among whom he travelled as creatures who had simply surrendered to or been overwhelmed by their frontier environment and thus as creatures not worthy of civilized consideration. However, the immediate sources of our tradition of the frontier character are not in such accounts as these. They are rather in the later eighteenth-century accounts of those hardy men who went into the Ohio country, made a new and special world for themselves, and so became the advance guard of that American civilization which was to follow them westward.

The two selections here printed exhibit two early stages in the creation of this frontier character. Weiser's diary is as direct an account of pre-civilized pioneering life as we likely could find— simple, straightforward, business-like, and realistic. The Boone narrative shows us what the American imagination was doing to an actual frontiersman—to a Boone who, though he was less a professional handler of Indians than Weiser, must have been fairly close to the actual Weiser. Cast in popular rhetoric, correctly religious, dramatically self-conscious, obviously doctored-up by its editor, it begins to make Boone into the ideal pioneer— the pioneer in whom more civilized and settled Americans believed, the pioneer who for them was bound to give up his life and new-found land to make way for their civilization. Here is the origin of the myth of Leatherstocking and of his sometimes heroic, sometimes villainous progeny—always men who at once create the law and are outside of it. Here, moreover, is one origin of the American obsession with the lonely hero, living dangerously, cut off from proper civilization. This Boone is not the "real" frontiersman, but rather the frontiersman whom Americans were creating so that they might comprehend themselves and what they might become as they moved west to clear the way for their new civilization.

Bibliographical Note. The classic essay on the meaning of the frontier in American culture is F. J. Turner's "The Significance of the Frontier in American History" (1920). Turner's essay is easily available, along with other essays pro and con, in *The Turner Thesis Concerning the Role of the Frontier in American History,* ed. G. R. Taylor (New York, 1949). R. W. G. Vail, *The Voice of the Old Frontier* (Philadelphia, 1950) is important for its exhaustive bibliography of frontier writings. A study of American feelings about the Indian and his relation to their mission as civilizers is R. H. Pearce, *The Savages of America* (Baltimore, 1953). Now the definitive study of the American understanding of the frontier is H. N. Smith, *Virgin Land* (Cambridge, 1950).

CONRAD WEISER

(*1696-1760*)

Bibliographical Note. The text which is printed below follows that in R. G. Thwaites, ed., *Early Western Travels,* I (Cleveland, 1904), 21-44; this text derives from the *Pennsylvania Colonial Records,* V, 348-358. On Weiser, see the wonderfully full biography by P. A. W. Wallace, *Conrad Weiser, 1696-1760* (Philadelphia, 1945).

THE JOURNAL OF CONRAD WEISER, ESQR., INDIAN INTERPRETER, TO THE OHIO (written 1748) *

"August 11, 1758." Set out from my House & came to James Galbreath that day, 30 Miles.

12th. Came to George Croghans, 15 Miles.

13th. To Robert Dunnings, 20 Miles.

14th. To the Tuscarroro Path, 30 Miles.

15th and 16th. Lay by on Account of the Men coming back Sick, & some other Affairs hindering us.

17th. Crossed the Tuscarroro Hill & came to the Sleeping Place called the Black Log, 20 Miles.

18th. Had a great rain in the afternoon; came within two Miles of the Standing Stone, 24 Miles.

19th. We travelled but 12 Miles; were obliged to dry our Things in the afternoon.

20th. Came to Franks Town, but saw no Houses or Cabins; here we overtook the Goods, because four of George Croghan's Hands fell sick, 26 Miles.

21st. Lay by, it raining all Day.

22d. Crossed Alleghany Hill & came to the Clear Fields, 16 Miles.

23d. Came to the Shawonese Cabbins, 34 Miles.

24th. Found a dead Man on the Road who had killed himself by Drinking too much Whisky; the Place being very stony we cou'd not dig a Grave; He smelling very strong we covered

* Reprinted by permission of the publishers, the Arthur H. Clark Company, from the Early Western Travel Series, 1748 to 1846, edited by Reuben G. Thwaites. Volume I.

him with Stones and Wood & went on our Journey; came to the 10 Mile Lick, 32 Miles.

25th. Crossed Kiskeminetoes Creek & came to Ohio that Day, 26 Miles.

26th. Hired a Cannoe; paid 1,000 Black Wampum for the loan of it to Logs Town. Our Horses being all tyred, we went by Water & came that Night to a Delaware Town; the Indians used us very kindly.

27th. Sett off again in the morning early; Rainy Wheather. We dined in a Seneka Town, where an old Seneka Woman Reigns with great Authority; we dined at her House, & they all used us very well; at this & the last-mentioned Delaware Town they received us by firing a great many Guns; especially at this last Place. We saluted the Town by firing off 4 pair of pistols; arrived that Evening at Logs Town, & Saluted the Town as before; the Indians returned about One hundred Guns; Great Joy appear'd in their Countenances. From the Place where we took Water, *i.e.* from the old Shawones Town, commonly called Chartier's Town to this Place is about 60 Miles by Water & but 35 or 40 by Land.

The Indian Council met this Evening to shake Hands with me & to shew their Satisfaction at my safe arrival; I desired of them to send a Couple of Canoes to fetch down the Goods from Chartier's old Town, where we had been oblig'd to leave them on account of our Horses being all tyred. I gave them a String of Wampum to enforce my Request.

28th. Lay still.

29th. The Indians sett off in three Canoes to fetch the Goods. I expected the Goods wou'd be all at Chartier's old Town by the time the Canoes wou'd get there, as we met about twenty Horses of George Groghan's at the Shawonese Cabbins in order to fetch the Goods that were then lying at Franks Town.

This Day news came to Town that the Six Nations were on the point of declaring War against the French, for reason the French had Imprison'd some of the Indian Deputies. A Council was held & all the Indians acquainted with the News, and it was said the Indian Messenger was by the way to give all the Indians Notice to make ready to fight the French. This Day my Companions went to Coscosky, a large Indian Town about 30 Miles off.

30th. I went to Beaver Creek, an Indian Town about 8 Miles off, chiefly Delawares, the rest Mohocks, to have some Belts of Wampum made. This afternoon Rainy Wheather set in which lasted above a Week. Andrew Montour came back from Coscosky with a Message from the Indians there to desire of me that the ensuing Council might be held at their Town. We both lodged at this Town at George Croghan's Trading House.

31st. Sent Andrew Montour back to Coscosky with a String of Wampum to let the Indians there know that it was an act of their own that the ensuing Council must be held at Logs Town, they had order'd it do last Spring when George Croghan was up, & at the last Treaty in Lancaster the Shawonese & Twightwees have been told so, & they stayed accordingly for that purpose, & both would be offended if the Council was to be held at Coscosky, besides my instructions binds me to Logs Town, & could not go further without giving offence.

Septr. 1. The Indians in Logs Town having heard of the Message from Coscosky sent for me to know what I was resolv'd to do, and told me that the Indians at Coscosky were no more Chiefs than themselves, & that last Spring they had nothing to eat, & expecting that they shou'd have nothing to eat at our arrival, order'd that the Council should be held here; now their Corn is ripe, they want to remove the Council, but they ought to stand by their word; we have kept the Twightwees here & our Brethren the Shawonese from below on that account, as I told them the Message that I had sent by Andrew Montour; they were content.

2d. Rain continued; the Indians brought in a good deal of Venison.

3d. Set up the Union Flagg on a long Pole. Treated all the Company with a Dram of Rum; The King's Health was drank by Indians & white men. Towards Night a great many Indians arrived to attend the Council. There was great firing on both sides; the Strangers first Saluted the Town at a quarter of a Mile distance, and at their Entry the Town's People return'd the fire, also the English Traders, of whom there were above twenty. At night, being very sick of the Cholick, I got bled.

4th. Was oblig'd to keep my bed all Day, being very weak.

5th. I found myself better. Scaiohady came to see me; had some discourse with him about the ensuing Council.

6th. Had a Council with the Wondats, otherways called Ionontady Hagas, they made a fine Speech to me to make me welcome, & appeared in the whole very friendly. Rainy Wheather continued.

7th. Being inform'd that the Wondats had a mind to go back again to the French, & had endeavour'd to take the Delawares with them to recommend them to the French, I sent Andrew Montour to Beaver Creek with a string of Wampum to inform himself of the Truth of the matter; they sent a String in answer to let me know they had no correspondence that way with the Wondats, and that the aforesaid Report was false.

8th. Had a Council with the Chiefs of the Wondats; enquired their number, & what occasion'd them to come away from the French, What Correspondence they had with the Six Nations, & whether or no they had ever had any Correspondence with the Government of New York; they inform'd me their coming away from the French was because of the hard Usage they received from them; That they wou'd always get their Young Men to go to War against their Enemies, and wou'd use them as their own People, that is like Slaves, & their Goods were so dear that they, the Indians, cou'd not buy them; that there was one hundred fighting Men that came over to join the English, seventy were left behind at another Town a good distance off, & they hoped they wou'd follow them; that they had a very good Correspondence with the Six Nations many Years, & were one People with them, that they cou'd wish the Six Nations wou'd act more brisker against the French; That above fifty Years ago they made a Treaty of Friendship with the Governor of

New York at Albany, & shewed me a large Belt of Wampum they received there from the said Governor, as from the King of Great Britain; the Belt was 25 Grains wide & 265 long, very Curiously wrought, there were seven Images of Men holding one another by the Hand, the 1st signifying the Governor of New York (or rather, as they said, the King of Great Britain), the 2d the Mohawks, the 3d the Oneidos, the 4th the Cajugas, the 5th the Onondagers, the 6th the Senekas, the 7th the Owandaets [Wyandots], the two Rows of black Wampum under their feet thro' the whole length of the Belt to signify the Road from Albany thro' the 5 Nations to the Owendaets; That 6 Years ago, they had sent Deputies with the same Belt to Albany to renew the Friendship.

I treated them with a quart of Whiskey & a Roll of Tobacco; they expressed their good Wishes to King George & all his Brethren of the English.

This Day I desir'd the Deputies of all the Nations of Indians People, & were mightily pleas'd that I look'd upon them as settled on the Waters of Ohio to give me a List of their fighting Men, which they promis'd to do. A great many of the Indians went away this Day because the Goods did not come, & the People in the Town cou'd not find Provision enough, the number was so great.

The following is the number of every Nation, given to me by their several Deputies in Council, in so many Sticks tied up in a Bundle:

The Senacas 163, Shawonese 162, Owendaets 100, Tisage-chroanu 40; Mohawks 74; Mohickons 15; Onondagers 35; Cajukas 20; Oneidos 15; Delawares 165; in all 789.

9th. I had a Council with the Senakas, & gave them a large String of Wampum, black & White, to acquaint them I had it in Charge from the President & Council in Philadelphia to enquire who it was that lately took the People Prisoners in Carolina, one thereof being a Great man, & that by what discovery I had already made I found it was some of the Senekas did it; I therefore desir'd them to give me their Reasons for doing so,

& as they had struck their Hatchet into their Brethren's Body they cou'd not expect that I could deliver my Message with a good heart before they gave me Satisfaction in that Respect, for they must consider the English, tho' living in several Provinces, are all one People, & doing Mischief to one is doing to the other; let me have a plain & direct answer.

10th. A great many of the Indians got drunk; one Henry Noland had brought near 30 Gallons of Whiskey to the Town. This Day I made a Present to the old Shawonese Chief Cacka-watcheky, of a Stroud, a Blanket, a Match Coat, a Shirt, a Pair of Stockings, & a large twist of Tobacco, & told him that the President & Council of Philadelphia remember'd their love to him as to their old & true Friend, & wou'd Cloath his Body once more, & wished he might weare them out so as to give them an opportunity to cloath him again. There was a great many Indians present, two of which were the big Hominy & the Pride, those that went off with Chartier, but protested against his proceedings against our Traders. Catchawatcheky return'd thanks, & some of the Six Nations did the same, & express'd their Satisfaction to see a true man taken Notice of, altho' he was now grown Childish.

11th. George Croghan & myself staved an 8 Gallon Cag of Liquor belonging to the aforesaid Henry Norland, who could not be prevail'd on to hide it in the Woods, but would sell it & get drunk himselfe.

I desir'd some of the Indians in Council to send some of their Young Men to meet our People with the Goods, and not to come back before they heard of or saw them. I begun to be afraid they had fallen into the Hands of the Enemy; so did the Indians.

Ten Warriors came to Town by Water from Niagara; We suspected them very much, & fear'd that some of their Parties went to meet our People by hearing of them.

12th. Two Indians and a white man went out to meet our People, & had Orders not to come back before they saw them, or go to Franks Town, where we left the Goods. The same Day the

Indians made answer to my Request concerning the Prisoners taken in Carolina: Thanayieson, a Speaker of the Senekas, spoke to the following purpose in the presence of all the Deputies of the other Nations (We were out of Doors): "Brethren, You came a great way to visit us, & many sorts of Evils might have befallen You by the way which might have been hurtful to your Eyes & your inward parts, for the Woods are full of Evil Spirits. We give You this String of Wampum to clear up your Eyes & Minds & to remove all bitterness of your Spirit, that you may hear us speak in good Chear." Then the Speaker took his Belt in his Hand & said: "Brethren, when we and you first saw one another at your first arrival at Albany we shook Hands together and became Brethren & we tyed your Ship to the Bushes, and after we had more acquaintance with you we lov'd you more and more, & perceiving that a Bush wou'd not hold your Vessel we then tyed her to a large Tree & ever after good Friendship continued between us; afterwards you, our Brethren, told us that a Tree might happen to fall down and the Rope rot where-with the Ship was tyed. You then proposed to make a Silver Chain & tye your Ship to the great Mountains in the five Nations' Country, & that Chain was called the Chain of Friendship; we were all tyed by our Arms together with it, & we the Indians of the five Nations heartily agreed to it, & ever since a very good Correspondence have been kept between us; but we are very sorry that at your coming here we are oblig'd to talk of the Accident that lately befell you in Carolina, where some of our Warriors, by the Instigation of the Evil Spirit, struck their Hatchet into our own Body like, for our Brethren the English & we are of one Body, & what was done we utterly abhor as a thing done by the Evil Spirit himself; we never expected any of our People wou'd ever do so to our Brethren. We therefore re-move our Hatchet which, by the influence of the Evil Spirit, was struck into your Body, and we desire that our Brethren the Gov[r]. of New York & Onas[1] may use their utmost endeavours

---

[1] "Onas" was the Indian term for the governor of Pennsylvania—first used for Penn in his treaty with the Delawares, in 1682.—*Thwaites*.

that the thing may be buried in the bottomless Pit, that it may never be seen again—that the Chain of Friendship which is of so long standing may be preserv'd bright & unhurt." Gave a Belt. The Speaker then took up a String of Wampum, mostly black, and said: "Brethren, as we have removed our Hatchet out of your Body, or properly speaking, out of our own, We now desire that the Air may be clear'd up again & the wound given may be healed, & every thing put in good understanding, as it was before, and we desire you will assist us to make up everything with the Govr. of Carolina; the Man that has been brought as a Prisoner we now deliver to You, he is yours" (lay'd down the String, and took the Prisoner by the Hand and delivered him to me). By way of discourse, the Speaker said, "the Six Nation Warriors often meet Englishmen trading to the Catawbas, & often found that the Englishmen betrayed them to their Enemy, & some of the English Traders had been spoke to by the Indian Speaker last Year in the Cherrykees Country & were told not to do so; that the Speaker & many others of the Six Nations had been afraid a long time that such a thing wou'd be done by some of their Warriors at one time or other."

13th. Had a Council with the Senekas and Onontagers about the Wandots, to receive them into our Union. I gave a large Belt of Wampum and the Indians gave two, & everything was agreed upon about what sho'd be said to the Wandots. The same Evening a full Council was appointed & met accordingly, & a Speech was made to the Wandots by Asserhartur, a Seneka, as follows:

"Brethren, the Ionontady Hagas:[2] last Spring you sent this Belt of Wampum to Us (having the Belt then in his hand) to desire us and our Brethren, the Shawonese & our Cousins the Delawares, to come & meet you in your retreat from the French, & we accordingly came to your Assistance & brought you here & received you as our own flesh. We desire you will think you now join us, & our Brethren, the English, & you are become one

---

[2] "Jonontady Hagas" was the Iroquois phrase for the Wyandot or Huron Indians.—*Thwaites*.

People with us"—then he lay'd that Belt by & gave them a very large String of Wampum.

The Speaker took up the Belt I gave & said: "Brethren: the English, our Brothers, bid you welcome & are glad you escaped out Captivity like: You have been kept as Slaves by Onontio,[3] notwithstanding he call'd You all along his Children, but now You have broke the Rope wherewith you have been tyed & become Freemen, & we, the united Six Nations, receive you to our Council Fire, & make you Members thereof, and we will secure your dwelling Place to You against all manner of danger." —Gave the Belt.

"Brethren: We the Six United Nations & all our Indian Allies, with our Brethren the English, look upon you as our Children, tho' you are our Brethren; we desire you will give no ear to the Evil Spirit that spreads lyes & wickedness, let your mind be easy & clear, & be of the same mind with us whatever you may hear, nothing shall befall you but what of necessity must befall us at the same time.

"Brethren: We are extremely pleased to see you here, as it happened just at the same time when our Brother Onas is with us. We jointly, by this Belt of Wampum, embrace you about your middle, & desire you to be strong in your minds & hearts, let nothing alter your minds, but live & dye with us." Gave a Belt— the Council broke up.

14th. A full Council was Summon'd & every thing repeated by me to all the Indians of what pass'd in Lancaster at the last Treaty with the Twightwees.

The News was confirm'd by a Belt of Wampum from the Six Nations, that the French had imprisoned some of the Six Nations Deputies, & 30 of the Wandots, including Women & Children.

The Indians that were sent to meet our People with the Goods came back & did not see any thing of them, but they had been no further than the old Shawonese Town.

---

[3] "Onontio" was the Indian term for the governor of Canada.—*Thwaites.*

15th. I let the Indians know that I wou'd deliver my Message to morrow, & the Goods I had, & that they must send Deputies with me on my returning homewards, & wherever we shou'd meet the rest of the Goods I wou'd send them to them if they were not taken by the Enemy, to which they agreed.

The same Day the Delawares made a Speech to me & presented a Beaver Coat & a string of Wampum, & said, "Brother: we let the President & Council of Phila. know that after the Death of our Chief Man, Olomipies, our Grand Children the Shawnese came to our own Town to condole with us over the loss of our good King, your Brother, & they wiped off our Tears & comforted our minds, & as the Delawares are the same People with the Pennsylvanians, & born in one & the same Country, we give some of the Present our Grand Children gave us to the President & Council of Philda. because the Death of their good Friend & Brother must have affected them as well as us."—Gave the Beaver Coat & a String of Wampum.

The same Day the Wandots sent for me & Andrew & presented us with 7 Beaver Skins about 10 lbs. weight, & said they gave us that to buy some refreshments for us after our arrival in Pennsylvania, wished we might get home safe, & lifted up their Hands & said they wou'd pray God to protect us & guide us the way home. I desir'd to know their names; they behav'd like People of good Sense & Sincerity; the most of them were grey headed; their Names are as follows: Totornihiades, Taganayesy, Sonachqua, Wanduny, Taruchiorus, their Speaker. The Chiefs of the Delawares that made the above Speech are Shawanasson & Achamanatainu.

16th. I made answer to the Delawares & said, "Brethren the Delawares: It is true what you said that the People of Pennsylvania are your Brethren & Countrymen; we are very well pleas'd of what your Children the Shawonese did to you; this is the first time we had publick Notice given us of the Death of our good Friend & Brother Olomipies. I take this opportunity to remove the remainder of your Troubles from your Hearts to enable you to attend in Council at the ensuing Treaty, & I assure you that the President & Council of Pennsylvania condoles with You over the loss of your King our good Friend and Brother."—Gave them 5 Strouds.

The two aforesaid Chiefs gave a String of Wampum & desir'd me to let their Brethren, the President & Council, know they intended a Journey next Spring to Philadelphia to consult with their Brethren over some Affairs of Moment; since they are now like Orphan Children, they hoped their Brethren wou'd let them have their good Advice and Assistance, as the People of Pennsylvania & the Delawares were like one Family.

The same Day the rest of the Goods arriv'd the Men said they had nine Days' Rain & the Creeks arose, & that they had been oblig'd to send a sick Man back from Franks Town to the Inhabitants with another to attend him.

The neighboring Indians being sent for again, the Council was appointed to meet to-morrow. It rain'd again.

17th. It rained very hard, but in the Afternoon it held up for about 3 hours; the Deputies of the several Nations met in Council & I delivered them what I had to say from the President & Council of Pennsylvania by Andrew Montour.

"Brethren, you that live on Ohio: I am sent to You by the President & Council of Pennsylvania, & I am now going to Speak to You on their behalf I desire You will take Notice & hear what I shall say."—Gave a String of Wampum.

"Brethren: Some of You have been in Philadelphia last Fall & acquainted us that You had taken up the English Hatchet, and that You had already made use of it against the French, & that the French had very hard heads, & your Country afforded nothing but Sticks & Hickerys which was not sufficient to break them. You desir'd your Brethren wou'd assist You with some Weapons sufficient to do it. Your Brethren the Presid^t. & Council promis'd you then to send something to You next Spring by Tharachiawagon,[4] but as some other Affairs prevented his Journey to Ohio, you receiv'd a Supply by George Croghan sent you

---

[4] This was Weiser's Indian name.—*Thwaites*.

by your said Brethren; but before George Croghan came back from Ohio News came from over the Great Lake that the King of Great Britain & the French King had agreed upon a Cessation of Arms for Six Months & that a Peace was very likely to follow. Your Brethren, the President & Council, were then in a manner at a loss what to do. It did not become them to act contrary to the command of the King, and it was out of their Power to encourage you in the War against the French; but as your Brethren never miss'd fulfilling their Promises, they have upon second Consideration thought proper to turn the intended Supply into a Civil & Brotherly Present, and have accordingly sent me with it, and here are the Goods before your Eyes, which I have, by your Brethren's Order, divided into 5 Shares & layd in 5 different heaps, one heap whereof your Brother Assaraquoa sent to You to remember his Friendship and Unity with You; & as you are all of the same Nations with whom we the English have been in League of Friendship, nothing need be said more than this, that the President & Council & Assaraquoa[5] have sent You this Present to serve to strengthen the Chain of Friendship between us the English & the several Nations of Indians to which You belong. A French Peace is a very uncertain One, they keep it no longer than their Interest permits, then they break it without provocation given them. The French King's People have been almost starv'd in old France for want of Provision, which made them wish & seek for Peace; but our wise People are of opinion that after their Bellies are full they will quarrel again & raise a War. All nations in Europe know that their Friendship is mix'd with Poison, & many that trusted too much on their Friendship have been ruin'd.

"I now conclude & say, that we the English are your true Brethren at all Events, In token whereof receive this Present." The Goods being then uncover'd I proceeded. "Brethren: You have of late settled the River of Ohio for the sake of Hunting,

---

[5] The Virginians were called by the Indians "Long Knives," or more literally "Big Knives." Ash-a-le-co-a is the Indian form of this word. . . .—*Thwaites*.

& our Traders followed you for the sake of Hunting also. You have invited them yourselves. Your Brethren, the President & Council, desire You will look upon them as your Brethren & see that they have justice done. Some of your Young Men have robbed our Traders, but you will be so honest as to compel them to make Satisfaction. You are now become a People of Note, & are grown very numerous of late Years, & there is no doubt some wise Men among you, it therefore becomes you to Act the part of wise men, & for the future be more regular than You have been for some Years past, when only a few Young Hunters lived here."—Gave a Belt.

"Brethren: You have of late made frequent Complaints against the Traders bringing so much Rum to your Towns, & desir'd it might be stop't; & your Brethren the President & Council made an Act accordingly & put a stop to it, & no Trader was to bring any Rum or strong Liquor to your Towns. I have the Act here with me & shall explain it to You before I leave you; But it seems it is out of your Brethren's Power to stop it entirely. You send down your own Skins by the Traders to buy Rum for you. You go yourselves & fetch Horse loads of strong Liquor. But the other Day an Indian came to this Town out of Maryland with 3 Horse loads of Liquor, so that it appears you love it so well that you cannot be without it. You know very well that the Country near the endless Mountain affords strong Liquor, & the moment the Traders buy it they are gone out of the Inhabitants & are travelling to this Place without being discover'd; besides this, you never agree about it—one will have it, the other won't (tho' very few), a third says we will have it cheaper; this last we believe is spoken from your Hearts (here they Laughed). Your Brethren, therefore, have order'd that every cask of Whiskey shall be sold to You for 5 Bucks in your Town, & if a Trader offers to sell Whiskey to You and will not let you have it at that Price, you may take it from him & drink it for nothing."—Gave a Belt.

"Brethren: Here is one of the Traders who you know to be a

very sober & honest Man; he has been robbed of the value of 300 Bucks, & you all know by whom; let, therefore, Satisfaction be made to the Trader."—Gave a String of Wampum.

"Brethren, I have no more to say."

I delivered the Goods to them, having first divided them into 5 Shares—a Share to the Senekas another to the Cajukas, Oneidos, the Onontagers, & Mohawks, another to the Delawares, another to the Owendaets, Tisagechroanu, & Mohickons, and the other to the Shawonese.

The Indians signified great Satisfaction & were well pleased with the Cessation of Arms. The Rainy Wheather hasted them away with the Goods into the Houses.

18th. The Speech was delivered to the Delawares in their own Language, & also to the Shawonese in their's, by Andrew Montour, in the presence of the Gentlemen that accompanied me. I acquainted the Indians I was determined to leave them tomorrow & return homewards.

19th. Scaiohady, Tannghrishon, Oniadagarehra, with a few more, came to my lodging & spoke as follows:

"Brother Onas, We desire you will hear what we are going to say to You in behalf of all the Indians on Ohio; their Deputies have sent us to You. We have heard what you have said to us, & we return you many thanks for your kindness in informing us of what pass'd between the King of Great Britain & the French King, and in particular we return you many thanks for the large Presents; the same we do to our Brother Assaraquoa, who joined our Brother Onas in making us a Present. Our Brethren have indeed tied our Hearts to their's. We at present can but return thanks with an empty hand till another oportunity serves to do it sufficiently. We must call a great Council & do every thing regular; in the mean time look upon us as your true Brothers.

"Brother: You said the other Day in Council if any thing befell us from the French we must let you know of it. We will let you know if we hear anything from the French, be it against us or yourself. You will have Peace, but it's most certain that the Six Nations & their Allies are upon the point of declaring War against the French. Let us keep up true Corrispondence & always hear of one another."—They gave a Belt.

Scaiohady & the half King, with two others, had inform'd me that they often must send Messengers to Indian Towns & Nations, & had nothing in their Council Bag, as they were new beginners, either to recompense a Messenger or to get Wampum to do the business, & begged I wou'd assist them with something. I had saved a Piece of Strowd, an half Barrell of Pow[d]er, 100 pounds of Lead, 10 Shirts, 6 Knives, & 1 Pound of Vermillion, & gave it to them for the aforesaid use; they return'd many thanks and were mightily pleased.

The same Day I set out for Pennsylvania in Rainy Weather, and arrived at George Croghan's on the 28th Instant.

CONRAD WEISER.

PENNSBURY, Sept. 29th, 1748.

JOHN FILSON
(c. 1747-1788)

The text given below, apparently Filson's rewriting of notes dictated by Boone, was first published as the Appendix to Filson's *Kentucke* (Wilmington, Delaware, 1784). The whole has been reprinted in facsimile, with notes appended, ed. W. R. Jilson (Louisville, 1930); the text here printed follows Jilson's facsimile, pp. 49-92. The best life of Boone is John Bakeless, *Daniel Boone* (New York, 1939).

THE ADVENTURES OF COL. DANIEL BOON; CONTAINING A NARRATIVE OF THE WARS OF KENTUCKE

Curiosity is natural to the soul of man, and interesting objects have a powerful influence on our affections. Let these influencing powers actuate, by the permission or disposal of Providence, from selfish or social views, yet in time the mysterious will of Heaven is unfolded, and we behold our conduct, from whatsoever motives excited, operating to answer the important designs of heaven. Thus we behold Kentucke, lately an howling wilderness, the habitation of savages and wild beasts, become a fruitful field; this region, so favourably distinguished by nature, now become the habitation of civilization, at a period unparalleled in history, in the midst of a raging war, and under all the disadvantages of emigration to a country so remote from the inhabited parts of the continent. Here; where the hand of violence shed the blood of the innocent; where the horrid yells of savages, and the groans of the distressed, sounded in our ears, we now hear the praises and adorations of our Creator; where wretched wigwams stood, the miserable abodes of savages, we behold the foundations of cities laid, that, in all probability, will rival the glory of the greatest upon earth. And we view Kentucke situated on the fertile banks of the great Ohio, rising from obscurity to shine with splendor, equal to any other of the stars of the American hemisphere.

The settling of this region well deserves a place in history. Most of the memorable events I have myself been exercised in;

and, for the satisfaction of the public, will briefly relate the circumstances of my adventures, and scenes of life, from my first movement to this country until this day.

It was on the first of May, in the year 1769, that I resigned my domestic happiness for a time, and left my family and peaceable habitation on the Yadkin River, in North-Carolina, to wander through the wilderness of America, in quest of the country of Kentucke, in company with John Finley, John Stewart, Joseph Holden, James Monay, and William Cool. We proceeded successfully, and after a long and fatiguing journey through a mountainous wilderness, in a westward direction, on the seventh day of June following, we found ourselves on Red-River, where John Finley had formerly been trading with the Indians, and, from the top of an eminence, saw with pleasure the beautiful level of Kentucke. Here let me observe, that for some time we had experienced the most uncomfortable weather as a prelibation of our future sufferings. At this place we encamped, and made a shelter to defend us from the inclement season, and began to hunt and reconnoitre the country. We found every where abundance of wild beasts of all sorts, through this vast forest. The buffaloes were more frequent than I have seen cattle in the settlements, browzing on the leaves of the cane, or croping the herbage on those extensive plains, fearless, because ignorant, of the violence of man. Sometimes we saw hundreds in a drove, and the numbers about the salt springs were amazing. In this forest, the habitation of beasts of every kind natural to America, we practiced hunting with great success until the twenty-second day of December following.

This day John Stewart and I had a pleasing ramble, but fortune changed the scene in the close of it. We had passed through a great forest, on which stood myriads of trees, some gay with blossoms, others rich with fruits. Nature was here a series of wonders, and a fund of delight. Here she displayed her ingenuity and industry in a variety of flowers and fruits, beautifully coloured, elegantly shaped, and charmingly flavoured; and we were diverted with innumerable animals presenting themselves per-

petually to our view.—In the decline of the day, near Kentucke
river, as we ascended the brow of a small hill, a number of
Indians rushed out of a thick cane-brake upon us, and made us
prisoners. The time of our sorrow was now arrived, and the
scene fully opened. The Indians plundered us of what we had,
and kept us in confinement seven days, treating us with common
savage usage. During this time we discovered no uneasiness or
desire to escape, which made them less suspicious of us; but in
the dead of night, as we lay in a thick cane brake by a large fire,
when sleep had locked up their senses, my situation not disposing me for rest, I touched my companion and gently awoke
him. We improved this favourable opportunity, and departed,
leaving them to take their rest, and speedily directed our course
towards our old camp, but found it plundered, and the company
dispersed and gone home. About this time my brother, Squire
Boon, with another adventurer, who came to explore the country
shortly after us, was wandering through the forest, determined
to find me, if possible, and accidentally found our camp. Notwithstanding the unfortunate circumstances of our company, and
our dangerous situation, as surrounded with hostile savages, our
meeting so fortunately in the wilderness made us reciprocally
sensible of the utmost satisfaction. So much does friendship
triumph over misfortune, that sorrows and sufferings vanish
at the meeting not only of real friends, but of the most distant
acquaintances, and substitutes happiness in their room.

Soon after this, my companion in captivity, John Stewart, was
killed by the savages, and the man that came with my brother
returned home by-himself. We were then in a dangerous, helpless situation, exposed daily to perils and death amongst savages
and wild beasts, not a white man in the country but ourselves.

Thus situated, many hundred miles from our families in the
howling wilderness, I believe few would have equally enjoyed the
happiness we experienced. I often observed to my brother, You see
now how little nature requires to be satisfied. Felicity, the companion of content, is rather found in our own breasts than in the
enjoyment of external things: And I firmly believe it requires but

a little philosophy to make a man happy in whatsoever state he is. This consists in a full resignation to the will of Providence; and a resigned soul finds pleasure in a path strewed with briars and thorns.

We continued not in a state of indolence, but hunted every day, and prepared a little cottage to defend us from the Winter storms. We remained there undisturbed during the Winter; and on the first day of May, 1770, my brother returned home to the settlement by himself, for a new recruit of horses and ammunition, leaving me by myself, without bread, salt or sugar, without company of my fellow creatures, or even a horse or dog. I confess I never before was under greater necessity of exercising philosophy and fortitude. A few days I passed uncomfortably. The idea of a beloved wife and family, and their anxiety upon the account of my absence and exposed situation, made sensible impressions on my heart. A thousand dreadful apprehensions presented themselves to my view, and had undoubtedly disposed me to melancholy, if further indulged.

One day I undertook a tour through the country, and the diversity and beauties of nature I met with in this charming season, expelled every gloomy and vexatious thought. Just at the close of day the gentle gales retired, and left the place to the disposal of a profound calm. Not a breeze shook the most tremulous leaf. I had gained the summit of a commanding ridge, and, looking round with astonishing delight, beheld the ample plains, the beauteous tracts below. On the other hand, I surveyed the famous river Ohio that rolled in silent dignity, marking the western boundary of Kentucke with inconceivable grandeur. At a vast distance I beheld the mountains lift their venerable brows, and penetrate the clouds. All things were still. I kindled a fire near a fountain of sweet water, and feasted on the loin of a buck, which a few hours before I had killed. The sullen shades of night soon overspread the whole hemisphere, and the earth seemed to gasp after the hovering moisture. My roving excursion this day had fatigued my body, and diverted my imagination. I laid me down to sleep, and I awoke not until the sun had chased away the night. I continued this tour, and in a few days explored a considerable part of the country, each day equally pleased as the first. I returned again to my old camp, which was not disturbed in my absence. I did not confine my lodging to it, but often reposed in thick cane-brakes, to avoid the savages, who, I believe, often visited my camp, but fortunately for me, in my absence. In this situation I was constantly exposed to danger, and death. How unhappy such a situation for a man tormented with fear, which is vain if no danger comes, and if it does, only augments the pain. It was my happiness to be destitute of this afflicting passion, with which I had the greatest reason to be affected. The prowling wolves diverted my nocturnal hours with perpetual howlings; and the various species of animals in this vast forest, in the daytime, were continually in my view.

Thus I was surrounded with plenty in the midst of want. I was happy in the midst of dangers and inconveniences. In such a diversity it was impossible I should be disposed to melancholy. No populous city, with all the varieties of commerce and stately structures, could afford so much pleasure to my mind, as the beauties of nature I found here.

Thus, through an uninterrupted scene of sylvan pleasures, I spent the time until the 27th day of July following, when my brother, to my great felicity, met me, according to appointment, at our old camp. Shortly after, we left this place, not thinking it safe to stay there longer, and proceeded to Cumberland river, reconnoitring that part of the country until March, 1771, and giving names to the different waters.

Soon after, I returned home to my family with a determination to bring them as soon as possible to live in Kentucke, which I esteemed a second paradise, at the risk of my life and fortune.

I returned safe to my old habitation, and found my family in happy circumstances. I sold my farm on the Yadkin, and what goods we could not carry with us; and on the twenty-fifth day of September, 1773, bade a farewell to our friends, and proceeded on our journey to Kentucke, in company with five families more, and forty men that joined us in Powel's Valley, which is one hundred and fifty miles from the now settled parts of Kentucke. This promising beginning was soon overcast with a cloud of adversity; for up on the tenth day of October, the rear of our company was attacked by a number of Indians, who killed six, and wounded one man. Of these my eldest son was one that fell in the action. Though we defended ourselves, and repulsed the enemy, yet this unhappy affair scattered our cattle, brought us into extreme difficulty, and so discouraged the whole company, that we retreated forty miles, to the settlement on Clench river. We had passed over two mountains, viz. Powels and Walden's, and were approaching Cumberland mountain when this adverse fortune overtook us. These mountains are in the wilderness, as we pass from the old settlements in Virginia to Kentucke, are ranged in a S. west and N. east direction, are of a great length and breadth, and not far distant from each other. Over these, nature hath formed passes, that are less difficult than might be expected from a view of such huge piles. The aspect of these cliffs is so wild and horrid, that it is impossible to behold them without terror. The spectator is apt to imagine that nature had formerly suffered some violent convulsion; and that these are the dismembered remains of the dreadful shock; the ruins, not of Persepolis or Palmyra, but of the world!

I remained with my family on Clench until the sixth of June, 1774, when I and one Michael Stoner were solicited by Governor Dunmore, of Virginia, to go to the Falls of the Ohio, to conduct into the settlement a number of surveyors that had been sent thither by him some months before; this country having about this time drawn the attention of many adventurers. We immediately complied with the Governor's request, and conducted in the surveyors, compleating a tour of eight hundred miles, through many difficulties, in sixty-two days.

Soon after I returned home, I was ordered to take the command of three garrisons during the campaign, which Governor Dunmore carried on against the Shawanese Indians: After the conclusion of which, the Militia was discharged from each garrison, and I being relieved from my post, was solicited by a

number of North-Carolina gentlemen, that were about purchasing
the lands lying on the S. side of Kentucke River, from the Cher-
okee Indians, to attend their treaty at Wataga, in March, 1775, to
negotiate with them, and, mention the boundaries of the purchase. This I accepted, and at the request of the same gentlemen,
undertook to mark out a road in the best passage from the
settlement through the wilderness to Kentucke, with such assistance as I thought necessary to employ for such an important
undertaking.

I soon began this work, having collected a number of enterprising men, well armed We proceeded with all possible expedition until we came within fifteen miles of where Boonsborough
now stands, and where we were fired upon by a party of Indians
that killed two, and wounded two of our number; yet, although
surprised and taken at a disadvantage, we stood our ground.
This was on the twentieth of March, 1775. Three days after, we
were fired upon again, and had two men killed, and three
wounded. Afterwards we proceeded on to Kentucke river without opposition; and on the first day of April began to erect the
fort of Boonsborough at a salt lick, about sixty yards from the
river, on the S. side.

On the fourth day, the Indians killed one of our men.—We
were busily employed in building this fort, until the fourteenth
day of June following, without any farther opposition from the
Indians; and having finished the works, I returned to my family,
on Clench.

In a short time, I proceeded to remove my family from Clench
to this garrison; where we arrived safe without any other difficulties than such as are common to this passage, my wife and
daughter being the first white women that ever stood on the
banks of Kentucke river.

On the twenty-fourth day of December following we had one
man killed, and one wounded, by the Indians, who seemed
determined to persecute us for erecting this fortification.

On the fourteenth day of July, 1776, two of Col. Calaway's
daughters, and one of mine, were taken prisoners near the fort.

I immediately pursued the Indians, with only eight men, and on the sixteenth overtook them, killed two of the party, and recovered the girls. The same day on which this attempt was made, the Indians divided themselves into different parties, and attacked several forts, which were shortly before this time erected, doing a great deal of mischief. This was extremely distressing to the new settlers. The innocent husbandman was shot down, while busy cultivating the soil for his family's supply. Most of the cattle around the stations were destroyed. They continued their hostilities in this manner until the fifteenth of April, 1777, when they attacked Boonsborough with a party of above one hundred in number, killed one man, and wounded four—Their loss in this attack was not certainly known to us.

On the fourth day of July following, a party of about two hundred Indians attacked Boonsborough, killed one man, and wounded two. They besieged us forty-eight hours; during which time seven of them were killed, and at last, finding themselves not likely to prevail, they raised the siege, and departed.

The Indians had disposed their warriors in different parties at this time, and attacked the different garrisons to prevent their assisting each other, and did much injury to the distressed inhabitants.

On the nineteenth day of this month, Col. Logan's fort was besieged by a party of about two hundred Indians. During this dreadful siege they did a great deal of mischief, distressed the garrison, in which were only fifteen men, killed two, and wounded one. The enemies loss was uncertain, from the common practice which the Indians have of carrying off their dead in time of battle. Col. Harrod's fort was then defended by only sixty-five men, and Boonsborough by twenty-two, there being no more forts or white men in the country, except at the Falls, a considerable distance from these, and all taken collectively, were but a handful to the numerous warriors that were every where dispersed through the country, intent upon doing all the mischief that savage barbarity could invent. Thus we passed through a scene of sufferings that exceeds description.

On the twenty-fifth of this month a reinforcement of forty-five men arrived from North-Carolina, and about the twentieth of August following, Col. Bowman arrived with one hundred men from Virginia. Now we began to strengthen, and from hence, for the space of six weeks, we had skirmishes with Indians, in one quarter or other, almost every day.

The savages now learned the superiority of the Long Knife, as they call the Virginians, by experience; being out-generalled in almost every battle. Our affairs began to wear a new aspect, and the enemy, not daring to venture on open war, practiced secret mischief at times.

On the first day of January, 1778, I went with a party of thirty men to the Blue Licks, on Licking River, to make salt for the different garrisons in the country.

On the seventh day of February, as I was hunting, to procure meat for the company, I met with a party of one hundred and two Indians, and two Frenchmen, on their march against Boonsborough, that place being particularly the object of the enemy.

They pursued, and took me; and brought me on the eighth day to the Licks, where twenty-seven of my party were, three of them having previously returned home with the salt. I knowing it was impossible for them to escape, capitulated with the enemy, and, at a distance in their view, gave notice to my men of their situation, with orders not to resist, but surrender themselves captives.

The generous usage the Indians had promised before in my capitulation, was afterwards fully complied with, and we proceeded with them as prisoners to old Chelicothe, the principal Indian town, on Little Miami, where we arrived, after an uncomfortable journey, in very severe weather, on the eighteenth day of February, and received as good treatment as prisoners could expect from savages—On the tenth day of March following, I, and ten of my men, were conducted by forty Indians to Detroit, where we arrived the thirtieth day, and were treated by Governor Hamilton, the British commander at that post, with great humanity.

During our travels, the Indians entertained me well; and their affection for me was so great, that they utterly refused to leave me there with the others, although the Governor offered them one hundred pounds Sterling for me, on purpose to give me a parole to go home. Several English gentlemen there, being sensible of my adverse fortune, and touched with human sympathy, generously offered a friendly supply for my wants, which I refused, with many thanks for their kindness; adding, that I never expected it would be in my power to recompense such unmerited generosity.

The Indians left my men in captivity with the British at Detroit, and on the tenth day of April brought me towards Old Chelicothe, where we arrived on the twenty-fifth day of the same month. This was a long and fatiguing march, through an exceeding fertile country, remarkable for fine springs and streams of water. At Chelicothe I spent my time as comfortably as I could expect; was adopted, accordin to their custom, into a family where I became a son, and had a great share in the affection of my new parents, brothers, sisters, and friends. I was exceedingly familiar and friendly with them, always appearing as chearful and satisfied as possible, and they put great confidence in me. I often went a hunting with them, and frequently gained their applause for my activity at our shooting-matches. I was careful not to exceed many of them in shooting; for no people are more envious than they in this sport. I could observe, in their countenances and gestures, the greatest expressions of joy when they exceeded me; and, when the reverse happened, of envy. The Shawanese king took great notice of me, and treated me with profound respect, and entire friendship, often entrusting me to hunt at my liberty. I frequently returned with the spoils of the woods, and as often presented some of what I had taken to him, expressive of duty to my sovereign. My food and lodging was, in common, with them, not so good indeed as I could desire, but necessity made every thing acceptable.

I now began to meditate an escape, and carefully avoided their suspicions, continuing with them at Old Chelicothe until the first day of June following, and then was taken by them to the salt springs on Sciotha, and kept there, making salt, ten days. During this time I hunted some for them, and found the land, for a great extent about this river, to exceed the soil of Kentucke, if possible, and remarkably well watered.

When I returned to Chelicothe, alarmed to see four hundred and fifty Indians, of their choicest warriors, painted and armed in a fearful manner, ready to march against Boonsborough, I determined to escape the first opportunity.

On the sixteenth, before sun-rise, I departed in the most secret manner, and arrived at Boonsborough on the twentieth, after a journey of one hundred and sixty miles; during which, I had but one meal.

I found our fortress in a bad state of defence, but we proceeded immediately to repair our flanks, strengthen our gates and posterns, and form double bastions, which we compleated in ten days. In this time we daily expected the arrival of the Indian army; and at length, one of my fellow prisoners, escaping from them, arrived, informing us that the enemy had an account of my departure, and postponed their expedition three weeks.—The Indians had spies out viewing our movements, and were greatly alarmed with our increase in number and fortifications. The Grand Councils of the nations were held frequently, and with more deliberation than usual. They evidently saw the approaching hour when the Long Knife would dispossess them of their desirable habitations; and anxiously concerned for futurity, determined utterly to extirpate the whites out of Kentucke. We were not intimidated by their movements, but frequently gave them proofs of our courage.

About the first of August, I made an incursion into the Indian country, with a party of nineteen men, in order to surprise a small town up Sciotha, called Paint-Creek-Town. We advanced within four miles thereof, where we met a party of thirty Indians, on their march against Boonsborough, intending to join the others from Chelicothe. A smart fight ensued betwixt us for some time: At length the savages gave way, and fled. We had no loss on our side: The enemy had one killed, and two wounded. We took from them three horses, and all their baggage; and being informed, by two of our number that went to their town, that the Indians had entirely evacuated it, we proceeded no further, and returned with all possible expedition to assist our garrison against the other party. We passed by them on the sixth day, and on the seventh, we arrived safe at Boonsborough.

On the eighth, the Indian army arrived, being four hundred and forty-four in number, commanded by Capt. Duquesne, eleven other Frenchmen, and some of their own chiefs, and marched up within view of our fort, with British and French colours flying; and having sent a summons to me, in his Britannick Majesty's name, to surrender the fort, I requested two days consideration, which was granted.

It was now a critical period with us.—We were a small number in the garrison:—A powerful army before our walls, whose appearance proclaimed inevitable death, fearfully painted, and marking their footsteps with desolation. Death was preferable to captivity; and if taken by storm, we must inevitably be devoted to destruction. In this situation we concluded to maintain our garrison, if possible. We immediately proceeded to collect what we could of our horses, and other cattle, and bring them through the posterns into the fort: And in the evening of the ninth, I returned answer, that we were determined to defend our fort while a man was living—Now, said I to their commander, who stood attentively hearing my sentiments, We laugh at all your formidable preparations: But thank you for giving us notice and time to provide for our defence. Your efforts will not prevail; for our gates shall for ever deny you admittance.—Whether this answer affected their courage, or not, I cannot tell; but, contrary to our expectations, they formed a scheme to deceive us, declaring it was their orders, from Governor Hamilton, to take us captives, and not to destroy us; but if nine of us would come out, and treat with them, they would immediately withdraw their forces from our walls, and return home peaceably. This sounded grateful in our ears; and we agreed to the proposal.

We held the treaty within sixty yards of the garrison, on purpose to divert them from a breach of honour, as we could not
avoid suspicions of the savages. In this situation the articles were
formally agreed to, and signed; and the Indians told us it was
customary with them, on such occasions, for two Indians to
shake hands with every white-man in the treaty, as an evidence
of entire friendship. We agreed to this also, but were soon convinced their policy was to take us prisoners.—They immediately
grappled us; but, although surrounded by hundreds of savages,
we extricated ourselves from them, and escaped all safe into the
garrison, except one that was wounded, through a heavy fire from
their army. They immediately attacked us on every side, and
a constant heavy fire ensued between us day and night for the
space of nine days.

In this time the enemy began to undermine our fort, which
was situated sixty yards from Kentucke river. They began at the
water-mark, and proceeded in the bank some distance, which we
understood by their making the water muddy with the clay; and
we immediately proceeded to disappoint their design, by cutting
a trench a-cross their subterranean passage. The enemy discovering our counter-mine, by the clay we threw out of the fort,
desisted from that stratagem: And experience now fully convincing them that neither their power nor policy could effect
their purpose, on the twentieth day of August they raised the
siege, and departed.

During this dreadful siege, which threatened death in every
form, we had two men killed, and four wounded, besides a
number of cattle. We killed of the enemy thirty-seven, and
wounded a great number. After they were gone, we picked up
one hundred and twenty-five pounds weight of bullets, besides
what stuck in the logs of our fort; which certainly is a great proof
of their industry. Soon after this, I went into the settlement, and
nothing worthy of a place in this account passed in my affairs for
some time.

During my absence from Kentucke, Col. Bowman carried on
an expedition against the Shawanese, at Old Chelicothe, with one

hundred and sixty men, in July, 1779. Here they arrived undiscovered, and a battle ensued, which lasted until ten o'clock, A. M. when Col. Bowman, finding he could not succeed at this time, retreated about thirty miles. The Indians, in the mean time, collecting all their forces, pursued and overtook him, when a smart fight continued near two hours, not to the advantage of Col. Bowman's party.

Col. Harrod proposed to mount a number of horse, and furiously to rush upon the savages, who at this time fought with remarkable fury. This desperate step had a happy effect, broke their line of battle, and the savages fled on all sides. In these two battles we had nine killed, and one wounded. The enemy's loss uncertain, only two scalps being taken.

On the twenty-second day of June, 1780, a large party of Indians and Canadians, about six hundred in number, commanded by Col. Bird, attacked Riddle's and Martin's stations, at the Forks of Licking River, with six pieces of artillery. They carried this expedition so secretly, that the unwary inhabitants did not discover them, until they fired upon the forts; and, not being prepared to oppose them, were obliged to surrender themselves miserable captives to barbarous savages, who immediately after tomahawked one man and two women, and loaded all the others with heavy baggage, forcing them along toward their towns, able or unable to march. Such as were weak and faint by the way, they tomahawked. The tender women, and helpless children, fell victims to their cruelty. This, and the savage treatment they received afterwards, is shocking to humanity, and too barbarous to relate.

The hostile disposition of the savages, and their allies, caused General Clark, the commandant at the Falls at the Ohio, immediately to begin an expedition with his own regiment, and the armed force of the country, against Pecaway, the principal town of the Shawanese, on a branch of Great Miami, which he finished with great success, took seventeen scalps, and burnt the town to ashes, with the loss of seventeen men.

About this time I returned to Kentucke with my family; and

here, to avoid an enquiry into my conduct, the reader being before informed of my bringing my family to Kentucke, I am under the necessity of informing him that, during my captivity with the Indians, my wife, who despaired of ever seeing me again, expecting the Indians had put a period to my life, oppressed with the distresses of the country, and bereaved of me, her only happiness, had, before I returned, transported my family and goods, on horses, through the wilderness, amidst a multitude of dangers, to her father's house, in North-Carolina.

Shortly after the troubles at Boonsborough, I went to them, and lived peaceably there until this time. The history of my going home, and returning with my family, forms a series of difficulties, an account of which would swell a volume, and being foreign to my purpose, I shall purposely omit them.

I settled my family in Boonsborough once more; and shortly after, on the sixth day of October, 1780, I went in company with my brother to the Blue Licks; and, on our return home, we were fired upon by a party of Indians. They shot him, and pursued me, by the scent of their dog, three miles; but I killed the dog, and escaped. The Winter soon came on, and was very severe, which confined the Indians to their wigwams.

The severity of this Winter caused great difficulties in Kentucke. The enemy had destroyed most of the corn, the Summer before. This necessary article was scarce, and dear; and the inhabitants lived chiefly on the flesh of buffaloes. The circumstances of many were very lamentable: However, being a hardy race of people, and accustomed to difficulties and necessities, they were wonderfully supported through all their sufferings, until the ensuing Fall, when we received abundance from the fertile soil.

Towards Spring, we were frequently harassed by Indians; and, in May, 1782, a party assaulted Ashton's station, killed one man, and took a Negro prisoner. Capt. Ashton, with twenty-five men, pursued, and overtook the savages, and a smart fight ensued, which lasted two hours; but they being superior in number, obliged Captain Ashton's party to retreat, with the loss of eight killed, and four mortally wounded; their brave commander himself being numbered among the dead.

The Indians continued their hostilities; and, about the tenth of August following, two boys were taken from Major Hoy's station. This party was pursued by Capt. Holder and seventeen men, who were also defeated, with the loss of four men killed, and one wounded. Our affairs became more and more alarming. Several stations which had lately been erected in the country were continually infested with savages, stealing their horses and killing the men at every opportunity. In a field, near Lexington, an Indian shot a man, and running to scalp him, was himself shot from the fort, and fell dead upon his enemy.

Every day we experienced recent mischiefs. The barbarous savage nations of Shawanese, Cherokees, Wyandots, Tawas, Delawares, and several others near Detroit, united in a war against us and assembled their choicest warriors at old Chelicothe, to go on the expedition, in order to destroy us, and entirely depopulate the country. Their savage minds were inflamed to mischief by two abandoned men, Captains McKee and Girty. These led them to execute every diabolical scheme; and, on the fifteenth day of August, commanded a party of Indians and Canadians, of about five hundred in number, against Briant's station, five miles from Lexington. Without demanding a surrender, they furiously assaulted the garrison, which was happily prepared to oppose them; and, after they had expended much ammunition in vain, and killed the cattle round the fort, not being likely to make themselves masters of this place, they raised the siege, and departed in the morning of the third day after they came, with the loss of about thirty killed, and the number of wounded uncertain.—Of the garrison four were killed, and three wounded.

On the eighteenth day Col. Todd, Col. Trigg, Major Harland, and myself, speedily collected one hundred and seventy-six men, well armed, and pursued the savages. They had marched beyond the Blue Licks to a remarkable bend of the main fork of Licking River, about forty-three miles from Lexington, as it is particularly represented in the map, where we overtook them on the nineteenth day. The savages observing us, gave way; and we, being ignorant of their numbers, passed the river. When the enemy saw our proceedings, having greatly the advantage of us in [our] situation, they formed the line of battle, as represented in the map, from one bend of Licking to the other, about a mile from the Blue Licks. An exceeding fierce battle immediately began, for about fifteen minutes, when we, being over-powered by numbers, were obliged to retreat, with the loss of sixty seven men; seven of whom were taken prisoners. The brave and much lamented Colonels Todd and Trigg, Major Harland and my second son, were among the dead. We were informed that the Indians, numbering their dead, found they had four killed more than we; and therefore, four of the prisoners they had taken, were, by general consent, ordered to be killed, in a most barbarous manner, by the young warriors, in order to train them up to cruelty; and then they proceeded to their towns.

On our retreat we were met by Col. Logan, hastening to join us, with a number of well armed men. This powerful assistance we unfortunately wanted in the battle; for, notwithstanding the enemy's superiority of numbers, they acknowledged that, if they had received one more fire from us, they should undoubtedly have given way. So valiantly did our small party fight, that, to the memory of those who unfortunately fell in the battle, enough of honour cannot be said. Had Col. Logan and his party been with us, it is highly probable we should have given the savages a total defeat.

I cannot reflect upon this dreadful scene, but sorrow fills my heart. A zeal for the defence of their country led these heroes to the scene of action, though with a few men to attack a powerful army of experienced warriors. When we gave way, they pursued us with the utmost eagerness, and in every quarter spread destruction. The river was difficult to cross, and many were killed in the flight, some just entering the river, some in the water, others after crossing in ascending the cliffs. Some escaped on horse-back, a few on foot; and, being dispersed every where, in a few hours, brought the melancholy news of this unfortunate battle to Lexington. Many widows were now made. The reader may guess what sorrow filled the hearts of the inhabitants, exceeding any thing that I am able to describe. Being reinforced, we returned to bury the dead, and found their bodies strewed every where, cut and mangled in a dreadful manner. This mournful scene exhibited a horror almost unparalleled: Some torn and eaten by wild beasts; those in the river eaten by fishes; all in such a putrified condition, that no one could be distinguished from another.

As soon as General Clark, then at the Falls of the Ohio, who was ever our ready friend, and merits the love and gratitude of all his country-men, understood the circumstances of this unfortunate action, he ordered an expedition, with all possible haste, to pursue the savages, which was so expeditiously effected, that we overtook them within two miles of their towns, and probably might have obtained a great victory, had not two of their number met us about two hundred poles before we come up. These returned quick as lightening to their camp with the alarming news of a mighty army in view. The savages fled in the utmost disorder, evacuated their towns, and reluctantly left their territory to our mercy. We immediately took possession of Old Chelicothe without opposition, being deserted by its inhabitants. We continued our pursuit through five towns on the Miami rivers, Old Chelicothe, Pecaway, New Chelicothe, Will's Towns, and Chelicothe, burnt them all to ashes, entirely destroyed their corn, and other fruits, and every where spread a scene of desolation in the country. In this expedition we took seven prisoners and five scalps, with the loss of only four men, two of whom were accidentally killed by our own army.

This campaign in some measure damped the spirits of the Indians, and made them sensible of our superiority. Their connections were dissolved, their armies scattered, and a future invasion put entirely out of their power; yet they continued to practice mischief secretly upon the inhabitants, in the exposed parts of the country.

In October following, a party made an excursion into that

district called the Crab Orchard, and one of them, being advanced some distance before the others, boldly entered the house of a poor defenceless family, in which was only a Negro man, a woman and her children, terrified with the apprehensions of immediate death. The savage, perceiving their defenceless situation, without offering violence to the family attempted to captivate the Negro, who, happily proved an over-match for him, threw him on the ground, and, in the struggle, the mother of the children drew an ax from a corner of the cottage, and cut his head off, while her little daughter shut the door. The savages instantly appeared, and applied their tomahawks to the door. An old rusty gun-barrel, without a lock, lay in a corner, which the mother put through a small crevice, and the savages, perceiving it, fled. In the mean time, the alarm spread through the neighbourhood; the armed men collected immediately, and pursued the savagers into the wilderness. Thus Providence, by the means of this Negro, saved the whole of the poor family from destruction. From that time, until the happy return of peace between the United States and Great-Britain, the Indians did us no mischief. Finding the great king beyond the water disappointed in his expectations, and conscious of the importance of the Long Knife, and their own wretchedness, some of the nations immediately desired peace; to which, at present, they seem universally disposed, and are sending ambassadors to General Clark, at the Falls of the Ohio, with the minutes of their Councils; a specimen of which, in the minutes of the Piankashaw Council, is subjoined.

To conclude, I can now say that I have verified the saying of an old Indian who signed Col. Henderson's deed. Taking me by the hand, at the delivery thereof, Brother, says he, we have given you a fine land, but I believe you will have much trouble in settling it.—My footsteps have often been marked with blood, and therefore I can truly subscribe to its original name. Two darling sons, and a brother, have I lost by savage hands, which have also taken from me forty valuable horses, and abundance of cattle. Many dark and sleepless nights have I been a companion for owls, separated from the chearful society of men, scorched by the Summer's sun, and pinched by the Winter's cold, an instrument ordained to settle the wilderness. But now the scene is changed: Peace crowns the sylvan shade.

What thanks, what ardent and ceaseless thanks are due to that all-superintending Providence which has turned a cruel war into peace, brought order out of confusion, made the fierce savages placid, and turned away their hostile weapons from our country! May the same Almighty Goodness banish the accursed monster, war, from all lands, with her hated associates, rapine and insatiable ambition. Let peace, descending from her native heaven, bid her olives spring amidst the joyful nations; and plenty, in league with commerce, scatter blessings from her copious hand.

This account of my adventures will inform the reader of the most remarkable events of this country.—I now live in peace and safety, enjoying the sweets of liberty, and the bounties of Providence, with my once fellow-sufferers, in this delightful country, which I have seen purchased with a vast expence of blood and treasure, delighting in the prospect of its being, in a short time, one of the most opulent and powerful states on the continent of North-America; which, with the love and gratitude of my country-men, I esteem a sufficient reward for all my toil and dangers.

DANIEL BOON

Fayette county, Kentucke.

Rinehart Editions